David Pugmire

£25

20062

2

Man and Society

VOLUME ONE

MAN AND SOCIETY

*A Critical Examination of
Some Important Social and Political Theories from
Machiavelli to Marx*

VOLUME ONE

JOHN PLAMENATZ
*Fellow of Nuffield College
Oxford*

LONGMANS

LONGMANS, GREEN AND CO LTD
48 Grosvenor Street, London w1

*Associated companies, branches and representatives
throughout the world*

*Printed in Great Britain by
Lowe and Brydone (Printers) Ltd., London*

To My Father

PREFACE

THIS book is not a history of political thought; it is, as its title implies, a critical examination of a number of important theories. It is not concerned to argue for some interpretations of these theories against others but to examine assumptions, ideas and attitudes.

The book is an expansion of lectures given at various times at three universities, Columbia, Harvard and Oxford. It is hoped that it will prove useful to students of social and political theory whose interest in the subject is more philosophical than historical; and the author has had in mind students in the United States as much as in Britain. He has aimed at lucidity but is aware that some parts of the book make difficult reading.

The most difficult part of all, which treats of Hegel, has been read by Professor H. L. A. Hart and Sir Isaiah Berlin, by Professor Herbert Deane of Columbia University, and by Mr William Weinstein and Mr John Torrance of Nuffield College, and the author is grateful to them for valuable comments and criticisms. He thanks Mr Alan Ryan of Balliol College for making the index. He also thanks his wife for reading the book in manuscript and suggesting improvements of grammar and style.

July 1961   J.P.

CONTENTS

INTRODUCTON

THE artist ploughs his own furrow; the scholar, even in the privacy of his study, cultivates a common field. He is responsible to others for what he does; he feels the need to explain his purpose, to justify his efforts.

There are many things well worth doing not attempted in this book. It is not a history of social and political thought; it does not enquire how one thinker influenced another, and compares them only to make clearer what they said. It scarcely looks at the circumstances in which this or that theory was produced. And it quite neglects several important thinkers. Althusius will get into the index only because he is mentioned on this page, and so too will Vico, who has been greatly and rightly admired. Grotius and Kant are mentioned only in passing. If my purpose had been to produce a history, however brief, of political thought from Machiavelli to Marx, this neglect or scanty treatment would have been without excuse.

Every thinker, even the most abstract, is deeply influenced by the circumstances of his day. To understand why Machiavelli or Hobbes or Rousseau wrote as he did, we must know something of social and political conditions in their day and country and of the controversies then to the fore. But this does not, I hope, mean that whoever discusses their theories must also discuss these conditions and controversies. Is there to be no division of labour? These conditions and controversies have often been described, and the writer who is primarily concerned with arguments and ideas need not discuss them except to make something clear which might otherwise be misunderstood. He must use his judgement: at times he may need to make a considerable digression, and at other times a passing reference or mere hint will be enough.

Those who say that to understand a theory we must understand the conditions in which it was produced sometimes put their case too strongly. They speak as if, to understand what a man is saying, we must know why he is saying it. But this is not true. We need understand only the sense in which he is using words. To understand Hobbes, we need not know what his purpose was in writing *Leviathan* or how he felt about the rival claims of Royalists and Parliamentarians; but we do need to know what he understood by such words as *law*, *right, liberty, covenant*, and *obligation*. And though it is true that even Hobbes, so 'rare' at definitions, does not always use a word in the sense which he defines, we are more likely to get the sense in which he does use it by a close study of his argument than by looking at the condition of England or at political controversies in his day.

These are, of course, well worth looking at on their own account. Nevertheless, we can go a long way in understanding Hobbes' argument and yet know very little about them.

No doubt, Hobbes is a special case. We can get more of his meaning by merely reading what he wrote than we can, say, of Machiavelli's or Montesquieu's or Burke's. It is a matter of degree. But, even in their case, we learn more about their arguments by weighing them over and over again than by extending our knowledge of the circumstances in which they wrote. Hobbes was not less a child of his times than they were. If we want to know why he wrote as he did, or why an argument such as his was produced and found exciting, we have to look at what was happening when he wrote; he was no more independent of his times than was Machiavelli or Burke. Of every really great thinker we can say that, compared with lesser men, he is idiosyncratic; he is, for a time, more liable than they are to be misunderstood because he has more to say that is unfamiliar. He uses the common language but uses it differently. But this is not more true of Hobbes than of Machiavelli. Hobbes belongs as completely to his age as Machiavelli does to his; and if, in order to understand him, we need take less notice of the circumstances in which he wrote, this is because his style and method are different. To understand the argument of *Leviathan* is one thing; to understand the age in which alone it could have been written is another. I do not deny that the second understanding may contribute to the first; I merely doubt whether the contribution is anything like as great as it is sometimes made out to be. Of course, it is of absorbing interest to see a great thinker in the setting of his age. How society and politics are related to political and social theory is as well worth studying as theory itself. Who would deny it? But that is another matter.

Students of society and government make use of ideas and assumptions inherited from the past. In this book I have not been concerned to trace the origins and evolution of these ideas, but rather to examine them critically by considering some of the most familiar and most famous theories which contain them. I have chosen these theories, rather than others, precisely because they are familiar, and because, between them, they contain most of the important ideas and assumptions still used or made, whether by students of society and politics or by persons engaged in political controversies. All these theories, in one way or another, are inadequate; they fail to explain satisfactorily what they set out to explain. They are also – though this is less important – 'out-of-fashion': by which, I am sorry to say, I mean no more than this, that sociologists and political scientists in many places (though not in all) now believe that they have less to learn from them than from one another.

These ideas and assumptions ought to be examined critically; and where can they be so examined to better advantage than in the context of well-known, long discussed and, in some cases, still influential theories? It is sometimes objected that the questions raised by, say, Hobbes or Locke are no longer relevant. But if we discuss social and political matters, we must still speak, as they did, of *law*, of *rights*, of *obligation* and of *consent*. By seeing how they used these words and what arguments they constructed, we learn to use them ourselves. By seeing where their explanations are inadequate, we learn something about what they sought to explain. To treat *right* as absence of obligation (which is what Hobbes did) may do for some purposes, but not for others. By examining critically the argument of *Leviathan* and *De Cive*, we learn why this is so. It may be true, as Locke said, that the authority of governments rests in some sense on the consent of the governed; but perhaps it cannot do so unless consent is understood in a sense different from his. By seeing where his argument goes wrong, we are better placed to construct another to take its place. If we do not get from Hobbes or Locke answers to the questions we now put, we do, by examining their theories, learn to put our own questions more clearly. And I take Hobbes and Locke for examples deliberately because they are among the most abstract of political theorists. Machiavelli, Bodin, Montesquieu, Hume, Burke, Hegel and Marx all take larger account than they do of history and of the machinery of government.

The great advantage of these old theories is that they are both rich in content and familiar. If our purpose is to examine ideas used to explain society and government, these theories provide them abundantly, vigorously and attractively. They are a fertile field for the exercise we have in mind. Everyone agrees that students of society and government need to look carefully at the assumptions they make and the ideas they use; that they, owing to the nature of their subject, are especially liable to be the dupes of words. Yet there are now many who question the use of a close study of theories produced long ago in circumstances widely different from our own. It is therefore a point worth making, that these ideas are nowhere better or more economically studied than in these old theories. Nowhere *better* because of the richness and variety they present, and nowhere *more economically* because they have been sifted again and again and we can get down quickly to essentials.

In some circles where the study of these theories is depreciated, there is nevertheless a keen interest taken in the ideas and assumptions used or made by the sociologist or the political scientist. There are sociologists and political scientists who put themselves to great trouble to define the terms they use and to state their assumptions. They do not always do it well. They wish to be lucid, precise and realistic; they aim at explaining the facts and are in search of a vocabulary adequate to their purpose. It is impossible not to sympathize with them. Yet, for all their efforts, they are often more obscure, or looser in their arguments, or more incoherent than the makers of the old theories which they neglect on the ground that they are irrelevant. A close study of these theories might be a good discipline for them.

Or the social scientist, though he does not know it, repeats what has been said as well, or better, long ago. Ideas very like his own have been used long before his time, and yet he thinks them new because he has coined new words to express them. It is sad to read a book for which it is claimed that it breaks new ground, and to find it thin and stale.

Not for a moment do I suggest that these old theories provide the social scientist with all that he is looking for. They are not a stock of ideas sufficient for his purposes. They are inadequate for all kinds of reasons, some of which are discussed in this book. I suggest only that the study of them is still amply rewarding, and to no one more so than to the student of society who feels that he lacks the ideas needed to explain what he studies. Of course, he will not find the ideas he wants ready made in these theories, but he will become more adept in the handling of ideas and a better judge of their uses. He will be more discriminating, more scrupulous, and perhaps also more severe with himself and his contemporaries. Bentham said that his purpose in writing *A Fragment on Government* was to teach the student ' to place more confidence in his own strength, and less in the infallibility of great names – to help him to emancipate his judgement from the shackles of authority'. An admirable purpose. But today, in some intellectual circles, the authority of great names is less oppressive than is fashion, which is an even worse guide. If we neither neglect great names nor defer to them, but seek, to the best of our ability, to take their measure, we are then better placed to take our own.

It is said that, in the past, it was difficult, if not impossible, to study the facts, social and political, whereas now it is much less difficult. There are vastly greater records than there were, more easily accessible; there are methods now used to get at the facts which could not have been used in earlier periods; it is easier than it was to test hypotheses, and we are more sophisticated in the making and testing of them. The social sciences may have no spectacular achievements to their credit, but then it is not to be expected that they should. It is admitted that they differ greatly from the natural sciences, that there are difficulties peculiar to them, that their conclusions are less precise and more open to question. Such is their nature that, though they call for no less imagination, no less intelligence, no smaller talents from their devotees than other sciences, they afford lesser opportunities; and we are not to expect from them hypotheses as precise, as impressive, as revolutionary and as widely acclaimed as those of, say, Copernicus or Newton or Darwin or Pasteur. And yet it is claimed for them that they do now deserve to be called *sciences* because those who practise them are seriously concerned to construct theories to explain the facts, and are self-critical and open-minded. As much as the natural scientists, they are imbued with the scientific spirit, even though their methods are more uncertain and their results looser and less well established. The social scientist is much more apt than the natural scientist to talk nonsense and to make a fool of himself. This is one of the hazards of his occupation. Yet his occupation is science.

But the occupation of the great social and political theorists of the past was not science. They did not study the facts or did so only at random; they did not construct hypotheses and test them. They deduced their conclusions from axioms *a priori* and from definitions, or they relied on what they chose to consider the common sense of mankind. They were not scientific but speculative. What is more, their aim was often less to explain than to justify or to condemn. That they seldom distinguished between their aims is only one proof the more that they were not scientists. And so it is sometimes held that their theories are much more impediments than helps to the social scientist, who need not rate his own achievements high to feel that, as compared with them, he is moving in the right direction, given that the object of the journey is to extend knowledge. Hence the need often felt by the social scientist to turn his back on these old and famous theories.

There is nothing arrogant about this attitude, with which it is easy to sympathize.[1] But there can be no real turning of the back on these old theories, whose ideas and assumptions still permeate our thinking about society and government, whether we know it or not. We are not free of them as the natural scientists are of the essences and entelechies of mediaeval and Aristotelian philosophy. We have still to come to terms with these thinkers of the past, to make up our minds about them, if we are to learn to think more clearly than they did.

Moreover, these theories were by no means entirely speculative, nor was their function always primarily to justify or to condemn. They were also, to a greater or a lesser extent, attempts to explain the facts; to explain what the social scientist aims at explaining. To examine them, as is still sometimes done, merely in order to establish how far they are internally consistent, is not an exercise of much use to the social scientist. Nor does it matter to him just which, among several different interpretations of a well-known doctrine, is the nearest to being correct. The enquiry perhaps most useful to him is an enquiry into the adequacy and relevance of these theories. How far do they provide a satisfactory explanation of what they seek to explain? How far are their assumptions and ideas useful for purposes of explanation?

---

[1] There is more that is arrogant about the disparagement of the social sciences still common in England than about the claims made for them in the United States.

Granted that the theories are in many ways inadequate or irrelevant, just why are they so? This book attempts, among other things, to answer these questions; and never more so than when it treats, sometimes at considerable length, of three among the more recent and still widely influential theories, those of Rousseau, Hegel and Marx.

The expositor and critic is bound to give what he honestly believes to be a fair interpretation of the doctrines he discusses. But, if his purpose is not to offer his own interpretation which he believes to be an improvement on others, or to pronounce in favour of one among several current versions, he is not bound to argue the case for his interpretation. Since I have been concerned much more to examine the adequacy and relevance of assumptions, ideas and arguments than to establish that Machiavelli or Hume or Marx meant this rather than that, I have refrained from defending my interpretations, except where it has seemed to me that they might strike the reader as unusual or not plausible.

Again, I have not considered every aspect of the most important theories; I have considered only those aspects which raised most sharply the issues I wanted to discuss. For example, I have not considered what Montesquieu has to say about religion and its social functions, though in fact he has a great deal to say about it and says it in the most interesting way. The points I wanted to make about religion, and its place in society, I have tried to make in discussing certain beliefs of Machiavelli and of Marx. It may well be that to someone whose field of study is the sociology of religion, Montesquieu has more to offer than either Machiavelli or Marx. Certainly, he treats of religion more elaborately and with greater subtlety than they do. But it seemed to me that their simpler and perhaps cruder treatment served my purpose better.

These theories are more than attempts to explain society and government, and more also than apologies for or attacks upon the established order. They are philosophies of life; and philosophies of this kind are often dismissed as useless or pernicious on the ground that they claim to be more than they really are.

They flourished, it is said, before the scientific study of man, of society and of government had properly begun; they pretended to a knowledge they did not possess. But now that men are beginning to see how to get this knowledge, how to study themselves and society to good purpose, they can do without these pretentious theories. When these theories are not, in the Marxian sense, *ideologies* (when their function is not to defend or challenge the interests of some class or group), they are merely personal statements. They express what somebody feels about man and man's condition in the world. Taken for what they are they may be interesting, but they must not be taken for more.

Certainly, the makers of these theories had illusions about them, and often claimed a knowledge they did not possess. I have already said in their defence that they took some account of the facts and made some attempt to explain them, and I do not suppose that the persons who call their theories 'ideologies' or 'fantasies' or 'mere personal statements' mean to deny this. I believe that these theorists took larger account of the facts and were more seriously concerned to explain them than their critics imply, but that is not what I now want to argue. Nor do I want to argue that the element of class or group *ideology* in these theories is smaller than Marxists have supposed. I want rather to insist that these theories, even when they are not attempts to explain the facts and do not serve to defend or challenge class or group interests, are more than mere personal statements; and that to call them so is grossly misleading. They do more than express personal preferences, even though preferences which many share.

Some of these theories are integral parts of a cosmology, of a sometimes elaborate theory about the universe and man's place in it; others are not. Hegel affirms that reality is an infinite Mind or Spirit seeking self-realization, an activity or process passing from level to level, and which is manifest, at its highest levels, in communities of finite selves; that is to say, in communities of men. His social and political theory is rooted in a philosophy which purports to explain everything; or alternatively (and this alternative is perhaps nearer the truth) his philosophy is an attempt to apply to all things ideas which make sense only when applied to human activities and social institutions. Others, as for example the Utilitarians, are more modest. The Utilitarians, for the most part, do not seek to improve upon or to add to the explanations of the physical and biological offered by science; with rare exceptions they say nothing about divine or immanent purposes. They confine themselves to explaining man and his social behaviour. They take man as they think he is, as a creature of desires who seeks to satisfy them as abundantly as he can at the least cost to himself. They seek to explain his behaviour and all social institutions on this and a few other assumptions about man and his environment; and in support of their assumptions they appeal above all to what they take to be the common sense of mankind. Yet they, too, are concerned to do much more than explain the facts; they too seek to criticize and to persuade. They too have a philosophy of life which is something more than an explanation (however inadequate) of how men live.

All these theories, no matter how 'pretentious' or 'modest' they may be, are elaborate philosophies which contain a large element which is not science or conceptual analysis or ideology in the Marxian sense. They are what I venture to call, for want of a better word, practical philosophies or philosophies of man; they are forms of self-expression of which it is lamentably inadequate to say that they are mere personal statements. They are neither mere exercises in psychology, statements about how men feel and think and behave, nor mere excursions into morals. They involve much more than the laying down of ultimate rules (as, for example, the 'greatest happiness' principle or the principle of 'self-realization') or even the construction of elaborate hierarchies of rules.

There is always a close connection between a philosopher's conception of what man is, what is peculiar to him, how he is placed in the world, and his doctrines about how man should behave, what he should strive for, and how society should be constituted. The connection is there, multiple and close, whether the philosopher is a Rousseau or a Hegel, who does not agree with Hume that there is no deriving an *ought* from an *is*, or whether he is Hume himself. For Hume, though he believes that no rule of conduct follows logically from any description of man and his condition in the world, offers to show how man, being the sort of creature he is, comes to accept certain rules. Man and the human condition are, in some respects, everywhere the same, and therefore there are some rules which are everywhere accepted. They are not the only rules which men accept, and are not always in keeping with the other rules. Indeed, these other rules are sometimes preferred to them. Nevertheless, there are some rules which men everywhere accept, or would accept if they understood themselves and their condition; therefore, we have only to understand what man is and how he is placed in the world to know what those rules are. This way of thinking is not confined to the natural law philosophers and Idealists; it is common to them and to the Utilitarians, and (as we shall see) there is a large dose of it even in Marxism.

In this book I am as much concerned to discuss these theories as *philosophies of life* as I am to examine critically the assumptions they make and the ideas they use in the attempt to explain the facts. And, here again, I confine myself almost entirely to what my authors have to say, attending hardly at all to the origins of their theories or the circumstances in which they were produced. I have already said enough, I hope, to show that this neglect does not come of a failure to appreciate the importance of what I have not tried to do. I have learnt much from many scholars, but the attempt to tread in all their footsteps would be absurd.

Man, as Machiavelli sees him, is self-assertive. He lives, not to seek God's favour or to serve some larger than human purpose, but to satisfy himself; he seeks security and something more, he seeks to make himself felt. He seeks reputation, to make his mark, to create some image of himself which is impressive to others. The stronger he is, the more he is willing to risk security for reputation. Man is both self-preserving and self-assertive; but Machiavelli sympathizes more with the second than the first of these needs. He values above all the two qualities which enable a man to assert himself; courage and intelligence. These are not just preferences which Machiavelli happens to have; they are rooted in his conception of what it is to be a man. Hobbes also sees man as self-assertive but sees him even more as in search of security in a world of self-seeking men; and he puts a high value on prudence and consistency of purpose. Organized society is a discipline which the prudent accept and the imprudent must be forced to submit to. Rousseau sees man as the victim of society, as a creature who has lost his integrity. Society derives from his needs, develops his faculties, and yet is oppressive to him. As a rational and moral being, man is at once the creature and the victim of society, and can be cured of the ills it produces in him only in a reformed society. Bentham sees man as a subject of desires who, unlike other animals, can compare and foresee; he sees him as a competitor and collaborator with other men in the procuring of what satisfies his desires. The proper function of rules and institutions is to ensure that competition and collaboration are as effective as possible; that they help and do not impede men in their efforts to satisfy their desires. Hegel sees man as a creature who becomes rational and moral in the process of coming to understand and master an environment; he sees him transformed and elevated by his own activities. He sees him as changing from age to age, and the course of this change as 'implicit' in his nature, in his capacity to reason and to will. Marx sees man as a creature whose image of himself and the world is a product of what he does to satisfy his basic needs; and yet he also sees him as a creature who comes in the end to know himself and the world, understanding his condition and accepting it, and who thereby attains freedom.

We have here six very different philosophies, even though there are elements common to several of them. And, though we can say of each of them that it was 'the product of its age', though we can give reasons for its appearing when and where it did, we cannot say of any one of them that it is obsolete or irrelevant. They are ways of looking at man and society which are of perennial interest; we can find traces of them in philosophies much older than the ones which now seem to us to give fullest expression to them. Man and his social condition do change from age to age but they also remain the same; and the different philosophies which men have produced reflect not only how they and their condition have changed but also the diversity of their reactions to what has not changed. Professor Whitehead once said that all later philosophies are footnotes to Plato. This may be extravagant but is not absurd, and is least extravagant when applied to Plato's views about man and society. Plato's theory of knowledge and Aristotle's logic have been superseded in a sense in which their political philosophies have not. This is not because epistemology and logic have made progress since their time as the study of man and society has not; it is because political philosophy has always aimed at something more than explanation. One explanation of what is involved in having knowledge or in reasoning may be an improvement on another. But with philosophy, in the sense in which I am now using the word, it is a different matter.

Today, in the social as in other studies, two kinds of enquiry find favour: the aim of one is to explain the facts, and when its methods are (or are held to be) adequate to its aim, it is called science; and the aim of the other is to examine the ideas and methods used in explanation and in other forms of discourse, and when those ideas and methods are of wide application, it is sometimes called analytical philosophy. The theories expounded and criticized in this book, though by no means unscientific and unphilosophical in these two senses, are also more than science and analytical philosophy. Moreover (as I have said already, though in different words) as science and analytical philosophy they are often grossly inadequate. Therefore, since science and this kind of philosophy are in favour, these theories, which are often indifferent specimens of both, are in disfavour. And even when it is conceded that there is a large element in them which is neither the one nor the other, this element is written off as an aberration, due to a failure to understand what is the proper business of science or philosophy.

The suggestion is that these theories aim at extending knowledge but do not know how it is to be extended, or that they confuse other things with the extension of knowledge. They have several purposes but fail to distinguish between them, or have purposes so vague that they are not really purposes at all. They aim at explaining the facts or at elucidating ideas or at defining rights and obligations or at persuasion; and move from one aim to the next without knowing that they have done so. They are uncertain of purpose. The present-day critic, coming upon this confusion and trained to make the distinctions these theories too often fail to make, easily concludes that, if they have some purpose beyond explanation, elucidation, definition or persuasion, beyond the purposes familiar to him (and which he does not quarrel with provided the man who has them knows what he is doing), that purpose is illusory, rooted in misunderstanding. By all means let a political writer explain or analyse or persuade, but let him know what he is doing. For, if he does not know what he is doing, he will aim at the impossible or will delude himself into believing he is contributing to knowledge when he is not or will unconsciously seek to pass off his peculiar preferences as eternal truths.

I have already conceded that most of the great political and social thinkers of the past failed to make certain distinctions now commonly made, and that they were under illusions about their theories. Yet it is a mistake to conclude that, to the extent that they aimed at more than explanation, analysis or persuasion, their efforts were pointless or useless. Their theories have another function besides these, and a function which is not less important than they are.

Sophisticated man has a need to 'place' himself in the world, to come to terms intellectually and emotionally with himself and his environment, to take his own and the world's measure. This need is not met by science. It is not enough for him to have only the knowledge which the sciences and ordinary experience provide. Or perhaps I should say, to avoid misunderstanding, it is not enough for him to have only knowledge; for I do not wish to suggest that what he needs and science and ordinary experience cannot provide is knowledge in the same sense as what they provide is so but merely comes to him from another source. Nor is it enough for him to have this knowledge together with a moral code and a set of preferences. He needs a conception of the world and man's place in it which is not merely scientific, a conception to which his moral code and preferences are integrally related. I have here in mind something more than the assumptions on which science and everyday experience themselves rest, assumptions which cannot be verified because they must first be accepted before it makes sense to speak of verification. This need is not felt by all men; and it is felt by some much more strongly than by others; but it is a persistent need. It is a need which can be met for some only by religion, but which for others can be met in other ways (unless any system of beliefs which meets it is to be called a religion). The theories examined in this book are systems of belief of this kind; or, rather, this is one aspect of them, and a very important aspect of some of them.

It would be profoundly misleading to speak of this aspect of them as if it were no more than a statement of preferences or a laying down of rules or a defining of goals. If it were only that, it would be possible to reduce it to a list; and this is not possible. A hostile or perverse critic may say that, as far as he can see, there is nothing more to it than that and a whole lot of verbiage besides, which to him means nothing. If he says this, there may be no arguing with him, beyond pointing out that it is perhaps a kind of verbiage in which he himself indulges when, momentarily, he forgets his opinions about it. When Rousseau or Hegel or Marx tells us what is involved in being a man, he is not, when what he says cannot be verified, either expressing preferences or laying down rules; he is not putting 'imperatives' in the indicative mood; he is not prescribing or persuading under the illusion that he is describing. He is not doing that or else talking nonsense. It might be said that he is telling his reader how he feels about man and the human predicament; or, more adequately and more fairly, that he is expressing some of the feelings that man has about himself and his condition. But he is not describing those feelings or just giving vent to them; he is *expressing* them, and the point to notice is that this expression takes the form of a theory about man and his condition. It could not take any other form. Thus, if it is an expression of feeling, the feeling requires systematic and conceptual expression. Only a self-conscious and rational creature could have such feelings about itself and its condition; and the theories which express these feelings, far from being statements of preference or rules of conduct passed off as if they were something different from what they really are, serve only to give 'meaning' to these statements and rules. Not that they are needed to make the statements and rules intelligible, to make it clear what the preferences are or what is involved in conforming to the rules; nor yet to justify the preferences or rules by pointing to their consequences. They give 'meaning' to them, not by explaining or justifying them, but by expressing an attitude to man and the human condition to which they are 'appropriate'; so that, even when we do not share the attitude, we understand how it is that those who do share it have those preferences and accept those rules. We do not infer the rules from the attitude, nor do we establish, in the manner of the scientist, a constant connection between the attitude and the rules and preferences; our understanding is different in kind from that of the scientist or the logician. It is neither an understanding of how things happen nor that some things follow from others; and yet it is an intellectual enterprise, a rational experience.

Man, being self-conscious and rational, has theories about himself and his social condition which profoundly affect his behaviour; theories which have not been, are not, and never will be merely scientific. They will always be more than explanations of how he behaves and how institutions (which are conventional modes of behaviour) function. And they will always be more than statements of preference or assertions of principle and attempts to justify them; they will be more than 'personal statements' and more than exercises in persuasion. I do not say that there cannot be theories about man and society which are merely scientific, nor yet that any social theory which is more than merely scientific must have this particular more to it; I say only that the need for this more is enduring, and is in no way weakened by the spread of the scientific spirit.

But, it may be asked, granted that this is so, is not the study of these old theories, insofar as they do not attempt to explain the facts or do not examine the ideas used in explanation, of merely historical interest? They may once have been persuasive but are not so today when the issues which inspired them are dead; and, to the extent that they do not seek to persuade but express what you have called attitudes to man and the human condition, our attitudes are no longer theirs. These theories, in this aspect of them, speak for their contemporaries and not for us; they belong to the past and the study of them is mere history.

To this there are two answers. Issues and attitudes change less than they seem to, for the language used to express them changes more than they do. These theories are products of their age but are also ageless; their diversity shows not only how epochs and countries differ from one another but also the variety of man's attitudes to himself and his condition. It has been said that all men (or is it all thinking men?) are either Platonists or Aristotelians; which, though not literally true, makes a point worth making. So too, in similar style, we can say that in all ages there are Machiavellians and Marxists and Utilitarians, and even men who, like poor Rousseau, despair of the future of mankind while protesting that man is naturally good.

Secondly, man is an object of thought to himself and would not have the capacities peculiar to his kind unless he were such an object. His being a person, his sense of his own identity, his feeling that he has a place in the world, depend on memory, his own and other men's, for he has rational intercourse with them and belongs to enduring communities. Man is more than just the product of his past; he is the product of memory. The past 'lives on' in him, and he would not be what he is unless it did so. Thus, for him, as for no other creature, to lose his past, to lose his memory, is to lose himself, to lose his identity. History is more than the record of how man became what he is; it is involved in man's present conception of what he is, it is the largest element in his self-knowledge.

Man, being rational and capable of self-knowledge, puts to himself two sorts of questions, and science answers only one of them. The sort of question which science answers he puts both of himself and of what is external to him; but the sort which science does not answer he puts only of himself or of creatures whom he believes to be in his own condition. And these questions which science does not answer are also not answered by analytical philosophy. They are questions which have no final answers; for the answers to them differ from age to age and, perhaps even more, from person to person. These questions which science cannot answer are often put in the same form as the questions which science can answer. We may ask, 'What is man?' meaning 'What sort of creature is man?' and look for answers to the biologist, the psychologist, and the social scientist. Or we can put the question which Pascal tried to answer in the *Pensées*, which is a different question altogether, though put in the same words. Pascal believed in God; but the need to put this question does not arise from this belief. An atheist may put it and find an answer which satisfies him, and yet remain an atheist. But the answer, whatever it is, is not a mere set of rules. The question, 'What is man?', as Pascal put it, a question which science cannot answer, is not to be reduced to the question, 'How ought man to behave?'

Political and social theories of the kind discussed in this book are

xxii   MAN AND SOCIETY · VOLUME ONE

not the only theories, nor even the most important, which attempt answers to this sort of question; and of course they also put questions of other sorts. But this is an important element in them, and still as much worth studying as any other. The putting and answering of questions of this sort is an activity not less rational and not less difficult than scientific enquiry, and neither more nor less useful. These theories have helped to form sophisticated man's image of himself. No doubt, in primitive and illiterate communities men make do without them; but then they also make do without science. To ask, as some have done, 'What is the use of these theories?' is as pointless as to put the same question of science.

Chapter 1

MACHIAVELLI

I. INTRODUCTORY

MACHIAVELLI stands outside the main tradition of European political thought. He thinks and speaks of society and government differently from the great mediaeval writers, and differently, too, from the great writers of the sixteenth and seventeenth centuries, men like Bodin and Hobbes, Hooker and Locke. The mediaeval writers were mostly concerned with problems of definition, and with deriving men's rights and obligations from these definitions. They put such questions as: 'What is the Church?' 'What is the Temporal Power?' 'What purposes do they serve?' Those purposes seemed to them to flow from the nature and present condition of man. They therefore also asked, 'What is the nature of man?' This last question was, in their eyes, equivalent to asking, 'What are God's intentions for man?' The rights and duties, both of magistrates and of subjects, derived, ultimately, from these intentions of God, from the limitations of human reason as created by God, from the condition of man following the sin and fall of Adam, and from God's conditional promise of forgiveness brought to the posterity of Adam by Christ. Mediaeval political theory was rooted in theology, and sought to explain the authority of Church and State and the limits of that authority by reference to the will of God and the nature of man as created by God.

The political theory of the sixteenth and seventeenth centuries was also, for the most part, rooted in theology. That theology was, of course, different from the theology of the Middle Ages: very obviously so in Protestant writers but also, though less so, in Catholic ones, for they too were affected by the Reformation. Yet, though the conclusions reached by these political theorists might differ greatly, they continued to use much the same methods as their predecessors had done in the Middle Ages. They put the same questions: 'What is the essential nature of man?' 'What are God's purposes for him?' And they derived their conclusions about Church and State, about the rights and duties of magistrates and priests, on the one hand, and of their subjects and flocks, on the other, from the answers they gave to these questions. They used the same method: they offered definitions, and from these definitions, they derived conclusions about men's rights and duties. These definitions were answers, not to questions about empirical facts, but to questions about the purposes of God and the essential nature of man. That is what makes them definitions: definitions in the Aristotelian sense. The political philosopher who defines the nature of man does not purport to tell us how man actually behaves but rather what his end or destiny is, what he is created for.

This method was not the only one used by political writers even in the Middle Ages, but it was the traditional method; the only method that many writers used, and the method that nearly all writers used, though they might use other methods as well. Even if we take an unusually worldly, untheological mediaeval writer like Marsilio of Padua, we find the same concern with definitions and the same belief that moral rules can be derived from them. It was a method brought to the highest point of subtlety and elaboration in a theological age, but it by no means appealed only to men who accepted what the theologians taught. And it lasted long after the Middle Ages.

Some who openly rejected the method were less well rid of it than they imagined. Hobbes spoke scornfully of the 'essences' of Aristotle and of definitions which purport to tell us what things are for, what their destiny is, what they tend towards, and do not merely point to those of their observable characteristics which distinguish them from other things. He had no use either for the definitions of Aristotle or for the mediaeval glosses upon them produced by Christian theology. Yet he too made definitions, albeit of a different kind, and drew conclusions from them about the rights and duties of rulers and subjects. His conception of human nature, so different from Aristotle's and different too from that of the theologians, is yet no more than theirs got from experience. Indeed, if we compare his idea of man with Aristotle's or even Aquinas's, it is more inadequate, less true to the facts. Hobbes puts another kind of definition in the place of the kind he rejects, and then proceeds to his conclusions. To some extent, despite his deliberate break with tradition, he uses a traditional method and even traditional ideas; he argues with the mediaeval thinkers and those who follow their example to some extent on their own terms. He tries to prove them wrong.

Machiavelli does nothing of the kind. He cares nothing for traditional arguments because he does not put traditional questions. He does not, as Hobbes and the Utilitarians do, no less than Aquinas, put these two questions: What is man? and What are his rights and duties? seeking in the answer to the first question a key to the answer to the second. He offers no definitions, and never seeks to explain why, and to what extent, subjects have a duty of obedience. He is not, in the same sense as Aquinas, Bodin, Hobbes, or Locke, a political philosopher. The question which to them seemed the most important, the question of political obligation, does not interest him. He wants to know what makes government strong, what makes freedom possible, how power is most easily obtained and preserved. In trying to answer these questions, his appeal is always to history; his books are full of examples. He seldom makes a generalization or gives a piece of advice without producing evidence in its favour.

Since he is so clearly not a political philosopher in the traditional sense, Machiavelli has sometimes been called a political scientist. He tries to support his conclusions by an appeal to the facts. He is interested in man, not as he ought to be, but as he is. True, he is concerned to do more than explain how governments function; he does not merely describe, he also prescribes; he gives advice about what should be done to create or to restore strong government. But he does not speak to men of their destiny or of ends which they, as rational creatures, are obliged to pursue. He takes it for granted that they want strong government, and confines himself to advising them how they can get it.

I think it misleading to call Machiavelli a political scientist. His indifference, when he speaks of government, to the destiny of man or to God's purposes for the 'most excellent' of His creatures, is not enough to make a political scientist of him. The Utilitarians share this indifference; they take it for granted that man in fact wants happiness, and confine themselves (so, at least, they think) to giving advice about how happiness is to be obtained. So, too, Hobbes takes it for granted that man wants security, and is chiefly concerned to advise him how he can get it. Hobbes and the Utilitarians both start from what they take to be the actual desires of mankind; they, too, are concerned with man as he is (or as they think he is) rather than as he ought to be, and the advice they give him is grounded in their estimate of what man actually is.

There is nothing specifically scientific about this attitude. A writer on politics is not scientific merely because he is interested in facts rather than ideals, and rests his advice on what he takes to be the facts. An account of what men want and what they ought to do in order to get it is not scientific merely because it is not an account of what they ought to want. It is scientific only if it uses suitable methods to establish what the facts are, what men actually do want and what experience has shown to be the most effective way of getting it. In this sense, Hobbes is not scientific, nor are the Utilitarians, nor is Machiavelli.

It is true that Machiavelli appeals to history as Hobbes and the Utilitarians do not. But he does so at random to support whatever conclusions he happens to be interested in. He has no conception of scientific method, of the making and testing of hypotheses. He never makes a systematic study of any one political order, let alone a comparative study of several. His generalizations about men and government, as also his practical advice, are the fruits of experience much more than of systematic study. They are the fruits of his experience as a civil servant in Florence and his reflections upon contemporary Italy. He uses history to support the conclusions reached by reflection on personal experience and observation. Machiavelli is shrewd, realistic, imaginative; he sees further than other men with as wide an experience as his own to reflect on. If this were not so, we should not be interested in him; we should not look upon him as one of the greatest of political writers. But to say all this is not to concede that he is a political scientist.

Of Machiavelli's two most famous books, one, *The Prince*, discusses a limited problem: how to acquire enduring and absolute power with the least effort. The other, the *Discourses*, is a commentary on another book, on the first decad of Livy's *History of Rome*. It is a series of reflections suggested by the reading of Livy, and is roughly divided into three main topics: how states are founded and governments organized; how states are enlarged by conquest and by other means; and how their inevitable decay can be prevented for as long as possible. Though these topics are discussed much more elaborately and realistically than they ever had been in the Middle Ages, they are not discussed systematically.

They are discussed for their own sake, and not in order to draw from them support for some kind of theory about the rights and duties of subjects and rulers. The discussion rests on assumptions not derived from theology and reaches conclusions which are not moral rules. Yet, untheological and morally neutral though the discussion is, it hardly deserves to be called scientific. The questions that Machiavelli puts are, of course, questions about matters of fact; the answers to them are not essential definitions in the Aristotelian sense, and they are not moral principles. They are empirical generalizations; they are based on observation. And yet they are not scientific because Machiavelli has no idea, however vague, that there are appropriate rules, that there is a proper method, for testing such generalizations. He does not do for the study of society what Galileo tries to do for the study of nature; he does not use, let alone define, methods appropriate to testing the sort of conclusions he reaches. It is only persons who follow such rules, who use such methods – or who feel, at least, the need for them and try to discover them – who deserve to be called scientists. Machiavelli felt no such need, and it is therefore misleading to call him, as some writers have done, the first political scientist – or the first since Aristotle. He was intelligent, original, penetrating and hard-headed; he had some of the qualities that go to make the good scientist. But he was not methodical and never aspired to be. Though the questions he put were new, he never seriously addressed himself to the problem of what is the best way of answering them. He wrote essays about politics, and not scientific studies, however rough, however inadequate.

When I say that Machiavelli is not scientific, I do not mean merely that many of his conclusions are questionable or even superficial. A writer who is not a scientist may sometimes be right where a scientist is mistaken. For example, I should say that Montesquieu comes much closer than Machiavelli to being a political scientist, though he too reaches many questionable and superficial conclusions. Montesquieu expresses opinions about a much wider variety of subjects, and is therefore probably much more often wrong than is Machiavelli. Though he, too, is imaginative and original, he is less hard-headed and more credulous than Machiavelli. But he does at least attempt to make a systematic study of different types of government; he takes many examples; he aims at an exhaustive classification; he is concerned about the methods he uses. We may say that his study is not as systematic as he thought it was, that his examples are not well chosen, that his classification is not exhaustive, and that his ideas about his methods are confused; we may say all this, and yet concede that he aims at making a scientific study of society, that he has some notion of what distinguishes a scientific from an unscientific study. But we cannot say this of Machiavelli. He is not, as Montesquieu is, a very imperfect social and political scientist; he is not a political scientist at all but a man of genius with considerable practical experience writing about politics.

If we compare Machiavelli, not only with mediaeval political writers but even with such writers as Hobbes and Locke, nothing is more striking than the keen interest he takes in history. Most of his arguments are supported by copious examples taken from the past and the present. But this interest in history has sometimes been misinterpreted. Some of his admirers claim for him that he was the first writer on politics to use what they call the 'historical method'. They may not claim for him that, because he uses this method, he is a political scientist; they may even avoid the term 'political scientist', perhaps because they think that only the natural sciences are truly scientific. There are many scholars, especially in England, who are reluctant to speak of the 'social sciences', preferring to call them the 'social studies'.

I no longer share this reluctance. Of course, the social studies do not use the same methods as the natural sciences, and they reach less precise and more questionable conclusions. Nevertheless, there are methods appropriate to the social studies, and I should call anyone who used these methods a social scientist. That there is still controversy about the methods does not make it improper to call the student of society a social scientist. Provided the student recognizes that his study is empirical and makes a real effort to use what he thinks are proper methods to test his conclusions, I should say that he deserves to be called a scientist. If Machiavelli had used a historical method to establish political conclusions, if he had had definite ideas about how history should be used to reach or to test such conclusions, I should not hesitate to call him a political scientist. But I find no evidence that he used such a method or had any such ideas. To support political principles with historical examples is not to use the historical method in the study of politics; it is merely to drive points home by selecting vivid illustrations.

True, Machiavelli is steeped in history. Yet, like nearly all his contemporaries, he lacks what, for want of a better word, I shall call ' a sense of history '; he lacks the sense that society changes from age to age, so that to see the past as it really was requires a great effort of the imagination. He sees history as little more than a kind of extended experience enabling the wise man to learn more about human nature than he could if he had to rely merely on his own personal experience, on his own memories. He uses the records of the past as he uses those of his own time; the historians speak to him as his contemporaries do; they tell him of what he could not see and hear for himself. He ponders what they tell him as he ponders his own memories; he is greatly indebted to them. But the past of which they speak seems to him very much like the present which he knows. Men, he thinks, find themselves again and again in similar predicaments. If their actions are recorded, others can learn from their examples and mistakes. Human nature, at bottom, is always and everywhere the same. Put a man in the same situation, and he will act the second time as he did the first, unless he remembers the consequences of the first action and decides to avoid them. History provides us with a much larger store of examples and warnings than we could otherwise have; it is the memory of mankind; it is a treasury on which any man can draw provided he has the wish to do so.

This is the use of history to Machiavelli; it is the abundant and fascinating source of practical wisdom, adding greatly to our understanding of ourselves and our neighbours. But he has almost no conception of moral and cultural change. The ancient Greeks and Romans are, in his eyes, much the same as the Italians of his own day. He does not deny that ancient Rome differs in many ways from Medicean Florence, but then so too do Venice and Milan. That the old Romans, belonging to a society profoundly different from all the states of Renaissance Italy, thought and felt in ways peculiar to themselves and difficult for him to appreciate, never really occurs to him. The old Romans are, in his eyes, merely better men than the modern Italians, braver and wiser and less corrupt. He speaks of Caesar and Alexander, and even of Moses, much as he speaks of any famous Italian of his own day whom he has not met. He might agree that men in antiquity were better than they now are, that there has been a sad falling away from the dignity, the manliness, and the courage of the past. But he does not see how different were their values, their philosophies, their conceptions of themselves and of the world.

Of necessity, by our standards Machiavelli knew little history. He knew most about ancient Rome and the Italian republics of his own day. He knew much less about the Greeks. There was little enough history in his time for anyone to know, and much of it was inaccurate. Most of it consisted of annals and not of descriptions of how institutions and custom had changed. Machiavelli could scarcely use it to deepen his understanding of how societies develop and institutions and ideas are transformed; he could use it only to deepen his knowledge of human nature.

Those who call Machiavelli a political scientist or who say that he was the first to use the historical method in the study of politics are moved to do so because they feel that he is, in some sense, an innovator. He breaks with tradition; and they are hard put to it to explain just how he breaks with it. They see that he is chiefly concerned to show how power is obtained and preserved, and that he abounds in examples taken from history. He wishes to explain the facts and uses history to help him do so. That, they think, is enough to make a scientist of him; or, if not a scientist, then a political theorist using the historical method.

They are right in saying that Machiavelli is an innovator, but they miss the sense in which he is one when they call him a scientist or a user of the historical method. I do not know what word to choose to mark how Machiavelli differs both from mediaeval political writers and the exponents of divine right and the contract theory. I might be tempted to call him a positivist, if that word were not already associated with the theories of Comte and his disciples. He does not consciously put forward any ultimate moral principles; he takes it for granted that men want security and need strong government, and he tells them how to get what they want and need, appealing always to the facts in support of his arguments. He is not to be placed in any category; he is neither Platonic nor Aristotelian, neither Stoic nor Epicurean; he cares nothing for theology and deals only in human purposes; and yet he does not, like Hobbes and the Utilitarians, rest his political theory on an explicit psychology. He does not first tell us what man is like and then argue that a certain type of government suits him best; he appeals, not to psychology, but to history. He is *sui generis*.

Machiavelli puts new questions; or rather he puts questions neglected for centuries, since Aristotle's time. What makes the State endure and government strong? How can a state already on the way to dissolution be reformed? What kinds of morality and religion strengthen the State? And he puts these questions, as even Aristotle had not done, for their own sake, and not because he needs the answers to help him solve a moral problem, to help him discover the political conditions of the good life. In putting these questions, and in trying to answer them, he makes assumptions which are either new or were never made so boldly and unequivocally before him.

It may be that he never sees clearly how these assumptions are related to one another, nor even what they are. Certainly, he does not make them explicit, nor does he use them to construct a systematic theory of government. Yet he makes them and holds fast to them. Together, they make up an attitude to life, to man and society and government, which is as little Greek as it is mediaeval. It is new in the intellectual history of Europe. In this sense alone does Machiavelli have a philosophy; he has a new way of looking at man and society rather than a new theory about them. It is so sharp and vivid, so clearly his own, so much the fruit of a single, strong, imaginative, and independent mind, that it deserves to be called a philosophy. It is a very personal criticism of life, which is the product of long reflection and great intelligence. Machiavelli's writings are not a random collection of second-hand ideas of the kind that any educated man picks up during the course of his life; they have a character peculiar to them, an aesthetic unity, because they are all the products of a highly idiosyncratic and vigorous mind. Machiavelli has a philosophy in the same sense as Montaigne has one, or even as Molière has one. Though there is no systematic theory, there is a consistent attitude, or a coherent set of attitudes. There are characteristic reactions that go easily together.

Machiavelli's philosophy is secular. This distinguishes it as much from Greek as from mediaeval philosophies. The Greeks did not distinguish the divine from the human, the sacred from the profane, as we have learnt to do since the emergence of Christianity. But by Machiavelli's time the distinction had been made, and his peculiarity is that he attends only to the human and the profane. The Greek, not less than the mediaeval, idea of man forms part of a conception of a universe in which are unfolded greater than merely human purposes. But Machiavelli is as entirely secular as Bentham or Bertrand Russell.

Machiavelli's philosophy is entirely secular, and to that extent, if you like, modern. Yet it is not entirely, nor even predominantly, modern; for Machiavelli is in some ways as foreign to us as he is to the Middle Ages and to Antiquity. His is the classic, the purest, the most self-assured, the most uncompromising, expression of an attitude to life – to human life, taken in the round, and not just to the political side of it – which is not mediaeval or ancient or modern, but belongs only to the Renaissance, and above all to Renaissance Italy, an Italy still untouched by the Reformation. It does not so much reject Christianity as turn its back upon it, and has no use either for the Greek notion of the good life or for modern faith in progress. Machiavelli is as indifferent to Christian morals as to Christian theology, whereas our morality, even when we are agnostics or atheists, still owes a great deal to the faith with which it was connected. Machiavelli is more completely un-Christian than any of the sceptical philosophers of our century. Even in the narrower field of politics, Machiavelli is as unmodern in some ways as he is modern in others. He is so partly because his moral assumptions are different from ours and partly because the kind of state with which he is most familiar, the small Italian republic, is neither feudal nor national. He is aware that there are states very different from the Italian republics, and he sometimes discusses them, and yet, when he speaks of the State, it is clear that he usually has in mind a polity essentially similar to the Florence or Milan or Venice of his own day. That is why, the better to understand his political theory, we must first take a look at the Italian republics of the fifteenth and early sixteenth centuries.

II. ITALY AND FLORENCE IN MACHIAVELLI'S TIME

Italy, in the early sixteenth century, was, and long had been, the least feudal of the civilized countries of Europe. Her towns were the largest, richest, and most independent; her civilization was the most urban and the most secular. The authority of the Emperor had worn so thin as scarcely to deserve the name of authority. The Emperor did not rule any part of Italy; he merely had better excuses than other princes beyond the Alps for meddling in Italian affairs. Less feudal than England or France, Italy was also less united, less close to becoming a single nation and a single state.

The Italian municipality or commune, when it first emerged as a privileged community, had been weak; its inhabitants had felt themselves more dependent on associations inside it, such as the guild and the family, than on the commune itself. But as the commune grew strong and developed into the city-state, these other ties weakened. The Florentine or Milanese learnt to regard himself as primarily a citizen of Florence or Milan and to set great store by such political rights as he had. The largest and most powerful community he belonged to, the city, was small; its rulers were much closer to him than would be to an Englishman or a Frenchman of that period the rulers of his country. The ordinary Florentine was more absorbed in the life of his State, better aware of what his rulers were doing, politically more restless and enterprising than the ordinary subject of the English or French King. He was much closer to thinking and feeling as a citizen. The ties that bound him to the largest community he belonged to were stronger. Even if he loved his country no better, he had more to fear and to hope for from the day-to-day actions of his rulers. He felt himself to be, as an individual, more important, precisely because his city was small and intimate. He was freer of lesser associations and also apt to be more self-centred. The Italian commune had not developed a representative system; it was no doubt too small to feel the need to do so. As it grew larger and more independent, direct government by free citizens became unmanageable unless the number of the citizens was kept small, because direct popular government must either be on a narrow basis or else must lapse into anarchy. At the same time, to maintain its growing independence, the Italian commune needed to increase its resources and to extend the territory under its control. It had therefore to multiply its subjects while restricting the number of its citizens; in other words, it had to become an oligarchy. Florence in 1494, when Savonarola restored what was called democracy, had 90,000 inhabitants but only some 3,200 citizens.

Restricted citizenship and the weakening of the old ties that bound men to guild and family caused great discontent, which one class of citizens could exploit against one another, or an adventurer against the whole body of citizens. Hence the weakness of the narrow regimes that fifteenth-century Italians called democratic, and the ease with which they were replaced by oligarchy or tyranny. Of the three greater Italian republics, Venice had by Machiavelli's time become, for good and all, an oligarchy, and Milan a tyranny. Only in Florence was there still reasonable hope of re-establishing democracy; that is to say, of making good the political rights of the less than twentieth part of the inhabitants of the city who had a hereditary claim to take part in its government and in the control of the territories subject to it.

During the greater part of the fifteenth century, Florence had been a tyranny, but an especially mild one. Her feudal nobility had long since lost most of their power, and the sharpest conflicts among the citizen body had, in the early fourteen hundreds, set the Major against the Minor Guilds, the rich merchants against the small tradesmen, the oligarchic party against the democratic. The Medici, though they belonged to one of the Major Guilds, took up the cause of the Minor ones, and used the conflict so cleverly that they got control of the State. They were not oligarchs but demagogues.

Variety and instability of government, deliberate change, remodelling of the machinery of State, were nowhere to be seen as much as in Italy. Any student of politics who, like Machiavelli, contemplated the recent histories of the Italian republic could discover more kinds of government and more frequent changes in forms of government than in all the other western countries put together. Florence had transformed her government several times in the hundred years before Machiavelli began to write about politics.

For thirty-five years, from 1429 to 1464, she had known the mild and disguised tyranny of Cosimo de Medici, who had preserved the forms of the constitution. Then, for twenty-three years, from 1469 to 1492, Lorenzo de Medici had continued to rule by Cosimo's methods, but more blatantly and arbitrarily. Lorenzo's son, Piero, fled in disgrace from Florence in 1494 when the French invaded Italy. Florentine democracy was restored that same year by the Dominican friar, Savonarola, a fearless and austere demagogue who attacked luxury and corruption. Machiavelli was twenty-five when Savonarola gained control of Florence and set the poor against the rich. He was both fascinated and repelled by Savonarola; fascinated by his ascendancy over the people, repelled by his fanaticism and political crudeness. Savonarola cared only for purifying morals; he did nothing to reform institutions or to consolidate his power. While the people listened to him, he was all-powerful; but as soon as they began to grow tired of him, the party of the rich easily contrived his downfall and death in 1498. But the rich were not strong enough to put an end to the democracy he had restored, which survived until 1512, when the Spaniards took Florence and brought back the Medici.

Two months after Savonarola's death, Machiavelli entered the State service; and it is worth bearing in mind that all his practical experience of politics was as a servant of democracy, or of what passed for democracy in sixteenth-century Italy. He was familiar by hearsay with the tyranny of the Medici, and had directly observed the fanatical omnipotence and sudden ruin of Savonarola.

III. MACHIAVELLI'S CAREER AND HIS WORKS

It would be quite beside my purpose to give an account, however brief, of Machiavelli's life. I am concerned with his ideas and not with his life or his character, except to the extent to which they throw light on his ideas. We do not ordinarily need to know how a man comes by his ideas to be able to understand what they are, but sometimes, in order to get the full significance of his theories, we need to know more than a man tells us about his purposes in constructing them. This is certainly true of Machiavelli, who was a civil servant for many years before he was a writer, and who learnt more from experience and observation than from books. Moreover, he wrote his books, and especially the most famous of them, in enforced retirement and to prepare the way, if possible, for a return to the active political life. Machiavelli wrote because he could not act; he took no pleasure in his withdrawal from politics, and was always as eager to affect a situation as to understand and describe it. Even as a historian, he put himself into other men's shoes, considering the alternatives open to them as if he were placed as they were and had to make a decision. No one was readier to praise and to blame than he was; and yet he passed his judgements nearly always as a politician and hardly ever as a moralist. He praised men for knowing what they wanted and knowing how to get it, and he blamed them for not knowing what to do or not daring to do it; he scarcely ever passed judgements on their ultimate purposes.

Until July 1498 Machiavelli was almost unknown, even in his native Florence. In that month, at the age of twenty-nine, he was appointed secretary to the Council of Ten, the second most important executive council in the Republic. The Council of Ten combined the functions of a War and a Home Office, and its secretary was therefore an important servant of the State. There were wars in Italy all the time that Machiavelli held office, and he was sent on many missions to Italian and foreign princes: to the Pope, to the King of France, to the Emperor Maximilian, to Caesar Borgia, and to other persons less well remembered by posterity. Four years after he had started his official career, it was decided that the Signoria, the chief executive council of the Florentine Republic, should have a President, or Gonfaloniere, elected for life. The man chosen to fill this post, Piero Soderini, was by way of being a friend of Machiavelli, who therefore, though only a civil servant, contrived to have a considerable say in the making of policy. Perhaps he was never as important as he later, in the days of his retirement, persuaded himself that he had been, but he was important. He was close to the centre of affairs, had strong opinions about them, and was able to get a hearing.

When the Medici returned to Florence in 1512, Machiavelli lost his job. He had served the republic for nearly fifteen years and had acquired a taste for the active political life. Though he knew that he could not aspire to govern, he still allowed himself to hope that he might be in the future what he had been in the past, an important official in close touch with the makers of policy. He tried hard to win the favour of the Medici and to get employment from them, but he was compromised by his long service of democracy. That service had not even weakened his preference for democracy. He blamed several persons – and not least Piero Soderini – for the disasters that befell the republic, but he was by no means convinced that the absolute rule of the Medici was the best suited to Florence. He merely accepted that rule because he believed that, in the circumstances, it was impossible to get rid of it; and since the Medici were restored and he wanted active employment and could get it only from them, he did what he could to win their favour. But he was never an admirer of their methods of government. He was never won over to them; his heart was never with them. He continued to believe that, where conditions allow it, democracy or free government is better than monarchy or princely rule, and he was by no means certain that nothing could have been done, before the return of the Medici, to ensure that Florence should be both free and strong enough to defend her free institutions. The Medici were right in not being persuaded of Machiavelli's devotion to their interests; they kept him out in the cold for fourteen years, merely encouraging him to write the history of Florence, and when at last he was partly restored to favour, he had only a year to live. He died in June 1527.

It was after 1512, during the years of his retirement, that Machiavelli wrote his four books on government, on war, and on history. The shortest and most famous, *The Prince*, was written in 1513, and Machiavelli hoped it would attract the attention of the Medici and induce them to employ him in affairs of State.

But *The Prince*, though its author hoped it might bring him employment, is not an insincere book; we cannot say of it that it does not contain Machiavelli's true opinions but only what he thought would please the Medici. The arguments of *The Prince* are perfectly consistent with the arguments of the much longer *Discourses*, in which Machiavelli expresses his strong preference for popular government. As has often been noticed, there is scarcely a maxim in *The Prince* whose equivalent is not to be found in the *Discourses*. *The Prince* contains only a part of Machiavelli's political thought, but that part is quite in harmony with the rest. It does not assume that princely rule is better than popular government; it merely confines itself to considering how princely rule is best established and preserved in the sort of conditions that prevailed in Italy at the time it was written. It is a well-made book, a treatise, terse and vigorous, on practical politics.

If Machiavelli had been a courtier by temperament, he would have written, to attract the favour of the Medici, a very different book from *The Prince*. He might have given the same advice but would have given it differently; he would have wrapped it up in soft words, he would have made it more palatable. Princes, not less than other men, like to think of themselves as high-minded; they like to disguise their motives and the true character of their actions, not least from themselves. The advice given in *The Prince* is too direct, too bold, too naked not to appear cynical even to persons who would be quite willing to act upon it if only they had the courage to do so. So lucid, so unadorned, so stark a book, such strong meat without sauces to soothe the delicate stomach, is not a fit offering for princes. Machiavelli was disappointed; his book did not dispose the Medici to employ him. He was, though perhaps he did not know it, above all a writer and an artist rather than a practical man; he lacked discretion, and was carried away by his theme.

Of the men whom Machiavelli visited on his various missions, none impressed him more than Caesar Borgia, an unscrupulous political adventurer and the son of Pope Alexander VI. Borgia had tried to carve out a principality for himself, and had stopped at nothing in the attempt. He had failed, not for lack of courage or skill, but because the odds against him were too great, and above all because his luck did not hold. When the Pope, his father, died, he was, at a critical moment of his career, taken ill, and was unable to do what he should have done to defend his interests. It has often been said that Machiavelli admired Caesar Borgia and took him for his model when he wrote *The Prince*.

Certainly, Machiavelli admired Borgia greatly, and the portrait of the Prince is taken from Borgia more than from anyone else. Yet Borgia was a tyrant, while Machiavelli was a partisan of popular government. Machiavelli did not believe that men like Borgia make the best rulers, or even nearly the best; he believed only that they are at times a desperate remedy for a desperate disease. And he believed that Italy suffered from that disease. The Italians had, he thought, become so depraved and corrupt that only a resolute, clear-headed, hard and unscrupulous prince could save them by uniting their country under one government. Machiavelli was too much a realist ever to have believed that Borgia could have united Italy; even if Borgia had succeeded in his enterprise, he would have made himself master of only a small part of Italy and would have had many Italian rivals to contend against. His success might have made Italian disunion even more painful to Italy than it already was. But, though Borgia could not have united Italy, anyone who could have done so would have needed to have (in Machiavelli's opinion) the qualities of Borgia; and among those qualities were several which we should call vices.

Machiavelli certainly admired Borgia, but the admiration was not unqualified. When he wrote *The Prince*, Machiavelli's feelings for Borgia were already more mixed than they had once been. Not because Borgia had failed in his enterprise, but because, when luck had turned against him, with the death of his father and his own illness, he had for a time lost his nerve. His illness had prevented his opposing the election of Pius III, and Machiavelli could not blame him for that; but Pius III had died soon after being elected, and Borgia, though at that time he was no longer ill, had allowed his partisans to vote for Cardinal della Rovere, who became Pope Julius II, and whose enmity Borgia should have foreseen. He had miscalculated from pusillanimity, and had not simply made a mistake; he had, in Machiavelli's opinion, shut his eyes to the dangers that faced him because he was too dispirited to take bold action. The portrait of the prince is not exactly the portrait of Borgia as he appeared to Machiavelli at the time that he wrote his most famous book; it is rather a portrait of what he had once believed that Borgia was. It is an idealized portrait, a deliberate embellishment, an image inspired by his reflections on what he had seen of Borgia rather than a sketch of what he really took Borgia to be. It is inspired to some extent by disappointment in Borgia, by the desire to improve on him, as well as by admiration for him.

That Machiavelli was an Italian patriot who was humiliated by the intrusion of foreigners into his country and who desired the union of Italy cannot be denied. But it would be a mistake to treat *The Prince* as a book inspired by simple patriotism. Though Machiavelli desired the union of Italy, he could hardly have believed that it was possible in his day. Did he suppose that the Medici were able to achieve it? We know that, in spite of his endeavours to win their favour, he did not admire them. They were too petty and too weak for so great a rôle. There is no evidence that Machiavelli believed that what Florence could not do might be achieved by Venice or Milan. He regarded the papacy more as an obstacle in the way of Italian union than a promoter of it. Machiavelli was a man of strong passions and vivid imagination; his zeal for Italy is unquestionable. But it is difficult to believe that he thought it possible that Italy as he knew it could be united. *The Prince* is inspired by more than the dreams of an Italian patriot; it is inspired by curiosity. Machiavelli took it for granted that strong government is desirable, and he knew that strong government is not always popular government. He was interested for its own sake in the main question posed in *The Prince*, which is this: What qualities must a man have and what methods must he use to establish a strong and enduring monarchy?

The Art of War treats of politics only in relation to war, and the *Florentine Histories* put forward no political opinions not to be found in *The Prince* and the *Discourses*. The entire political theory of Machiavelli is therefore to be found in just two works; and not only the political theory but also the philosophy of life implicit in it. *The Prince* and the *Discourses* are important not only for what they tell us about how power is to be gained and preserved; they are also important for the philosophy contained in them but never made explicit. I shall be as much concerned to expound and criticize that philosophy as the political theory which goes with it.

Machiavelli's character is of a kind that is easily misunderstood because it is so uncommon, so free from the sentimentalities and illusions in which most men take comfort. His intelligence is keen; he lays bare our baser motives with a matter-of-factness which makes us uneasy. He is imaginative and lucid. His lucidity and cynicism make him seem cold to persons accustomed to look at the world through a comfortable haze. But he is not cold; he is as much capable of passion as of cynicism. He is not a man of very wide sympathies; but what he sees, he sees clearly and in sharp outline. He has few illusions about himself and still fewer about his friends. His terse, direct, exact descriptions are disturbing to those who like the warmth of ordinary make-believe. Neither his detachment nor his passions appeal to the modern taste, especially the northern taste; he is too cold when his intelligence alone is at work, and his passions are no longer ours. What excited his admiration does not excite ours, or excites it much less. He admired singleness of purpose, intelligence, courage, and pride above all other qualities. We are more often struck by his cynicism than his admirations; for his style appears to us more the style of the cynic than of the admirer. The northern admirer is apt to enthuse, and enthusiasm is apt to be long-winded. By temperament Machiavelli is perhaps further removed from us than any of the other great political writers since the Middle Ages.

Many have found it difficult to believe that a man who could speak so cynically, and even coarsely, of his love affairs, who could describe so precisely the faults of his friends, who could discuss his own ambitions with so little reserve, could be anything but heartless or selfish. But all this may well have been an effect of pride, of a determination never to be deceived by anyone, not even by himself; and also, in part, of the bitterness of a disappointed man. He was, in fact, sincere and clear-sighted and therefore rather more loyal to his principles than most men are; and also, I suspect, (unless loyalty consists merely in a disposition to praise) not less loyal to his friends.

IV. MACHIAVELLI'S POLITICAL THEORY AND HIS PHILOSOPHY OF LIFE

I have denied that Machiavelli was a systematic thinker and that he had an orderly and well-constructed political theory. To extract a comprehensive and neat system of ideas out of his writings would be to force those ideas into a frame which was not his own. At the best we should have, not a structure designed by him, but a structure of our own built out of his materials. I have also said that he had no explicit philosophy of life, no set of opinions about man and his place in the world which he ever troubled to put together into a system. That philosophy, though it has in fact an inner consistency and a definite character, is merely implicit in *The Prince* and the *Discourses*, and is never there expounded.

I shall consider Machiavelli's political theory and his philosophy or attitude to life by discussing in turn those of his assumptions, beliefs, and preferences which seem to me most characteristic of him: his conception of the State, his belief that men are to a considerable extent masters of their environment, his interest in the psychology of rulers and the ruled, his concern for morality as a social force, his alleged lack of morality, his opinions about religion, and his preference for popular or free government.

We have seen that Machiavelli neglects the problems which seemed the most important to political thinkers before him, mediaeval and Greek. He never undertakes to analyse the concepts that politics uses; he never puts or answers such questions as 'What is the State?' 'What is law?' 'What are rights?' If we want to discover what he understands by these words, we have to see how he uses them. It is obvious that he speaks of society, government, and law differently from the mediaeval writers, and differently also from Plato, Aristotle, the Stoics and the Sceptics. But he is not himself aware of these differences, and therefore never feels the need to explain the terms he uses or to prove them more adequate than others. Though, no doubt, he uses them much as they were currently used in his own day, he gives no sign of being aware that, by doing so, he is marking himself off from the great thinkers of the past.

Though Machiavelli says nothing about the duty of obedience and the limits of authority, though he entirely neglects this perennial theme of political philosophy, he is by no means – as we shall soon see – morally neutral. He has strong preferences. The idea that he has not is an illusion created in the unwary by the tone he often affects to discuss what he likes and dislikes. Some men are better able than others to look at their own preferences dispassionately; to speak of them as if they were not their own but someone else's. Machiavelli has this ability more than most men. He has it, not because he is cold or morally indifferent, but because his sympathies, though they are not wide, are strong. He can put himself in other men's shoes, he can appreciate what it feels like not to feel as he does himself; and with this capacity there goes the ability to see himself, as it were, from the outside. He expresses his own preferences clearly and vigorously, and very often does so without attempting to justify them. He is not without deep moral preferences, but also he is not a moralizer.

1. Machiavelli's Conception of the State

In the Middle Ages political writers spoke of the Temporal Power more often than of the State. They conceived of the whole of Christendom as one vast community with two kinds of authority established in it, the Spiritual and the Temporal. By the Temporal Power they understood the whole body of magistrates exercising authority outside the Church. They saw the Temporal Power as a hierarchy of persons standing to one another in many kinds of often rather loose relations, defined by custom and not easily changed. They often spoke as if all the civil magistrates in Christendom formed one hierarchy, with the Emperor at the top, though they also knew, what was indeed obvious, that the Emperor's authority did not in fact extend over the whole of Christendom, there being other Christian princes as supreme in their dominions as he in his. All Christendom formed, in theory, one community, and yet there were acknowledged to be in practice several kingdoms inside it independent of the Emperor. Within the Temporal Power, whether it was conceived of as a single Empire or as many separate kingdoms, nobody had absolute power. Not only was the authority of the Temporal Power, taken as a whole, limited by the authority of the Church, but the authority of every magistrate within it was limited by custom and also – so it was argued – by the Law of Nature, the same for all men everywhere though modified by custom to suit the circumstances of particular peoples.

From the thirteenth century onward, these ideas were considerably altered by the study of Aristotle's *Politics* and of Roman Law, and also by the continual growth of royal power, especially in the western kingdoms. Already in the fourteenth and fifteenth centuries, we have the beginnings of the modern conception of the State. Yet the feudal idea of temporal authority as a kind of private property still persisted; as, too, of course, did the claims of the Church, the Spiritual Power, and the old conception of civil government as primarily a remedy for sin. No political thinker of the Middle Ages, except perhaps Marsilio of Padua, spoke of the State as we do now: as an all-embracing and supreme authority; as a compact, precisely articulated, centralized body, with so strong a hold on its members' loyalties that it almost seems natural to speak of it as having a mind or will of its own. The modern State, even in its federal form, is highly centralized if we compare it with the strongest mediaeval kingdom; every part of it responds much more quickly to impulses received from the centre. The rights and duties of officials and citizens are more definite and elaborate. There is either a single system of courts enforcing a uniform law; or, if there is more than one system, the spheres of their competence are strictly defined.

Machiavelli's conception of the State is already ours. He does not think of it as a hierarchy of magistrates whose authority and relations to one another are defined by custom, but as a single structure, closely-knit and all-controlling, all of whose parts respond to one centre. The State is not, for him, co-ordinate with the Church; it contains within itself (or, at least, ought to contain) all the authority there is within the territory it embraces. Only the family is prior to the State, and nothing is superior to it or not to be questioned by it. This conception of the State squares with the notion of sovereignty, as we find it fully developed by Hobbes; but it squares also with the even more modern notion of federalism, which allows of no Hobbesian sovereign. The pillar of a federal state is its constitution, which divides, deliberately and carefully, a whole mass of power among bodies whose mutual relations are defined by law. There is nothing left out of account, nothing that lies outside the sphere of the State; all authority is exercised either by the State or with its permission. From the point of view of the State, the Church is either a part of itself, a State Church, or a voluntary association whose rights are defined by it.

Of course, we do not find in Machiavelli the explicit notion of sovereignty that we find in Bodin and Hobbes; we find only the conception of the State which eventually gave birth to that notion. For the doctrine of sovereignty is a deliberate rejection of mediaeval ideas about the limited authority of government, ideas which Machiavelli not so much repudiated as ignored. Machiavelli took it for granted that the well-constructed State is all-powerful within its frontiers, enjoying the undisputed loyalty of all its citizens. He did not openly contest the authority of the Church; he merely spoke of the State as if all public authority belonged properly to it alone.

The modern, the Machiavellian, conception of the State, is not just an old Greek idea revived. Unlike the Platonic and Aristotelian *polis*, Machiavelli's State is morally neutral. It is an organized mass of power used by those who control it for the pursuit of whatever ends seem good to them. It is not thought of by Machiavelli, as the *polis* was by Plato and Aristotle, as forming the minds of its citizens, as the means to their moral improvement, as the environment enabling them to develop their faculties harmoniously. Machiavelli was not indifferent to morals; he often insisted that the State cannot be strong if its citizens are pusillanimous and dishonest. But he never tried to explain or justify it as the condition of their perfection or improvement. Indeed, he never tried to justify it in any way. He took it for granted that nearly everyone wants to belong to a powerful and respected political community. It may not be all that he wants, or even what he wants most intensely, but it is the one wish he shares with the great majority of his compatriots. The State is the society which, above all others, excites men's loyalties and ambitions. It is also, in a different but related sense, the complex of institutions which gives to that society its cohesion, its individuality, and its power. The State has a structure, and the better constructed it is, the greater its stability and its strength. Machiavelli's conception of the State is more Roman than Greek; but above all it is modern.

2. Machiavelli's Faith in Man's Ability to Change his Environment

In the Middle Ages it was taken for granted that institutions rest on custom, that time has made them what they are, and that they are not to be changed. The Temporal and the Spiritual Powers were explained as instituted by God for the preservation and redemption of man. Man's nature and his needs are unchanging, as are also God's purposes for him. The institutions of Church and State are adapted to his nature and destiny, for man is a sinful creature who may yet be saved by the grace of a merciful God. Because man's predicament is always the same, so too is the frame of his world, his institutions. The purpose of all civil institutions, of government, law and property, is to preserve man from the consequences of the evil in him; he needs to be restrained, to be saved from his own and other people's unbridled passions. To restrain him is the function of the Temporal Power. The function of the Spiritual Power, the Church, is to bring God's Word to him, offering him the sacraments and so putting him in the way of salvation. The order of the world, the structure of authority inside it, Spiritual and Temporal, is unchanging.

When mediaeval writers call institutions like government and property *conventional*, they mean that they are consequences of the Fall, of the corruption of man's nature by Adam's sin, and would never have come to exist if man had remained true to his nature as God first made him. Though they admit that government and property rest on custom and serve human needs, they do not allow that men, having made them for their use, may change them as they please. For, though they arose among men to protect them from one another, and are therefore means to security, they are also remedies for sin divinely instituted. The condition they are meant to remedy is permanent, and so too are they. They are adapted to what is enduring in the fallen nature of man.

It is enough to read only a few pages of Machiavelli to see how differently he looks at law and government. He does not deny the obvious; he knows that habits change slowly. He does not despise custom or deplore its hold on man. He even believes that states and nations decay, and that the process, if it has gone far, cannot be stayed. He is very much aware of the many obstacles in the way of anyone who, wants to make great political changes. Yet he greatly admires the man who wants to make them and knows how to set about doing so. The only purposes he takes account of are men's own purposes for themselves; and all institutions are, in his eyes, human contrivances for human ends. What man has established to suit himself, he can also change, provided he knows how.

Hence the intensely practical and yet broad and deep interest that Machiavelli takes in politics. He invites us to be enterprising and cautious. We are not, as citizens and social creatures, caught up in purposes larger and more sacred than our own; we are men living among our own kind, each with only one life to live and make the best of. We cannot attain our purposes unless we study ourselves and our social world, unless we know what is possible and what is not. Arrogance is foolish, but so too is the tame acceptance of our lot.

Men cannot do what they please with their institutions. What they can do is limited by the character of what they work with. But they can take thought and refashion what they have inherited from their ancestors; they are not bound to accept it unchanged. They must take large account of custom, and ought always to build upon it where it offers a secure foundation. Machiavelli was too much a realist to suppose that men can remodel the State as they like to achieve whatever purposes they have in mind. He knew that innovators and reformers are exceptional men, apt to be misunderstood by their contemporaries and frustrated by the inertia and stupidity of the herd. Yet he believed that they could, if they chose the right moment and the right methods, achieve a great deal.

For all his caution, Machiavelli exaggerated the extent to which men can change their institutions to suit their ambitions and ideals. He took the Roman and Greek historians literally; he believed what they told him about Lycurgus, Solon, Romulus, and Numa Pompilius; he had no means of separating the mythical from the true in their stories. The founders of states are, he said, to be counted among the greatest of men, if the states they found endure. He believed that history provides many examples of founders and restorers of states, of men who, almost single-handed, set up new political societies or transformed old ones. He seems also to have believed that, at least in the parts of the world best known to him, in the Mediterranean countries, the power of the elect, of heroic natures, to create and to reform had been greater in the past than it had since become. There men had grown corrupt, and, the more corrupt men are, the more difficult it is to find a remedy for whatever weakens the State.

Machiavelli's ideas about how states are created and reformed may seem to us rather too simple. We may protest that the deliberate creation or reform of a political system is much more likely in an advanced than a primitive society, and that it is truer today than ever it was in early Greece and Rome that systems of government are human contrivances for human ends. We may also be readier to admit than he was that our ability to make exactly the changes we want is severely limited, that political reforms always have consequences not foreseen by their makers, that achievement always falls far short of intention. The social structure is more complicated than Machiavelli imagined it to be, and the political structure is only a part of it; our understanding of it is imperfect, and when we act upon it, we can never rely on getting from it precisely the reactions we want. Nevertheless, we are still perpetual reformers, trying to adapt our institutions to our purposes; though with different and perhaps larger reservations, we still share the faith which Machiavelli was the first among modern political writers to take for granted.

M. Renaudet has noticed that Machiavelli was interested only in political reforms.[1] To explain the disorders to which states are liable he often pointed to rivalries between the rich and the poor. Indeed, it would have been difficult for a Florentine not to do so. But he proposed no social reforms; he did not think it important to keep inequalities of wealth within limits. He had no strong feelings for or against any class, with only one exception – the feudal nobles, whom he abominated. Thus, on the whole, he accepted the social order as it was. He noticed that a prince, to increase or preserve his power, must treat different classes differently; their attitudes to government differ and so too must the attitudes of government to them. He was not unaware that forms of government and types of social order are closely connected; he could see that a wealthy commercial city cannot be governed in the same way as a poor and simple agricultural community. Yet he sought only political remedies for whatever seemed to him defective or evil in the State.

He disliked the feudal nobles, not because they were rich or raised up high above other classes, but because they weakened the State; they were not, as he saw them, a privileged class inside the State so much as a privileged class against the State. They had usurped some of the prerogatives of the State; they had rights of private jurisdiction and private war, and as long as they had them, there could not be a powerful State. Machiavelli disliked the feudal nobles only because they had made private rights of what belonged, or should have belonged, to the State. He thought it desirable that they should lose these rights, but he did not want to deprive them of anything more.

There is also another way in which the modern reformer differs from Machiavelli. He often believes, as Machiavelli does not, in progress. He believes in more than the remedy of abuses; he believes in indefinite progress. He is not primarily interested in strengthening the State or in putting off, for as long as possible, its inevitable decay. He has some conception, more or less vague, of a desirable social and political order, and, though he admits that men may never reach it, or not for a long time to come, he believes that they can approach indefinitely nearer to it. He may or may not believe that this progress is inevitable, but he believes that it is at least possible. Whereas Machiavelli, like several of the philosophers and historians before the Christian era, believed in cyclical change.

No doubt, there are men today who are reformers and who yet do not believe in indefinite progress. They may reject the very idea of progress, or they may, without rejecting it, think that indefinite pro-

[1] Augustin Renaudet: *Machiavel.* 2nd edition. Paris, 1956.

gress is unlikely. If they do not reject the very idea of it, they may hold that the forces likely to impede it are stronger than the forces likely to favour it. Yet they may still be reformers. They may hold, quite reasonably, that they ought to do their best to improve the world even though it is unlikely, in the long run, to be a better place than it is now. They may, by their efforts, ensure that, at least for a time, it is better than it would have been without those efforts.

But they may reject the very idea of indefinite progress. They may hold that, as society changes, so too do men's values. They may argue something like this: 'If one generation act to improve society by certain standards, they help to bring into existence other standards which move their descendants to make changes which by the earlier standards are not improvements. Though, no doubt, there are some standards common to all epochs and all societies, it is seldom by reference to them that an epoch or society which claims to be superior to another can justify its claim. By the standards common to Englishmen in the tenth and twentieth centuries, modern England is no better than the England of a thousand years ago.' And yet even those who argue like this can still be reformers, and not unreasonably; they can have their own standards, and can seek to live by them as well as they can, leaving it to later generations to look after themselves.

These reformers who, for one reason or another, do not believe in indefinite progress still differ greatly from Machiavelli. Their scepticism rests on a conception of social change quite foreign to him; they think of it as going on endlessly, neither repeating itself nor coming indefinitely closer to some desirable goal. They do not believe, as he did, in cyclical change; they do not believe that there is a natural or *normal* course of growth and decay through which all states move unless some force external to them prevents their doing so. In the last two hundred years, most believers in a *normal* course of social and political change have also been believers in indefinite progress; they have seldom been attracted to the idea that social change is cyclical.

It may be that one reason for this is the great accumulation of historical knowledge; we know too much about too many very different types of society to believe that there is a normal cycle of change which they would all complete if external causes did not destroy them prematurely. We know too much to believe that long ago other societies passed through the phases through which our societies are now passing. But history does not, in the same way, prevent our believing in progress. It may be that the more steeped we are in history, the less inclined we are to believe in progress. I do not say that it is so, but I suggest that it may be. And yet history does not, in this case, clearly refute us, as it does in the other. There is overwhelming evidence against the belief that all social and political change is cyclical except when the community involved in it comes to an untimely end; there is nothing like the same clear evidence against the belief in indefinite progress.

Since Machiavelli believed that all states, unless external causes disrupt them, pass through the same cycle of change, from youth through maturity to decay, he thought it the mark of a great statesman that he gave his State a solid constitution, prolonging its maturity for as long as possible. He saw this maturity as the period of the State's greatest strength and vigour, when it is least likely to succumb to external blows. Just as a man may be struck down in his prime, so too may a state, if it is exposed to destructive forces of exceptional power; but the greater its vigour, the greater its expectation of life.

Machiavelli took this idea of cyclical change from Polybius. It is easy to see what makes it attractive. Renewal and decay are the law of life, of the vegetable and animal kingdoms, and men have always been apt to argue by analogy from the biological to the political. Though there is nothing about political change, as they experience it, to suggest that it is cyclical, they are ready to apply to it ideas suggested to them by the changes they see in themselves. There are some beliefs which, given the state of our knowledge, come easily to us, though there is no real evidence of their truth, and which we later abandon only with difficulty, after we have accumulated overwhelming evidence against them and have come to understand the significance of that evidence. It is now easy to see that one belief of this kind is belief in cyclical change, and perhaps in the future it will be as easy to see that another is belief in indefinite progress.

Today we have a conception of political and social change foreign to Machiavelli; we see it as unending, unrepetitive, and all-embracing, transforming all communities. This conception does not logically require belief in indefinite progress, but is compatible with it.

3. The Psychology of Rulers and the Ruled

Machiavelli does not enquire, as Hobbes and so many other political thinkers were to do, into the psychology of natural man, into human nature as it might have been outside organized society. There is, with him, no argument from the psychological to the social and the political. He is not concerned to show, as Hobbes is, that man, since he has by nature such and such characteristics, can get security only under a certain type of government, nor yet to prove, as Locke tries to do, that man, by reason of his nature, has rights which can be made good only if he is governed with his own consent. Nor does he hold, with Aristotle, that man has a nature which is fully realized only in the State, where he becomes actually what he is potentially. We never find Machiavelli speaking as if man were somehow more true to his essen-

tial nature in society and the State than outside it. Though he sometimes hazards opinions about universal human nature, they are with
him merely remarks made by the way. No important political conclusions are derived from them. He takes it for granted that men,
without the discipline of government, would know nothing of justice
and honesty, but he does not labour the point or use it to justify
government.

Machiavelli is interested, not in natural man, but in social man; man
as citizen, soldier, prince and public official. He is interested, above all,
in political psychology, in the passions and opinions which inspire
political behaviour. He is interested both in individual and in mass
psychology. In this respect, he is a precursor, not of Hobbes, Locke and
Rousseau, but of Montesquieu, Burke and Tocqueville.

There is nothing specifically modern about this interest in political
psychology. When I say that Machiavelli was, in this respect, a precursor of Montesquieu and Burke, and not of Hobbes and Locke, I am
merely pointing to something about him that distinguishes him from
the political theorists of the Middle Ages and of the sixteenth and
seventeenth centuries. Both Plato and Aristotle were interested in political psychology, as well as in essential human nature. They saw that the
passions and prejudices that inspire political behaviour differ in different types of State. So, too, did several of the Greek and Roman
historians.

Given the questions which Machiavelli was concerned to answer, it
is easy to see why he should have been so much interested in political
psychology. He wanted to know how states are established, how they
grow strong, and what causes them to decay. To ask 'How ought this
State to be governed?' was, in his eyes, equivalent to asking 'What sort
of government should it have to make it enduring and strong?' At
the same time, he knew that conditions are not everywhere and at all
times the same; he knew that what makes some states strong weakens
others. He saw connections between political institutions and political
psychology. He took it for granted that men are, at bottom, very much
alike in all societies, or at least that, though they differ considerably as
individuals, much the same types are to be found everywhere. Your
Caesar differs from your Pompey, and yet you must expect to find men
of their types in any society. Machiavelli did not trouble to consider
how far what is common to all mankind is due to all societies being in
many respects alike and how far it consists of inborn characteristics; he
merely took it for granted that much the same types of men are to be
found in all societies. He took this for granted, and yet at the same
time, and not inconsistently, believed that the passions and motives
inspiring political behaviour differ considerably from State to State.
Where there is popular government the type of man that gets power
is apt to be different from the type that gets it in a closed oligarchy or

monarchy. The attitude of the citizen to public affairs and to his government is different in a democracy and a dictatorship, though men in both communities can be sorted out into much the same psychological types. We can imagine some men – as, for example, Savonarola or Hitler – getting power only where certain quite exceptional conditions hold, and we can imagine others – Caesar, perhaps, or Washington – getting it under much more varied circumstances. Different circumstances bring out different sides of a man's character; and so we can say that the qualities needed to make a Roman dictator and a President of the United States are different, even though we believe that Caesar had them all.

I am tempted to say that Machiavelli was the most political of all the great political theorists, that he confined his interest almost entirely to man's political behaviour. As we shall see, he was not indifferent to morals or to religion. Quite the contrary. But he was more concerned to discover what makes the good citizen than what makes the good man, and cared more for the political effects of religion than for what it is in itself. As I hope to show later, his concern for religion was closer to being exclusively political than his concern for morality, and yet his concern for both was primarily political.

We cannot blame a man for confining his interest to one part of human and of social life, but we can blame him if he speaks as if it were the whole of it or the most important part. Machiavelli is one-sided, not because his interest in man and society is limited, but because he seems not to understand how limited it is. He is more than one-sided; he is also untouched by much that is human. Man, as he depicts him, is a creature concerned above all to impose his will on other men or to impress them; he is primarily a political animal, though in a sense different from Aristotle's. He is not political as being capable of realizing his potentialities only in a political community; he is political as being a lover of power and reputation, as being self-assertive, as being a creature who strives to achieve his ends by controlling others, and whose dearest wish is to raise himself above them. No doubt, these qualities are much more to the fore among leaders than among the people generally. But, then, Machiavelli, to the extent that he is interested in the individual for his own sake, is interested in the man who achieves · or aspires to political greatness. Though he does not say, as Nietzsche was to do, that ordinary men exist only to give scope for the activities of heroes, his interest is confined mostly to heroes and would-be heroes, and his heroes are not poets or artists or philosophers but only men of action. He does not exactly despise the humble; he merely ignores them, except in the mass, when they begin to count politically. He does not ask what the State does for them, beyond giving them security; he is not interested in the sort of men they are or the lives they lead. And yet he is interested in the men he thinks of as great or as aspiring to greatness; he is interested in them because of what they are in themselves and not only because of the political consequences of what they do. He admires Borgia for being the sort of man he is as well as for trying to establish a powerful State.

4. Machiavelli's Concern with Morality as a Social Force

It is to *The Prince* that Machiavelli owes his reputation, and especially his evil reputation. At the worst, *The Prince* has been called a wicked book; at the best, a book not concerned with morality. And yet, as Villari and others have shown, there is no unscrupulous maxim or repulsive advice in *The Prince* whose equivalent is not to be found in the *Discourses*, a milder, fuller, and less offensive book. It is easy to accuse Machiavelli of immorality or of cynicism. No doubt, he sometimes was immoral, in the sense that he advocated courses which must be condemned by anyone who accepts certain very common beliefs about how people should behave. No doubt, too, he was often indifferent about matters which most people think morally important. It is not only useless, it is even impertinent, to try to defend him against some of the charges levelled at him. He had rather a good opinion of himself, and also an acute sense of the ridiculous. If he had lived to hear his accusers, he would have been indifferent to most of them, and amused by some. Frederick the Great, who both took his advice and denounced him for giving it, would probably have been a favourite with him. He would probably have found most ridiculous of all the people who have taken it upon themselves to defend him. It was no part of his ambition to be thought a good man by respectable persons.

I certainly do not wish to defend Machiavelli against the charges of immorality or cynicism. It is a charge that can be brought, on occasion, against many important politicians and political writers; and its being brought more often against Machiavelli than against others seems to me not to matter very much. It is, I think, more important to notice that few writers about government and society have had as much as Machiavelli to say about society's need of good morals; he had some new and also true ideas about the social functions of morality.

In the second chapter of the first book of the *Discourses*, Machiavelli, discussing the origins of states, says that the sentiments of justice and honesty arose among men after they had chosen to live under chiefs for their common protection. Though this argument is not repeated in his other works, it is nowhere denied; and it would, I think, be fair to say that he believed that there is no morality prior to society. He believed that men, if subject to no discipline, would seek to satisfy their appetites by every means open to them, restrained only by fear. Before law and government have bridled them, men are creatures of passion and reason; but they are neither moral nor immoral. It is the discipline of law that makes them honest and just. Take this discipline away, and they soon lapse into selfishness, dishonesty, and injustice.

It often happens, when men are observed to share one belief, that they are taken to share another, because the observer mistakenly supposes that the two beliefs are logically connected. It has been noticed that Machiavelli and Hobbes both look upon justice as an effect of law; and therefore, since Hobbes (so it is said) believed that men are always self-regarding and that positive law is the *only* measure of the just and unjust, it has sometimes been taken for granted that Machiavelli did so too. The assumption is gratuitous; the first belief does not entail the second, and there is no evidence that Machiavelli held them both.

Hobbes went to great trouble to make his meaning clear, to prove that, from first to last, man, savage or civilized, amoral or moral, is entirely self-regarding. Man is just and honest in civil society because it is there made worth his while to be so; but his purpose is always the same, the pursuit of his own good, which is peace for the sake of felicity; and felicity is continuous success in satisfying desire. From first to last, man lives for himself alone. We can know that Hobbes thought this because he went out of his way to drive the point home.

Machiavelli tells us only that men are by nature immoderate, and that, without the discipline of law, they are neither just nor honest. He never undertakes to show, nor anywhere takes it for granted, that honesty and justice are refined forms of egoism. To hold that morality is an effect of law and social discipline is not to be committed to hold that man, by necessity of his nature, is always selfish, or that there is no difference between merely obeying the law and having a sense of justice. For example, Rousseau believed that man in the state of nature is a mere creature of appetite, and that only life in society, by putting him under the discipline of law and opinion, makes him capable of justice; and yet Rousseau was emphatically not a psychological egoist. Nor did he equate justice with legality.

But I must take care not to suggest that Machiavelli stands closer to Rousseau than to Hobbes. In Rousseau's writings there are, as there are not in Machiavelli's, several arguments meant to show how the discipline of social life makes man moral and just. Where Hobbes and Rousseau are explicit, coming to opposite conclusions, Machiavelli is silent. The state of nature, which means so much to them, means nothing to him. Machiavelli is no more to be classed with Rousseau than with Hobbes. All that can be fairly said of him is that he believes that honesty and justice, and their opposites, are qualities acquired by men in society, and that he always speaks of these qualities, as we all do when we have no theoretical axe to grind, in ways which do not imply that they are refined forms of egoism or that justice is merely obedience to positive law.

Yet the critics who say that morality, to Machiavelli, is something different from what it is to most people, are not entirely wrong. There is some truth in what they say, but they exaggerate. They do so because they misunderstand the distinction he makes between what he calls 'virtu' and ordinary goodness. Since Machiavelli thinks 'virtu' indispensable to the citizen and the State, and sometimes says that goodness is harmful to them, it is easy to conclude that he makes a sharp distinction between private and public morality, between what makes good men and what makes good citizens. This, I am sure, is a mistake; there is a distinction, but less sharp and more subtle than is often supposed.

By 'virtu' Machiavelli means vitality, or energy and courage without regard to their objects, energy and courage both for good and evil; and by goodness he means what most people of his time meant by it, namely, the qualities generally admired in European society. Most of these qualities – honesty, justice, devotion to duty, loyalty, and patriotism – are, he thinks, necessary to the good citizen. So that the 'virtu' proper to the citizen is not energy and courage for good and evil indifferently, but for good alone; that is to say, displayed in honest and just causes for the public good.

That Machiavelli thinks a high level of private morality necessary to the State is shown by what he says about the Swiss and the Romans. Of the peoples of his own time, he admires the Swiss most; he argues that they are free and formidable because they have a high sense of duty to their neighbours as well as to their country. The Romans, he says, lost their liberty because they neglected their duties as citizens; but it was the same causes that made bad citizens of them and that corrupted their morals. Nobody is more interested than Machiavelli in the moral causes of political strength and weakness. This is what we should expect, for no one with his interest in psychology could neglect the moral factor or suppose that private and public virtues are not closely related.

But Machiavelli is not a Christian moralist. He is, as he has often been called, a pagan. He dislikes some of the qualities most admired by the whole-hearted Christian. He dislikes excessive humility; he dislikes asceticism, and patience under injustice; he likes a man to have a proper sense of his own dignity, to resent an insult even more than an injury; he has a high notion of what man owes to himself as well as to his neighbour. Meekness is an invitation to others to be unjust, and therefore a bad quality in a citizen. He approves of ambition, of the passion for worldly fame, because he takes it for a mark of vitality; and the State needs strong men. All citizens should be honest, just and patriotic; but the ablest of them are most likely to make full use of their talents under the spur of ambition. Ambition is dangerous; but it is also necessary, if the State is to be well served. The problem is not to destroy it but to direct it into proper channels. In the independent and self-governing State, the State whose citizens are free, ambition and public spirit sustain one another. Machiavelli believes that the desire for fame increases men's fortitude and courage. Hence a certain distaste for Christianity, the religion that teaches humility and unwordliness.

It is the *worldliness* of Machiavelli, much more than his belief that the end justifies the means, which makes the morality he commends so unmediaeval and unchristian. He admires the ancient Romans more than any other people. What he admires most about them is their fortitude in adversity, their strong sense of public duty, their readiness to make great sacrifices for the republic; and all this, not for the sake of eternal happiness, but from motives of honour and patriotism. The Roman felt that he owed it to himself and to others to live with courage and dignity, and when he sought fame, he sought it in serving his country. Machiavelli does not admire the man more occupied with the condition of his own soul than with his neighbours and his country.

The qualities admired by Machiavelli are, for the most part, the qualities in men which make for strong political communities. But it would be a mistake to suppose that he admires these qualities only for their political effects. That is not the impression that his writings, taken as a whole, create on the unprejudiced reader. He admires the Romans for being the sort of men they were, and not only because Rome was powerful. Because he is at pains to show how their virtues made Rome formidable, it does not follow that he cares for the virtues only for their political effects; any more than it follows that Christian moralists who tell us that the reward of virtue is heaven approve of what they call virtue only on account of its reward. Machiavelli admires the greatness of Rome and the virtues of the Romans; he believes that the virtues produced the greatness, and perhaps also that the greatness encouraged the virtues. Since he speaks of both with admiration, it is to read more into his words than he puts there to suppose that he cares for the virtues only for the sake of the greatness they produce.

The truth is that the order of Machiavelli's moral preferences is different from ours, and even more different from that of the mediaeval Christian. How he differs from the mediaeval Christian I have already tried to explain; and now, in order to make his position, as I see it, clearer, I shall try to show how he differs from us. He admired courage, intelligence, and resourcefulness much more than we do, and kindness and modesty much less. He liked men who are true to the passions they really feel, who dare to live the lives that seem good to them, who are not slaves of opinion. He despised the man who is honest and mild, not from principle, but from timidity. He did not say, with Shakespeare, that conscience makes cowards of us, but he did believe that we often think we are acting conscientiously when in fact we are merely afraid. He was apt to speak contemptuously of persons who refrain from crime only because they fear the consequences of it; and this has too often been mistaken for approval of crime. He admired courage, intelligence, and tenacity of purpose wherever he found them, even in the criminal, and he expressed his admiration boldly, as people no longer care to do.

In saying all this, I am not seeking to make him out better than he was. My only concern is to make his position clear. He was, I dare say, too ready to mistake the promptings of conscience for cowardice. Whether a man is courageous or cowardly, he will more readily do something dangerous which he believes to be good than something dangerous which he believes to be evil. The horror that a man feels at the thought of committing what he believes to be a great crime, even when he is strongly tempted to commit it, ought not to be confused with fear of the consequences. Though this horror has something of fear in it, it is fear of a special kind. It is fear of the act more than of its consequences. If we compare him with Plato or with any of the great tragedians, ancient or modern, we cannot say that Machiavelli had a deep insight into the mind of the criminal. But that, after all, is not a harsh judgement to pass on a mere political theorist.

Machiavelli, who set no great store by veracity, seems to have admired people who have no illusions about themselves, who can themselves face the truth even though, from policy, they hide it from others. And he had no pity for those who fail because they are poor in spirit, whether their ambition is noble or criminal; he had no pity for them, not because he worshipped success, no matter how obtained – for he was never as vulgar as that – but because he admired singleness of purpose, and the courage, subtlety, and resourcefulness which so often bring victory when to the timid defeat seems inevitable. He could speak of failure with sympathy and respect, provided it was not an effect of cowardice or stupidity. He could also condemn success (as he did Caesar's) when a man gets power for himself by destroying freedom and corrupting the State. He was not interested in an eternal or universal morality; he approved the most strongly the moral qualities that make political societies free and strong, and individuals enterprising, bold, and public-spirited.

5. Machiavelli's Attitude to Religion

Nothing separates Machiavelli more sharply from his mediaeval predecessors than his attitude to religion. He was concerned with it only as an influence on political and social behaviour, as a system of beliefs and ceremonies strengthening some motives and weakening others. He put founders of religions even higher on the roll of honour than founders of states. All founders of religion are, in his eyes, worthy of honour, provided the religions they found support the kind of morality he admires or finds useful. His attitude to religion, unlike his attitude to certain moral qualities, is entirely utilitarian. We have seen that he valued honesty, justice, courage and patriotism for their own sake as well as because they make the State strong, but religion he valued only for what it brings, for the morality it promotes. The man who cares more for his relations with God than with men, the man who is truly pious in the Christian sense, was distasteful and perhaps incomprehensible to him.

He approved of the religion of the Romans because, in his opinion, it encouraged virtues useful to the republic and created ties to draw citizens closer together, producing supplementary loyalties to strengthen their patriotism. He even claimed for the Romans that they had been more religious than other peoples, and therefore less easily corrupted and more devoted to the State. Roman piety bridled the passions and directed them to ends useful to the republic; it kept morals pure and strengthened social ties, reminding men of their duties to their families, their neighbours, and the community. Though Machiavelli cared little for Christian piety, he cared a great deal for the old Roman kind; for the kind which is not reverence for a Being infinitely greater than oneself but a decent respect for the forms of worship and sacred myths of one's own people. This kind of piety is more a matter of practice than of faith.

Since Machiavelli's time, we have learnt to distinguish between dogmatic and undogmatic religions; between religions preaching doctrines which their adherents are required to accept and religions which impose no doctrines and require little more of their adherents than their taking part in certain ceremonies. No doubt, for many of its adherents even a dogmatic religion consists mostly of ceremony and ritual; they pay lip service to the doctrines without understanding them and without admitting, even to themselves, that they do not understand them. They are comforted and encouraged, not by doctrines which mean nothing to them, but by forms of worship. And yet, where religion is dogmatic, though there are many who take part in it in the same spirit as they would do if it were undogmatic, there are others who take the doctrines seriously. In their case, religion does not serve merely to strengthen loyalties and affections useful to the community; it may, and often does, bring them into conflict with the community, or it absorbs spiritual energies which else might be devoted to it. Machiavelli did not distinguish, as we do now, between dogmatic and undogmatic religions, but he did have a sense of the difference between them, as his different attitudes to Christian and Roman piety show. And he preferred undogmatic to dogmatic religions.

Yet his conception of religion, even of undogmatic religion, is inadequate. He speaks with great respect of founders of religion; they are more to be admired even than founders of states. But it is the dogmatic religions, rather than the undogmatic, that have founders: Buddha, Christ, and Mohammed. The origins of the older, pre-dogmatic religions are unknown to us. They may in fact serve to strengthen communal loyalties but they were not deliberately created for this purpose. The dogmatic religions arose when men had become more sophisticated; they arose along with philosophy; they were attempts of man, no longer satisfied with the simple pieties and amorphous beliefs of primitive societies, to provide himself with a coherent and comprehensive picture of the world and of his place in it. Dogmatic religion is a response to a need which arises in man when he has become self-conscious and self-critical, and critical also of the society in which he lives; it is essentially ' unworldly '.

Even men for whom religion is much more a matter of practice than of doctrine, if they are truly pious, do not share Machiavelli's attitude to religion. Religion is, to them, something valued for its own sake and not for its political effects. It is a communion with others which is deeply moving, even when it has little or nothing to do with explicit beliefs. They see in religious ceremonies the solemn expression of feelings which they deeply respect. No doubt, they also see religion as something which brings men closer to one another, deepening the emotional ties between them, adding colour and dignity to their lives, and filling them with a sense of awe for what is permanent in the human condition. Yet they value this communion for its own sake without asking themselves whether it strengthens the State. Men need ceremony; they need to come together to give ritual expression to emotions shared in common. They need to hold up to outward reverence certain common aspects of life; they need to honour the ties that bind them to one another; they need to clothe life in ceremony.

It may be that Machiavelli understood these needs; he certainly understood how greatly men are governed by the imagination. And yet, though he understood the need for undogmatic religion, he does not appear to have shared the piety even of the undogmatic. He believed that Roman piety was useful to the republic, but he does not seem to have admired piety, even of the Roman kind, for its own sake, as he admired courage, intelligence, tenacity and public spirit. He was by temperament almost entirely irreligious. Certainly, he was quite without sympathy for the man who feels intensely the need for a faith to live by and a personal relation with God. He knew, of course, that there are such men, but he did not understand their need.

When Machiavelli died in June 1527, ten full years had not elapsed since Luther had nailed his theses to the church door at Wittenberg. Both *The Prince* and the *Discourses* were written before Europe had heard of Luther. We do not know how Machiavelli would have reacted to the Reformation if he had lived long enough to take account of it. Yet it is not pointless to make a guess. Machiavelli was nothing if not definite in his opinions, and his attitude to religion is clear enough to make it worth while considering how he might have reacted to Luther's attack on the Church and the Papacy.

Though Machiavelli was repelled by Savonarola's fanaticism, he approved of his condemnation of corrupt and worldly priests. Religion, if it is to do what it ought to do, if it is to strengthen social ties and encourage virtues useful to the State, must be held in respect, and it will not be respected unless priests live exemplary lives. Machiavelli would almost certainly have sympathized with Luther's denunciation of papal and ecclesiastical abuses. Nor did he care, for its own sake, for papal supremacy inside the Church. He was concerned only with the social and political effects of religion, and not with the organization of the Church, and there is nothing in his writings to indicate how he believed that the Church should be organized so as best to ensure that religion had the desired effects.

Machiavelli would probably have condemned Luther for challenging old beliefs. He would not have done so because he was attached to those beliefs, but because he disliked disputes which might weaken the State. Religion should draw men together and not divide them. If Machiavelli had found that men could in practice differ in their religious beliefs and yet share a common devotion to the State, he would presumably not have minded how much they differed. The old Romans had not all shared the same beliefs; they had taken part in the same religious observances in spite of considerable differences in their personal beliefs. Machiavelli presumably cared nothing for uniformity of belief, merely as such. He would not have blamed Luther for not sharing established beliefs. But he probably would have blamed him for the sort of attack he made on those beliefs, for helping to create an atmosphere where it was difficult for men to have different religious beliefs without coming to blows. Luther was not content to abandon the old faith; he felt the need to denounce it. He raised passions which weakened what were, in the eyes of Machiavelli, the primary loyalties, to the family and (above all) to the State. He may not have intended to do this, but that is what in fact he did. It was not enough for Luther that he should abide by his own opinions; he wanted to proclaim them to the world and to pour contempt on the opinions he rejected, thus confusing men and bringing them into conflict with one another and with their rulers. To denounce abuses which debase religion is praiseworthy, to hold privately to beliefs different from the established ones is allowable; but to set people quarrelling furiously over obscure points of doctrine unintelligible to most of them is both absurd and dangerous. This, I suspect, would have been Machiavelli's reaction to Luther.

Though Machiavelli, who did not care what people believed provided their beliefs were not harmful to the State, was not intolerant, he was not a believer in liberty of conscience. He neither asserted nor denied it, for the issue was never brought home to him. It would no doubt have seemed absurd to him to try to force beliefs on others on the ground that they are necessary to salvation. He says nothing to suggest that he would have condoned persecuting beliefs on any other ground than their being harmful to society. Yet he does not assert man's right to hold and publish whatever beliefs he chooses, short of committing slander or libel or inciting to violence. He says nothing about freedom of thought and speech and publication, and there is no evidence that he cared for it either for its own sake or for its consequences. We can say that in practice he was not intolerant; but we cannot say that, as a matter of principle, he was either for or against toleration. He lived before the era of religious wars and dissensions, and so we must not speak of him as if he had taken a stand on an issue which was gradually raised to the point of being a clear issue only during that era.

Machiavelli disliked the Papacy entirely for political and Italian reasons. He was too much a realist to suppose that Christianity could be replaced by the undogmatic national cults of antiquity, by anything like the religion of the virile and public-spirited old Romans whom he admired so much. Though he said that Christianity made virtues of some qualities harmful to the State, he admitted that it encouraged others indispensable to it. Men need some religion, and in Europe they could scarcely have any other than Christianity. Machiavelli did not object to the claim of the Roman Catholic Church to be the one true Church, the universal Church. Whatever he may have thought privately of the claim, he was not concerned to deny it publicly. He did not contest the Pope's spiritual authority over all Western Christendom, though he strongly disliked papal or priestly interference in temporal affairs and always spoke of the State as if its authority within its own territory were unlimited. Yet he never troubled to put forward any theory about the proper relations between Church and State. There was no need for him to do so; the issue was not a live one in Italy in his time.

The popes of his day were not perhaps to be taken seriously as spiritual rulers trying to extend the authority of the universal Church at the expense of princes and republics. They were formidable in Italy much less as rulers of the Church than as rulers of the papal states. Machiavelli disliked the Papacy because he saw in it the chief obstacle to the union of Italy. The popes were too weak to unite the country, and yet were unwilling to let anyone else unite it. He resented their political influence, which was so much greater than the size and resources of the papal states gave them a right to. If he resented their spiritual authority, it was not because they were using it to limit the Temporal Power (for they had never been less inclined to use it for that purpose); it was because they were using it to push the interest of the papal states at the expense of other states in Italy. They held a trump card denied to the other players competing for political supremacy in Italy; and this Machiavelli objected to, not because he wanted fair play, but because he thought that the Pope's ambitions, as a temporal ruler, were bad for Italy.

Machiavelli, though himself probably without religious beliefs, was clearly not an enemy of religion – not even of dogmatic religion. Christianity, by his standards, was by no means the best of religions; but that does not mean that he wanted to weaken its hold on men, for he had no hope of anything better taking its place. He was personally without religion but not therefore against religion. He saw in religion chiefly a means of discipline, and what to many people is the heart of religion meant nothing to him. There have been avowed atheists who have understood better than he did what Christianity and the other great dogmatic religions mean to the faithful.

6. Machiavelli's Preference for Popular or Free Government

Machiavelli's severest critics, who have accused him of immorality, cynicism, and even superficiality, have not denied his strong preference for popular or, as it was often called, free government. He admired the Roman Republic, not the Roman Empire. As democracy was understood in his own day, he was a democrat. He did not want every adult male in Florence to take a part in government, but he did want the artisans and small traders to do so as much as the great merchants and the nobles. Popular government or political freedom meant, in his day and country, government responsible to the whole body of citizens and not to all adults within the State. Within the citizen body were included most native Florentines carrying on an independent business, and the excluded, apart from women and children, were mostly foreigners, servants, and other dependents. Thus the citizens, though only a minority of the people, included most of the native-born men with (to use an expression once popular in England) 'a stake of their own' in the country, and who could therefore be expected to be patriotic and independent, and to take a keen interest in public affairs.

Freedom, as it was understood in Machiavelli's time, did not include liberty of conscience. Champions of freedom in his day were not much concerned to protect the rights of dissident minorities or of individuals who rejected commonly received principles. There is a wide difference between the freedom desired by Machiavelli and the liberty expounded by John Stuart Mill. Yet Machiavelli had a high regard for personal dignity and independence. We have seen that he greatly admired the Swiss because they were free and uncorrupt. He ascribed their freedom to their self-respect and independence of spirit combined with a strong sense of duty to their neighbours and their country.

Many people who have not shared our concern for liberty of conscience, who have not even conceived of such a liberty, have put a high value on independence of spirit. The Athenians, in the fifth and fourth centuries before Christ, the Romans under the republic, the English long before they had learnt to be liberal and tolerant, were remarkable for their love of independence. They respected a man who stands for his principles, who does not bow to the multitude, who has the courage of his convictions. It is important to distinguish this respect from concern for liberty of conscience. The Romans had no tenderness for purveyors of what they took to be perverse or immoral opinions; they did not admire the man who rejects principles respected in his community time out of mind; they abhorred the iconoclast. They did not respect the man who, for conscience' sake, challenges the most cherished beliefs and principles of his community; they respected only the man who stands by those principles when most other men, swayed by passion, have lost sight of them. They admired integrity; they admired moral courage; they admired the man able to stand alone against the multitude. They could do all this without caring in the least, or even having any idea of, what we call liberty of conscience. This is the independence of a free people, as Machiavelli understood it. It is to be found wherever there is a strong tradition of popular government or of popular participation in government; it is even to be found among many primitive peoples, whereas concern for liberty of conscience is something altogether more sophisticated and more rare.

We have seen that the man who could write *The Prince* could also count Julius Caesar among the worst of tyrants. Now Caesar, as much as any man that ever lived, possessed 'virtu' in the Machiavellian sense; he had energy and courage enough to serve the greatest ambition. He was intelligent and resourceful; he could easily deceive others but had few illusions about himself; he desired fame and strove to make the world suit his purposes. He, if anyone, should be a hero to an admirer of power and of unscrupulous courage used to establish a strong and enduring empire. Yet we find Machiavelli, who could praise a petty adventurer like Caesar Borgia, condemning an incomparably greater and more important man. Machiavelli's reason for condemning Caesar is that he destroyed Roman liberty when he might have saved it. A man aspiring to fame should, he said, wish to be born in a corrupted State, not utterly to spoil and subvert it, as Caesar did, but to new-model and restore it. Caesar's crime was that he took advantage of corruption to get power at a time when it was still possible to restore liberty; and liberty cannot be restored except by destroying corruption. If Caesar had lived in Renaissance Italy and had used the same methods to get power, Machiavelli would not have condemned him, as he did not condemn Borgia.

It is astonishing what large claims Machiavelli makes for free government. We are told in the second chapter of Book Two of the *Discourses* that 'experience shows that no state ever extended its dominion or increased its revenues, any longer than it continued free'. This claim is bold to the point of extravagance; history does not bear it out. Machiavelli's argument in support of it is worth noticing, for it is more typical of the late eighteenth century than of the early sixteenth. What makes a state powerful, enterprising, and prosperous is, he says, the citizens' steady preference for the public good; but this preference is nowhere as likely as in a republic, because the public good is the advantage of the majority, whose will, in a republic, must always prevail. This perhaps too simple argument reads almost as if it came straight from Rousseau.

Machiavelli makes other and more modest claims for the people. Unrestrained by law, they are capable of enormities; but not more than princes are. They are good judges of men; better usually than princes, who often prefer servility to independence of judgement. Easily misled when they hear only one side of a question, the people are good judges of the merits of alternative policies put to them by rival orators. They are impetuous and need guidance; they must have good leaders whom they trust. They are less often moved by avarice than princes, and less given to jealousy and suspicion. Popular government, in the eyes of Machiavelli, is clearly something nobler, more generous, more enterprising than monarchy or oligarchy. It is the form of government best suited to a vigorous and healthy people.

Though Machiavelli says nothing about the rights of the individual or of minorities, he does say that freedom thrives on controversy. Now, controversy will not thrive except where there is real independence of judgement. Roman liberty, he said, was preserved for centuries by the unceasing conflict between patricians and plebeians. That conflict turned on the Agrarian Law, on the question of how property in land should be distributed; and the disputes it led to in the end destroyed

liberty. This, says Machiavelli, has led many people to conclude that
faction destroys liberty; but the conclusion is facile, and only partly
true. Faction can destroy liberty, and in the end did destroy it in
Rome; but Roman liberty would never have survived so long if the
plebs had not successfully challenged patrician supremacy. Anyone
can understand that faction easily grows bitter, and that if it grows
too bitter freedom is destroyed. What is equally true, but less obvious,
is that, where there are no disputes to divide men and make them
rivals for power, there cannot be freedom.

Machiavelli, when he used this argument, was not thinking of the
competition for power between rival parties, the competition which is
supposed to preserve freedom' in modern democracies; he was thinking rather of a division of offices between different classes in the community, with each class jealous of its rights and critical of the others.
Yet, at bottom, his conception is not very different from ours. Freedom
is preserved by a competition for power kept within bounds by respect
for law, and also by a common loyalty to the State. This competition,
so long as the law is respected, does not weaken the State but makes it
stronger, because it requires vigilance, energy, and courage in the
competitors.

Though Machiavelli preferred popular government to any other
kind, he thought it difficult to establish, and almost impossible to
revive, once corruption had destroyed it. It is the best and strongest
of governments, but not therefore the most common or the best suited
to most states. When a people have become corrupt, the mere revival
among them of the institutions they had when they were free will not
restore their freedom; because a corrupt people will misuse the instruments of freedom. The institutions needed to reform a corrupt state –
and reform, for Machiavelli, means the restoration of freedom – are
different from those that maintain freedom in an uncorrupt State.

Freedom can, he said, be restored either gradually or by violence;
gradually, when some wise and farseeing person guides the State
slowly back to freedom, persuading the people of the need for change;
and by violence, when the change is made all at once and the opponents
of democracy are ruthlessly cut down. Machiavelli thought it unlikely,
though not impossible, that either method would succeed. The rulers
of a corrupt State profit too much from the power they hold to allow
a reformer to take it away from them peacefully and by degrees. Moreover, the kind of men most apt to use violence are not likely to use it
to restore freedom. Freedom is their pretext rather than their aim.

Machiavelli therefore did not condemn monarchy. When a people
are corrupt, they must, for their own good, be subject to a single
powerful ruler. Incapable of freedom, they must still have order, and
must therefore get it in the only way open to them. Machiavelli preferred an absolute to a feudal monarchy, thinking it better that the

people should have one master than many. As a citizen of a great mercantile city, which had long been the cultural as well as the financial centre of Europe, he heartily disliked the feudal nobility. He approved of the efforts of the kings of France to increase their power at the expense of the nobles. Yet, even here, he was moderate; for he also approved of the supreme courts of law in France, the *parlements*, whose activities very considerably limited the royal power. For the States-General, the French equivalent of the English Parliament, he had no sympathy. As the French *parlements* were hereditary corporations of lawyers and the States-General were the nearest thing in France to a body representing the whole nation, this preference may seem odd in an avowed admirer of popular government. It is not, however, as odd as it seems, for the *parlements*, while they restrained the monarchy, sympathized with its endeavours to make France law-abiding, united, and strong, whereas the States-General were dominated by the nobles and the priests, who cared more for the privileges of their class or order than for the good of the State.

7. *Machiavelli's Reputation for Immorality*

I have tried to explain just how much and for what reasons Machiavelli cared for morality, why he thought religion necessary and also why he preferred popular government to every other kind. How then did he acquire his world-wide reputation as an immoral writer? How is it that the word 'Machiavellian' is nearly always used in a pejorative sense? Is it really possible that for centuries people have so misunderstood Machiavelli as to take him for the opposite of what he was – as to take him for a cynical apologist of tyranny?

No doubt, Machiavelli has been misunderstood; and partly by his own fault. It is not his fault, of course, that most people who have read him have read only *The Prince*, which gives a much stronger impression of cynicism than the *Discourses*.[1] It is also not his fault that his preferences are not ours, that he is hard where we are soft, cold where we are sentimental, awed and fascinated by what we grudgingly admire. He had not our respect for the over-tender conscience, nor our patience with the well-meaning fool. He felt a strong sympathy for the man of principle, capable of heroic self-sacrifice, but not for the man tormented by scruples. It is often said that the West is no longer truly Christian. This may well be true as regards our beliefs (or lack of them) about God and the universal order. But our morals are still largely Christian, much more so than our beliefs; and it is there that we

---

[1] There is no advice, however unscrupulous, given in *The Prince* that is not repeated in the *Discourses*. But in the *Discourses* there is much more besides, to reconcile Machiavelli with the modern reader.

differ most from Machiavelli. He was not much repelled by Christian theology, for he gave little thought to it; he was repelled by Christian morals, which seemed to him to rob men of the pride and self-assertiveness needed for a full life. It takes some imagination and even an effort of will on our part to persuade ourselves that Machiavelli was perhaps not less concerned than we are that men should behave well but merely had different ideas about what constitutes good behaviour. Though we can, by taking thought, come to realize this, it is still not easy, when we come upon some of his opinions in all their nakedness, to avoid being shocked by them. Machiavelli is so explicit, so bold, so eager to drive home conclusions repulsive to us that the impression of cynicism remains even after reason has sought to dispel it. Of course, by our standards he sometimes was immoral; but he had his own standards which mattered as much to him as ours do to us.

Yet there is another, a more specific and damaging, charge of immorality brought against him: that he excused in the powerful, in those who rule, actions which, when others do them, are plainly wrong, even by his own standards. This charge is not that he was mild where we are severe, or treated as innocent what we condemn; it is that he argued that what is wrong for most people might be right for some. This charge has been generalized (and weakened) into the accusation that he held that the end justifies the means.

There is nothing really vicious about the doctrine that the end justifies the means. It all depends on the end. The Utilitarians, for instance, taught that an action is right if it promotes the greatest happiness of all whose happiness is in question; and this, of course, is to say that a particular end (the greatest happiness) justifies any means to it. Many people have thought the Utilitarians wrong-headed, and some have found them dull; but scarcely anyone has accused them of immorality. We may hold that some actions are wrong no matter how good their consequences, and yet not be shocked by someone who holds the contrary opinion.

Nor is it vicious to argue that some people, because of their special position in society, may do things which it would be wrong for any-one, not in that position, to do.

Our trouble with Machiavelli is that the end he puts forward as justifying all means to it seems to us lamentably inadequate. To say with Bentham, 'Do anything that promotes happiness', sounds well enough; we may not agree but we are not shocked. But to say, with Machiavelli, 'Do anything that establishes the State's power more firmly or increases its extent', sounds downright wicked. It would have sounded wicked in the Middle Ages, and at almost any other period of European history; and it still sounds wicked today.

But, in justice to Machiavelli, we ought to remember that, in his opinion, the *only* end that justifies any means to it is the establishment or preservation or enlargement of effective power, of the State, which is, he thinks, the first condition of order, and also, under favourable (though admittedly rare) circumstances, of freedom as well. Machiavelli admired the man who gets power, by whatever means, to make a weak and corrupt State strong; but he condemned the man who gets it by weakening the State, by corrupting it, or by taking advantage of its corruption when it is still possible to restore freedom.

Where, as in sixteenth-century Italy, there was almost no freedom to destroy and almost no hope of restoring it, Machiavelli was willing to support a tyrant in all his wickedness, provided that the wickedness was really needed to bring order and unity to the country. Hence the portrait of the single-minded, bold, subtle, unscrupulous prince, who will stop at nothing to get what he wants, and who is justified (in the eyes of Machiavelli) because what he wants is to bring all Italy under his rule and to drive the barbarian invaders out. The prince may be ambitious and evil, more concerned to get power for himself than to do good to Italy; and yet he ought to be supported and his crimes condoned, because, if he gets what he wants, Italy will have domestic peace and orderly government.

It is true that Machiavelli cared for national greatness for its own sake, as well as for its good effects. He wanted Italy united, not only that Italians might be saved from anarchy, and from the miseries and humiliations that anarchy brings, but also that Italy might be great. This ideal of national greatness, which meant so little in the Middle Ages, has been important among nations of European stock since the sixteenth century; and Machiavelli was the first great exponent of it. His maxims were, with rare exceptions, accepted almost without question by sixteenth-century governments. Deceit, treachery, and cruelty were common in high places, not only in Italy, but also in the northern countries; though the Italians were perhaps bolder in their crimes and less hypocritical about them. There was nothing Machiavelli wanted his prince to do that had not already been done many times over. He did not corrupt the rulers of Europe but merely found excuses for their corruption. And we must not forget that he condemned their stupidity, which caused them to commit many unprofitable and therefore unnecessary crimes. It is the clever tyrant who can most often afford to be mild, because, when he is severe, he is so to good purpose. He makes each crime go further, and so can afford to commit fewer crimes.

Machiavelli was not much condemned until the seventeenth century. By that time the hold of many governments over their subjects had been greatly strengthened; the modern State was more solidly organized and relations between states more regular, and therefore more honest. Richelieu, who wanted national greatness for France just as much as Machiavelli wanted it for Italy, found that he could achieve it without resorting to many of the crimes committed by Italian tyrants in the early sixteenth century. The *Political Testament*, attributed to him, condemns what Machiavelli excused. Princes, it says, ought to keep faith with one another, even when it is not their interest to do so. France was by this time so united and powerful a kingdom that her rulers could more easily distinguish between immediate and permanent interests; they could see that it was worth while, in the long run, making considerable sacrifices to preserve France's good name. The predicament of an Italian ruler of the early sixteenth century, fighting for survival against unscrupulous enemies, was altogether different. Honesty was a rather better policy in Richelieu's Europe than in Machiavelli's Italy. By Richelieu's time, Europe was almost ready to accept a new version of the law of nations from the hands of Grotius; to admire it in theory and to try to make the facts look as if they were in keeping with it. Machiavelli's advice was still sometimes taken, but his reasons for giving it were roundly condemned. He had become the whipping-boy of philosophic statesmen.

8. *Machiavelli's Great Omission*

I have not, I hope, neglected any important aspect of Machiavelli's political theory. That theory is not a systematic whole, but a set of assumptions and opinions about man, society, and government which reveal what is, taking it all in all, an extraordinarily fresh, sharp, intelligent, secular, many-sided, and realistic philosophy of life. Machiavelli had precursors, no doubt, as all great thinkers and writers have; the further we carry our researches, the clearer it becomes that no man is as original as at first sight he may appear. Nevertheless, it is with Machiavelli that modern social and political theory really begins. Indeed, he is often more modern in outlook, more untheological, less *a priori*, and more down-to-earth than many of the great men who come after him.

But there is one omission which cannot help but strike anyone who has studied his writings at all closely. Though Machiavelli knew that the future lay with the larger States and therefore wanted Italy to become one of them, he gave almost no thought to the problem of how a great State should be governed. His scattered comments on the government of France, the only great State he knew at all well, shrewd though they are, amount to little. Still less did he consider what institutions might be necessary to establish or preserve or restore freedom in a large State. The kind of popular government he had in mind and approved of had never existed except in small republics. He was not interested in representative government, which alone makes popular government possible in large States. Though he loved free-

c

dom, the only free institutions he took serious account of could work only on a small scale. And yet he also loved Italy, and wanted her to be great. We never find him, like Rousseau, arguing that popular government is possible only in small States; nor did he prefer small to large States. Yet, though he knew that small States could not survive in face of the large ones, he was not made anxious for freedom by this knowledge. He never succeeded in reconciling his two strongest passions: for political freedom and for the independence of Italy. Indeed, he never even felt the need to reconcile them.

Chapter 2

LIBERTY OF CONSCIENCE

EUROPEANS, on both sides of the Atlantic, are apt to speak of freedom as if it were something peculiarly European, or at least of European origin, though the peoples of Asia and Africa are now also coming to understand and desire it. They speak as if the concept of freedom, born in Greece, perfected in Christianity, and realized in practice through institutions developed by the English, the French, the Americans and other western peoples were Europe's gift to the world. They speak also as if the attainment of freedom were the supreme achievement of mankind; from which it seems to follow that the liberal peoples of European stock are, if not inherently superior to others, at least more advanced than they are.

The sophisticated Chinese or Indian, learned in the traditions of his own country, will perhaps be struck by the arrogance of this claim. He will perhaps be moved to protest that freedom has been valued by other than European peoples long before they began to be influenced by Europe. Freedom is as much Asian, as much African, as it is European; it is human. Men have set store by it in all kinds of communities; it is, and long has been, a value acknowledged everywhere, though not everywhere in quite the same terms. Europeans are merely being provincial when they claim that freedom is now thought desirable in Asia and Africa only because the Europeans have taught other peoples to know and desire it. The world now speaks of freedom much as the Europeans first learned to speak of it; the modern vocabulary of freedom is largely European. But freedom, though it now wears European dress, is not therefore peculiarly, or even originally, European.

This protest against European arrogance and provincialism is not misplaced. The Europeans, in this matter of freedom, have made altogether too large and too simple a claim for themselves. The love of freedom is rooted in sentiments and habits to be found everywhere in the world; it is, in essence and origin, no more European than Asian or African. Those who say that man is by nature free because he is rational are, I think, right, though they sometimes read more into this dictum than is acceptable. It may not follow that man ought to be free because he is rational; but it canot be denied that, unless he were rational, he would not put a value on freedom. He is provident and critical and self-critical; he organizes his life; he becomes attached to a way of life or strives to achieve an ideal, and makes a claim against

45

other men that they should allow him to live as seems good to him or to strive for what he finds desirable. He does this in Asia and Africa as well as in Europe and America.

All this is true. The peoples of European stock have made too large and too simple a claim. And yet there is a claim which they could make, and which perhaps they intend to make, even though they seldom find the right words for it. Freedom is not a simple idea. Or perhaps it would be better to say that the word is used to cover several ideas, which are closely connected and easily confused, but which need to be distinguished from one another. I think it can be claimed for the Europeans that they have done more than other peoples to define and elaborate these different, though closely connected, ideas of freedom, and also that they have produced most of the institutions which make it possible to realize them in large and complex communities. Moreover, it can be claimed for one of these ideas, much more confidently than for the others, that it is originally European; I mean the idea of liberty of conscience, which is scarcely to be found even among the Greeks. It is an idea which slowly emerges in the West in the course of the sixteenth and seventeenth centuries; and yet to-day, in the eyes of the liberal, it is this liberty which is the most precious of all.

This revised claim made for the Europeans is more modest than the other. But it is not quite as modest as it may at first appear. The definition and elaboration of moral concepts is not a mere exercise in lexicography and logic; it is not even a merely intellectual operation. In the process of examining our values critically, we enlarge and refine upon them; and we do this also in the process of acquiring the institutions which help us to realize them. For example, we cannot say that what the English-speaking peoples understood by freedom in the sixteenth century is precisely what they now understand by it, except that they now use different words to define it and different institutions to preserve it. By applying their minds to it, by disputing about it, and by aiming deliberately at its preservation and enlargement when reforming their institutions, they have, for better or worse, greatly changed their conceptions of it.

Though my present purpose is to explain how the idea of liberty of conscience emerged in Western Europe in the sixteenth and seventeenth centuries, I am not interested, for its own sake, in the question of origins. It is merely that I believe that one of the best – and sometimes even *the* best – method of getting a firm grip on a moral idea is by seeing how it arose and by contrasting it with the other ideas closely related to it. There were champions of freedom and martyrs for it long before anyone stood up for liberty of conscience, and these were also advocates of toleration. How then does liberty of conscience differ from other forms of freedom? And how does it differ from mere toleration?

In all societies there are limits to what men will put up with from one another and from those set in authority over them; in all societies it is admitted that men ought not to be prevented from doing what the law, in the broadest sense, does not forbid, and ought not to be compelled to do what the law does not require. As Hobbes insisted, law and freedom are correlative terms. We can agree with him here without also agreeing that law is properly defined, as he defines it, as command. Wherever there are accepted rules of conduct, there is some idea of freedom; or, in other words, wherever men recognize obligations, they also ordinarily claim that they ought not to be compelled where they are not obliged. It is not merely, as Hobbes said, that they are in fact free to do what the law does not forbid; it is also that they are held to have the right to do it, in the sense that any attempt to prevent them is condemned. Freedom, in this sense, is not the mere fact that there is no obligation or compulsion within a given sphere; it involves the notion that interference is wrong. Freedom is therefore the right to do what is not forbidden and to refrain from doing what is not required. In this obvious and important sense, there is freedom wherever there are obligations, or accepted rules of conduct; and there are such obligations or rules in all societies.

Again, in all societies the authority of rulers is held to be limited. Either it is not recognized that they have authority to make laws, or it is held that, if they have it, the authority is limited, legally or morally. In primitive societies rulers are bound by custom; their functions are judicial and executive rather than legislative. If they disregard custom, they are held to have acted oppressively. Where the ruler's legislative authority is admitted, it is nearly always held to be limited by a higher law. The doctrine that the ruler has a legally unlimited right to make law is scarcely older than the seventeenth century, and is in any case confined mostly to philosophers and lawyers. And even they, with rare exceptions, admit that the right, though legally without limit, is not unlimited morally. Everywhere, among non-Europeans as much as among European peoples, it has been widely held that rulers do not make but merely enforce the law, or that their right to make law is limited by a higher and unchanging law, or (where law and morality are distinguished) that it is their moral duty not to make laws which are immoral. These doctrines, since they set limits to the authority of rulers, are assertions of freedom.

In all societies man has a sense of his own dignity. He feels himself entitled to certain courtesies, he resents insults, he resents interference. He resents it, not only because it frustrates his desires, but because it humiliates him. As a social creature, he is both dependent and independent; he cannot live without others, and must serve them and be served by them. But his dependence is regular; it is subject to rules which both bind and protect him. Outside the sphere of his depend-

ence, he is independent and is jealous of that independence; he is
watchful to preserve it, more for the sake of his dignity than because
he expects material advantages. This is as true of primitive as of
civilized man, and as true of civilized man in the East as in the West;
it is true of him in all kinds of communities and under all forms of
government. If we bear this in mind, we can give some meaning to
the assertion often made that man is 'by nature' a lover of freedom.
True, he is 'by nature' other things as well which often prevent his
being free.

By freedom is also meant a man's right to take part, directly or
indirectly, in running the affairs of his community. This is political
freedom. There is nothing specifically European about it. Among
primitive peoples all over the world, there has quite often existed a
form of tribal democracy. Or perhaps it would be nearer the truth to
say that in simple societies, government, such as it is, is apt to be
mixed; it often has elements of monarchy, oligarchy, and democracy
about it. Nor is the popular element in government confined, except
in Europe or where European influence is strong, to primitive societies.
Indians claim that in their country, before the coming of the British,
there were powerful village communities in which oligarchy was often
very much tempered by democracy. There is nothing surprising about
this. In non-industrial societies, the village is often almost self-supporting, and is also, to a considerable extent, self-governing. The local
rulers, who are not mere agents of the central government but enjoy a
considerable autonomy, may, of course, be oligarchs, but they need
not be. Authority may be widely diffused in the community, and the
men who have it may be quickly responsive to popular opinion. The
central government of a great empire may be despotic and yet allow
a considerable measure of popular control at the village level. Ottoman
rule was not merely despotic, it was also arbitrary and oppressive, and
yet the Christian village communities subject to the Turk were largely
self-governing and to some extent democratic. The Turk was chiefly
interested in gathering taxes, in money and in kind; and, provided he
got what he asked for, he cared little enough what the Christians did
with themselves. Even in the West, in the mediaeval manor, the serfs
had some powers of self-government; there were some matters which
they decided for themselves or in consultation with their lord or his
officers, and the same was true in Russia before the great emancipation
of 1861. There is nothing peculiarly western about popular government
in this rudimentary sense.

The most that can be claimed for the West – and it is a large claim –
is that it has evolved institutions and ideas making possible popular
government and the protection of individual rights in very large and
complex communities. The western peoples, by their subtle and careful
analyses of moral, legal, and political ideas, by their systematic and

lucid codifications of law, and above all by developing courts having strict procedures and high professional standards, courts of law independent of the other branches of government, have made possible the precise definition of rights and their scrupulous and impartial protection. Custom alone, or custom combined with a rudimentary judicial process, may protect the individual and the family adequately in simple and slow-changing societies; but where society is complex and changes quickly, where men depend for the necessities of life, not on a small village community most of whose members are known to them, but on a vast and intricate economy, freedom, in the sense of the secure enjoyment of rights, must be precarious, unless judicial processes are elaborate, refined, scrupulous, and free from interference by the executive. There must be what western jurists have called the rule of law.

The rule of law, in this sense, is also necessary if democracy is to be possible on a large scale, if intimidation and corruption are to be prevented, if the ordinary citizen is to have a truly independent vote.

I have spoken of two kinds of freedom, the secure enjoyment of established rights (or freedom from arbitrary interference) and the right to take part in running the affairs of the community (or political freedom), which are not specifically European, even though it is nations of European stock who have evolved the ideas and institutions making possible their realization in vast and complex communities. I have also spoken of a third kind of freedom, liberty of conscience, which is peculiarly European in a sense in which the other two are not. By calling it European, I do not mean to imply that only Europeans desire it and set a value upon it, or that only Europeans are capable of realizing it. I mean only that, for a variety of reasons which have (so far as I know) nothing to do with any racial or inherited characteristics peculiar to peoples of European stock, it first emerged among them. It is the least common, the most recent, and the least easily understood and established form of freedom. And yet, where it is established, it is apt to be considered the most precious of all freedoms. Precious above all for its own sake, though precious also for the sake of the other two kinds. For in the modern world, where the power of governments over the bodies and minds of their subjects is so enormously greater than ever before, neither political freedom nor the enjoyment of established rights can be really secure where there is no liberty of conscience.

Liberty of conscience is the right to hold and profess what principles we choose, and to live in accordance with them. Like any other right, it is not unconditional; it is limited, as all rights are, by other rights and duties, and also by the need to ensure that some people do not so use it as to deprive others of it. The liberal admits that I can rightly be forbidden to live according to my principles, when by doing so I injure other people, and that I am not entitled to obtrude my principles upon them when they would rather not listen to me. I can also sometimes be rightly forbidden to give public expression to my principles, if by so doing I provoke violence, even though I have no intention of provoking it. Whatever the right we exercise, we have a duty to consider the consequences to others of what we do. But they too have a duty to act so as to enable us to exercise our right. For example, where a decision has to be taken in common, and our principles are relevant to that decision, they ought to listen to us when we expound those principles, and ought not to turn deaf ears to us on the ground that they find our principles shocking. The right to profess what principles we choose implies the right to criticize the principles we reject, and both these rights are limited in similar ways.

Liberty of conscience was not admitted in the Middle Ages, and even the Athenians, for all their passion for freedom, scarcely knew it. The Greeks were a highly critical and intellectual people; they discussed many problems quite freely, and were capable at times of remarkable tolerance. So, too, though in a lesser degree, were the Romans, especially after they had absorbed Greek influences. Indeed, the Romans, though less inventive, less imaginative, less critical and intellectual than the Greeks, were not less open-minded. Scepticism and tolerance were at times as widespread among the educated classes in the ancient world as ever they have been in the West. Yet the ancients did not value liberty of conscience as we have learnt to do. Why was this so?

I cannot give a confident answer to this question. But I am struck by the fact that, if we consider how liberty of conscience came to be valued in the West, we notice that it was first asserted and cherished in an age of strong beliefs. It was first asserted among peoples who adhered, as the Greeks and Romans did not, to dogmatic religions, among peoples who had been taught for centuries that nothing was more important than to have the right beliefs, and who had recently become divided in their beliefs beyond hope of ever again reaching agreement. To Europeans in the West it seemed to matter enormously, not merely how men behaved, but what they believed. It mattered that they should hold sincerely the right beliefs and not merely that they should speak respectfully of traditional beliefs. This was, no doubt, the source of fanaticism and persecution, but it was also, I suggest, the source of a new conception of freedom. Liberty of conscience was born, not of indifference, not of scepticism, not of mere open-mindedness, but of faith. 'Faith is supremely important, and therefore all men must have the one true faith.' 'Faith is supremely important, and therefore every man must be allowed to live by the faith which seems true to him.' These are two quite different arguments, and yet it is not difficult to see how the first gradually gave way to the second in a part of the world which had long been accustomed to think of itself as a single community of the faithful and now found itself divided into several. This new conception of freedom emerged out of controversies which raged in a divided Christendom about the limits of toleration. These controversies, in their turn, were closely connected with disputes about the proper relations between Church and State in the only part of the world where such disputes were possible. The idea that men could belong to two communities, separate from one another and each supreme in its own sphere, was peculiar to the West; it was not accepted in the eastern part of Christendom, where the Spiritual was subordinate to the Temporal Power, and it was inconceivable outside Christendom. I want now to consider these disputes about the relations between Church and State and about the limits of toleration, and to show how a new conception of freedom slowly emerged out of them. I must go back for a moment to mediaeval times, but only for a moment.

I. TRADITIONAL CONCEPTIONS AND THE REFORMATION

1. The Middle Ages

In the Middle Ages the rights of the Christian against authority were often and vigorously asserted, but those rights did not amount to what we should call liberty of conscience. The Christian was held not to be bound to obey commands contrary to the Word of God; he was said to be bound in conscience to obey God rather than man. Yet this claim on his behalf did not go so far as to say that he was responsible to God alone for his interpretation of that Word; it did not make him the final judge. In practice, the claim was made against the Temporal Power, and was a weapon used by champions of the Church against that Power. It was never made against the Church. No doubt, both Popes and lesser priests were often criticized. There were also disputes about where final authority in matters spiritual lay inside the Church. But it was not disputed that it did lie in the Church. God's Word is above all human laws, but the only authoritative interpreter of the Word is the Church.

The authority of the Pope inside the Church was often challenged. The mediaeval Church had grown strong under the wing of the papacy, and had done great service, cultural and moral, to the peoples of western Europe. But in the fourteenth century, owing first to the removal of the Popes to Avignon and then to the Great Schism, the prestige of the papacy had declined rapidly. The Church had grown corrupt and the Popes seemed unable or unwilling to reform it. Men therefore reverted to a belief of the early Christians, a belief that had

c*

never quite died out, that the authority of the Church belongs properly to the whole community of the faithful, laymen as well as priests. The Church, the entire Christian community, must reform itself; it must meet together through its spokesmen in the General Council of the Church and consider how best to put an end to corruption and to schism. Marsiglio of Padua and William of Occam were the two ablest exponents of this doctrine.

The two General Councils that actually met in the fifteenth century were far indeed from being the bodies representative of all Christendom, lay and clerical, that Marsiglio and Occam had wanted; and, in any case, the Councils did not succeed in reforming the Church or abridging the Pope's authority. But I am not concerned with those Councils, with what they attempted and why they failed. I want to point out only that the opponents of the papacy were not asserting the right of the individual Christian against the Church; they were asserting the right of the Church, a community of laymen and priests, against the papacy. They were not even claiming for every Christian the right to take part in running the Christian community. The delegates they had in mind, who were to meet together in General Council to speak authoritatively for the whole Church, were not to be chosen by the Christian population generally, but were merely the eminent and the powerful, both churchmen and laymen, from all parts of Christendom, the ' natural' leaders of society, the persons who by custom had the right to speak on behalf of their local communities. William of Occam's idea of Church government was in fact more aristocratic than democratic. If it had come to anything, it might have made the Church easier to reform and more tolerant. There would probably have been considerable diversity of opinion in a General Council consisting of laymen and priests from every part of western Europe, and the system could not have endured unless they had learnt to make compromises and to tolerate one another. But, as we shall see, there can be toleration and willingness to compromise within fairly broad limits without there being true liberty of conscience.

2. Luther

Luther, who asserted the priesthood of all believers, who said that every Christian can interpret God's Word for himself, and that faith alone is enough for salvation; Luther, who said these things, must surely have believed in liberty of conscience! That is the claim sometimes made for him. Now, it is true that these doctrines can be understood in a sense which implies liberty of conscience. It was therefore an important step towards the attainment of that liberty when Luther published those doctrines with a force and eloquence unique among reformers. Luther was one of the greatest, one of the most fervent and colourful, pamphleteers and propagandists that ever lived, and the seed that he scattered so widely has had an immense and, on the whole, a liberating influence. But that does not mean that Luther himself understood liberty of conscience as we do now; not even when he first defied the papacy and before the excesses of the Anabaptists and the Peasants' Revolt made him a fierce and even brutal champion of authority.

Luther certainly defied authority for conscience' sake. At the beginning of his quarrel with Rome, in October 1518, when there was still hope of healing the breach, he wrote to Cardinal Cajetan: 'I know that neither the command nor the advice nor the influence of anyone ought to make me do anything against conscience or can do so. For the arguments of Aquinas and others are not convincing to me, although I have read them over . . . and have thoroughly understood them . . . The only thing left is to overcome me with better reasons.' In the tract on *The Liberty of a Christian Man*, published in November 1520, Luther said: 'One thing only is needful in a good life and Christian liberty, the gospel of Christ . . . Perhaps you ask: What is this Word of God and how is it to be used, for there are many words of God? . . . Faith is the sole salutary and efficacious use of God's Word, for the Word is not to be grasped . . . but with faith only.' And in a sermon at Wittenberg, in March 1522: 'Compel or force anyone with power I will not, for faith must be gentle and unforced. Take example by me. I opposed indulgences and all the papists, but not with force: I only wrote, preached, used God's Word, and nothing else. That Word, while I slept and drank beer with Melancthon and Amsdorf, has broken the papacy more than any king or emperor ever broke it.'

These things Luther said within five years of his first defiance of Rome and before Anabaptists and rebellious peasants had brought home to him the dangers of excessive freedom. They belong to the first and most liberal phase of his public career. Later on, he greatly modified his opinions. But not, I think, as greatly as may appear at first sight. For we are apt to read more into his early pronouncements than he put into them, to interpret them in too liberal a sense. If anyone now were to say what I have quoted Luther as saying, we should infer that he believed in liberty of conscience, and our inference would probably be correct. But if we make the same inference in Luther's case, we are probably wrong. For many things that are now taken for granted were not so taken in his time, and he made assumptions we no longer make. That Luther was more liberal before 1525 than he was afterwards is certainly true; but that he began by believing in liberty of conscience and afterwards gave up that belief is almost certainly false. Or, to put it another way, he understood by liberty of conscience something different from what we understand by it.

All Christians are, he says, priests; and this implies that every Christian can understand the gospel. But, then, who is a Christian? Not, clearly not, *any* man who can read the gospel and claims to understand it. For an atheist can do that. The Christian must have faith; he must accept what the gospel teaches, if he is really to understand it. That much Luther certainly believed. To assert the priesthood of all believers does not therefore imply that anyone who rejects the gospel has the right to do so. Liberty of conscience is only for believers. And what exactly is the extent of this liberty? Have believers the right to read anything they like into the gospel? Or must their interpretations of it be reasonable? And if that stipulation is made, who is to decide what interpretations are reasonable?

Again, faith is presumably sincere. What is to prevent a man who has no faith from pretending that he has it, and from reading into the gospel whatever he chooses to find in it? And who can put himself forward as an infallible judge of the sincerity of others? The closer we look at this formula about the priesthood of all believers, the more obscure and the less liberal it looks. Used as Luther used it in defiance of the Pope, it has great emotional force. Luther believed in the gospel, and on that belief rested all his hope of salvation. We can argue, in the light of what history we know, that his act of defiance served the cause of liberty. But we have no warrant for saying that, at any time of his life, Luther asserted what we now understand by liberty of conscience.

Luther believed, at least before 1525, that we ought not to use force to compel belief, 'for faith must be gentle and unforced'. It is, however, quite possible, quite consistent, to hold this belief and yet deny that anyone has the right to profess what faith he pleases. Everyone ought to believe the truth sincerely, and therefore it is wrong to use force to compel belief; but it does not follow that it is wrong to forbid the profession or teaching of false doctrines. In a letter to Joseph Metsch, in August 1529, Luther wrote: 'No one is to be compelled to profess the faith, but no one must be allowed to injure it. Let our opponents give their objections and hear our answers. If they are thus converted, well and good; if not, let them hold their tongues and believe what they please. . . . Even unbelievers should be forced to obey the Ten Commandments, attend church, and outwardly conform.' These sentiments and others like them Luther mostly uttered after the Anabaptist and Peasant troubles, but they are not inconsistent with the doctrines he preached during the first years after the breach with Rome. While Luther was a rebel, his arguments were devised to justify his rebellion; later on, when he had to consider how order should be preserved in Germany, he used other arguments. Though the early arguments do not imply the later ones, they are quite compatible with them. It is possible to hold them simultaneously without contradiction.

If we look at what Luther taught about the organization of the Church and its relations to the Temporal Power, we can see how far he was from understanding what liberty of conscience implies in practice, what institutions must exist to make it good. The Church, not long before Luther's time, in the fifteenth century at the General Councils, had made a half-hearted and abortive attempt to reorganize and cleanse itself. Luther, like Wyclif before him, despaired of the Church's ability to reform itself, and thus looked to the princes, the Temporal Power, to reform it. He therefore argued that the clergy are as entirely subject as the rest of the people to the secular magistrates. They have no coercive power, for Christ gave none to them, and their function is merely to instruct in the faith. To carry out this function, they need property, which they receive from the Prince. It is the right of the Prince to appoint to all benefices within his dominions, and to see to the moral discipline of the clergy. Yet the Church is not a mere fellowship of believers, an association of persons who instruct and sustain one another in the faith. It is a mystical body, divinely instituted, through which God, by means of the sacraments, gives His grace to the faithful. There is no faith outside the Church, and no salvation without faith. But neither is there, inside the Church, any order of persons, any priesthood in the Catholic sense, to whom God gives special powers which He does not give to all true believers. The clergy are merely instructors in the faith, and their selection, training, and discipline are matters for the Prince to decide. The Church, as a community of the faithful and an organ of grace, is a divine institution, but as an organization of pastors, of instructors in the faith, it is merely human, and no one, in virtue of his place in that organization, can be any the less subject to his prince.

Though Luther taught that it is for the prince to organize the ministry, to appoint pastors, to provide for them, and to ensure good discipline among them, he also denied that the prince has authority in matters of conscience and faith. Not for him to decide how the Scriptures, which contain God's Word, shall be interpreted. To us it seems odd that Luther should not have seen that whoever appoints to the ministry and provides for it will in fact decide what it shall teach. How can the Church depend on the secular power in matters of discipline and organization, and yet retain its spiritual independence? Luther seems also to have believed that the Church, the community of the faithful, is universal, so that there never can be more than one true Church. Yet he knew that there were many independent princes, and he wanted each prince to organize the ministry in his own dominions. How could a Church be only one body if there were inside it many separate ministries controlled by as many independent princes? And why should Luther assume that princes would care more than bishops and popes for the purity and good discipline of the Church?

Luther's opinions about the relations of Church and State hardly deserve to be called a political theory; they leave too much out of account, they make too many too simple assumptions. Yet Luther must not be set down for a crude German worshipper of power. He leant on the princes because he felt he had nothing else to lean on. He had reacted violently against the old Church order, which was independent and yet (in his opinion) worldly, corrupt, and incapable of reforming itself. By his defiance of the Pope he had made a great stir in the world; but he had also made powerful enemies and needed powerful friends to protect him. He found them among the German princes.

Luther had an even stronger motive for clinging hard to the princes. His example was catching, and there were soon people willing to carry his principles much further than he had done. Why, these people asked, if God's Word is contained entire in the Scriptures, which every faithful Christian can interpret for himself, why have an organized Church at all? Why have any discipline in matters of faith? The Church is the community of the faithful, but only God can know who the truly faithful are. The true Church is therefore invisible except to God, and there is no need for a visible Church organized by men. Others went less far, admitting that the faithful ought to form voluntary associations to sustain one another in the faith, but also denying the need for a Church as Luther understood it. Some denied the two sacraments, Baptism and the Eucharist, which Luther still retained; some condemned property, marriage, and other institutions; some denied the legitimacy of any kind of authority of man over man, spiritual or temporal. These people, who formed not one sect but many, were called Anabaptists, because many of them believed in adult baptism. Most of them were harmless, though some were aggressive and violent. Their theories were denounced as subversive, and Luther was anxious to dissociate himself from them.

Luther saw the danger of allowing anyone, no matter how ignorant or fanatical, to preach what doctrines he pleased. Yet, lacking a true conception of liberty of conscience, he did not know how to reconcile the claims of faith with the need for order. He proclaimed both the priesthood of all believers and the need for strong discipline in Church as well as State. His defiance of Rome had excited the Anabaptists, who used his principles and authority to reach conclusions abominable to him. Socially and politically, he was, as most of them were not, deeply conservative. Not, as some hostile critics have said, because he worshipped power, but because he believed that, without the social peace which rests securely on custom, men are distracted from God. It does not much matter, he thought, what kind of order there is in the world; what matters is that what order there is shall be secure, so that men can take the world for granted and turn their thoughts to God. A man as deeply religious as Luther (and no one denies the strength and sincerity of his faith) is not inclined to worship power, even when his anger is hottest against disturbers of the peace.

As Luther saw it, it was the Anabaptists who were worldly, and not he; for they were concerned, as he was not, about how worldly power and wealth were distributed. Luther wanted worldly discipline for the sake of spiritual freedom, and could not see how this freedom could be made more secure by changing the social and political order. He lacked a political sense; he had no idea how to get what he wanted, how State and Church should be organized to make possible the quality of life most precious to him. He longed for freedom but did not know how to make freedom at home in the world. The Anabaptists frightened him, and he clung the more closely to the order familiar to him.

Luther preached total submission to established authority, excepting only that commands contrary to God's Word must not be obeyed. The Christian must never actively resist his prince or combine with others against him. He must disobey only when obedience involves sin, and never for the purpose of weakening the authority of the prince. The Christian has only one right against established Power, the right meekly to suffer unjust punishment, bearing witness to the truth as Christ did on the cross.

3. Calvin

Calvin was even less inclined to liberty than Luther. In his political and social theories, he was not a deep or subtle thinker, a questioner of accepted principles, a framer of new concepts and hypotheses. He was almost entirely derivative. This is true, apparently, even of his theology, which mostly comes from Luther, though it emphasizes some aspects of Luther's teaching much more than Luther did, and neglects others. Troeltsch, in his great book on the *Social Teaching of the Christian Churches*, says that Calvin was a more lucid, consistent, and systematic theologian than Luther, but also speaks of his ' doctrinaire logic peculiar to men of the second generation, due to their sense of possessing a secure inheritance '.

Calvin's theology does not concern us, but his political theory has all the qualities that Troeltsch ascribes to his theology: it is lucid, consistent, systematic, and entirely second-hand. It comes, however, not from Luther, who really had no political theory, but from mediaeval and early Christian sources. To be more precise, his conception of the relation between Church and State is essentially mediaeval, while his theory about the internal government of the Church is early Christian rather than mediaeval. In any case, his political theory, whatever its sources, is illiberal; it scarcely leaves room for liberty of conscience.

There is not in Calvin, as there is in Luther, a yearning for liberty which finds no adequate political expression.

According to Calvin, the Bible, which takes precedence over custom and all man-made laws, prescribes how the Church, the community of the faithful, is to be governed. It is not for the Temporal Power to govern it. The Church alone has authority to declare true doctrine, and also to control the moral life of the community. Temporal rulers do not derive their authority from the Church; they too get it from God, either through the people or directly. Church and State are therefore separate, and neither is subordinate to the other. Now this, as we have seen, is the typical doctrine of the Middle Ages, though extremer champions of Papal or Imperial claims had denied it.

Temporal rulers – and this too is good mediaeval doctrine – are obliged to support the Church, to favour the true doctrine and worship against all others, and to extirpate heresy, if necessary by force. But this doctrine, in Calvin's time, had different practical implications. In the Middle Ages there had been only one Church, and temporal rulers, though they might have doubts how far to go in supporting the Church, did at least know what Church to support. After the Reformation, matters stood differently; it was no longer as obvious as it had been which Church was worthy of support. It might be obvious to Calvin or to the Pope, but in the minds of temporal rulers there was more room for doubt.

Calvin declared that the Church is independent of the State, and also admitted that the State is independent of the Church. There is, he said, only one true Church, which it is the duty of the State to support. But how, in a Europe where there were already several Churches claiming to be the one true Church; how ensure that the State shall support *the* true Church? It can hardly be done unless the true Church makes the State subordinate to it. This, at least, was the conclusion that Calvin was driven to in practice, though he never admitted it in theory. In Geneva he set about making the Church supreme. Without, for a moment, denying the independence of the State, he so contrived matters that the Church should be certain of the State's support. And certain it could not be unless the State was in fact subordinate to it. In Calvin's Geneva, though supreme civil authority belonged to the City Council, and supreme ecclesiastical authority to the Consistory, in fact both bodies were dominated by the Congregation of Pastors. This may seem odd, when we consider that, according to Calvin, authority in the Church belongs to the entire community, laymen as well as pastors; but in no other way could he have achieved his object. In no part of Catholic Europe, outside the Papal states, was the hold of the Church over the State as great as in Geneva. The Roman Church scarcely needed such a hold, for its claims on the State had long been admitted. It could rely on old loyalties and old habits.

Calvin preached the doctrine of obedience to established civil authority almost as fervently as Luther. It could not endanger his position in Geneva; for where the Church in fact dominates the State, there is no need for it to contest the State's authority. Calvin knew that, outside Geneva, the position of his adherents was precarious; especially in his native France, where the most the Calvinists could hope for, for a long time to come, was toleration. To earn this toleration, they had to avoid appearing dangerous to the king, and had also to strengthen their influence at court, which they could best do by admitting as unreservedly as possible their duty of obedience. There is therefore a surface resemblance between Luther's and Calvin's teaching about the obligations of subjects to their rulers. They both tell men to obey God rather than man, and also never actively to resist established authority, because, in the words of Saint Paul to the Romans, ' the powers that be are ordained of God '. To resist the prince is to resist God.

This resemblance, masking a difference between two almost opposite conceptions of how Church and State should be organized, did not last long. As soon as Calvin saw that the Huguenots could not get the support they needed at the French Court to enable them to get secure privileges for themselves, and so work peacefully to bring the whole country over to their way of thinking, he added a rider to the doctrine of non-resistance which quite changed its character. He argued, in a letter to the Huguenot leader, Coligny, that though, in general, subjects must never actively resist their rulers, yet, if Princes of the Blood, supported by the *Parlements*, gave the lead, it was allowable, on the authority of these magistrates, to take up arms in defence of legal rights, even against the legitimate sovereign. This doctrine was suited to the special needs of the Huguenots. Though they were only a minority in France and could not hope to control the Estates-General, many of them were noblemen or wealthy merchants, who held the chief magistracies and controlled the highest courts of their own provinces. Calvin's doctrine of active resistance by lesser magistrates to the sovereign or supreme magistrate justified their using their local privileges in defence of their faith. They needed a right of resistance they could use wherever they were socially predominant, but which could not be used to stir up against them the lower classes who were strongly Catholic in almost every part of France. Yet Calvin's doctrine, slightly altered to meet the needs of the Huguenots, was at bottom only the old mediaeval theory of resistance, as we find it in Aquinas, which asserts, not a right of individual or even popular resistance, but a right of official or privileged resistance. According to this theory, only those who already have authority have the right to resist authority. The mere citizen or subject has no such right.

Calvin and the Huguenots had to be careful; they had to prove just enough to suit their rather special needs. But Calvin had, in Scotland, a disciple who could afford to be less cautious in advocating open resistance to established authority; who was not content to argue that, under certain circumstances, lesser magistrates can use force to defend established rights against higher magistrates; who boldly affirmed that, no matter what the established rights might be, the people can always set them aside on the authority of the Bible, if these rights are used against the true religion. This is the argument of John Knox's *First Blast of the Trumpet Against the Monstrous Regiment of Women.* It was the duty of the English people, he said, to depose Mary Tudor, who was persecuting the true faith. Though her title to the throne might be good by English Law, that law stood for nothing against the authority of Holy Scripture, which has placed woman under the government of man. The *First Blast* is an attack on a very restricted class of persons, on women who happen to be queens regnant and who persecute the faith of John Knox. In his later writings, Knox broadened his argument, taking it to its logical conclusion. It is everywhere the duty of the faithful to depose impious rulers and to establish the true faith. Knox went further, much further, than Calvin had done; he was a more violent and reckless controversialist. It was not, however, mere recklessness that carried him on, for the Calvinists were stronger in Scotland than in France, and could afford to be bolder. Knox's doctrine of resistance is entirely in keeping with Calvin's conception of the proper relations between Church and State.

The right of resistance is confined by Knox to the faithful, to those who believe in the true doctrine. Sincere believers in false doctrines have no right of resistance against true believers seeking to establish uniformity of worship. Knox was no respecter of persons. No matter how humble a true believer, he has the right to resist. The privilege of fighting for the faith is not confined to the well-born and powerful. Knox was, if you like, a democrat. But he cared nothing for liberty as such; he cared only for the liberty of people who agreed with him. He believed in liberty of conscience about as much as the Communists do today.

The early Calvinists, in Geneva, in France, in Scotland, and in England too, were quite unambiguous. We cannot say of them, as some people (though, in my opinion, mistakenly) have said of Luther, that they put forward a claim to liberty of conscience, which they then belied by making other claims incompatible with it, without noticing the incompatibility: or that they began by believing in it and afterwards gave up the belief. They never believed in it, and were never any closer to doing so than the Pope.

4. The Jesuits

It is instructive to compare the Calvinist position with that of the Jesuits, as we find it especially in the writings of Molina and Suarez.[1] Although the Jesuits were the Pope's most devoted servants in the struggle to reunite Christendom under the authority of Rome, their conception of the proper relations between Church and State is at bottom the old mediaeval conception as we find it, not in the extreme Papalist writers, but in Aquinas. It is merely adapted to the new situation created by the reformers. The Jesuits stand out among the political controversialists of the sixteenth century by their lucidity, their respect for logic, and their better manners.

They distinguished sharply between the authority of the Pope and the authority of temporal rulers. The Pope's authority comes directly from Christ; it does not come from the Church, the community of the faithful. But the authority of temporal rulers is vested in them by the community they govern; though it also comes from God, as all legisimate authority must do, it comes from God through the people. Princes and other temporal rulers are the delegates of their peoples, and their authority is therefore limited. What the people have created for their convenience and happiness, they may resist or remove when it does not serve the purposes it was meant to serve. Both Molina and Suarez asserted the people's right to depose their rulers for misgovernment.

The Jesuits admitted that temporal authority is in origin independent of the Church, and that the Pope has no right to interfere with purely temporal matters. But it is his duty to see to it that men are not governed in such a way that their salvation is imperilled. Though the Temporal Power is independent of the Church, it has no right to obstruct the end and purpose of man's life, which is spiritual as well as temporal. The Pope, *ad finem spiritualem*, may depose a prince, or at least may excommunicate him, and his subjects are then released from obedience to him.

The Jesuit doctrine in this matter is at bottom the same as the Calvinist, except that, where Jesuits speak of the Pope, Calvinists speak of the Church, meaning in practice the morally respectable and the godly, led by their pastors. Arguing from first principles, the Jesuits, who had not to suit their doctrine to the conditions of any particular country, always insisted on the popular origins of temporal power, and never confined the right of resistance to inferior magistrates. The Church, for them, was essentially a monarchy, but the State could have whatever form its people had chosen to give it; whereas the

[1] Molina. *De Iure et Iustitia* (1599).
Suarez. *Tractatus de Legibus ac Deo Legislatore* (1612).

Calvinist ideal, in both Church and State, was aristocratic, the rule of the godly. There were other differences between them, but their conceptions of the relations of Church and State were broadly similar. Neither allowed room for anything like true liberty of conscience. To them the liberty of the faithful meant only the rights of the Church against the State.

5. The Sects

The Catholics, the Lutherans, the Anglicans, the Calvinists, all had this in common: they believed that there could be only one true Church. Whatever their views about the internal government of the Church and its relations to the State, they all agreed that the Church is not a voluntary association of believers, a merely human institution which men may or may not join as they please. It is through the Church that God's Word is brought to man, and through it also that man receives from God the gift of grace without which he cannot be saved. Though Luther and Calvin proclaimed the priesthood of all believers, and said that the Bible alone contains the whole Word of God, the entire truth necessary to salvation, they did not believe that men could receive the Word and be saved outside the Church, or that there could be several Churches, each interpreting the Word differently from the others, and yet all equally acceptable to God. Luther and Calvin, no less than the Catholics and Anglicans, believed in uniformity of faith and worship.

We have so long been used to there being several Christian Churches that it is difficult for us to enter into the minds of persons who took it for granted that there could be only one. Indeed, in this matter, the Catholic argument, that a single Church can have only one head, is perhaps the most easily intelligible to us, even when we are Protestants, because it is more in keeping with modern ways of thinking about what constitutes a community. How can there be only one Church for all Christians unless they all recognize one authority as supreme over them? How could Luther, who left it to each prince to organize and provide for the ministry within his own dominions, believe in only one Church? How could the Anglicans do so, and yet recognize the king of England, whose kingdom included only a small part of all the Christians in the world, as supreme governor of their Church? Calvin, at least, appears rather more logical to us. Though he held that it is for the faithful in every locality to establish their own Church, which, if it is truly based on God's Word, will have full spiritual authority, he also wanted to have a kind of federation of Protestant Churches united against Rome.

Christians in the sixteenth century did not think of the Church as a society which owes its unity to being under a single government. Nor did they think of it as merely a group of persons having the same religious beliefs. They thought of it as a divinely instituted community, a brotherhood in Christ, possessing in the Bible, in the sacraments, in certain forms of worship, the means of faith and of union with God. I am not a theologian, and I must take care not to get out of my depth, but I believe that to be united in the faith with other people is not just to share their convictions or to be under the same Church government. It is to stand to God in the same relation as they do, a relation that no man can stand in unless he receives God's grace, which he can do only through the means to grace provided by God, which are the Word and the Sacraments. Catholics, Lutherans, and Calvinists might disagree about what Holy Scripture meant and about who had the right to interpret it, and also about the number, character, and effects of the sacraments, but they all agreed that there were specific means to grace provided by God, without which no man could be saved. These means were provided through the Church, the only true Church; so that nothing should matter more to any man than that he should belong to that Church.

Let us try to see how this conception of the Church, even when combined with the doctrine of the priesthood of all believers, stands in the way of liberty of conscience. Like the Catholics, the Lutherans and Calvinists thought it the duty of the one true Church to bring the Word and the sacraments to all men, and so put them in the way of receiving God's grace. But, while the Catholics believed that the head of the Church had divine authority to interpret the Word to all men, Luther and Calvin held that Holy Scripture is such that any man of good will, sound intelligence, and sufficient knowledge cannot help but understand its plain meaning. But this Protestant idea, that the correct interpretation of the Word somehow comes of itself, through the mere power of the Word, had in practice to be modified; for the very simple reason that there cannot in practice be uniformity of belief unless it is imposed from above. There is no salvation without the truth, and there is only one truth, revealed in Holy Scripture. How then is it to be contrived that all men of good will, sound intelligence, and sufficient knowledge shall interpret Holy Scripture in the same way? If they interpret it differently, how can it be known who possesses the truth? How can there be only one truth acceptable to God and only one true Church, and yet all believers be priests?

Luther and Calvin denied that Holy Scripture, in fundamental matters, can be honestly and reasonably interpreted in more than one way, and also implied that every man of good will, sound intelligence and sufficient knowledge will interpret it aright. Now, this denial and this assertion, taken together, must lead to great difficulties, logical and practical. The logical difficulties are perhaps insuperable, but the practical difficulties can be got over after a fashion. There is, *ex hypothesi*, no need for a single authorized interpreter of Holy Scripture, since anyone possessing certain qualities can be relied upon to interpret it correctly. All that is needed is some authority to decide whether or not a man possesses these qualities. In Calvin's Geneva, this authority was the Consistory. Since it contained only men of good will, sound intelligence, and sufficient knowledge, it felt justified in concluding that anyone who understood Holy Scripture in a way not acceptable to itself did not possess these qualities, and was either malicious or incompetent. It was as simple as that. Though not in so many words, yet implicitly, a claim was made which I believe I do not distort if I put it thus: 'Any morally and intellectually competent person can understand the Scriptures as well as we can; but since we are competent, anyone who understands them differently from us proves himself incompetent, either morally or intellectually.' There could be no question of setting up other criteria for testing good will, intelligence, and knowledge, that is to say, for testing moral and intellectual competence; for then it might happen that people who passed the same tests differed fundamentally about Holy Scripture. The only safe criterion, if there is to be one only true Church and one true doctrine, is the criterion used by the Genevan Consistory. Any competent person can know the truth, but the only mark of his competence is that he agrees with us who also know it. Those who, like the Consistory, are strong enough to coerce others need only assume their own competence to feel justified in concluding that anyone who does not agree with them does not know the truth, and is therefore incompetent and deserves to be silenced. How much more modest this claim than the one made on the Pope's behalf! And yet, in practice, it comes to much the same thing! No one, no man or group of men, assumes supreme authority from God to interpret God's Word; nobody assumes anything more than that he is morally and intellectually competent.

No doubt, it is not self-contradictory to hold that there is only one true Church teaching the doctrine necessary to salvation and yet to allow full liberty of conscience. It is not illogical to hold that no one will be saved unless he accepts certain beliefs and belongs to a certain community, and at the same time to admit everyone's right to believe what he pleases and to join any community. But this position, though there is nothing inconsistent about it, is not attractive to people who believe that there is only one true church. They are driven back upon it only when experience has taught them that there is no hope of bringing everyone into their Church and that the cost in suffering of trying to force them in is altogether excessive. It is the position they gradually fall back on the longer they have to put up with several Churches, each claiming to be the one true Church.

Not everyone adhered to this idea that there can be only one true Church because, of its very nature, the Church is universal. Even in the Middle Ages there had been people who denied the need for a universal Church, who rejected the sacraments as means to salvation, and who had no more use for an organized ministry than for priests in the Catholic sense. These people, the Catharists and Waldensians in the north of Italy and the south of France, had been persecuted without pity and their heresies almost rooted out. At the Reformation the Anabaptists adopted very similar beliefs, and this time there was no longer one only Church over the whole of Western Europe strong enough to put them down. Among the Anabaptists there were some who denied the need for any kind of organized Church, but most of them were content to say that a Church is only a voluntary association of believers, so that there can be any number of Churches, each as truly a Church as any other. Anabaptist ideas passed from Germany to Holland, and thence to England, and eventually to the English colonies across the Atlantic, either directly from Holland or through the mother country. By the middle of the seventeenth century the sectarian conception of a Church as a voluntary association had taken firm hold among politically important minorities both in England and America. People for whom their Church is merely a voluntary association of believers, and who therefore do not look to the State to provide for one only true Church, need evolve no elaborate theory about relations betwen Church and State. All they need ask of the State is that it should let them alone, provided they do nothing to disturb the peace. All they need ask for is toleration.

Not only Catholics, but Lutherans, Anglicans, and Calvinists asked for more than this. Yet, in a Europe permanently divided among several Churches, they could not continue asking for it indefinitely, and everywhere. Somewhere or other, each of these Churches was weaker than the others, and therefore found it expedient to abate its claim. As might be expected, it was the weakest among them that made the first concessions. The Calvinists were both more widely and more thinly spread over Europe than the Lutherans and the Anglicans. They were therefore the least well placed, except in one or two countries, to induce the State to do what they wanted. They were less numerous and powerful than the Catholics, and less congenial to princes than the Lutherans and Anglicans. In several countries, they had to reconcile themselves to being, for a long time to come, a small minority, and were therefore disposed to give up the claim that the State should support the one true Church against all others. They adopted what came to be called the 'free church' principle. The Church must rely on itself alone to maintain faith and good discipline among its members, and can require no more of the State than to be tolerated. The first English Calvinists to adopt this principle were the

Congregationalists. There were not many of them, and the most they could hope for was to be let alone. But the Calvinists were driven back on the 'free church' principle by their weakness; whereas the sects, rejecting the traditional conception of a universal Church, were from the first more inclined to toleration.

Old ideas die hard. Even the Congregationalists, though they wanted no support from the State, still expected it to suppress what they called idolatry and blasphemy; which meant in practice any forms of worship very unlike their own. They were prepared to admit that other people could differ from them, provided they did not differ too much. The weakness of this early Calvinist belief in toleration is plainly shown by what happened to the Congregationalists when they got to America. When they found themselves a majority in some of the New England colonies, they became as eager as Calvin had been to use the civil power to make their Church supreme.

Though the 'free church' principle, once firmly established, leads inevitably to toleration, it took the Calvinists a long time to accept its implications. Belief in toleration among the religious comes more easily to groups who either, like the Anabaptists in Germany and Holland and their Baptist and other successors in England and America, from the first conceive of the Church as merely a voluntary association of believers, or who, like the Socinians, though they think a universal Church desirable, do not require uniformity of belief. Toleration and liberty of conscience are not, as I shall try to show, by any means the same; but they are intimately related. I want now to consider them more closely: how they differ, how they are connected, and how they spread.

II. THE GROWTH OF TOLERATION AND LIBERTY OF CONSCIENCE

So far I have been considering traditional ideas about the nature of the Church, its relations to the State, and the rights of the Christian conscience. I have tried to show how equivocal the great reformers were, how what they gave with one hand they took away with the other, and how far they really were from the conception of full liberty of conscience. Yet their very equivocation was a service to freedom. No doubt, they did not concede in practice what they seemed to offer in theory; but they did seem to offer it. They spoke of the individual Christian's competence in matters of faith as the mediaeval Church had not done, and they successfully defied authority, spiritual as well as temporal. They helped indirectly to prepare Europe for intellectual freedom, far though they themselves were from understanding and desiring it. I now want to consider how the full conception of this freedom gradually emerged, and what arguments were used in its favour. By the end of the seventeenth century it had fully emerged. Of course, the fight against intolerance continued long afterwards, and still continues today. The right to profess and practise the religion of one's choice was still far from universal in Europe in Locke's time. It was indeed still the exception and not the rule. But by Locke's time, the case for liberty of conscience had been clearly put; though not all its implications had been drawn, the assumptions the case rested on had been clearly stated. Moreover, it had ceased to be primarily a theological argument. The right asserted was not mere freedom of worship and religious belief; it was the right to hold and profess any opinions. Religion was in those days held so important that to allow people to hold what religious beliefs they wanted was virtually to concede full intellectual freedom. If men were free to accept or reject beliefs long held necessary to salvation, why should they be bound in lesser things? So the doctrine was put about that a man is not responsible to other men for the opinions he holds, and may profess them freely, provided that by so doing he does not promote disorder. This is essentially the doctrine of Locke's first *Letter on Toleration*, published in 1689. Not long afterwards we come to the age of Voltaire, when the champions of religious and intellectual freedom could afford to take the offensive and believers in persecution first began to look more foolish than dangerous. By that time freedom of thought and expression, understood as we now understand it, was already widely, though not yet often legally, acknowledged in the West as among the most precious of the rights of man. It was also widely disputed, but much less confidently than before.

1. Arguments for Mere Toleration

Long before Locke there were many advocates of toleration. But we must not confuse what they understood by toleration with positive belief in liberty of conscience. It is possible, for all sorts of reasons, to condemn persecution without conceding that men have a right to hold (and express) what opinions they choose and to order their lives accordingly, provided they do no harm to others. To forbear from persecution, and even to advocate such forbearance, is not to assert a right to freedom of thought and expression.

People can believe in persecution or toleration for two quite different kinds of reason: political and religious. They can hold that uniformity of belief is necessary to the security of society or the State, or at least that the suppression of some kinds of belief is necessary to that end; or they can hold that the attempt to establish uniformity of belief will be so costly or painful as not to be worth while. These are political reasons for advocating persecution and toleration. With them only in mind, we can quite consistently advocate persecuting some beliefs and tolerating others, or persecuting some beliefs at one time and tolerating them at another. The party in France known as the *Politiques*, though most of them thought uniformity of belief desirable, were against persecuting the Huguenots because they believed that the Huguenots could not easily be suppressed by force; and so they argued that to tolerate them was better than to continue the civil war. Queen Elizabeth, in England, persecuted the Catholics and the Puritans, not because she was offended by their religious beliefs or because she cared overmuch for the state of their souls, but because she thought them dangerous to the State. [The Catholics, she feared, might put their allegiance to the Pope above their allegiance to herself, and the Puritans, she thought, wanted to set up in England forms of worship, Church government, and moral discipline which most of her subjects disliked.] Political motives for toleration and for persecution were frequent in the sixteenth century, and some historians, Professor J. W. Allen among them, have been inclined to think that they were the most frequent of all. Perhaps they were, among the persons whose motives mattered most politically; among the actual rulers of states, who alone could decide whether to persecute or not. Among their subjects other motives were probably stronger; and the feelings of their subjects must have had a large influence on the decisions of the rulers. Some kings, who might have been glad to be tolerant, could not afford to be for fear of losing the loyalty of their subjects or of offending some powerful group. The greatest crime of the sixteenth century, the St Bartholomew massacre, was forced on a reluctant king by persons and groups he was too weak to defy.

Political arguments for the persecution or toleration of beliefs, even though they are the most frequent in high places, are always, in a sense, derivative and secondary. For, unless it is supposed that men's beliefs affect their political behaviour, there are no political grounds for deciding to persecute or tolerate these beliefs. Faith must affect, or be thought to affect, politics before politics takes notice of faith. The religious motives for persecution or toleration are not derivative in the same way; they spring from concern with the nature and quality of men's beliefs and of human life generally, with what is believed and how it is believed, and with the consequences to the individual himself of faith or the lack of it, and not from concern with the political effects of belief. It was, as I shall try to show, from religious arguments for toleration that the conception of full liberty of conscience gradually emerged. These arguments were first put by the smaller sects that did not accept the idea of only one true Church or only one set of beliefs acceptable to God.

If God has a purpose for man, a purpose which must be attained if man is to get eternal happiness and to escape eternal misery, and if it cannot be attained unless man stands in a certain relation to God, which he cannot do unless he has the true faith, it must matter enormously that he should have that faith. He may not want to have it; he may not understand its value, or he may not believe that it has the value attributed to it by those who have it. But if the faith has that value, he should have it; and it is therefore the duty of those who already have it and know its value to do their utmost to see that he gets it. They may not succeed, but they should at least try.

Everyone who values faith believes that it should be sincere. Indeed, unless it is sincere, it is not faith; for to pretend to believe is clearly not the same thing as to believe. From this premise those who, from religious motives, believe in toleration derive their strongest arguments. They do not admit that it does not matter what a man believes; they do not deny that it is the duty of those who have faith to bring it to those who do not have it. But certain methods, they say, are ruled out by the very nature of the end to be achieved. You cannot force belief, and it is therefore absurd to try. Not only absurd but harmful. For to pretend to believe when you do not is an even worse condition than not to believe. Where force is used, it is impossible to tell the sincere from the false believer, the faithful from the hypocrite. Even among the persecutors there may be hypocrites, who persecute not for the faith but to serve their own ends. If error is made dangerous, faith itself shines the less brightly, for it cannot be distinguished from hypocrisy.

This argument for toleration was quite familiar to the sixteenth century, though it was perhaps less frequently used than the political arguments. To some people it seems so obvious and so strong that they cannot understand how it has come to be so often rejected. Yet there have been persons who, having used it themselves, have afterwards abandoned it; who have seen the force of it and have found that force not enough. Saint Augustine began by condemning persecution on the ground that it makes hypocrites rather than believers, and ended by admitting its necessity; and so too, over a thousand years later, did Martin Luther. They came to believe that the persecution of heretics discourages the propagation of false doctrines, that it silences error and thus prevents the seduction of the weak-minded. The heretic has always been persecuted, less for his own sake than for the sake of others. It was not to force the truth upon him that he was tortured and burned, nor even to add a little agony in this world to the everlasting torments he would endure in the next; it was rather to purge society in a striking and solemn manner of a seducer and corrupter of souls.

Liberal critics of persecution have sometimes argued that persecutors would not resort to terror if they really believed that reason was on their side. Why persecute if you can convince? This argument is not sound. Men are not merely rational creatures, they are sensual, lazy, and passionate as well. It is a doubtful assumption that the best arguments must in the end convince. The zealous persecutor of the sixteenth century was certain that reason was on his side, but he knew that men are not always amenable to reason—not so much from lack of intelligence as from pride or because the flesh is weak. It is notoriously a hard thing to be a good Christian; it requires self-discipline, self-sacrifice, and humility. It is hard for the lazy and the restless, and still harder for the proud. The ordinary, sensual, lazy man is easily tempted away from a religion requiring so much of him, and the restless man quickly falls a victim to new and strange doctrines, to anything that encourages him to throw off the accustomed burdens. The proud man loves to defy authority, to take the measure of his own courage, to prove himself better and wiser than other people.

The obdurate heretic—so thinks the persecutor—is the most dangerous heretic of all; he is the peculiar victim of pride. His virtues may be greater than other men's, but he has also, much more than they have, the sin of pride, the sin which can turn even a man's virtue to evil purpose. The zealous persecutor, when he destroys the obdurate heretic, is not using force to make up for the weakness of his arguments; his arguments, he thinks, are rejected, not because they are weak, but because men who have fallen a prey to evil passions will not listen to reason when reason points to conclusions they dislike. It is therefore right to silence the proud, even by death, if the lazy, the weak, and the restless, who are the great majority, may thereby escape corruption. To the conscientious persecutor, the argument that, where thought is free, the truth must in the end prevail, seems paltry and sentimental; an argument attractive only to men lacking courage to exert themselves in defence of the truth.

2. The Socinians and Castellion

Belief in true liberty of conscience, in man's right to hold and profess what opinions he pleases, limited by the need to protect the same right in others, scarcely existed in the sixteenth century. It is a belief which emerged, slowly and painfully, out of disputes about toleration, and did not find clear and adequate expression until the seventeenth century. At the same time, belief in toleration, inspired by political motives, was quite common in the sixteenth century. Fairly common, too, was belief in toleration inspired by concern for the purity and sincerity of religious belief. We find it in Erasmus, in some of the early tracts and letters of Luther, in Bodin, in Montaigne, and in

Hooker. I mention these names only to show how wide was the diversity of beliefs held by men who, for one reason or another, advocated a fairly wide toleration. They cared not only for domestic peace but also (and sometimes much more) for the quality of men's beliefs; they wanted to put as little strain as possible on tender consciences. 'God,' said Luther, 'desires to be alone in our consciences, and desires that his Word alone should prevail.' We are not to suppose this opinion less typical of the age than the opinions of the persecutors. Luther could say this, and then take up other positions putting him in the camp of the intolerant.

The friends of toleration, especially when they defended it from religious rather than political motives, were seldom leaders of strong parties; they were not, for the most part, demagogues but quiet and scholarly men. It may be—and we certainly have no good reason for supposing the contrary—that their sentiments found an echo in many hearts; but these champions of toleration were more isolated from one another and less vociferous than the persecutors, and they lacked organized support. To consider only the men I have already mentioned (and there were many more): Erasmus was concerned to prevent religious disputes rather than to stand up for toleration as a principle; Luther was equivocal and confused; Bodin never dared publish the book which was his ablest defence of religious liberty; Montaigne disliked controversy too much ever to wish to engage in it, and had little faith in the power of argument; Hooker was scholarly and abstruse. There were many believers in toleration, and yet there was widespread persecution. To get toleration it was necessary to fight for it, to engage in active and sometimes dangerous controversy; and these great men, among the greatest writers and thinkers of their age, were mostly not fighters. Luther, of course, was a great fighter, brave and stubborn, but he was also moody and muddle-headed and more often intolerant than tolerant. The others were either not fighters by temperament or else gave the best of their energies to other causes.

The cause of toleration in the sixteenth century, and the first half of the seventeenth, was sustained less by these great men than by some of the sects and by liberal groups inside one or two of the larger Churches; by the Socinians and Unitarians, by the Anabaptists and Baptists, by the Arminians in Holland, and by the Latitudinarians in the Church of England. They argued the case for toleration before the triumph of rationalism in the West, before Spinoza, Locke and Bayle, before the argument was refined and brought back to first principles, before it was cleared of biblical and historical encumbrances and received the simple, untheological, and universal form which made it popular in the eighteenth and nineteenth centuries; that is to say, before it ceased to be merely an argument for religious toleration and became an argument for full liberty of conscience. These early champions of toleration were moved, not by political motives, but by a deep concern for the quality of religious belief.

The Socinians or Antitrinitarians were originally a small group of Italian reformers who took refuge in Switzerland. Less dogmatic, more scholarly, and more gentle than most of the northern reformers, they had already, before they left Italy, made converts among the German Anabaptists. But they did not exert their greatest influence until after they had moved to Switzerland.

Most prominent among them were Laelius Socinus, from whom the group got the name Socinians, George Blandrata, and Bernard Ochino. Calvin was quick to notice the moderation of these men whom he called 'academic sceptics'. His attacks obliged Blandrata and Ochino to flee to Poland, and Socinus contrived to stay in Switzerland only by keeping very quiet. From Poland Blandrata moved to Transylvania where he was joined in 1578 by the nephew of Laelius Socinus, Faustus, who had inherited his uncle's unpublished writings. Laelius was the gentle and retiring thinker, and his nephew Faustus the active disciple.

In the sixteenth century Poland, till the Jesuits got control of it, was among the most tolerant countries in Europe, and Transylvania was even more so. It was in these two countries that the Italian Socinians, together with their disciples, came to be known as Unitarians.

The Unitarians and the Anabaptists were strongly attracted to one another by a common belief in toleration. But there were also profound differences of opinion and temperament between them. The Anabaptists disliked most kinds of external discipline; they inclined to anarchy in both social and religious matters. In Germany some of them had attacked property and had used force to overthrow the established order. Most of them were not revolutionaries, but they were, or affected to be, indifferent to worldly affairs; they wanted to withdraw themselves from the ordinary run of men, either into spiritual isolation or into fellowship with the few who shared their own beliefs. The world was an oppression or a snare to them; and when they were not rebels (as most of them were not) they were inclined to be escapists. They were mystics or quietists or believers in the simple life. They disliked hierarchy, complexity, and ceremony, as much in society as in religion. They cared little or nothing for letters or tradition and were almost untouched by the humanism of the Renaissance. Let the faithful, they said, form communities or churches if they feel the need to do so; but let them ask nothing of governments except to be let alone.

The Socinians were not at all inclined to anarchy; they accepted the need for hierarchy and organized discipline. They had a sense of history and respect for tradition; they believed that primitive simplicity was no longer possible, that men must accept society and make the best of it. They were, especially the Italians among them, humanists.

In the religious sphere, they made a sharp distinction between Church affairs and matters of faith. It is not for temporal rulers, or for any-one else, to decide what men shall believe. From this, however, it does not follow that temporal rulers must have nothing to do with the government of the Church. On the contrary, it is their duty to establish a Church, make adequate provision for it, and see to it that it carries out its duties. But the Church should be as broad, as all-inclusive, as hospitable to all forms of Christian belief as possible; it should teach doctrines acceptable to all or to nearly all Christians, for though Christians now passionately disagree about some things, they agree about many others. What they agree about is all that is really essential to the Christian faith. There should be one Church opening its doors wide to all believers, but no one who refuses to enter should be per-secuted. The Socinians did not want many small sects or Churches, narrow and perhaps ephemeral, each separate from the others and lacking sympathy for them; they wanted to preserve the old mediaeval sense of a universal brotherhood in Christ. They cared for toleration as much as the Anabaptists did, but they cared for other things as well; there is about their conception of the Church a generosity and a breadth which is in sharp contrast to the rather narrow sectarianism of the Anabaptists. Their device was not 'Let each of us go his own way', but rather 'Let us agree to differ and yet still remain united in Christ.'

The Socinians believed that the essentials of Christianity are con-tained entire in the New Testament, and that only those parts of the Testament accessible to reason can be matters of faith. There may be, in the New Testament, matters beyond human understanding, but nothing in it can be contrary to human reason or to the common sense of mankind. Every man must therefore be allowed to judge Holy Scripture for himself. So far the Socinians were of one mind with Luther and Calvin. But they drew from these premises conclusions that neither Luther nor Calvin would accept. Where every man judges for himself, they said, there must be diversity of opinion; and this diversity, since it is inevitable, must be accepted with a good grace. The first Socinian *Confession of Faith*, published in 1574, roundly condemns the persecution of dissidents. The famous *Catechism of Rakau*, published in Poland of 1605, comes nearer to proclaiming full liberty of religious belief than any earlier manifesto issued by an organized body of Christians: 'Let each man be free to judge of religion: this is required by the New Testament and by the example of the primitive Church. Who art thou, miserable man, who would smother and extinguish in others the fire of the divine spirit which God has kindled in them?'

Long before the *Catechism of Rakau*, there had appeared an im-portant book arguing for toleration on purely religious grounds,

Castellion's *De Haereticis An Sint Persequendi,* published in 1554 under a pseudonym. The book was so markedly Socinian in character that it was widely attributed to Laelius Socinus himself, though the author was actually a Frenchman who had once been attached to Calvin but had afterwards turned against him. The book, which was an open attack on Calvin, was inspired by the burning as a heretic in Geneva of the Spaniard Servetus. The dispute between Castellion and Calvin is worth studying because it reveals just how far one of the noblest champions of toleration in the sixteenth century still was from arguing on broad principles for full liberty of conscience.

Castellion never once said that man has a right to profess what beliefs he pleases; he never asserted full liberty of conscience. He spoke *against* persecution rather than *for* liberty. Christians, he said, are all agreed about some things, while about others they have disputed for centuries. But what has always been disputed cannot be known for certain, and what cannot be known for certain is not necessary for salvation. Since God is good and just, He must have made it possible for men to know for certain whatever is necessary for salvation. Therefore, the only beliefs necessary for salvation are those that Christians have always agreed about. We must accept frequent disputes as evidence that the beliefs they relate to are not necessary for salvation. For otherwise, since the people we dispute with may be right, we risk persecuting them for the truth; and even if they are wrong, we should still be persecuting them for holding to what they honestly believe to be true. God cannot wish us to force others to assent to what they believe is false, even when it happens to be true.

Though we sympathize with Castellion's motives, we must admit that his argument is weak. For he did not say, any more than Calvin did, that every man has the right to believe what he chooses and to assert his belief. He believed as Calvin did, that a man, to be saved, must be a good Christian; that is to say, not just a good man, but a man having certain beliefs. Now, the beliefs that Christians disputed about in Castellion's time seemed to them just as plain and important as the beliefs they held in common. Calvin did not for a moment deny that the beliefs necessary for salvation had been made plain to men by God; he merely denied that what is often disputed cannot be plainly true. And surely, on this point, he was right. It is notorious that men are often led by their passions and prejudices to reject the plain truth. Calvin's argument is just as well grounded as Castellion's. Holy Scripture, being the Word of God, must, he assumed, have a plain meaning; for we cannot suppose, either that it is beyond God's ability to make His meaning clear, or that He could wish to confuse His creatures. Since we cannot deny either God's lucidity or the fact that men have quarrelled about the meaning of Holy Scripture, we cannot conclude that what they have quarrelled about is not necessary to salvation. Calvin believed that the meaning of Holy Scripture is plain to every reasonable and literate man, unless his reason is obstructed by his passions.

Towards the end of the century, Bodin, in a manuscript not meant for publication and in fact not published until long after he was dead, went further even than Castellion and the Unitarians; he was for tolerating all religions, Moslem and Jewish as well as Christian, on the ground that all sincere belief and worship are acceptable to God. He used rather better arguments to reach conclusions even more liberal than Castellion's, and there may well have been thousands who thought like him without troubling to set down in writing what they could not safely publish.

Yet even this argument, which condemns persecution, not for its harmful social effects, but because it attacks sincere belief, does not amount to a fully conscious respect for freedom as such. I do not mean merely that the people who used it set limits to toleration: that Bodin would have no truck with atheism, and that Castellion never made it clear what should be done to people who reject Christianity altogether. I mean rather that to condemn persecution as wrong is still not to assert men's right to full liberty of conscience. It is still not to assert that men may hold, publish, and propagate what opinions they choose provided they do not threaten the peace or destroy one another's reputations. There is a difference between saying that it is wrong to make people suffer for their opinions and saying that it is their right to hold and teach what opinions they choose. There was still a considerable difference between the most tolerant published opinions of the sixteenth century and the sentiment attributed to Voltaire: 'I do not agree with you, but I shall defend to the death your right to say so.'[1] Voltaire was not, perhaps, the stuff that martyrs are made of; but the assumption behind the words put into his mouth is clear. Voltaire may have seen himself, for a moment, as a possible martyr for freedom; but in the sixteenth century there were martyrs only for faith.

It is not my purpose to describe the spread of toleration; I am concerned not so much with the propagation of ideas as with ideas themselves. The counter-reformation drove the champions of religious liberty out of Hungary and Poland, and the sects fared badly in Germany. In the seventeenth century, it was in Holland, in England, and in some of the English colonies across the Atlantic that this kind of liberty made the greatest progress. Most of its advocates were Protestants, because in Protestant countries, where religious minorities were more varied and vociferous, there were more people with little

---

[1] I have not come across these words in anything I have read of Voltaire's; and I do not know who first attributed them to him. Voltaire did believe in freedom of speech, though how far he would have gone in defending another man's right to it, I do not know.

hope of imposing their beliefs on the majority. Bitter experience taught them that they had more to gain than to lose by allowing to others a liberty which they claimed for themselves. The Catholic Church, the largest and most international of Christian Churches, was the least interested in toleration because the most hopeful of supremacy. Catholics, where they were in a minority, might demand toleration, not only for themselves, but Christians of all kinds, and might even come to believe in it sincerely; but most Catholics lived in countries where they were the majority. Moreover, the Catholic Church had for centuries been the only Church in the West, and it was peculiarly difficult for Catholics to reconcile themselves to the loss of this monopoly. It was only to be expected that the organized bodies of Christians pressing the most strongly for a wide toleration, and eventually for complete religious liberty, should be Protestant and not Catholic.

It is, however, important to notice that the attitudes of the different Churches to toleration and liberty of conscience depended almost entirely on their relative sizes and hopes of predominance. Calvinists were not by temperament more tolerant than Lutherans and Anglicans; they were merely more thinly distributed over a wide area and were everywhere in a minority except in a few small states and distant colonies. Toleration and persecution are social doctrines and practices, and have no clear logical connection with purely theological beliefs. If we knew only how Catholic theology differs from the Lutheran and Calvinist varieties, we should have no good reason for supposing that Catholics would be less inclined to be tolerant than Lutherans and Calvinists. Even the doctrine that there is no salvation outside the Church does not logically imply that it is right to persecute unbelievers. If we are to understand why some varieties of Christians were more inclined than others to be tolerant, or came more easily to believe in liberty of conscience, we must look, not at their religious beliefs, but at the position of their Church or sect in relation to the State and to other Churches. And, in the case of the Catholics, we must look at the traditions of their Church in its dealings with the Temporal Power and with heretics, traditions built up over the centuries, and owing more to history than to theology.

As a matter of fact, many good Catholics were tolerant, even in the sixteenth and seventeenth centuries; and some of them proved it when occasion offered. While the colony of Maryland was predominantly Catholic, every form of Christianity was tolerated there. Anglicans and Puritans oppressed in other colonies flocked to Maryland, until the flood of immigrants made the colony more Protestant than Catholic and toleration came to an end.

3. Liberty of Conscience and the Philosophers

In the sixteenth century political arguments for toleration were the most frequent, and next after them religious arguments; but, as time passed, a third type of argument, broader in scope, came to the fore, a type which, for want of a better word, I shall call *philosophical*. It rests, not on considerations of expediency, nor on concern for the sincerity of religious beliefs, but on an ultimate principle: that every man has a right to hold and profess what opinions he chooses, provided the opinions are not seditious. Princes and parliaments got used to having subjects with different religions, and learnt by experience that they could rely on their loyalty provided they did not ill-treat them; and private persons got used to having neighbours who, though they did not share their most cherished beliefs, were yet found to be trustworthy and benevolent. As princes and peoples got used to toleration, from putting up with it because they could not safely do otherwise, or from inertia or indifference, or because they feared the spread of hypocrisy, they passed gradually to approval of it for its own sake. They passed gradually from the practice of toleration to a positive belief in liberty of conscience. Let a man hold and profess any opinion, as long as he does not stir up disorder or promote treason. There were already, by the end of the seventeenth century, many educated persons who accepted this principle.

They were not content, in supporting this principle, merely to quote Holy Scripture or to argue that persecution is ineffective or weakens the State or promotes hypocrisy. They continued to use the old arguments for toleration, and sometimes even improved on them, as Locke did in his *Letter Concerning Toleration*, but they also put liberty of conscience forward as a natural right. They asserted it, either as a part of the law of nature or as a valid inference from it. True, they did not all understand natural law and natural right in the same way. Spinoza, for example, did not understand them as Locke did. Yet they both produced, for allowing men to profess any opinion which is not seditious or subversive, arguments derived from what they took to be fundamental law, which men can discover by the use of their reason. It is arguments of this type which, to distinguish them from the others, I call philosophical, not because philosophers who believe in liberty of conscience have always used such arguments (for many would not use them today) nor because the philosophers who used them in the seventeenth century used only them, but because the arguments rest on assumptions essential to their philosophical systems. Though Spinoza's argument for liberty of conscience, if we compare it with Locke's, is more abstract and owes less to the Socinians and other sixteenth-century religious champions of toleration, the principle that liberty of conscience is a natural right is as clearly affirmed by Locke as by Spinoza, and in a form more generally acceptable, because Locke, unlike Spinoza, does not give a peculiar sense to the term *natural right*.

The principle of liberty of conscience was clearly and boldly asserted. by Spinoza and Locke, and by other writers too, in the second half of the seventeenth century; but this does not mean that all the conclusions later drawn from the principle were already drawn in their time. It usually takes considerable time for the main implications of an important doctrine to be drawn. Even the philosophers who advocated freedom of thought in the seventeenth century were chiefly interested in religious freedom, though they did not qualify their principle in such a way as to confine it to religious opinions. They spoke of man's right to profess any opinion which is not seditious, and not merely of his right to profess any religious opinion. But they did not trouble to make a distinction between the seditious and what offends against commonly received ideas about morality, and they therefore did not assert a right to profess beliefs which offend against such ideas but are not seditious. We should certainly be going further than we have any right to go if we were to say, for example, of Locke, that, because he argued that men should be allowed to profess any opinion which is not seditious, he would have admitted that they ought not to be prevented from professing beliefs which are morally offensive. He may even have thought that such beliefs are always seditious in the sense that they advocate or condone practices which subvert public order. Or it may be that, if it had been brought home to him that beliefs might be morally offensive without being seditious, he would have been moved to say that man has a natural right to profess only opinions which are neither seditious nor immoral. We should certainly be wide of the truth if we supposed that the *Letter Concerning Toleration* is as liberal as J. S. Mill's *Liberty*. Yet Locke is already closer in spirit to Mill than to Castellion and Bodin and the other sixteenth-century champions of toleration. He asserts man's fundamental right to profess what opinions he chooses. He clearly asserts that right, though he may set limits to it that Mill would not set, and that we should not set. And we all agree, including even Mill (who would not have tolerated slander and libel), that this right, like every other, must be limited.

The ablest exponents, in the seventeenth century, of what I have called the philosophical case for toleration, or the case for liberty of conscience, were undoubtedly Spinoza and Locke. Spinoza's argument is to be found chiefly in the twentieth chapter of the *Tractatus Theologico-politicus*, published in 1670, fifteen years before Locke wrote his first *Letter Concerning Toleration*. But, apart from these two arguments, there is a third which also deserves attention because it raises issues not raised by Locke and because it had a profound influence in France, the country where, in the next century, the attack of the philosophers on religious intolerance set a model for all Europe. Pierre Bayle's *Philosophical Commentary on these Words of Jesus Christ, Compel Them to Come In* was published in 1686 in Amsterdam, one year after Locke, while he was in hiding in Holland to avoid extradition to England, had written his *Letter*, which he did not venture to publish until 1689, after the revolution which brought Dutch William to the English throne.

Spinoza, as an advocate of liberty of conscience, is less attractive than Locke, not because he believes less strongly in what he advocates, but because the assumptions on which he rests his arguments are less familiar. Locke's conceptions of natural law and natural right are traditional, Spinoza's are not. For Spinoza natural law is not prescriptive, it does not consist of maxims of prudence or of moral rules or of divine commands. It consists of scientific laws, which are, for Spinoza, necessary uniformities of behaviour. The laws of nature, as they apply to man, do not differ from the laws of nature as they apply to the rest of the universe; they are ways in which man necessarily behaves. Man is both passionate and rational; but, whereas he shares the passionate side of his nature with other animals, he alone among them is rational. When therefore he acts rationally, he acts in accordance with the nature peculiar to him, and when he does this, he is free. It is a law of nature that man does what he believes to be in his own best interest. Reason is merely the power to form adequate ideas and to grasp necessary connexions; and therefore to act rationally involves having an adequate idea of one's interest and of the means to it. If a man has this adequate idea, he necessarily acts in what is truly his own best interest; but even if he does not have it, he necessarily acts in what he believes to be his own best interest.

For Spinoza natural law and natural right are not correlative but identical terms. Man has a natural right to do whatever he does necessarily, by the law of his nature, and all his actions are necessary. Since man is rational, or in other words reasons by necessity of his nature, he has a natural right to do so. And so we find Spinoza saying:

It is impossible for thought to be completely subject to another's control, because no one can give up to another his natural right to reason freely and form his own judgement about everything, nor can he be compelled to do so. This is why . . . a sovereign is thought to wrong its subjects, and to usurp their right, if it seeks to tell them what they should embrace as true and reject as false, and to prescribe the beliefs which should inspire their minds with devotion to God; for in such matters an individual cannot alienate his right even if he wishes.[1]

[1] *Tractatus Theologico-Politicus*, p. 227 in *Spinoza, The Political Works*, edited and translated by A. G. Wernham. Oxford, 1958.

The 'natural' and 'inalienable' right to reason freely and form judgements about everything, as Spinoza conceives it, is by no means a natural and inalienable right in the ordinary sense. It is merely a power of which man cannot in fact divest himself, even should he wish to do so; it is not a right that other people are obliged to respect. That is why Spinoza has to admit that a ruler 'has the right to treat as enemies all who are not in complete agreement with him on every point'.[1] He has the right to do it provided he has the power, and he may have the power to treat them as enemies even though he lacks the power to compel them to agree with him. Moreover, Spinoza greatly underestimates both the extent to which beliefs can be controlled and also man's capacity to abandon the power to reason freely. The man who habitually submits to another's judgements may freely decide on this submission, but if he does decide on it and acts accordingly, there is an important sense, not discussed by Spinoza, in which he gives up the right to 'reason freely and to form his own judgement'. And submission need not be voluntary; a man may pass, without ever having decided to do so, very much under the influence of other men. A complete submission may perhaps be impossible, except in extreme pathological cases, where a man is so inert and suggestible that he is incapable of any but 'reflex actions' unless someone else has put ideas into his head. But there are many degrees of submission short of these extreme and rare cases.

So far, given the peculiar sense in which he uses the terms *natural law* and *natural right,* Spinoza's assertion of man's natural right to reason freely and form his own judgements may not, from the point of view of the ordinary believer in liberty of conscience, amount to much. For Spinoza, power and right are identical, whereas the believer in liberty of conscience is not asserting a power but a right, and therefore understands by right something different from what Spinoza understood by it. But the matter is not as simple as that. Spinoza did not arbitrarily choose to use the word *right* in a sense peculiar to himself; he did not believe that he was telling other people how he proposed to use a word, but rather that he was explaining to them the true nature of what they, as well as he, called by that word. And though he did not conclude, as the ordinary believer in liberty of conscience would do, that since man has a natural right to reason freely and to form his own judgements, the sovereign has no right to punish his subjects for professing opinions different from his own, he did conclude that he is acting against sound reason when he does so. Though we may say of Spinoza, even more confidently than of Hobbes, that his philosophy leaves no room for moral obligation as it is ordinarily understood, that philosophy does not prevent his showing that the attempt to

[1] Ibid., p. 229.

establish uniformity of belief is unreasonable. The sovereign would not make the attempt if he had an adequate idea of his own interest and of the means to it. Spinoza's philosophy being what it is, when he calls an action reasonable or unreasonable, he is getting as close as he can to what is ordinarily meant by calling it right or wrong. Moreover, though a philosopher constructs a theory which fails to take proper account of an important element in common experience, his theory is not therefore free of that element. Though rights and duties, as commonly understood, have no place, logically, in his theory, they still have a place in his thinking; he continues to use arguments which are conclusive only if there are rights and duties in some ordinary sense, which is different from the sense he has defined, though he may not know it. Spinoza argues that the sovereign acts unreasonably if he attempts to establish uniformity of belief, and that he acts reasonably if he allows his subjects openly to express all opinions which are not seditious. If we substitute 'wrongly' for 'unreasonably' and 'rightly' for 'reasonably', we have here the creed of the believers in liberty of conscience.

Unlike Hobbes, Spinoza does not believe that the purpose of the State is merely to give security to its members, to liberate them from the constant fear of death; its purpose is to enable men to 'live in harmony' and 'to enjoy peace', which 'is not mere absence of war, but a virtue based on strength of mind'. He says that 'a commonwealth whose peace depends on the apathy of its subjects, who are led like sheep because they learn nothing but servility, may more properly be called a desert than a commonwealth'.[1] No State is solidly established unless it serves its members' interests; but men, by necessity of their nature, seek more than merely to keep alive, they seek also to reason freely and to form their own judgements. For, as we have seen, to say that they have the natural right to do this is, for Spinoza, the same as to say that they have the power (which here includes both the will and the ability) to do it. Or, as we might put it, using the idiom of Rousseau, man is by nature free, and the political order which promotes that freedom is the more solid for doing so. Spinoza does not believe in a God who offers men salvation on condition that they hold certain beliefs sincerely; he does not advocate toleration primarily because he fears that intolerance will encourage hypocrisy, nor yet because he fears that the attempt to achieve uniformity of belief will incite more conflicts than it appeases; he advocates it because he puts a high value on freedom of thought.

Locke was much more directly influenced than Spinoza by the arguments of the Socinians and other pious champions of toleration. He was no pantheist but a practising Christian who believed in a

---

[1] *Tractatus Politicus*, p. 311, in *Spinoza, Political Works*, A. G. Wernham.

personal God. In one place in the *Letter Concerning Toleration* he even admits that there are beliefs necessary to salvation. 'Every man', he says, 'has an immortal soul, capable of eternal happiness or misery; whose happiness depends on his believing and doing those things in this life which are necessary to the obtaining of God's favour, and are prescribed by God to that end.'[1] But he believes, as Castellion had done, that only a sincere faith is acceptable to God, and that such faith cannot be compelled. 'Whatsoever may be doubtful in religion, yet this at least is certain, that no religion which I believe not to be true can be either true or profitable unto me. In vain, therefore, do princes compel their subjects to come into their church communion, under pretence of saving their souls.'[2] The doctrines imposed on men as being true and necessary to salvation differ from country to country; and so, since there is only one body of truth which really is necessary to that end, it follows that many are persecuted for refusing to profess erroneous doctrines.

Such arguments as these – and they make up a considerable part of the *Letter* – though perhaps put more simply and persuasively, go no further than the Socinians had already gone. They are arguments congenial to the lover of liberty, but, as we have seen, they take no account of some of the strongest arguments put on the other side. Those who persecute the purveyors of what they think are false and damnable beliefs do so less to bring true and sincere faith to their victims than to prevent their corrupting the still uncorrupt. They hold that, since there is a truth necessary to salvation, God must have made it plain to His creatures, for it is unthinkable that a benevolent God should make salvation conditional on true belief and yet leave it open to reasonable doubt as to what that belief is. It is absurd to suppose that the beliefs necessary to salvation are those about which all men are agreed, because since there are atheists in the world, we must conclude either that there are no such beliefs or that, if there are, they do not relate to God.

But Locke has other arguments than these old ones inherited from the Socinians. His conception of the State enables him to deny that it has authority to concern itself with men's souls. 'The commonwealth seems to me to be a society of men constituted only for the procuring, preserving, and advancing their own civil interest.'[3] And by men's civil interests Locke means those things for the preservation of which they have put themselves under government, such as life, liberty, health and external possessions. We have here another version of the same doctrine that we find in the *Second Treatise of Civil Government*:

---

[1] *A Letter Concerning Toleration*, edited by J. W. Gough. Blackwell's Political Texts, p. 151.
[2] Ibid., p. 141.
[3] Ibid., p. 126.

the authority of government is limited by the nature of the end which it is established to serve, and it is established by men to preserve life, liberty, and property. Government may use force to preserve these things but may not use it for any other purpose. Any man who believes that something is true and important has a right to try to persuade other men of its truth. But this is no more the right of rulers than of their subjects. 'Every man has commission to admonish, exhort, convince another of error, and, by reasoning, to draw him into truth; but to give laws, receive obedience, and compel with the sword belongs to none but the magistrate. And upon this ground, I affirm that the magistrate's power extends not to the establishing of any articles of faith, or forms of worship, by the force of his laws.'[1]

Locke has the same conception of a Church as the Anabaptists in Germany and the Independents in England. It is a free and voluntary society whose members have joined it of their own accord to worship God in the manner which they think acceptable to Him. It follows from this that no Church has any authority directly from God to teach the true faith. Yet every association, no matter what its purpose, needs some discipline, some rules, if it is to endure and to have any hope of doing what it is established to do. To maintain its discipline it may admonish and exhort its members, and if any of them persist in disobeying its rules, it may expel them. Expulsion or (as Churches like to put it) excommunication is the ultimate sanction; it is the severest penalty that any Church can impose. No Church is entitled to deprive its members of any of their civil rights or to call upon the civil magistrate to do so. Expulsion from a Church deprives a man of no more than the rights he acquired by joining it, and he acquired them on condition of respecting its rules. 'Nobody, therefore, in fine, neither single persons nor Churches, nay, nor even commonwealths, have any just title to invade the civil rights and worldly goods of each other upon pretence of religion.'[2] Locke says here on *pretence of religion* because the intolerance he is attacking happens to be religious; but it clearly follows, from what he says about States and Churches and the limits of their authority, that no one is entitled to injure anyone merely on account of his beliefs.

Just as the magistrate has no right to suppress beliefs which he considers heretical, so he has no right to suppress practices which he considers idolatrous. Anything which is lawful in the ordinary course of life is lawful as a form of worship. 'Melibeeus, whose calf it is, may lawfully kill his calf at home, and burn any part of it he thinks fit . . . And for the same reason he may kill his calf also in a religious

[1] Ibid., p. 128.
[2] Ibid., p. 135.

meeting.'¹ But infanticide is unlawful in ordinary life, and is therefore intolerable as a religious practice. If idolatry is in fact offensive to God, it is undoubtedly a sin; but it does not follow that the magistrate ought to punish it. It is sinful to tell lies, but a lie is not punishable merely as such; it is punishable only when the liar, by his lie, injures other men or the commonwealth. The argument of the *Letter Concerning Toleration*, like that of the *Second Treatise*, is that no man is to be punished unless he has offended other men, unless he has injured them in their rights. Now, logically, it follows from this that no man ought to be punished for any action which is merely immoral and not injurious. Yet Locke did not actually draw this conclusion, as Mill was to do in *Liberty*. We can only say that it follows from what he said, we cannot say that he said it; and experience teaches us that men do not always accept what follows logically from their own principles. Locke's peculiar concern in the *Letter* is to argue that men may profess what opinions they choose, especially in matters of religion, provided the opinions are not seditious, and that they may, in any association which they form, and especially at religious meetings, do anything which it would not be unlawful for them to do outside it.

The word *seditious* is scarcely used in the *Letter Concerning Toleration*; I use it because it seems to me as well suited as any other to convey Locke's meaning. I might have used the word *subversive*, which conveys Locke's meaning just as well; but I have avoided it because it has been so much used in recent controversies. Locke is laying down a very general principle: all opinions are to be tolerated unless they are dangerous to society, or, as he puts it, 'unless they are contrary to human society or to those moral rules which are necessary to the preservation of civil society'.² Locke's periphrasis conveys no more precise impression than the single word *seditious*. What opinions are 'contrary to human society'? What moral rules are 'necessary to the preservation of civil society'? Is a man to be punished for professing any opinion which would be dangerous to society if more than a few men acted on it? Is he to be punished, for example, for condemning the use of violence under all circumstances, even though he is so little listened to that the government can recruit all the soldiers and policemen needed to defend the country from invasion and to maintain order? Or, is an opinion only to be punished if there are enough persons likely to act on it to constitute a public danger? Are opinions to be tolerated which excite deep and widespread indignation but which would not be dangerous if they did not excite it? These are all issues which Locke does not raise. I do not criticize him for not raising them; there was no need for him to do so in a discourse whose object

---

1 Ibid., p. 145.
2 Ibid., p. 154.

was to condemn religious persecution. It was enough that he should have asserted, as clearly and boldly as he did, so important a general principle. Mill, in *Liberty*, does not improve upon it; he merely works out some of its implications, raising issues that Locke, for his purpose, had no need to raise.

Locke believed that it was rare indeed for a Church to profess opinions 'contrary to human society' or to 'moral rules necessary to the preservation of civil society'. He believed that scarcely any of the opinions for which men were punished in his day were dangerous to society. It would, he thought, be folly for any Church or sect to put forward, as religious doctrines, opinions which manifestly 'undermine the foundations of society'. But, nevertheless, on rare occasions, what they dare not say plainly and nakedly, men will say covertly. For example, no Church teaches openly that men are not obliged to keep their promises, but some do teach that faith is not to be kept with heretics. Or again, though no Church teaches that a king may be dethroned by those who differ from him in religion, some do teach that an excommunicated king forfeits his crown and kingdom. These, Locke tells us, are doctrines dangerous to society and are not to be tolerated. No Church has a right to be tolerated whose members admit an allegiance to a foreign prince, for to tolerate it is to allow a foreign jurisdiction to be set up in one's own country. Lastly, atheism is intolerable because atheists, being without fear of a God in whom they do not believe, cannot be trusted to keep their promises.

It would appear, then, that Locke would not have tolerated atheists or the Catholic Church. True, Locke does not actually say in the *Letter*, that the Catholic Church ought not to be tolerated, but he clearly has that Church in mind when he speaks of a Church teaching that faith is not to be kept with heretics and that an excommunicated prince forfeits his crown, and whose members admit an allegiance to a foreign ruler. Locke, a Protestant, was not unprejudiced in his attitude to the Catholic Church, nor was he careful to distinguish between the authoritative doctrines which every Catholic was required to accept and doctrines taught by the Jesuits and by others, which a man might reject and still remain a good Catholic. The great majority of English Catholics probably did not accept the doctrines to which Locke objected. The Catholic is, of course, obliged to put what he considers to be the law of God before man-made law, but then so, too, is any other Christian. He admits the authority of his Church to pronounce on moral issues as well as on questions of theology, but then so, too, in practice, do most other Christians. The Lutheran or the Calvinist is just as likely as the Catholic to look to his Church for moral support when he refuses to obey a law made by men on the ground that it is contrary to God's law. That the Catholic believes, as the Calvinist and Lutheran do not, that his Church, when it pronounces on certain matters, is infallible, does not really make it more likely that he will refuse to obey the law of his country on religious grounds.

Locke's intolerance of atheism is inspired by the same doubtful beliefs as Rousseau's advocacy, in the last chapter of the *Social Contract*, of a civil religion. A man cannot be a good citizen, thinks Rousseau, unless he believes in God, and so any man who lacks this belief is to be banished from the State, not because he is an unbeliever, but because he is unfit for society. The assertion that a man who does not believe in God is unfit for society purports to be a statement of fact, and may be refuted by producing the true facts.

The limits which Locke places on toleration are narrower than most people now think proper. His imputations against Catholics and atheists may strike us as false to the point of absurdity. But at least they are charges that can be easily rebutted. They detract nothing from Locke's principle that a man's beliefs are his own concern, and that government must allow him to give free expression to them, unless they are seditious, unless they advocate or provoke conduct dangerous to society. The modern liberal disagrees with Locke, not about his principle, but about the facts: he denies that atheists do not keep their promises or that Catholics cannot be relied upon to be loyal.

Pierre Bayle's *Philosophical Commentary on these Words of Jesus Christ, Compel Them to Come In* is much longer than Locke's *Letter Concerning Toleration*; it is more polemical, more personal, more highly coloured, and goes much more into the details of the controversies of the period. Yet it is not less philosophical than the *Letter*, because it too rests its arguments on clearly enunciated first principles of universal application; it too treats liberty of conscience as a right that men have everywhere merely by virtue of being rational creatures. But inevitably, since the book is diffuse and polemical, and goes minutely into controversies that have long ceased to be interesting, the general argument stands out less sharply than it does with Locke and Spinoza.

I would not say that Bayle believed more strongly in toleration than either Locke or Spinoza, but he was less interested than they were in the problem of how public order is to be maintained, and was therefore less concerned to set limits to toleration than to argue against the limits proposed by other people. He was also, perhaps, by temperament bolder than Locke and less apt to see dangers where there were none. He argued that, if you want to put an end to error, you defeat your own purpose by resorting to force, which may silence your opponent but will not convince him. To fight error with blows is as absurd as to try to take bastions with speeches or syllogisms. Moreover, Christ never used force to compel belief, and those who speak in His name should follow His example. Coercion has been used to turn Catholics into Protestants, and Protestants into Catholics, to turn Christians into Moslems and Moslems into Christians. It is incredible that God should have authorized the use, in the service of truth, of a means used to such diverse effect. Bayle would not, like Locke, exclude atheists from toleration. The man who errs has as good a right to his opinions as the man who possesses the truth. Bayle was no unbeliever; nor did he reject Christianity. But he attacked those he called the 'half-tolerant', who would allow a considerable diversity of beliefs but would not tolerate anyone who denied what they took to be the fundamentals of Christianity. If any belief is open to criticism, then all beliefs are so. There is nothing which it is wrong for men to call in question, not even the truth about God.

Bayle even says, as Locke does not, that diversity of faith may be pleasing to God, just as a choir of many voices may be more pleasing than a lone voice singing. And to say this is to come close to suggesting that there are no minimal beliefs necessary to salvation; that, though there are true beliefs about God, a man may find favour with God without holding them. If men hold incompatible beliefs about God, then some of these beliefs must be false. If men who hold false beliefs about God are acceptable to Him, why should not unbelievers be so too? Locke, for all his advocacy of toleration, seems to have accepted the notion that there are beliefs necessary to salvation. He speaks, in the Letter, of 'there being but one truth, one way to heaven',[1] and says that 'if any man err from the right way, it is his own misfortune'.[2] It is true that, in one place,[3] he admits that, if there were several ways to heaven, there would be no excuse left for religious persecution, but the general impression conveyed by the Letter is that he accepted the orthodox notion of a truth necessary to salvation. Bayle, who was no less a believer than Locke, came much nearer to rejecting it.[4] Now, to reject this notion, as even Locke for one moment admitted, is to reject the assumption on which the whole case for persecution in order to save men's souls rests.

Bayle excluded only the Catholics from toleration. They are not to be tolerated because they are themselves intolerant. This exception, made at a time when the Huguenots in France were being cruelly persecuted, is not surprising. Bayle's concern with large questions of principle combined with a keen interest in the controversies of his own day, a combination which made him 'philosophical' without being remote or arid, his freshness and pungency, his combativeness

---

[1] Letter Concerning Toleration. Blackwell's Political Texts, p. 128.
[2] Ibid., p. 132.
[3] Ibid., p. 138.
[4] How far Bayle and Locke were believing Christians is a matter of dispute which does not concern us here.

and generosity, his vivacity and irony, attracted Voltaire and the Encyclopaedists, who borrowed heavily from him during their prolonged assault on the Church. They put some of his arguments with greater economy and elegance than he was master of, but they added little that was substantial to them.

Bayle's belief that the intolerant ought not to be tolerated still has its adherents today among people who call themselves liberals; it seems to them eminently just. But they are, I think, mistaken. If we believe in liberty of conscience, if we assert every man's right to hold and profess what opinions he chooses, then we ought, logically, to tolerate the intolerant, provided their intolerance is not dangerous. A man's right to profess whatever faith he chooses does not depend on the content of his faith, not even when part of that faith is that other faiths ought to be suppressed. His right is limited only by the need to protect the rights of others. If, in a particular situation, the profession of that faith is dangerous to others, and if the danger can be averted only by preventing those who hold it from professing it, then it is right to prevent them. We have no right to punish or obstruct the intolerant merely because they are intolerant; we have the right to do it only when their activities are in fact dangerous to freedom or otherwise injurious, and it is incumbent upon us to make sure that there is no other likely way of averting the danger or injury. The liberal is committed to the view that the enemies of freedom have as much right to it as its friends, that right being in all cases limited by the need to protect freedom and to prevent injury. No doubt, the enemies of freedom are usually – though by no means always – more dangerous to it than its friends; but that does not affect the point at issue.

By the end of the seventeenth century the new faith in intellectual freedom, in liberty of conscience, had found adequate and bold expression, though many of the implications of that faith still stood in need of elaboration – as indeed they still do today. The origins of that faith were not Dutch but European generally, but it was in Holland, then the freest country in Europe, that a Jew, an Englishman, and a Frenchman gave to it the form it still, essentially, wears today.

Chapter 3

BODIN

I. HIS PHILOSOPHY IN GENERAL

MY purpose is not biographical or historical; I do not want to explain how Bodin came by his opinions or to show the place of his theory in the political, social or intellectual history of his time. I am concerned with expounding and criticizing a political and social theory which is certainly interesting in itself, but which is also something more. It is also important because it introduces into political and social thought, or provides good examples of, ideas which we still use to describe society and government or whose criticism increases our ability to think clearly about them. But sometimes a political theorist is so much wrapped up in the affairs of his country that it is scarcely possible to consider his theory without also considering, however briefly, the political circumstances in which it was produced. This is especially true of Machiavelli and Bodin.

The two great political theorists of the sixteenth century have several things in common which distinguish them from many of their successors. They were both for a considerable time servants of the State, and their political thought was deeply affected by their practical experience. Bodin had been in the royal service for several years before his greatest book was published in 1576. He was elected that same year a deputy by the Third Estate of Vermandois to the Estates-General meeting at Blois, and later he was in the service of the Duke of Alençon, whom he twice accompanied to England. Bodin did not, like Machiavelli, write his books after he had left the public service; he wrote them while he was still active in public affairs. When he wrote about politics, however generally, he had the situation and the needs of his own country very much in mind. Much more so, for example, than Hobbes. True, Hobbes would not have written as he did had he not been an Englishman reflecting on government at a time when his country was on the brink of, or plunged into, civil war; and yet we can take in and appreciate the message of *Leviathan* without considering its historical setting. But some of the distinctions made by Bodin seem pointless, and some of his conclusions absurd, unless we see him as the champion of the royal power in France during the wars of religion.

Bodin is like Machiavelli also in this, that he is a political theorist immersed in history. Indeed, he read more widely than did Machiavelli, and was a more learned man. In 1548, when he was eighteen or nineteen (the exact date of his birth is unknown), he left his native Anjou for Toulouse, where he remained, first as a student and then as a teacher of law, some twelve years. He even succeeded in getting a Chair in Roman Law shortly before he gave up academic life and moved to Paris to practise at the Bar. At Toulouse, being an opinionated and pugnacious (and perhaps even a jealous) man, he had come to look upon himself as a rival of Cujas, the greatest Roman lawyer of his day, the man who first expounded Roman Law as the law of a unique society very unlike the countries of western Europe in the sixteenth century. Though Bodin never acknowledged a debt to Cujas, he did treat law much as Cujas treated it; he explained it historically and socially, always bearing in mind the type of society where it flourished. He possessed, though in smaller measure, one of the great qualities of Cujas, a sense of history.

He possessed this quality probably in greater measure even than Machiavelli. No doubt, Machiavelli was an artist and a great writer, as Bodin conspicuously was not. This, indeed, is one reason, and perhaps the most important, why Machiavelli is still remembered, and Bodin is not, except by academic students of political theory. Machiavelli had much more imagination than Bodin. When he speaks of Caesar or of any other historical person, he brings before us a live man; at least, he comes much closer than Bodin to doing so. His understanding of human nature, though limited, is much more sure, and his ability to recreate character much greater. But a man may have this kind of imagination and yet lack historical imagination, a sense of history. He may present us with an image of a Caesar or a Pompey which is psychologically convincing, and yet may see him more or less as he would see one of his own contemporaries, without understanding how greatly Caesar's environment differed, socially and morally, from his own. And conversely, a man without much insight into individual character, a man like Bodin, may have historical imagination. He may have a lively sense that societies differ greatly in both structure and ethos from one another, and that the past must not be recreated in the image of the present. Clearly, if he has this kind of imagination, it is likely to affect his political and social theory; he will not suppose that what is best for his own country is also best for others.

Today, of course, we are very much aware that societies differ greatly, and we need not be more than ordinarily imaginative to have this awareness. We have been copiously warned against attributing our own ideas and values to men in countries and ages remote from ours. We live at a time when man's image of himself and his environment has been deeply influenced both by the study of history and by the comparative study of widely different societies. But in Bodin's time it was not so.

Bodin was less narrowly *political* than Machiavelli. He had larger intellectual ambitions. He aimed, as it still seemed possible to do in the sixteenth century, at universal knowledge. He was a student of theology as well as of law, history, and government; he took an interest in mathematics, astronomy, physics and medicine. He could read Hebrew, Greek and Latin, and among modern languages, Italian, Spanish and German. He wanted to explain the universe and man's place in it; he aimed, as Machiavelli never did, at systematic and comprehensive knowledge. Evidently, with such wide ambitions as these, he failed of his purpose. He never constructed a systematic theory out of such knowledge as he did acquire; he merely aimed at system without achieving it. Yet he had some ideas worth noticing both about how the sciences differ from one another, and about the use of history to the political and legal theorist. In the *Methodus ad facilem historiarum cognitionem*, published in 1566, he claimed that it was possible, by comparing the laws and institutions of different countries, to reach a set of principles which could serve as a universal standard of criticism. It was possible to discover what standards and purposes were common to men everywhere, and then to estimate what institutions and what laws would come nearest to realizing them under varying conditions. For Bodin never supposed that any one political or social system could be the best for all peoples at all places and at all times. But, though he recognized that peoples differ in their environments and even in their inborn qualities and dispositions, he thought it possible, by the comparative method, to discover principles accepted by them all. He thought it possible to make the discovery, but it can hardly be said that he went far towards making it.

Nevertheless, he did use history for a different purpose from Machiavelli's; he did not use it merely as a store of examples from which he could select those needed to illustrate his maxims; he used it to show how much one political community can differ both in structure and ethos from another, or how a system of government gradually emerges.

Bodin, as might be expected of a sixteenth-century philosopher and jurist, went further than to say that there are important principles accepted by all mankind, principles discoverable by the method he advocated. He took it for granted that these principles are not merely universal but are also rational in a sense in which principles peculiar to only a few peoples and ages are not, because reason can show them to be adapted to man's essential nature. They are the laws of nature, manifestations in man of the divine wisdom. Bodin, despite his advocacy of the comparative method, was in many ways more traditional than Machiavelli. He was not content to find out what all men actually want or actually think good; he wanted to know what is good absolutely, and believed that his comparative method could help him to discover it.

He attempted what Machiavelli attempted, but also had other aims more like those of the mediaeval philosophers. He too wanted to know how to strengthen the State and how to prevent its decay; he too was aware that a political or social remedy must be adapted to a system which already exists and which cannot be greatly changed. But he was also interested in questions of legitimacy, which he did not distinguish from questions of fact. In his day political theorists had not yet learned to make this distinction. Not even Machiavelli made it. He merely happened to be interested only in questions of the one type and not the other. But Bodin was interested in both, and his meaning is sometimes difficult to seize because he did not make distinctions which we are in the habit of making and think important.

Bodin is more comprehensive, more traditional, and more systematic, at least in intention, than Machiavelli, and at the same time less direct, less lucid, and less persuasive. By the standards of his day, he was a man of vast erudition, and by any standards he was a man of immense intellectual energy. Though it was more than he could do to put his ideas into good order, he was continually excited by them. He never gives the impression, as learned men quite often do, of being weighed down by a burden of knowledge too heavy for them; he is seldom flat or dull or weary. But he is tortuous, obscure, repetitious and disorderly. He lacks elegance; he is scholastic and pedantic. He often gets lost in the labyrinths he has created, little though he may know it. In these respects and others, he reminds me very much of Marx; there is the same irrepressible energy, the same power of rapid assimilation, the same claim to competence in many different spheres, the same impatience of criticism, the same boldness of conjecture, the same recklessness, the same preoccupation with questions of method. Both Bodin and Marx claim to know how society should be studied, and yet neither explains his method clearly nor uses it consistently. It is almost as if they cannot bear not to be able to give an immediate answer to any question which occurs to them; as if they cannot put up with ignorance, however temporary, as if their minds, like the nature of the mediaeval philosophers, abhor a vacuum. Where they do not know and cannot easily discover by using the methods they advocate and misdescribe, they promptly make a guess and support it by whatever reasons seem at the moment to serve their purpose.

Bodin was aware – much more so than most learned men of his time – that different methods are appropriate to different fields of study, that some are deductive while others are based on experience. Politics he put very definitely in the second category. Yet he could not in practice bring himself to accept the limitations which he placed on this empirical study. Sometimes he used the method he advocated, but at other times he reverted to other methods which he had himself condemned as inappropriate. He remained in some ways very much a mediaeval philosopher, with a passion for definitions, multiple distinctions, *a priori* principles, and teleological arguments. He often cared more for symmetry than for logic or for facts. If there were three of one thing, there must be three of another to suit the arrangement which he had decided upon for reasons often left obscure.

He could use the oddest and most irrelevant arguments. To prove that men are the superior and governing sex, he thought it enough to observe that Nature had given them beards to make them more honourable. Though he divided the sciences into the deductive and the empirical, he never lost his respect for what he called the ' occult sciences ' and the wise men of the East who practised them. Though he told his readers that they must put up with ignorance where they could not get properly attested knowledge, his passion for omniscience prevented his taking his own advice. Though he warned them that they must not take an opinion on trust merely because it was to be found in the works of Aristotle or in some other book venerated for centuries, he made one of the interlocutors in his dialogue on religion argue that we can accept Christ's being born of a virgin on the ground that in the Old Testament there is talk of the spontaneous generation of birds and fishes, that Plato speaks of earth-bound men, and Virgil of mares that become full by turning their nostrils to the wind. Bodin was a mixture of scepticism and credulity, as so many learned men were in the sixteenth century. But what is remarkable about him is not his being credulous; it is rather the breadth of his scepticism. And yet he is not as free as Machiavelli or Montaigne or Rabelais of the superstitions of his age. We cannot imagine any of them writing, in perfect good faith and eager to save his fellow mortals from a pressing danger, a book like the *Demonomania of Sorcerers*, where Bodin describes how those who have sold themselves to the Devil and who seduce others to him may be known by their behaviour, and how legal action may most conveniently be taken against them. This learned treatise, which Bodin published towards the end of his life, was immediately translated into Latin and, thus raised in dignity, was used by the courts as a legal text-book for several generations.

Bodin was not as narrowly political and practical as Machiavelli, and not as consistently sceptical as Montaigne and Rabelais. But he had his moments of rare insight, and he was eminently constructive. He was a philosopher, in two different senses of that word, as Machiavelli was not. His political theory is only part of a larger theory about the universe and man's place in it; it is a political theory attached to a cosmology, as most political theories had been in the Middle Ages. That is to say, though the mediaeval producer of a political theory may not himself have produced his own version of a theory of the universe, he usually took for granted some traditional version and related his political theory to it. Again, Bodin asked what knowledge is and what are the proper methods of acquiring it. He was, in his own very tentative and inadequate way, a philosopher in the manner of Descartes as much as in that of the mediaeval theologians. No doubt, he is not important as a philosopher; it is perhaps no loss to philosophy, in either of these senses, that his contribution to it is not studied. But it is important that he was a philosopher, that he reflected, however inadequately, on how politics should be studied. For, had he not reflected on this matter, he might never have attempted to produce the sort of political theory which he did produce. He tried to do what he believed had not been attempted before him; he tried to compare political systems, not merely in order to classify them, but to discover which are best suited to what conditions.

Chauviré, whose excellent book about Bodin was published as long ago as 1914, lamented that Bodin was forgotten. 'Evidently' he said, 'it is Montesquieu who has killed him, by saying the same things better than he did, and other things besides.' This verdict was premature. Bodin is no longer forgotten, at least not by historians and political theorists, and many competent judges would agree with J. W. Allen that he is, with Machiavelli, one of the two great political thinkers of the sixteenth century.

Bodin is famous as a champion of royal power. Yet his greatest work, *Six Books on the Republic*, was attacked for not being royalist enough as well as for being excessively royalist. In 1576, the year in which he published his great argument for the absolute sovereignty of the French monarch, Bodin, as a deputy in the Third Estate, persuaded that body to refuse a subsidy for which the king was asking. No doubt, it was mere chance that Bodin's own defiance of the royal will should have coincided with the appearance of his most vigorous defence of monarchy. But it is worth considering why Bodin persuaded the Third Estate to refuse the king's request. The three Estates had voted in favour of a motion calling for religious uniformity, and Henry III was asking for a subsidy to enable him to establish that uniformity by force of arms. Bodin could not persuade the Third Estate to reject a motion which he thought dangerous to peace, but he was able to persuade it not to vote the money which would enable the king to enforce what the motion called for. He defied the king for the sake of religious toleration and peace. Moreover, he believed that Henry III, by attacking the Huguenots, would weaken his authority. He would not only drive the Huguenots into open rebellion, he would also put himself in the power of the extremer Catholics. The king could best strengthen his authority by refusing to lead one part of the nation in arms against the other. He could save France by raising the monarchy above the religious factions.

In England in the seventeenth century the king was a party to civil war; he defended his prerogatives against the encroachments of the two houses of Parliament. In France, in the sixteenth century, the king was not, in the same obvious sense, a party to the religious wars. The Huguenots were not, to begin with, any more concerned than anyone else to challenge the royal authority; they came to challenge it only because the kings of France took up the cause of the extremer Catholics. And the Huguenots, as soon as their leader, Henry of Navarre, became the legitimate heir to the throne, quickly forgot all their arguments for limiting the royal power; they were suddenly transformed into ardent royalists. Neither Charles IX nor Henry III had been a fanatical Catholic; they had taken up the Catholic cause partly because it was the more popular and partly because they had feared the Catholic League. The real initiative against the Huguenots had not come from them.

Bodin, soon after his arrival in Paris from Toulouse in 1561, had made friends with men who were later to form a group opposed to both the main parties to the civil wars. These men – the brothers Pithou and Etienne Pasquier prominent among them – came to be known as the *Politiques*; they were champions of religious toleration and of royal power. They believed that religious uniformity could not be achieved in France by force of arms, and that there could not be enduring domestic peace unless the Huguenots were tolerated. Only the king, if he made bold use of the authority traditionally vested in his office, could be strong enough to impose toleration and to maintain peace. The Estates-General could not do it; they lacked the authority of the monarch, and in any case, having come to be dominated by the Catholic party, were unwilling to come to terms with the Protestants. So the champions of religious toleration tended also to be champions of royal power.

II. HIS VIEWS ON TOLERATION

Some of the *Politiques* were lukewarm in matters of religion, but Bodin was not. He remained throughout his life a deeply religious man. He was born a Catholic and died an ardent champion of religion, though probably without being strongly attracted to any form of Christianity. At one time he may have been a professing Calvinist, for he seems to have gone to Geneva in 1552, staying there for several months—an unlikely journey for a young Frenchman in those days unless it were made from religious motives. There also survives from him a letter which reveals strong leanings towards Protestantism. But Calvinism, if ever he adhered fully to it, can have been only the religion of his early manhood. In his last years he was very probably a deist rejecting all forms of Christianity. Yet his deism, if deist he was, was not the mild sentiment of some of the eighteenth-century philosophers. The god of his old age, if no longer the Christian God, was never a remote deity uninterested in human affairs, the god of Voltaire. He was much more than an hypothesis which Bodin could not bring himself to reject or a still undiscarded remnant of childhood piety. God, for Bodin, was always a real person, omnipotent and omnipresent, a God to be worshipped, feared and loved, a God close to man, the most excellent of His creatures made in His own image.

Of the complaints made against *Six Books on the Republic*, perhaps the most bitter was that it advocated religious toleration. Yet the views expressed in that work are mild indeed compared with those which Bodin reached in his old age. By 1593 – some three years before he died – he had completed a dialogue about religion called *Heptaplomeres*, which he dared not publish and which first saw the light of day long after his death.

Heptaplomeres is an imaginary conversation about religion between seven people: A Catholic, two kinds of Protestants, a Moslem, a Jew, an adherent of natural religion, and a broad-minded friend of all religions which are not fanatical. We may take it that the last two come closest to sharing Bodin's own beliefs, for he puts most of the best arguments into their mouths. They dispose of myths and dogmas in the name of reason, and yet, like Bodin himself, are sometimes unreasonable. The most consistent of the seven is the broad-minded Senamus, who distrusts revelation, rejects most dogmas as absurd or meaningless, and will have nothing to do with miracles; he is Bodin at his most sceptical. Senamus believes in a single, eternal and benevolent God, in the freedom of the will, and in a life after death, which does not last for ever but only long enough to ensure that virtue is rewarded and that those who have suffered unjustly in this world are compensated in the next. These, according to Senamus, are the only beliefs attested by reason; and no others are needed to support morality.

The three Christians in the dialogue get the worst of it, and are the most often reduced to silence. Bodin's attitude to them reveals his distaste for the theological disputes of his age. But the Christians are not roughly handled; and above all – and this is what really matters – they are *not* converted. The seven champions of seven creeds, when they separate, are left with the beliefs they brought to their meeting; their arguments have given them, not new religious convictions, but a greater tolerance and good will. The moral of *Heptaplomeres* is clear: all religions are acceptable to God if they are sincere, and if they admit the truths attested by reason and necessary to good morals.

Bodin, towards the end of his life, was very probably a deist friendly to Christianity but sceptical of all specifically Christian dogmas.

Chauviré suggests that Senamus, the most sceptical and light-hearted of the seven interlocutors, expresses only one side of Bodin's attitude to religion. Toralba, the adherent of natural religion, who thinks it possible to defend the divinity of Christ on purely rational grounds, is almost as formidable in argument as Senamus; and it is clear that Bodin has great respect for his views. Solomon the Jew is also gently handled, and none of the interlocutors challenge the authority of the Old Testament, of which Solomon is admitted to be the most competent interpreter. Bodin, in his attitude to religion as in other aspects of his thought, reveals an equivocation much less uncommon among intellectuals in the sixteenth century than it is now: a bold scepticism alternating with submission to the authority of sacred texts. He had a special affection and respect for the Old Testament, partly perhaps because he was proud of his knowledge of Hebrew, a rare accomplishment in his age. Bodin, if ever he ceased to be a Christian, which he probably did, must have given up the ancestral faith reluctantly.

All things considered, Bodin's attitude to religion is not unlike that expressed some two hundred years later by Rousseau's Savoyard vicar. Like the vicar, Bodin values religion for two reasons: because it is a support to good morals, and because without it man does not feel at home in the world. Bodin takes it for granted, as Locke and Rousseau (and many others) were to do, that man can scarcely have adequate motives for behaving well unless he believes in an after-life and an omniscient Being aware of his inmost thoughts. He also takes it for granted that man needs the sense of living in a world shaped by much larger than human purposes if he is not to be cynical and hopeless, if he is not to feel lost in a mindless universe, if life is not to lose its savour. Like the Savoyard vicar, Bodin has a horror of atheism and materialism, which seem to him both demoralizing and depressing. Man is hopeful, brave, benevolent, and capable of self-sacrifice because he sees himself living in a world governed by a Being infinitely greater than himself, a Being to whom he, man, is important. This horror of atheism is far removed from Machiavelli's approval of religion on purely utilitarian grounds; it is a sentiment perhaps unknown to Machiavelli. It is like the fear of death but also unlike it; it is the fear of insignificance. It is not a man's fear that he may cease to exist; it is the fear that, though he exists, there is no point to his existence. It is a feeling, strong in some men and perhaps unknown to others, that, unless there is a God, it is unbearable to be a man.

III. HIS POLITICAL THEORY

Bodin's *Republic*, like almost everything he wrote, is badly arranged and repetitious. It would be absurd to follow his order in discussing his political theory. It is perhaps best to begin by discussing some of the concepts he uses, above all the concept of sovereignty, passing on to consider his views about the various forms of government, their advantages and defects, and ending with a brief look at his defence of the French monarchy.

1. Power, Right, and Sovereignty

Bodin does not begin his treatise on politics, as Hobbes and Locke were to do, with an account of rights. He does not speak of a state of nature and says very little about the first origins of government. He thinks it probable that most states were created by force, though some grew out of the family or were set up by agreement. He does not use the notion of covenant or contract to explain what are the functions of government or what makes it legitimate. He takes it for granted that a government, no matter how it arose, is legitimate provided it maintains order and acts for the good of its subjects.

The doctrine of the social contract is, no doubt, artificial and misleading. If we suppose that the allegiance of a subject arises from a contract or a promise, from an act having the juridical or moral character connoted by one or other of these terms, we get involved in all sorts of difficulties, verbal and real. But, as a matter of history, the doctrine did bring to the fore the question of political obligation, and did incline the thinkers who used it to distinguish rather more sharply between questions of fact and questions of right. Admittedly, the contract theorists often failed to distinguish between these two types of question, but at least they came closer to doing so than mediaeval political thinkers had done. Moreover, the inadequacies of their theories in the end brought home the need to make this distinction clearly. It is not an accident that Hume and the Utilitarians, who between them killed and buried the contract theory, were among the first to explain this need.

Bodin, writing before the social contract had become a fashionable device of explanation, seldom (if ever) troubles to distinguish between what makes government effective and what makes it legitimate. He does not argue, as Hobbes has been accused of doing, that might makes right; he does not try to show that government is legitimate to the extent that it is effective. To argue as Hobbes does, or as he has been accused of doing, a philosopher would need to be aware of the distinction he is denying or treating as unimportant. If his critics are right, Hobbes is either saying that others have made a distinction where there is no difference or that they have drawn improper conclusions from that distinction. But Bodin, because he does not distinguish might from right, must not be supposed to have held that might makes right. Certainly, the mere failure to make this distinction does not imply that he held this opinion.

There is no evidence that Bodin believed that anyone strong enough to get obedience is for that reason alone entitled to it. But he does seem to have believed that enduring power is probably being exercised for the benefit of the persons subject to it. Power used capriciously is unlikely to endure because men will not long submit to it. Thus Bodin presumed, as Burke did, that, if a ruler has enduring power, he has a good title to it because he uses it for the common good. He either makes a wise use of it or he follows custom, which has become what it is because it has been found useful. Bodin venerated whatever in society is long established and regular in operation; he believed that it conforms with men's more permanent needs as determined by their nature, and therefore also with the will of God, who created that nature. 'True wisdom', says Chauviré, interpreting Bodin, 'is to study facts objectively and in their wholeness; to determine their order, which, owing to God's goodness, conforms with the general good, and to follow that order in one's theories and actions.'[1] Things can be as they ought not to be; for God has given to men the power to choose, and they may make evil or mistaken choices. But they suffer the consequences of evil and error, and wish to be rid of them. Therefore whatever is long acceptable to them is very probably for their good. Lasting authority and wisdom are closely allied, not because those who have authority are necessarily wise, but because their authority is exercised in traditional ways adapted to human nature and to the peculiar circumstances of those subject to them.

This kind of argument was apt to be more convincing in the past than it is now. All governments in the sixteenth century, if we compare them with ours, were weak. Law-breakers escaped justice more easily than they do now, and it was almost impossible to enforce a widely unpopular law. Central governments depended, if they were to have effective authority, on the loyalty of local bodies and potentates whom they would have been hard put to it to coerce. If, then, their authority was effective and enduring, the presumption was that it was exercised in ways which seemed just, if not to the illiterate and the poor, then at least to the better-to-do and the locally prominent, who were taken to be spokesmen for the people generally. The authority of kings, to be effective and enduring, had to be exercised in ways approved of by this part of the people, who were assumed to be virtually the whole people, though numerically only a small part of them. And it was further taken for granted that the authority of this part over the rest of the people, if it was enduring, was so because it too was exercised for the common good.

[1] R. Chauviré, *Bodin, Auteur de la République*. Paris, 1914, p. 290. The translation is mine.

Writers on politics in Bodin's time and for nearly two hundred years afterwards were much less concerned with the attitude of the poor and the illiterate to the classes above them, of whom they spoke as if they were the whole people, than with the attitude of these classes to the central government. If the 'people', in this narrow sense, did not contest the authority of the government, then, since the government's power to *oppress* them (that is to say, to govern them in ways which seemed to them contrary to the common good) was slight, the presumption was that the government was not oppressive. The people, thus conceived, were not incapable of judgement or of taking action against their rulers. Their acquiescence was not the acquiescence of the ignorant, and their obedience was not the obedience of the impotent. Therefore their acquiescence and obedience could be taken to be a virtual consent, which was free, though tacit, to the authority of their rulers. And, of course, it never occurred to Bodin to ask whether the acquiescence and obedience of the poor and the illiterate were of the same kind, whether the unquestioned authority of the socially superior classes over their inferiors was also good evidence that that authority was exercised for the common good.

Though the assumption implicit in much that Bodin says is that enduring power is legitimate because its endurance is evidence that it is exercised for the common good, he sometimes uses arguments inconsistent with this assumption. For example, he does not hold that the authority of conquerors over the conquered becomes legitimate only by being used for their good; he accepts the commonly held opinion that, since victors in war have the right to kill the vanquished, they can rightfully become their rulers by offering them their lives in return for obedience. Even when victors are aggressors, even when they make war from no other motive except the desire to extend their dominion, their victory gives them a right to rule over the vanquished, and even to deprive them of their property and their personal freedom. This was allowed by the *ius gentium*, as academic lawyers interpreted it in the sixteenth century, and that is enough for Bodin, the one-time professor of law. There were property and freedom, he admits, before there were governments. He dislikes slavery[1] and sets great store by the right of property, but that does not move him to question the teaching of the jurists that conquerors, though they are also aggressors, can rightly deprive the conquered of their freedom and their estates. He does not pretend that it is for the common good that they should do so; on the contrary, he admits that it is not. Thus he admits, at

---

[1] When he objects to slavery he does so more from the master's point of view than the slave's. The slave, he says, hates his master and is therefore his enemy. He is the most dangerous enemy of all, the enemy in the household; and yet he is little use to his master unless the master keeps him close to him. The slave is less profitable to his master than a free servant working for a wage.

least by implication, that force can be legitimate even when it is not exercised for the common good. Thus there is not in Bodin's political theory one consistent doctrine of legitimacy.

Bodin treated the family, not the individual, as the basic unit of social life. He defined it as 'a right government over several subjects under obedience to a head of the family, and over what belongs to them'; and he said of it that it is 'the true source and origin of every republic, and the principal member thereof'. He found it weakened by the immorality and insubordination resulting from civil war, and wanted to strengthen it by increasing paternal authority, even to the point of giving a father the right of life and death over his children.

Property, being an institution older than the State, ought to be respected by the State. The family, the primary community on whose solidity and health all other communities depend, rests upon it. Who destroys property weakens the family, and therefore the State also, which is made up of families.

The State Bodin defined as 'the right government of several families, and of what is common to them, with sovereign power'. The word 'right', in this definition, implies that the power is exercised for the common good or in accordance with the laws of nature. Sovereignty is defined as 'the absolute and perpetual power in a republic'. It is 'perpetual' because, whoever has it, though he acts through agents, does not lose it; it is perpetual in the sense of *inalienable*. It is absolute because whoever has it 'holds it, after God, only by the sword'; it is absolute in the sense of *unconditional*. The sovereign makes the law, which is his mere command, and himself is not subject to the law which he makes. Law is defined as the 'command of the sovereign touching all his subjects generally on general matters'.

The sovereign acts necessarily through agents; but, no matter how extensive the powers he delegates, no matter what rules he lays down or permits to arise concerning the passing of these powers from one person to another, they are always exercised on his behalf. The authority is always entirely his, even though others exercise it in his place, and he cannot be held to have lost any part of it merely because he has allowed them to exercise it for a long time. In other words, those who exercise authority under the sovereign have no prescriptive right to that authority which they can appeal to against the sovereign if he decides to deprive them of it. The right of the subject to his external possessions does not derive from the sovereign, nor does his authority within his own family. But all temporal authority which is not paternal belongs properly to the sovereign and is exercised by him directly or through agents. Whoever holds authority of the sovereign and claims it for his own offends against the sovereign.

The doctrine that the sovereign's authority is inalienable was directed against the feudal lords, both temporal or spiritual, who claimed rights of jurisdiction in temporal matters otherwise than as agents of the sovereign. The temporal lords claimed that these rights were hereditary, that they were inherited from their ancestors along with their estates. The bishops and abbots claimed that they were rights attached to their benefices. Bodin protested strongly against this assimilation of rights of jurisdiction with rights of property. He insisted that they are quite different in kind, since the first kind are exercised for the protection of the second. Kings may in the past have found it convenient to grant rights of jurisdiction to holders of certain properties, and may have allowed these rights to pass to their heirs or successors; but this could never convert authority into property, because the two are by nature different. No public office can be a part of any man's private estate, and whoever has rights of jurisdiction holds a public office. To hold any public office, except the highest, is to be an agent of whoever holds the highest office, of whoever is the sovereign.

Bodin did not want to deprive the lords temporal and spiritual of their jurisdictions; he knew that in practice it would be impossible to do so. He could not, as a Frenchman who had been in the king's service, echo Machiavelli's almost unqualified condemnation of the feudal nobility; he knew that the king, to make his power effective, needed the support of the nobles. They were part of the established order, and there was no civil service capable of taking over their functions. The most that Bodin could hope for was that the nobles would acknowledge that they held such authority as was theirs in trust from the king.

Bodin is given the credit of being the first to put forward clearly the conception of sovereignty as the legally unlimited power of making law. That power, he said, is perpetual (i.e. inalienable) and absolute; and he also suggested that it is indivisible, for he denied that there could be a mixed state, that is, one in which the supreme law-making power belongs to more than one person or assembly. He distinguished custom from law, saying that law is the sovereign's command and always takes precedence over custom. Now, the modern idea of sovereignty is precisely that it is supreme legislative power, 'absolute', 'inalienable', and 'indivisible'. When sovereignty is vested in an assembly, it is not thought of as divided between its members, but as belonging to the whole body.

Yet the conception of sovereignty, as we find it in Bodin, is still, for all its modernity, in some respects very unlike what it has since become. Bodin had nothing like Hobbes' gift for disentangling his ideas; whatever is new in him is stuck fast in the old, and takes much of its colour from its surroundings.

Though Bodin called sovereignty absolute, he also said that it is limited in three ways: by divine and natural law; by the law of succession (the law in virtue of which sovereignty is acquired by whoever rightly possesses it); and by the right to private property. Hobbes also spoke of laws of nature existing before there was sovereign power, and called them the commands of God; but he did not think of them as limiting the sovereign's authority. He went out of his way to argue that they must be taken to be whatever the sovereign says they are. Indeed, he even went so far as to suggest that they are not laws, properly so called, until there is a sovereign to enforce them. Whereas Bodin thought of them as somehow limiting the sovereign's authority, even though no one could justly use them as an excuse for actively resisting him.

It might be objected that this is making a distinction where there is no difference. Bodin said that the sovereign is responsible to God alone for how he uses his authority, and denied that subjects may resist him on the ground that he has broken the law of nature. To make this objection is, I think, rather to miss the point. We are discussing a political idea and not the practical consequences drawn from it. Bodin never suggested that the laws of nature, though binding on the sovereign, are not properly laws unless there is a sovereign to enforce them, nor yet that they are whatever the sovereign says they are. He did not distinguish, as Bentham was to do, moral principles from positive laws. He always spoke of the laws of nature as they were traditionally spoken of, as divine commands superior to the sovereign's commands and not always in keeping with them. He saw no contradiction between speaking in this way and calling the sovereign's authority absolute, and made no distinction between legal and moral obligation.

Bodin did not believe that subjects are bound to assume that every command of the sovereign is in keeping with the laws of nature; he forbade only active resistance to the sovereign, and allowed the subject to disobey only if he was convinced in conscience that what the sovereign commanded was contrary to God's law. He also said that the sovereign has no right to take his subjects' property without their consent, or to change the law of succession. The rule that establishes his right to govern is a rule he cannot change.

Hobbes, of course, knew as well as Bodin did that no human power is in fact absolute. But his purpose was to show how what must, of its very nature, be limited in fact, can be without limits in law. His purpose was different from Bodin's, and his conception of sovereignty clearer and closer to the modern one. Yet Bodin's originality was considerable; he was the first who clearly ascribed to sovereignty the attributes of inalienability and indivisibility, and who first classified states according to where supreme legislative authority lay within them. By monarchy he meant, not the government of one man whose authority is primarily executive and judicial (though he may also take part in making law), but the government of one man who by tradition alone has the right to make law. Aristocracy and democracy he re-defined on the same principle.

2. *Forms of Government*

Like other political philosophers, Bodin unconsciously passed off some of his own preferences as statements of fact. There are, he said, only three basic types of state or republic: monarchy, aristocracy, and democracy. Because sovereignty is indivisible, there cannot be a fourth type. Sovereignty must belong either to one person, or to a minority, or to a majority of the people. Even when it belongs to more than one person, it belongs entire to the whole group that has it, and is not shared among them. To say this is to imply that, where there is no sovereign, there is no state; for Bodin makes sovereignty part of his definition of the state.

Yet, in spite of his definition and would-be exhaustive classification of states into three main types, Bodin knew that in fact the power he called sovereign is sometimes shared by several persons and bodies; he knew that there are mixed types of states, and therefore states without sovereignty as he defined it. When he said that there are no mixed types, he really meant that there ought not to be any. He believed that states where the supreme legislative power is divided cannot perform their proper function, which is to afford security. Denmark, he said, has never enjoyed secure peace since the king was forced to share sovereign power with the nobles. Bodin made full use of the old prerogative of the political philosopher; he could annihilate something by definition, and then calmly go on to discuss what was wrong with it where it existed.

This tactic, though logically indefensible, is rhetorically effective. To speak of what ought not to be as if it could not be, though in fact it is, is somehow to make the condemnation more absolute. By putting the concept of sovereignty into the definition of the State, Bodin adds weight to his argument that the State cannot be stable nor its members secure unless supreme legislative authority belongs entire to one person or one body of persons. He also suggests, what he appears to have believed was true, that there is everywhere a tendency for this authority to be concentrated in the hands of one person or assembly. This, presumably, for two reasons: because every person and body among whom the powers which constitute sovereignty are divided will strive unceasingly to increase his or its share until one of them succeeds in engrossing the whole, and because it is the common interest that this should happen and the people will come to see that it is so and to acquiesce in it. Men need the State to give them security, and this it can best do when there is a sovereign inside it. There is therefore a strong bias towards sovereignty, and the bias is good. The State tends to become what it ought to be. This is not exactly what Bodin says, but it is, I think, suggested by his making sovereignty, as he defined it, an essential characteristic of the State.

Bodin distinguishes three kinds of monarchy: the royal and legitimate, the seigneurial or lordly, and the tyrannical. In the first the prince respects the laws of nature and does not interfere with his subjects' property; in the second he has rights over the persons and properties of his subjects and yet rules them for their good as well as his own; and in the third he disregards the laws of nature and treats his subjects as if their persons and estates belonged to him. These distinctions which are primarily moral illustrate a confusion, or at least an inconsistency, in Bodin's mind as to what makes human authority legitimate.

How, we may ask, does the seigneurial monarchy differ from the tyrannical? Bodin is ambiguous. Does the seigneurial monarch ruling his subjects for their own good exercise his rights over their persons and properties? Or does he, though the rights are his legally, refrain from exercising them? Does the tyrant's tyranny consist in his exercising rights which he does not have, or in his not ruling his subjects for their own good? In what does ruling subjects for their own good consist, if not in giving them security of person and property? Certainly, in the sixteenth century, to provide this security was thought to be the essential function of the temporal power. That being so, it would seem that the seigneurial monarch, when he rules his subjects for their own good, gives them security of person and property; it would seem that he rules in the same manner as the royal and legitimate monarch. Getting his power by conquest, he has a right not to rule his subjects for their own good, not to give them security of person and property; but he chooses not to exercise his right. If he did exercise it, he would be a bad ruler, though not a tyrant. For the tyrant is not merely the ruler who fails to give his subjects security of person and property; he is the ruler who fails to give it to them when he has no right to withhold it. He is the ruler who treats his subjects as if he had over them the right of a victor over the vanquished, when in fact he has no such right. It might seem that, logically, Bodin should have allowed for four, and not just three, types of monarchy; he should have distinguished the seigneurial monarch who chooses not to exercise the right which conquest gives him from the one who does exercise it.

Why then did Bodin not do this? Presumably because he was loth to admit that the ruler, no matter how he comes by his power, has the right to disregard the good of his subjects and to rule them entirely for his own good. But, since he accepted what the jurists had taught about the *ius gentium*, he could not bring himself to deny that the conqueror acquires a right over the persons and properties of the conquered. So he spoke as if the conqueror, while exercising this right, while ruling his subjects as the father of a family rules his slaves, might yet be ruling them for their own good, even when he disposed of their persons and properties as if they were his own. He spoke as if government might be good, might be in the interest of the governed, even though it did not give them security of person and property. But, if the function of government is to provide this security, if the good of the governed consists in their having it, how can a ruler govern for his subjects' good if he treats their persons and property as if they were his own? This is a question which Bodin could not answer. He did not reject the assumption commonly made in his day, and indeed for long afterwards, that the proper business of government is to give this security to the governed, that the public good consists in their having it; he did not suppose that political authority serves the same purpose as paternal authority. Nor did he hold that some men are by nature slaves and that therefore it is for their good to be treated as such. He could not reconcile his belief that what makes power legitimate is that it is exercised for the good of those subject to it with what he had learned from the jurists about the *ius gentium*. So he persuaded himself that it was possible to rule men for their good while depriving them of their personal freedom and property, and never troubled to ask what that good could then be. He found it possible to assert both that the seigneurial monarch, treating his subjects as slaves, could act for their good, and that the tyrant, by so treating them, must harm them. Unprovoked aggression against foreigners, if successful, creates a right to treat them as slaves, while unprovoked aggression against one's own subjects or compatriots does not. Clearly, the moralist and the lawyer in Bodin never came to terms.

Bodin, loving symmetry, having distinguished three forms of monarchy, goes on to distinguish three forms of aristocracy and three of democracy; but he speaks of them so perfunctorily that there is little to be gained by considering them in detail. What he says about the three main types of government is more interesting than what he says about the three forms within each type.

Each type of government has its distinctive devices, customs and merits, which the statesman must understand if he is to preserve it and them. He must learn to distinguish the customs and devices which strengthen a form of government from those which weaken it. Bodin, despite his preference for monarchy, could see the virtues of other kinds of government. Popular government, he said, is prolific in great men, and its civil laws are closest to natural justice. The advantage of aristocracy is that it rests on what is permanent among men, natural inequality. It gives authority to those most worthy of it, to the able, to the rich, to the well born. Bodin seems to have believed that nobility and riches are usually effects of character and talent, that men who rise to high places mostly deserve to do so. Even when the heirs to wealth and honours are the most ordinary of men, their privileges are not unjust; for their ancestors excelled in some way or other, and it is right and expedient that able men should be rewarded in their posterity. Bodin could see virtues in both popular government and aristocracy. He prided himself on his open mind. There is not a trace in the *Republic* of the doctrine of the divine right of kings.

Yet Bodin's standard of good government was monarchy and, above all, French monarchy. The king of France seemed to him the best of all royal and legitimate monarchs. Not necessarily the actual king, the man who happened to be on the throne, but the king as he might be if he made full and wise use of the authority that tradition gave him. Popular government, even at its best, is unstable. It stimulates all ambitions, and therefore all talents, but it also gives opportunities to the selfish, unscrupulous, or foolish. It is not true that the people are good judges of men; the qualities they most admire are not the qualities that make good rulers. To give control to the people is to hope for wisdom from what is by nature superficial and impetuous. Though aristocracy avoids some of the evils of democracy, it encourages others as much or more. It is by nature factious. When the nobles quarrel, one party seeks the support of the common people against the other, to the great damage of the State. Aristocracy, almost as much as democracy, lacks secrecy and despatch in the conduct of public affairs. It creates a wider gulf than either monarchy or democracy between the privileged and unprivileged, and so makes it dangerous to arm the people, thus weakening the State militarily.

Monarchy has its disadvantages: sudden changes of policy when one prince succeeds another, disputed successions, regencies, the corrupting influences of undisputed power. But it is, take it all in all, the best of possible governments. When the monarch is hereditary, reverence for him grows from generation to generation; he knows that his authority is lasting and will pass after him to his natural heirs, and is therefore strongly inclined to work for posterity. Getting power without seeking it, he values it less for itself than for what he can do with it. To live in his people's memory, he must use power well; he must care for all classes of his subjects, and stands only to lose by allowing one class to oppress another. He can protect small groups against the people, and in the public interest can prefer their advice to the clamour of louder and more powerful factions. Though Bodin admitted that unlimited power corrupts, he thought it so necessary to public security that the risk was worth taking. His own belief in God was strong, and he probably took it for granted that kings, unless they were foolish or wicked, would feel their responsibility to God. The fear of God, he thought, is a reasonable fear, and therefore a considerable motive with every properly educated man. The modern argument, that responsibility to God alone is virtual irresponsibility, would probably have seemed impious to him, as it would have to most people in the sixteenth century.

E

Bodin distinguished between three kinds of justice: the commutative or arithmetic, the geometric, and the harmonious. The first, which is proper to popular governments, treats all men alike, whatever their personal qualities and social standing. It treats every offence or claim or contract on its intrinsic merits, as a situation which might affect any man; it treats the individual, whoever he may be, as an abstract possessor of rights and duties. 'Geometric' justice, which is aristocratic, takes account of the social standing of the offender or plaintiff, treating him differently according to his circumstances, his wealth, and the class he belongs to. The best justice is neither 'arithmetic' nor 'geometric' but harmonious, taking into account the nature of the act or claim, the wealth and standing of the agent or claimant, and the needs of society. This 'harmonious' justice, which accepts inequality but keeps it in bounds, is proper to monarchy.

These distinctions are not quite as clear as Bodin takes them to be. He treats harmonious justice as a kind of happy combination of the other two, and implies that each of the others is one-sided. Geometric justice takes account of the wealth and social standing of the offender or claimant, and so too does harmonious justice. How then do the two differ? Clearly, geometric justice, just as much as the others must take account of the nature of any offence or claim on which it has to pronounce; it cannot refuse to consider whether the offence is murder or larceny or whether the claim is for money or for the restitution of conjugal rights. Every kind of justice, whether it is proper to democracy, aristocracy or monarchy, necessarily takes into account the nature of the offences and claims submitted to it; so that the second and third kinds must differ from the first by taking something else into account as well, and this something, Bodin tells us, is the wealth and social standing of offenders and claimants. But, in that case, harmonious justice, proper to monarchy, is not a combination of the other two, it is merely a milder form of geometric or aristocratic justice, taking account of the same things but not attaching the same weight to them.

Moreover, the justice proper to democracy is not really *arithmetic* in the sense defined by Bodin; it does not impose the same penalties for the same offences regardless of the wealth of the offenders. It imposes heavier fines on the rich than on the poor. It aims at maintaining a certain type of social order, and imposes penalties which are adequate deterrents for that purpose. A fine sufficient to deter a poor man will not deter a rich one, while other forms of punishment may bear more heavily on the rich than on the poor. Only where there is complete equality of wealth and social standing can arithmetic justice achieve its purpose. But Bodin tells us that complete equality is impossible, even though democracy is not. It follows therefore that strictly arithmetic justice is not suited to any possible society, not even to a democracy.

Nevertheless, it is worth taking a closer look at the social philosophy which seems to lie behind Bodin's conception of 'harmonious' justice. He believed that there never had been and never could be a society where there was complete equality of wealth and social standing. If an attempt were made to create this equality artificially, it could not last but would immediately begin to disappear, if only because men's talents differ and some men have more children than others. To maintain equality it would be necessary, at frequent intervals, to put an end to the inequalities which had appeared in the meantime. Every so many years those who had outdistanced their fellows would have to be put back on a level with them. There would have to be periodic cancellations of debts and annulments of contracts, or otherwise creditors would grow rich and important and rise superior to debtors. But this would destroy good faith and therefore undermine the security which government exists to provide. The attempt to maintain equality, if it is seriously and persistently made, must in the long run destroy society.

This argument, unless I am mistaken, implies that, whatever the legal system, whatever the structure of rights and obligations, some people will always contrive to do better than others, becoming much richer and more powerful than their neighbours, so that, if equality is to be maintained, it will always be necessary to change the laws and to tamper with rights and obligations to the detriment of the rich and the exalted and to the advantage of the poor and the lowly. The argument takes it for granted that no stable system of law can be devised which will keep inequalities within fairly narrow limits. This assumption, at a time when no one had thought of death duties or of a graduated income tax, seemed plausible. That taxation could be used to offset the tendency for inequality to grow always greater simply did not occur to Bodin, whose respect for property rights was as great as Locke's. Taxes could be rightly levied, so he thought, only to meet the expenses of government. With such ideas fixed in his head it is not surprising that he could imagine no other way of maintaining equality than by the cancellation of debts and the annulment of contracts.

Bodin was not content to argue that equality is impossible; he also thought it undesirable. He put forward what he believed to be strong arguments in favour of inequality and inherited privileges. It is not enough, he said, to ensure that men are rewarded according to their talents, if they are not allowed to pass on their rewards to their children. For men ordinarily work for their children as well as for themselves; they hope to live on in their posterity. Deprive them of this hope, and you weaken society by weakening a motive that causes men to make the best of their talents. The ablest of them devote their energies to getting glory, power and wealth; to getting whatever raises them above their neighbours and proves their superiority. They also look forward beyond their own lives; they wish to be honoured in their children, to perpetuate themselves and their greatness. A man's concern for his posterity, as Bodin saw it, is clearly not a pure form of altruism; it has a large element of self-love in it. But he believed that self-love, when it works in this way, works for the good of the community.

Bodin admitted that inequality can be excessive and distinctions of class too rigid. Not only do the poor need to be protected from the rich and the powerful, but men of humble birth ought not to be excluded from the highest honours. Society ought to provide men both with security and with opportunities of bettering themselves. Democracy, insisting on an impossible equality, must, in the endeavour to attain it, weaken the bonds that hold society together and the motives that enrich and strengthen it; while aristocracy divides society too much and too rigidly. Monarchy alone both maintains and moderates inequality; it keeps the social hierarchy firmly in place, and yet also enables men of talent to climb to high places. It makes for social harmony, which equality does not; for equals are jealous of equals, whereas, where privileges are inherited or acquired by merit, ordinary people respect their superiors. Conventional inequalities are irksome chiefly to persons of inferior birth and superior talents, but monarchy provides an outlet for their ambitions.

Though Bodin believed that what he called royal and legitimate monarchy is the best of all governments, he did not think it suited to all peoples. Governments must, he thought, vary with the peoples subject to them. A whole chapter of the *Republic* is taken up with a discussion of the effects of climate and physical environment on peoples. Northerners are tougher, more active physically, and also more chaste than other people; southerners are physically weaker, more thoughtful, and more sensual. The people in between, living in the middle regions, are less tough but quicker-witted than the northerners, and also tougher and more active than the southerners; they excel in the political arts, and it is among them that we must expect to find the best governments. The southerners excel in the abstract and occult sciences, in mathematics, theology, and astronomy; they have founded all the great religions; but politically they are weak.

Mountain peoples, even when they live in southern regions, incline to northern characteristics; whereas plainsmen, wherever they live, are apt to be like southerners. The further west we move, at whatever altitude, the more northern in type the people we find; the further east, the more southern. Bodin did not adhere rigidly to these generalities; he admitted that men of exceptional talent, no matter where they are born, rise superior to a national character largely determined by climate and geography. He also admitted that society can change even when climate does not; for he noticed that Roman society had changed from age to age. Bodin's reflections on the social effects of climate and geography were neglected for nearly two centuries, until Montesquieu took them up again to form one of the major themes of his largest work.

In *De l'Esprit des Lois*, there is not only a theory about the social effects of climate, there are also arguments favourable to monarchy very like those to be found in Bodin's *Republic*. Bodin's affinities with Montesquieu are obvious, as are also his affinities with Hobbes. There is, however, another great political thinker with whom he has as much in common as with either of them. By Burke's time, Bodin was almost forgotten, and it is improbable that Burke ever studied him. But there are remarkable similarities between them. Both are impressed by the variety of social and political institutions, which they are more inclined to justify than condemn. Both approve of inequality, and go out of their way to explain how it holds society together; both are respecters of tradition and admit the need for reform; both believe that society is weakened unless the claims of birth and talent are alike respected; both see in religion the best preservative of the social order, and yet value it more for its own sake than for its social effects; and for both freedom is an acquired rather than a natural right. Bodin is certainly to be counted among the greater conservative political philosophers.

3. Limitations on Power: The French Monarchy

Bodin believed in a sovereign monarchy, and yet also wanted royal power limited in all sorts of ways. This might be thought a weakness in him when he is compared with Hobbes. He was certainly less consistent than the English philosopher; but he had, what Hobbes had not, a considerable experience of government. He was more realistic, though less lucid, and he appears more inconsistent than in fact he was. He thought it dangerous to allow that anyone had a legal right to set a limit to royal authority, but he knew that the king could not rule efficiently without devices to retard his actions. Bodin wanted royal edicts subjected to close scrutiny; he wanted them responsibly criticized and their defects brought respectfully to the king's notice. He feared not delay but deadlock. No one must have power to challenge the king's authority; no one must thwart him when his mind is quite made up. The appeal must always be from the king to the king better advised. The king's will must prevail in the end; but the king, when making up his mind, should take account of the opinions of those who, by tradition, have the right to advise him. The king's will must be established in traditional ways and with the help of competent persons. His power depends on the loyalty, the independent judgment, and the trust of his advisers and officials, and also on his people's love. His power is legally absolute but not arbitrary; it should be exercised after proper deliberation.

Bodin did not reach this position immediately. In the *Methodus*, published in 1566 ten years before the *Republic*, he was still arguing that the king is bound by the laws, not of his own good will, but of right, and that he cannot oblige the *parlements* to register his edicts. It was the religious wars that changed his mind, causing him to say unequivocally that the monarch, as their author, is superior to the civil laws, and that the *parlements*, despite their right of remonstrance, cannot refuse to register royal edicts if the king, having considered their objections, still insists on their doing so. The authority of the *parlements* and of the estates, general and provincial, comes from the king, just as do the jurisdictions granted to dukes, marquises and barons. What the king has given, he may take away. Indeed, he never really gave it, for his authority, being supreme, is inalienable; he cannot give away any part of it, he can only appoint agents to use it in his name. All who have rights of jurisdiction, all who declare the law and apply it within his dominions are his officers, and an office is never the property of the man who holds it.

But though Bodin had by 1576 come to hold this position, he by no means wanted to reduce either the *parlements* or the estates to impotence. He thought of the estates less as legislatures than as assemblies where popular needs and grievances could be discussed and brought to to the king's notice. A meeting of the estates-general was a meeting of the sovereign with the representatives of his people. Such meetings were, in Bodin's eyes, not only useful but indispensable; the sovereign must keep contact with his subjects, and must not deal with them only through officials. Meetings of the estates enhance the king's majesty and strengthen the people's devotion to him. They are a form of political intercourse making for good government. They are also necessary if the people are to vote subsidies to the king, who, being obliged to respect his subjects' property, cannot lay new taxes on them without their consent. Bodin was perfectly well aware that the need to get his subjects' consent to new taxes limited the sovereign's power. He had himself, in the very year when the *Republic* was published, induced the Third Estate to refuse a subsidy, hoping thereby to thwart the royal will. But the need for consent to taxation detracted nothing, in Bodin's eyes, from the sovereignty of the French king. This need provided the king with strong motives for not making widely unpopular laws and for not pursuing policies strongly condemned by his subjects. Bodin saw no harm in this. The king was still sovereign; there were no legal limits to his right to make law. No one had the right to resist him on the ground that he had abused his authority. It is one thing to provide the king with strong motives for not using his authority in ways which seem dangerous or wicked to his subjects, and quite another to admit their right to resist him on the ground that he has broken a law superior to his will.

Bodin preferred the *parlements* to the estates. Being himself a lawyer, he saw in these hereditary corporations consisting of lawyers a useful and responsible check on the royal will. He cites with approval many cases of kings giving way to them. They could not claim to be representative of the people; they were royal courts exercising justice in the sovereign's name. They could hardly aspire to be more than guardians of the law and keepers of the king's conscience. Bodin, who had no faith in popular wisdom, had considerable respect for the sagacity and moderation of professional bodies. He exalts the rôle of the lawyer in preventing abuses of authority, just as Montesquieu was to do after him.

Bodin would have liked the king to establish a new kind of army, recruited and paid by the Crown; he would have liked the army to be more professional and less feudal. He distrusted the nobles, and his preference for the *parlements* over the estates may have been due as much to fear of feudal pretensions as to contempt for popular wisdom. He sympathized with the lawyers in their efforts to curtail feudal privileges for the benefit of the monarchy. He argued that the nobles, unless they served their king in time of war without payment, should lose their tax immunities. But he was too conservative, too respectful of tradition, to be whole-heartedly opposed to what was still the most powerful class in France.

Bodin wanted the royal power legally absolute but in practice limited in traditional ways. He appealed to history, and therefore, since (though he might not know it himself) he wanted a stronger monarchy than France had in fact ever had, he interpreted the past to suit his argument. Nevertheless, he wanted to preserve much that had long existed. He wanted to preserve corporate bodies of many kinds, because they, more easily than individuals, can defend themselves against arbitrary power, not by violence, but by making their influence felt. Such bodies must never act conspiratorially, and must never challenge the sovereign's laws. But their very existence, their moderation, their prestige, their number, encourage the sovereign to consider carefully what laws he shall make for the common good, and also provide him with powerful motives for respecting his own laws. Bodin wanted many obstacles to the royal will, but none that was insurmountable. There ought always to be some final authority, some person or persons whose decisions cannot be legally challenged, whom persistently to disobey is to be guilty of a punishable offence. In France that authority could, he thought, belong only to the king, who could not in practice exercise it just as he pleased, for no authority – not even sovereign power – is absolute in fact as well as in law. What is required for good government is, on the one hand, that no one should be in a position to place his veto on whoever has the highest authority in the State, and on the other, that the obstacles to that authority (and in practice there will always be some, good or bad) should serve to direct it to the common good.[1]

Bodin had been too long in the royal service to have much admiration for kings. He was a patriot before he was a royalist. The civil wars seemed to him to prove that the nobles, when not under discipline, were too selfish and turbulent to carry out public duties conscientiously; France needed their spirit and their talents but could use them best in the royal service. For the common people, Bodin felt much sympathy but little respect. He found them too ignorant and unreflective to help themselves effectively, and their passions and prejudices made it easy for unscrupulous persons to excite and mislead them. Their anger might be dangerous to order but was likely to be of little advantage to themselves. To Bodin the common people seemed (if I may so put it) a blind and foolish, but not evil, monster, to be firmly led, decently treated, and kept quiet by all suitable means. Distrusting the French nobles and believing that the lower classes were politically helpless, he had no alternative but to be a champion of monarchy. He saw his country in danger and thought that the king alone could save it.

Though Bodin did not admire kings, he idealized the French monarchy. He saw it as an elaborate structure, with the king at its centre, surrounded by the great institutions of State, so disposed about the monarch that he could hardly in practice abuse his authority. Surrounded by conscientious, intelligent, and loyal servants, he would have powerful motives for governing well. There was, while Bodin lived, less danger of the king's abusing his power than of its being challenged by unscrupulous factions for selfish ends. Bodin's ideal was the king well served, the monarch supported by an apparatus of power

---

[1] Bodin did not look upon the Church as a useful brake on the royal will. Writing in a country which was overwhelmingly Catholic, he could not deny the autonomy of the Church within its own sphere. He wanted ecclesiastical jurisdiction limited to maintaining discipline within the Church, and argued that clerks should answer to the ordinary courts for all temporal offences. The Church should be prevented from growing too rich, and should be obliged to provide a decent living for everyone in holy orders, no matter how humble his office. Religious unity is desirable provided it can be maintained without violence and without strong measures against dissenters. The prince is right to forbid attacks on the Established Church, but ought to use only gentle methods to persuade his subjects to adhere to it. Strong action is justified only against atheism, which deprives men of the most powerful motive for acting justly.

Bodin, believing strongly in God and in society's need of religion, would not have the prince indifferent to it, nor equally favourable to all forms of it. It is the duty of the prince to promote religion by suitable means, and to preserve religious unity if he can do so without recourse to violent or severe measures. Religious unity is desirable, not because God requires it, but because it makes for social peace.

whose regular and smooth working would tend of itself to elaborate and purify his will, making him reasonable and public-spirited.

Chauviré ascribes two great qualities to Bodin: originality and good sen.e. He then goes on to explain how it is that, in spite of these qualities, Bodin is seldom read. His greatest book is ill-constructed, digressive, repetitious, bizarre and verbose; his style is dull and facile, typical of the civil servant and the politician, his similes are mostly borrowed and ordinary, though sometimes fresh and striking; he is frank and naïve, he has considerable vigour (*verve*) and some imagination but lacks order and polish and lucidity. Chauviré, whose excellent book is clearly a labour of love, speaks of Bodin as of a man destined to be eclipsed by men more brilliant and more gifted than himself. He makes, in the course of his book, every point he can in favour of Bodin, and then in the end passes a verdict on him which, though essentially just, is so cautious as to be almost severe. Perhaps he is afraid of making too large a claim on behalf of a fellow Angevin, perhaps he is afraid of being led astray by local patriotism.

Chauviré might have been less cautious. As an apologist for royal supremacy Bodin is less eloquent, less lucid, less splendid than Bossuet, but he is also more original and more ingenious. He is a less subtle reasoner than Hobbes but reveals a greater understanding of how government operates. He is less brilliant than Montesquieu but shrewder and less carried away by his own ideas. If we look only at the content of his arguments and not at how they are presented, he produced what was perhaps the ablest case ever made for monarchy, as Europe knew it in the sixteenth, seventeenth and eighteenth centuries. Not the most impressive or persuasive case, especially at the first reading, but the case which makes the most realistic assumptions and stands up best to criticism.

He was not a practical innovator; he proposed no great changes. His originality consists, above all, in a new way of looking at what men were already familiar with: the great monarchies of the West. To explain these monarchies he put forward new ideas, which he did not perhaps define as clearly as they were to be defined after him, but which he used consistently enough to make his contemporaries see what was familiar with fresh eyes. And the State which absorbed his attention and his loyalty was more complicated and more difficult to understand than the small republics of Machiavelli's Italy. He was less narrow, more elaborate and more moderate, more imaginative and more adequate in his views, than anyone else moved to write about politics by the spectacle of a France in the throes of civil war.

E*

Chapter 4

HOBBES

I. INTRODUCTORY

LIKE the *Vindiciae*, like Bodin's *Republic*, like the theory of the divine right of kings, Hobbes' political philosophy is a product of civil strife and war. But, unlike these others, it does not take sides. On personal grounds, as a tutor in noble houses, Hobbes might prefer the Royalists to their opponents; he might even, on political grounds, prefer the sovereignty of one man to the sovereignty of a whole parliament of men. The Puritans were not congenial to him. His sympathies inclined him to one side rather than the other, but he did not allow them to affect his arguments. His fundamental position was different from that of either party to the civil war.

The Royalists and Parliamentarians quarrelled about the proper limits of the legislative and executive powers; they quarrelled about what tradition allowed, and also, though to a lesser extent, about what was naturally just. Their knowledge of history was slight; they had the most one-sided and inadequate ideas about their country's past. They talked a great deal about fundamental law, and accused one another of subverting it; but they had only vague and confused ideas about it. Both sides wanted what we should call constitutional monarchy. Unfortunately, neither side could give a clear account of how that monarchy should be organized. Both sides were so busy making and resisting particular demands, so immersed in the conflict, that neither could see the system of government as a whole or understand how it had been affected by the early reforms of the Long Parliament – reforms accepted by most of the Royalists as well as by their opponents. The old monarchy – the system created by the Tudors and inherited from them by James and Charles – ceased to exist in 1641, killed by the Long Parliament. But neither of the factions into which that Parliament split understood what had happened. They both believed they were fighting to maintain something traditional, something that had worked well for centuries and was now threatened by the other side.

Hobbes found nothing to attract him in the arguments of either side. They were arguing about how power should be divided, about what tradition allowed and what was required by natural justice. He cared nothing for tradition and had his own peculiar account of natural law. He put two questions that did not interest the belligerents: What is the essential function of government? and: What kind of government can best perform it? His answer to the first question was: Government exists to give as much security as possible to individuals; and to the second: It cannot do so effectively unless supreme authority is all in the same hands. The belligerents were agreed that power must be divided; they quarrelled about the division of it, and yet were not clear in their own minds just how they wanted it divided. But Hobbes knew his own mind perfectly: Power ought not to be divided. If he was right, the war was not worth fighting, and the quarrel that led to it was absurd.

Hobbes, as you can see, was a very superior person, very much *au dessus de la mêlée*. Here were people drifting into an unnecessary war only because they could not think clearly, because they put irrelevant questions and busied themselves about unimportant matters. He would put the right questions and give the true answers; he would enlighten his generation. Hobbes had great faith in the persuasive power of reason, and also in his own powers as a reasoner. Like many of his contemporaries, he believed that the quarrel that led to war was merely an argument about principles, an intellectual dispute; and thought himself wiser than the quarrellers for seeing that their dispute rested on misconceptions. The clash of interests that lay behind the dispute was invisible to him.

Hobbes took little notice of politics until the approach of civil war turned his mind to it. He was a philosopher before he became a political theorist, and he applied philosophical methods acquired independently of the study of politics to the solution of political problems. On a prolonged visit to Paris, he had made the acquaintance of Mersenne, Descartes' friend, and of Gassendi, a materialist philosopher. Hobbes professed not to admire the Cartesian philosophy; he rejected Descartes' sharp distinction between matter and mind, and was attracted by the materialism of Gassendi. But his method was like Descartes'; he too began with definitions and with simple and distinct ideas, and erected a whole philosophy on them. It is not always the men we admire most who most influence us.

It was after his return from Paris in 1637, when he was already in his fiftieth year, that Hobbes decided to apply his newly discovered philosophic method to politics. He was stimulated to do so by the already bitter controversies going on around him. His first political treatise, *The Elements of Law*, was completed just before the Long Parliament met in November 1640. Hobbes, who seems to have prided himself on his timidity as other men do on their courage, decided that Parliament would not like his treatise; and so he fled to France. He was the first émigré, and he did not return to England for eleven years.

Hobbes' first political treatise was a plea for absolute monarchy. It sought to prove more than the king had ever claimed. But Hobbes was not really more Royalist than the king. His argument for absolute monarchy could easily be, and very soon was, transformed into a general argument for absolute government. Hobbes never really abandoned the position he took up in 1640. In his two greatest works on politics, in *De Cive* and in *Leviathan*, he merely elaborated doctrines already put forward before the civil war began. The first edition of *De Cive* appeared in 1642; the considerably enlarged and altered edition in 1647. The first English translation of *De Cive*, made by Hobbes himself, was published in 1651, the same year as Leviathan. This translation, entitled *Philosophical Rudiments Concerning Government and Society*, forms the second volume of the Molesworth Edition of Hobbes' *English Works*.

II. HOBBES' ACCOUNT OF HUMAN NATURE

Hobbes' account of human nature is simple. Whatever a man desires he calls good, and whatever he is averse to he calls evil; so that good and evil are not qualities inherent in things but are only signs revealing how the persons who use the signs feel about the things they apply them to. Will is not different from desire but is ' the last appetite in deliberating'. When a man has more than one desire and yet can satisfy only one, he contemplates the objects of his desires and compares them with one another, until at last one desire conquers the others and he acts. Continual success in getting what a man desires is felicity; and his power is his ability to get whatever he may desire. Man, unlike the other animals, is rational; he is aware of himself as a creature liable to many desires and can discover the best means of satisfying them. He has therefore not only his natural appetites to satisfy, but also acquires an appetite for power and for whatever power depends on: riches, honour, and command. This appetite, unlike the natural appetites which are quickly satisfied when they recur, is insatiable. A man can never have too much power; he therefore becomes a competitor with all other men for it, and so their enemy. 'Competition of Riches, Honour, Command, or other power, enclineth to Contention, Enmity and War. Because the way of one Competitor, to the attaining his desire, is to kill, subdue, supplant, or repel the others.'

'The proper object of every man's Will', says Hobbes, 'is some Good to himself.' Imagination can make him interested in another's good, but only because he feels pleasure or pain at the thought of himself situated as that other is. Pity is the grief we feel for the calamity of another arising from the imagination of the like calamity befalling ourselves. Hobbes therefore implies that man is by nature self-regarding and can never be otherwise.

Now, this doctrine, this psychological egoism, which so many of

Hobbes' critics have fastened on, is not really necessary to his political theory. Even if Hobbes had described pity and benevolence differently and had not reduced them to manifestations of self-pity and self-love, his political conclusions might have been the same. For pity and benevolence, even if we suppose them genuinely altruistic, are not emotions strong enough to explain the existence of political society. Even Hume, who was so far from being a psychological egoist that he went out of his way to refute that way of thinking, thought that men's purely self-regarding feelings go almost the whole way in explaining their political behaviour. It is in a stable society that benevolent feelings have the largest scope, and they are therefore much more effects than causes of the stability it was Hobbes' purpose to account for. The less orderly and secure men's lives, and the less they are bound by rules, the more ruthless, narrow, and selfish they are. On this point, most modern psychologists would, I think, agree with Hobbes. The human child, in his earliest relations with others, is almost entirely selfish; he has to be taught to think of others. In other words, he has to be disciplined. We may quarrel with Hobbes for supposing that men ever were in a state of nature, or for misunderstanding how social discipline affects them and creates new motives in them; but he was surely much nearer being right than wrong when he assumed that men who had never been under any kind of social discipline would be wholly selfish.

Hobbes denied that society is natural. It is important to get clear just what he meant by the denial, for it has often been misinterpreted. In a note to Chapter I of his own English version of *De Cive*, he says, commenting on his much criticized assertion that man is not born fit for society:

Wherefore I deny not that men (even nature compelling) *desire* to come together. But civil societies are not mere meetings, but bonds, to the making whereof faith and compacts are necessary; the virtue whereof to children and fools, and the profit whereof to those who have not yet tasted the miseries which accompany its defects, is altogether unknown; whence it happens that those, because they know not what society is, cannot enter into it; these, because ignorant of the benefits it brings, care not for it. Manifest therefore it is, that all men, because they are born in infancy, are born unapt for society ... wherefore man is made fit for society not by nature but by education.

In other words, it is education that makes us 'apt for society', which means, not desirous of company, but fit for society; and men in the state of nature are, *ex hypothesi*, without education. It may be that they never were in a state of nature, and therefore never without a social environment moulding their characters – which is education in the largest sense. But if, in order to discover what men gain from society, we imagine them in a state of nature, we must divest them of the qualities they acquire by being subject to social discipline. We need not suppose that nothing in their nature draws them into society, but we must suppose them unfit for society.

Much breath and ink have been wasted denouncing the cynicism of Hobbes. No doubt, men are not as self-regarding as he thought them, and his accounts of several of their passions will not bear examination. His definitions are often too simple. But he was not, by the standards of his time, either cynical or severe. Nobody in the seventeenth century believed that man, untouched by society, is good. Most theologians agreed that man is born evil, with the taint of Adam upon him, and that only by God's grace is he able to attain merit. The peculiarity of Hobbes is not that he asserted man's natural selfishness – for moralists had been busy asserting and denouncing it for centuries – but that he denied his essential wickedness. There is not a word in Hobbes about original sin. On the contrary, he says that ' the Desires, and other Passions of Man, are in themselves no Sin. No more are the Actions that proceed from those Passions, till they know a Law that forbids them.' His contemporaries were not much disturbed by Hobbes' cynicism or his low opinion of human nature. In the writings of religious men they could find much harsher and more terrible judgements. Nearly all the Puritans thought much worse than Hobbes did of human nature; but he, unlike them, did not set himself up above the common run of mankind as one of the elect.

What his contemporaries really disliked about Hobbes was his peculiar attitude to God, which many took for atheism, and his being satisfied with human nature as he found it. This and this, he said, is the stuff of human nature, which in itself is neither good nor bad. Without the discipline of law, men cannot help but behave in ways that make them miserable; but, put them under that discipline, and there is nothing about them that need prevent their happiness. At bottom, they remain always the same, passionate and rational, with reason serving their passions; their real nature does not change, and there is nothing inherently evil about that nature. Create the proper environment, and their nature will do them no harm.

Hobbes did not leave God out of his picture of the world, but he did give the impression that he had first painted the picture without God, and had then put God in afterwards, to save the appearances. His contemporaries were not altogether deceived. Hobbes was saying that men could, by their own devices, get for themselves all the happiness they wanted. In a still theological age the sin of this worldly and complacent philosopher was not cynicism but pride.

' And this much for the ill condition, which man by meer Nature is actually placed in; though with a possibility to come out of it, consisting partly in the Passions, partly in his Reason.' Reason gains no victory over the passions. It is merely that, as a result of the terrible experiences of the state of nature, the passions that incline men to peace grow in the end stronger than the passions that incline them to war. This condition is not enduring, and men cannot get peace except by the use of their reason. The office of reason is to serve the passions by discovering the best means of satisfying them. Thus it is that reason suggests 'convenient articles of peace'. It can only suggest but not impose them. Man always remains a passionate creature. His actions are determined primarily by his desires and emotions and only secondarily by reason. While the passions that incline men to war are the stronger there is no hope of peace; for reason always serves the stronger passions; but the state of continual war is so terrible that the passions that incline men to peace must in the end grow strong enough to cause them to seek peace. It is then only that reason, always in the service of the passions, teaches them the way to get peace. The precepts it teaches are what men otherwise call the laws of nature.

Hobbes' account of the relations between reason and the passions is open to criticism on two grounds: it does not sufficiently allow that reason can affect the quality of men's passions, and it supposes that men are more purposeful and consistent than they in fact are. In other words, it makes too little of reason in one way, and too much of it in another.

It is misleading to say that reason merely serves the passions, that it does not prescribe ends but only discovers the means to them. Hobbes sometimes speaks as if man would still have the same passions even if he were not rational; as if all reason does for him is to enable him to satisfy his passions more easily. But a rational creature has passions he would not have if he lacked reason; he has, through his reason, conceptions of himself, his environment, and his relations with other creatures like himself, which he could not have unless he were rational. All his emotions, all his desires, are deeply affected by these conceptions. The whole quality of his life is altered by them. Hobbes admits that men come to desire some things because they are rational; they desire power, for instance, because it is a means to felicity, and they could not know this unless they were rational. He even admits that power, which is desired at first for what it brings, comes in the end to be desired for its own sake, and often more strongly than any other thing. But he does not see how these admissions undermine his account of how reason stands to the passions. Man can know himself and his surroundings, and can also have illusions about the world and himself, as no animal without reason could do. To speak of him, as Hobbes does, as if he were just a creature of passions like the other animals, and differed from them only in being able to use reason to satisfy his passions, is lamentably inadequate. This shallow psychology was later taken over by some of the Utilitarians, and helps to explain much that is flat and poor about their philosophies.

Man is more deeply affected by reason than Hobbes supposed, and yet also less reasonable in the pursuit of his ends. Hobbes speaks of man as if he were clear in his mind what he wanted, and were therefore easily persuadable by reason. Look, Hobbes says to him, this is what you want, and these are the ways to get it. Take careful stock of your position, and it will then be obvious to you what you should do. Hobbes would have us believe that all men's troubles come from their not knowing how best to get what they want; it seldom occurred to him that they might come from their not knowing what they want, from confusions of thought and feeling too deep to be unravelled and which yet only creatures endowed with reason are liable to. And so Hobbes, who disparaged reason, also made too much of it; and in this also some of the Utilitarians followed him.

III. THE LAWS OF NATURE

Hobbes' conception of the laws of nature is difficult and requires careful elucidation. He calls these laws maxims of prudence and also divine commands. If they were only the first, they would clearly not be moral laws; at least not in any usual sense of moral. If they were the second, they might be moral laws. Whether we conclude that they are or not depends, of course, on how we interpret Hobbes' meaning.

The laws of nature, as they were ordinarily conceived in Hobbes' time, were supposed to be binding on men even in the absence of all authority of man over man, even in the state of nature. They were both descriptive and prescriptive; they were thought of partly as psychological and partly as moral laws, though the difference between the two kinds of law was seldom made clear. For example, self-preservation was usually treated as a natural law, and yet also as a mode of behaviour and not as a rule of conduct. It was observed that man does, as a matter of fact, seek to preserve himself, and his doing so was called a law of nature. It was also commonly supposed to be his duty not to interfere with other men in what they did to preserve themselves, and this duty too was called a law of nature. The laws of nature, as they were traditionally understood, in part described ends which it was taken for granted that men did pursue, even outside society, merely because they were the sort of creatures they were (or, as it was often put, 'by necessity of their nature'), and in part laid down the rules that they ought to follow, as creatures pursuing these ends, in their dealings with one another. You and all other men, in virtue of your humanity, have certain needs and aspirations. Since you are rational, you can know that other people have these needs as well as you do, and can discover the rules all men ought to follow in order not to prevent one another from achieving the purposes common to their kind. Men are God's creatures. He made them what they are. By endowing them with reason, He enabled them to pursue their ends differently from other animals. Traditionally, both the needs attributed to men in virtue of their humanity and the rules which it was supposed reason required them to follow in their dealings with one another were treated as effects of God's will. The laws of nature were therefore also laws of God, and were supposed to hold good in the state of nature as much as in political society. It was thought that men, because there are rules which they ought to conform to even in the absence of all human government, have natural rights against one another; rights which governments can make secure but do not create. Everyone has a right to require of others that they should keep to the rules in their dealings with him; he would have this right even in the state of nature, and he has it in political society.

It was usually supposed that the ground of natural obligation, of the duty to follow the rules which all must follow if men are to achieve their natural purposes, is the will of God. Our duty in the first place is to God, and to other men only because God has commanded us to love one another. Thus, we do our duty when we do what God requires of us. Now, in itself, this doctrine does not imply that obligation arises either from fear or from self-interest. True, Christian writers delighted to speak of God's power and to repeat that the fear of God is the beginning of wisdom. But they did not put forward God's omnipotence as the only or chief ground of obligation. We ought to obey God, not because we are completely in His power, but because He made us and desires our good. He also threatens to punish our disobedience, and so provides us with a strong motive for obeying Him; but the duty of obedience is not therefore grounded only in His power. The doctrine that the ultimate ground of all obligation is the will of an omnipotent God is not to be reduced to a special case of the principle that 'might is right'.

Though it was usually held that the law of nature is obligatory because it is the will of God, it was also insisted that the will of God is not arbitrary. If it were arbitrary, it could not be discovered by reason. God wills the good of His creatures; and the rules making for this good are the laws of nature. Reason discovers the content of these rules, and God's command that men shall obey them makes them obligatory.

Already, a whole generation before *Leviathan* was published, a Christian philosopher had denied that the ground of the obligation to obey the laws of nature lay in God's will. Suarez had argued that it follows, merely from man's being the sort of creature he is, that he ought to behave in some ways and not in others. The difference between right and wrong is not an effect of anyone's will, not even God's, though God necessarily commands what is right and forbids what is wrong. A few years after Suarez, we find the same argument in Grotius. 'The law of nature', he says, 'is a dictate of right reason, which points out that an act, according as it is or is not in conformity with rational nature, has in it a quality of moral baseness or moral necessity; and that, in consequence, such an act is either forbidden or enjoined by the author of nature, God.' The law of nature is thus not obligatory because it is the will of God; it is grounded in reason, and God commands us to obey it because it is right that we should do so.[1]

If we compare Hobbes' with the traditional account of the law of nature, and also with the views of Suarez and Grotius, certain differences are immediately apparent. Hobbes does not put together psychological laws or uniformities of behaviour and rules of conduct. His laws of nature are all prescriptive; they tell us what men should do and not how they in fact behave. Again, though the laws of nature, for Hobbes as for Suarez and Grotius and everyone else, are discovered by reason, the discovery is differently conceived. Reason, in Hobbes' account of the matter, does not tell us that, because men are rational and are capable of deliberate choice, it follows that they ought to observe certain rules in their behaviour to one another; reason does not infer the laws of nature from the nature of man or from God's purposes for men. Nor yet does reason directly apprehend without inference that man ought to keep these laws. According to Hobbes, man, by reflecting on his experience, discovers that, if he is to have peace, he ought to observe certain rules in his dealings with other men whenever he has sufficient grounds for believing that they will do so too. Hobbes' laws of nature are precepts of reason; they are rules of conduct. The question is, are they moral rules?

Hobbes says that a law of nature 'is a Precept, or general rule, found out by Reason, by which a man is forbidden to do that, which is destructive of his life, or taketh away the means of preserving the same; and to omit that, by which he thinketh it may be best preserved'. He also calls the laws of nature 'maxims of prudence'. As a mere precept or general rule found out by reason, as a maxim of prudence, a law of nature is not a moral rule. For a precept of reason or maxim of prudence, merely as such, is only a rule which it is our interest to

---

[1] The laws of nature, as precepts discovered by reason, were treated either as inferences from man's essential nature or as self-evident truths. It was sometimes said that, because man is rational and provident and aware that there are other creatures like himself, he ought to keep certain rules in his behaviour towards these creatures. Or else it was put forward as a self-evident truth, directly apprehended by reason, that a rational creature ought to keep these rules. That is to say, the rules were not inferred from statements about man's nature but were treated as ultimate principles not requiring further justification, being themselves self-evident. That moral principles cannot be true or false was, of course, an idea foreign to the natural law philosophers of the seventeenth century.

follow, and is therefore not obligatory in the sense that a moral rule is so. Nor is it obligatory in the peculiar sense in which Hobbes understands moral obligation; for he speaks as if, where there was no law 'properly so called', there could be no moral obligation. And he says that law, *properly*, is 'the words of him that by right hath command over others'. As mere precepts of reason, the laws of nature are 'but Conclusions or Theorems concerning what conduceth to the conservation and defence' of those who reach the conclusions. Or, to speak more accurately, they are conclusions about what, given certain conditions, would conduce to their conservation. If then it is said that they ought, if they can, to create those conditions, nothing more is meant than that it is reasonable that they should. The *ought* does not here refer to what anyone, even Hobbes, would call a moral obligation. For Hobbes does not assert the morality of the laws of nature until after he has explained that it is only as commands of God that they can be *properly* laws, even where there is as yet no human sovereign to enforce them.

Speaking of law 'properly so called', Hobbes says that it is not counsel but command, and is *obligatory* (in some stronger sense than a mere precept of reason is so) only because it is a command. And what makes it a command is not its being couched in the imperative but the commander's power to compel obedience.

Though Hobbes defines law as the word of him that by right has command over others, he uses arguments which imply, not only that there is no right of command without effective power, but also that where there is such power there is always a right of command. For example, he holds that the subjects of a conqueror, as much as those of a ruler established by express consent, are obliged to obey him.

Hobbes also says that all allegiance, at least of man to man, rests on consent, on a covenant express or tacit. Even the conqueror has the consent of his subjects, who must be presumed to have promised obedience to him in return for his not having killed them, which he, having the power to do it, could rightfully have done. Now, if this is consent, it surely follows that a man consents whenever he obeys because he thinks that he has more to lose than to gain by not doing so. If, then, consent, thus conceived, creates a duty of obedience, anyone who can contrive that others have more to lose than to gain by obeying him (and according to Hobbes they will obey him if they see that it is so, for such is their nature) acquires a right of command over them. In other words, where there is effective power to command, there is consent to that power, and therefore a duty of obedience and a right of command.

But if this is consent, it would seem to follow that God's authority, no less than man's, rests on consent; for surely God's position in relation to those who believe in Him is the same, in all relevant respects, as the conqueror's in relation to the conquered. True, God's power is not created by men's submitting to His will because they see they have more to gain than to lose by submission, but then neither is the conqueror's created by the submission of the conquered. In both cases, submission is an effect of power and not a cause of it. Therefore, if submission is an act of consent which bestows authority in the one case, it must surely be so in the other.

Hobbes says or implies in several places that authority springs from the consent of those subject to it, and he does so in contexts which do not always suggest that he has only human authority in mind. Indeed, in one or two places, it would seem that he is speaking of divine as well as of human authority.[1] But why, we may ask, does he speak of

[1] Mr. Warrender, in the first part of the tenth chapter of his book, *The Political Philosophy of Hobbes*, though he does not deny that Hobbes sometimes speaks as if all obligation rested on covenant, says that this is not his true position. Hobbes, he says, does not really hold that even obligations under natural law rest on consent. Yet there are arguments in Hobbes which clearly imply the contrary, as for example the argument that atheism is no sin. (See *De Cive*, in the English translation, Hobbes's *English Works* Vol. II. pp. 197-9). According to Hobbes, sin, as distinguished from mere crime, is an offence against God's law, though, of course, since God commands those who believe in Him to obey the civil law, any believer who offends against that law is guilty of both sin and crime. But how, asks Hobbes, can a man sin who denies that there is a God, or that He governs the world? For such a man can say that he never submitted his will to God's, not conceiving Him so much as to exist. Though atheists are in God's power, He cannot command them or receive obedience from them; for there can be command and obedience only where the commander makes his will known to those he requires to obey him, which he cannot do if they do not believe he exists. Atheists are *enemies* but not *subjects* of God, for they have not submitted to Him, acknowledging His existence and His power. Now, in Hobbes' view (peculiar though it may be), to submit to power is to consent to it and to oblige yourself to obey its possessor. Indeed, strictly speaking, submission also creates the *power to command* as distinct from the *power to use*. No one, no matter how great his power, can have command over me unless I choose to obey him on account of his power. He may use me as a tool but may not command me unless I submit to his power. Not even if He is God and omnipotent; though, being God and omnipotent, He can, if He chooses, cause me to submit to His power.

It is true that Hobbes distinguishes between God's peculiar authority over the Jews, which was established by express covenant, and His general authority over all men who believe in Him. For this general authority to exist, it is enough that there should be a God who commands men on pain of punishment if they disobey Him, and that men should believe He does so. Authority, as Hobbes conceives of it, requires no more than that those subject to it submit to a power which they believe is great enough to ensure that they stand to lose more than they gain by disobedience to it; and this submission is a tacit covenant as distinct from an express one. But if men are so situated that there is no one already powerful enough to make it worth their while to submit to him, and if they think it their interest that there should be, a tacit covenant is no longer enough. They must then choose someone to submit to and must ensure that he has the power to compel obedience; they must set up a ruler by express covenant, who will be a sovereign by institution.

consent at all in this connection? Why is he not content to say, without more ado, that effective power creates an obligation to obey and therefore a right of command? Partly, perhaps, because he wants to turn the tables on writers who, arguing that authority rests on consent, conclude that it is wrong to compel obedience where there has been no consent. Hobbes' reply to them is that, wherever power is effective, it is to men's advantage to submit to it, and that when they submit from this motive (and they cannot submit from any other) the submission is consent. And partly perhaps (and it is then that he has specifically human authority clearly in mind) because it occurs to him that no man can compel obedience of a multitude of subjects unless there are some men willing to comply with his wishes without being compelled. Human power depends on human willingness to obey as divine power does not. But Hobbes, if he had distinguished more clearly between power and authority, could have admitted this readily without needing to argue that authority (even the human kind) always springs from the consent of those subject to it.

It is perhaps not important to decide whether Hobbes believed that all authority, or only the human kind, is established by consent. For what he says about consent does not explain what he means by obligation, in the stronger sense in which a maxim of prudence is not a rule which men are obliged to obey, nor yet what he means by *law*, the concept to which he relates *obligation* in this stronger sense. But it is important to notice that Hobbes, when he calls the laws of nature 'laws properly so called', and treats them as *obligatory* in a stronger sense, always thinks of them as commands. Sometimes he speaks as if they were not properly laws until there is a human ruler to enforce obedience to them, and at other times says that they are laws 'properly so called' merely as commands of God. And it is also to be noticed that Hobbes, though he sometimes says of the laws of nature that, as commands of God, they are moral laws, and calls the obligation to obey them a moral obligation, does not speak of that obligation as if it were different in kind from what the obligation to obey merely civil laws would be in a world where there was no God. For all that he *sometimes*[1] seems to be arguing that men by consent or covenant can oblige themselves to obey a human ruler only because they are already obliged by God's law to perform their covenants, he never distinguishes between moral and legal obligation. By which I mean both that he fails to explain how they differ and that nothing like an adequate distinction between them is implicit in what he says.

For Hobbes, as for Bentham after him, a man is not obliged to conform to a rule, in the stronger sense of obligation, unless breach of it

---

[1] I say *sometimes* deliberately because Hobbes, when he speaks of the covenant establishing a human sovereign, often treats the laws of nature as mere maxims of prudence, forgetting that they are also commands of God.

makes him liable to punishment either by God or by man. But to call a rule *moral* (as Hobbes does) when the breach of it makes us liable to divine punishment, or (as Bentham does) when it exposes us to the ill-will or disapproval of others, is not to distinguish between properly moral obligation and other kinds. It is characteristic of a moral rule that the breaker of it, if he recognizes that it is a moral rule and that he has broken it, *condemns himself* for doing so. No doubt, others may blame him for breaking the rule, but he will not look upon it as a moral rule merely on that account. This *self-condemnation* is quite different from the fear, regret, irritation or embarrassment he may feel when he breaks a rule of some other kind. And if he merely uses a rule to guide his own conduct or to influence the behaviour of others, that is no sign that he takes it for a moral rule; for he may so use what he thinks of as no more than a maxim of prudence. Where there is a moral rule there is an internal censor. And though this aspect of moral rules, being difficult to explain, was not much enlarged upon by moral philosophers before the time of Rousseau and Kant, it was already implicit in the notion of conscience. From Rousseau's time to Freud's many theories have been produced to explain this internal censorship and its social and psychological causes and functions, but no theory which quite neglects it takes account of what is properly moral obligation.

How, according to Hobbes, are men obliged to obey God's laws? 'To those therefore whose power is irresistible, the dominion of all men adhereth naturally by this excellence of power; and consequently it is from that power that the kingdom over men . . . belongeth naturally to God almighty; not as Creator, and gracious, but as omnipotent.'[1] According to Hobbes, men are so made that they always act from hope of advantage (or fear of hurt) to themselves. If then there is an omnipotent God who commands and forbids them on pain of punishment if they disobey, they cannot help but obey him while they actually have in mind how they stand in relation to him. For they then know that their every thought and action is open to him and that he can do what he pleases with them. Whenever God is truly present to their minds, they, being the sort of creatures they are, necessarily obey him. This, I take it, is what Hobbes understands by man's obligation to God, for it is what follows logically from what he says. But, as I hope to show in a moment, in order that men should be so placed in relation to someone that, while they have in mind what that relation is, they necessarily obey him, there is no need for him to be omnipotent. The obligation to obey God, as Hobbes conceives of it, does not differ in kind, but only in extent, from the obligation which some men could have to others even in a godless world.

[1] *Leviathan*, Ch. 31, p. 234. Blackwell edition.

Long before Hobbes' time, it had been said that men are obliged to obey God because he is omnipotent. This way of speaking was traditional. But it was only a part of the tradition. It had also, and often, been said that men are obliged to obey God because he made and loves them, and desires their good. Thus, to borrow the words of Hobbes, 'the kingdom over men' belongs 'naturally' to God, not merely (or even primarily) as 'omnipotent', but 'as Creator and gracious'. Now *obligation* in this sense (though the writers who speak of it do not define it) is clearly not obligation in the sense understood by Hobbes. If I am obliged to obey God because he made me and loves me (and not only me, but other men, whose brother I am as sharing in this love) my obligation clearly does not consist in my necessarily choosing to obey Him whenever His Omnipotence is truly present to my mind because I happen to be the sort of creature who always acts from hope of benefit or fear of hurt to himself. Hobbes' peculiar sense of obligation is not moral obligation as we ordinarily understand it, whereas the traditional conception of man's duty to God may be so, at least in part. I do not mean that we can find in writers before Hobbes an account that we should find satisfactory of what moral obligation is, but only that they habitually speak of man's obligation to obey God in ways that suggest that it is, or may be, a genuine moral obligation.

It has been questioned whether Hobbes seriously considered the laws of nature to be divine commands. He has often been accused of atheism. Whether he was an atheist or not, I do not know. Though God is given a conspicuous part in his political philosophy, that part is equivocal. The laws of nature are properly laws, says Hobbes, only because they are the commands of God; for it is their being so that makes them obligatory. One of the laws of nature is that men should keep their covenants; and temporal authority is established by covenant. It would therefore seem that Hobbes wants to derive the obligation to obey the holder of temporal authority, the sovereign, from a prior obligation to obey God. Yet he also says that in the state of nature the laws of nature oblige only *in foro interno* and not *in foro externo*; or, as he puts it, 'they bind to a desire they should take place: but . . . to the putting them in act, not alwayes'. This seems to mean that in the state of nature we are always obliged to desire that the laws of nature, which are God's laws, should be obeyed, but are not always obliged to obey them. It is odd to speak of our being obliged to desire that something should be done, when nobody may be obliged to do it. And Hobbes is putting it far too mildly when he says that the laws of nature, in the state of nature, oblige *in foro externo* 'not alwayes'. If he had said 'scarcely ever', or even 'not at all', he would have come closer to saying what he meant. For he also says that, in the state of nature, men have a right to all things, even to one another's bodies, which is surely to imply that they have no obligation, at least *in foro externo.*

Mr Warrender, in a book recently published on the *Political Philosophy of Hobbes*, suggests that by obligation *in foro interno* Hobbes meant something more than just the duty to desire or to intend keeping God's law; that he meant the duty to be always prepared to keep it when it can be kept safely, and to be always seeking for ways to create the conditions which make it safe to keep it. This is a generous interpretation of Hobbes' actual words; but let us not quarrel with generosity. We are always obliged to obey the laws of nature if it is safe to do so; we are obliged *in foro externo* on this condition; but unfortunately the condition almost never holds in the state of nature, for it is almost never safe for us actually to do what the laws enjoin. What, however, we always can do, even in the state of nature, is hold ourselves in readiness to obey the laws when obedience is safe and also seek the means of making it safe. There is, as Mr Warrender points out, a real difference between just desiring that something should happen, and being always prepared to do whatever is needed to make it happen as soon as occasion serves.

According to Mr Warrender, we must, if we are to do justice to Hobbes, distinguish between what makes an action a duty and the conditions which provide a sufficient motive for doing it. Thus, we can say both that it is our duty to obey the laws of nature when we can safely do so only because God has commanded obedience on that condition, and that it is the sovereign who makes it safe for us to obey them. That is, we can say that God lays our natural duties upon us while the sovereign provides us with a sufficient motive for doing them. Therefore, even though it is the sovereign who maintains the social order in which alone nearly all our duties hold, we would have no duty to the sovereign unless we had a prior duty to God. It is my duty to do X under conditions Y only because God commands it, but it is the sovereign who creates these conditions. This is what Mr Warrender understands Hobbes to mean.

To show that Mr Warrender is reading more into Hobbes than is there would be a laborious task requiring close scrutiny of several difficult passages in *Leviathan* and *De Cive*. It would also be wasted labour. Perhaps Hobbes did believe that there could be no genuine obligation to the sovereign unless there were a prior obligation to God. But, if he did, he ought not to have done so, for it is a belief that does not square with his own account of obligation. If obligation is what Hobbes says it is, there is no need whatever to derive our duty to man from our duty to God.

According to Hobbes, we are obliged to obey another person when we are so related to him that, if we see that relation clearly, we cannot help but choose to do what he commands. But we can be so related to man and not only to God. True, God alone is omnipotent and omnis-cient, so that we can say only of Him that we are always obliged to obey *all* His commands. For it must always be true that, if we see clearly how we are related to God, we cannot choose but obey Him. No sovereign is omniscient or omnipotent; no sovereign's punishments are inescapable. It cannot therefore be true of any sovereign that we are always so related to him that, if we see the relation clearly, we can never choose to disobey. But that does not mean that we cannot often be so related to him that, if we see the relation clearly, we must choose to obey. Whenever I stand to gain more than I lose by obeying the sovereign, I am, in Hobbes' sense of obligation, obliged to obey; for if I saw clearly how I stood, I would necessarily choose to obey. Man is so made, Hobbes tells us, that he always acts from hope of benefit or fear of hurt to himself. No more is required to create obligation, in Hobbes' sense, than that someone should be powerful enough to ensure that someone else has more to gain than to lose by obeying his commands. Thus, if we accept Hobbes' account of obligation, we simply cannot say that the duty to obey man must always derive ultimately from the duty to obey God. We can say, of course, that we have a perfect duty of obedience only to God, in the sense that we ought to do whatever He commands; for, being omniscient, He will never command what we cannot do, and being omnipotent can always punish us for disobedience. We can say that the obligation to obey man is limited in ways in which the obligation to obey God is not. But that does not make it a different kind of obligation, or require that it should derive from a prior obligation to obey God.

Suppose we leave God out of Hobbes' political philosophy, and treat the laws of nature as no more than maxims of prudence, can we then explain how men could come to make a covenant setting up a sovereign and to have an adequate motive for keeping it? It has often been denied that we can explain it, both by defenders of Hobbes who have wanted to put the most favourable interpretation on his theory, and by detractors. The defenders have therefore been inclined to make as much as they could of his doctrine that the laws of nature are com-mands of God, while the detractors have sometimes treated it as a piece of hypocrisy to mask the true nature of his philosophy. But the truth is that it is not at all difficult to explain how, even in a godless world, complete egoists come to make and keep an agreement to set up a ruler over them. It may be that Hobbes never saw clearly how this could be done; and yet all the elements that go to make up this explanation are to be found in *Leviathan* and *De Cive*, though they are there so mixed up with other things that it is not easy to see how they fit together into a consistent whole.

I want now to try to fit that explanation together, and to show that every part of it is to be found in what Hobbes actually wrote. But before I do this, I must utter a word of warning. Though the explanation is all to be found in Hobbes, it is not to be taken for Hobbes' political philosophy or to be treated as the essential part of it. It is merely extracted from that philosophy, and was probably never seen by Hobbes himself as a single and consistent argument. It would be a solecism to treat it as the core of his theory and what is mixed up with it as padding. It is, however, important historically, because it is the elements in his theory that go to make it up that have attracted the most attention. For it is not as a natural law philosopher in the traditional sense that Hobbes is remembered; it is rather as the writer who tried to explain men's political behaviour entirely in terms of self-interest.

IV. THE MAKING AND KEEPING OF THE COVENANT

Even if we suppose that the laws of nature are not commands of God, and that therefore no one in the state of nature is obliged, even in Hobbes' sense of obligation, to keep them, we can still say that men ought to keep them when it is safe to do so. The 'ought' here refers neither to moral obligation as ordinarily understood nor to obligation in Hobbes' sense; it is not their duty to keep these laws, it is only their interest.

The first two among Hobbes' nineteen laws of nature are rules that men ought to keep, in this sense of ought, even in the state of nature. The first law is the precept or rule, 'That everyman ought to endeavour Peace, as farre as he has hope of obtaining it; and when he cannot obtain it, that he may seek, and use, all helps and advantages of Warre.' This is a precept which men can follow even in the absence of government; and as it is their obvious interest to follow it, they ought to do so. Now, in the state of nature, as Hobbes describes it, men cannot get peace. The rule that they ought to seek peace is therefore equivalent to the rule that they ought to try to put an end to the state of nature. They have tasted in full the miseries of that state, and have conceived of something incomparably better, which is peace. Being rational and inventive creatures who can learn from experience, men are able both to imagine a condition different from the one in which they find themselves and to devise means of bringing it about. The first rule does not tell them to desire peace (for their miseries in the state of nature make them do that) but to endeavour it: to look out for ways of getting it, and to be prepared to do whatever has to be done to obtain it.

Though the rule, as a maxim of prudence, is only a piece of advice, there is really as much force to it as if men were obliged, *in foro in-*

terno, to keep it. Their condition in the state of nature is desperate, and their desire to put an end to that state is urgent and strong. By leaving God out of the picture, and doing away with all obligation, even in Hobbes' sense, in the state of nature, we have not really weakened men's motives for getting themselves out of that state. For the state of nature, as Hobbes depicts it, is to all practical intents and purposes a godless state; because men, when they are in it, stand so little in awe of God that they cannot even trust one another to keep God's laws. It is not the urge to obey God but to keep themselves alive which impels them to endeavour peace. Hobbes makes this abundantly clear, for all that he speaks so often of God and of obligation *in foro interno*.

The second law of nature is also a rule which men, in their own interest, ought to keep, even in the state of nature. It is the rule, 'That a man be willing, when others are so too, as farre forth, as for Peace, and defence of himselfe he shall think it necessary, to lay down this right to all things (which he has in the state of nature), and be contented with so much liberty against other men, as he would allow other men against himselfe.' Anyone who, in the state of nature, in fact renounced his right to anything unless others did so too would be a simpleton, a fool, and would pay dearly for his folly by placing himself at the mercy of others. But if he refused to lay down his right when others were willing to lay down theirs, they would combine against him and destroy him as an obstacle in the way of their getting peace. The second law of nature is a corollary of the first: it tells us what is actually involved in the endeavour to seek peace. As a piece of advice, as a maxim of prudence, it is every bit as strong as the first law. Though it is true that in the state of nature men are profoundly distrustful of one another, and for that reason reluctant to make concessions, it is also true that their condition is intolerable and that they are desperately anxious to get out of it. Every man knows that the fears and miseries which are his lot are also the lot of others, and that the others must be as eager as he is to put an end to them. Admittedly, Hobbes' picture of the state of nature is pure fantasy. Yet if we are to see the force of his argument, we must look at the whole of that picture. If men were deeply mistrustful of one another without also being deeply afraid, they would have no strong motive for endeavouring peace and laying down their rights conditionally. Or if each man were afraid without knowing that the others were so too, no one could reckon on other people's desiring peace as strongly as he himself desires it. But that is not the condition of men 'in meer Nature'; for though they are afraid and mistrustful, they also long for peace, and know that others do so too.

Hobbes says of the laws of nature, that 'they have been contracted into one easy sum, intelligible even to the meanest capacity; and that is, *Do not that to another which thou wouldest not have done to thy-self.* All that a man need do to feel the force of the laws of nature is to put himself in other men's shoes, considering their predicament as if it were his own. The first two laws are preliminary to the rest: they require men in the state of nature to endeavour to create the conditions which make it reasonable for them to keep the other laws. They are equivalent to the precept, *Try to make it safe for everyone to follow the rule, Do not that to another, which thou wouldest not have done to thyself.*

It is with the third law of nature, *That men perform their Covenants made,* that our difficulties begin. Can men keep it in the state of nature? Hobbes tells us that covenants without a power strong enough to enforce them are void, and that in the state of nature there is no such power. And yet a covenant is needed to create that power; for in the state of nature men are equal, and can therefore set up a power strong enough to coerce them only by agreement. It would appear, then, at first sight, that the covenant is both necessary and impossible.

Is this a genuine dilemma? Or can the covenant establishing civil society of itself create the power needed to enforce it? That, certainly, is what Hobbes would have us believe. Hobbes distinguishes between two kinds of covenant: those in which the contracting parties do not simultaneously perform what they promise, and those in which they do. Covenants of the first kind require mutual trust, which Hobbes thinks is nearly always unreasonable in the state of nature, there being no power to enforce covenants. For, says Hobbes, 'he that performeth first, has no assurance that the other will performe after; because the bonds of words are too weak to bridle men's ambition, avarice, and other Passions, without the fear of some Coercive Power; which in the condition of meer Nature . . . cannot possibly be supposed.'

Covenants of the second kind do not require mutual trust, because the parties to them all keep their promises at the same time. It looks therefore as if the covenant setting up the sovereign, if it is really to set him up, must be a covenant of this second kind. Hobbes clearly thought that it was, for he spoke of all men renouncing their natural rights at the same time. This renunciation somehow creates the power which makes it impossible for those who renounce their rights to take them back again. Having said that 'Covenants, without the Sword, are but Words, and of no strength to compel a man at all', Hobbes, a little further on, continues thus: 'The only way to erect such a Common Power . . . is [for all men] to conferre all their power and strength upon one Man, or upon one Assembly of Men, that may reduce all their Wills, by plurality of voices, unto one Will.' The covenant can set up the sovereign needed to enforce it because its actual making consists in a simultaneous renunciation of their rights by all parties to it in favour of some man or assembly that is not a party to it; and this renunciation of rights is a conferring of power. That is how Hobbes presents the matter; and there can be no doubt that he found his argument convincing. But really it will do! Let us begin by asking: What is involved in all men's conferring power on some one man, in their renouncing rights in his favour? Power and right, after all, are not physical objects which can be handed over at one stroke, on a single occasion, by some persons to others. They are not weapons whose surrender gives overwhelming strength to whoever takes them. A grant of power is a promise made by one man in favour of another, whereby he undertakes so to behave *in the future* that the other will be able to do what he could not do before. If ten men promise one another to obey an eleventh man, that man has no greater power over them than they have over each other, unless they in fact keep their promises. It is not their making the promises but their keeping them that gives him power. If his power alone can make them keep their promises, and yet he has no power unless they keep them, their condition does not change; they remain in the state of nature and have no sovereign over them. Hobbes has confused himself and his readers by taking it for granted that a simultaneous renunciation of natural rights in favour of a particular person or assembly is equivalent to a grant of power to him or them, even when the persons who renounce the rights have no good reason to trust one another until there is a common power over them. The renunciation of these rights is not the *present* performance of the covenant required to make Hobbes' argument valid; it is merely a promise of *future* behaviour which, unless most of the people who make the promise keep it, can create no power capable of coercing the few who may choose to break it. Hobbes tried to show that there can be no confidence where there is no power to force the unwilling to keep their promises. What he failed to see is that there can be no power where there is no confidence.

Are we therefore left with an insoluble dilemma? Only if we pose the problem as Hobbes posed it; only if we insist on saying that in the state of mere nature 'covenants without the sword are but words'. But we do not need to say this even if we accept Hobbes' doctrine of the irremediable egoism of man and his account of the state of nature. No doubt, covenants without the sword are of no strength to *compel* a man; and no doubt, too, covenants, of themselves, while no one is strong enough to enforce them, can create no obligation, in Hobbes' sense of the word. If there were an obligation to keep a covenant in the state of nature, it could be only an obligation to God; and in any case, in Hobbes' opinion, if the covenant involved future performance, the obligation could only be *in foro interno* and not to 'putting it in act'. But we have agreed to take no account of God, and therefore must not speak of obligation, even in Hobbes' peculiar sense (and there is no question of any other) in the state of nature. It is a state without obligation, and also without power, since Hobbes tells us that all men are equal in it. And yet, though no one has obligations or power, men can still have an adequate motive for keeping their covenants. I am speaking, of course, of men as Hobbes described them in the state of nature: of creatures entirely self-regarding, without benevolence, honour or pity, and whose passions are apt to get the better of their reason.

Men like that could not, of course, trust one another to keep a covenant when it was to their immediate advantage to break it; they could not trust one another to keep it merely because they had more to gain than to lose in the long run by keeping it. For Hobbes, though he supposes that reason in men is strong enough to enable them to discover what is in their enduring interest, also supposes that they are liable to strong passions which shut their eyes to that interest. They will often be tempted to break the covenant, and the mere belief that it is, in the long run, to their advantage to keep it will not often move them to resist the temptation. Some men, no doubt, are cooler and wiser than others, but, unfortunately, it is not to their advantage to keep the covenant unless they are assured that the others will also keep it. If the unwise and improvident do not keep the covenant, they defeat the purpose for which the covenant was made, so that it is no longer the interest, even of the wise and provident, to keep it. That is why Hobbes insists so much that unless the foolish are frightened into keeping the covenant when they have a mind to break it, the wise would be foolish to keep it.

Hobbes was right to insist on this, but he was wrong to speak of the covenant as involving an immediate keeping of their promises by the parties to it. He was wrong to speak as if obedience and trust were effects of the sovereign's power and not also causes of it. He forgot, at least in this part of his argument, an important fact. Even though no man may trust another to keep the covenant when the other stands to gain by breaking it, he can rely on his sympathy and assistance against any third man who breaks it. For, given the situation as Hobbes describes it, it is the interest of every man that every other man should keep the covenant. It is therefore his interest that the sovereign should have the power to punish any law-breaker except himself. Though he may not trust anyone to keep the covenant who is sorely tempted to break it, he can rely on everyone else being against the breaker of it. The covenant makes the sovereign powerful, not at all because it involves an immediate keeping of promises, but because it creates a situation in which it becomes everyone's interest that some definite person (the sovereign) should get the better of anyone else he seeks to coerce. I want the sovereign to be able to coerce everyone except me, and everyone else has a desire similar to mine. This is enough to ensure that the covenant makes the sovereign powerful enough to be able to punish anyone who breaks the covenant. The sovereign is powerful because he can ordinarily rely on the support of all his subjects except the law-breaker against the law-breaker; his power is not, in the first instance, a cause of trust but an effect of it.

Thus, though it may be true to say that covenants without the sword are of no strength to *compel* a man, it is false that without the sword they are *but words*, if by this is meant that they do not change the situation. There can be no sword, no power, unless they do change the situation. The mere designation of the sovereign creates an interest which did not exist before, an interest which is not an effect of the sovereign's power but a condition of it; it makes it every man's interest that every other man should be obedient to some definite person. Hobbes mistakenly supposes that his two assertions, *covenants without the sword are of no strength to compel* and *covenants without the sword are but words*, are equivalent. But they are not so in the least, though they may seem to be so to the hasty reader. The covenant creates an alliance, which is nonetheless effective because the parties to it are entirely self-regarding and cannot trust one another to keep their word when they are strongly tempted to break it; it makes every man an ally of the sovereign against the law-breaker except when it is himself that breaks the law.

The makers of the covenant, when they promise to obey the sovereign, undertake not only to keep his laws but also to help him enforce them, if he requires their help; for both undertakings are clearly involved in the promise of complete obedience. Though the passions of an entirely selfish creature may often move him to break the laws, unless he is held in check by fear of punishment, they will hardly ever move him to obstruct the sovereign when he seeks to punish someone else. If the sovereign, as he must, appoints officers to give effect to his commands, he can rely on their loyalty, partly because he rewards their services and partly because it is everyone's interest that everyone else should obey the sovereign and his officers. No more than this is needed to make the sovereign's power effective. No one need trust anyone to be wise enough always to prefer social peace, his greatest good, to some immediate advantage, and there need not be (as indeed there cannot be) any simultaneous transferring of right or granting of power, any present performance of the covenant by all the parties to it.

There are passages in Hobbes that show that he knew this; that he knew that men's passions, though often tempting them to break the laws themselves, seldom prevent their siding with the law against other people. He did not, however, see the full implications of this fact, and therefore did not use it as he might have done to support his own theory. By saying that 'Covenants without the Sword are but Words', by insisting so much that confidence is an effect of power and forgetting that it is also a cause of it, by suggesting that completely selfish and imperfectly reasonable men cannot be relied upon to keep their promises except where there is a force strong enough to compel them, by treating the covenant as a simultaneous surrender of rights which of itself establishes an authority able to force people to keep their promises, Hobbes misled both himself and his readers. He quite unnecessarily posed the problem in a way that made it insoluble, and then undertook to solve it by treating the covenant as if it were an act involving a *present* performance of their promises by all the parties to it; whereas what it in fact involves is merely their all simultaneously making the same promise about future behaviour. I surrender, you surrender, he surrenders, we all surrender our rights at exactly the same moment and to the same person or assembly; nobody trusts anybody, and there is no simple-minded reliance on people's not breaking promises they cannot be compelled to keep. 'This', we are told, 'is the Generation of that great Leviathan, or rather (to speak more reverently) of that Mortall God, to which we owe, under the Immortal God, our peace and defence.'

This is magnificent, but it is not good sense.

V. HOBBES' CONCEPTION OF NATURAL RIGHT AND THE USE HE MAKES OF IT

About Hobbes' conception of law there is no ambiguity; it may be inadequate but at least it is clear. Law, properly so called, is 'the word of him, that by right hath command over others'. And it follows from Hobbes' account of obligation that anyone who can get himself obeyed has the right of command; for if any man can so place others in relation to him that, when they understand that relation, they cannot choose but do what he tells them, they are obliged to obedience and he has a right of command. But, as we shall see, this sense of right, which is enough to make clear Hobbes' definition of law, is not the sense he uses when he speaks of natural right. It is true that Hobbes speaks with two voices of the laws of nature, sometimes calling them maxims of prudence and sometimes divine commands; and that he does not make it clear just how far men are obliged to obey them in the state of nature. This alternation and this obscurity do not, however, affect his definition of law, which is clear enough.

With natural right it is quite different. Hobbes' definition of it is not clear, and in any case offers no clue to either of the senses in which he most frequently uses the term. I shall try to show that Hobbes cannot afford to be clear about natural right; that he has, when he describes the state of nature, to use the term natural right in a sense different from the sense he has to use to explain what makes the sovereign's authority legitimate and absolute. I am not suggesting that Hobbes meant to be obscure; he was merely, as we all so often are, driven to obscurity by the unconscious need to cover up the defects of his argument.

Let us notice the extent of his confusion. 'The Right of Nature . . . is the Liberty each man hath, to use his own power, as he will him-selfe, for the preservation of his own Nature.' 'By Liberty is under-stood . . . the absence of external impediments.' In the state of nature, a man has a right to everything, even to another's body. Yet this right can be laid aside; it can be renounced or transferred. When a man transfers or renounces a right, he is obliged or bound not to hinder whoever gets the right from the benefit of it. The transference or renunciation of a right is a voluntary act, and the object of every such act is some good to the doer of it. Therefore there are some rights which no man can renounce or transfer even though he goes through the motions of doing it. A man cannot, for example, lay down his right of resisting anyone who tries to kill or wound or imprison him; for he can have nothing to gain by laying it down. If he promises not to resist, the promise is void.

All this is wonderfully confused. We are told that in the state of nature man has a right to all things. This means, perhaps, that he has a right to anything which he deems necessary to his security, and that he is sole judge of his need. This is the interpretation most favourable to Hobbes, though it is not the only one possible or even the one most in keeping with what Hobbes most often says.[1] But, however that may be, we can see that the word *right* cannot, in this sense, mean *power*, because the right to all things is not a power over all things. In the perilous state of nature, where man is said to have a right to all things, he very clearly is not able to get whatever he wants, or even whatever he deems necessary to his security. And yet, if natural right is called a liberty, and liberty is defined as absence of external impediments, it follows that natural right is a power. The natural right to all things is then the power to get all things; which is absurd, since no man can have this power, and least of all in the state of nature.

Those who say, without qualification, that Hobbes equates natural right and power are mistaken, but so too are those who insist that he distinguishes between them. He sometimes does the one and sometimes the other. No doubt, he does not say, in so many words, that natural

---

[1] Ordinarily – and I shall discuss this point again later – Hobbes, when he speaks of the natural right to all things, does not trouble to say 'all things necessary to security'. Moreover, he does say that man, when he acts, *always* seeks his own good and not other people's. Therefore man has a natural right to whatever he thinks beneficial to himself, no matter how much it harms others, provided that what harms them does not also harm him. But my purpose here is to examine how Hobbes uses social and political concepts, and so I do not consider the difficulties he gets into by assuming that man always acts from hope of benefit or fear of hurt to himself.

F

right is merely a power, because he wants to set very wide limits to natural right, and indeed usually speaks of it as if it were unlimited, which power clearly is not; and yet, when he calls natural right a liberty he does suggest that it is a mere power, for that is what follows from his definition of liberty. Though he is aware that power is always limited, and never more so than in the state of nature, Hobbes, at least in his unguarded moments, suggests that, in that state, natural right is unlimited; and even when he speaks more cautiously, he still suggests that it is limited only by the obligation not to harm other people unreasonably – that is to say, not to harm them when by so doing we add nothing to our own security. Hobbes seeks to derive the sovereign's authority from natural right, and also wants to make that authority virtually absolute. He wants to show that the sovereign's authority is both absolute and legitimate because it derives from a transference or renunciation of natural rights which are virtually unlimited.

As a matter of fact, there is a sense of the word 'right' which does allow us to say that all men have a right to all things, though we nearly always use it for a much more limited purpose. Sometimes, when we say that a man has a right to something, we do so without implying that other people have duties to him. When we do this, all that we mean is that there is no law or rule which prescribes what he shall do. Now, it is precisely because we normally think of man as a creature who has obligations that we sometimes feel the need to say that, in a particular situation, there is nothing which he is obliged to do; and sometimes we say this by saying that he has the right to do whatever he pleases. When we speak in this way, we are putting what is essentially a negative statement in a positive form. What we mean is that he has *no* obligation, and what we say is that he has an unlimited right. In this sense, Robinson Crusoe, while he was alone on his island, had a right to everything. This is not an unusual, and is even a quite proper, use of the word 'right'. But it is worth noticing that when we speak in this way, we are nearly always speaking about moral persons in unusual situations; about persons who, though they normally do have obligations to other people, have none for the time being, situated as they are. We are not inclined to say that the wild beasts in the jungle have a right to everything merely because they have no duties.

Still, we could extend this negative use of the word 'right' to serve a wider purpose than it usually serves. We could imagine a condition of mankind where there were no rules of conduct, positive or moral, and therefore no duties; and we could then say that all men, being in that condition, had a right to everything. It may be that this is what Hobbes was saying, at least part of the time, when he was speaking of natural right. In the fourteenth chapter of *Leviathan* he warns us that we must not confuse *jus* and *lex*, *right* and *law*; because 'law and right differ as much as obligation and liberty, which in one end and the same matter are inconsistent.' It may well be that, in this passage, Hobbes meant by liberty not absence of external impediments, but absence of law and obligation.

Thus we have in *Leviathan* at least two senses of natural right; the first equates it with power and the second with absence of obligation. The first, as we have seen, clearly will not serve Hobbes' purpose; for a man's power is never more limited than in the state of nature, whereas Hobbes wants to say, at least some of the time, that natural right is unlimited. The second makes better sense on the face of it; for it is not absurd to speak of a complete absence of obligation as an unlimited right, and we can, without formal contradiction, attribute this right to everybody.

But this second sense, though it does not make it nonsense to speak of everyone's having a right to everything, will not do for Hobbes' purpose any better than the first. For Hobbes' purpose is to explain how the covenant, which he calls a mutual *transferring* of right, makes it the duty of subjects to obey the sovereign. Nor does this second sense square with Hobbes' account of the laws of nature as commands of God.

If the laws of nature really are commands of God, we must have obligations even in Hobbes' state of nature. These obligations may be small but are none the less obligations for that. They are mostly obligations *in foro interno*; they require us, as we have seen, to endeavour peace and to be prepared, as soon as we can safely do so, to treat others as we would have them treat us. We may, in the state of nature, do anything that we think necessary to our self-preservation, and we alone can be judges of what is necessary. But we may do nothing to hurt anyone unless we do it to preserve ourselves; for we are obliged to endeavour peace, and this we cannot do unless, as far as we safely can, we so behave to others as to cause them to trust us. If, for instance, in the state of nature, we make a promise which we can keep at slight risk to ourselves, we ought to keep it; for by so doing we teach other people to trust us in greater things. If the laws of nature are commands of God, it follows that we have duties even in the state of nature, and therefore do not have a right to everything.

It has been suggested[1] that Hobbes, when he speaks of everyone's right to everything, does not mean to deny that men have obligations in the state of nature, but means only that, in that state, every man is always judge in his own case. God lays down the laws of nature but does not otherwise intervene in human affairs. He leaves it to everyone to decide for himself how these laws apply to particular cases. Until there is a sovereign, there is no one to judge between men. The natural right to all things is not therefore a complete absence of obligation; it is only absence of all responsibility of man to man. In the state

[1] By Mr Warrender, and perhaps also by others.

of nature, man is responsible to God alone for what he does under divine law. Yet God gives man only the bare law; He neither interprets nor administers it in this world, so that each man must rely only on his own judgment until there is a human judge between him and other men. Therefore a man's right, in the state of nature, is whatever he honestly thinks it is; and this, we are sometimes told, is all that Hobbes means when he says that, in the absence of a common human superior, every man has a natural right to everything.

This argument is ingenious, but it is, I think, straining to do more than justice to Hobbes. It takes for granted that Hobbes ordinarily means, not what he most often says, but what he ought to say (and only sometimes implies) to make his account of natural right square with his account of natural law as divine command. The fact is that, nearly always, when Hobbes speaks of natural right, he does so as if he had forgotten all about the laws of nature being commands of God. We can, if we like, be charitable and put this down to mere carelessness, and so accept a not altogether convincing argument in Hobbes' defence. But, even then, we are left with a conception of natural right which cannot be reconciled with some of the things he says about the covenant establishing the sovereign's authority.

Hobbes speaks in two voices about this covenant. Sometimes, and more often, he speaks as if the makers of it *transferred* their rights to the sovereign, and sometimes, and less often, as if they merely renounced them. He feels the need to speak of it in the second way whenever he takes literally what he says about all men having a natural right to all things. If everyone has all the rights he can have, no one can possibly add to those rights. Thus we find Hobbes saying: 'For he that renounceth, or passeth away his right, giveth not to any other man a right which he had not before; because there is nothing to which every man had not a right by nature; but only standeth out of his way, that he may enjoy his own original right, without hindrance from him.' Thus the makers of a covenant, by agreeing not to exercise their own natural rights as they have done hitherto, make it possible for the sovereign to exercise his right much more effectively. They cannot add to the sovereign's right; they can do no more than add to his power.

Now, this account of the covenant simply does not make sense if man's natural right to all things is taken to mean his responsibility to God alone for how he interprets and keeps the laws of nature. Natural right, thus understood, does not include the right to interpret the laws of nature on behalf of other people. If the man chosen to be sovereign did no more than retain his natural right, he would have no authority over others, and therefore would not be sovereign. To be sovereign he must have the right to interpret the laws of nature on behalf of other people; he must acquire a right he did not have before.

He acquires it by means of the covenant only because his subjects have agreed that he shall have it. Each of them has agreed with the others that the person chosen to be sovereign shall interpret the laws of nature on his behalf.

Moreover, no man's direct responsibility to God for keeping God's law can cease with the setting up of the sovereign. If I owe it to God to keep His law, I may reasonably conclude that I shall be more likely to keep it, if I can agree with other men on a common superior to interpret and enforce that law on behalf of us all; but I am still obliged to obey that superior only if what he enforces is God's law or a law in keeping with it, and I can never divest myself of my prior responsibility to God. If, for example, I undertake to obey the sovereign whatever he commands, and reserve the right to resist him only when he threatens my life or liberty, I may be failing in my duty to God. I can do my duty to God to keep His law by unquestioning obedience to the sovereign only if this obedience is the best means of keeping God's law. But whether or not it is the best means is a question, not of right, but of fact. If I have one duty, and then, the better to perform it, I undertake another duty, I cannot put the second duty so entirely in the place of the first as to take it for granted that in doing the second I am also always doing the first; I can do the first in doing the second only if I have reasonable grounds for believing that the second is *in fact* a means to the first.

It might be argued that, on the assumptions made by Hobbes, I do have reasonable grounds for believing that by always obeying the sovereign I am also obeying God. For God, according to Hobbes, in requiring me to obey His laws, requires no more of me than that I should act wisely for my own preservation; and this I do if I never resist the sovereign except when he tries to destroy or imprison me. But this is by no means obvious. By not resisting the sovereign now, when he is ill-treating other people but not me, I may make it more likely that he will destroy or imprison me in the future. To obey God's law I must estimate the danger to myself of the sovereign's action even when he does not now threaten me.

I conclude, therefore, that if we hold that Hobbes, by man's natural right to everything, means his being responsible to God alone for interpreting and keeping God's law, we must also hold that Hobbes is logically bound to say that the covenant does give to the sovereign rights which he does not already have, and also that the subject can never divest himself of the duty to prefer God's law to the sovereign's, even when the sovereign is not trying to destroy or imprison him. But both these things Hobbes denied, the first sometimes and the second always.

However, I do not believe that this is the correct interpretation of what Hobbes meant by man's natural right to all things. I think it much more likely that he did not know exactly what he meant. It may sound presumptuous to say this about a philosopher who has often been praised for lucidity; but lucid though Hobbes may often have been, he was not so when he spoke of natural right. Even if we suppose that he meant by it merely the complete absence of all obligation, we are still left without a sense of natural right which can be reconciled with his account of the covenant and its effects. Let us see why this is so.

It is obvious that right, if it is mere absence of obligation, cannot be transferred, and Hobbes admits in several places that no right is transferred when the covenant is made. So far, so good. He does, however, say that when the covenant is made, rights are 'laid down' or renounced. What is involved in this renunciation? Hobbes speaks of the covenant as putting the parties to it under obligation. Therefore, to renounce a natural right is to lay oneself under an obligation. But this, too, is an odd way of speaking, for in a situation where there are no obligations of any kind, it is difficult to see how anyone could lay himself under an obligation merely by agreeing to something. As Hobbes himself puts it, 'covenants without the sword are but words, and of no strength to compel a man at all'; and, as we have seen already, it is not until the makers of the covenant keep it that there is a force strong enough to compel them to keep it. Unless there is a prior duty to obey God – which there cannot be if the natural right to all things means the complete absence of all obligation – no one in the state of nature can lay a duty on himself merely by being a party to a covenant. All he can do, if he and the others actually do what they say they intend to do, is help create a power which can coerce the recalcitrant; but it is only after the power has come into being that he can be said to have a duty to keep the covenant. All that happens when the covenant is made is that everyone agrees so to behave in the future that the person chosen for sovereign shall be able to compel obedience, and no obligation arises unless the parties to the covenant first keep it without being obliged to do so.[1] This is how we must speak of the covenant and its effects if we assume that the natural right to all things means the complete absence of obligation.

This is not how Hobbes speaks of it. Though he says that there are no rights actually transferred by the covenant, the effects of the covenant, as he describes them, imply the opposite. The covenant, Hobbes tells us, makes the sovereign the 'bearer' of his subjects' per-

---

[1] If they keep the covenant, they create the power able to compel them on those occasions when they are tempted to break it; they create the situation where there are commands which, if they see their interest clearly, they necessarily choose to obey and are therefore (in Hobbes' sense) *obliged* to obey. But, if the situation arose without their creating it, they would also be obliged.

sons and their 'representative', and makes them the 'authors' of everything he does. Now, if natural right is only the complete absence of obligation, the covenant cannot have this effect. All that it can do, if the parties to it keep their word, is to make one man or body of men incomparably more powerful than anyone else. The sovereign can be his subjects' 'representative' and they the 'authors' of all his sovereign acts only if he has acquired from them a right, which he did not have already, to act on their behalf. This is implied by the ordinary sense of these words, and also, as the contexts prove, by the sense in which Hobbes uses them.

It is my belief that Hobbes gives at least three senses to 'natural right'. When he calls it a liberty and says that liberty is the absence of external impediments, he implies that a natural right is a power. But this first sense, though worth noticing, is not important; it merely follows from Hobbes' definitions, and is not a sense in which he actually uses the word when he describes the covenant or its effects. Nor is it a sense in which the word is ordinarily used; it is merely an abberration, something implied by certain words actually used by Hobbes but perhaps never seriously meant by him. Hobbes, I think, uses the word in the second sense, which is the complete absence of obligation, *only* when he describes the covenant; though not always even then. He uses it (but without realizing quite what the use commits him to) whenever he insists that there is no transferring of rights when the covenant is made; for it is only if right is absence of obligation that it makes sense to say that, because everyone has a right to everything, no right can be acquired by covenant. As soon, however, as Hobbes moves on to discuss the *effects* of the covenant, he switches to a third sense of right, the most usual sense in which one man's right implies other men's duty. This is the sense that makes it possible for Hobbes to speak of the sovereign as his subjects' 'representative' and of subjects as the 'authors' of all the sovereign's public acts.

Hobbes makes great play with this notion that the sovereign is his subjects' representative. 'A Multitude of men', he says, 'are made One Person, when they are by one man, or one Person, Represented. . . . For it is the Unity of the Representer, not the Unity of the Represented, that maketh the Person One.' That is to say, a multitude are made one people, distinct from other peoples, by being represented by one man or body of men. We are also told that 'the Essence of the Commonwealth . . . is One Person, of whose Acts a great Multitude, by mutual Covenants one with another, have made themselves everyone the Author.' The multitude make no covenant with the sovereign, but by their agreements one with another give him the right to speak and decide for them all, authorizing his every public action as if it were their own.

From this argument, that the sovereign, though no party to the covenant, becomes in virtue of it his subjects' representative and they the authors of his sovereign acts, Hobbes draws his two most important practical conclusions: *firstly*, that subjects never have the right to change the form of their government, because they have bound themselves to obey a particular sovereign and acknowledge all his public acts for their own, and have thereby abandoned the right to put themselves, without his permission, under a similar obligation to anyone else; and *secondly*, that subjects, because they make the covenant with one another and not with the sovereign, can never 'by any pretence of forfeiture' on his part 'be freed from his subjection'. The sovereign cannot injure though he can hurt them; for an injury is an injustice, and no man can injure himself. As subjects are authors of all the sovereign's acts, nothing that he does can be an injury and so give them the right to throw off his authority. Now, all this makes no sense if natural right is complete absence of obligation; it begins to make sense only if natural right is something that can be granted or transferred, which mere absence of obligation cannot be. The only kind of right that can be granted or transferred is the kind that implies obligation. Only if a house is mine, in the sense that I alone have the right to use it because other people are obliged to keep out of it, can I grant or transfer the right to use it to someone else. But rights, in this sense, cannot be unlimited and universal; if everyone has them, then no one can have a right to all things.

There is really no avoiding the conclusion that Hobbes, in his account of the covenant and its effects, shifts from one sense of natural right to another quite different from it. At one stage of his argument he admits that there can be no actual transfer of natural right, since everyone has a natural right to everything, and yet at all other stages uses arguments which make no sense unless natural right can be transferred; and this it can be only if it implies obligation, and is therefore not a right to all things. Not content to show that it is always inexpedient or dangerous for subjects to try to change the system of government, or that they have no legal right to do so, Hobbes is eager to prove that they have no natural right to change it. Arguments about legitimacy ought to mean nothing to a man who takes natural right for absence of obligation.[1] But Hobbes is never more insistent than when he tries to prove that every established government, whatever it does, is always legitimate.

When I say that Hobbes' arguments about the effects of the covenant

---

[1] Or, rather, his position ought to be that the legitimacy of a government consists only in its being reasonable for its subjects to obey it because its power is in fact effective. This, too, is a position taken up by Hobbes. But he also, especially when he spoke of the covenant's making the sovereign the 'representative' of his subjects, was trying to prove that government is legitimate in a more usual sense.

make sense only if natural right can be transferred, I do not mean that they are, on this condition, valid and conclusive. Even if natural right could be transferred, it still would not follow that, when a number of people agree with one another to obey unconditionally some person to whom they make no promise, they would have no right to release each other from the agreement merely because the person to be obeyed was no party to it. However we define right, this argument (which Hobbes makes so much of) is bad. We might as well argue that, if we all agree never to speak to someone whom we all dislike, we are forever bound by the agreement because the object of our dislike was not a party to it. In this trivial case, the argument is clearly defective; and is not the less so when used to settle an important question.

Perhaps Hobbes would have done better had he explained political obedience entirely as an effect of self-interest and fear, had he spoken only of maxims of prudence in the state of nature and never of divine laws, and had he always spoken of natural right as complete absence of obligation. The only ground of obedience would then have been the private interest of the person called upon to obey. Covenants made before the sovereign's power was effective could then create neither duty nor right; for duty and right (in the sense of right that implies duty) could exist only where there was a sovereign. If Hobbes had spoken in this way, he would have had to treat the virtually absolute subjection of the subject, not as something entailed by the sovereign's unlimited right, but as the subject's interest; he would have had to say that it is the subject's interest always to obey the sovereign except when the sovereign seeks to destroy him, and that it is never his interest to resist the sovereign whatever he may do to other people. Of course, Hobbes did say this. But he was not content to say *only* this; he also felt the need to use arguments which make no sense unless natural right is more than mere absence of obligation.

If Hobbes has correctly described the subject's interest, then, so long as most subjects see their interest and act upon it, the sovereign's power is as great as it can be or need be. For, in that case, anyone who disobeys the sovereign will find his fellow-subjects arrayed against him as a law breaker. The more enlightened the community, the greater the sovereign's power.

If Hobbes had reduced his argument to this, he would have been more consistent but perhaps less persuasive. The argument, put in this way, is too naked, too cynical, to appeal to many people at any time. In the seventeenth century, when most people still believed in God, it would have been deeply shocking. Hobbes was as much concerned to prove the legitimacy as the expediency of sovereign power, unrestricted except by the subject's claim to resist attack on his life or person; and we do him less than justice if we fail to recognize this. He tried to prove two things at once, and was probably as sincere in the one

F*

endeavour as in the other. Certainly, we have no reason to believe that he himself was convinced only by the arguments for the expediency of absolute government and put the others in because he thought they would be more acceptable. He was probably quite honest with his readers, and marshalled his arguments in good faith.

Therefore we must not treat his arguments for the legitimacy of sovereign power as if they were supplementary to the others; they are just as much a part of Hobbes' political philosophy. But they are, as I have tried to show, unusually confused; much more so, I think, than most writers on Hobbes have been inclined to admit. They are also less new and less striking than the arguments for expediency. It is as the man who tried to prove that absolute government is always expedient that Hobbes stands out among political thinkers. He spent as much time discussing right as expediency, but it is what he said about expediency that is best remembered. Indeed, he has often been accused of reducing right to expediency. Though the accusation is scarcely just, it is true that Hobbes came nearer to doing this than any other political writer of his importance.

It is worth while isolating Hobbes' arguments for the expediency of absolute power from the rest of his doctrine in order to see what they amount to and how far they hold.

VI. HOBBES' ARGUMENT FOR ABSOLUTE GOVERNMENT

Suppose we eliminate from Hobbes' theory all mention of natural right, and all talk of the sovereign being his subjects' representative and they the authors of his acts. What then remains of his argument for absolute government? And government absolute in just what sense? For power, as Hobbes knew, is never unlimited. No man or body has ever stood, or could in the real world stand, to other men in such a relation that whatever he or it commanded they would do.

Hobbes insists that men in fact obey only from hope of benefit or fear of hurt to themselves, only while it is their interest to do so; and he admits that it is not always their interest. A subject may defend himself against a sovereign who seeks to destroy or imprison him. As Hobbes puts it, he has 'a natural right' to resist his sovereign; but we, having for the moment agreed to make no mention of natural right, must say that the subject is well advised to resist whenever it is his interest to do so, which it clearly is when the sovereign seeks to destroy or imprison him.

There is a sense, as obvious as it is important, in which every man is always a judge in his own case; for he alone can decide whether or not to submit quietly to another's judgment. Far from denying this,

Hobbes often insists upon it. It is a fact that necessarily limits sovereign power. It is inevitable and not to be regretted because it is a product of the same instinct of self-preservation which ordinarily disposes men to obedience. Creatures so indifferent to life that they would not even defend themselves from someone seeking to destroy them would care so little for security that we cannot imagine them setting up government in the hope of getting it. The sovereign has power only because his subjects obey him, and they obey him for the sake of security; but the sovereign's power also depends on his invading the security of the law-breaker, who therefore resists the sovereign from the same motive that causes other people to obey him.

What then, this being admitted, can Hobbes mean by arguing that authority must be absolute? He can only, as I see it. mean that it is never men's interest that there should be rules or conventions limiting their obedience to government; and also never their interest that supreme governmental authority should be divided. They must never undertake to obey the sovereign only on condition that he governs according to such and such principles, and must never have more than one centre of supreme authority. To assert moral or customary or legal limits to the ruler's authority is to give notice that you will not obey him if he transgresses those limits, and it is also to encourage disobedience in others. It is to do much more than just defend yourself against him when he seeks to destroy or imprison you; it is to put forward the claim to judge between him and anyone who defies him. If the sovereign's power is limited, not merely by the inevitable fact that (human nature being what it is) anyone he seeks to destroy will resist him, but on grounds of principle, then it is possible for anyone to appeal to principle against the sovereign. There is then a law which the sovereign may break and which others may claim the right to enforce. There are then two kinds of law, and the sovereign makes only one of them. But Hobbes' position is that, if there is more than one maker and enforcer of law, there cannot be real security.

Security is threatened, not by everyone's inevitably resisting whoever would destroy him, but by the claim made on general grounds that the sovereign shall be resisted or disobeyed when he does not respect conditions supposedly laid down for the benefit of all his subjects. When subjects obey conditionally, disputes must arise about precisely what actions of the sovereign infringe the conditions laid down. If the sovereign is the final judge in such disputes, conditions might as well not be laid down, for he will interpret them to suit himself. If another authority is set up to decide the dispute, there is danger of civil strife. If the people generally set themselves up for judges, there must be anarchy. There must therefore be no resisting the sovereign on general grounds, as a matter of principle, or for the sake of justice. Resist him, by all means, when he seeks to destroy you, but do not offer to resist him when he seeks to destroy others. The chances are that he is seeking to destroy them in order to maintain his authority, and it is your interest that he should maintain it. Never seek to impose for the general good any conventional or legal limit to the sovereign's power, for it is not your interest to do so. That, I think, is the real substance of Hobbes' argument for absolute government, if all talk of natural right is shorn away from it.

The argument is certainly plausible. The merely selfish law-breaker who resists arrest is not particularly dangerous to society. The police will probably catch him in the end, and almost everyone will consider him a public enemy. It is the man who, like John Hampden, defies the sovereign in the name of justice, resisting him as a matter of principle, who threatens the foundations of social peace. The thief often has property which he wants to hold in security; he is therefore anxious that other people should keep the law which he, from time to time, for his own profit, breaks. And in any case, all who know him for a thief are against him. But a John Hampden wants other people to follow his example, and they may well do so; for what encourages him to take his stand is the expectation or hope that others will do as he does. He is not a furtive criminal but a defier of authority. He asserts everyone's right against the sovereign. He makes a challenge which the sovereign must take up even at the price of war.

Hobbes seems to have believed that all agreement about principles or rules to limit authority is at bottom illusory, lasting only as long as the rules are not applied. As soon as the need is felt to apply them, they are variously interpreted. Unless it is agreed whose interpretation is final, there is always danger to peace. But if there is this agreement, then the final interpreter, whoever he may be, can make what he likes of the rules; he is the true sovereign. There was therefore no need to make the rules in the first place, for in practice they must be whatever the final interpreter says they are. His authority is unlimited, and the rules have failed of their purpose. On the other hand, if there is no final interpreter, the rules are a source of contention between all the parties that interpret them differently to suit their different interests. The rules are either useless or else are occasions of strife and even of war. It is impossible that a large number of persons should always agree about the application of general principles to particular cases. But, fortunately, it is easy enough for them to understand that it is their interest that all disputes should be quickly, peacefully, and finally decided; and experience must in the end teach them that this can be so only if the final decision of them is left to one person or one body of persons.

Hobbes' argument for absolute government therefore rests on the assumption that, unless supreme authority is undivided, there cannot be a final and generally accepted arbiter in all cases, including disputes about the limits of authority. Now, this assumption is just not true. It is possible so to divide authority between different bodies and persons that none is sovereign in Hobbes' sense and yet no dispute can arise which somebody has not the right to settle finally. In the United States, for example, ultimate authority of different kinds is vested in the President, in Congress, in the Supreme Court, and in each of fifty states. Of these fifty-three centres of authority, none is subordinate to any of the others. They all limit one another, but none has the authority which is properly its own by permission of the others. They have it because their authority is in fact generally recognized as long as they use it according to the principles laid down in the constitution. They have it for precisely the same reason as Hobbes' sovereign has his authority; they are in fact obeyed because it is admitted that they should be. If the limits of their authority were set by the people, in the sense that private citizens could properly refuse obedience whenever they decided that those limits were overstepped, there would soon be anarchy. But the constitution (both the written part of it and the conventions that have gathered round it) provides methods for settling all disputes peacefully, even disputes about the constitution. Since all who have authority have it under the constitution, they all have a general interest that the constitution should be obeyed. They have exactly the same interest in relation to it as the subordinates of a Hobbesian sovereign have in relation to him. Their power depends on the constitution's being respected, and its being respected limits their power. Nor can we say that the constitution is sovereign, for if there is a sense in which a constitution can be sovereign, it is clearly not the Hobbesian sense.[1]

Whether there is a sovereign or not, there is always, where government is stable, a constitution; there are always rules governing the use of power which are in fact obeyed by those who exercise power. Louis XIV was absolute ruler of France only because all persons having authority in France observed a highly complicated set of rules whose general observance made Louis absolute. His authority was absolute but his power was not unlimited, for he – like all other rulers – was even more dependent on his subordinates than they on him. Power is always in fact divided, for the very simple reason that government is always a form of collaboration. Those who have power in the State must observe some rules in their dealings with one another; for unless they do so, they cannot govern. Government, of its very nature, is a regular activity; a system of behaviour determined by rules.

Hobbes' argument for the expediency of absolute government or sovereign power therefore comes down to this: the rules governing the

[1] Nor are the bodies which, between them, have the right to amend the constitution sovereign, for the only authority they share is the right to amend the constitution.

use of power are more likely to be respected when they place the final right of decision in all spheres of government (in other words, supreme authority) in the hands of one man or assembly than when they divide it between several. If the argument is put in this way, which seems to me a fair way of putting it, it does not look convincing. No doubt, if there is to be domestic peace, the rules governing the use of power must be understood by the persons required to obey them; and no doubt also, whenever disputes arise about what the rules are, there must always be an agreed method for settling them. In Hobbes' England these conditions did not hold: there was great confusion about what the fundamental laws were, there were disputes about them, and there was no agreed method for settling the disputes. As Hobbes saw it, the disputes could only be settled by war, and in fact the victors exercised what could fairly be called absolute authority. But though these conditions did not hold in England in Hobbes' day, it is not true that they hold only where there is a sovereign in the Hobbesian sense. Supreme authority can either all be placed in the same hands, or it can be divided between several persons and bodies and rules laid down for settling disputes between them. Which is the better method depends on circumstances.

Hobbes argued that the body whose function is to decide disputes between other bodies must in fact be sovereign. But clearly this is not true; not if we take his sense of sovereignty. If the United States Supreme Court, as the guardian of the constitution, has the last word in settling disputes about the limits of executive and legislative authority, that is not enough to make it sovereign in Hobbes' sense. It cannot itself exercise the powers of the President or of Congress, and if it tried to do so would not be obeyed. To settle disputes about the limits of other people's authority is clearly not to do what they do; it is to do something else which is quite different, it is to exercise another kind of authority. Congress and President are no more subordinate to the Supreme Court than that Court is to them merely because it has the last word in interpreting a constitution under which all three hold their powers.

Whether or not there is a sovereign, the common interest of all persons taking part in government is ordinarily that the rules, which make the structure of government what it is, should be respected; because it is on this structure that their power depends. If, for any reason, some of them want to increase their share of power at the expense of others, and try to break or to change the rules, they are not the less likely to do so merely because there is a sovereign. So long as the rules are coherent and so long as they are obeyed, the system works well enough. People may want to change the rules for all kinds of reasons: because they want to get more power for themselves, because they believe that thereby the efficiency of government will be improved, or because they want to increase or decrease the influence on government of some part or other of the people. Whatever their reasons or motives, they are as likely to be strong where there is a sovereign as where there is not.

In early Tudor times the House of Commons accepted a body of customs governing the use of power which gave the king greater authority than Charles I had when Parliament went to war with him. The Tudor constitution was unwritten and some of its conventions were vague; it was, like all constitutions, in process of change. There was nothing about it, if we look at it merely as a body of customary rules governing the use of power, that explains why it was more acceptable than the system (which was in fact largely the same) challenged by the Long Parliament. Apart from the specific interests and motives of the defenders and challengers of a political system, we cannot explain why it should be acceptable at one time and not at another. But Hobbes would have us believe that the system which provides a sole final authority in all spheres of government is always the most suitable, whatever men's interests. He took it for granted that, where there is no such authority, there will inevitably arise disputes that cannot be settled except by war. He could not see that, where there are several final authorities, each in a different field, there may yet be a settled procedure for deciding any dispute that may arise; nor yet that, where there is such a procedure, men have precisely the same interest in accepting it as they have in accepting the authority of the sovereign.

VII. CONCLUSION

Many of the weaknesses of Hobbes' political philosophy derive from his too narrow assumptions and definitions. He treats law as primarily command, not taking sufficient notice of the fact that the power to command derives from the habit of obedience. Before there can be political power, there must be rules that men follow, not from fear of government, but from other motives. Law in the broadest sense is prior to government, which is impossible without it. Hobbes does, of course, speak of a law of nature, which is the command of God, prior to government. But he speaks of it equivocally. Though God's power is irresistible, He does not provide His creatures with adequate motives for keeping His law until there is a human sovereign to enforce it. And if obligation is what Hobbes says it is, there is really no need, given his account of the state of nature and the covenant, to assert a prior obligation to obey God in order to explain the duty of obedience to the sovereign. Hobbes does not discard the old tradition of a law of nature which is also the will of God, but makes so odd a use of it that in his hands it can no longer serve the old purposes. God is very much present in his scheme of things, but is also, at bottom, superfluous.

Again, Hobbes begins by giving such an account of natural right as reduces it to mere power or else, more plausibly, to complete absence of obligation. Then, having defined the covenant setting up the sovereign as a laying down of natural right by the parties to it, he tries to use it to prove the legitimacy of sovereign power. But this he cannot do if natural right is only the absence of obligation; and so he passes, without noticing it, to a more adequate and ordinary conception of right, but a conception not in keeping with his own account of the state of nature. Hobbes, I suggest, was a more confused thinker than he is usually taken to be.

Yet his merits are greater than his faults. He understood that men are not born but are made sociable, that there is no justice without law, and no law without discipline, and no discipline without sanctions. It is under the pressure of authority that man becomes a creature who learns to respect in others the claims he makes for himself. But Hobbes made the mistake of supposing that all authority is at bottom political, and so he could not see that even human law (as custom) is prior to government. And yet, in spite of his calling the law of nature the command of God, and his speaking of obligation *in foro interno* even in the unsocial state of nature, I think that Hobbes came close to believing that morality is something that appears only in society. He spoke, as I have said, in two voices; he used the old conception of a law of nature valid even outside society, and yet made a lame and halting use of it. Perhaps the dissatisfaction sprang from a half-formed belief that it is only as a social creature, as a creature subject to a discipline externally imposed, that man becomes moral. If Hobbes had seen clearly what this belief implied, he might have rejected altogether the conception of a law of nature prior to all forms of social discipline; he might have done, in the seventeenth century, what Hume was to do in the eighteenth. As it is, *Leviathan*, much more powerfully than anything written before it, brings to our notice what man might be like if he were subject to no discipline, if he were included in no social order. *Leviathan*, more than any political treatise before it, compels us to reflect on what is involved in man's being a social and a moral creature.

Hobbes was mistaken in supposing that all social discipline outside the family is political. But this mistake was not peculiar to him; it was almost universal among political thinkers in his day. It was not corrected until the next century, in France by Montesquieu and in England by Hume.

Chapter 5

DIVINE RIGHT AND ABSOLUTE MONARCHY

I. THE ORIGINS OF THE DOCTRINE

PERHAPS no important doctrine has flourished for so short a time as the doctrine that the authority of kings is absolute because it comes to them from God. Yet the doctrine is more than an historical curiosity; it is one among several answers to the everlasting problem of European political philosophy, the problem of political obligation. If this particular answer was found attractive for only a few generations, it was not because, in itself, it was inferior to the others. It is no more far fetched than the theory that government was established by a contract defining the rights and obligations of rulers and ruled; it puts no greater strain on credulity, and is perhaps simpler and less confused. It was short-lived, not because the arguments used to support it were unusually weak, but because the circumstances which made it attractive did not long endure. The doctrine flourished in the seventeenth century, and its ablest exponents were English or French, or were Scotsmen settled in France; it flourished in two out of the three most powerful monarchies of the West at a time when they were either in the throes of civil war or had lately emerged from it. 'In the censure of kingdoms,' says Filmer, 'the King of Spain is said to be the King of men, because of his subjects' willing obedience; the King of France, King of asses, because of their infinite taxes and impositions; but the King of England is said to be the King of Devils, because of his subjects' often insurrections against, and depositions of, their Princes.'[1] But when Andrew Blackwood, a gallicized Scot, and Pierre de Belloy were claiming absolute power by right divine for the king of France, he too was a king of devils. Not that the devils of France had turned into asses by Filmer's time, for in the late sixteenth and early seventeenth century, the king's rebellious subjects, in both France and England, were the well-to-do and the privileged, who weighed as heavily on the asses as ever the king did.

The argument for absolute monarchy by divine right, in France and in England, was a product of civil war; it was an argument attractive to men who sought an absolute and unquestionable authority at a time when it seemed easiest to find it in the king. The theory of the social

[1] Filmer. *Patriarcha*. B. Blackwell, 1949, edited by P. Laslett, p. 95.

contract, as elaborated by Huguenots and Jesuits, was a challenge to a type of authority unknown in the high Middle Ages, a central and extensive authority making all other authorities subordinate to itself; it was a challenge made on behalf of subjects whose religion differed from that of their prince. To such subjects as these the growing power of the monarchy, in an age when religious uniformity was everywhere thought desirable, naturally seemed dangerous. But then to others their challenge to it also seemed dangerous; and the doctrine of absolute monarchy by divine right was an answer to that challenge. This doctrine is therefore as unmediaeval as the doctrine it answers; and yet, like the contract theory, it has roots which go back into the Middle Ages and beyond. It is a new theory containing old ingredients. Like nearly all political doctrines, it has a long ancestry, even though it denies an almost universal belief of the Middle Ages, that all human authority is limited and may, if abused, be justly resisted.

In the Middle Ages it was generally held that all authority of man over man, whether spiritual or temporal, comes from God and is limited. Though there were plentiful disputes about the limits of spiritual and temporal authority, and extravagant claims were sometimes made by champions of the one or the other, it was almost universally admitted that the two were separate, and that neither should encroach on the other. Not even the most extreme champions of the Pope, not even those who ascribed to him the fullness of power, *plenitudo potestatis*, literally claimed for him what Hobbes was to understand by sovereign authority; and the claim which was never made on the Pope's behalf was also never made on behalf of the Emperor or any other temporal prince. Just as the Pope's claims were resisted, and variously understood, both inside the Church and by the Temporal Power, so the claims made by Emperors or Kings were resisted and variously understood both by their temporal subordinates and by the Spiritual Power.

To say that all human authority comes from God is not to deny that it may come also from the people; it is to deny only that it can come from the people alone. Though in the Middle Ages it was much more usual to speak of temporal than of spiritual authority as coming from both God and men, there were some who were willing to speak in this way of both types of authority. For though everyone believed that the Church having spiritual authority over the faithful was established by Christ, and would have no authority if it had not been so established, the tradition was not entirely lost that the first bishops, the first overseers, had been chosen by their flocks.

God, the creator, has full authority over His creatures, and therefore no creature can have authority over another unless God has allowed it. But God need not, and ordinarily does not, grant authority directly to those that have it. He has endowed man with reason, and therefore with the capacity to provide for his needs in ways impossible to crea-tures not endowed with reason. Men need to be governed in this world, and where God does not Himself undertake to govern them or to appoint rulers over them, He allows them to provide for themselves. Communities of men have authority from God to make provision for their government, and thus it is that the authority of man over man, at least in the temporal sphere, can be both divine and popular in origin; it must be from God and it can be, and ordinarily is, from the people also.

Those who held that temporal authority comes from the people as well as from God usually had little to say about its origin. For the most part, they were content to argue that those who have temporal power have a customary right to it, and that what rests on custom has the people's consent; or later, as Roman law came to be studied more widely, they spoke more often of a grant of authority made long ago by the people to their rulers just as the Roman jurists had spoken of a grant by the Roman people to the Emperor. Some held that the grant was irrevocable, and others that it could be revoked.

The authority of the prince or supreme temporal ruler was thought to be limited in a variety of ways. Every man was held obliged to prefer divine to human law, and must therefore disobey anyone, lay-man or priest, who commanded what God forbade or who forbade what God commanded. Secondly, there was the acknowledged duty of obedience to the Spiritual as well as to the Temporal Power. Lastly, there were other magistrates besides the Emperor or King, besides the prince, magistrates whose authority rested on custom and whose right to defend their authority, even against the prince, was widely recognized. In the feudal hierarchy, lesser magistrates were not the mere agents of their superiors; they were not related, either in theory or in practice, to the suzerain, to the lord paramount, as all having authority under the sovereign are related to him according to either Bodin or Hobbes.

Thus the authority of the supreme temporal ruler was limited in several ways, and could be effectively resisted; for he was supreme only in the sense that there was no one above him in the hierarchy. Indeed, we may say that, in the Middle Ages, all authority, temporal and spiritual, was severely but not precisely circumscribed; it was loosely defined and subject, within uncertain limits, to considerable fluctua-tions. There were rights in plenty to invoke against anyone having authority. But this does not mean that the right of subjects to resist authority was widely asserted in the sense that Locke or Bentham asserted it. The Spiritual Power had rights against the Temporal Power, and the Temporal against the Spiritual; the Church had rights against the Pope, and a variety of privileged orders and corporations had rights against the King. Men might differ widely about the extent of these rights, but few, if any, denied them altogether. But these rights, insofar as they were effective, were the rights of the privileged against one another. In the Middle Ages the right of resistance to authority was confined, more or less, to persons having authority, and so we can say that, though all authority was limited, the right of the mere individual against those in authority was hardly asserted.

Though it was hardly asserted, it was seldom denied as explicitly and fervently as it came to be in later centuries. It was neglected rather than denied. True, even the always moderate Aquinas taught that there is no duty of obedience to a usurper nor yet to a legitimate ruler when he commands what is unjust; what is contrary to divine or natural law, or even to human law (which he thought of as mostly custom) where the ruler has no authority to alter it or set it aside. Aquinas preferred a system where there are customary methods of restraining the supreme holder of temporal power, but he admitted that, where there are no such methods or they are ineffective, it may be necessary to resort to other methods, not sanctioned by custom, against a ruler who persists in tyranny; that is to say, who claims and attempts to exert an authority which is not his. Yet the admission is not evidence against what I have said, for Aquinas believed that these other methods, when the common good requires their use, should be used by established orders and corporations. Thus we may say that, though Aquinas allows any man a right to disobey, he confines the right of active resistance to holders of authority. But, as we shall see, the right merely to disobey was never denied even by the most extreme champion of the much later doctrine that the authority of princes is absolute and comes to them from God alone and not also from the people.

By early mediaeval custom, the Emperor or King was not even above the law, *legibus solutus*, in the sense of not having to answer for his actions; there was a court to decide between him and those who complained against him, and if he refused to accept its decisions, they might be enforced against him by a withdrawal of allegiance or even by force of arms. But these methods were difficult and dangerous, and so attempts were made to put the king under more effective control; as, for example, by the barons of England in 1258 who imposed the Provisions of Oxford on Henry III. Later, as kings felt a greater need to consult the people (or, rather, the privileged orders and corporations) through their representatives in order to explain royal intentions and needs to them, and to get subsidies from them, Parliaments and Estates served both to make the royal power more effective and to limit it. The Roman conception of the Emperor as above the law, as *legibus solutus*, was applied more and more generally to all princes, to all who, in the temporal hierarchy, had no superior. So, too, from the thirteenth to the fifteenth century, the idea of human law as an expression of conscious will steadily gained ground at the expense of the idea of it as primarily custom. Mediaeval writers repeated more and more frequently the sentence of the Roman lawyers, that what pleases the prince has the force of law. But this sentence, as they uttered it, was still not a claim that the prince was sovereign as Bodin or Hobbes understood sovereignty; for they did not go on to assert that the prince had the right to declare or make law without consulting the people, nor yet that, when he acted against natural or divine law, he might not be resisted. As late as the fifteenth century, Nicholas of Cusa was teaching that human law is the law of the entire community, and that the prince is bound by it; and this was also the doctrine of Gerson in France and of Fortescue in England. The sentences which the champions of absolute monarchy by divine right were to rely on so much were already in wide circulation, but were seldom understood in the sense later ascribed to them by those champions.

In both France and England it was widely admitted in the fifteenth century that ' what concerns all should be approved by all '; that is to say, by the body supposed to speak for the entire community. Parliament in England was already consulted more often and about more matters than the States-General in France, but the provincial Estates in France met quite frequently. In both countries the king often made decisions (which we should call laws) by ordinance or by order-in-council, without consulting Parliament or the Estates, for no clear distinction was made between the executive and legislative functions. Yet what was widely admitted was not so much that the king could not make laws without consulting his people as that he ought not to take important decisions without doing so. And those who declared that what concerns all should be approved by all did not feel committed thereby to deny that what pleases the prince has the force of law. These two assertions, as they understood them, were not contradictory.

In the early Middle Ages, when both the Spiritual and the Temporal Power were loosely and weakly organized, each interfered in the sphere of the other with very little friction; or rather, no serious attempt was made to define the two spheres. Later, as the two Powers came to be better organized, each resented the ' interference ' of the other; and each defined and re-defined its authority in the endeavour to enlarge it. For a variety of reasons, the Church set itself in order more quickly than the ' State ', and the Pope acquired greater authority inside it than the temporal princes in their kingdoms. Until the fourteenth century it was the Spiritual rather than the Temporal Power which took the offensive. To support its pretensions, the Church pointed partly to its superior dignity, and partly to what it took to be history. The function of the Church, as churchmen saw it, was to give men the instruction and guidance they needed to find God; which they claimed was a higher function than that of temporal rulers, which was merely to maintain the peace. The Church, which helps men to achieve their highest end, is necessarily superior to the Temporal Power, which looks after their lesser ends. Thus, though both Powers are divinely instituted, the lesser power is subordinate to the higher in the sense that, though the Church does not itself exercise temporal power, it has a duty to see that those who exercise it do so worthily; and its most powerful instrument in carrying out this duty is excommunication, for when a prince is excommunicated his subjects no longer owe him obedience. These conclusions were supported by other arguments: it was alleged that by the donation of Constantine, the empire of the West was given to the Papacy, which later made it over to the Germans; that the authority of temporal rulers is not properly theirs until they have been anointed by the Church; that Christ, being God, had *de iure* both temporal and spiritual authority while He was on earth and had granted both to St Peter and his successors.[1]

The claim of the Church that temporal power, though divinely instituted, comes to its actual possessors through the Church was firmly rejected by the Emperor and the other princes. They and their apologists asserted that the authority of princes comes to them as directly from God as the authority of the Pope and the Church. But this assertion, at that time, was not a denial that authority also comes to them from the people; it was merely a refusal to admit that the divine origin of temporal authority implied any subordination of the Temporal to the Spiritual Power. The Emperor, on whose behalf papal and ecclesiastical pretensions were most vigorously contested, was not even an hereditary but an elected prince; there was no question but that his authority was limited. The other prince whose quarrel with the Pope was the fiercest, the King of France, did rule by hereditary right and was already, by the time that the boldest claims were made on the Pope's behalf, much more powerful in France than the Emperor in the empire, but his authority also was far from absolute.

In the early Middle Ages it was not admitted that a king came to his throne by mere hereditary right, on no other ground than that he was his predecessor's closest descendant according to some fixed rule; though the king was usually closely related to his predecessor, the claim of an elder son or of the person whose right would have been undoubted, if the rule of succession had been what it later became, was not infrequently set aside in favour of a younger brother or someone else deemed more worthy. The coronation was then no mere formal ceremony; it was an act of investiture, a bestowal of authority. In

---

[1] The text most often quoted to support this argument was from the Gospel of St Matthew, 16:19; where Christ says to Peter, 'I will give unto thee the keys of the kingdom of heaven: and whatsoever thou shalt bind on earth shall be bound in heaven: and whatsoever thou shalt loose on earth shall be loosed in heaven.'

England it was not till the fourteenth century that succession by mere hereditary right was firmly established. As the power vested in the king grew, it came to seem more important that there should be no disputes as to who had the right to be king; and so it came to be held that whoever succeeds by hereditary right is truly and fully king from the moment that his predecessor dies. Yet this assertion did not imply that temporal authority was not of popular origin; for the rule of succession was customary, and custom was held to imply popular consent.

It was yet another step from asserting succession by hereditary right to saying that that right is indefeasible, that whoever has it cannot lose it whatever he does. This particular doctrine, though sometimes widely held, was never generally accepted in England. It was popular among Yorkists but was denied by Lancastrians. Even as late as Elizabeth's reign, while Mary Stuart was still alive and there were people willing to argue that she had a better title to the English throne than Elizabeth, an act was passed making it high treason for anyone to question Parliament's right to alter the succession to the throne. After Mary's execution, Elizabeth's title was less questionable, and the doctrine of indefeasible right was for a time widely popular, largely because it was denied by the Jesuits who hoped to see a Catholic prince on Elizabeth's throne. In France the doctrine first became popular during the Hundred Years War, and was used to contest English claims. Though the English might by force make themselves masters of France, though a French king might be bullied into recognizing Henry of England as his heir, the law of succession remained unchanged. No English victories, no concessions extorted from defeated Frenchmen, could make a difference; there was only one rightful heir to the throne of France. Henry of England could never be King of France; no power on earth, not even the French king, not even the States-General, could give him that title. This French assertion of indefeasible right was originally a declaration of independence; to those who asserted it, it was a doctrine standing for domestic peace, for the unity of France, for resistance to the invader. It did not imply that the power of the rightful king was absolute, nor even that it was not derived originally from the people; but it did imply that what the people had once bestowed, they could no longer take away.

Before the sixteenth century, neither the doctrine that the authority of kings comes from God nor the doctrine that a legitimate king is so by indefeasible hereditary right was used to resist claims made on behalf of the people; these doctrines came to be used for this purpose only after the Reformation. For the reformers, though their defiance of the Church could hardly have succeeded had they not been supported by princes and kings, started a movement which eventually produced a new type of resistance to princely and royal power. Hitherto the authority of princes had been challenged only by the Church or by the feudal lords; it was soon to be challenged by, or on behalf of, religious minorities, of groups unknown to mediaeval society. These groups often could not assert traditional rights or use traditional methods. They often could not, as the mediaeval Church had been able to do, use rights long recognized and doctrines long familiar to resist the Temporal Power or to attempt encroachments upon it; they often could not, as the feudal lords had long been able to do, use an assembly like the States-General or Parliament, an assembly dominated by their order, to restrain the king. They could not appeal to customary rights to justify resistance. At least, they could nowhere do so effectively until in England by the seventeenth century they had acquired a considerable influence in the lower house of Parliament, the house which in mediaeval times had been much the less important of the two, but which had recently gained greatly in power and prestige, largely owing to the use made of it by Tudor monarchs.

The theory of the social contract was first used in the sixteenth century in the interest of religious minorities.[1] It does not place customary limits on temporal authority, nor assert a merely customary right of resistance; it asserts, as mediaeval political thinkers (for all their insistence that all human authority is limited) did not do, that the people, having agreed to set up rulers over them for certain purposes, therefore have the right to resist or remove them if they persist in courses which defeat those purposes. A contract is essentially a voluntary and deliberate agreement; the parties to it are presumed to be free not to make it, and also to understand what they are doing when they make it. It is odd to speak of great multitudes making contracts; it looks like fantasy or, if the contract is assumed to be tacit, like an abuse of language. The mediaeval idea that popular consent to temporal authority is implied by the general acceptance of what is customary seems much closer to the truth. Yet the language of contract, which seems so obviously out of place when it is a question of explaining the origins of government, was deliberately chosen. Those who used it wanted to suggest that political authority rests on the deliberate consent of the governed. The suggestion is so wide of the mark that, as one difficulty after another faced them, they hedged or took back at later stages of their argument what they had said before. That is why, of all political theories, theirs is perhaps the most equivocal and vacillating. Yet the theory was inspired by the need to make, on behalf of minorities, claims of a kind not made before. The Huguenots could not hope to use the States-General to resist the King of France, for they were too few in number. At a time when the States-General still seemed bent on averting civil war, a Huguenot

[1] There are references to a social contract in theories earlier than the sixteenth century, but it was then that the idea of such a contract first became popular and, as it were, *central* to political theory.

writer, Hotman, could produce a book like *Franco-Gallia*, arguing that supreme authority in France belongs by custom to the States-General, the sole body representing the entire French people; but as soon as it was clear that the States-General would support the Catholic cause, the Huguenots resorted to a different type of argument.[1] Hence the appearance in 1579 of one of the earliest versions of the contract theory: Hubert Languet's *Vindiciae contra Tyrannos*. And the Jesuits, who also produced versions of that theory, were concerned to justify Catholic resistance and conspiracy in countries where not only princes, but parliaments and Estates as well, favoured one or other of the reformed religions.

Admittedly, the main purpose of the contractualists was not to assert a popular right of resistance to misgovernment. They were primarily concerned to defend one particular right, the right of free worship; and even this one right was not the right to adhere to *any* religion; it was the right to adhere to the religion which those who claimed the right believed to be alone true. The Huguenots did not believe that Catholics should be allowed to practise their religion freely in Protestant countries, nor the Jesuits that Protestants should be allowed to do so in Catholic countries. But theories often have implications wider than the particular concerns of the men who produce them. In practice, it was scarcely possible to use the contract theory to assert man's inalienable right to practise the true religion without admitting that men have other rights which they may need to defend against their rulers. Moreover, the right which both Huguenots and Jesuits wanted above all to assert was not a right of the Church against the State; it was the right of every man to worship God in the only way acceptable to God. It was an individual right: it was the right, not of an order or corporation, but a right of man. It was not put forward as a customary right.

The contract theory, as we find it in the sixteenth and early seventeenth centuries, is a logically (and historically) indefensible but

---

[1] Hotman's argument has much in common with arguments used in England some two generations later by the Parliamentary leaders. Just as Eliot and Pym appealed to the historic rights of Englishmen and of Parliament, so Hotman appealed to the historic rights of Frenchmen and of the States-General. No doubt, the States-General never became the formidable and effective body that Parliament had already become in late Tudor and early Stuart times, and in particular the Third State was less solid and self-reliant than the House of Commons. But, above all, the Huguenots soon found that they could achieve nothing through the States-General, whereas the opponents of Charles I's religious policy were powerful in the House of Commons. The Huguenots could not make a persuasive case for resistance on mainly historical grounds (even by using bad history, as both Hotman and Pym did); they therefore, for a time (till their leader, Henry of Navarre, became legitimate heir to the throne), found it their interest to let history alone and use a more abstract form of argument.

rhetorically effective way of insisting that the authority of rulers rests, not only on the will of God and not on mere custom, but on its being used to defend the interests and rights of the people: their supreme interest and right being to have and to practise the true religion. It also asserts, though ambiguously and hesitantly, that rulers are answerable to their subjects for the use they make of their authority. The Jesuits were less ambiguous and less hesitant than the Huguenots, perhaps because they were a religious order to whom the authority of the Church mattered greatly but the authority of princes much less, whereas the Huguenots had more peculiar and less stable needs, and were strong only in parts of France.[1] Mariana, in *De Rege et Regis Institutione* (1599), taught that temporal authority is granted to whoever possesses it by those who thereby become subject to it, and is always

[1] According to the author of the *Vindiciae*, the right of resistance belongs to the people collectively and not to *any* subject who believes that the prince has broken the covenant. But how are the people to exercise their collective right? The people, says the *Vindiciae*, act through their representatives. If the people, taken collectively, are one party to the covenant, it would seem that their representatives, whoever they are, must speak for the entire community; that they must be national and not merely local. But this is not how the *Vindiciae* describes them; for the magistrates to whom it grants the right of resistance are leaders in their local communities, city magistrates, noblemen, officers of the crown, provincial courts, and so on. These 'representatives', most of them holding office by hereditary right and not by election, have the right to resist the prince in the people's name, but apparently the people have no right to resist them! Now, the idea that the privileged, though only a small part of the community, have the right to speak for the whole of it had long been widely accepted. Indeed, it was not seriously challenged, except by the Levellers, until the rise of radicalism towards the end of the eighteenth century. Locke, for example, took it for granted that in 1688 Parliament spoke for the people of England, even though he knew that the great majority of Englishmen had no vote. The peculiarity of the *Vindiciae* is not that it confines to a part of the community, to a privileged order, the right to speak and to act for the whole of it, but that it does not confine it to that order throughout the community. It allows a minority of the privileged to defy, in the name of the people, a ruler whose authority is not contested by the majority of their order. The Huguenots, strong in some parts of France and weak in others, and stronger everywhere among the upper than the lower classes, needed a theory to justify a resistance which was neither nation-wide nor truly popular, and they could not invoke customary rights. Hence the crabbed and peculiar argument of the *Vindiciae*, which aims at justifying the resistance of a scattered minority among the privileged, and yet makes use of an abstract doctrine better suited to justify a resistance which is nation-wide, either because all classes support it or because it is supported in all parts of the community by classes whose claim to speak for the entire community has not yet been seriously challenged. Were the Huguenots in 1579 so much smaller a minority than the Whigs for whom Locke spoke some hundred years later? Perhaps not. But they were not, in the same sense, a *national* minority, they controlled no great national institution, and they were also widely hated and feared. Their resistance to the Crown threatened their country's unity as the resistance of the Whigs did not.

granted conditionally. Of its very nature, temporal authority cannot be absolute, nor can anyone, man or body, have an indefeasible right to it; for what is set up by the people for their convenience may be put down or altered by them from the same motive. The authority of temporal rulers depends on the *continuing* will of their subjects, and is limited by the purpose which moved their ancestors to establish it and for whose sake they now recognize it. To avoid tyranny, the people must reserve to themselves the right to legislate and to vote taxes, a right which they must exercise through a representative assembly, for otherwise they have no means of giving expression to their will. Though Mariana admits that it is for this assembly, and not for individuals, to resist the ruler when he misrules his subjects, he does not suggest (as, for example, Aquinas does) that where there is no such body with a customary right to speak for the people, active resistance is not permissible. He implies that the people have a right to be represented by some such body, and even allows tyrannicide where the prince defies the assembly or prevents its meeting. According to Suarez, in his *Tractatus de Legibus ac Deo Legislatore* (1611), a state is formed when a collection of people by common consent first form themselves into a community having the right to provide for their own government, and then go on to make a covenant binding on whoever is granted the right to rule and on his legitimate successors. While the ruler and his successors govern according to this covenant, their subjects are obliged to obey, for they are as much bound by the covenant as their rulers; but should any ruler break it, they have the right to resist him. Though Suarez does not make it clear how a people are to determine that their ruler has broken the covenant or how they are to resist him, he does assert a right of popular resistance.

Just as some writers were moved to put forward a new type of argument to justify resistance to temporal rulers, so others, who were not concerned with the fate of minorities but with dangers to the peace, were moved to make exceptional claims for those rulers, or for the most highly placed among them. There were others before Bodin who had said that the king of France had sovereign power, but they had not defined sovereignty as he was to do. They had not argued, as he did, that all others having temporal authority in France were mere officers of the king, having only as much authority as he was pleased to grant them, and which he could take away from them whenever he saw fit to do so; they had not claimed for him the sole right of making or declaring law, saying that he consulted the people's representatives, not because he was obliged to do so, but only because he found it useful; they had not insisted that the king was responsible to God alone for how he used his authority, and that no one, no matter what his official capacity, could rightfully refuse to obey him except when what he commanded was contrary to the command of God. It had long been held that the mere subject must not refuse obedience to his prince except when to obey him would involve disobedience to God; but this prohibition had not been understood to apply to every person or body having temporal authority within his dominions. Bodin's conception of sovereignty was as new as the arguments of the contract theorists.

But Bodin was not an exponent of the doctrine that kings have absolute power by divine right. Though he believed, in the sense of the mediaeval writers, that all authority of man over man comes ultimately from God, he did not make a special case for kings. He thought that, in every well-ordered state, there must be a sovereign, but he did not hold that the sovereign must be a king. He preferred monarchy to other types of government, and thought it best suited to a country like France. Further than that he did not go; he did not say that God had blessed monarchy above other forms of government, nor did he forbid resistance to the King of France on the express ground that he was God's deputy in a certain part of the world. He thought it enough to produce what he thought was good historical evidence that in France sovereignty belonged by tradition to the king, and he rejoiced that it should be so.

Yet Bodin's idea of sovereignty was taken over by the first exponents in France of the doctrine of absolute monarchy by divine right. They claimed, not only for the King of France, but for all kings, that they are God's deputies on earth and therefore have absolute authority over their subjects; they claimed for them, and for them alone, what Bodin understood by sovereignty. The theory of the divine right of kings, as we find it first in France and then in England, puts forward these propositions: that temporal authority comes to princes from God alone and not also from the people; that it belongs entirely to them and to such persons as they appoint to exercise it and from whom they can withdraw it when they please; that they acquire it by indefeasible hereditary right, and are accountable only to God for how they use it and not to their subjects or to any man or body of men holding authority, of whatever kind, spiritual or temporal. Exponents of the theory, though they do not exactly deny that forms of government other than monarchy are legitimate, usually neglect them, and are at pains to show that monarchy is divinely instituted in some special sense. They appeal to Holy Scripture to show that it was monarchy, and not some other form of government, which God gave to His chosen people; and they also argue that monarchy is a form or extension of paternal authority, which was the first to exist among men and is the most natural, and may therefore be presumed to enjoy the peculiar favour of God. God is the Father of mankind, and the king is the father of his people, and so is to that extent Godlike.

II. THE POPULARITY AND SIGNIFICANCE OF THE DOCTRINE

The doctrine became popular because it met a need which was peculiarly strong in countries in the throes of, or threatened by, civil war. It was in many ways better suited to meet that need than the theories of either Bodin or Hobbes. It was simpler, cruder and less elaborately argued than Bodin's defence of the French monarchy; it appealed in a religious age to some of the most deeply and widely held beliefs. Bodin was interested in forms of government other than monarchy; he believed that different forms are suited to different peoples; he was aware that institutions change and are adapted to circumstances, he appealed to precedents often not easy to interpret. If he was not always a clear thinker, he was certainly a subtle one. His argument for absolute monarchy in France rested partly on an appeal to tradition and partly on an appeal to the common interest; it was an intricate and a difficult argument, best appreciated by the learned and by men experienced in government. Whereas the argument of, say, Pierre de Belloy was bold and simple: the king must be obeyed unconditionally because his authority comes from God, who has made him answerable to Himself alone for how he uses it. The king's authority is absolute and legitimate, not by long tradition or because its being so is ultimately for the people's good, but because Almighty God, in His wisdom and mercy, has made it so.

To the man who appreciates clear thinking and well-constructed argument, Hobbes' account of sovereignty and his apology for it appear more admirable even than Bodin's. Hobbes will always be a favourite among intellectuals. He is a robust, bold, resourceful, and at times close reasoner; he uses his arguments with the assurance of an all-seeing general winning a complete victory in a large and intricate battle; he is the most pungent of political philosophers, and has a sharp wit, though he is not bitter or waspish. He is a remedy for dullness; to read him is to be put in a better humour. From a certain point of view, he made the best of all cases for absolute authority. But he did not make a case likely to attract the unsophisticated. He has had, no doubt, a great and a long influence; he has had a distinguished intellectual posterity. Many have borrowed from him, including the two most famous among the champions of absolute monarchy by divine right, Filmer and Bossuet. Yet he has been more admired than persuasive; those best able to appreciate his merits, the intellectuals, have also been the best equipped to take from him what they needed without swallowing his arguments whole. To others he has seemed perverse or cynical, and even when they have liked his conclusions, they have wanted to reach them by other roads than he took. He ascribed to the sovereign as much authority as any believer in absolute monarchy by divine right claimed for the king, but he allowed that men had by common agreement set up government for their own benefit. He allowed that the people, when they made this agreement, might place sovereignty where they pleased, and merely expressed, on grounds of convenience, a preference for monarchy over other forms of government. He did not believe in indefeasible right, for he argued that the possessor of sovereignty loses it altogether as soon as he can no longer enforce obedience. Though he argued for absolute authority, and elucidated the idea of it as no one before him had done, he used arguments which offended the prejudices of those who most craved for that authority; his doctrine, to the extent that they took notice of it, was distasteful and disturbing to them. Neither Bodin nor Hobbes, the two ablest apologists of absolute authority, produced a doctrine satisfying to the many who feared civil war and anarchy above all things and looked for a sure refuge against them. The doctrine which came closest to satisfying them, though it owed much, first to Bodin and later to Hobbes, was different. It was simpler and looser, resting on familiar and widely received assumptions and calling for no great intellectual effort from those to whom it was addressed. It also relied heavily on Holy Scripture, on texts and examples which were familiar and venerable; it rested, much more obviously than the theories of Bodin and Hobbes, on a religious foundation. If it was a simple, it was not a bare or bleak doctrine; it was profusely illustrated from the Bible, it made ample use of ideas and stories which Christians had not yet learnt to question or to treat as allegory or parable.

Yet it needed years of civil war and anarchy to bring this doctrine to birth. For, though it made use of the familiar and the venerable, it also denied what had been asserted or implied by the great majority of political writers in the Middle Ages: that the authority of temporal rulers, though divinely instituted, also comes to them from the people and is always limited. At first, even the most fervent champions of royal power and legitimacy in France, though they insist that the king's authority is ' absolute ', take care to explain that it is also limited. When they call it absolute, they mean that there is no authority on earth superior to it, that the king is answerable to no court when he breaks the law, that it is always wrong to take up arms against him; but they do not claim for him what Bodin understood by sovereignty, they do not claim for him that no one can make or declare law in France except the king or whoever has authority from him to do so, and they do not forbid all resistance to his will other than passive disobedience when he commands what is contrary to the command of God. So much reluctance, so much beating about the bush of sovereignty, bears strong witness to the hold over men's minds of the old mediaeval idea that human authority is limited by the purpose it serves. The royalists in

France were driven to more extreme opinions only by the extremity of their country's need.

The doctrine of absolute monarchy by divine right appeared earlier in France than in England because domestic war came first to France; and the doctrine was more widely accepted for a longer time, partly no doubt because the wars of religion brought France much nearer to anarchy than the civil war brought England, but above all because the royalists in England were defeated. The defeat and eventual execution of the English king, far from producing anarchy, gave England the strongest government she had ever had, whereas in France, though royal authority was repeatedly challenged and brought to nothing in several provinces, the rebels were never able to set up an effective government in any part of the country. Besides, the parties to the war, the Catholic League and the Huguenots, were not fighting, as both Royalists and Parliamentarians were in England, for some idea of how their country should be governed. They challenged or supported the royal power according to circumstances; they defended it when they thought they could use it for their own purposes, and challenged it when they feared that their enemies might use it. Though they were engaged in a struggle which was not merely religious, though they were fighting for power and influence and not only to preserve or extend the faith, they were not engaged, as the parties to the English civil war were, in a constitutional struggle. The civil war in England was won by one of the parties to it, the party that wanted still further to limit the royal power, whereas the religious wars in France were won by neither party to them. They merely served to strengthen the royal power, which both parties had sought in vain to control or to emasculate. Hence the earlier and wider and more enduring popularity in France of the doctrine of absolute monarchy by divine right.

Indeed, the doctrine was respectable in England for only a short time. Even the Royalists were not attracted to it during the civil war, for they were not fighting for absolute monarchy. They were fighting, as also were the Parliamentarians, for constitutional monarchy, though they had a different conception of what it should be. If England ceased for a time to be a monarchy, it was certainly not because Parliament had challenged the royal power in order to destroy it; it was because the victors found they could not come to a satisfactory settlement with Charles I, and there was no one to put in his place. Filmer's *Patriarcha*, the most famous English version of the doctrine of absolute monarchy by divine right, though inspired by the quarrel which led to civil war, and perhaps written before the war started, was not published until 1680, twenty-seven years after its author's death. So the doctrine, in English history, belongs to the period of the restored monarchy, and of a renewed and bitter struggle between Charles II and Parliament; it owed its brief popularity, not to actual civil war, but to a fear that the country might again be plunged into civil war. It seemed to many people that the country could avoid a repetition of the troubles it had lived through only if the King's authority were recognized to be absolute. Much the same causes made the doctrine popular in England as in France, but in France they were more urgent and more lasting.

It has been suggested that the theory of absolute monarchy by divine right, though it was not less widely popular in Catholic than in Protestant countries, found fuller or less qualified expression in Protestant countries.[1] For in Catholic countries it was impossible to deny that the Church was independent of the royal power. The King of France could not aspire to be what the King of England was, supreme head of the Church as well as of the State; nor could it even be claimed on behalf of Catholic princes that, although they had no authority to decide what men should believe in matters of religion, it was for them to see to it that the Church was properly organized, to appoint to benefices inside it, and to maintain ecclesiastical discipline. It was impossible for a Catholic to claim for his king the authority within the Church attributed by Luther to princes, not to speak of the supremacy accorded to the English King. As early as Henry VIII's reign, it had been argued (for example, by Christopher St Germain[2]), that, though the Church alone can expound the Scriptures, can declare the truth concerning faith, the Church in England must be taken to be the professing Christians of England, whose head and representative is the king. This was to unite spiritual and temporal authority in one person just as clearly as Hobbes united it, and it was something that no Catholic prince could allow anyone to do on his behalf.

Yet the Catholic apologists of absolute monarchy by divine right, in their zeal against the champions of limited monarchy and the right of resistance, by no means forgot the old quarrel of the Temporal with the Spiritual Power. Both Belloy and Barclay, two of the earlier exponents of the doctrine,[3] denied that the Pope, by excommunicating a prince, could release his subjects from allegiance to him. No act of the Pope, said Belloy, could touch Henry of Navarre's right to the French throne, for he was heir to it by virtue of a rule established by God. The Pope, said Barclay, has the right to excommunicate anyone, even a king; but his action can have no political effects. The end of temporal authority is men's security and felicity in this world, whereas the end of spiritual authority is to bring men to God in the next world. Therefore it can never be true that the Pope can help save the souls of the

[1] See J. N. Figgis, *The Divine Right of Kings*, ch. VI.
[2] See J. W. Allen, *Political Theory in the Sixteenth Century*, Part Two, ch. IV.
[3] Belloy in *Apologie Catholique* (1585) and Barclay in *De Potestate Papae* (1609).

king's subjects by destroying the king's authority over them, and so he cannot have the right to destroy it; he cannot depose a king by putting an end to his subjects' allegiance. Barclay assumes that men's spiritual and temporal needs can be precisely distinguished and quite separately provided for, so that the Pope, whose duty is to care for the first, must never interfere with the king, whose duty is to care for the second; he implies that it can never be necessary, for the good of men's souls, to interfere with the exercise of temporal authority. This assumption and this implication are both doubtful, if not false; but a Catholic had to make them if he was to hold fast to the doctrine of absolute monarchy by divine right. Barclay could not assert that all authority of man over man, no matter what its kind, belongs only to the king, and so he was moved to argue that the temporal sphere is completely separate, so that no exercise of temporal authority can prevent the Church carrying out its mission.

In France, as in England, the kings were faced with two kinds of opposition on religious grounds. In England there were the Catholics, on the one hand, and the Protestant sects on the other. There were many in England who, even though they did not believe in absolute monarchy, sympathized strongly with the king while he resisted the ambitions and demands of both Catholics and sectaries. So, too, in France, there were many who sympathized with the king in his resistance both to the Catholic League and to the Huguenots, and who deplored his falling under the sway of either. To many in both England and France it seemed that the royal power was a moderating influence, that what the king stood for, in Church and State, was more truly popular and more for the common good than what he resisted. To them, not only in theory but in practice, the king came closer than anyone to being the 'representative' of his people. This feeling was to be found among both the laity and the clergy, in France as well as in England. Just as in England the Established Church was ardently loyal to the king, so too in France were the Gallicans. Though the French Church never broke with Rome, there were bishops and lesser priests in it eager to assert its 'liberties' against the Pope; and, like the Established Church across the water, they looked to the king to support them against enemies on both their flanks, against both papal and Calvinist pretensions. The motives and quality of Gallican and Anglican devotion to the throne were not unlike. Bossuet, the most vigorous champion of Gallican liberties, was also the most eloquent of all exponents of the theory of the divine right of kings. Of course, most English royalists devoted to the Established Church did not believe in absolute monarchy by divine right, and this is true also of some French royalists who were strong Gallicans; but those who did believe in it were not markedly less moderate and tolerant in matters of religion than those who did not.

G

In the sixteenth and seventeenth centuries two questions which are now acknowledged to be very different from one another were not clearly distinguished: How does political authority arise? and, What makes it legitimate? The contract theorists argued that political authority was, or must be supposed to have been, set up by agreement between those who became subject to it, and is therefore limited by the purpose which the agreement was intended to achieve. The idea of contract was used to explain the origin of government mostly by persons who wanted to justify resistance to government. But Hobbes used it for the opposite purpose; he sought to show that only an agreement to give unconditional obedience to some person or body of persons could provide the parties to the agreement with the security they wanted. Bodin appealed to tradition, to long establishment, more in the spirit of Burke than of mediaeval political thinkers: time makes authority legitimate, not so much because it is evidence of popular consent as because it is evidence that power is exercised for the public good. In France sovereignty belongs properly to the king: it has long been so and therefore ought to be so. But Bodin's account of the French system, as indeed any similar account of any other system, could always be challenged; it is always possible to appeal to tradition, to history, against the use of it made by defenders of any particular interpretation of it. The champions of absolute monarchy by divine right felt the need to rest their claims on what seemed to them more solid foundations. Hence their argument that monarchy is the most *natural* form of government because it arises out of paternal authority, or because it is a copy on earth of God's kingdom in heaven or of His sole dominion over all things. Hence too their close scrutiny of the history of the Jews, God's chosen people, as recorded in the Old Testament. For where is God's will more clearly manifest than in the history of that people on whose behalf He has intervened directly in human affairs?

The champions of absolute monarchy by divine right, like other political writers engaged in continual controversy, were as much concerned to show up the absurdities of rival doctrines as to state their own persuasively; and it has been suggested that they were more successful in the first aim than in the second.[1] Perhaps they were. At least, it is likely to seem so to us, for we now reject both their theory and the theories they criticized, and so we are apt to be more impressed by their reasons for disagreeing with their rivals than by what they had to say in support of their own doctrine. Yet I suspect that this verdict is inspired largely by seeing the doctrine in its English context. And in England it was popular only for a short time, and during that time

[1] This is the impression created on the reader by Mr Laslett in his Introduction to Filmer's *Patriarcha and Other Political Works* (Blackwell, 1949) and by Dr Figgis in his *Divine Right of Kings*.

was vigorously contested. The best English version of it, Filmer's *Patriarcha*, was written long before the doctrine became popular; it was writen by someone as much concerned to attack rival (and more popular) doctrines as to put forward his own. Of Filmer, more truly than of any other exponent of the doctrine, we can say that he is more impressive when he attacks others than when he defends himself. The earlier exponents of the doctrine – for example, Pierre de Belloy and William Barclay in France – were mere controversialists. If they are important at all they are so only as early champions of a doctrine more ably stated after their time. Their works are no longer read, except by scholars interested in French political controversies arising out of the wars of religion. Whereas Filmer is still read and is worth reading; for though he, too, was a controversialist, he was so on a higher level. He was not content to make assertions and to support them with texts; he tried to construct an argument, and got into difficulties in the attempt. Dr Figgis has suggested that Filmer's virtues were the undoing of the doctrine he defended; he drew men's attention to what is the essence of it, and so made it easier for them to detect its flaws. By his method he invited them, not to a war of quotations from Holy Scripture (though he used them freely), but to rational argument; and rational argument (so Dr Figgis implies) was just what the doctrine could not withstand. All unconsciously, Filmer prepared the doctrine of absolute monarchy by divine right to be a fitting sacrifice to Reason (or perhaps I should say, to Common Sense) under the knife of John Locke.

It is a pretty picture and is not altogether untrue; for it was certainly Locke's attack on the doctrine which ruined it in educated circles, first in England and later in France (where no other English political philosopher has enjoyed anything like Locke's reputation), and it was Filmer's version of it that Locke attacked. But we ought not to take the measure of a doctrine in the version of it which has remained famous precisely because it was attacked by a man greater than its author. Not that Filmer is worth reading only because Locke attacked him; he would still be worth reading even if Locke had never attacked him. Yet the fact remains that he lives on in our memories because he was Locke's victim. Indeed, there are many who have read Locke's attack without reading what he attacked. Those who have argued that Filmer is intellectually much more respectable than Locke's treatment of him might lead one to expect have not been concerned to defend his doctrine; they have been closer to accepting Locke's political philosophy than Filmer's, and so have been more impressed by Filmer's criticisms of others than by his positive beliefs.

No political theory is more completely dead than the doctrine of absolute monarchy by divine right. But it was once very much alive; and, if we want to see what it meant to those who accepted it, we had better look at it, not only in Filmer's version, but in Bossuet's as well. For in France the doctrine was triumphant as it never was in England. It was, in the France of the seventeenth century, as widely accepted, as near to being orthodox, as the political philosophy of Locke in eighteenth-century England. Bossuet expounds it with an assurance, a serenity, and a moderation which lend dignity to it; he expounds it even more than he argues for it. He, too, no doubt, is a controversialist, but he is more than just inwardly convinced that he possesses the truth; he also speaks like a man sure of his audience. Bossuet's *Politique Tirée des Propres Paroles de l'Ecriture Sainte*, though it preaches a doctrine in many ways similar to Filmer's *Patriarcha*, is altogether different in tone and effect. Not that Bossuet is preaching to the converted, for his purpose is to instruct and persuade; it is rather that he is preaching what he believes must persuade if his listeners have not closed their minds to reason. What makes Bossuet impressive is that his confidence in the truth of what he teaches is free of arrogance; it is the confidence of the man who both has faith and has never doubted that faith and reason can be perfectly reconciled. His version of the doctrine is not more impressive than Filmer's merely because, being more moderate, it is not open to some of the attacks that Locke made on Filmer. Nor is it more impressive merely for being the work of one of the greatest of French writers. It is more impressive because it brings home to us, whose beliefs about political authority differ so greatly from his, what the doctrine of divine right meant to those who accepted it whole-heartedly. Bossuet speaks, as no one else does, for a now defunct but once important political order; he speaks for it with the authority that Aquinas spoke with for the social and political order of the thirteenth century.

The earlier and cruder versions of the doctrine were produced in the late sixteenth century, the later and more sophisticated versions, by Filmer and by Bossuet, in the middle of the seventeenth. The influence of Bodin and of Hobbes is apparent in all their writings. For Filmer, though he wrote his best-known work, *Patriarcha*, before Hobbes had published any of his reflections on government, came afterwards to read both *De Cive* and *Leviathan*, finding them much to his taste. The first sentences of Filmer's preface to his *Observations Concerning the Originall of Government* make it clear what he accepted and rejected in Hobbes:

With no small content I read Hobbes' book *De Cive*, and his *Leviathan*, about the rights of sovereignty, which no man, that I know, hath so amply and judiciously handled: I consent with him about the rights of exercising government, but I cannot agree to his means of acquiring it. It may seem strange that I should praise his building and yet mislike his foundation; but so it is, his *Jus Naturae*, and his

Regnum Institutivum, will not down with me: they appear full of contradiction and impossibilities; a few short notes about them, I here offer, wishing he would consider whether his building would not stand firmer upon the principles of *Regnum Patrimoniale* (as he calls it) both according to scripture and reason.[1]

To put the building constructed by Bodin and perfected by Hobbes on a firmer foundation: this is the purpose common to Filmer and to Bossuet. ' According to scripture and reason ', says Filmer, believing that the two are perfectly in keeping with each other. ' I cannot but reverence that form of government which was allowed and made use of for God's own people, and for all other nations. It were impiety to think that God, who was careful to appoint judicial laws for His chosen people, would not furnish them with the best form of government: or to imagine that the rules given in divers places in the gospel by our blessed Saviour and His Apostles for obedience to Kings should now, like almanacs out of date, be of no use to us.'[2] The assumption of Filmer and Bossuet is that the political teaching of Holy Scripture is clear and unequivocal. As we look back on the political controversies of the sixteenth and seventeenth centuries, when the Scriptures were quoted to such diverse and even bizarre effect, this may seem to us an assumption reckless to the point of absurdity. But is it more absurd than Burke's faith in tradition, in what he called ' the general bank and capital of nations and of ages '? It is only another example of the perennial need felt for a store of wisdom, a body of doctrine on which all men may rely as a sure guide for action. If even the most important matters are never to be regarded as settled, if everything is always to be open to question, how are men ever to have security and peace of mind? But, unfortunately, the store of wisdom does not consist of hard coins which keep their shape as they pass from hand to hand; it consists of ideas and doctrines whose meanings change with the minds that entertain them.

III. FILMER

Before we consider the doctrine which Filmer offers his readers for true, let us look at what he has to say against the opinions which he is most concerned to demolish: that, men being free by nature and at liberty to choose what government they please, the right to govern was granted to those who first had it by those who thereby became subject to it; and that the authority of kings is limited by the terms of that

---

[1] Filmer. *Patriarcha and Other Political Works.* Ed. Laslett, p. 239.
[2] From the preface to *The Anarchy of a Limited or Mixed Monarchy*, Filmer, op. cit., p. 278.

grant. Against these opinions he advances two kinds of arguments, historical and abstract. For example, in the second chapter of *Patriarcha* he accuses Bellarmine of contradicting his own assertion, that men are by nature equal, when he admits that the patriarchs of the Old Testament were 'endowed with kingly power'. In the Bible we can read how the first man was created, how he acquired a wife and children, and what happened to his posterity; and the account we find there is proof conclusive that in the beginning men were not equal. It was, so Filmer thought, above all the Jesuits and 'some zealous favourers of the Geneva discipline' who were putting about this doctrine of the natural freedom and equality of men. But the Jesuits and followers of Calvin were presumably as certain as was Filmer that the Bible is authentic history. He was producing against the doctrine of natural equality facts which those who asserted it were bound to accept as true. Again, in *The Freeholder's Grand Inquest Touching our Soveraigne Lord the King and His Parliament*,[1] Filmer appeals to history to show that the legislative power in England belongs only to the king and is not shared by him with the two Houses of Parliament, though by custom he consults with them when he exercises that power. This is a different kind of appeal to history, for Filmer cites many precedents and quotes amply from documents; but still it is an appeal to history. Filmer here makes the same claims for the King of England as Bodin made for the King of France. If we neglect this part of his argument, it is not because it is in itself bad, for Filmer's use (or abuse) of history is not unusually one-sided or superficial by the standards of his day; it is because it raises no issues of much concern to the political theorist.

To those who say that men are by nature free Filmer objects that they are in fact born dependent. In his *Observations on Mr Hobbes' Leviathan* he says: 'I cannot understand how this right of nature can be conceived without imagining a company of men at the very first to have been all created together without any dependency one of another, or as mushrooms (*fungorum more*) they all on a sudden were sprung out of the earth without any obligation one to another.'[2] But men are born of women and into families, whose members have obligations towards one another; and children owe obedience to their parents. Nor can it be said that children become free by nature when they cease to be under age, for 'in nature there is no *nonage*; if a man be not born free, she doth not assign him any other time when he shall attain his freedom '.[3]

It would be unjust to Filmer to say that this argument misses the essential point because those who hold that man is by nature free are

---

[1] Laslett's edition of Filmer's *Political Works*, pp. 133-84.
[2] Ibid., p. 241.
[3] From *The Anarchy of a Limited or Mixed Monarchy*, in Laslett's edition of Filmer's *Political Works*, p. 287.

not to be taken literally, the essence of their doctrine being, not that men were once free and then voluntarily placed themselves under obligations, but rather that men are born to freedom, in the sense that, given their nature, given that they are rational and can make choices, the obligations which they recognize, when they attain the age of reason, are related to the ends they pursue, to what they desire or find desirable. Only creatures capable of freedom can have obligations. We must remember that, in Filmer's time, those who spoke of man's being naturally free meant to convey more than what we may choose to call the 'essence' of their doctrine because it seems to us the most valuable part of it. No doubt, the more prudent of them did not mean to be taken quite literally. As Filmer himself recognized, Hobbes did not believe that, as a matter of fact, men had once lived in a state of nature. But he did mean to convey that all authority of man over man rests on consent. He meant, as did all the others who spoke of man's being naturally free, to convey something that is not true, and which Filmer could see was not true. Admittedly, there is something valuable in the doctrine that he attacked which Filmer failed to see. There is a point which he missed. But, we may ask, how clearly did the upholders of the doctrine themselves see the point? They certainly failed to state it, for it is only implicit in what they said. The doctrine that man is naturally free, as it was expounded in the seventeenth century, has some implications which are acceptable and others which are not. At least it can be said for Filmer that he saw the defects of the doctrine more clearly than its exponents saw what was valuable in it.

The idea that men's primary obligations, the obligations on which the social and political order rests, derive from consent seemed absurd to Filmer. He was not hard put to it to demolish the arguments of those who, like Hobbes, contended that even the right of the conqueror is established by covenant because the conquered must be supposed to agree to obey him on condition that he allows them life and liberty. If the conqueror, when he makes his conquest, is in what Hobbes calls a state of nature, he has (as Hobbes admits) the right to subject others to his will provided he has the power, and so has no need of their consent; and if he is not in the state of nature, he is subject to some sovereign, and so has no right to conquer others and force them into subjection. To another assertion of Hobbes, that even paternal authority rests on 'the child's consent, either express or by other sufficient arguments declared', Filmer merely objects that it is not to be understood how a child can express consent or 'by other sufficient arguments declare it' before it has reached the age of discretion.[1] Those who held that political authority rests on the consent of the governed did not deny that many governments were in fact established by

[1] From *Observations Concerning the Originale of Government*, Laslett, p. 240 and p. 245.

conquest or arose gradually out of paternal rule; they were concerned rather to assert that, no matter how they were established or arose, their authority rests on the consent of the persons subject to them. But it seemed to them that they could not reach this conclusion unless they could show that even conquerors and parents rule by consent. They laid themselves open to such criticisms as Filmer's partly because they failed to distinguish questions of origin from questions of right and partly because they persisted in speaking of consent as if it implied some kind of contract.

According to the contract theorists, it is the *people* who have the right to provide for their own security, and therefore the right to set up government to give them security. But who, asks Filmer, are to be reckoned as the people? Who, in the absence of all government, of all authority of man over man, are the people? Are they the whole of mankind? If they are not, how did this come about? If there are several or many peoples in the world, each with the right to set up a separate government, how did they acquire this right? Did all mankind divest themselves of a right which belonged to them collectively in favour of separate multitudes?[1] Do the writers who claim this right for the people understand the nature of their claim? Do they know on whose behalf they are making it? 'Literally, and in the largest sense, the word signifies the whole of mankind; but figuratively . . . , it notes many times the major part of a multitude, or sometimes the better, or the richer, or the wiser, or some other part; and oftentimes a very small part of the people, if there be no other apparent party, hath the name of the people by presumption.' When we use the word *people* in the senses which Filmer calls figurative, we are not speaking of men in the state of nature, for 'by nature all mankind in the world makes but one people, who they [i.e. those against whom Filmer is arguing] suppose to be born alike to an equal freedom from subjection; and where such freedom is, there all things must of necessity be common: and therefore without a joint consent of the whole people of the world, no one thing can be made proper to any one man, but it will be an injury, and a usurpation upon the common right of all others. From whence it follows that natural freedom being once granted, there cannot be any one man chosen a king without the universal consent of all the people of the world at one instant, *nemine contradicente.*'[2]

Filmer's point is simple enough. What makes one part of mankind distinct from the others, what makes them collectively one people, is that they are under one government. Community is not prior to authority. Just as a family consists of all who are subject to the same

[1] See *Patriarcha*, Ch. XIII; Laslett, pp. 81-2.
[2] This passage and the one before are from *The Anarchy of a Limited or Mixed Monarchy*, Laslett, p. 285.

father, so a people consists of all who are subject to the same government. They are a distinct community because there is an authority to which they are all in fact subject. If we assume the contrary, if we assume that they are a community who by agreement establish an authority over themselves, we have to explain how they came to be a community. And this, says Filmer, we cannot do. For, if by nature all men are equal and free, and all things belong to them in common, no section of mankind can set up a government in any part of the world without injury to the rest of mankind, without curtailing their natural freedom. If all things are by nature common to all men, and all men are by nature free, how can any number of men, short of the whole number, lay it down that there shall be among them (in the part of the world where they happen to be) either government or private property? For by their action they claim to exclude all other men from that part of the world which they have appropriated, which is a clear invasion of natural freedom. Must we then suppose that mankind unanimously divided themselves into separate multitudes, giving to each a right to set up a government? The supposition is not only fantastic, it is also inadequate. 'Mankind is like the sea, ever ebbing or flowing, every minute one is born another dies; those that are the people this minute, are not the people the next minute, in every instant and point of time there is a variation.'[1] And we cannot say the acts of parents bind their children, for 'then farewell the doctrine of natural freedom'.[2] Nor yet can we say that the decision of the majority binds the rest, 'for the major part never binds, but where men at first either agree to be so bound, or where a higher power so commands',[3] and in the case supposed, in the state of nature, no higher power does so command. 'No one man, nor a multitude, can give away the natural right of another. The law of nature is unchangeable, and howsoever one man may hinder another in the use or exercise of his natural right, yet thereby no man loseth the right itself . . . Therefore, unless it can be proved by some law of nature that the major, or some other part, have power to overrule the rest of the multitude, it must follow that the acts of multitudes not entire are not binding to all, but only to such as consent unto them.'[4]

Just as those who seek to derive the obligation to obey rulers from the consent of their subjects are inclined to use the word *consent* broadly and loosely, so those who contest their doctrine are inclined to use it strictly. Filmer attacks the notion of tacit consent which Locke was to use so freely.

---

[1] Ibid., p. 287.
[2] Ibid., p. 287.
[3] Ibid., p. 286.
[4] From *Patriarcha*, Ch. XIII, Laslett, p. 82.

If the silent acceptation of a governor by part of the people be an argument of their concurring in the election of him, by the same reason the tacit assent of the whole commonwealth may be maintained. From whence it follows that every Prince that comes to a crown, whether by succession, conquest or usurpation, may be said to be elected by the people. Which inference is too ridiculous, for in such cases the people are so far from the liberty of *specification* that they want even that of *contradiction*.[1]

That is to say, in such cases, the people, far from being able to choose who shall rule over them, cannot even refuse to accept the ruler who puts himself upon them.

No government, says Filmer, ever was set up by the people subject to it. To this it may be objected that in some countries kings come to the throne by election and not by hereditary right. But even in these countries they are elected by only a small part of the people; by nobles or by 'great men' or by princes of the blood. Wherever we look, we never see rulers chosen by even the major part of their subjects, let alone by all of them. And the bodies which claim to represent the entire people are very far indeed from doing so. In England the Commons are no doubt reputed to represent the people, but in fact represent only 'a part of the lower or inferior part of the body of the people, which are the freeholders, worth 40s. by the year, and the Commons or freemen of cities and boroughs, or the major part of them. All of which are not one-quarter, nay, not a tenth part of the Commons of the Kingdom.' This is a kind of turning of the tables on those who wished to limit the authority of kings by an appeal to popular rights. Why should a body representing only a tenth part of the people think themselves entitled to challenge the king in the name of the whole people? This is a question which Locke, when he comes to 'demolish' Filmer, never troubles to answer. It is a question not taken seriously, except by the Levellers, until the second half of the eighteenth century.[2] It is interesting to see a champion of divine right using arguments later used by radicals.

Filmer wins many neat victories over the men who affect to make the people's cause their own. It is not he but Grotius who says that by nature men are free, and yet it is Grotius and not he who speaks of a right to rule established by conquest. True, Grotius speaks of a just war; but how can a man who wages a just war acquire by victory a right to rule the vanquished, if he did not have that right before the war began? For a war of conquest to be just, it must be waged in order

---

[1] Ibid., p. 82.
[2] And even the Levellers did not want manhood suffrage. They did not want *servants* to have the vote, and half the adult males in England were then *servants* as the word was understood in those days.

to enforce a title which is good independently of the outcome of the war.

> For if a King come in by conquest, he must either conquer them that have a governor, or those people that have none; if they have no governor, then they are a free people, and so the war will be unjust to conquer those that are free, especially if the freedom of the people be by the primary law of nature as Grotius teacheth: but if the people conquered have a governor, that governor hath either a title or not; if he hath a title, it is an unjust war that takes the kingdom from him: if he hath no title, but only the possession of a kingdom, yet it is unjust for any other man that wants a title also, to conquer him that is but in possession, for it is a just rule, that where the cases are alike, he that is in possession is in the better condition.[1]

Filmer, when he argues that political authority does not rest on consent, is often forceful and ingenious; he is much less so when he denies that the authority of kings is limited. I have in mind not his arguments from history to show that the authority of the King of England is unlimited, for they need not concern the political theorist; I have in mind only the general arguments which apply to royal authority everywhere. The best of them are to be found in *The Anarchy of a Limited or Mixed Monarchy*, which appeared in 1648, and is for the most part a criticism of Philip Hunton's *Treatise of Monarchy* (1643); and they amount to little more than was better said by Hobbes.

Filmer asks who is to judge between the king and any of his subjects in a limited monarchy.

> For instance, the King commands me, or gives judgement against me: I reply, his commands are illegal, and his judgement not according to law; who must judge? If the monarch himself judge, then you destroy the frame of the state, and make it absolute, saith our author [i.e. Hunton]; and he gives his reason: for to define a monarch to a law, and then to make him judge of his own deviations from that law, is to absolve him from all law. On the other side, if any, or all the people may judge, then you put the sovereignty in the whole body, or part of it, and destroy the being of a monarchy. Thus our author has caught himself in a plain dilemma: if the King be judge, then he is no limited monarch; if the people be judge, then he is no monarch at all. So farewell limited monarchy, nay farewell all government, if there be no judge.[2]

[1] From *Observations Upon H. Grotius*, Laslett, p. 270.
[2] From *The Anarchy of a Limited or Mixed Monarchy*, Laslett, p. 295.

That is to say, if there is to be effective government, there must be a final judge of what the law is, and the final judge is the only true maker of the law, the sovereign whose precept, in the words of Hobbes, 'contains in it the reason of obedience'. Government affords security only because it provides those subject to it with a common judge. If, then, subjects challenge the decisions of the common judge, they destroy or threaten this security. For then 'every man must oppose or not oppose the monarch according to his own conscience. Thus at the last, every man is brought, by this doctrine of our authors, to be his own judge. And I also appeal to the consciences of all mankind, whether the end of this be not utter confusion and anarchy.'[1] The argument against limited monarchy is more forcefully put in this later treatise than in the twentieth chapter of *Patriarcha*, no doubt because Filmer in the meantime had read Hobbes.

Of Filmer's views about what makes government legitimate we need not take long notice. They are simple, and they are less ingenious and persuasive than his criticisms of the doctrines he disliked. God gave Adam complete authority over his children and therefore over his children's children, which authority, when Adam died, passed to his successor by a fixed rule of succession. As Filmer puts it, 'civil power, not only in general is by Divine institution, but even the assigning of it specifically to the eldest parent'.[2] It would seem to follow, on the assumption that all men are the posterity of Adam, that there is always only one man in the world having absolute authority over all other men, one king of men, one heir of Adam. Filmer does not deny this, but he has to explain how it comes about that there are many independent kingdoms in the world. He tells us that Noah, after the flood, divided the world up among his three sons, and that after the confusion of Babel some seventy-two separate nations were established, each a distinct family with one man in it having paternal and absolute authority over the whole family. We may ask by what authority Noah deprived his eldest son of the monarchy of the world to which he was entitled by a rule established by God? Presumably, in the confusion of Babel, the thread of legitimacy was lost. Men no longer knew who was the sole heir of Adam, or (if we suppose that Noah had authority from God to divide the world into three kingdoms) who were the three heirs of Noah's sons. There were presumably seventy-two men each with a clearer title than any other man to paternal authority over a part of mankind, and the seventy-two parts made up the whole of mankind. There was no longer one undoubted king of men, but there were seventy-two kings, to one or other of whom all that were not kings owed obedience, and there was no doubt who owed obedience to whom. And all this by the providence of God!

[1] *Ibid.*, p. 297.
[2] From *Patriarcha*, Laslett, p. 57.

Filmer does not claim anything so absurd as that the hereditary kings of his day are the heirs of the seventy-two who emerged from the confusion of Babel. Nor does he even claim for every king of his day that he is the father of his people, in the sense of being the heir by primogeniture of the parental authority of their common ancestor. 'It is true, all kings be not the natural parents of their subjects, yet they all either are, *or are reputed*, as the next heirs of those progenitors who were at first the natural parents of the whole people, and in their right succeed to the exercise of the supreme jurisdiction.'[1] Does this mean that, in Filmer's opinion, every separate people have a common ancestor, even though they have lost all memory of him and their actual king is not his heir by the rule of succession established by God? How far is this taking kings for other than they are to go? Are a people under one king to be reputed to have a common ancestor, even when they have not? Or is the king to be reputed the heir of a common ancestor only where there really was such an ancestor? Filmer does not explain.

Where it is not known who is the legitimate heir, then the independent heads of families 'have power to consent in the uniting or conferring of their fatherly right of sovereign authority on whom they please. And he that is so elected claims not his power as a donative from the people, but as being substituted properly by God, from whom he receives his royal charter of an universal Father, though testified by the ministry of the heads of the people.'[2] At this point Filmer has not chosen his words carefully. If the heads of families *are conferring their own fatherly right* on whom they please, they are performing an act of the same kind as the covenant whereby, according to Hobbes or Locke, men in the state of nature put themselves under an obligation to obey a common superior; they are renouncing a right which is theirs in favour of somebody else. In this case, of course, the right is different; it is paternal authority and not what either Hobbes or Locke would regard as a natural right whose renunciation could create political authority. But though the right is different, the transaction, if it is a conferring of their own fatherly authority, is similar; it is a setting up of authority by covenant. Filmer would have done better to have said that, there being no claimant known to be legitimate to an authority to which the whole people are undoubtedly subject, it devolves on the heads of families to find a substitute for the legitimate heir. In other words, where it is not known who is the king by the rule of succession established by God, it becomes the duty of those whose authority in its own sphere is undoubted (i.e. the heads of families) to choose a king. But, in that case, it must be certain that the people

---

[1] From *Patriarcha*, Laslett, pp. 60-4, our italics.
[2] Ibid., p. 62.

really are one people, that they have a common ancestor, that there is someone whose title to rule would be undoubted if the line of descent from that ancestor were certainly known. For otherwise the heads of families would not be providing a substitute for the true though undiscoverable king; they would be creating a king by transferring or renouncing their own rights. They would be setting up authority by covenant, in the manner described by the men whose doctrine *Patriarcha* was intended to refute.

What if the actual ruler is a usurper? What if he is neither the legitimate heir, nor a substitute for him provided in the manner which Filmer describes? This is a question not answered in *Patriarcha*, and in *The Anarchy of a Limited or Mixed Monarchy* Filmer says only this: 'many times by the act either of a usurper himself, or of those that set him up, the true heir of a crown is dispossessed, God using the ministry of the wickedest men for the removing and setting up of Kings: in such cases the subjects' obedience to the fatherly power must go along and wait upon God's providence, who only hath a right to give and take away kingdoms.'[1] This means, presumably, that where an usurper makes his power effective, those whom he compels to obedience ought to obey him because his success is evidence that God is using him for some purpose of His own. But what if the dispossessors of a legitimate king change the form of government? What if they abolish monarchy? The authority they set up in the place of what they have brought down is not paternal. They are not usurpers of royal authority (which in Filmer's opinion is merely paternal authority exercised over a large number of people), but creators of another kind of authority, which, so Filmer tells us, is not divinely instituted. Yet their action is as much allowed by God as a successful usurpation of kingly power. To this Filmer has nothing to say, for he says only that 'if those who live under a monarchy can justify the form they live under to be God's ordinance, they are not bound to forbear their own justification, because others cannot do the like for the form they live under; let others look to the defence of their own government'.[2] It would appear then that monarchy is like the Jews; it is the chosen of God, though every now and again God allows what He has not chosen to prevail over it.

Large claims have been made on Filmer's behalf. J. W. Allen thought him more profound and more original than Locke. Dr Figgis praised him and those who shared his views for conceiving of society as *organic* and not *artificial*, which was how Locke and others thought of it. But these commendations are misplaced. Filmer's views about the origins of society are no more and no less adequate than Locke's; and the important difference between them is, in any case, not about the

[1] Ibid., p. 289.
[2] Ibid., p. 284.

origins of society, but about the ground of political obligation. Locke
had not neglected to read Aristotle's *Politics*; and he probably did not
disagree with Aristotle that villages arose out of families and states
out of villages. He was not concerned to argue that political authority
did not, as a matter of history, often arise out of paternal authority; he
was concerned only to argue that it is different in kind and rests, as
paternal authority does not, on the *consent* of the persons subject to it.
No doubt, he did not properly explain the nature of this *consent*; nor
did he succeed in making it clear just what rights he was conceding
to subjects and what obligations he was laying upon them. But that is
another matter. If he did not see that the problem of political obligation cannot be settled by an enquiry into the origins of government, he
was no blinder in this respect than Filmer. Whenever Locke's immediate object was to show that the authority of rulers rested on the
consent of the ruled, he was inclined to speak as if men had, some time
in the past, deliberately set up government; but when he reflected on
the probable origins of government, as he did in the sixth chapter of
the *Second Treatise*, he was willing to admit that it may often have
happened that 'the natural fathers of families, by an insensible change,
became the politic monarchs of them too'.

Filmer comes no closer than Locke to seeing that the obligations on
which the social order rests are themselves the product of men's living
together in society. To have a deeper sense than Locke had of what is
involved in man's being a social creature it is not enough to deny,
with Filmer, that the primary obligations arise from consent. Locke
himself admits (and indeed insists) that men have obligations which
do not arise from consent; for he says that in the state of nature there
is a law of nature which men are obliged to obey. If there were not
obligations which do not arise from consent, consent could create no
obligations. This is as much admitted by Locke as by Filmer. What
Locke does not admit, or rather does not notice, is that man is made
moral by education, in the widest sense of that word; that he comes
to conceive of himself as a bearer of rights and obligations by being
involved in social relations with other creatures of his own kind. There
is nothing in *Patriarcha* or in Filmer's other writings to suggest that
he takes serious account of what Locke does not notice.

Dr Figgis fails to make it clear just what he is claiming for Filmer
when he says that he conceives of society as *organic*. Where Figgis
speaks of the *organic* others speak of the *natural*. Locke explains the
political order, the State, as if men had created it for their own
convenience, whereas Filmer (so it is said on his behalf) speaks of it as
if it had *grown naturally* out of the family; and this is accounted a
merit in Filmer. I must confess that I fail to see that the advantage
would lie with Filmer, even if what is claimed for him were true. No
doubt, it is always misleading to speak of a system of government (or

of the social order generally) as if men had deliberately established it for certain ends. Even the boldest reformers change only a part of the existing social and political order, and are in any case themselves born into a social environment which they have not reformed and which profoundly affects their modes of thought and feeling. But then it is no less misleading to speak of the State as if it grew 'naturally' out of the family. Social evolution is no more like growth than it is like contrivance; like the deliberate adaptation of means to ends. A social and political order is partly the unintended and partly the intended product of human activities. It may be, except very rarely, much more the first than the second; but, whichever it is, the activities which bring it about are activities of rational creatures capable of deliberate choice. To speak of the change which results from such activities, even when it is unforeseen and unintended, as *natural* or *organic* is surely as misleading as to speak of it as if it were contrivance.

But it is doubtful whether the claim made for Filmer is true; it is doubtful whether he conceived of the process whereby kingdoms arise out of families as being *organic* or *natural* as those words are understood by those who ascribe to him, in this respect, a deeper insight than Locke's. Though Filmer was a shrewd critic of doctrines he disliked, he was not a deep thinker. Long before Hume (though less neatly) he demolished the theory that political authority derives from a social contract, but he put nothing satisfactory in the place of what he demolished.

IV. BOSSUET

Nor, as a political theorist, is Bossuet a deep thinker. But he has certain advantages over Filmer. He does not attempt to reduce all authority of man over man to one type; he does not argue that to be truly legitimate authority must be paternal. Filmer, like the contract theorists whom he belabours, rests all on a single principle; just as they insist that all legitimate human authority arises from consent so he insists that it is always paternal. And just as they are reduced to some odd shifts to show that there is consent where to the man with no theoretical axe to grind it would seem obvious that there is not, so he is reduced to others no less odd to show that authority is paternal though the possessor of it is not the natural heir of a common ancestor. Bossuet is reduced to no such shifts. Monarchy is, he thinks, the best form of government, and is the only form which God has established among men by open intervention in their affairs. Yet Bossuet does not hold that monarchy is the only legitimate form. All established rulers are legitimate (all have authority from God), provided they are not recent usurpers. Thus Bossuet does not agree with Hobbes that any ruler, from the moment he has made his power effective, has legitimate authority. It is long continuance which makes effective power legitimate, converting it into authority, no matter how it was first acquired: not because its survival is evidence of its being popular but because it is a mark that it comes from God. No doubt, its survival is some evidence of its being popular, and also of its being exercised for the common good, but what makes it legitimate is its coming from God.

It cannot be said for Bossuet that he is even as original as Filmer. He is altogether a borrower; but, given his purpose, he is a discriminating, an intelligent borrower. His largest debt is to Hobbes and his next largest to Bodin, but where Aristotle suits his purpose better, he borrows from him. Moreover, he fits his borrowings together into a more or less consistent whole; and is therefore less open to criticism than is Filmer. Or perhaps I should say that he is seriously vulnerable only when his assumptions are questioned, whereas Filmer, like Locke, is open to criticism even when they are not. Bossuet's apology for absolute monarchy is magnificent and compelling, as Filmer's is not, for two reasons: because it is eloquent, dignified, and well presented, and because it is simple and full of good sense. There is no need to expatiate on the first reason. The gifts which make Bossuet the greatest of French orators do not desert him when he turns from the pulpit to politics.

To us, until we have translated ourselves in imagination into another age, the doctrine of absolute monarchy by divine right seems extravagant. The repeated appeals to Holy Scripture strike us as irrelevant. We are no longer impressed by an immense display of Biblical and Patristic texts, and we see no divinity in kings. There is no political doctrine less congenial to us; and so when we come to read the works of a writer of small talents, a Filmer, we are impressed, not by the doctrine he teaches, but by his shrewd attacks on rival creeds. His exposition of his own beliefs is the price we pay for what we really value, his criticisms of others; we feel about him what someone who preferred his prefaces to his plays felt about Bernard Shaw. But with Bossuet the play's the thing. He can, while we read him, take us out of ourselves; he can show us what monarchy meant to Frenchmen in an age not less respectful of reason and not less discriminating than our own. Bossuet has as strong a preference as Descartes for clarity and order, which is a preference as much aesthetic as intellectual.

In the next century, which Frenchmen sometimes call 'the century of Voltaire', the Church of Bossuet was attacked by the intellectuals, and the monarchy lost prestige, and so Bossuet, the ablest champion of Church and monarchy in France, came to be regarded as an enemy by the philosophers. The very title of his *Politique Tirée des Propres Paroles de l'Écriture Sainte* came to seem ridiculous. Who, in an age which prided itself on its enlightenment, would go to the Bible to get his political theory? But, as Lanson has pointed out, Bossuet did not really get his political theory from that source; he merely made a show of doing so. He whole-heartedly accepted the established order in France, the monarchy called 'absolute', and he found in Hobbes (also well versed in the Scriptures), in Bodin, and in Aristotle all his strongest arguments for it. And in the Bible he found texts to support those arguments and stories to illustrate them. Lanson quotes a sentence from Bossuet which he says is the key to his book: 'Aristotle has said it, but the Holy Ghost has uttered it with greater force.'[1] Bossuet's texts and illustrations are always well chosen; they add colour and charm to his argument.

The *Politique Tirée de l'Écriture Sainte* was written by Bossuet for the dauphin; it is a work of instruction and not of controversy. It is admirably clear; it proceeds carefully, step by step, and each step is simple though the whole argument is elaborate. It is not in the *Politique*, but in the fifth of his *Avertissements aux Protestants sur les Lettres du Ministre Jurieu*, that Bossuet engages in controversy with those who hold that the authority of rulers rests on the consent of their subjects. Jurieu, a Protestant pastor, in the course of a general attack on Bossuet's *Histoire des Variations des Églises Protestantes*, had put forward this particular doctrine, and Bossuet devotes the fifth *Avertissement* to demolishing it. Bossuet is formidable in controversy, and this work is as good an example as any of his method and style; but it offers little that is new to the political theorist. It is as an exponent of political 'orthodoxy' rather than as a critic of political 'heresy' that Bossuet is incomparable. It is the Bossuet of the *Politique* and, to a lesser extent, of the *Panegyric on St Thomas of Canterbury* who is our present business.

Since Bossuet admits that the authority of all established governments is from God, he need not deny that governments have sometimes been set up by consent of the persons subject to them. He is content to say that, in the beginning, the authority of man over man was paternal. Abraham, he says, has been called a king, but his life was pastoral and he ruled only his family; his 'empire' was domestic. It was only later that true kings arose, either with the consent of their subjects or without it. Thus for Bossuet, as for Hobbes and Locke, political authority differs in kind from paternal, and is no mere extension of it. But, whether it is established by consent or by force of arms, it is equally legitimate; it is legitimate because God allows it to endure and requires obedience to it. All authority, paternal and political, comes equally from God; and yet political authority differs

---

[1] Bossuet: *Politique Tirée*, etc., Book III. Article 3, Proposition V. The translations from the French are my own.

from paternal, not because it rests on consent, but because it arises among men in a different way and serves different ends. There have been forms of government other than monarchy, yet monarchy is the commonest, oldest, and most natural form. It is the most natural because, though established by consent or by force of arms, it most closely resembles paternal rule. Bossuet goes so far as to say that the *foundation* and *model* of monarchy is paternal rule.[1] But this does not mean that he agrees with Filmer. He does not say that whoever possesses royal power is (or is to be reputed as being) the heir of the common ancestor of his people, exercising over them the same kind of authority as the ancestor exercised over his family; he says rather that monarchy was the first form of political authority because at the time that it arose among men they were familiar only with paternal rule. He says that the very first governments were established gently, not by conquest but by consent; and the examples he gives suggest that the earliest political rulers, who were kings, were often chosen by their peoples. The earliest kings were the 'fathers' of their people, though in a sense different from Filmer's; they were 'fathers' because their feelings for their subjects were paternal and their subjects' feelings for them were filial. The idea that, where there is a common ancestor, one of his descendants, his heir by the rule of primogeniture, possesses over his entire posterity the same authority as he had over his wife and children is quite foreign to Bossuet. So far is Bossuet from thinking that royal and paternal authority are in principle the same that he claims only for the first and not the second that it is absolute. He says that, since Abraham was not truly a king, Adam was not one either; and therefore the authority of kings does not come to them from Adam, and is not to be assimilated to the authority which God gave to Adam over his wife and children.

Hereditary monarchy has three principal advantages. It is 'self-perpetuating'; that is to say, there is no need to find a new king to take the place of the old one when he dies, for the king has one only heir by the rule of succession. That form of government is best which avoids contests for supreme power and disputes about who is the rightful possessor of it. That government is best which is the furthest removed from anarchy, where it is certain who has supreme authority and who is entitled to succeed to it. A second advantage of hereditary monarchy is that, more than any other form of government, it makes the conservation of the State the interest of the persons who govern it. A prince who works for his State works for his children, and in him love of country and of family run together. A third advantage is that it provides the people with men who are born to authority, who are the descendants of kings, who are invested thereby with a dignity which

---

[1] Ibid., Book II, Art. 2, Prop. vii.

belongs to a family which has been great for generations. They are heirs of the past as no man raised from obscurity can be; they are the sons and grandsons of men whose achievements are part of the history of their country.

'Government', says Bossuet, 'ought to be mild';[1] and 'princes are made to be loved'.[2] He means that, because they are born to greatness, their subjects are well disposed to them. They have only to behave well to get ready obedience. It is those who come by authority with difficulty, those whose title is most apt to be questioned, who must resort to harsh measures to maintain it. And who better than a hereditary prince can take advice without loss of dignity? The king should be more ready to listen than to speak, for he has the last word. Not for him to argue but to weigh the arguments put before him. He competes with nobody and nobody competes with him. Who is better placed to benefit from the ability and wisdom of others than the man who need fear no comparison with them? Yet Bossuet, who is ready to see all the advantages of an hereditary monarch, sees also the temptations to arrogance and obstinacy which beset him. Absolute power, however it is come by, has a tendency to corrupt; but (so thinks Bossuet) there must be such power if government is to be effective, if it is to provide men with security. He asserts without troubling to argue the matter that disputes about power are more harmful to the people generally than the abuses of power to which absolute rulers are tempted. Perhaps he is impressed by the testimony of Hobbes and by the example of what had recently happened in Hobbes' native land.

Disputes about power can be of two kinds: they can be about the extent of authority or they can be about who is the rightful possessor of an authority whose extent is not questioned. To a patriotic Frenchman of Bossuet's time, well read in history and well versed in contemporary affairs, it might seem that hereditary monarchy, as France then knew it, was best placed to avoid both kinds of disputes: the kind which brought civil war to England and the kind which so often brought insecurity to Rome at the death of an emperor.

To the sceptics of the next century Bossuet, as a writer on politics, appeared little more than a flatterer of kings. 'Majesty is the image of the greatness of God in the prince. God is infinite, God is everything. The prince . . . is a public personage, the whole State is in him; the will of the entire people is enclosed in his will. As all perfection and every virtue are united in God, so all the power of particular persons is united in the person of the prince.' 'See an immense people united in one only person; see this sacred, paternal and absolute power; see reason enclosed in one only head secretly governing the

[1] Ibid., Bk. III, Art. 3, Prop. xii.
[2] Ibid., Bk. III, Art. 3, Prop xiii.

body of the State: and you see the image of God in kings, you have
the idea of royal majesty.'[1] 'The title of christ is given to kings; and
so everywhere we see them called christs, the anointed of the Lord.'[2] 'It
is so great, this majesty, that it cannot be in the prince as in its source;
it is borrowed from God who gives it to him for the good of the people,
for it is good that they should be contained by a higher power.'[3] To
later philosophers, who found Louis XV insignificant or even con-
temptible, it seemed absurd that in the reign of his predecessor a
bishop could use such language of a king.

But Bossuet was no flatterer. His attitude to kings is the same as his
attitude to priests. Kings are in themselves no better than other men;
they are merely instruments of God. They are not set apart from
other men, or raised above them, by their merits; and we respect in
them, not what they are in themselves, but only their character as
agents of God. Those whom God calls to His service are not an
aristocracy in the Aristotelian sense, they are not the natural superiors
of other men. And yet, because God works through them as He does
not work through others, He sets them apart from others; He lends
them a dignity which is not theirs by nature. The majesty of kings is
a borrowed majesty, bestowed upon them for their people's good.
Authority should come easily to those that have it, and obedience to
those that owe it; and therefore it is good that the ruler should be
raised high above his subjects. But the ruler is a man like other men,
just as the priest is; and if he is to be raised above them, it must be by
virtue of some excellence which is not part of his nature. It must be by
virtue of a borrowed excellence, of a majesty which is not in him as in
its source but comes to him from God. 'For it is good that [the people]
should be contained by a higher power.' Not by sheer power, but by a
higher power; that is to say, by a power which to those subject to it
seems of a higher nature than anything they see in themselves.

And the reason 'enclosed in one only head secretly governing the
body of the State' is not the unaided intelligence of one man; it is a
borrowed wisdom, though borrowed, this time, not from God but
from the king's advisers. Bossuet, like Bodin, knows that, whether the
king is absolute or not, many heads go to the making of policy. There
are many men taking part in the government of an absolute monarchy,
and it can rarely happen that the wisest of them is the absolute
monarch. And yet, for the good of the people, there must be one man
whose decision is final, and that man must be set apart from the
others from the beginning; he is the listener, the taker of advice, the
supreme governor, who is not answerable to man but only to God for

[1] Ibid., Bk. V, Art. 4, Prop. i.
[2] Bk. III, Art. 2, Prop. ii.
[3] Bk. V, Art. 4, Prop. i.

how he rules. Others give their reasons to him, but he need not give his to them: this is the sense in which he governs 'secretly'.

Both Hobbes and Filmer play down the dangers of tyranny. Tyranny, says Hobbes, is merely monarchy 'misliked', it is a word which men use to express their feelings. Filmer denies that any King of England since the Conquest has been a tyrant. More people, he says, were put to death for political reasons in the last hundred years of the Roman republic than under all of the worst emperors put together, and he concludes that 'there is no tyranny to be compared to the tyranny of the multitude'.[1] Bossuet has greater misgivings. There is, he thinks, no truth better attested by the Holy Ghost (that is to say, by the Bible) than that wealth and power expose their possessors to great temptations. Some have sought a remedy by placing obstacles in the way of royal power, and Bossuet does not speak of them as if they had acted unreasonably. Without going into detail, he seems to conclude that all governments have grave defects, and that absolute monarchy is merely the least defective. God first established an absolute monarch in the person of Saul. 'We have not forgotten', he says at the end of the second book of the *Politique*, 'that there appear in antiquity other forms of government, about which God has prescribed nothing to mankind: so that every people must accept, as a divine order, the government established in their country, because God is a God of peace, who desires tranquillity in human affairs'.

Bossuet makes a distinction between absolute and arbitrary government which is not unlike the distinction later made by Montesquieu between monarchy and despotism. Where there is absolute government, there is a sovereign who cannot be legally compelled, who is free of all human authority, who is under no law except the law of God, and is responsible to God alone for his actions. And yet in practice there are laws such that 'whatever is done contrary to them is legally invalid (*nul de droit*).'[2] Bossuet, in the passage from which these words are quoted, is unusually obscure. He probably means that, where government is absolute but not arbitrary, the sovereign (whom he thinks of as a king), though he is not responsible at law for what he does, in fact respects the law in his dealings with his subjects. He rules a people accustomed to impartial justice. Therefore, though his authority to alter the law is uncontested, though no one has authority to declare any public act of his invalid, though he cannot be sued or punished for his private acts, he is expected to act justly; he is expected, in his dealings with all men, to respect the laws which are enforced in his name. If he does not respect them, he is held to have acted unjustly, and there is a wrong to be redressed. His subjects are acknowledged possessors of rights which it is the sovereign's acknowledged duty to

---

[1] From *Patriarcha*, Chapter XIX, Laslett, p. 93.
[2] Ibid., Book. I, Art. 4, Prop. viii.

define and to enforce. Hence the idea that the sovereign, though his authority is absolute, may act unjustly and even illegally; hence the readiness of subjects to seek redress from the sovereign against himself. The sovereign is sovereign, not because he can do no wrong, but because he alone can redress the wrong he does. The prince who, like the King of France, recognizes that his own laws bind him and who is expected by his subjects to respect them, is an absolute but not an arbitrary sovereign.

Bossuet is less apt than either Hobbes or Filmer to treat the law as the command of the sovereign. He even says that all who have spoken well about law have regarded it as a treaty or pact between men, who are agreed about what is needed for the good of their society. This, he hastens to add, does not mean 'that the authority of the laws depends on the consent and acquiescence of the peoples, but only that the prince . . . is assisted by the wisest heads in the nation, and leans upon the experience of past centuries'.[1] And 'there are fundamental laws which cannot be changed'.[2] Only the prince has authority to declare what the law is, only he may alter it, and there is no one with authority to deny that the law is what he says it is. And yet the prince, whose legislative authority is supreme, is in practice only to a small extent a maker of law. There are laws which he could not change without destroying the social order on which his own power rests. Law serves the needs of men, and that is why it is obeyed; and every ruler's power, even when his authority is absolute, is limited by the character of the social order in which he exercises it, by the needs of his subjects, by the structure of law. Thus the power of the absolute sovereign is in practice greatly limited, even when he happens not to fear God.

Lanson, who takes every opportunity he can to praise Bossuet, says that the force of his argument depends very much on the fear of God being a powerful motive with both rulers and ruled. No doubt, Bossuet everywhere takes it for granted that this motive is strong, or can be made strong by education. Yet he claims no more for the sovereign than Hobbes claimed for him, and we may wonder how much importance Hobbes attached to this motive. Is there no case for absolute monarchy except among men whose faith in God is strong? No less of a case, surely, than for absolute government which is not monarchy; of which we have had several examples in the twentieth century. If absolute government is more dangerous now than it was in Bossuet's time, it is not because (as Lanson suggests) belief in God is now much weaker; it is more dangerous because the power of all governments is enormously greater.

'The mighty', says Bossuet, 'will be mightily tormented', while the humble will be treated gently. Yet he appeals to utility as much as to

[1] *Politique*, Bk. I, Art. 4, Prop. vi.
[2] Ibid., Bk. I, Art. 4, Prop. viii.

the fear of God. In the fifth *Avertissement*, in reply to Jurieu who has said that rulers have no right to misgovern, he answers that what is at issue 'is not whether the prince has the right to do wrong, which nobody has dreamed of [asserting], but whether, if he does do it . . . it is reasonable for private persons to take up arms against him, and whether it is not more useful to mankind that they should retain no right against the public power.'[1] The true interest of subjects is not that there should be set limits to supreme authority but that the holder of that authority should have powerful motives for exercising it for their good, which he is most likely to have if he is an hereditary monarch.

The duty of subjects to a heretic or infidel ruler is as great as to a Catholic prince. Bossuet says of St Thomas of Canterbury that he never forgot that he was a subject, that he never treated his king disdainfully nor sought in any way to make him odious to his people, to stir up disaffection against him. To explain the nature and limits of the archbishop's defiance, he quotes Tertullian's words to a magistrate: *Non te terremus, qui nec timemus.* '*Non te terremus*, there speaks the subject, submissive and respectful always; *qui nec timemus*, there speaks the bishop, firm and unshakeable always. *Non te terremus*, I meditate nothing against the State; *qui nec timemus*, I am ready to suffer all for the Church.'[2] If the clergy have privileges, it is in order that religion may be honoured; if they possess goods, it is in order to carry on their sacred ministry; if they have authority it is to use it as a curb on the licentious and a support to discipline. A Catholic prince should be jealous for the privileges of the Church, having nothing to fear and much to gain from its influence on the faithful.

Bossuet, whose life was spent largely in the fight against heresy, took it for granted that the Church, to carry out its sacred mission, needs no authority which can be a threat to the authority of princes. If the prince is not of the true faith, the Church cannot release his subjects from their allegiance to him, and nothing in its doctrine (for the false claims made on its behalf by enthusiasts are no part of that doctrine) serves to weaken his authority; and if he is of the true faith, the Church is a pillar of his authority. Though the Church is not subordinate to the State, its independence cannot be a threat to the temporal ruler, whatever his faith; for he need never attack its independence to assert his legitimate authority. If he does attack it, the Church must defend itself, not by setting his subjects against him, but by refusing to admit that he has authority in the sphere reserved to it. The resistance of the priest, like that of the humblest layman, is

---

[1] *Cinquième Avertissement aux Protestants. Oeuvres de Bossuet*, Paris, 1841, Vol. 4, p. 394(2).

[2] *Panegyric on St Thomas of Canterbury*. Pléiade edition, p. 644.

passive; he prefers God's law to man's, he refuses to obey the prince when he cannot do so without disobeying God. Since God requires more of the priest than of the layman, there are likely to be more occasions when it is his duty to disobey his prince; but the disobedience is essentially the same. Not only must it never be active resistance, it must also never be an attempt to subvert the authority which belongs properly to the prince.

In matters of religion Bossuet was intolerant, but not conspicuously so in an intolerant age. More so than Henry IV and his English grand-son Charles II, but less so than the Jesuits or the Catholic League, and not more so than the Huguenots in France or the Long Parliament in England; not more so than the groups eager, at one time or another, to set limits to royal power. The prince, he says, must use his authority to destroy 'false religions' in his State, but must use severe methods only in the last resort. Christian princes have banished the authors of heresies but have dealt gently with their followers in the endeavour to bring them back to the faith. Bossuet, when he speaks of princes, some-times attributes to them qualities which he would wish them to have; and, no doubt, he does so here.[1] But at least he makes it plain what he takes those qualities to be. He does not deny that Christian princes have put heretics to death, but says not a word in their defence. The early Church, he tells us, always begged the Christian Roman Emperors not to apply the extreme penalty to heretics, unless they were guilty of treachery or sedition.[2]

The doctrine which Bossuet and Filmer contested, the doctrine that the authority of rulers rests on the consent of the ruled, is so much more congenial to us than is their doctrine that it is difficult for us to realize that in the sixteenth and seventeenth centuries most advocates of government by consent were no more liberal than the champions of absolute monarchy. The advocacy which we now remember best is, of course, that of Locke, who was certainly more liberal than either Bossuet or Filmer; but the earlier exponents of the doctrine that

---

[1] *Politique*, Bk. VII, Art. 3, Prop. x.

[2] That Bossuet should have welcomed the Revocation of the Edict of Nantes is not surprising, for the privileges granted to the Huguenots by that edict amounted to much more than toleration of their faith. The edict gave them a large measure of autonomy in over a hundred towns; it put them virtually out of reach of the sort of influences to which Bossuet wanted to expose them; it insulated them from the faith which alone in his opinion was true. If Bossuet did not openly condemn the *dragonnades* and other cruel methods used against the Huguenots, he never said a word in approval of them. Bossuet was never really powerful at court, and certainly was not so at the time of the worst excesses against the Protestants; though to later generations, this great champion of absolute monarchy has seemed guilty of the atrocities permitted by the absolute monarch whose subject he was.

legitimate authority rests on consent[1] were not much concerned for liberty of conscience or for other rights of the mere individual, as distinct from the rights of parliaments or their own co-religionists. Both among the advocates of absolute and of limited monarchy we can find wide divergences of opinion: we can find bigots intent on forcing others to share their beliefs and we can find men of larger views. Indeed, Bodin, perhaps the earliest champion of absolute monarchy as the seventeenth century was to understand it, was every bit as tolerant as John Locke.

This is not to deny that the idea of a social contract has implications which its first users did not see. The idea was first used to make, on behalf of religious minorities, claims of a kind not made before. Neither the Jesuits nor the Huguenots were greatly concerned that government should be carried on with the consent of the governed, or that the individual should be able to live as seemed good to him provided he did no harm to his neighbours: they cared, not for the freedom of the individual, but for the freedom of worship of those who shared their faith. In a Europe no longer united in one faith, in a Europe where there were minorities claiming to have the one true faith which their rulers did not share, they found it expedient to make bold and elaborate use of an idea which, if not new to their age, had been little used before it. That idea had larger implications than they knew. But it was not until the second half of the seventeenth century that these implications came to be seen more clearly, by Locke and by others. The earlier users of the idea of a social contract, the men whom Filmer and Bossuet attacked, cared no more for the freedom of the individual than did the advocates of absolute monarchy.

Bossuet says that, if there is to be security, there must be nothing in the State, no body and no person, able to challenge what he calls the 'public power'. The State being one, there can be only one public power inside it; that is to say, though there may be many persons and bodies of persons taking part in government, they constitute one public power because there is one person whose subordinates all the others are. Unless all persons except one exercising public authority are the subordinates of that one person, there is no cohesive, no united public power, and men lack the security which government exists to provide.

Bossuet and Hobbes both speak as if the unity of the State consisted in its having only one sovereign, only one person in whom all political authority ultimately resides. The difference between them is merely

---

[1] Hobbes also argued that the authority of rulers rests on the consent of the ruled, and used the model of a social contract to explain his views about political obligation; but his purpose was quite the opposite of Locke's and of his Jesuit and Huguenot precursors. He wanted to establish that the authority of rulers is unlimited.

that, whereas Bossuet more or less takes it for granted that the sovereign is a single man, a natural person, Hobbes allows that he may be an 'artificial' person, a body of men. Two conceptions are absent from their thinking: the idea of a system of government where there is no sovereign, no person (natural or artificial) whose right to make law is legally unlimited, but where, none the less, authority is so distributed among its possessors that there is always some person (or body) competent to give a final decision in any matter, not excluding disputes about how authority is distributed; and, secondly, the idea of a system where there is a sovereign, in the sense of a legally unlimited legislator, and at the same time a separation of powers. These two conceptions are foreign to the political thought of the sixteenth and seventeenth centuries. Political authority in Hobbes' England was so distributed that there was no recognized way of settling disputes about its distribution, and so it seemed obvious to Hobbes that, if these disputes were not to lead to civil war, supreme authority must all be concentrated in the hands of one person, natural or artificial; and Bossuet agreed with Hobbes. Of course, what was true of political authority in Hobbes' England had also been true of it not long before in France; indeed in the Middle Ages it had been true of it in all Europe. But, then, in the Middle Ages, there had not been felt the same need for a strong central government. In the Middle Ages there had been neither absolute monarchy as France knew it in the seventeenth century, nor constitutional government, as first England and then America came to know it in the eighteenth. The two ideas which I said are absent from the political thought of Bossuet and Hobbes are both ideas of constitutional government.

The first is realized, more or less, in the United States, where political authority is so distributed that there is no sovereign and yet there is always some person or body competent to give a final decision in all important matters, including disputes about how authority is distributed. The second is realized, more or less, in Britain, where there is a sovereign, a legally unlimited legislature, and also a separation of powers. That there is a sovereign in Britain is widely accepted, but not that there is a separation of powers. And yet there is one, at least of the kind forbidden by Hobbes and Bossuet, if not of the kind described by Montesquieu.[1] The absolute king, according to Bossuet, is both the supreme lawmaker and the supreme executive, while Hobbes takes it for granted that whoever has the legally unlimited power to make law stands to all others who take part in government as a superior to a subordinate. The supreme executive power belongs in Britain, in fact if not in name, to the Cabinet, which is not a body subordinate to the supreme legislature, though nearly all its members are also in fact

---

[1] Montesquieu's position has, I believe, been seriously misunderstood, as I try to argue in the chapter devoted to his political theory.

members of that legislature. Now that the royal assent to bills is a mere formality and the House of Lords can hold them up for no more than a year (a residual power which the lower House, if it were determined to do so, could abolish), the House of Commons is virtually a sovereign legislature. But the Cabinet is not a committee of the House of Commons; nor yet, despite the Cabinet's control of a parliamentary majority, is the House of Commons its mere agent. Neither the sense in which the executive is responsible to the House of Commons nor the sense in which the work of that House is directed by the executive allows us to call either body subordinate to the other. Nor are the two bodies identical, even though nearly all the members of one are also members of the other. We have in Britain a sovereign legislature and a separation of powers; we have something unimagined by either the champions of absolute or of limited monarchy in the days of Hobbes and Bossuet.

The assembly supposedly representative of the people, which in England alone in the seventeenth and eighteenth centuries came to be regarded as an integral part of the machinery of government, was not so regarded in earlier ages, even in England. The king from time to time 'met his people' assembled in Parliament or the States-General, and it was thought good that he should do so, but there was no question of his governing his people through ministers responsible to these bodies, which were not thought of as partaking in government. In an age when men were coming to feel a much stronger need for effective central government, these bodies, which privileged orders and corporations had long used to defend their interests against the royal power, were apt to be regarded as hindrances rather than helps to good government. This was especially so in France.

Bossuet, speaking of the public power, had in mind only the king's government; it never occurred to him to think of the States-General (which had not met since 1614) nor yet of the provincial estates (which were still meeting in his day) as parts of the public power. The idea of Montesquieu, the idea of the public power as a system whose parts check one another, did not occur to him; and the idea of Locke, of mere subjects setting themselves up as judges to decide when the public power has overstepped its bounds, seemed to him (as to Hobbes) an invitation to anarchy.

V. PASCAL

Pascal wrote no treatise on politics; he produced no theory of political obligation. He was indifferent to the two questions which excited the political philosophers of his day: How does government first arise among men? and, What makes it legitimate? In the *Pensées*, which contain nearly all his reflections on man in society, on law, and on government, he barely hints at an answer to the first question and takes no notice of the second. He says not a word to suggest that the authority of kings comes to them from God or from the people; he is certainly not a champion of absolute monarchy by divine right. Yet the pages of the *Pensées* which treat of matters interesting to the political theorist are not the least moving, the least original, in that incomparable book. Pascal lived under an absolute monarchy and saw nothing to prefer to it.

Pascal has affinities with Hobbes and with Hume. Like Hobbes he sees in government a curb for the unbridled passions and pride of men, and like Hume he sees men governed by habit and imagination more than by reason. But, unlike both Hobbes and Hume, he is interested much more in man than in government; he is interested in how man feels and thinks about law and government rather than in what they are in themselves.

Hobbes takes man as he finds him or thinks he finds him; he affects to speak of him as he might of some species to which he did not himself belong. He expresses no sense of either the pathos or the dignity of man. Man has appetites which he seeks to satisfy, and comes to desire power as a means to satisfying them; his pride arises from his concupiscence. He must compete with other men to satisfy his desires, and so comes to put a value on whatever gives him an advantage over them: on power in all its forms, as command, wealth and reputation. He strives for superiority and is moved by pride. If he were without government his situation would be intolerable, for, other men having the same passions as he has, he would be their enemy and they his; but, fortunately for himself and others, he is under government, and can pursue felicity (or the satisfaction of his desires) in conditions which promise success. There is nothing wrong with human nature, as Hobbes sees it: if there were no government, that nature would make life intolerable to the creature afflicted with it, but in fact there is government; for man's nature includes the capacity (reason) which enables him to avert the sufferings which his unbridled passions would bring upon him.

Pascal has different, and perhaps deeper, ideas about the passions which afflict man. He does not see pride arising in man because, in the endeavour to get the means of satisfying his natural desires, in the struggle for power, man seeks to dominate other men. 'The self', he says, 'has two qualities: it is inherently unjust, in that it makes itself the centre of everything; it is irksome to others in that it wishes to enslave them: for every self is the enemy of all the others and aspires to tyranny over them'.[1] But this yearning of the self to be the centre of all things does not arise from a striving for power, for the

---

[1] *Pensées*, Pléiade edition of Pascal's *Oeuvres*, p. 863, § 136.

means to the easier and fuller satisfaction of the natural appetites; it is of the essence of the self. It arises from an attitude of the self to itself possible only to a being which thinks. 'Everyone is a universe [*un tout*] to himself, for, he being dead, everything is dead to him. Hence it is that everyone believes that he is everything to everyone else.'[1] This is true only of man, who alone knows himself. When Pascal says that man knows himself he does not mean that he has true opinions about himself; he means rather that he is an object of thought to himself, that he is aware of himself. He is aware of himself and of others; he appraises himself and others. 'The beasts do not admire one another. The horse does not admire his companion; not that there is no emulation between them at a race, but it is of no consequence.'[2] Other animals are sometimes drawn into conflict by their appetites, but man alone is truly the rival and the enemy of his companions. He is so, not because, being rational, he can compete with them for the means of satisfying desire in ways impossible to the beasts, but because, being by nature a creature that thinks and is therefore self-centred, he is everything to himself and aspires to be everything to others.

Hence the inordinate vanity of man, who spends his life in the endeavour to create, preserve, and embellish some image of himself in the minds of others; who seeks satisfaction in an imaginary life, in his life as he wishes it to appear to others and not as it really is. Yet this concern for reputation, which is a cause of man's wretchedness, is also a mark of his dignity; it is a tribute to opinion, to the product of thought, to reason, to the peculiar excellence of man: 'He [man] rates human reason so high that, no matter what other advantage he may have on earth, if he is not also placed to his advantage in the reason of man, he is not satisfied. It is the finest place in the world: nothing can divert him from the desire for it.' Even when we despise men, we desire their good opinion, and so belie our own contempt; we desire their good opinion because they are men, because they are creatures who think, who pass judgements, and we recognize in them the dignity of their kind, the dignity of man. We look for happiness and find misery, we look for certainty and find doubt: we look for what only we, being capable of reason, can look for; and so our wretchedness comes of what is most excellent in us.

Man who aspires to be everything has also a sense of his own insignificance. He cannot bear to be alone with himself, to take stock of himself, to contemplate himself as he really is in the infinity of space and time; and so he seeks to divert himself from himself. Hence his love of noise and movement; he pretends to himself that he is active in the pursuit of what is worth having, of what will satisfy

[1] Ibid., p. 863, § 139.
[2] Ibid., p. 897, § 277.
[3] Ibid., p. 897, § 276.

him. But he is active only to escape from himself, to fill the void. Man aspires to be what he cannot be, and yet has reason enough to know that what he aspires to is out of his reach. If he were like other animals, if he had no reason, he would not aspire to be everything, and yet it is also reason in him which makes him aware of his insignificance. Man alone knows that he must die and feels the need to escape the thought of death; man alone can know himself and feel the need to escape from himself. The deliberate pursuit of one object of desire after another which, for Hobbes and the Utilitarians, is the proper business of mankind, an activity which *can* be successful and which brings happiness when it succeeds, becomes, for Pascal, an effect of man's need to hide from himself. Pascal is appalled by the triviality of man, which he ascribes, not to his stupidity, but to his fear of truth.

Man, if he is to escape the wretched condition into which he is driven by vanity and fear of truth, must learn to see himself as he really is; he must accept himself for what he is, despising what is weak in himself and respecting what is excellent, his capacity for thought and knowledge. 'I blame equally those who choose to praise man, and those who choose to blame him, and those who look for amusement; and can approve only those who painfully seek the truth [*qui cherchent en gémissant*].'[1] The search for truth leads ultimately to God, through whom alone man finds what he is impelled by his nature to seek, a knowledge which satisfies. But we are not, as mere students of social and political theory, concerned with what is most important to Pascal in his own philosophy, his conception of man's relation to God; we are concerned only with what he says about man's condition before he has found God. Man, in that condition, is afflicted by vanity and by the need to escape from himself in the pursuit of pleasure and ambition. This is the condition of man for which the social order and government are remedies. In this condition, for Pascal as for Hobbes, man is the enemy of man; and he is so by nature, though this is not the whole truth about his nature. Nor is the remedy remedial in the same sense as it is for Hobbes; it is not the only remedy, and is far indeed from being sufficient. It merely protects men from one another but does not enable them to find happiness. The sufficient remedy is not the order maintained by government; it is the discovery of truth and of God. For Hobbes, who thinks of 'felicity' as merely the successful pursuit of objects of desire, all that is needed to deliver man from wretchedness and put him in the way of happiness is that his environment should be changed. For Pascal, men are not only by nature one another's enemies; they are also their own. Government can save them only from the consequences of the first enmity; from the consequences of the second, which is the worse and in which the other is rooted, they must save themselves by the grace of God.

[1] Ibid., p. 909, § 333.

Pascal says that at one time he believed that human justice was essentially just; but he has now learnt better. Theft, incest, infanticide and parricide have all been counted among virtuous actions. Justice has been defined in several ways, and the definition which pleases Pascal best is that the just is the customary, the commonly received. Nothing, according to mere reason, is in itself just; there are no rules discoverable by reason which we can use to appraise the rules actually accepted and enforced.[1] Montaigne is wrong when he says that custom must not be followed merely because it is custom but because it is reasonable or just. Yet Pascal admits that people follow custom because they believe it to be just. They wish to be subject only to reason or justice; and custom, if it were not thought reasonable or just, would be thought tyrannical. That what is customary is just, in some sense of justice which does not make *just* and *customary* synonyms, is apparently a belief that men cannot do without. At least Pascal suggests that it is so, though he does not attempt to explain why it should be. No doubt he believes that there is after all an ' essential justice', to which men aspire though they cannot discover it; so that they must have something which can pass for justice among them, something which they believe is other than it is without really knowing what they take it for. In the social philosophy of Pascal, the role of justice is not unlike that of the *thing-in-itself* in Kant's theory of knowledge; it is something of which nothing can be known except that it exists, and so men take what they can know (justice as it appears to them) to be justice as it really is.

In a work which is not a finished treatise, which consists only of materials brought together for a book and never built into one, Pascal does not trouble to explain how men come to have the customs they do have. He does not anticipate Hume (who abandons the notion of an essential justice discoverable by reason even more completely than he does) by suggesting that, men's capacities and needs being broadly similar all over the world, they come everywhere to accept certain rules which experience teaches them are in everyone's interest, rules without which no society could subsist. He produces no universal rules as substitutes for the law of nature as traditionally conceived. Nor does he suggest that government first arose because it was found generally convenient. He says merely that there must be inequality among men, since they all wish to dominate, though only some can do so. He imagines a struggle between men which ends with the stronger bending the weaker to their wills, the masters deciding how

---

[1] Pascal does not hold consistently to this position. Sometimes he speaks as if he believed that rules of conduct are merely accepted or rejected, so that it is absurd to enquire whether they are true or valid in themselves; while at other times he speaks as if there were an essential justice, though men cannot discover it.

'force' shall pass from their hands into those of their successors. It is then that 'imagination' begins to take the place of 'force', presumably because men come to believe that what is established is as it ought to be. But Pascal is so little interested in the origins of the social and political order that he gives little thought to the matter.[1]

In his opinion it matters much more that laws and forms of government should go unquestioned than what they are. What, he asks, appears more unreasonable than to choose the eldest son of a queen to govern a State? If the traveller of noblest birth were chosen to captain a ship, it would be thought ridiculous. And yet, given the perversity, the unruliness of man, the unreasonable becomes reasonable. Should the most virtuous man and the most able govern the State? But anyone may claim to be that. Therefore let the rule be that he is to govern who has something about him that cannot be disputed: let him govern who is the eldest son of the king, of the man who ruled before him. What rule is less hurtful to vanity than one which accords superiority without pretence of merit? The other advantages of hereditary monarchy, so conspicuous to Bodin and Bossuet, count for nothing with Pascal, who does not mention them. If Pascal is right, it is a waste of time to look for the form of government which provides the best rulers. Hereditary monarchy is not to be preferred because those who come to power under it are likely to rule better than those who come to it in some other way, but only because, human nature being what it is, it is easier to contrive that the title to supreme authority is uncontested than that the authority is wisely exercised.

Pascal's scepticism goes further even than Hume's. Hume not only supposes that there are some very general rules accepted by men everywhere because they are everywhere found convenient (the rules which men call, to mark their importance, *laws of nature*, the rules which experience has shown to be well adapted to the needs of a creature having the nature of man in the world as it actually is); he also prefers some systems of government (for example, limited monarchy of the English kind) to others (democracy and absolute monarchy) on the ground that they are the most likely to provide security without being oppressive. Hume is more inclined to believe that customs and forms of government differ from country to country because men's needs differ. In general, he is less given than Pascal to suggesting that

[1] He is so much struck by the diversity of customs that it never occurs to him to enquire whether there are not some to be found everywhere, men's condition being in some respects everywhere the same. Nor does he ask how it is that some men can come to dominate others where there is not already a social order, where there are not already established conventions. It does not occur to him, as it does to Hume and to Rousseau, that rules must be prior to dominion; that men must already be respecters of customary rules before some among them can acquire power over others.

H

it matters almost not at all what custom or authority is established providing that whoever is required to obey it does so willingly. Yet he too is more concerned to advise men to accept what is established than to argue for one system in preference to another; he too wishes to leave men undisturbed in their submission to what they are used to and what has long been received, to custom and prejudice. Pascal asks: 'Why do men follow old laws and old opinions? Is it because they are the soundest? No, but they are unique, and so remove from us the root of diversity.'[1] Hume would perhaps qualify Pascal's answer thus: Old laws and old opinions are likely to be the soundest, but most men are unable to show that they are, and never dream of making the attempt. They accept them unquestioningly as standards of what is right; and it is good that they should do so because the stability of the social order depends on most people's accepting without question what is commonly received, and what they are not competent to question.

Pascal and Hume come closest to complete agreement about the laws of property; they both suggest that, though it is necessary that there should be some rules, it is indifferent what they are. In the first of the *Trois Discours sur la Condition des Grands*, which Pascal prepared for the instruction of the eldest son of the Duc de Luynes, he tells his pupil that he is not to imagine that there is a law of nature requiring that he should inherit the property of his ancestors. If the rule were that a man's estate must revert, after his death, to the republic, it would not be a whit less just than the rule which secures his estate to his eldest son. God allows communities to make what rules of property they please, and no matter what the rules are, they ought to be respected. The heir to great wealth owes his wealth to mere chance: to his being born the son of his parents in a community happening to have a certain rule of inheritance. He is raised above his fellows because the social order is what it is, and it might, no less justly, no less reasonably, be entirely different. There is not a word in Pascal, so far as I know, to suggest that some rules of property are better adapted than others to the needs or feelings of the generality of men.[2]

<hr />

1 *Pensées*, Pléiade edition. p. 889, § 240. The diversity Pascal has in mind consists in differences of opinion about what is just or right, which he thinks must arise if the appeal is to reason and not to custom.

2 No doubt, Pascal would admit that whatever rules of property do arise in a community do not do so by mere chance. There are reasons why just those rules and not others did arise. But he says nothing to suggest *either* that there are some rules which arise everywhere because they are everywhere found convenient, *or* that the rules which arise in some particular community do so because they are found to be generally convenient in that community. On the other hand, he does suggest in one place (*Pensées*, p. 900, § 289) that organized society results from the victory of the strong over the weak, so that what is first established by force, presumably for the benefit of the strong, comes to be generally accepted as *imagination* underpins what *force* has set up.

In the second of the *Trois Discours*[1] Pascal distinguishes two kinds of greatness: greatness by convention (*d'établissement*) and greatness grounded in nature. Dignities and noble rank are of the first kind, and are achieved in one place in one way and in another place in another. It has pleased men that it should be so; and that is all that Pascal has to say about it. Greatness of the second kind consists in such things as intelligence, virtue, health and strength; it belongs *by nature* to whoever possesses it, presumably because it consists of qualities of mind or body, developed by exercise and education. We have obligations to both kinds of greatness. To the first we owe only outward respect or deference. We owe it, not because it is our interest to show it, but because it is right that we should do so; it is right that we should accept what is established. To greatness of the second kind we owe esteem. It is foolish to refuse outward respect to the first kind on the ground that it is not the second, or to expect for the second what is owing only to the first. The superiorities recognized by the world have nothing to do with merit; and it is as simple-minded to suppose that they could rest on merit as that they do. Men are so made that they cannot have peace except in a society of unequals; and therefore, since inequality has nothing to do with merit, the wise man does not refuse to high rank the deference it expects. Pascal invites the heir of the Duc de Luynes to think of himself as of a man wrecked in a storm on an unknown island whose people have lost their king. The stranger looks like the king and the people take him for the king; and the stranger, though at first with reluctance, assumes the role which chance has thrust upon him. He acts as if he were a king and yet knows that he is not one; he allows himself to be elevated in the eyes of the people, though in his own he remains what he truly is, no better than they are. Their illusion is salutary and he need not destroy it; but he ought not to share it, for if he does, he will abuse the position which has come to him by accident.

The people, Pascal tells us in the *Pensées*, have some very sound opinions: for example, that pursuit is better than capture, or that men are to be honoured for such external qualities as noble birth and wealth, or that a blow is to be deeply resented. The pursuit of what we think we want diverts us from ourselves while its capture proves that it is not worth having; honouring men for external qualities preserves the social order; and to receive a blow without resentment is to lose reputation on which solid advantages depend. Yet these sound opinions

---

[1] M. Jacques Chevalier, the editor of the Pléiade edition of Pascal's *Oeuvres* says that Nicole, 'who has preserved the memory' of the *Trois Discours* in his *Education d'un Prince* (1670) assures his readers that, though they may not consist of Pascal's actual words, they are true to his thoughts and sentiments. *The Trois Discours* make up only six pages (pp. 387-92) of the Pléiade edition.

rest on illusion, for those who hold them usually do not know why they are sound. Thus, they honour persons of noble birth believing in the superiority of the nobly born. The generality of men honour the nobly born, the half intelligent despise them on the ground that the advantages of birth come by chance and not by merit, while the truly intelligent honour them, though not for the reason that the others do. 'True Christians bow to folly notwithstanding; not that they respect it, but the order of God, who, to punish men, has subjected them to this folly: ' *Omnis creatura subjecta est vanitati. Liberabitur.*'[1] But never to become quite free in this world where the man who has overcome vanity in himself still belongs to a social order which magnifies it in others!

There are questions left unanswered by Pascal. How, in a world where essential justice is unknown, are even the wise to distinguish between the two kinds of greatness? How do they recognize virtue? In what does it consist? Is it no more than obedience to custom? And what makes intelligence or health or strength estimable? True, they are not qualities *external* to their possessors; but then neither are stupidity, ill-health and weakness. What causes men to esteem one another for having these qualities? Hume, who would no doubt agree with Pascal that the value of what is valuable to man is not determined by his reason but his passions and his will, attempts to answer these questions, but Pascal does not do so. It is not to be expected that he should in a work which is not a book but the raw materials for a book, and which treats of man in society only in passing to other (and in the author's eyes) higher matters. Man, until he finds God, is a creature intolerable to himself, and society provides no remedy for the worst evils which afflict him; it merely preserves him from some of the outward manifestations of these evils provided he accepts established authority unquestioningly.

In the next century men came to believe in progress; they came to believe that men could discover (and indeed, to a great extent, already had discovered) in their environment and in themselves the causes of unhappiness, and could remove them. Either, like the Utilitarians, they conceived of happiness as the successful pursuit of pleasure, or they thought of it as a way of life suited to what is enduring in man's nature. In either case, it was something which men might hope to achieve in this world, something which they could get for themselves from one another without troubling their heads over much about their relations with God or their fate after death. The greater men's knowledge, the better they could adapt their means to their ends. Whether these believers in progress took the simple Utilitarian view, which likens the pursuit of worldly happiness to the accumulation of wealth,

---

[1] *Pensées*, Pléiade edition, p. 905, § 313.

or preferred a more subtle conception of it, they took it for granted that this pursuit is the proper business of man. To them Pascal seemed merely perverse. To his 'the last act is bloody, no matter how fine the comedy in all the rest', they might have answered that the last act appears bloody only to those who have not known how to enjoy the comedy.

It may be that, on this last point, they were right. At least we must hope so, for today, when so few can find consolation where Pascal looked for it, it is good that faith in the possibility of worldly happiness should be strong. And, in any case, we do not get from Pascal a balanced account of man's condition in society; we get only a deeper insight into some aspects of it.

Pascal, who differs so greatly from the believers in progress of the next century, differs also from Bossuet. He is altogether without reverence for kings or for the established order; they are, to him, objects of neither esteem nor contempt. He looks at worldly society with the eyes of St Augustine, without hatred and without pleasure. The established social order accords with the will of God, and yet it is a part of creation in which the Creator apparently takes no delight. It is a remedy for sin but not a means to the good life; it protects man from some of the effects of evil but contributes nothing to his perfection. It is not educative in any important sense. Whereas Bossuet, following Aquinas and Aristotle, sees the social order as essentially a moral order. Man has a nature which is improved by life in society; his reason and affections find an outlet in it. Man grows into manhood as a member of society. He cannot become all that he ought to be as a mere partaker in social life, for his relations with God are more important than his relations with other men; but he is brought nearer even to his ultimate goal by being a partaker in it. Not merely because the Temporal Power maintains the peace needed to make possible the ministrations of the Church, but also because man learns what it is to need and to love God through his need and love for creatures like himself. Thus, for Bossuet as for Aquinas, worldly institutions are the handiwork of God in a larger and more hopeful sense than they are for Pascal. There are lesser and higher ends for man, and the way to the higher is through the lesser. The hand of God in every part of his universe is a loving hand.

The common motive of all the champions of absolute monarchy, whether, like Filmer and Bossuet, they make kings in a special sense the agents of God or, like Bodin and Hobbes, they do not, is fear of anarchy. This fear takes different forms, and in no one is more acute and all-pervasive than in Pascal. But what he fears most is not the 'war of all against all', the absence of government among men; what he fears above all is a spiritual anarchy, which needs more than government to cure it. Man who aspires to be everything, who wishes to be

God, feels the emptiness in himself, the anarchy at the heart of his being, and therefore dare not face himself. His worldly ambitions occupy his mind without satisfying him, and hierarchy and government are needed to impose an external discipline on a creature full of vanity and incapable of happiness, and therefore dangerous to himself and his neighbours. This is the condition into which man's nature necessarily impels him, and the only cure for it is that he should find God. The established social order protects him from the effects of his own and other men's passions, and it also provides the external peace he needs if he is to have the courage and the strength to face his predicament, if he is to undertake the painful search which, if it succeeds, leads him to God. The established order is an order proper to a madhouse, because man, until he has found God, does not know himself or what to do with himself; he is either appalled by the senselessness of life or takes refuge in illusion.

This condition of man, which Pascal imputes to his nature before he has found God, was later imputed to society by Rousseau; and sociology began to take the place of theology. The maladies to be accounted for remain largely the same but the causes ascribed to them are widely different. Man is so situated that he cannot or dare not become what he must be to come to terms with himself and thereby find happiness: this is the theme common to Pascal and Rousseau.

Chapter 6

LOCKE

I. INTRODUCTORY

IT has been disputed whether or not John Locke wrote the second *Treatise of Civil Government* to justify the revolution of 1688. The political theorist, primarily interested in the content of the theories he examines and not in what moved their authors to produce them, will not wish to take sides in this dispute. Whatever moved Locke to write his *Treatise*, there is no doubt that he approved of the revolution and also of the form of government and social order he found in England. That government, in Locke's day, was a mixture of monarchy and aristocracy, and there is no reason to suppose that Locke found fault with it. Wealth was very unequally distributed, and Locke appears to have been satisfied that it should be so. We may take it for granted that, at least in his opinion, the doctrines expounded in the *Treatise* were perfectly consistent with the established social order and form of government.

Yet Locke's *Treatise* is clearly not an apology for a particular form of government or society. It is much too abstract for that. No one who read the *Treatise* could learn from it how England was governed at the time it was written. No one could guess that the revolution of which its author approved was the work of a small and wealthy part of the nation which dominated a legislature consisting of an hereditary house of Lords and another house elected on a very narrow franchise. The argument of the *Treatise* is that government is not legitimate unless it is carried on with the consent of the governed. But the *Treatise* says little indeed about how government should be organized in order to have the consent of the governed. Indeed, as we shall see, if consent can be given in the ways described by Locke, any form of government has the consent of its subjects provided they obey it.

The revolution of 1688 which Locke's second *Treatise* is supposed to justify did not set up a new system of government; it was merely the final victory, in a struggle which had lasted nearly a hundred years, between classes that had grown strong under the wing of the Tudor monarchy against the monarchy that came after it. One great issue was settled; the supremacy of Parliament was established once for all. The king must govern in broad conformity with Parliament's wishes. But how exactly was he to do so? What precise relations must exist between Crown and Parliament to enable the king to govern effectively and yet responsibly? This second issue, not less important than the first, was not settled by the revolution of 1688. That is not surprising. Civil wars and revolutions do not often decide how a country shall be governed; they often do little more than make it impossible to govern it in the old ways. The period of readjustment comes afterwards. Just as the English colonists in America, having won their independence, still had a long way to go before achieving effective self-government, so the classes which asserted Parliament's supremacy by driving James II into exile needed at least a generation to discover how to reconcile royal government with parliamentary supremacy. The complicated system of Crown and aristocratic patronage which enabled eighteenth-century governments to find and maintain parliamentary majorities was not well established until Walpole's time. What a later age was to call parliamentary monarchy, with the king's ministers unable to govern unless they enjoyed the confidence of parliament, was unknown to Locke just as it was to the parties to the constitutional struggle culminating in the revolution of 1688. It is much less Locke than Montesquieu or Hume or Burke who deserves to be called a champion of that type of government. Chapter VI of Book XI of the *Spirit of the Laws* is a powerful argument for the English form of monarchy, an argument of a kind that Locke never produced. Locke's *Treatise* is not concerned to justify any form of government; it is concerned rather to assert the right of the people to resist their rulers when they are misruled by them.

But having said this, I immediately feel the need to qualify what I have said. Though Locke allows that any government carrying out its trust is governing with the consent of its subjects, he does say that it is best for the executive and legislative powers to be in separate hands, and that a government cannot rightfully tax its subjects except with their consent given through their representatives. Where he expresses a preference for any particular institution or device, it is almost always clear that he has been strongly influenced by established practice in his own country. Moreover, he puts forward his highly abstract argument in such a way as to avoid coming to conclusions which could be used to condemn the English system of government and social order of his day.

Locke was not a believer in equality, either political or social. Yet the modern reader can scarcely fail to notice that some of the assumptions made in the *Treatise* were also made by Tom Paine at the end of the next century, and were used by him to justify democracy; while others were made by the early socialists, who used them to condemn the existing distribution of property. Paine agreed with Locke that, since man is by nature free, no man can have authority over another except with his consent, and then went on to argue that therefore, if there must be government, it ought to be democratic. Several of the early English socialists agreed with Locke that, since every man owns his own labour, he is entitled to whatever he produces with his labour, and then went on to argue that the existing system of property, which deprives labourers of a great part of what they produce, is unjust. Locke did not come to these conclusions. I have said that he avoided them. I do not suggest that he did so deliberately. Almost nobody in Locke's time believed in equality, political or social, as Paine or the early socialists understood it. I suggest only that Locke's preference for the established order in England had a strong, though negative and unconscious, influence on the way he developed his argument. Though the *Treatise* is not a defence of Whig aristocracy, it would not be what it is if its author had not approved of that dispensation. It may be that many of the ambiguities and false reasonings which spoil the second *Treatise* arise from Locke's unconscious need to avoid unwelcome conclusions.

They spoil the *Treatise*, of course, for us and not for Locke's contemporaries; we are accustomed to seeing conclusions drawn from Locke's premises different from those which he drew, and which seem to us to follow more logically from them. When we come across anyone saying that he believes in government by consent, we expect him to prefer democracy to other forms of government. Locke's contemporaries, having no such expectations, were not struck, as we are, by the looseness of the terms he uses and his passing, without himself noticing it, from one sense of a word to another. All through the *Treatise*, Locke, though he uses the word *consent* in several senses, seems to be unaware that he does so; he uses it as if he believed that he were using it always in the same sense. He begins by using it in the sense of voluntary agreement, and then, later, creates the impression that he is consistently using it in this one sense, though in fact he is not; he unconsciously creates this impression by first insisting that it is only consent, in the sense of voluntary agreement, which makes authority legitimate and then going on to speak of other forms of consent, which he does not distinguish from voluntary agreement, as if they too had the same effect. If our sympathies are with the author and his methods of argument are traditional and are widely accepted as appropriate to his purpose, we are not on our guard and we follow uncritically where he leads. We are first told that only voluntary agreement makes political authority legitimate, and then afterwards that other actions, also called acts of consent, have this same effect, and so we are disposed to believe that they too are tantamount to voluntary agreement. This was the condition of Locke's contemporaries who found his argument logically sound and were strongly attracted to his conclusions. They had not seen Paine reach quite different conclusions from the same premises, and they had not been taught by Hume and the more conservative Utilitarians that Locke's conclu-

H*

sions could be derived from other premises, less apt to be misused by radicals.

Locke uses a form of argument fashionable in his day. To explain the use of government and also its legitimacy, he first imagines men without government and then enquires what their motives must have been for setting it up. But, because he uses such traditional concepts as natural law and natural right, and also the myth of a social contract, he is not content to say that rulers are entitled to obedience so long as they carry out the essential functions of government, so long as they do what men in an imaginary state of nature may be supposed to have required of their rulers when they first agreed to have any. He feels obliged to say more than this, to say that they are entitled to obedience only if their subjects have actually consented to obey, and so is committed to showing that they have consented, that they have voluntarily agreed, even when it looks as if they have not. Hence the difficulties he gets into, which he slides out of by what to us appear to be mere verbal tricks, though both he and his contemporaries took them for good arguments.

Yet his *Treatise*, despite the inconsistencies and confusions which strike us so forcibly, was very well suited to the public at whom it was aimed. It was well suited to them both because it reached conclusions they liked and because it used forms of argument with which they were familiar and which seemed appropriate to them. Locke's *Treatise* was popular because it suited the social aspirations and also the intellectual prejudices of classes growing in importance, classes living on rents and profits and employing wage-labourers. It is a theory made up of old ingredients presented in a more secular and modern, and therefore attractive, form. In the Middle Ages it had usually been held that the authority of princes and magistrates comes ultimately from God and secondarily from the people, and it had also been argued that what is customary and traditional has the people's consent. But the Huguenots and Jesuits had wanted to justify resistance to rulers whose authority clearly rested on custom and tradition, and had used the myth of a social contract to achieve their purpose. By so doing they had given to the notion of popular consent, the consent deemed necessary to make temporal authority legitimate, a rather different content from what it had had in the Middle Ages; they spoke of it as if it were more than mere acquiescence, as if it were something closer to voluntary and deliberate agreement. Or, to speak more accurately, though they continued, when it suited them, to use the term *popular consent* in a mediaeval sense, they also used it in another sense, which they did not clearly distinguish from the older one. They set an example that Locke followed.

The idea that true consent is personal and deliberate (though not necessarily express) was common among seventeenth-century political writers. We find it in Hobbes and Pufendorf. It could be argued that Hobbes' initial assumptions make the social compact redundant; but the fact remains that he thought of it as a covenant of every man with every man, as a voluntary agreement between equals. It is not, like the consent of the mediaeval philosophers, something revealed in the mere prevalence of custom. Pufendorf, born in the same year as Locke, went further than Locke did in using the notions of consent and contract. He tried to explain all human authority as an effect of contract. Even the slave consents to the authority of his master, for either he is a poor man who, in return for subsistence, engages his services in perpetuity, or he is a captive taken in war whose life is forfeit and who buys the right to live at the price of his freedom. Paternal authority also rests on contract, though the contract here is presumed rather than actual. The child needs, in its own interest, to be looked after by its father, and if it were old enough to know this, would agree to be subject to paternal authority. If the notions of contract and consent are pushed as far as Pufendorf (and others) pushed them, we are forced to this conclusion: that anyone capable of knowing that something is his interest or, when he looks back on the past, of recognizing that it was his interest, may be taken to be consenting to what is done in his interest, even where there is no question of his exercising a choice. Locke never went as far as this: he made a more modest use of the notion of consent than some of his contemporaries.

Locke's *Second Treatise of Government* is a re-statement of doctrines current for centuries or else put forward since the Reformation in the interest of minorities liable to persecution. It is simple, attractive, untheological, and persuasive. It is the sort of book that strengthens people in opinions they already hold or are beginning to hold; it persuades them of the truth of what they are already inclined to believe. It is not, at a first glance, a puzzling or difficult or disquieting book. The author carries his readers along with him, easily and comfortably. That is, of course, provided they wish to be carried. If they insist on probing his meaning, if they refuse to take what he says at its face value, then difficulties arise inevitably; but it is easy enough, at his own level of discussion, to understand and to be persuaded by Locke.

He demands from the acquiescent reader no great effort. This is not an effect of lucidity. Hume was more lucid than Locke, and yet it needs a greater effort to follow his meaning. An exact and consistent writer requires the close attention of his readers; and close attention is never easy. With Locke, the case is rather the opposite. Too often, the more carefully we attend to his arguments, the less intelligible they appear. I speak of him, of course, only as a political writer; it is not my present business to do more.

Locke's political theory has been called superficial. In a sense it is so. He was by no means a strict reasoner, and the frequent weakness of his arguments is not compensated for, as it is with Montesquieu, Rousseau and Burke, by novelty of method, largeness of design, or unusual penetration. Locke confined himself to ordinary problems and reached by easy methods conclusions that many people found attractive. It was his competence and persuasiveness, rather than his opinions, that were out of the ordinary.

Locke was interested primarily in the problem of political obligation. We can learn almost nothing from him about the nature of power, of the State, of law, or of government. This is not just an effect of his non-empirical method. Hobbes, whose method was as little empirical as Locke's, does teach us to think in new ways about law and the State. His ideas about them may now seem inadequate, but we still recognize their importance. By defining moral and political terms in his own peculiar and vigorous way, Hobbes obliged his successors to think again about the things those terms were used to describe and helped them to acquire a vocabulary better suited to describe them. His strictly deductive method enabled him to make a contribution of the greatest importance to political and even social theory; though, of course, a contribution of a different kind from those made by men like Hume or Montesquieu, who used different methods.

Locke made no such major contribution. Our understanding of political and social concepts or institutions is not appreciably greater for anything he wrote which is not also to be found elsewhere. He was not much interested in the facts, and he made no new and important assumptions. That does not mean, of course, that there is little to learn from a close study of his political theory. There is a great deal. But that is primarily because it is a good example of a certain type of theory. In examining Locke's theory, we are examining ways of thought common to many philosophers in his day. Locke's abstract and moralizing political philosophy, though neither markedly original nor carefully argued, was so convincing, so much in keeping with feelings and hopes common among the educated classes in western Europe (and later in North America), that it was for generations widely accepted as substantially true. Locke, more than any other writer on politics, has been the representative, the most acceptable, accomplished, and respectable interpreter of the liberal philosophy of the West. Old ideas, inherited through the Christian fathers from the Stoics, about natural law and the essential equality of men, together with other ideas, derived from more purely mediaeval sources, about the limited authority of government and the need for popular consent, receive from him the form which made them look convincing to a secular Europe destined to found new nations in other continents and to dominate the world intellectually. Locke used these ideas to justify responsible government and popular rebellion against tyranny. That was a use they could be put to more easily in England than elsewhere; for in England, alone among the great European nations, there existed a representative assembly strong enough to produce a national – and not a feudal, ecclesiastical, or sectarian – opposition to monarchy. In England, more than anywhere else, it was possible to limit royal power without threatening national unity.

II. A SUMMARY OF LOCKE'S POLITICAL THEORY

In the state of nature all men are free to dispose of themselves and their possessions as they think fit, and their only obligation is to respect the same freedom in others. They are rational creatures and can see that when they deal with other creatures like themselves they ought to treat them as equals. It is in this sense that men, even in the state of nature, are bound by law; they are bound by the law of nature, by rules of conduct which reason teaches them they ought to observe in their dealings with one another.

This right of every man in the state of nature to dispose of himself and his possessions as he thinks fit, Locke calls property. So that a man's property, in this large sense, is co-extensive with his rights. Every man, says Locke, has a property in his own person; by which he means that he has a natural right, limited only by God's purposes and by the obligation to respect the same right in others, to do as he pleases. He may not destroy himself, for he is God's creature and his property in himself is not independent of God's will; and he is not free to invade the freedom of others. But otherwise there are, in the state of nature, no limits to his freedom or his property. And property, in this larger sense, is the same as freedom.

Locke also uses the word property in the ordinary sense, to mean the right to the exclusive use of external objects. Property in this narrower sense he derives from property in the larger sense. Natural man has the right to do anything he pleases except to destroy himself or to invade the right of others; he therefore has the right to set aside for his own use whatever he has a mind to, provided, of course, that someone else has not already taken it.

The state of nature is not a state of war, for it has, as we have seen, a law of nature to govern it. But law, if there is no one to enforce it, is in vain. Therefore, says Locke, ' the execution of the law of nature is in that state put into everyman's hands, whereby everyone has a right to punish the transgressors of that law to such a degree as may hinder its violation '.[1] This is a right of punishment and not merely a right of self-defence. If it were merely a right of self-defence, no one in the

---

[1] *Second Treatise of Government*, Chapter II, § 7.

state of nature could rightly use force except against persons invading his own rights. But what Locke says is that everyone in the state of nature has a right to punish anyone who offends against the law of nature, whether he is himself the victim of that offence or not. It is only because all men have this right in the beginning that they can afterwards transfer it to magistrates when civil society is established.

Notice how strong a case Locke makes for freedom at the beginning of his treatise. Property in the larger sense, which makes it equivalent to freedom, is prior to government; it is man's right, under God, to dispose of himself and of what he sets aside for his own use in whatever ways seem best to him. This right is limited only by the obligation to respect the same right in others, and it cannot be further limited except with the consent of its possessors. The law of nature allows interference only with aggressors; it does not allow the generality of men to require more of any man than that he should respect that law, which means only that he should respect in others the freedom he claims for himself. They cannot legislate for him. The only law to which all men are subject, whether they like it or not, is not a law made by men; it is not even the undeliberate product of their living in society with one another. It is not custom or convention but the law of reason, which defines the rights and duties that constitute and sustain freedom. The law of nature is therefore the law of freedom. It is a law that men do not make but only discover. The maker of law requires of others that they should submit to his will, and no man can rightly require this of another man without his consent. In the state of nature, the right of command belongs only to God, who commands only that men deal justly with one another; or, in other words, that they obey the law of nature, which is obligatory independent of God's will.

For Locke, the supreme question in politics is, What makes government legitimate? Nothing, he thinks, can make it so except the consent of the governed; and that consent, to be genuine, must be personal, deliberate and free. 'All men', says Locke, 'are naturally in that state [of nature], and remain so till, by their own consents, they make themselves members of some politic society.' Notice the words 'by their own consents'. Locke would not have put 'consent' into the plural if he had not meant us to understand that every man must consent for himself alone, because only his own act can bind him.

This was Locke's initial position. In later chapters of his book, as, one after another, he came upon the difficulties it led to, he went a long way in modifying it – a much longer way, indeed, than he ever knew. But in the beginning he was bold; he pushed freedom almost to the farthest limit. No grown man owes a duty of obedience to any other man except by his own consent, and that consent must be free. The authority of government arises, not from men's needs, but from their freely given consents. No doubt, men establish government in the first place because they feel a need for it, but it is the consent, and not the need, which makes government legitimate.

To drive his point home, Locke distinguishes between two kinds of authority. He admits that one kind, limited in extent and duration, rests on need alone and not on consent, but he insists that it is not political. Children cannot look after themselves and must therefore be ruled by their parents. They owe a duty of obedience to their parents while they are cherished, fed, and educated by them, but this duty ceases as soon as they can fend for themselves. Paternal authority is different from political, arising from other causes and serving other ends. Men, of course, need government just as children need parental care, though the need is less pressing; but it does not follow that, because they need government, they cannot take care of themselves. On the contrary, they take care of themselves by establishing government; they are the only judges of their needs and of what they must do to meet them.

Locke is quite ready to admit that political government may have arisen from paternal power. 'Thus', he says, 'it was easy and almost natural for children by a tacit and almost natural consent, to make way for the father's authority and government. They had been accustomed in their childhood to follow his direction . . . and when they were men, who was fitter to rule them?'[1] Nevertheless, though the first magistrate may have been a father, his political authority differed essentially from his paternal power. For true political authority rests only on consent.

Men put themselves under government to preserve their property; that is, their lives, liberties, and estates. In the state of nature they had the law of nature to guide them. But they must, from time to time, have differed about the law or about its application to particular cases. They must therefore have felt a need for 'an established, settled known law, received and allowed by common consent to be the standard of right and wrong', and also for 'a known and indifferent judge, with authority to determine all differences according to the established law', and lastly for a 'power to back and support the sentence when right, and to give it due execution'.[2] By putting themselves under government, men do not give up *all* their rights, but only those which must be surrendered for the common good, which is the preservation of freedom or property in the larger sense. In particular, they give up their right to punish.

No government has absolute authority, but only as much as it needs for the common good. 'Thus the law of nature', says Locke, 'stands

[1] Ibid., Ch. VI, § 75.
[2] Ibid., Ch. IX, §§ 124-6.

an eternal rule to all men, legislators as well as others.'[1] It is for the
people to decide whether or not the government is exercising power
properly 'to the public good of society'.[2] The legislative power, which
for Locke is supreme in every civil society, is 'only a fiduciary power
to act for certain ends',[2] so that the people always retain the right to
remove or alter the legislature should they find it untrue to the trust
reposed in it. How, exactly, are they to exercise this right? Apparently,
by rebellion; for against an abuse of trust by their rulers 'the people
have no remedy . . . but to appeal to Heaven';[3] that is to say, to
force.

Though the right of rebellion is the ultimate sanction against abuse
of power, it is possible to take precautions to make such abuse less
likely. The legislative and executive powers ought to be placed in
separate hands, for 'it may be too great a temptation to human
frailty, apt to grasp at power, for the same persons who have the
power of making laws to have also in their hands the power to
execute them'.[4] But, though Locke thinks it desirable for these two
powers to be separate, he does not insist that they must be so, if
government is to be by consent of the governed. About the judicial
power, which presumably he includes in the executive, Locke says
nothing. The legislative power is unalterable in the hands where the
people have once placed it, for no one not authorized to do so by the
people should have the power to make law.

We have seen that Locke, in the early chapters of the *Second
Treatise*, conceived of consent as something free, deliberate, and personal. This stronger sense of it survives into the eighth chapter, where
we find him saying: 'Whatever engagements or promises any one
made for himself, he is under the obligation of them, but cannot by
any compact whatsoever bind his children or posterity.'[5] Then, suddenly, after this clear and bold statement, we find an abrupt transition
to a much weaker sense of consent; we find Locke arguing that a man,
when he inherits his father's property, 'by that act alone gives consent
to the government his father owed obedience to'. 'And thus', he
continues, 'the consent of free men, born under government . . . being
given separately in their turns, as each comes to be of age, and not in
a multitude together, people take no notice of it, and thinking it not
done at all, or not necessary, conclude they are naturally subjects as
they are men'.[6] It is enough, for the moment, to notice that this
argument involves an abrupt retreat from the bold position that

[1] Ibid., Ch. XI, § 135.
[2] Ibid., Ch. XIII, § 149.
[3] Ibid., Ch. XIV, § 168.
[4] Ibid., Ch. XII, § 143.
[5] Ibid., Ch. VIII, § 116.
[6] Ibid., Ch. VIII, § 117.

Locke first took up; its implications for his general theory of government I shall consider in a moment.

Locke's account of property, in the narrower and more usual sense of external possessions, is almost as important a part of his political theory as his notion of consent. God, he says, gave the world to all men in common to make use of to the best advantage to preserve life and liberty. But what God provides is not often, in its natural form, immediately useful to men; it has to be made useful by their labour. Since man has an original property in his own person, his labour belongs to himself. Therefore, whatever he mixes his labour with, he takes out of the common store and makes it his own, so that no one but himself has the right to use it, except with his permission. 'Whatsoever, then, he removes out of the state that Nature hath provided and left it in, he hath mixed his labour with it, and joined to it something that is his own, and thereby makes it his property.'[1]

The law of nature, which gives man the right to acquire property by mixing his labour with what God provides for all men's use, also sets limits to what he can acquire. 'As much as anyone can make use of to any advantage of life before it spoils, so much he may by his labour fix a property in.'[2] If he takes more, he 'invades his neighbour's share'; that is to say, he takes what he cannot use, and so prevents someone else taking it who could use it. Included in the notion of spoiling is allowing anything to go to waste; for Locke says that 'as much land as a man tills, plants, improves, cultivates, and can use the product of, so much is his property'.[3] Notice that Locke says that a man can, by his labour, take as much from the common store as he can use 'to any advantage of life'. This would seem to imply that every man is the sole judge of what he can use to advantage. He may not take more than he can use, for God has given the world to all men in common for their use; but so long as he uses it, he is not accountable to other men for the use he makes of it. This is, I think, implied by Locke's answer to the question: how can we know that anyone has taken more than he can use; that he has, to use Locke's own words, 'invaded his neighbour's share'? The only answer given is that he has allowed it to spoil or, if it is land, has allowed it to go to waste. Provided you do not allow what you have mixed your labour with to spoil, and provided you go on mixing labour with it, if such mixing is needed to prevent spoiling or waste (e.g. provided you keep cultivable land in cultivation), you are presumably using your property to some advantage; and thus you retain your right to it against all comers.

When what you make your own is perishable, you can usefully take only a small amount; but when it is not perishable and does not

1 Ibid., Ch. V, § 26.
2 Ibid., Ch. V, § 30.
3 Ibid., Ch. V, § 31.

require regular cultivation to prevent its going to waste, you can accumulate as much as you like. Locke tells us that men invented money for their mutual convenience, and thereby created something that could be accumulated in any amount without spoiling or going to waste. Money was adopted by a general tacit consent, for its usefulness was soon apparent to everyone. Locke has not a word to say against the vast accumulations of wealth and the inequalities made possible by the invention of money.

III. LOCKE'S CONCEPTION OF SOCIETY AND OF CONSENT

I have deliberately summarized Locke's theory in a way that brings out sharply the two most important parts of it: the doctrine that all legitimate political authority rests on consent, and the account of how property, in the sense of the right to external possessions, arises. These two parts of his theory are closely connected; for Locke, though he thinks it the duty of rulers to protect their subjects' natural rights, their property in the larger sense, also supposes that political authority was established by consent largely for the preservation of property in the narrower sense, and believes that valid consent can often be inferred when property is inherited. The son who inherits his father's estate thereby consents to the government recognized by his father.

Locke, unlike Hobbes, supposes that property, the exclusive right to external possessions, can exist and valid contracts be made even where there is no government to protect or enforce them. This has rightly been taken for an attack on Hobbes, who held that covenants involving mutual confidence are unreasonable until there is a power strong enough to enforce them. But it is, I think, more than an attack on Hobbes; it is also a denial that it is as social creatures, as creatures formed and disciplined by society, that men come to have rights and obligations.

It has often been said that Locke, by allowing that there can be genuine rights and obligations between men even in the absence of government, shows that he has a more adequate notion than Hobbes of what society is. Unlike Hobbes, he does not suppose that all society is political. His state of nature is a kind of society. That, indeed, is why his account of how legitimate government is established by contract is the more plausible of the two. This is the claim often made for Locke.

The claim, to my mind, is misleading. No doubt, Locke's account of how legitimate government arises from contract is more plausible than Hobbes'. But it does not follow that he has a more adequate conception of society. Admittedly, if human nature and man's condition without government were as Hobbes described them, no agreement could of itself make government legitimate; and admittedly too, if that nature and that condition were as Locke described them, it does make sense to use the notion of contract to show what makes government legitimate. But to say this is not to admit that Locke had a more adequate conception of society than Hobbes had.

To have an adequate idea of society without government it is not enough merely to ascribe rights which entail duties to men in the state of nature. Society, even without government, is more than just a number of people who, quite independently of the influence of society on them, come to see themselves as having rights and duties; who owe their morality only to the light of reason in them. Society is essentially a moral order, and men are moral only because they have been disciplined in society. They are made moral in the process of adapting themselves to society, and this always involves some compulsion. But Locke tells us that they are moral merely as men and not as members of society. He does not trouble to inquire how their living together affects them psychologically and morally. Man, as a moral being, as a bearer of duties and rights, is not, for Locke, essentially a creature of society. Locke has, no more than Hobbes, a conception of a social structure, a settled environment, which, even in the absence of government, can form men's minds. Of social institutions prior to government he says not a word. Property, in his account of it, is not really a social institution; it does not exist in virtue of rules and conventions that arise only in society. It is a natural right. Locke's men in the state of nature, no less than Hobbes', are as nature and not as society makes them. They are rational creatures who are liable to get in each other's way and who set up government to avoid the inconveniences of the state of nature. They may not be by nature enemies, as Hobbes' natural men are, but this is by no means enough to make social beings of them. For Locke, as for Hobbes, natural man is a creature loose from all social discipline; he is autonomous and self-contained, and belongs to no social order, no community. There is no sense at all in Locke that it is the pressure of society on man, his being brought up to conform with established ways, which makes him sociable and moral.

It could, I think, be argued that it was precisely because Hobbes came rather nearer than Locke to having an adequate conception of society that he got himself into greater difficulties. It is sometimes more disturbing to get a glimpse of the truth than to be altogether blind to it. As I pointed out when I discussed his political theory, Hobbes believed that man is not by nature sociable; and by sociable he meant something more than 'inclined to enjoy other men's company', he meant 'fit for society'. He spoke of man's being made fit for society by education. He understood that it needs social discipline of some kind to teach men to be sociable and law-abiding. Unfortunately, he was too ready to assume either that all effective discipline is political, or perhaps that no other kind of discipline can be effective except where there is government. He also had too narrow and mean a conception of what is involved in being social and law-abiding. But, for all that, he came closer than Locke to understanding that society is a form of discipline, and that a long process of education or adjustment is needed to make anyone sociable.

It was perhaps because he did come closer to this understanding that he was less inclined than Locke to attribute to natural man some of the qualities which are only acquired in society. For instance, he denied what Locke afterwards asserted, that 'keeping of faith belongs to men as men and not as members of society'.[1] Since Hobbes took it for granted that all society involves government, he had perforce to conclude that it is only under government that men can rely on one another's doing what they agree to do. At the same time, to explain the legitimacy of government, he chose to use the fiction of a social contract. Thus he put himself in a quandary that Locke avoided; he tried to show how the right of the sovereign to obedience derives from an agreement made between persons having no obligation to obey unless the sovereign is strong enough to enforce obedience.

Locke, of course, had a more usual and more plausible conception of rights and duties than Hobbes had. His rights entail duties, even in the state of nature. His laws of nature impose genuine obligations, not only to God, but also to men; whereas Hobbes' natural right is only absence of obligation, and his laws of nature are the commands of a God who scarcely requires obedience until there is a human power strong enough to enforce it. Locke was more plausible in this respect because he accepted more traditional and perhaps less sophisticated ideas about morality. He believed that men are moral because they are by nature rational, and can therefore discover, merely by reflecting on what is involved in being human, how they ought to behave. Now Hobbes, albeit confusedly, was inclined to deny that men are moral by nature, and therefore felt the need to look more closely at what Locke took for granted. Unfortunately, he did not look closely enough, and instead of explaining morality, explained it away. Yet Locke's more adequate (and also more orthodox) conception of morality does not reveal a better understanding either of what social life involves or of human nature. If Hobbes was wrong in treating morality as obedience to positive law, human or divine, Locke was no less wrong when he said that men are moral merely as men and not as members of society.

Locke, like Suarez, Grotius, and Pufendorf, begins by treating con-

---

[1] Ibid., Ch. II, § 14.

sent as something personal and deliberate. It is here that he and they differ from the general run of mediaeval political philosophers, who had justified the supremacy of custom on the ground that it is generally accepted and therefore expresses the permanent will of the community. Custom, according to their view, rests on natural law but, unlike that law, is not universal; it contains the natural law within it but adapted to the circumstances of particular peoples. Men do not decide what custom is; they do not consciously accept it. They scarcely ever call it in question; they merely do what is expected of them, and have a sense that they are acting rightly when they do so. Consent, so conceived, is not deliberate and voluntary. But for the seventeenth-century philosophers of natural law, Locke among them, it is of the essence of consent that it is an act of choice, whereby the chooser lays an obligation on himself. No doubt, this conception of it gets them into all kinds of difficulties, and they resort to all kinds of shifts to get out of the difficulties. They repeatedly go back on their own assumptions, though without themselves noticing that they do so. They speak of 'virtual' or 'tacit' or 'presumed' consent, without ever admitting that consent so qualified is no longer an act of choice. Some of them, in spite of their belief in natural freedom and the necessity of consent, are apologists of absolute government. Yet the notion of consent they begin with is clear enough, whatever may become of it afterwards as they strive to accommodate their doctrine that all legitimate human authority rests on consent to the actual facts. Consent, for them, is always the act of a person who knows, or may be presumed to know, what he is committing himself to by that act. The mediaeval idea was that the authority of custom rests on its being generally accepted, because this general acceptance shows that custom is adapted to men's needs and conforms to their sense of right. Custom is not arbitrary; it is not imposed by some men on others, and yet its authority does not rest on its being separately accepted by each person bound by it. Whether a man likes it or not, he must in practice accept it, not because he has agreed to do so, but because it is generally accepted; because it is the 'permanent will' of the community he belongs to. Locke's notion of consent, as he expounds it in the early chapters of his book, goes clean contrary to this mediaeval position.

According to Locke, the only natural obligation of an adult man to other men, the only obligation he is under whether he likes it or not, is not to injure them; or in other words, to respect in them the rights he claims for himself. Every other obligation he must take upon himself voluntarily. He need not marry, but if he does he must support his wife. He need not have children, but if he does he must protect and educate them. He need not enter into civil society, but if he does, he must keep his part of the bargain. Becoming a member of society is, indeed, conceived of by Locke as something very much akin to making a bargain.

Locke took this extreme position because it seemed to him to follow from what he said about man's natural freedom. If man has natural rights which are prior to government and has no obligation in the state of nature except to respect the same rights in others (that is to say, to obey the laws of nature), then surely he can owe no duty of obedience to any man unless he has agreed to obey? Government exists to secure our freedom, our natural rights. How, then, can it be legitimate unless its authority rests on our consent? To Locke it seemed obvious that it could not be.

He was, I think, mistaken. It is not obvious, and only seems to be so if we do what Locke did: if we run two quite different questions together without noticing that they are different: if we ask, how could government be rightfully established among creatures without government and having no obligation except to respect each other's natural rights? and then suppose that the answer to this question will tell us what is needed to make *any established government* legitimate. Where there is no government and no one has any obligation to another man except to respect his natural rights, it is difficult to see how anyone could rightfully impose government on anyone else without his consent. Government is then an untried device; it may or may not do what is intended of it, which is to preserve natural rights more effectively than they are preserved in the state of nature. In a situation of that kind, it is difficult to see how those who want government could rightfully impose it on those who do not. But where government already exists, the situation is no longer the same. Where government in fact protects men's rights, they ought to obey it whether or not they have consented to do so.

Locke says that it is everyone's duty to respect the rights of other people, and also that everyone has a natural right to punish offences against the law of nature. This right to punish is, as we have seen, more than a right of self-defence; it implies a right to take action to ensure that the law of nature is respected. Government, if it really does ensure that the law of nature is respected, is a proper exercise of this right. What does it matter how the institutions that protect freedom (i.e. natural right) were first established? If it is my right to preserve my own freedom and my duty to respect the freedom of others, then it is my duty to accept these institutions, even though I never agreed to do so. The right of everyone to be consulted at the imagined first setting up of government does not arise merely from everyone's having natural rights; it arises from those rights and the imagined situation. There is then no government, and it is proposed to set one up. The issue and effects are uncertain. Therefore everyone ought to be consulted.

Even in this imaginary situation, it does not follow that the decision to set up government, to be valid, must be unanimous: that those who want to try the experiment have no right to do so unless everyone agrees that it should be tried. Those who want government have a right against those who do not that they shall make reasonable provision to enable them to get it; and those who do not want it have a right against those who do that they shall make reasonable provision to allow them to escape it. What is reasonable provision must depend on the circumstances. If most people want government and only a few do not, then the few ought to move away from the place where it is proposed to establish it and accept fair compensation for any property they cannot take with them. But if most people do not want it, then those who do must either make up their minds to do without it or else remove themselves and establish it elsewhere. In either case, there is no need for all who are consulted to come to the same decision. Provided that all are consulted, and that reasonable provision is made for the minority to get their way without preventing the majority from getting theirs, everyone's natural right to freedom has been respected. We can then say that the political community is established with the deliberate consent of everyone who joins it. But the need for this consent arises only because there is no government, and a decision has therefore to be taken to set one up. Where there already is a government, where there is no need to set one up, it does not follow, merely because everyone is by nature free (i.e., has certain natural rights), that he cannot be required to obey unless he has agreed to do so.

If Locke had seen this, he would not have argued, as he did, from everyone's having a right not to have government imposed on him against his will when it is first proposed to establish it, to no one's having a duty to obey it unless he has agreed to obey. But, unfortunately, he did not see it, and so was driven to some odd expedients to show that men have agreed to obey even when they appear not to have done so. Just as it is easy, once you have imagined a state of nature, to go on to imagine people freely and deliberately joining together to form a political society, so it is difficult to explain how, once that society is long established, every adult person subject to it consents to the subjection. Locke, to get over the difficulty, argued that consent can be tacit; indeed, so tacit, that the people who give it do not notice that they have done so.

According to Locke, a man consents tacitly to obey the government whenever he inherits property. Let us examine his argument more closely. 'Commonwealths not permitting any part of their dominions to be dismembered, nor to be enjoyed by any but those of their community, the son cannot ordinarily enjoy the possessions of his father but under the same terms his father did, by becoming a member of the society, whereby he puts himself presently under the government he finds there established, as much as any other subject of that commonwealth.'[1] In other words, because governments lay down certain conditions for the enjoyment of property within their dominions, anyone who inherits property consents to the authority of the government within whose dominions that property is situated. He could refuse his inheritance. If he accepts it, he also accepts the conditions laid down by the government for the holding of property within its dominions, and this acceptance is a tacit consent to the government's authority.

Now, this argument does not square with Locke's account of property. Property, he says, is a natural right *prior* to government. What I own is mine by a right not created by government. Suppose I am not under government and then by my own free choice put myself under it. I pledge myself to obey as long as the government protects my natural rights, including my property. It is not, however, from my owning property that my duty of obedience arises but from my consent. The government protects my property because I have promised obedience; but my right to bequeath that property to my son and his right to inherit it were not created by the government. The rights of bequest and inheritance are both natural rights. My consenting to obey the government so long as it protects my property does not of itself lay upon me the obligation not to bequeath my property to my son except on the condition that he too obeys the government.

In support of the argument I have just considered, Locke puts forward another. He says: 'By the same act, therefore, whereby any one unites his person, which was before free, to any commonwealth, by the same he unites his possessions, which were before free, to it also; and they become both of them, person and possessions, subject to the government and dominion of the commonwealth as long as it hath a being.'[2] Notice that Locke says 'as long as *it*' (the commonwealth) and not as long as *he* (the person) 'hath a being'. The person dies, but because his possessions continue in being after his death they are, for some mysterious reason, still subject to the commonwealth. Just what is meant by saying that possessions are 'subject to the commonwealth'? Being inanimate, they clearly do not owe a duty of obedience. To say they are subject to the commonwealth is only to say that the commonwealth has a right to regulate their use. As they can only be used by persons, this amounts to saying that those persons are subject to the commonwealth. Thus, the first holder of a piece of property, who by his consent makes it 'subject to the commonwealth', by that same consent binds his heirs to subjection if they decide to exercise their right to inherit what is bequeathed to them. But this argument is clearly no better than the first. The right of bequest and the right

[1] Ibid., Ch. VIII, § 117.
[2] Ibid., Ch. VIII, § 120.

of inheritance (being rights of property) are natural rights, and there-fore a man does not hold them only on conditions which a government chooses to lay down, merely because an ancestor once promised to obey that government while it protected his natural rights. If a government were to say to a man's heirs: 'You cannot take what is bequeathed to you unless you admit that you are as much subject to our authority as your father was', it would be invading a natural right, and therefore breaking its trust. Indeed, this argument of Locke's denies one of his basic assumptions: that a man's consent can never bind his children and posterity. If I promise to obey a government while it protects my property, I do not thereby bind my son to obey it if he inherits that property, for I have a natural right to bequeath my property to him and he has a natural right to take his inheritance.[1]

Of course, it is true that a man, by inheriting property, does put himself under an obligation to obey government. Government protects property and makes possible its peaceful transference from one person to another, and anyone who benefits from government owes a duty of obedience to it. Locke is right in holding that even a man who takes lodging for a week or who travels freely on the highway has a duty to obey the laws that make safe lodging and travel possible. Everyone admits the duty in all these cases. But the duty does not arise from consent, either open or tacit; not at least if consent is taken to be (and Locke so took it) a voluntary act intended by the doer of it to give other people a right they would otherwise not have.

It might be objected that this is pressing Locke too hard. He was sometimes a careless reasoner, and if we take him up whenever he gives us a chance of doing so, we can reckon up against him a long account of confusion and poor logic. The word consent has many meanings; and surely it is sheer pedantry to insist that Locke should have stuck all through his book to the one he began with. But that is not in the least what I want to do. I want to say no more than this: since it was Locke's purpose to distinguish between legitimate government and tyranny, and since he believed that it is the consent of the governed that makes government legitimate, he ought to have used the word consent in ways which make it possible to distinguish between legitimate government and tyranny. Let him by all means

---

[1] In Chapter VIII, § 116, Locke speaks of a father making it a condition of his son's enjoying the possessions left to him that he should 'be of the community'. In the same chapter, in §§ 121 and 122, he distinguishes between the 'express promise and compact' which make a man a 'perpetual subject' of a commonwealth and the tacit consent which binds him to obey its laws only while he enjoys its protection. Neither of these points really touches my argument. Moreover, the second point, if we take it literally, obliges us to conclude that, while all naturalized citizens are 'perpetual subjects' and members of the commonwealth, the native-born for the most part are not.

use the word in more than one sense; let him speak, if he wishes, of open and tacit consent. All that is required of him is that he should so use the word that we can know when government has the consent of the governed and when it has not. After all, his purpose was not to show that no government has this consent, nor yet that every government has it; his purpose was to discriminate between governments that have it and governments that do not have it. He wanted to put consent forward as a criterion of legitimacy.

The case against Locke is that he failed in his own purpose. If a man's consent is his deliberate and voluntary agreement, and if nothing but a man's consent can make it his duty to obey government, then most people at most times and in most places have no duty of obedience. This was a conclusion that Locke rightly wanted to avoid. He therefore felt the need to abandon the position he took up to begin with and to use the word consent in other and weaker senses. Unfortunately he went to the other extreme, and gave the name consent to almost any action that creates an obligation to obey. It was perhaps inevitable, given the initial bias of his doctrine, that he should do so. If you begin by assuming that only consent creates a duty of obedience, you are only too ready to conclude that whatever creates that duty must be consent.

Whatever a man does which involves his taking advantage of the order maintained by government puts him under an obligation to obey it. The obligation is not, of course, unconditional, but is not the less real for that. Every government, however bad, maintains some kind of order, and everyone living under it benefits, in one way or another, from that order. Everybody is clearly obliged to obey the government in many things, even when he is rightly plotting to overthrow it by force. Therefore, if there really is no duty of obedience except where there has been consent, everyone has always consented to any government in whose dominions he finds himself.

We have seen that Locke, when he elaborated his doctrine that political obligation arises from consent, took not much interest in the actual machinery of government. He never seriously attempted to link up his doctrine of consent with a theory of parliamentary representation. I am not blaming him for the omission, which is typical of political theory in his day in spite of the great play made with man's natural freedom and the popular origins of governmental authority. But I do suggest that if Locke had taken a serious interest in the structure of government by consent, he would not have begun, as he did, with an impossibly stringent and narrow sense of consent and then passed on to a uselessly wide one.

True, Locke thought it best that legislative authority should be vested in collective bodies[1] and also strongly advised the separation

[1] See Ch. VII, § 94.

of the executive and legislative powers.[1] But he did not insist that an elected legislature is indispensable to government by consent. He was ready to admit that the people may, when they first set up government, place the legislative power, which he calls supreme, wherever they like; they may even, if they are so disposed, place it in the hands of an hereditary monarch.[2] Monarchy, aristocracy, and demoncracy are all, on Locke's assumptions, equally legitimate, equally government by consent, provided they are established in the first place by common agreement and that everyone who afterwards becomes subject to them gives his tacit consent in any of the ways that Locke describes. As we have seen already, since these ways include not only inheriting property, but even taking lodgings or travelling on the roads, this almost comes down to saying that a man gives his tacit consent whenever he does anything he could not safely or conveniently do in the absence of government. If even an hereditary monarch, with no elected parliament to assist him, can have authority to make laws, it follows that no special device, no general election or other method of consulting the people, is needed to make consent possible. Consent is given whenever subjects go about the ordinary lawful business of their lives.

Locke requires more than tacit consent in only one case. In the eleventh chapter of the *Treatise,* he says that the prince or senate 'can never have a power to take to themselves the whole, or any part of their subjects' property, without their own consent'.[3] The context makes it clear that consent, in this case, is something more than can be given by merely inheriting property or travelling on the highway. Locke makes a point of distinguishing between the power of the prince or the senate to make regulations controlling the use subjects may make of their property (which is an ordinary legislative power which need not be exercised by an elected body, unless it was stipulated that it should be when the form of government was decided), and the power to levy taxes. Only the second power, to be legitimate, *always* requires a form of consent which is not given in the mere process of living a law-abiding life. It always requires more than mere tacit consent. The right to tax property must always be expressly granted by the people to their rulers. Without troubling to consult you, the government may have your consent to anything it does for the common good, except when it requires you to pay taxes. You need not pay them unless they have been voted by your representatives.

No doubt, a good case can be made, on historical and practical grounds, for holding that people ought not to be taxed without their consent. 'No taxation without representation' is not even a peculiarly

---

[1] Ch. XII, § 143 and Ch. XIV, § 159.
[2] Ch. X, § 132.
[3] Ibid., Ch. XI, § 139, also § 140.

English principle; it is rooted in mediaeval conceptions of good government. You will find as ardent a champion of unlimited royal power as Bodin admitting that the King of France, despite his sovereignty, cannot take away his subjects' property without their consent. Clearly, if the king needs his subjects' consent to tax them, he cannot go nearly as far as he otherwise might in imposing his will on them. Bodin understood this as well as Locke. Yet Bodin was far indeed from believing that governmental authority is legitimate only if it is exercised with the people's consent. Locke's views about taxation are quite sensible in themselves and rest on an old and venerable and justifiable tradition, but they do not fit in with the rest of his theory. If the prince can make laws with his subjects' consent without troubling to consult them, why need he consult them to get their consent to taxation? Or, to put the opposite and more pointed question, if he needs to consult them to get their consent to taxation, how can he have their consent in other matters unless he consults them?

If the people's consent can be had without consulting them, the question must arise, How do we know that they *do not* consent? How do we know when authority has ceased to be legitimate and has become oppressive? We can find in Locke's *Treatise* no direct answer to this question. We can, however, venture to give one. We have seen that, if we accept his examples of what constitutes tacit consent, we virtually have to conclude that a man gives his consent to government merely by going lawfully about his business. If this is so, we are left with only one possible answer to our question: we can know that people do not consent only when they cease to obey on the ground that government is oppressive. They withdraw their consent by challenging the authority of the government. What Locke understands by tacit consent is so wide that in practice it leaves the subject with no means of withholding his consent except by civil disobedience or resistance.[1] Locke's purpose is to show that the duty of obedience arises from consent, and yet he stretches the notion of consent so far that in the end he virtually makes obedience imply consent. We consent to obey by obeying. Obedience creates the obligation to obey. But this is absurd.

In saying all this, I have not lost sight of Locke's strong preference for a separation of the legislative and executive powers, nor the passages in the *Treatise* where he speaks of the 'Legislative' as if it were an assembly. In one place, with England clearly in mind, he even suggests that, where the Legislative consists partly of representatives chosen by the people and representation has become grossly unequal as between different parts of the country, the Executive, having the

---

[1] The man who commits a crime from hope of private gain does not withhold consent. He withholds it only if he justifies his disobedience on the ground that the government has abused its authority.

power to convoke the Legislative, might remedy this defect.[1] But the fact remains that Locke nowhere makes it a *condition* of there being government by consent that authority to make laws should belong to an elected assembly. Where, as in Chapter VII, § 90, he condemns absolute monarchy as inconsistent with civil society and says that the absolute prince is in a state of nature in relation to his subjects, he is only attacking the doctrine that the prince is above the law and his subjects owe him unconditional obedience; he is not suggesting that, except where legislative power belongs to an elected assembly, there is no government by consent. The argument of the *Treatise* is emphatically not that political power is only legitimate where there is what, since Locke's time, we have learnt to call representative government; it is rather that political power is legitimate only when it is exercised with the consent of the governed. Today it may seem to many that the second argument, if it is to amount to anything definite, must be equivalent to the first; but at the end of the seventeenth century it did not seem so, even to the author of the *Second Treatise*.

Certainly, Locke thought it best that legislative power should be vested in an assembly; and, though he did not say that the assembly (or any part of it) should be elected, he did argue that, where it is elected, it is a breach of trust in the executive to corrupt the representatives or to bribe or intimidate the voters.[2] There are several indications in the *Treatise* that Locke greatly preferred the English system of government of his day to, say, the French. But we must not allow this strong preference to mislead us. Nowhere in the *Treatise*, except when he speaks of taxation, does he attempt to establish a connection between the giving of consent and the choosing of representatives. He does not use the notion of consent to make a case for representative government; he uses it only to argue that political authority is always limited by the ends it ought to serve, so that, where those who have this authority do not serve those ends, their subjects have a right to resist them or to get rid of them.

It has been said – I think rightly – that, when Locke's *Second Treatise* is thoroughly sifted, what we are left with is not so much a doctrine of consent as a doctrine of resistance. The duty of obedience is conditional: government exists, not for the benefit of those who govern, but for the good of their subjects, who have the right to resist their rulers when they are oppressive. Now, there is nothing startling about this doctrine, which to most people today seems both commonplace and true. The doctrine, taken in itself, has no logical connection with the notion of consent. Logically, there is no difficulty about holding that subjects may rightfully resist an oppressive government, whether or not they have consented to its authority. Yet Locke

---

[1] Ch. XIII, §§ 147-158.
[2] Ch. XIX, § 222.

felt the need to derive the conclusion that oppressive government may be rightfully resisted from the premise that it is the consent of the governed that makes government legitimate.

Why did he feel this need? Simply because what now seems obvious to us did not seem so in his day. Everyone agreed, then as now, that government exists for the good of the governed, but not everyone concluded that therefore subjects have a right to overthrow oppressive government. Even Filmer, against whom Locke wrote his first *Treatise*, was ready to admit that the king ought to rule for his subjects' good; but the king, he said, is responsible to God alone for how he rules, because his authority comes from God. Locke's reply is that the king is also responsible to the people, because his authority also comes from them, and is not legitimate unless he rules with their consent. The connection between Locke's doctrine of consent and his doctrine of resistance is less logical than historical. If Locke had not argued as he did, his argument would probably have carried less weight with his contemporaries. It was only natural that Locke, writing when it was still widely denied that government could be rightfully resisted merely for being oppressive, should have felt the need to argue that allegiance is always conditional, because government holds its power in trust from the people to govern them well. If it breaks its trust, the people may rise against it; and it is for them alone to decide when the trust has been broken. It was not enough for Locke to say bluntly, 'the people, when they are oppressed, have the right to revolt'; he felt impelled to add, 'because they consented to obey only while their rulers governed them well'. Logically an unnecessary addition, but, at the time it was made, a persuasive one; and all the more persuasive for being sincere.

If we take it by itself, apart from his doctrine of consent, Locke's doctrine of resistance is clear, forceful, and adequate. In his fourteenth chapter he says: 'And where the body of the people or any single man, are deprived of their right, or are under the exercise of a power without right, having no appeal on earth, they have a liberty to appeal to Heaven whenever they judge the cause of sufficient moment.'[1] The appeal to heaven here referred to is, of course, not prayer but rebellion. Any man may rebel if he judges the cause of sufficient moment, whether the injury complained of is done to himself or to other people; and he may also rebel, even though no injury is done to private persons, if the ruler exercises a power he has no right to.

I do not see how it is possible to object to this argument. The right of resistance cannot be confined, as it was by mediaeval writers and by the author of the *Vindiciae*, to parliaments, courts of law, or lesser magistrates. For these may themselves be oppressive. Nor can it be restricted to the people generally or to large groups. If I believe that

---

[1] Ibid., Ch. XIV, § 168.

the government is oppressive and yet have no right to rebel unless most people share by belief, how can I know whether or not I have that right? If I set about trying to discover how much support I am likely to get, the government may stop me. Have I then the right to rebel? But for all I know, most people may want the government to stop me. The right of rebellion is, *ex hypothesi,* not a legal right, and can therefore never be confined to some definite proportion of the people; for any government worth the name will see to it that would-be rebels cannot make sure beforehand just how much support they can count on. Rebel leaders get most of the recruits coming to them after they have started operations. Rebellion is always something of a leap in the dark, and is apt to be the more so the more oppressive the government.

It has been said that Locke confines the right of active resistance to the people generally and does not allow it to the lone citizen or to a minority, except in self-defence. I must confess that I was once inclined to believe this myself on the strength of three paragraphs in the eighteenth chapter of the *Second Treatise.*[1] There Locke first argues that resistance by only a few people is useless, and then goes on to say that he does not see how resistance is to be prevented when misgovernment affects the majority, nor yet when, though it affects only a few, it seems to threaten all, and all are persuaded in their consciences that there is a general danger. Though, taken literally, these are only opinions about the probable consequences of certain actions or about what people are likely to do, it may be that Locke meant them to be more than just this; it may be that he meant to confine the right of rebellion to the majority of the people. But, though this is possible, it is unlikely. It is probable that Locke was saying no more than that no one ought to resist government by force, except in self-defence, unless he is persuaded in his conscience that there is widespread oppression or the danger of it. And this is surely a reasonable doctrine.

No doubt, the would-be rebel ought, *so far as he can,* to take account of other people's opinions and feelings. He ought to count the cost of his enterprise and to make a sober estimate of his chances of success. The less other people resent what he condemns as oppression, the more he should hesitate about taking drastic action, not only because such action is then less likely to succeed, but also because he ought not to risk other people's security lightly in a cause that means little or nothing to them. For one or more of several reasons, it may be wrong for a man to rebel when most other people think there is no cause for rebellion. The less others sympathize with him, the more he risks doing a great deal of harm and almost no good. He is liable to error, and is more likely to be misjudging the government when

[1] Ch. XVIII, §§ 208-210. See also Ch. XIX, § 230 and § 240.

most people disagree with him than when they agree. These are all good reasons, but none implies that a man has no right to rebel unless most people agree with him. Though many people before Locke asserted the right of rebellion, most of them hedged it about in ways that confined it to particular bodies and officials, making a sort of privilege of it. That is essentially the mediaeval or feudal conception of it. Locke placed it firmly in the hands of every man, requiring only that he should use it conscientiously for the common good and with a decent respect for the opinions of others. His doctrine of resistance is perhaps the most valuable part of his political theory.

It may seem from what I have been saying that I find no virtue at all in Locke's case for government by consent. I hope that is not the impression I have created, for I have not wished to do so. With Locke's central purpose, I have the strongest sympathy. He was concerned to safeguard freedom, which he conceived of, not as Hobbes had done, as absence of obligation in the state of nature or as the right to do what the law does not forbid in civil society, but as a moral right which it is the duty of governments to protect. Believing in freedom, he concluded that no man can have a right to command another man except with his consent; because if he had that right, the other man's freedom would be abridged as his own freedom was not, which would contravene the basic principle that all men are by nature equal. This argument, which satisfied Rousseau, Paine, Jefferson, and countless other radicals, is, as I have tried to show, not convincing. If freedom is not adequately preserved except under government, then everyone ought to obey the government while it preserves freedom, no matter whether he has consented or not.

Locke, having mistakenly decided that freedom, or the exercise of certain rights, which he called natural, requires universal consent to government, found himself obliged first to put forward a strong notion of consent, and then, in order to avoid difficulties, to replace it by a much weaker notion useless for his original purpose – which was to distinguish rightful government from tyranny. If consent is taken in his strong sense, nothing less than universal suffrage will do; and even that is not enough, for it does not ensure that everyone consents all the time. Yet Locke, as we know, was satisfied with the English Parliament of his day; he neither wanted to extend the franchise nor attempted to show how his theory could be used to justify the English system of government or to condemn James II.

Again, though there is much to be said for the principle 'no taxation without representation', it is difficult to see how that principle fits logically into Locke's general argument for government by consent. If all government, to be legitimate, requires the consent of the governed, why *must* that consent be express when it is consent to taxation but not necessarily otherwise? And lastly, acceptable though Locke's thesis is that the subject has a right to resist government if he is convinced in conscience that resistance is for the public good, it is impossible to agree with him that the subject has this right because he has no duty to obey government unless he has consented to do so. Locke did not even put himself to the trouble of showing that government by consent is unlikely to be oppressive, and thus unlikely to give just cause for resistance.

Yet, I would not deny that there is plenty to agree with in Locke's *Second Treatise*; I would say only that this plenty does not add up to a lucid and consistent political philosophy. Inspired by love of freedom and hatred of tyranny, Locke speaks out boldly, and we get his stronger sense of consent and his admirable doctrine of resistance; but he also accepts the established order, and to avoid conclusions inconsistent with it, quickly withdraws from a difficult position. As so often happens in such cases, he tries to withdraw without appearing to do so, without admitting it even to himself. That is why he ordinarily speaks of consent in his weaker sense as if it were really exactly the same as consent in his stronger sense; as if the difference lay, not in the nature of the consent, but in the manner of giving it; as if, by calling it *tacit*, he were saying only that it is not expressed in words. Just as consent can be given by writing or by word of mouth, so it can be express or tacit; it is always the same consent, however it is given. This is the impression that Locke creates during the course of his argument, and it is a false impression.

This is not to say that there is no connection between government by consent and the preservation of freedom, understood as the exercise of rights not created by government; it is to say only that this connection is not made clear by Locke's use of the notion of consent.

To see how government by consent and the preservation of freedom are connected, we must bear in mind that men need two kinds of protection. They need protection from one another as individuals; and this protection any effective government, whether or not it has their consent, can give them. Government can define men's rights and defend them adequately even though it is not responsible to them. If it does this, then its subjects have civil liberty as Hobbes understood it: they know what their rights are, they know what the law is, what it requires and what it forbids, and they can rely on the impartiality of those in authority over them. They then have security, which is the first condition of freedom: they know what they must do and must refrain from doing, and their rulers, who define these limits to their freedom, also protect their freedom inside these limits. Government, to use Hobbes' metaphor, sets hedges about us, not to impede our motion but to direct it, so that we may, as we go about our business, be as little as possible obstacles in one another's way.

There is little evidence that government is more likely to afford security to its subjects when it is responsible to them than when it is not. Its ability to do so ordinarily depends more on other things: on the power at its disposal, on the independence of the judiciary, on the principles generally accepted in governing circles. A weak government, even though it is responsible to its subjects, is likely to be timid or corrupt, or both together, and is therefore unlikely to be a scrupulous protector of rights. The condition of the people may be such that only an irresponsible government can be strong; for the people may be politically immature and not know what standards they and their rulers must respect if rights are to be impartially and effectively protected. Sometimes rights are best protected where government is virtually irresponsible, at other times where it is responsible to the wealthy and educated, and at still other times where it is responsible to the people generally.

But men may want more than the impartial enforcement of legal rights, more than protection from one another as private citizens or as servants of government. They may also want security against their rulers' governing them in ways that do violence to their sense of right, their sense of what is owing to them as rational and moral persons. Clearly, Locke thought that they do want this security also; for he, unlike Hobbes, insisted that men have rights which their rulers do not sufficiently protect merely by making their own authority effective, rights which even a strong government can infringe. If freedom is more than the secure enjoyment of legal rights, if it matters that men should be able to live as seems good to them provided they do no harm to others, then it is wrong for governments, however impartial their enforcement of legal rights, to violate their subjects' sense of justice or of right. If freedom is (as Locke thought it was) the supreme good, then it is wrong, however excellent your motive, to rule people in ways which offend deeply against their moral principles.

Now, it is reasonable to suppose that the more rulers are responsible to their subjects, the less likely it is that they will make laws or pursue policies which are offensive in this way. Moreover, the stronger the government, the greater the danger that it may make laws morally repugnant to its subjects. A government which is weak, even though it may be irresponsible, will take care not to offend its subjects, whereas a government which is both strong and irresponsible will be much less concerned not to offend them. Therefore, if subjects are to be secure from this kind of offence, the stronger the government, the more important it is that it should be responsible to the governed. If we understand by freedom under government no more than Hobbes understood by it, we may agree that the stronger the government, the more secure the freedom of its subjects; but if we understand by freedom what Locke understood by it, we need to go further, we need to insist that, the stronger a government, the more it matters that it should be responsible to its subjects if their freedom is to be preserved.

No doubt, the responsibility of rulers to their subjects where government is strong is not a sufficient condition of freedom, for the people may be ignorant and may lack political capacity. We can easily imagine situations in which responsible government would not protect freedom, even in Locke's sense of it, better than irresponsible government. Or, rather – and this, I think, is a better way of putting it – we can easily imagine situations in which the attempt to make government responsible to its subjects must fail because genuine responsibility requires in the people habits and qualities which they do not possess. Nevertheless, while conceding all this, we can still say that, where government is strong, freedom, as Locke conceived of it, unlikely to be secure except where the rulers are responsible to their subjects.

Now government, all over Western Europe, had been growing stronger for several hundred years before Locke wrote his *Treatise*. The doctrine that government is not legitimate unless it is carried on with the consent of the governed, a doctrine much more prominent in the seventeenth century than it had been in, say, the thirteenth, was itself a product of a greater fear of government, a fear due partly to the growing power of the State and partly to a deeper concern for individual freedom. It was a concern shared by Locke, and it moved him to produce his argument that rulers are answerable to their subjects for how they rule.

But, unfortunately, owing to the way in which Locke uses the notion of consent to establish his conclusion, his doctrine that rulers are responsible to their subjects is reduced to the mere assertion that subjects have the right to rebel against their rulers when they honestly believe that they are being seriously misgoverned. This assertion is by no means unimportant, and makes much better sense than many older doctrines of resistance; but it is not enough. The stronger government is, the more dangerous it is to rebel, and the less likely that rebellion will be effective. Therefore, the argument that rulers are answerable to their subjects for how they rule, where it is inspired by concern for a freedom which is more than mere security under the law, is seriously defective if it does not argue for a form of government which reduces the risk that rulers will tamper with the freedom of their subjects. Locke does suggest that rulers are less likely to do this where there is an elected legislature, but he does not insist that there must be one. He allows that there can be government by consent which is not representative government.

Of course, it is not to be held against Locke that he did not argue for democracy. Indeed, it is probable that, in his England, a legislature representing only a small part of the people was much more likely than a truly popular assembly to protect freedom. Democracy at the end of the seventeenth century, if it had been attempted, might well have proved fatal to liberty. Monarchy tempered by aristocracy may have been, in Locke's day, the form of government most favourable to liberty, the form securing it to as large a section of the people as could effectively enjoy it.

But, though it is not to be held against Locke that he did not argue for democracy, it is to be held against him that he argued for no particular form of government. From his doctrine that government is legitimate when it has the consent of its subjects, we cannot argue for one form of government in preference to another. If we take consent in his stronger sense, democracy alone is legitimate; and if we take it in its weaker sense, any government is legitimate while no one rebels against it, because rebellion is the only sufficient sign that consent is lacking. Indeed, if we take Locke's stronger sense of consent, even democracy is imperfectly justified; for if consent is personal and deliberate, no government has the consent of all its subjects. If it is true that no man can be rightfully governed except with his own freely given consent, then every government, even the most democratic, is almost certain to be to some extent oppressive.

Two things are, I hope, by this time clear: that we cannot follow Locke in holding that the duty to obey government arises from consent alone except at the cost of reducing the notion of consent to virtually nothing; and that we cannot use his doctrine of consent to distinguish between responsible and irresponsible government. True, Locke did not want to make precisely this distinction, but he did want to make another which he thought was closely allied to it, between legitimate government and tyranny. He believed that when rulers are answerable to their subjects they are less likely to oppress them, to behave like tyrants. If then Locke's account of consent will not do, what account must we substitute for it to enable us to distinguish between responsible and irresponsible government? Let me attempt an answer to this question.

We must retain Locke's stronger sense of consent, admitting that by doing so we abandon all hope of getting universal consent to any government. But in the place of his weaker sense we must put another quite different from it. Locke was not wrong to speak of two kinds of consent, though he mistook the connection between them and made the second kind too broad to serve his purpose. There is a difference between the consent which grants authority or establishes or alters a system of government and the consent which does not; and there is also a close connection between them. The difference does not lie in the manner of expression. The second kind is not the same as the first, though differently conveyed; it is not agreement presumed when silence can be fairly taken to be a mark of agreement. It may or may not involve making a deliberate choice; but what makes it an act of consent is that it is an action or failure to act which is political and creates a duty of obedience. This second kind of consent is, if you like, tacit; but that is not the important respect in which it differs from the first. For the first kind, though usually express, may also be tacit, as when those who favour a proposal which is carried are asked to keep silent. Where there is a definite choice to be made, and the convention is that silence or inaction is to be understood as preference for one alternative, there can be tacit consent even in the strong sense to the alternative actually adopted.

To mark the difference between these two kinds of consent, I shall call the first kind *direct* and the second *indirect*. Direct consent can be either express or tacit; whereas indirect consent is always tacit. These two kinds of consent are thus not the same thing differently expressed; they differ in themselves. Yet they are closely related, because only where the first kind exists do we have the conditions making possible the second kind. There is clearly a difference between consent to the government of particular persons, or to a constitution adopted by plebiscite or by an elected assembly, and consent to a political system long established; and yet both deserve to be called consent, as the tacit consent of Locke does not.

The present generation of Englishmen have not been consulted about the system of government they live under; they have inherited it from their ancestors. Yet they can, I think, be said to consent to it. Not because they own property in England or in any other way enjoy the protection of English law, nor because they put up with the system or even like it, but because they can, if they so wish, change it legally and peacefully. It does not follow, of course, that because no one tries to change it, everyone consents to it. There may be people who detest the system but do not try to change it because they despair of success, knowing that the majority are so strongly attached to it that they cannot be persuaded to change it. However democratic a system of government and however large the initiative it leaves to the ordinary citizen, we can never know for certain that everyone subject to it consents indirectly to the subjection. We can, however, assume that most people give this kind of consent. And this consent has a good deal more to it than Locke's tacit consent; it is more than mere acceptance of what you are powerless to reject.

When you vote for a person or a party that wins an election, you directly consent to his or to their authority, and you also consent indirectly to the system of government. Even when your vote is cast for persons who intend to change the system, you consent to it until it is changed. For you make use of the system in order to change it. Furthermore, by taking part in the election you consent indirectly to the authority of the persons that win it, even if you vote against them. This last consent does not depend on your approval of the system, on your thinking it right that whoever gets power under it should have power, whether or not you voted for him. Even if you dislike the system and wish to change it, you put yourself by your vote under an obligation to obey whatever government comes legally to power under the system, and this can properly be called giving consent. For the purpose of an election is to give authority to the people who win it, and if you vote knowing what you are doing and without being compelled to do it, you voluntarily take part in the process which gives authority to those people. It does not matter what your motive for voting is, any more than it matters what your motive is in making a promise. If you make a promise to someone with the intention of *not* keeping it, you are not the less bound by it because of your intention. If you make your promise voluntarily, and if you know what you are doing when you make it, your promise lays an obligation on you. Just as it is sometimes right to break a promise, so it may sometimes be right to use force against an elected government, even when you have voted for it. But that is merely to say that the obligation created by a promise or an act of consent is not absolute.

Consent, even when it is indirect, is not *any* action or failure to act which creates a duty of obedience. No doubt, whoever benefits from government is, to that extent, obliged to obey it; but this obligation does not arise from consent. Only when an action involves taking part in an election or decision is it a direct or indirect consent: a direct consent to the authority of the person or to the proposal you vote for and an indirect consent to the system you voluntarily take part in and to the result of the vote when it goes against you. A failure to act is an indirect consent only when it is abstention from voting or from legal opposition to the system when such opposition is safe and easy and might be effective. The abstention must not be enforced: it must be due either to indifference or to a man's freely choosing not to do what he easily could do. Indirect consent is not a granting of authority or permission, as direct consent is, and therefore differs from direct consent in what it is and not only in the way it is given. Yet it deserves to be called political consent because it is a free political action or failure to act which creates a duty of obedience. Admittedly, when I travel on the highroad or take lodging for a week or inherit my father's estate, I voluntarily do something that makes it my duty to respect established authority. But that much I do whenever I in any way benefit from the order maintained by government. It is only when the obligation to obey arises from something I freely do or freely abstain from doing, not just *under* government, but *about* government, to help decide who shall govern or what the political system shall be, that it can be said to arise from consent.

The argument against Locke is at bottom simple enough. No government can be said to rule with the people's consent, direct or indirect, express or tacit, unless the people can safely and legally put an end to its authority; that is to say, unless there are devices ensuring that it is in fact responsible to them. There cannot be indirect consent except where there are also direct consent and dissent. I can be said to consent to something indirectly only when I have the right to reject or to try to change it; or when I freely take part in a process of decision knowing that the decision may go against me. There cannot be indirect consent except where direct consent is safe and easy. Therefore, to give substance to the notion of indirect consent we must relate it to some established process of choosing or getting rid of governments, or of changing the political system; we must take into account the devices that make government responsible or representative.

Political consent, direct or indirect, must not be treated as a kind of contract, express or implied. Even direct political consent is not a conditional promise of obedience; its significance, the rights conferred by it and the duties undertaken, depend on the political system as a whole. Both the forms of political consent and the moral relations arising from it make it a transaction different in kind from a contract or treaty. How can we explain these differences except by taking account of the process of election and the conventions connected with it? How can we explain them except by taking account of what Locke almost completely ignored?

Locke was one of the most abstract of political philosophers, and at the same time one of the most moderate and sensible. He was abstract in his assumptions and moderate in his conclusions. There is nothing wrong with that. Political wisdom, with all deference to Burke, is not the prerogative of people who have no use for abstract reasoning. The fault of Locke's theory is that there seems to be no clear lines of argument leading from the assumptions to the conclusions. There is a great middle region left out of the *Second Treatise*. It may be that the ideas to fill it were in Locke's mind. If they were, he failed to get them down on paper.

IV. LOCKE'S ACCOUNT OF PROPERTY

We have seen that Locke uses the word property in a wider and a narrower sense: to mean the sum of a man's rights to life, liberty, and external possessions, and also to mean the right to external possessions alone. It is what he says about property in the second, the narrower, sense that I now want to consider.

Property, as Locke explains it, rests on two natural rights: the right to use what you need to preserve life and liberty, and the right to set aside for your exclusive use whatever you mix your labour with, provided it does not already belong to someone else. These two rights, as Locke defines and elaborates upon them, are not always compatible, and most of the difficulties in his account of property arise from his not having noticed this.

There are three major defects in Locke's theory of property. In the first place, the limit he sets on appropriation, the injunction to let nothing spoil or go to waste, is either irrelevant or inadequate, for it makes sense only under conditions which are in fact rare; secondly, the right of bequest, which Locke tacitly includes in the right of property, does not derive either from the right to preserve life and liberty or from the right to set aside for your own exclusive use what you have mixed your labour with; and thirdly, it does not follow, even if your mixing your labour with something gives you a right to use it to the exclusion of people who have not mixed their labour with it, that your being the *first* to mix labour with something gives you the right not to share it with anyone who subsequently mixes his labour with it. Let me consider these three points in turn.

(a). The injunction to let nothing spoil or go to waste is either irrelevant or inadequate, except under the most unlikely conditions. If natural resources were unlimited in quantity and fit for immediate use, there would be no need for anyone to mix his labour with anything, and therefore no need for property. Property arises because man has to work on what nature provides to make it fit for his use. If natural resources were unlimited, and yet not fit for immediate use, there would still be a need for rules of property; or otherwise the lazy could exploit the industrious by seizing the fruits of their industry. But, in that case, though there would have to be rules of property, the injunction about letting nothing spoil or waste would be useless. For if natural resources are unlimited, however much I spoil or let go to waste of what I have mixed my labour with, there is always enough for other people to mix their labour with. I cannot, by my waste, 'invade my neighbour's share'.

But if what nature provides is exhaustible, why should the right to acquire property through labour be limited *only* by the injunction to let nothing spoil or waste? Why should it not be limited by the duty to leave enough over for other people to make their own? Why take it for granted that, if nobody takes more than he can use without letting it spoil or waste, there will always be enough left over for everyone to be able to take as much as he can use to his own advantage? To limit the right of appropriation in this peculiar way makes sense only where natural resources are just scarce enough to ensure that, if they are wasted, some people will get less than they can use to advantage, and just abundant enough to ensure that, if they are not wasted, everyone will get as much as he can use to advantage. But this is a most unlikely situation.

As a matter of fact, Locke never troubled to enquire what conditions must hold to make sense of his rule about letting nothing spoil or waste. He probably condemned waste because he did not like it, without looking closely into its social consequences. According to the fashion of his day, he thought he could justify an institution like property by explaining how it arose or why men first needed it. Not unreasonably, he took it for granted that property first arose in sparsely populated countries among men whose needs were not great, where the work any man could do *or get done* was very limited, because he could in practice appropriate little more than the fruits of his own and his family's labour. In such a situation, a man who took too much land would soon find some of it going to waste. And since men are greedy, it might easily happen that, even if land were abundant, there would not be enough for everyone, unless there were a rule that no man might take more land than he could use to some advantage. And yet (and this is the crux of the matter) even in this case, takers of land, if they let it go to waste, would be 'invading their neighbour's share', not because they wasted land, not because they took more than they could use to advantage, but because they took what other people needed more than they did.

In itself, the rule about not taking more than you can use, about not wasting or spoiling, takes into account only your own interest and not other people's. Since you could spoil and waste, even when there was more than enough left over for other people, the true ground of the rule, *Let nothing waste or spoil*, is your own advantage. Why exert yourself to produce more than you need? Why labour in vain?

This rule of Locke's is well enough suited to simple farmers living in a fertile and thinly populated country, where every family works to maintain itself, taking almost nothing to market, and where there is no labour to hire. But in a densely populated country where there are many people without land, a man can easily accumulate a vast estate without letting an acre of it waste or allowing any of its produce to spoil. He can use every part of his estate to some advantage, either his own or other people's. He can hire labour and cultivate his land intensively, using part of the produce to feed the men he hires and exchanging the rest against other products. However luxurious his style of living, however much richer he is than other people, he wastes nothing and lets nothing spoil.

Even in a natural economy, where no money is used, some men can become vastly richer than others; and can do so, not because they work harder, but because they own land and the others do not. All this they can do without wasting anything or letting it spoil. There need be no fertile acre left uncultivated nor anything produced on their estates which is not used to someone's advantage, their own or other people's.

Indeed, even in a sparsely populated and very fertile and rich
I*

country, a few men could appropriate all the land and other natural resources and still keep Locke's rule about letting nothing waste or spoil. They could do it provided they had enough capital to attract and hire labour and could find a market for their produce. True, it is in long-settled and densely populated countries that capital first accumulates and large-scale production for the market first appears; but as soon as there is capital and there are markets, rich men can move into fertile and empty lands, and can take possession of immense natural resources without wasting or spoiling anything. It is only in a primitive subsistence economy that the amount of land a man can take is seriously limited by Locke's rule.

(b). It seemed so obvious to Locke that the natural right of property includes the right of bequest that he did not bother to prove his point. But if property arises as he says it does, this is by no means obvious. It clearly does not follow from the mere definition of property as the right of exclusive use. A man's right to use something to the exclusion of other people does not logically include the right to decide who shall use it after he is dead. The right of exclusive use and the right of bequest are different rights. They may both be called rights of property, and it may be usual for whoever has the first to have the second as well; but the second is not included in the first. A man's right of exclusive use is in no way curtailed if he has not also the right of bequest.

Locke derives the right to appropriate external objects from two other rights: the right of self-preservation and man's right of property in his own body. This first right includes, for Locke, more than the bare right to keep yourself alive; it includes the right to make provision for living commodiously, or in other words, for living as it suits you to live, provided you respect the same right in others. If you are to make adequate provision for keeping yourself alive and for living commodiously, you must be able to set things aside for your own future use, and you must be able to rely on their being to hand when you need them. You must have secure possession; you must have the right of exclusive use. This security is also a condition of freedom; for, unless you have it, you cannot live as you please, you cannot organize your life to suit yourself. There is a clear connection between the right to keep yourself alive and to live commodiously, which is the right of self-preservation, as Locke understands it, and the right to acquire things for your own exclusive use. But there is no such clear connection between the right of self-preservation and the right of bequest. It is not in the least obvious that you cannot keep alive and live commodiously and freely unless you can decide who is to have your property after you are dead.

The other source from which Locke derives the right to external possessions is man's property in his own body. His body is his, and therefore whatever he mixes the labour of his body with is his also. This argument is quaint and obscure. A man's body may be said to be his in two quite different senses: it is his as being part of him, and it is his in the same sense as his external possessions are, as something that he alone has the right to use. In whichever of these two senses we take it, it simply does not follow that, because a man's body is his, nobody else has the right to use what he has set aside or transformed with the labour of his body. This is clearly so if we take the first sense. 'His body is a part of him' is a statement of fact, whereas 'nobody else ought to use what he has set aside or transformed with the labour of his body' is a moral rule; and a moral rule cannot be derived in this simple way from a statement of fact. But even if we take the second sense, which is almost certainly what Locke meant us to do, the argument, though it may look more convincing, is not really better grounded. It is by no means obvious that, because a man has the sole right to use his own body, nobody else has the right to use what he has set aside or transformed with the labour of his body. On grounds of expediency, or because a man has the right to make adequate provision for himself, this may be a good rule; but the rule, good or bad, does not follow merely from a man's body being 'his', whether as part of him or as something which he alone has the right to use. 'My body belongs to me, and therefore what I have made with it belongs to me' is as much a *non sequitur* as 'my body is a part of me, and therefore what I have made with it belongs to me'. And, in any case, even if these arguments were valid, even if we could infer rules of property from a man's body being a part of him or from his having the sole right to use it, these rules of property would not include the right of bequest. If the right of bequest is to be justified, it must be, I think, largely on the ground that, in the long run, it promotes the general interest, but Locke never refers to any such ground. He considers only the advantage or the situation of the man who first acquires the property. It is because he has acquired it to preserve himself or because he has mixed the labour of his body with it that it belongs to him.

The right of exclusive use is only one of the several rights commonly called rights of property; the right of bequest is another, and there are still others. What Locke has done is this: he has derived one of these rights, the right of exclusive use, from the right of self-preservation, and has then taken it for granted that this right carries the others with it. This is a mistake easily made. If you take any society, you will find that certain rights, related to the same things, usually go together, so that whoever has one of them also has the others. These associated rights are all given the same name, and are treated as if they necessarily involved one another. An argument devised to establish one of them is taken to establish them all; and though, in strict logic, it does not do so, it is not the less convincing for that. Often, it is not until a demand arises for altering or abolishing some of these rights, that the argument is subjected to close scrutiny, and is either rejected or seen to have consequences more limited than was at first supposed. The contested rights are then defended, and new arguments are found to support them. The other rights which Locke ran together with the right of exclusive use to constitute the right of property have often been contested since his time by socialists; and none more so than the right of bequest. My purpose has not been to suggest that the right of bequest is or is not less defensible than other property rights, but only to show that Locke failed to explain or justify it, though he was convinced that he had done both.

(c). My third criticism of Locke's theory of property is that he passes, without seeming to notice it, from the position that what a man has mixed his labour with is his own, to the exclusion of other people who have not mixed theirs, to the quite different position, that what a man was the *first* to mix his labour with is his own even to the exclusion of other people who later mix their labour with it. The second position neither follows from the first, nor can be derived separately from the right of self-preservation, not even if we include in that right (as Locke did) more than the mere right to maintain one's life. To keep himself alive and to live commodiously, a man needs external goods for his own exclusive use, and has the right to acquire them by mixing his labour with what nature provides and no one else has appropriated. So far, so good. But, just as the right to self-preservation even thus widely understood does not allow him to appropriate as much as he pleases without caring what is left over for others, whose right to acquire property by their labour is as good as his, so it does not establish his exclusive right to what he was the *first* to appropriate against people who have no choice but to mix their labour with his property because there is nothing else left for them to mix it with. If labour has this power of creating titles to property, why only some labour and not all? Whence the privilege of the first labourers denied to those who come after them?[1]

[1] It might be objected in Locke's favour that, since every man's labour is his own, he has the right to sell it for a wage. This is true but does not affect my argument. His having the right to sell his labour does not deprive him of the right to appropriate what he mixes his labour with; he cannot justly lose this second right merely because others have appropriated all that there is to appropriate, for by so doing they have invaded his (their neighbour's) share. Were he to choose to appropriate what he produces (or were he to claim his share of a joint product), no one could rightfully deny him what he claimed. This must be so, if the right of appropriation by labour is, as Locke says it is, a natural right; for a natural right is a right which everyone possesses, and which government must therefore secure to everyone. Of course, we may insist on the labourer's right to sell his labour because we need to justify a social order where he has no choice but to sell it in order to get a living. The

Consider the case of the owner of a large estate who finds it profitable to use other men's labour on it. Why should not the labourers, by their mere labour, acquire a title to a share in his estate? Unless they worked for him, his land would go to waste; and to let something go to waste, says Locke, is to lose the right to it. The labourers cannot refuse their labour to the landowner, because there is no virgin land left for them to acquire. Yet they have the right, no less than the landowner, to preserve life and liberty; and the right to appropriate by labour derives from this right. How, then, can the work of the labourers, while it preserves the landowner's right to his land by preventing its going to waste, create no right of property in them? Can the landowner, merely because he owns the land, maintain his title to it through the work of others, even though he does not work himself? This is an odd conclusion to reach if you hold, as Locke does, that God gave all things in common to all men to use to keep themselves alive and to live commodiously, and that property, the right of exclusive use, originates in the mixing of labour with external goods.

Locke ought not to have said that a man has a right to the exclusive use of what he was the *first* to mix his labour with; he ought to have said, rather, that he has a right to the exclusive use of what he *alone* has mixed his labour with. If there is not enough left over for other people, a man cannot justly forbid them to work on what he has appropriated; for if he does, he violates their right to self-preservation. Nor do I see how he can justly refuse to share his property with them if he allows them to mix their labour with it. For they, no less than he, have a right to acquire property by their labour. No doubt, this second right derives from the right to self-preservation, but it is, none the less, a universal right. Locke calls it a 'natural right' and a natural right, by definition, is a right that everyone has. If the landless say to those who have all the land: 'let us work on your land and share it with you', they are not by that claim contesting anyone's right to acquire property by labour, but are only asserting that their right is as good as other people's. But suppose the owners of the land say to the land-less: 'Everything has been taken, and there is nothing left for you to take; you may, if you like, sell your labour to us for a wage, and so keep yourselves alive, but you may not by your labour acquire

need is plain enough, but the argument is not sound. We cannot justify the loss of one natural right by showing that those who lose it retain another right – not even if this other right is also natural.

Nor does Locke strengthen his case by saying that money, which enables men to appropriate much more than they can consume without danger of letting it spoil, came to be used by common consent. It is perfectly consistent with the natural right of appropriation by labour that men should use money if they find it convenient to do so, but it is *not* consistent with that right that they should so use money as to enable the propertied to deprive the property-less of the right.

property'; then, on Locke's premises, they act unjustly. They act unjustly because they implicitly deny that the right to acquire property by labour is a natural right, a right which belongs to everyone, so that no one can justly assert it in such a way as to deprive another person of it. The landowners could justly refuse to share their land with the landless only if by sharing it they risked starvation; only if there were not enough land to support the entire population.

The right of self-preservation and the right to acquire property by labour do not, of course, exclude all inequalities. Those who labour more have the right to more property, provided they do not by their labour deprive other people of the chance to appropriate. The right of bequest, though it does not follow from these two prior rights, is not excluded by them; it is only limited. People may, on perfectly good grounds not discussed by Locke, bequeath what they have appropriated, as long as they do so without curtailing other people's rights of self-preservation and of acquiring property by their labour. In certain unlikely conditions, it would be possible for all men to have the fundamental rights ascribed to them by Locke, and for some to be rightfully very much richer than others. But just how much inequality is compatible with these rights must depend on circumstances.

Locke's account of property was widely accepted in Europe and America even after Hume had produced a more lucid and consistent alternative to it. For Hume, like Locke, did not criticize the system of property that existed; his purpose was merely to explain it. Though Hume's explanation might be more convincing to people with a taste for abstract reasoning and sound logic, it accorded less with current conceptions. Property, for Hume, is a conventional or customary and not a natural right. But convention and custom change, as natural law and natural right do not; so that what is grounded in them is not as firmly grounded as it might be. Locke's defence of property was more reassuring than Hume's, and therefore, for all its defects, more popular.

The real challenge to Locke's theory of property came with the rise of socialism. Hume rejected Locke's initial assumption that property is a natural right, but accepted the system that assumption was meant to justify; whereas the early socialists mostly did not reject the assumption, but used it to attack what Locke was concerned to defend. They mostly admitted the right of self-preservation, as Locke had described it, and also his rule that whatever a man has applied his labour to ought to belong to him to the exclusion of others; but they demanded that these rights be carried to their logical conclusions. By seeing where Locke's arguments are defective, we can understand how it was that the early socialists could use his assumptions to reach conclusions very different from his own. That is why I have gone rather more minutely into his arguments than I would have done otherwise.

There is one great virtue in what Locke says about property. He does not justify it only as a means to security or happiness, or because it encourages industry; he also sees it as a means to liberty. This is a side of it that meant much more to him than it did, for instance, to most of the Utilitarians. It is not absurd, it is even helpful, to speak of a natural right to property, in the sense of a right that every society ought to secure to its members: a man's right to acquire by his labour an exclusive domain, an area of privacy, a degree of material independence to serve as a cushion against the outside world. Even if we are socialists, we can agree with Locke so far. To have nothing to fall back on when you are odds with your neighbours or with authority, to have nothing to sell but your labour when it is for other people to decide how you shall labour, is to be curtailed in your freedom, whether your employer is a private person or a public body.

V. CONCLUSION

I have been more critical, perhaps, of Locke's theory than of some others. If that is so, it has not been because, in my opinion, there is less that is true in it, but because so much that is true is supported by bad arguments. For all its weaknesses, Locke's political philosophy is supremely important, not only because it was so influential for a hundred years or more after he produced it, but because so much that seemed valuable to him still seems valuable to us.

Locke was deeply concerned about two things, property and freedom. He believed that they are closely connected with one another. In the wider of the two senses in which he uses the word *property*, property includes freedom, and in the narrower of the two senses, property is a means to freedom. Locke accepted the established social order whole-heartedly, though within that order most men lacked the property which he believed to be a condition of freedom. Presumably Locke knew this, and yet was not interested in redistributing the wealth so unequally distributed. In practice, therefore, he was concerned only for the freedom of a small part of the community. His desire to make property secure was so strong, and his sympathies for the class which Saint-Simon was later to call the most numerous and the most poor were so slight, that some of his critics have been loth to admit that he cared much for freedom. They see him much more as a champion of property than as a champion of freedom.

They do less than justice to him. There was no question, when he lived, of redistributing property, and he merely took for granted what almost everyone accepted. Whoever, in his day, put a value on freedom put a value on what in practice could be enjoyed fully only by a small part of the community. Locke claimed for all men what he could hardly have denied, had he been seriously challenged, was still within the reach of only a few. Only the well-to-do, only men of property, could hope, in his day, to take effective action against the abuse of authority; only their conception of a moral law superior to civil law could set a limit to the power of governments. Locke was content that it should be so. It seemed natural to him, as it seemed to nearly all his contemporaries, that the right to resist rulers who have abused their authority should in practice be confined to the educated and propertied classes, to the section of the community alone capable of passing an intelligent and responsible judgement in such a matter. ' Property is a means to freedom, and only those who have property are able or much concerned to defend freedom.' Though Locke never said this, in so many words, he almost certainly believed it. But his believing it at a time when most men had little or no property is no evidence that he cared for property more than for freedom or that he understood by freedom little more than security of external possessions. The man who wrote the *Letter on Toleration* as well as the two *Treatises of Civil Government* understood by freedom something larger than that, something much closer to what we now understand by it, even though we no longer speak, as he did, of natural rights. Locke did not, as Hobbes did, equate freedom with the right to do what the civil laws do not forbid, nor, as Machiavelli did, with the right to participate in government, nor yet, as Bodin did, with security of external possessions and family rights. Freedom, as Locke understood it, is man's right to live as seems good to him provided he respects the same right in others.

Since Locke's time we have become acutely aware of how much the freedom of the propertyless can be curtailed by the unrestricted exercise by the wealthy of their rights of property. We have therefore gone a long way in restricting these rights. We have also transferred many rights of property from private into public hands. Almost the whole business of government, as Locke and his contemporaries saw it, was to make secure private property as a means to personal freedom; whereas, as we see it, a large part of its business is to administer public property and to restrict the rights of owners of private property. We justify this great extension in the business of government partly on the ground that it makes for a more smooth and efficient production of wealth and partly on the ground that it extends to all classes some of the freedom which used in practice to be confined to the well-to-do. To Locke it seemed obvious that private property is the condition of freedom, just as to us it seems obvious that private property must be greatly restricted if more than a minority are to have freedom. But Locke was no more guilty than we are of confusing rights of property with personal freedom. He saw the two as closely connected, as indeed they are. Nobody disputes the closeness of the connection. The freedom men have must depend, in any society, very largely on how property is distributed. We have sought to extend freedom less by ensuring that all men have private property than by transferring rights of property from private to public persons; and now it is being brought home to us that property rights vested in the community can sometimes be as much a threat to the freedom of all classes as the wealth of the rich was to the freedom of the poor.

Locke, at a time when only the wealthy could have much freedom, made a bolder and larger claim for the individual against public authority than anyone, except a few of the extremer sects whose doctrines seemed to threaten the social order, had done before him. He made freedom, conceived more broadly than it had been in the past, seem desirable to a minority strong enough to get it for themselves; he made it seem desirable without making it seem dangerous. Had he foreseen the conclusions to be drawn from his premises by later critics of the political and social order which he cherished, he might have made different assumptions and have aimed at producing a political doctrine justifying aristocracy and condemning democracy. But he did not foresee them, and therefore was not afraid of claiming for all mankind what only a small number could then enjoy.

His political philosophy is, if I may so put it, the soul of liberalism, still confused and inadequate, still far from self-knowledge, strong in its faith and yet ignorant of much that that faith implies. More emphatically than anyone before him, Locke makes freedom a supreme end of government. It is a man's right, he tells us, merely because he is a man, to be allowed to make the best of his life according to his own notion of what is good. Government has nothing better to do than to help him achieve his end, not by giving him what he wants, but by making it possible for him to get it by his own efforts. Coercion is justified, not as a means to national greatness, nor for the sake of heaven, nor to enable men to attain virtue, nor to increase happiness, nor in the service of a common good transcending individual rights, but only because freedom is not to be had in this world without it. Power held on trust to secure freedom: this, since Locke's time, has been the most persistent of European political doctrines, especially in the liberal West. It was the doctrine of Montesquieu and of several of the French rationalist philosophers, of Kant and even (in some moods) of Hegel, of both the Whigs and the radicals in England, and of the founders of the American republic.

Though Locke, if we take account only of his political philosophy, was not a profound or subtle thinker, that philosophy was and still is strongly attractive. Much more so, indeed, than many others which are logically sounder. Though Locke does not tell us how power should be organized to preserve freedom, his is the first of the great political philosophies to make freedom, conceived in a larger sense than the ability to do what the law allows or what God commands, its central theme. It is freedom which is precious above all things, and not security or salvation or virtue or happiness or national greatness.

The system of government which he preferred to all others was not mere aristocracy, it was liberal aristocracy. His ideal was at bottom much the same as that of Burke and Alexander Hamilton, but he felt no need to condemn democracy since no one was asking for it when he wrote. Thus, though he was certainly no democrat, the principles which he proclaimed in an era of aristocratic resistance to absolute monarchy are still used in the West to justify liberal democracy. We may find many of Locke's arguments inconclusive; we may think him too often careless and superficial. But his heart, we feel, is in the right place; for that place is pretty much where our heart in the West is today. Locke was the first of the great liberals of our era, the first to speak the political language still the most familiar to us. It is a secular, an untheological language, without being materialist and without excluding God. It is, on the contrary, on easy terms with religion. Yet it explains government, not as an instrument of the divine will, but as a device of human wisdom to meet the needs of men taken as rational and moral beings.

Chapter 7

MONTESQUIEU

A LAWYER and a man of letters, Montesquieu was for nine years a 'président à mortier' or judge at the *Parlement* of Bordeaux, an office left to him by his uncle, together with other property and the name of Montesquieu. Montesquieu sold his office in 1725, when he was only thirty-six years old, intending to devote the rest of his life to literature. He had by then already published, in 1721, the *Persian Letters*, supposedly written by two travelling Persians to their friends at home giving their impressions of France. In 1728 and 1729, Montesquieu visited Germany, Austria, Italy, and Holland, and then, in the company of Lord Chesterfield, came to England, where he stayed another two years. Being well-to-do and well-connected, he was everywhere on his travels received in the best houses, where public affairs were discussed with a knowledge and candour scarcely possible at that time in other places. For the whole of his life Montesquieu remained a traveller in imagination, if not in fact; his curiosity about foreign countries was insatiable. And it was mostly a well-bred curiosity – detached, uncensorious, and urbane.

Returning to France, Montesquieu lived either in his home at La Brède near Bordeaux or in Paris, and devoted his energies chiefly to preparing *De l'Esprit des Lois*, though he also found time to write a lesser work, *The Considerations on the Greatness and Decadence of the Romans*, which appeared in 1734. *The Spirit of the Laws* was published anonymously in 1748, and was at once immensely successful.'[1] It was accepted as the political masterpiece of the age. Voltaire said harsh things about it and Frederick of Prussia was moderate in his praise, but most of the philosophers and princes admired it. Men as different from one another as Hume, Rousseau, and Burke paid warm tribute to it as to the greatest work of its kind produced in their century. Catherine the Great called it her 'breviary'; she was delighted to find in it the argument that to hold it together a large empire requires unlimited power in the ruler. Montesquieu was very much the fashion for about two generations, until it was discovered that his erudition was not always to be trusted, and that no one had ever before been misinformed about as wide a variety of subjects. In the beginning of the next century Macaulay could treat him almost as a kind of clever

---

[1] I have used the Pléiade edition of Montesquieu's works, and the passages quoted are my own translations from the French.

fool assiduously and uncritically collecting every piece of information that came his way.

It is true that Montesquieu was uncritical. He was a considerable traveller when still young and a great reader all his life; he put down on paper a prodigious number of what he took for well-authenticated facts, and had little opportunity to test the accuracy of his sources. He believed whatever the ancient historians told him; all their testimonies were, to him, of almost equal value. He took it for granted that the early history of Rome was more or less as Livy described it; he accepted what he found in Chardin about contemporary Persia, and in du Halde about China. Having been a traveller himself, observant and truthful, he was ready to believe any other traveller who wrote intelligently and well. He did not distinguish carefully between observation and surmise, and was too little aware how difficult it is for travellers to interpret correctly what they see. For all his scepticism and detachment, he was often credulous. A rationalist who would not believe in miracles, he found it easy to swallow quite tall stories provided they were not told in the interest of religion.

Montesquieu was a master of style and wit, but not of method and exposition. His greatest work is badly planned and loosely put together. It is as if he had taken great care over each part separately, and had afterwards made careless decisions about what order to put them in. *The Spirit of the Laws* is a long book, but not nearly as long as it seems. It is divided into thirty-one books, with anything from twenty to thirty chapters in each book; the chapters are too short, too compact; the longest have seldom more than ten pages, the shortest often less than one. No theme is sufficiently elaborated, and too much is left to the reader's imagination. The style is too brilliant, too concise, too aphoristic. No book so well written, and with so much that is excellent in it, was ever so liable to weary the reader.

How then has Montesquieu acquired his great reputation as a social and political theorist? A gift for satire, a beautiful style, wit and elegance, generalities supported by travellers' tales, examples taken from not always reliable historians: these are not the stuff to make a masterpiece of social and political theory. But Montesquieu had other gifts, less easily noticed but more excellent and rare. He had the kind of imagination that puts new questions and makes new assumptions; he had originality. But, like many other original thinkers, he was not himself fully aware of the significance of his own assumptions. He relapsed into the old ways of thinking and speaking; and, when he did so, was sometimes worse than other people. He was often derivative, shoddy and superficial. Though he always wrote well, his thinking was at times commonplace.

It is worth remembering that Montesquieu has had two quite different reputations: the first and more superficial in his own century, as an immensely learned and wise man, whose opinions were respected by absolute monarchs, by parliamentary leaders, by liberal philosophers, and by the makers of the American constitution; and a second and more solid reputation in later times, as the father of sociology, as the inventor of a new method and the framer of new hypotheses, as a man who is important more for what he attempted than for what he achieved. The element common to both reputations is admiration for him as a master of satire and one of the greatest of French prose writers. Macaulay, who did not admire him, caught him. as it were, between reputations, when his learning was already suspect and his wisdom beginning to wear thin, and the novelty of his method and assumptions was not yet recognized.

I. MONTESQUIEU'S CONCEPTION
OF SOCIETY

Long before he wrote anything that could properly be called social or political theory, Montesquieu had already proved that he had remarkable gifts as an observer of society; that he was as keenly interested in the social influences forming character as in actual behaviour and motives. He did not take social facts, established usages and opinions, for granted; he felt the need to explain them, to see the connections between them, and to enquire into their origins.

Even as a young man, he had found it easy to look at French society as if he did not belong to it, placing himself in imagination outside it, questioning what had hitherto seemed beyond question. The two Persians in the *Persian Letters* are perhaps not quite true to life. Montesquieu had never been to Persia, and relied on other people's books for what he knew of that country. His Persians are more European than Persian, but they do at least look at France through the eyes of strangers. They know nothing of French ways and have to puzzle them out as they go along. Montesquieu, when he wrote the *Persian Letters*, had chiefly a moral purpose in mind; the book is a satire castigating Frenchmen and Europeans generally. It is not, however, a direct and savage satire in the manner of Swift; for Montesquieu was seldom exasperated by his fellow-men, though he was often sharp and cut deep. The book is much more than satire; it is inspired by curiosity even more than by the desire to expose vice and folly; and it reveals as great an interest in institutions as in men. Some of the letters are no more than witty and malicious, but others are serious discussions of politics, religion, and literature as aspects of French life.

The Considerations on the Causes of the Greatness and Decadence of the Romans (1734) is an historical essay written by an ardent admirer of Rome and of the Roman historians. Though it accepts uncritically the facts given by those historians, and is therefore full of mistakes, it is not a catalogue of events or a literary piece. It is a brief history of Roman institutions, an attempt to explain how they arose, developed, and eventually decayed. It is perhaps the first serious attempt of its kind. It treats Roman society as a complicated whole, describes the social and political causes of Rome's career of victory and conquest, and explains how these conquests, by forcing the Romans to change their system of government, led inevitably to decay and to final collapse. Montesquieu is concerned to show why the Romans succeeded where others had failed, and how their success so altered the entire structure of their society that it destroyed the very institutions and virtues which made them successful in the first place. The book is short, some one hundred and thirty pages in all; but its argument is carefully elaborated and always clear. It is much easier to read than his masterpiece, and reveals Montesquieu's peculiar gifts more immediately. *De l'Esprit des Lois* is certainly the greater work, but, at a first reading, often baffles the reader more than it enlightens him.

Already in the *Persian Letters* and the *Considerations on the Greatness and Decadence of the Romans* we see how close for Montesquieu is the connection between forms of thought and feeling and social institutions; we already find him enquiring how laws, customs, and governments are affected by and affect men's opinions, loyalties, and ideas of right and wrong. We already find him looking at a people, not as a multitude of individuals under one government, but as a community distinguishable from others by their manners and institutions. All institutions, political, religious, domestic, economic, and artistic, are, in his eyes, intricately related to one another, so that any considerable change in one is bound to affect the others. He did not – as I shall try to explain when I consider his theory of climates – treat any of these influences as paramount, as of its nature always stronger than any of the others. He took them all equally into account, together with their effects on one another and on government. This is not to say that Montesquieu had what is called an ' organic ' conception of society. For to have this conception is to have much more than a lively sense of the interdependence of all aspects of social life; it is to assume that society has a self-maintaining structure which determines how it develops. I do not believe that Montesquieu makes this assumption. Nor can we find in Montesquieu a *philosophy of history* of the kind that became popular in France and Germany in the beginning of the next century. What is peculiar to Montesquieu, if we compare him with, say, Hobbes or Locke, is the assumption that government is not to be understood except as one aspect of a people's life intimately bound up with all other aspects. Society, he tells us, is vastly more intricate than we ordinarily have any idea of, and forms our minds in ways unsuspected by us until we begin to study it.

II. MONTESQUIEU'S THEORY
OF CLIMATES

After the doctrine of the separation of powers, nothing about Montesquieu is better remembered than his interest in the influence of climate on social institutions. Yet the scope of that interest has been misunderstood. Montesquieu was interested in much more than climate; he was interested in the physical environment generally, of which climate is only a part. You will find a great deal in the *Spirit of the Laws* about how the quality of the soil, the abundance or scarcity of water, the distribution of mountains, rivers and plains, the nearness or distance of the sea, and the presence or absence of good natural harbours, affect the ways in which men live. To take only one example. No writer before Montesquieu went as far as he did in explaining English institutions and national character as things peculiar to an insular, seafaring, and commercial people. This part of Montesquieu's theory has attracted less attention than his discussion of the physiological and social effects of climate, though it is often more plausible and better argued. 'The laws', Montesquieu tells us, 'have a lot to do with the manner in which different peoples procure their subsistence';[1] and of course how peoples procure their subsistence has as much to do with geography as with climate.

It has sometimes been assumed that Montesquieu believed in a kind of climatic or physical determinism analogous to the economic determinism of the Marxists. This assumption usually goes with a failure to understand what economic determinism really amounts to, or at least what it must be taken to amount to if it is to be more than a quite arbitrary decision to treat some kinds of social behaviour as more important than others.

The economic factor is part of the social process; it is a part of the system of human behaviour which constitutes a form of social life. Marx thinks of it as being autonomous in some sense in which the other factors are not; he supposes that how it changes is determined by its own nature and not by other factors. It is continually changing and thereby causing change in all other aspects of social life. It is called fundamental because all, or nearly all, important social changes are supposed to originate in it. It is true that Marx – and Engels even more than Marx – sometimes, in the face of criticism, retreats from this position. Nevertheless, it is the only position that even begins to make sense of their theory; it is the essence of economic determinism.

Montesquieu's position is entirely different. Climate and geography

[1] *Esprit des Lois*, Bk. XVIII, Ch. 8.

are not parts of the social process; they are only the unchanging physical environment. They cannot therefore stand to social life as, in the Marxist theory, the production of wealth stands to all other social activities. Since climate and geography do not change, they cannot determine the course of social change; they can do no more than set limits to it. They cannot be treated, as Marx could plausibly treat changes in the production and distribution of wealth, as ultimate determinants of all other large social changes. Montesquieu never attempted so to treat them. Indeed, he never conceived of a course of social change; of societies passing through successive stages in a course of development. He was concerned only to compare different types of society, and to explain how they come to be different. The physical environment (including climate) is, he thought, always an important part of the explanation. Not the whole of it, nor even the larger part; for Montesquieu never invites us to believe that the major differences between one society and another all derive from differences of climate and geography. The physical environment is unchanging and its influence inescapable; it is, of all influences on social behaviour, the most enduring. It is fundamental in that sense alone. There is, I think, no evidence that Montesquieu believed that the physical environment, because it is fundamental in this sense, determines all aspects of social life. The people who have ascribed this belief to him have allowed themselves to be misled by some nineteenth-century social theories, and have interpreted Montesquieu as if he were feeling his way towards an idea which was in fact quite foreign to him: the idea of a single cause (or, rather, causal factor) determining the entire structure of society.

Montesquieu liked to use strong and striking phrases. His words often suggest more than he perhaps meant to convey by them, and it is therefore easy to misinterpret him. He did sometimes lay heavy stress on the influence of climate and geography, but he also made much of other things. I think it fair to say that he believed that the physical environment, decisive in some respects, goes only part of the way in determining how people live. The further people are, so to speak, from nature – or, in other words, the more elaborate and sophisticated their institutions and methods of work and thought – the less these institutions and methods can be explained as effects of climate and geography. This is perhaps the fairest inference from what Montesquieu said, and also very probably true.

Montesquieu's account of the social effects of the physical environment, taken as a whole, makes good enough sense. The examples he gives are not always convincing, but his general conclusion stands. It is what he says about only one part of the physical environment, about climate and its influence on man, which is more open to question, not only in matters of detail, but in principle.

Montesquieu takes account of two kinds of human reaction to climate: how men react to it physiologically and psychologically, which might be called the *primary* reaction, and how they adapt their environment to it – the houses they make to protect themselves from it, the customs and habits they acquire because of it – which might be called the *secondary* reaction. Montesquieu pays more attention to the primary reaction than to the secondary, although the secondary reaction is probably the more important of the two. He also misconceives the nature of the primary reaction; his account of it is both simple and simple-minded.

Heat, he tells us, expands the ends of our nerve fibres, and cold contracts them, so that people who live in hot climates are apt to be sensitive, lazy, and timid, while people who live in cold climates are apt to be tough, brave, and hard-working. It is not clear whether Montesquieu believed that the physical and moral qualities thus acquired are passed on by parents to their children or are merely effects of the separate action of heat and cold on each person. We may assume that he knew that black and brown parents have black and brown children, just as white parents have white ones, but whether he believed that distended and contracted nerve fibres are inherited is not to be known. Of natural selection, as Darwin understood it, he had, of course, no inkling. He seems to have taken it for granted that man has been essentially the same at all times and places, though climate has everywhere had a considerable effect on him, especially on his nervous system, and so has made him to some extent different, physically and mentally, in different parts of the world. He did not consider whether climate has affected man directly in other ways than by the action of heat and cold on his nerve fibres and the moral qualities that come of this action.

It would be absurd to blame Montesquieu for not knowing what everyone knows today: that racial differences are not to be explained in this simple way by the direct action of heat and cold on the human body. The process of physiological, or rather biological, adaptation to climate is quite different from anything he had in mind. And yet Montesquieu was probably right in believing that the direct action of climate on our bodies and minds is of considerable importance. This we may admit even if we reject his account of the action of heat and cold on our nerve fibres. Heat and cold, dryness and humidity, probably do affect us directly, in mind and in body, quite apart from what we may do to protect ourselves from them or to use them. It would be rash to deny this direct influence or to dismiss it as unimportant. The difficulty is to estimate its importance and to distinguish it from other influences. We know too little about it, though probably enough to incline us *not* to believe most of what Montesquieu tells us about the physical and moral qualities of various peoples.

The secondary influence of climate, which Montesquieu does not neglect though he pays less attention to it, is not only more important than the primary in explaining how some peoples differ from others; it is also easier to describe and to measure. It is often easy to see how, in order to protect themselves against heat and cold, wind and rain, or to make the best use of them in supplying their needs, men have come to live as they do. The secondary influences of climate Montesquieu could have studied, not unprofitably, even with the information at his disposal, meagre though it was by modern standards and not always reliable. That study, even in his day, would not have been purely speculative. Though, as I have said, he did not neglect it, he did choose to spend more of his time on something less rewarding. And in doing so he was not remarkably ingenious or imaginative. Others before him – among them Bodin – had made large and loose generalizations about the influence of climate on the bodies and minds of different peoples. These precursors had usually taken care to show that climate does most to improve the stuff of human nature in their own part of the world; and Montesquieu, the cool and judicious Montesquieu, followed their example, even in this. Indeed he was less generous to the over-heated peoples of Asia than Bodin was; for Bodin, though he found them sensitive and timid, also ascribed to them greater wisdom and understanding, a larger and more speculative intelligence, than to the Europeans.

III. MONTESQUIEU'S CONCEPTION OF LAW

Of the many chapters of *The Spirit of the Laws*, only six seek to define and classify law; and they are among the worst in the book.[1] It could never be said of Montesquieu, as it was of Hobbes, that he was 'rare at definitions'. He had little talent for the lucid analysis of concepts, and has contributed almost nothing to the abstract theory of law. That is not to say that his conceptions of law are not important; it is to say only that what is important about them is revealed, not in the analytical chapters, but in the rest of the book. These six chapters are snares and delusions. They lead to nothing. They throw no light on what comes after them or on what has gone before; they neither introduce nor summarize.

In the first sentence of his book Montesquieu defines laws as 'necessary relations deriving from the nature of things'. This definition is meant to cover *all* uniformities of behaviour as well as moral rules, customs, and civil laws; it therefore treats descriptive and prescriptive laws as if they were of the same general type. This much is clear,

[1] *Esprit*, Bk. I, Chs. 1-3; Bk. XXVI, Chs. 1-3.

though otherwise Montesquieu is so brief and develops his ideas so little, that it is impossible to be sure of his meaning. For example, what had he in mind when he said that all laws derive from the nature of things? Did he believe, even of a physical object, that we distinguish its nature from its behaviour, and then infer how it behaves from its nature and the natures of other objects which impinge upon it? But we make no such inferences. Some aspects of its behaviour we include in our account of its nature, and the aspects we do not include we discover by observation. Did he believe that we can infer how even a physical object will behave from the qualities belonging to it? No doubt, we often define it partly in terms of its behaviour, and whatever we put into our definition we call its nature. But we do not actually infer its behaviour from its nature; we either include its behaviour in our definition or we discover it by observation. Did Montesquieu believe that we can infer how men *ought* to behave from what they are and from how they do behave? Though he sometimes speaks as if this were what he believed, he never really explains what it is that can be thus inferred; what the rules are which follow logically from man's nature. He seems, in his definitions, often to play with words, but in such a way that it is not possible even to guess at what he is trying to do.

Montesquieu devotes the whole of the second chapter of his book, about one and a half pages, to discussing the laws of nature. Speaking of one of these laws, he assures us that it 'impresses' upon us the idea of a creator and brings us to him; another 'inspires' us to seek food; while a third is the need we have of one another's company, especially when we belong to different sexes. Though this second chapter is as obscure as it is short, we can at least make bold to say that the laws of nature, as Montesquieu here describes them, are not normative rules; they are merely ways in which men in fact behave.

In his first chapter, Montesquieu speaks of rules (or, as he puts it, *rapports* or relations) of equity prior to positive law; but he does not call these rules *laws of nature*. The examples he gives are: that, if there were societies of men, it would be right to conform to their laws; that, if there were intelligent beings who had received a benefit from another being, they ought to be grateful; that, if an intelligent being had created another intelligent being, the creature ought to depend on the creator; that an intelligent being who has hurt another such being deserves to have the same hurt done to himself. Some of these rules, or others like them, have often been called laws of nature, and I do not know why Montesquieu refrained from so calling them. Presumably, he believed them to be laws falling within his general definition of law; he believed them to be 'necessary relations deriving from the nature of things', the things in question being, of course, in this case, men. Presumably, he believed that these rules derive logically from the nature of man as distinguished from other animals; from the capacities peculiar to man. That would be enough to make them laws of nature in the traditional sense. Presumably, too, Montesquieu believed that these rules are in fact common to all societies, no matter what their customs and civil laws; though this was probably not all that he meant to convey when he said that they were prior to positive law.[1] Yet he refrained from calling them *laws of nature*, preferring to give that name to descriptions of actual behaviour.

I shall not go minutely into Montesquieu's definitions of law or try to weigh carefully what he said about the laws of nature or the rules of equity. He spoke so loosely that his words will bear several different and equally plausible interpretations. And yet it is not this looseness which makes me reluctant to take these parts of his theory seriously. Confusion is often worth unravelling, especially in political and social theory, because the most original and suggestive writers are not always the most lucid. But in this case the attempt is not worth while, simply because Montesquieu makes no use, in the body of his work, of his pre-liminary definitions and classifications. For example, he tells us that law is human reason, and that the laws and customs of a nation are, or ought to be, applications of this reason to its circumstances.[2] Others besides Montesquieu have spoken in this way; and though the assertion, taken by itself, is too meagre to be clear and cries out for elaboration, it has in fact often been a prelude to important statements about law. With Montesquieu it is not so. This not very lucid utterance commits him to precisely nothing; for he never, in any part of *De l'Esprit des Lois*, attempts to show how the laws and customs of any people derive from 'rules of reason' universally accepted. When he discusses what he calls the *spirit* of any system of law, he is never concerned to show how it is connected with universal principles. His general definitions of law lead to nothing, and are probably brought in only out of def-erence to a traditional theory which he could neither bring himself to discard nor knew how to make use of for the purposes of his own theory.

What Montesquieu calls the *spirit* of the laws is not 'reason' or any-thing corresponding to the traditional Law of Nature; it is whatever gives to a system of law its distinctive character. It is the way in which the laws that make up the system are related to one another and to the whole complex of institutions that make a distinct community out of the people living in a particular region. Montesquieu is concerned to

---

[1] It could be argued that there are some rules implicit in the idea of a social order or community held together by conformity to established norms, no matter what these norms are: as, for instance, the rule of impartiality, that what is required of one person in a given situation should be required of another in a like situation; or the rule that, if some people are exempted from a conformity required of others, there must be a principle to justify the exemption. But this is not what Montesquieu had in mind.

[2] Ibid., Bk. I, Ch. 3.

explain how laws are related to one another, and not how they arise from any supposedly pre-social needs or aspirations of man. We can discover what he understands by law, not from his definitions of it, but from his social theory as a whole. When he uses the word *law* without trying to define it, he says nothing to suggest that there are laws which derive logically from the nature of man. When he uses it in a broad sense, he seems to have in mind any rule of conduct supported by sanctions, any rule the breach of which makes a man liable to punishment or disposes other men to behave in ways likely to deter would-be breakers of the rule. He also uses it in narrower senses, either to mean rules defining rights and obligations which the courts protect or enforce, or rules which those who exercise power must conform to if their acts are to be authoritative. If we compare Montesquieu's *definitions* of law with, say, Hobbes', we have to admit that he is much the more obscure and inconsistent of the two. But if we see how he uses the concept which he defines so inadequately, we can claim for him that he has a better understanding of the social functions of law. Though, in the fashion of his day, he sometimes calls the laws of nature commands of God, he does not, as Hobbes does, treat all civil laws as commands of a human superior strong enough to enforce the commands. As we shall see later, when we come to consider what he says about political power, he is much nearer than either Hobbes or Locke to recognizing that those who govern are necessarily subject to rules; not merely in the sense that there is a higher law, natural and divine, which they are required to obey, but because government (as distinct from the occasional coercion of some persons by others) is an activity involving procedure, an activity governed by rules and which is effective only because it is so governed. Though Montesquieu does not, any more than Hobbes or Locke, speak of *constitutional laws* or conventions, he takes much larger notice than they do of the fact that government is a systematic and 'public' or official activity. Wherever there is political power there are conventions regulating its use.[1]

Writers like Hobbes, Locke or Bentham, who seek (as far as they can) to explain all institutions as instruments to serve human purposes, are much more apt than a writer like Montesquieu to treat civil laws, if not always as commands (for they sometimes retreat from their more

---

[1] Montesquieu sometimes loses sight of this fact, especially when he speaks of despotism. And it would be unfair to Hobbes and Locke to suggest that they never took notice of it. Hobbes distinguished the sovereign's public acts from his behaviour as a private person, and this distinction has implications which are inconsistent with some of the things he said about absolute or sovereign power. But then it seldom happens, at least in political theory, that what is obvious to a later age because it has come to be so much insisted upon was altogether neglected in earlier periods. Bodin recognized that there were rules, other than God's laws, rules inherent in the French system of government, on which the French king's authority rested.

extreme positions when they find themselves in difficulties), then at least as effects of power. Indeed, Bentham, who has no use for such concepts as the state of nature and natural law, ordinarily speaks as if rules and institutions were either made deliberately or else emerged to satisfy needs not affected by them. This is his usual assumption, though sometimes he has to admit facts inconsistent with it. But Montesquieu's concern is exclusively with the needs and ambitions of man considered as a social creature. Laws and other institutions are, for him, rules or modes of behaviour seldom deliberately adopted and often not understood by the persons who follow them or to whom they apply. No doubt, society, as he sees it, is entirely human; its institutions and laws are no more than ways in which men actually do or are required to behave. Though only creatures having the capacities of man could be in society together, it is in society alone that men could be as they are. This, I think, is implicit in what Montesquieu says about man in society.

It is easy to pull Montesquieu's theory of law to pieces; not only his definitions, but also his facts and his generalizations from them. It is so vulnerable a theory, and vulnerable at so many points, that the hostile critic, absorbed in the task of destruction, can easily overlook what is true and valuable. If you consider Montesquieu's definitions and some of his favourite conclusions, it is too often obvious that the conclusions are inconsistent with the definitions, and even that both are false. Take a certain line with him, and you reduce him almost to nothing. For the greater part of what is really valuable in his theory of law consists of ideas and assumptions which are not defined or made explicit but are merely used. And, since they have nothing to do with the definitions, they are easily overlooked.

I must, however, take care not to exaggerate Montesquieu's mistakes or the weakness of his arguments. Many of his innumerable 'facts' and conclusions have proved true or close to the truth. Yet he was so often careless that a long list of errors and even absurdities can be reckoned against him. Voltaire, who disliked him, and perhaps disliked his reputation even more, repeatedly found fault with him, and spoke of him almost with contempt. Where he disagreed with Montesquieu, Voltaire was often right; he had more common sense than Montesquieu, and was less easily taken in. But he had also, though he did not know it, less insight and less imagination, and so failed to do justice to what was new and important in Montesquieu's treatment of custom and law.

In Rousseau we find a better understanding of Montesquieu, and in Burke a still better. Burke, too, was impressed by the intricacy and variety of laws and customs, by the close connections between them, by their being the slow products of time and experience, by their power to affect our minds, and by our ignorance about them. We cannot do what we like with laws and customs; we cannot easily change them to suit ourselves. What we can do with them is limited by what they are; for they are the context of our lives and purposes, the social environment we are born into, which we take for granted but do not therefore understand. Their spirit is around us and in us, expressed in our habits and our prejudices, in our unthinking responses, in the assumptions we make without even being aware that we make them. We are creatures of law more even than creators of law.

To get a clear notion of Montesquieu's originality, it is not enough to consider his methods and assumptions in a general way, which is all I have done so far. It is better to consider how he treated certain questions often treated before him. He too classified governments, discussed men's motives for obeying them, and enquired how power might be limited. If we see how differently he treated these topics, we can see better just what he contributed to social and political theory.

We must, however, remember this: that a political theorist who has no marked gift for making fine distinctions, for analysing the terms he uses, for clear and rigorous argument, is apt, if he is original, to seem less so than he is. We must remember, too, that a political theorist, if he is brilliant and has a turn for making fine phrases, will often have imputed to him for originality what is not so. There have been political and social theorists who have made reputations for themselves merely by putting old ideas and arguments into a new dress. They too have done useful service, for their admirers might never have had the ideas and arguments brought home to them unless they had come across them in that dress. These people, brilliant but without originality, are often, in the end, seen for what they really are, and their reputations suffer greatly. They come to seem pretentious. And yet probably they were never as pretentious as they come to appear; they only claimed for themselves what they honestly believed was their due, being merely the first to be misled by their own brilliance.

Montesquieu was original and brilliant, but his brilliance now serves rather to obscure his originality, often hiding it even from those who are not taken in by his brilliance.

IV. MONTESQUIEU'S CLASSIFICATION OF GOVERNMENTS

Montesquieu distinguished between three main types of government: republics, monarchies, and despotisms. He has been criticized for substituting this classification for the older one which derives ultimately from the Greeks – the classification into monarchies, aristocracies, and democracies. The principle behind the traditional classification is simple and obvious: it relates to number. It considers whether supreme authority belongs to one person, or to part of the community, or to the whole of it, acting directly or through representatives; or whether it is shared between them in what is called mixed government. These distinctions are important and easy to make. Monarchy really is a different kind of government from aristocracy, and aristocracy from democracy. Nor is it just a question of the number of people who have authority, for from these differences in number follow other more important differences of structure and spirit. The criterion of number is easily applied. What proportion of a community has political authority is something that can be discovered and that people can readily agree about.

Montesquieu's classification appears at first sight less useful, less clear, and less easily applied. What, after all, is the difference between monarchy and despotism? Is despotism anything more than monarchy 'misliked', as Hobbes put it? Where supreme authority belongs to the whole community or to a considerable part of it, we have, according to Montesquieu, a republic. But is not this to create confusion by using two criteria, one numerical and the other moral, instead of the traditional single criterion of number? The moral criterion is used to distinguish between despotisms and monarchies; and the numerical to distinguish republics from the other two kinds of government. Montesquieu's classification, by putting democracies and aristocracies together into the same class, seems to imply that the difference between them is less important than how they both differ from monarchy; and this is not at all obvious.

This criticism of Montesquieu does not, I think, do justice to him. No doubt, he was not seldom confused, and it may be that he was so even when he was distinguishing between the three main types of government. Certainly, in making these distinctions, he sometimes uses a moral criterion, and sometimes does not. The difference he makes between monarchy and despotism is partly a moral difference, whereas the difference between monarchy and a republic is not.

Yet Montesquieu's distinction between monarchy and despotism is not wholly, nor even primarily, moral. Nor is he, when he puts democracies and aristocracies together as forms of republic, neglecting or belittling the great and obvious differences between them. He is merely drawing attention to something important which is common to them, to something obscured by the traditional classification. Admittedly, this is not as plain as it should be. Montesquieu, when he classifies governments, is both using traditional ideas clumsily and pointing to differences neglected before him. His classification, confusing though it may be in some ways, is important because it turns largely on differences in the machinery of government. Let us see how this is so.

Though aristocracy and democracy differ very much, they have, if we contrast them with monarchy, two things in common: the laws are made by an assembly having elaborate rules of procedure, and there is a clear distinction made between the executive and legislative functions of government, even though there may be some persons who have a share in both. In a monarchy in Montesquieu's sense, in a monarchy as distinguished from a despotism, in (say) eighteenth-century France, the King-in-Council is both the supreme legislature and the supreme executive. It is not just that some people who take executive decisions also belong to the body which makes the law; it is one and the same body which is supreme in both spheres. Whereas in an aristocracy, as England was in Montesquieu's time, the body that makes executive decisions is clearly separate from the body that makes the law. The King-in-Council is not the King-in-Parliament. It may be that the same persons make executive decisions and also introduce the more important proposals of law; but they do not do so in the same place and in the same way. If the king's ministers could have made laws as they made decisions of policy, without the co-operation of Parliament, the laws that got on to the Statute Book in eighteenth-century England would have been very different from what they were.

We must also remember that in England in Montesquieu's time the king's ministers still owed their power as much (and indeed more) to the monarch's confidence in them as to the two Houses. We may think that Montesquieu misunderstood the English system of government, that the legislative and executive powers were not really separate. I believe that he misunderstood the system less than his critics suppose; but that is not the point I now want to make. Whatever the relations between executive and legislature in England in the early eighteenth century, they were very different from what they were in France, precisely because England had a parliament and France had not. Whether or not they were separate in quite the way imagined by Montesquieu, they were clearly separate in a way in which they were not in France.

A monarch, of course, has official advisers; as lawmaker and supreme executive he acts in council. But his advisers are appointed by him and are his subordinates. A monarch in council consulting his ministers about the laws he shall make is not a legislative assembly. When the ultimate legislative power belongs to a deliberative assembly, the machinery of government is essentially different from what it is when that power belongs to one man, even though that one man has advisers. The assembly may include or represent all the citizens, or only a part of them; but it is, in law, an assembly of equals making its decisions by a process of free debate and voting.

England, once an aristocracy and now a democracy, has in both capacities needed a parliament; whereas France, when she became an absolute monarchy, could do without the States-General. Montesquieu

K

knew that aristocracy and democracy are very different forms of government, but he was impressed by the fact that the institutions they use, especially in large states and the legislative branch, are broadly similar.

Monarchy is not, for Montesquieu, merely despotism without the more obvious attendant evils. The traditional classification of governments, which would put China and Persia into the same category as eighteenth-century France, seemed to him more misleading than his own. France and England, the one a monarchy and the other an aristocracy tempered by monarchy, seemed to him more alike, even in their forms of government, than France and Persia. Monarchy, according to Montesquieu, is a kind of government where supreme authority, legislative and executive, though it belongs to one man, is exercised in a traditional, public, and orderly manner. Where there is monarchy, a careful distinction is made between the ruler as king and the ruler as man. The monarch is a public person, whose acts are attested and whose commands are executed in accordance with a procedure laid down by custom. His decisions are final, but they are accepted only because they are made in the prescribed way. Where there is monarchy, there is a constitution, in the sense of a well-defined body of rules regulating the exercise of power.

If men are to have security, if they are to know what they may and may not do, if their rights and duties are to be exactly defined, the law must be certain and coherent. New laws must be promulgated and registered, they must be carefully devised to fit into the whole body of existing law. And justice must be done, both to criminals and between litigants, by independent courts. Where the law is stable, certain, coherent, and administered by independent courts, the ordinary subject, even if he takes no part in government, enjoys a precious liberty. He is a citizen and not a slave. He knows where he stands, both in his relations with his neighbours and with those set in authority over him. He knows his rights and duties, what he can demand of others and others can demand of him. Where such conditions obtain, there is the rule of law.

Montesquieu believed that these conditions obtained in France, making that country a monarchy and not a despotism. Under the French king there were subordinate and dependent authorities, long established, and with high professional standards. Government was elaborate and regular. The responsibilities of subordinates to their superiors were definite. 'Intermediary, subordinate and dependent powers' says Montesquieu, 'are of the essence of monarchic government, that is to say, of the kind where one person alone governs by means of fundamental laws . . . These fundamental laws necessarily require channels through which power flows: for, if there is nothing in the state beyond the momentary and capricious will of a single person, nothing can be stable, and therefore there can be no fundamental law.'[1]

One such intermediary power is the nobility, which Montesquieu thinks so necessary to monarchy that he puts forward the maxim, *point de noblesse, point de monarque.* In a monarchy there are classes whose privileges are so well established that the king, though his power is sovereign, cannot in practice touch them. Apart from the privileged classes, there must also be what Montesquieu calls ' *un dépôt de lois* ', a depository of laws, 'which is to be found only in political bodies that announce the laws when they are made and call attention to them when they are forgotten '.[2] When he considered his own country, the bodies Montesquieu had principally in mind were the *parlements* or sovereign courts, especially the *parlement* of Paris, which registered royal edicts and had the right to present remonstrances. Royal edicts had not the force of law until the *parlement* of Paris had registered them, and that court had the right to delay registration to give the king time to reconsider his decision. Lastly, where there is monarchy, the king never acts as a judge; justice is enforced by regular courts administering a known law and free from royal interference.

The king's council is not, according to Montesquieu, a suitable depository of law. For it expresses the monarch's momentary and executive will, not his permanent will which is embodied in the law. So that even where there is monarchy, though the supreme executive and legislative powers are in the same hands, they are to some extent differently exercised. They are, in a way, kept separate; their difference is officially recognized. Monarchy is orderly and coherent government, it keeps to well-defined rules which prescribe how it shall function. It is not arbitrary. We can find ideas like these in Bodin, in the distinctions he makes between the different kinds of monarchy. What to Montesquieu is simply ' monarchy ' to Bodin is ' monarchy royal and legitimate '. But Bodin habitually confuses a moral distinction with a political one; whereas Montesquieu not only does so much less often but makes the political distinction clearer by relating it to differences in the structure of government. Montesquieu may prefer monarchy to despotism, but his purpose is not just to express this preference. The point he is trying to make is that, while monarchy is a form of constitutional government, despotism is not.

Montesquieu thinks of despotism as arbitrary government limited, though loosely and uncertainly, by religion and custom. In a despotism no clear distinction is made between the ruler as a public and as a private person. There are no ' depositories ' of law, no professional and independent bodies whose duty is to register the ruler's decisions and to consider how they fit into the whole system of law, and who have a right to appeal publicly to his better judgement. There is no order

1 Bk. II, Ch. 4.
2 Bk. II, Ch. 4.

of nobles whose privileges the ruler cannot touch. The despot can make or mar anyone according to his pleasure. The monarch is bound by custom to choose many of his advisers and officers from among the nobility, whose status is secure; he is therefore surrounded by men of independent judgement, whom he has to treat considerately. Though his power is formally absolute, it is limited by the need to retain the confidence of an independent and educated class. But in a despotism no man's social status is secure, and there is, properly speaking, no informed public opinion independent of the despot. The despot, when he so chooses, acts as a judge, or else interferes with the justice dispensed by the courts. In his private relations with other men, he does not submit to law. The courts are not professional bodies learned in the law; they are venal and arbitrary. There is nothing to restrain them except loosely defined custom and the despot's edicts, which they interpret as it suits the momentary interest of the ruler or their own. Only where there is an independent judiciary are there definite canons of interpretation; so that from customs loosely and variously understood there can emerge a coherent and elaborate body of law, making for adequate, impartial, and consistent justice. The despot's power is not unlimited, but it is arbitrary. Even where the despot happens to be just by temperament, the chances are that many of his subordinates will not be so, because the structure of despotic government does not make for impartial justice.

This picture is, of course, overdrawn. Montesquieu could speak well of monarchy because he knew it well; he was a lawyer and a nobleman, and therefore belonged to the two classes whose privileges in fact limited the theoretically absolute power of the French King. About the eastern world, where what he called 'despotism' flourished, he knew much less. His conception of an almost entirely arbitrary power is unrealistic. Political power is essentially regular. Wherever there is government, there is a system of rules in accordance with which power is in fact exercised. The observance of these rules places power in the hands of its possessors, and also limits their power. Completely arbitrary political power is impossible; it is, indeed, a contradiction in terms.

We could, I think, refute Montesquieu out of his own mouth, for there are passages in *The Spirit of the Laws* which imply that all government is to a large extent regular and customary; that before there can be abuse of political power there must be political power, which of its very nature implies status and procedure. The ruler is different from his subjects, not naturally, but conventionally; he is so in virtue of customary distinctions and rules which are in fact obeyed. Government is always, in this minimal sense, the rule of law; it is always to some exent constitutional. As Montesquieu himself admitted, the power of the despot and of his servants is limited by custom and religion. Montesquieu, like other people with a turn for fine phrases, was prone to exaggerate; not so much because his prejudices got the better of him as because he was carried away by his own eloquence. Of the order maintained by despots, he said, 'it is not peace, it is the silence of towns which the enemy is about to occupy'.[1] As if, in countries like China and Persia before they were open to western influences, countries which he called despotisms, there were no such thing as justice!

Nevertheless, Montesquieu's distinction between monarchy and despotism is important. Where there is a precise and elaborate system of law administered by courts independent of the monarch, where new laws are carefully promulgated and liable to expert and public criticism, where social status is firmly grounded in rights and duties recognized by the courts and by the ruler, the system of government is very different from what it is where these conditions do not hold or hold much less. There was, in fact, a much greater difference between the French monarchy and, say, the Ottoman Empire than between the French monarchy and the eighteenth-century government of England. France, like England and unlike Turkey, was what the Germans call a *Rechtstaat*, a constitutional state.

V. THE SPRINGS OF POLITICAL ACTION

Each of the three main types of government has its characteristic motive, its spring of political action, what Montesquieu calls its *principe*. This characteristic motive is not what led to the establishment of the particular type of government; Montesquieu does not explain institutions by their psychological causes. He is not interested in their origins but in how they function. The *principe* of a government explains, not how it arose, but why it works. It is something like what Burke was later to call prejudice; it is what makes people behave as they must if certain institutions are to function properly. As Montesquieu puts it: 'There is this difference between the nature of the government and its *principe*, that its nature makes it what it is, and its *principe* makes it work. The one is the structure peculiar to it, and the other the human passions that cause it to function.'[2]

The characteristic political motive of republics is *virtue*, of monarchies *honour*, and of despotisms *fear*. By virtue Montesquieu means public spirit and patriotism. The virtuous man respects the law and has a deep sense of his duty to the state. By calling virtue the characteristic political motive of republics, Montesquieu does not mean to

[1] Ibid., Bk. V, Ch. 14.
[2] Ibid., Bk. III, Ch. 1.

imply that it cannot be found in monarchies. He means only that it is a motive indispensable to republics, because, unless citizens have it, republican institutions cannot function. He admits that honour and fear are also motives for action in republics, but they are not *characteristic*; they do not explain what keeps republican institutions, as distinguished from other kinds, working properly. Aristocratic republics apparently need virtue less than democracies; they have corporate interests to guard against the unprivileged classes, and this serves to bind the privileged closer together. Moderation is essential to aristocracies or otherwise the masses will rise against them. But democracy is peculiarly dependent on virtue; it cannot survive unless respect for law is general, and loyalty to the whole community stronger than loyalty to any class or person inside it. 'Virtue', said Montesquieu, 'is love of the republic, it is a sentiment and not a matter of knowledge [*une suite de connaissances*]. . . . When once the people have good maxims, they keep hold of them longer than what are called the polite classes [*les honnêtes gens*]. It is rare that corruption begins with them. They often derive from the slenderness of their understandings a stronger attachment to what is established.'[1] Virtue, as Montesquieu conceives of it, is made up of loyalties and sentiments which men acquire in a certain type of society simply by growing up inside it and learning to do what is expected of them. They learn to behave and to feel as they ought to do if the society is to survive; and to do that they need not understand the society.

The place of virtue, of public spirit, in republics is taken in monarchies by honour, which is a lively sense of what is due to oneself. Honour can inspire actions for the common good, but they are done less for the sake of that good than for the sake of glory or self-esteem or from loyalty to the prince. There can be, and there usually is, a good deal of virtue or public spirit in monarchies, but they can survive without much of it, provided that there is a lively sense of honour among the classes from which the monarch draws his officials and the officers of his army. The man of honour does his duty because it is beneath him to do otherwise; he owes it to himself to do it; if he fails in it he is disgraced in his own and other people's eyes. The man of honour takes care to keep up his position, to do nothing unworthy of himself or of the class or profession he belongs to. He owes allegiance to his king. He is a loyal subject rather than a patriotic citizen. His primary loyalties are to his king, his class, and his profession, and not to the State.

When he distinguished monarchies from republics, Montesquieu had in mind ideal types as much as realities. He did not suppose that all governments belong entirely to one or other of his three classes. The

[1] Ibid., Bk. V, Ch. 2.

English Government (which he greatly admired) was, he thought, partly an aristocracy and partly a monarchy, and he even found a democratic element in it. He would have agreed that virtue and honour were both strong motives of obedience among the upper classes in England, and fear, too, especially among the lower classes with no political rights. Mixed governments were not uncommon. Montesquieu's purpose was rather to distinguish between types of institutions and to describe the moral attitudes that go with them than to define categories among which all actual governments could be neatly distributed.

Just as Montesquieu is least plausible when discussing the nature of despotism, so is he weakest when describing its characteristic motive. It is, he says, fear. Under the oriental great king, there are innumerable petty despots, who, because the law is uncertain and control irregular, can, provided they are servile to their superiors, do pretty much what they please to their inferiors. Peculation, corruption, and tyranny flourish at all levels of government; there is little security and revolts are frequent. Not only do the common people obey mostly from fear (which is with them a considerable motive even under other types of government), but so too do the great despot's despotic subordinates. They are merely his servants, whose offices and privileges are entirely at his mercy. They have no secure status. They may be raised high at one moment and utterly cast down at another. There is a sense in which all men, under a despot, are equals; but they are equal as servants or slaves, not citizens. The great among them are so only as favourites of the prince; they have no secure social status which gives them prestige and influence independently of his will. They cannot resist him, except as rebels. They are therefore either servile or rebellious, and their motive for being the one or the other is usually fear.

This is obviously too dark a picture. Europeans travelling in Asia, because they did not find there the institutions they were used to at home, were too ready to conclude that everyone (except the most humble who were beneath notice) was subject to the caprice of a despot; and Montesquieu took his opinions from them. Not all the political virtues are essentially European. Nevertheless, there is such a thing as despotism, and it has many of the qualities ascribed to it by Montesquieu. He chose to take his examples of it from the East; he might have looked nearer home and found what he wanted. He would then have had the advantage of being better able to verify his facts.

The real virtue of Montesquieu's account of the three main types of government and of the characteristic motives that make them function lies less in what he has to say about particular matters than in the conception that inspires him. Machiavelli also thought virtue proper to democracy, but he did not consider several types of government and the mental and moral attitudes that go with them. He never made a comprehensive study of institutions, and of the habits and sentiments that make them function. He did not treat all that goes to make up the life of a society, both institutions and prevalent ways of thinking and feeling, as mutually dependent facts. He was concerned with less general, less theoretical matters: with giving advice to a single-minded ruler willing to unite Italy at whatever cost, with the causes of Roman greatness and Roman decadence, with the virtues of republics. Machiavelli was an acute, and even a profound, observer who liked to draw large conclusions from the study of history and contemporary affairs. Though he liked to draw attention to certain connections between different sides of social life, he had no conception of a social system, of a complicated structure of institutions, political and social, so closely bound up with one another that the system is not so much resistant to novelty as pervasive of it, imposing its own character on what is brought into it from outside; and he never made a comparative study of several types of social system, as Montesquieu tried to do. Montesquieu may have done it crudely and too often carelessly, but he did it deliberately.

Moreover, he did not, as others had done before him, consider man primarily as a creator of society, as a bearer of natural rights or a subject of natural needs devising with other men the means to protect those rights and make easier the satisfaction of those needs; he considered him primarily as a social creature; he considered his customs, laws, and institutions, together with the socially induced motives which cause him to conform to them.

VI. MONTESQUIEU ON POWER AND FREEDOM

That is not to say that Montesquieu was interested only in how society functions, in the facts; he also had his own strong preferences which he hardly troubled to disguise. There are indeed two Montesquieus in *De l'Esprit des Lois*: there is the unprejudiced, though sometimes credulous and careless, student of society, and there is the lover of freedom insistently pointing to the advantages of the political forms which best preserve freedom. Few writers on politics can match his dispassionate curiosity about institutions which he does not like and his frank approval of the institutions he does like. He is not cold or indifferent, any more than his compatriot Montaigne was; and he is, like Montaigne, both tolerant and discriminating in his praise.

Montesquieu never undertook to justify his preference for limited government; he merely enquired how freedom could be made secure politically.

It is interesting, in this respect, to compare Montesquieu with Locke.

They both care deeply for freedom; they are among the most completely, the most whole-heartedly, liberal of the great political thinkers. Yet their manner of advocating freedom differs greatly. Locke devotes a few paragraphs of his *Treatise* to showing that the legislative and executive powers ought to be kept separate to prevent abuses dangerous to liberty, and he also argues that subjects must not be deprived of any part of their property to help defray the cost of government except with their express consent, mere tacit consent not being enough. But this is almost the full stretch of his concern with practical devices to secure freedom. Much more than in the machinery of liberal government, he is interested in proving that all human authority is held in trust, and that when the trust is betrayed, subjects may rightfully resist their rulers. But with Montesquieu, this is not so. He takes no notice of the right of resistance, either to assert or deny it. He does not ask what subjects are entitled to do to preserve their freedom; he asks only how government should be organized the better to secure it. How should power be distributed among the persons and bodies that have it to ensure that the subject is as free as he can be under government?

Montesquieu, in his account of freedom and how it is to be secured, made a false beginning. In the *Spirit of the Laws* he puts forward within a few lines of one another two definitions of freedom: he says that it can consist only in the power to do what one ought to will and not to be constrained to do what one ought not to will and he also says that it is the right to do all that the laws permit.[1] Since the second of these definitions follows so closely on the first, it is fair to assume that Montesquieu took them to be equivalent. Certainly, in this chapter, he says nothing to suggest that men might be constrained by law to do what they ought not to will or prevented from doing what they ought to will. If, then, the two definitions are equivalent, it seems to follow that men ought to will what the law requires and ought not to will what the law forbids; and if this is so, Montesquieu's conception is at bottom the same as Hobbes' when he speaks of civil liberty. Judging Montesquieu merely by this chapter, which is the only one in which he is specifically concerned to define freedom, it would seem that, as much as Hobbes, he treats morality and legality as if they were the same thing.

But we have seen already that Montesquieu has little skill in defining his terms. He no more uses the term *freedom* consistently in the sense in which he defines it than he does the term *law*. His account of how the separation of powers makes for freedom suggests that when he speaks of freedom he has more in mind than what Hobbes calls civil liberty; it suggests that he has in mind both the power to do what the laws permit, and freedom in some other sense, which he fails to dis-

[1] Ibid., Bk. XI, Ch. 3.

K*

tinguish from this power. This failure to distinguish between two different senses of freedom, both of them involved in his account of how the separation of powers makes for freedom, is a fertile source of confusion, as we shall see.

Much more than either Hobbes or Locke Montesquieu insists that the power of every government is limited in two ways: by the manner in which it is distributed among the persons who exercise it and by the traditions and beliefs on which authority rests. 'Rome', he tells us, 'was a ship held by two anchors in the storm, religion and *mores*.'[1] Though Montesquieu admired Rome, and especially republican Rome, more even than he admired the England of his day, he did not think that these anchors were peculiar to Rome. Even the power of a despot is limited, and often greatly limited, by religious beliefs and popular conceptions of what is right and proper. Yet in a despotic state men are not free as they were in republican Rome; they do not have either security under the law or freedom in the other sense which Montesquieu fails to distinguish from this security. Men are not free merely because the power of their rulers is limited by religious beliefs and popular ideas about right conduct. It is not so much this limitation as the other, the way in which power is distributed among the persons who exercise it, which makes for freedom. Political power, of course, is always distributed; it is distributed under a despot as much as in a republic. Montesquieu does not deny this. Since all power is limited by the way in which it is organized or distributed, what matters, if there is to be freedom, is that it should be organized or distributed in a certain way. The despot, Montesquieu tells us, actually has less power than the monarch; his power is smaller but so too is the freedom enjoyed by his subjects. Freedom is not the greater because the ruler's power is small; freedom depends on how power is limited, on how it is distributed, on the rules that govern its use.

This idea, that power, if it is effectively to secure freedom, must not merely be limited (for that it always is) but limited in appropriate ways, is one of the most important and interesting in Montesquieu. Despotism, he thinks, is weak because it is arbitrary, because it is, of all the forms of power, the most uncertainly distributed, the least subject to precise and effective rules. Where power is not exercised according to precise rules, subordinates do not know what is expected of them. In theory they are servants of the despot, obeying him in everything; but in practice, they can, within uncertain limits, do what they please. They have no rights against the despot, and are therefore perpetually in danger from him; but he, though his authority is in theory unlimited, is also their victim, because he is thwarted at every turn by their clumsiness, dishonesty, and stupidity. Since his real power is small, his unlimited authority becomes a cloak for the petty tyrannies

[1] Ibid., Bk. VIII, Ch. 13.

of thousands of subordinates. The remedy, which both strengthens government and safeguards liberty, is power exercised under fixed, elaborate, and precise rules; it is, to use a modern phrase not used by Montesquieu, *constitutional government*. Strong government is orderly government, and can protect men's rights the more effectively for being itself subject to rules. Political power is like flowing water, which must be properly harnessed before it can exert strong pressure. The first condition of liberty is the rule of law, which can exist under any government except a despotism.

We must remember that Montesquieu, when he spoke of despotism, always had in mind the oriental kingdoms of his day. That is why he took it for granted that despotism must be weak. We must not confuse despotism as he understood it with the dictatorships, fascist and communist, of our age. We know how immensely strong these dictatorships can be. But they are strong because, structurally and morally, they are quite different from the Asiatic despotisms of the eighteenth century. They are highly elaborate political machines; they require the strictest discipline among the immense political army of persons who exercise power. Power inside them, to the extent that it is arbitrary, is so mostly at the top; and if the power is great, it is so because, everywhere except at the top, it is mostly not arbitrary. And even at the top, it is much less arbitrary than it seems; the dictator must, in practice, conform to the ideology, the social and political faith, which he has built up and on which his power largely rests. The modern dictatorship, fascist or communist, is a *revolutionary state*, even though it uses many institutions and practices first developed in liberal and constitutional countries, but later transformed and put to other uses. It is a form of government that Montesquieu could not imagine, let alone allow for. His ideas about power and its relation to law and custom would need to be considerably modified to allow for it, but would not, I think, need to be changed in essentials.

So far, Montesquieu's position is clear enough. All power is limited. The condition of freedom is not that power should be slight or precarious, but that it should be limited in some ways and not in others. How then should it be limited?

Montesquieu makes a distinction, which he thinks important, between *laws making for freedom as they relate to the constitution* and *laws making for freedom as they relate to the individual*. He likes to speak of *free constitutions* as well as of the freedom of citizens; and in one place[1] he utters the paradox that 'a constitution may be free, and the citizen not be so: or the citizen may be free and the constitution not be so'. This paradox is misleading, if not absurd, and I shall have more to say about it in a moment because it is connected with Montesquieu's definition of freedom as the power to do what the

[1] Bk. XI, Ch. 6.

laws permit. But I want first to consider these two kinds of law making for liberty.

About the second kind, the laws making for freedom as they relate to the individual, there is no special difficulty. Montesquieu discusses them in the twelfth book of the *Spirit of the Laws*. They are the laws and processes ensuring that no one is punished except for a breach of known law; that he is properly indicted, tried and sentenced, in accordance with rules which serve to protect the innocent as much as to discover and condemn the guilty; that he can assert his rights effectively both against other citizens and against the executive branch of government. These laws and processes, if they are to achieve their purpose, require that the courts should be independent of the ruler, in fact if not in name. In short, by the laws making for freedom as they relate to the citizen, Montesquieu means what is usually meant by the phrase *the rule of law*.

The nature of the other kind of laws, the laws that make for freedom as they relate to the constitution, is also easily enough understood. They are the laws prescribing how authority is distributed among those who have it. In other words, they are constitutional laws; and in practice there always are such laws or conventions, even where there is no written constitution. Montesquieu tells us that they do not make effectively for freedom unless they establish a separation of powers.

Clearly, both these kinds of law aim at preventing abuse of authority, and they both prescribe how power shall be exercised. The citizen cannot get a fair trial, cannot make good his rights, unless the courts exercise their powers according to rules established for his protection. It could be argued that all rules governing the use of authority, and thus also the rules which bind the courts, are in the broad sense constitutional. We could therefore say that Montesquieu's two kinds of law making for freedom are both laws making for freedom as they relate to the constitution. Yet the distinction between the two kinds of law is real and important. Rules which prescribe how those in authority shall deal with one another, how they shall stand to one another in their official capacities, are different from rules which prescribe how persons in authority shall deal with ordinary citizens. Both these kinds of rules make for freedom, and they make for it in different ways.

So far, so good. The distinction between these two kinds of law is worth making, and has to be made if we are to explain how power is to be organized to preserve freedom. Yet we have to admit that Montesquieu does not make as lucid and good use of it as he might for his purpose. If both kinds of law make for liberty, why say, as Montesquieu does, that the citizens may be free and yet the constitution not be free? What can be meant by calling the constitution free except that it makes for the freedom of the citizen? Strictly speaking, it is only individuals that can be free. To say that a constitution is free is only a roundabout way of saying that it helps to secure freedom to the individual; that political power is so distributed among its possessors as to enable the individual to enjoy the rights which constitute his freedom. Montesquieu really had no freedom in mind except the freedom of the citizen, and when he called the constitution free, he meant only that it was a means to individual freedom. Why then did he say that the constitution might be free and the citizen not be so? Or that the citizen might be free and the constitution not be so? He was, I think, in the paradoxical and misleading fashion he was too fond of, saying two things: that the separation of powers, though a necessary condition of freedom, is not a sufficient condition; and also that, even where there is no *formal* separation of powers, the citizen can possess a precious kind of freedom – the kind which is the impartial and scrupulous enforcement of a body of carefully formulated laws. France did not have what Montesquieu, following an eighteenth-century fashion, called a free constitution; for in France the legislative, executive, and judicial powers all belonged, at least nominally, to the king. Yet Montesquieu believed – though with reservations – that, though France lacked a free constitution, Frenchmen enjoyed real freedom – the kind of freedom secured by what he called 'the laws making for freedom as they relate to the citizen'.

These points are worth making, but they do not excuse Montesquieu's paradox, which is grossly misleading. A free constitution, according to Montesquieu, is one in which the three powers, executive, legislative, and judicial, are separate. Now, if Montesquieu's own account of the French system of government is true, France had a constitution which, though nominally unfree, was in reality at least partly free. Though all authority belonged in name to the king, the courts of law were in fact independent of him; and it was because they were independent that in France the laws making for freedom as they relate to the citizen were in practice effective. More than anything else, it was this independence of the courts which made France, in the eyes of Montesquieu, a monarchy and not a despotism. The laws making for liberty as they relate to the citizen are not, of course, the same thing as the independence of the courts; but Montesquieu clearly believed that, unless the courts are independent, there either will not be any such laws or they will be a dead letter.

Montesquieu ought not to have said that the citizen can be free when the constitution is not free; that is to say, when none of the powers is separate from the others. He ought rather to have said that, though the separation of powers is not in itself enough to make the citizen free, he cannot have freedom unless at least one of the three powers, the judicial power, is separate from the other two, in fact if not in name. That, I take it, is what he meant to say. It is certainly what is implied by what he did say; by what he did say, except, of course, for the unlucky paradox about the citizen's being sometimes free when the constitution is not, and the constitution free when the citizen is not.

If all that is needed to ensure that the laws making for freedom as they relate to the citizen are not a dead letter is that the judicial branch should be independent of the other two, why need the other two branches be independent of one another? Why should the constitution of eighteenth-century England be more 'free' than the constitution of eighteenth-century France? The only freedom in question, the only freedom that could possibly be in question, is the freedom of the citizen, of the individual. Since all that is meant by calling a constitution free is that it makes for the freedom of the citizen, why should a constitution in which all three powers are separate be more free than one in which the judicial power alone is separate from the other two? It is difficult to answer these questions within the limits of Montesquieu's theory. Yet, clearly, he thought the separation of all three powers necessary to the enlargement and security of freedom.

The difficulty arises, I think, from his inadequate definition of freedom as the right to do whatever the laws permit. It is inadequate not so much because it does not define what most people mean by freedom as because it does not define what Montesquieu meant by it. If he had really meant by freedom no more than the right to do what the laws permit, he would have been satisfied with no greater separation of powers than sufficed to secure freedom in this sense. He would have been satisfied with the independence of the judiciary, which he thought enough to ensure respect for the laws making for liberty as they relate to the citizen; or, in other words, to ensure the scrupulous and impartial application of the laws to all members of the community. That he was not satisfied with the independence of the judiciary suggests that he had a larger conception of freedom than was covered by his own definition.

It was clear to him that there could be no freedom apart from law, and he could not imagine how there might be freedom against the law. Yet he could not dismiss the possibility that the law itself might be oppressive, even though this assumption does not square with his definition of freedom. If Montesquieu had been as obstinately logical as Hobbes, if he had had the same respect for his own definitions, he might have been tempted to deny that the laws could be oppressive. But Montesquieu had some of the saving grace of John Locke: he would not press a point home when it led him to a conclusion repugnant to common sense. It was clear to him that citizens may be oppressed, not only against the law, but also by means of the law; and he wanted to prevent that oppression, even though, if his own definition of freedom were adequate, there could be no such oppression.

The laws making for liberty as they relate to the citizen clearly do not prevent oppression by means of the law; they prevent only *illegal* oppression. The independence of the courts serves only to make these laws effective. If the laws themselves are not to be oppressive, other precautions must be taken; the executive and legislative powers must be kept separate. The makers of policy must not also be makers of law, or they will make laws to serve their own ambitions. 'Experience has always shown,' says Montesquieu, 'that every man who has power is inclined to abuse it; he goes on until he finds limits. . . . That there should be no abuse of power, matters must be so arranged that power checks power.' Abuse of power means, not just unlawful action, but legal oppression as well.

Montesquieu is doubly confusing: because he offers a definition of freedom which does not accord fully with his own conception of it, and because the distinction he makes between the two kinds of law making for freedom is not clearly related to his doctrine of the separation of powers. By saying that the citizen can be free when the constitution is not free, he implies that the laws making for freedom as they relate to the citizen can be effective even where there is no separation of powers; whereas his true position seems to be that they require, to make them effective, that at least the judicial branch should be separate, in fact if not in name. And he does not explain, as clearly as he might, why the separation of the other two powers makes for freedom; it does so, not by preventing illegal oppression, but by making legal oppression much less likely than it would otherwise be. And how can law be oppressive except by offending against commonly accepted notions of justice and decency?

Montesquieu puts the separation of all three powers on the same footing, whereas his own general argument requires that he should not do so. The separation of the judiciary from the other two powers does not serve the same purpose as their separation from one another. The independence of the judiciary prevents oppression in contempt of law; while the separation of the executive and legislature greatly discourages, if it does not entirely prevent, oppression by means of the law. Those who make the law, if they do not also administer it, will not be tempted to make oppressive laws for their own benefit. This much is, I think, implied by Montesquieu's distinction between the two kinds of law making for liberty and his doctrine of the separation of powers. The confusion arises because the connection between the separation of powers and these two kinds of law is left obscure; and it is left obscure because Montesquieu's definition of freedom is defective, being both inadequate to the ordinary conception of it and too narrow for his own purpose. If freedom is merely the right to do what the laws permit, there can be no oppresive laws; and if legal oppression is impossible there is no need for the three powers to be separate. The independence of the judiciary is then enough.

Freedom is primarily a moral rather than a legal notion, and is so, I suspect, as much in primitive societies, where morality and law are not clearly distinguished, as in more sophisticated societies, where they are. Primitive peoples who do not distinguish between the legal and the moral do not use the word law as we use it, and as Montesquieu ordinarily used it, to refer above all to rules enforced by the courts; they use it to refer to any rules to which obedience is required. Law, as they see it, is neither quite what we mean by a moral principle nor quite what we mean by a law; though it is probably closer to the first than to the second. Where the moral and the legal are not distinguished, freedom is perhaps well enough defined as the right to do what the laws permit. But where they are distinguished, as they were in Montesquieu's time, that definition is inadequate. Freedom is then not the right to do what the laws permit, but the right to do what is not wrong. It includes the right to do what the law wrongfully forbids, and the right to refrain from doing what the law wrongfully commands. It implies that rulers have a duty not to make laws which infringe certain moral principles. In primitive societies, where there are neither legislatures nor regular courts, there is not the same need felt to assert freedom against law; to distinguish the moral from the legal. But Montesquieu felt this need, and was therefore at times embarrassed by his own definition of freedom. And yet he failed to provide a better one. He was not tempted to go back to the notion of natural freedom, as we find it in Locke, for the whole spirit of his philosophy is that freedom has no meaning outside society; that is to say, outside the context of laws, customs, and manners which make a community what it is. Not being a very clear thinker, he failed to express his belief in the social nature of freedom in a way that made it possible to explain how the law itself could be oppressive.

VII. MONTESQUIEU AND LOCKE ON THE SEPARATION OF POWERS

It has been said that Montesquieu's doctrine of the separation of powers is merely an elaboration of ideas found in the twelfth chapter of Locke's *Second Treatise*. This is not true.

The idea that power ought not to be gathered entire into the hands of one man or body is much older than Locke's *Treatise*. It is traditional; and in the time of Bodin and Hobbes, it was more a novelty to attack than to uphold it. In England, in Charles I's time, while Parliament had seemed to be merely defending its rights against the king, most sympathies had been with Parliament; but after September 1641 when, led by Pym, Parliament went on to claim a right to control the executive, it lost the support of moderate men, because it seemed to be aiming at a monopoly of power. There was, of course, no systematic theory about the separation of powers; but it had long been taken for granted that the King-in-Parliament, the supreme interpreter of law, was separate from the King-in-Council, who actually governed. Locke was content to repeat the traditional doctrine, making no more of it than had traditionally been made. Though he distinguished between three governmental powers, the legislative, the executive, and the federative (by which last he meant the control of relations with other states), the third is nowadays included in the second; and, in any case, he did not advise that it should be in separate hands. The only separation that seemed to him to matter was between the legislative and the other two powers. Locke did not even mention the judicial power, which he no doubt thought of as part of the executive.

Now, we have seen that, with Montesquieu, it is precisely the power that Locke *did not mention* which it is supremely important to keep separate from the others. It was chiefly because the judicial power was in fact independent in eighteenth-century France, that Montesquieu thought of France as being a monarchy and not a despotism. The rule of law, which is the first condition of freedom, is made possible by that independence.

No doubt, France was not a perfect example of monarchy, as Montesquieu defined it. In a monarchy there is security under the law, and in a country like France, where a man might be deprived of his liberty indefinitely without being brought to trial, if he were arrested on the warrant known as *lettre de cachet*, there was not full security under the law. Montesquieu approved of *habeas corpus* and regretted its absence in France. The law prescribing its use is an excellent example of what he understood by a 'law making for liberty as it relates to the individual'. Montesquieu knew that the once formidable *Parlement* of Paris had been humbled by the monarch; he knew also that the nobles, by becoming courtiers, had lost much of their old independence. France, in his day, was not as good an example of monarchy as it had been before the reign of Louis XIV. If we apply Montesquieu's criteria impartially, we have to admit that France in the eighteenth century verged on despotism.

Nevertheless, the institutions which Montesquieu thought proper to monarchy existed in France, and he was familiar with them in their French forms. There were courts of law with a long tradition of independence and impartiality, there were nobles who were still much more that creatures of the monarch, and there were *dépôts de lois*. France, by the standards of Montesquieu, was not a despotism but a defective monarchy, and perhaps even a monarchy in process of decay. Yet what Montesquieu, when he was defining an ideal type and not describing an actual government, called by the name of monarchy is very like what Bodin dignified by the title of *monarchy royal and legitimate.* And the best example of this form of government, in Bodin's eyes, was the French monarchy; not as it actually was in his day, but as it was entitled to be, as it would be if it were in full possession of its traditional authority.

Though Montesquieu was never, in the same sense as Bodin, a champion of monarchy; though he did not prefer it to all other types of government, reckoning those nations the happiest which were capable of having it, he did find many virtues in it, and his conception of it owes a great deal to the 'idea' of French monarchy as elaborated by Bodin and other fervent royalists. Montesquieu was steeped in the laws and traditions of French monarchy long before he became an admirer of the English political system. I am tempted to make two claims for him: that he understood how England was governed much better than those who accuse him of making a gross mistake about the English system imagine, and that his conceptions and doctrines owe at least as much to French as to English examples. In the sixth chapter of Book XI, the famous chapter describing the English system of government, Montesquieu says, speaking not only of France but of most of the kingdoms of Europe, that in them government is moderate because the prince, though he exercises the executive and legislative powers, does not exercise the third, the judicial power. But in Turkey, where the Sultan exercises all three powers, there is a terrible despotism. Clearly then, the defects of the French government, serious though they are in the eyes of Montesquieu, are not enough to make it a despotism.

Montesquieu, for the sake of freedom, wanted all three powers kept separate; indeed, he insisted more strongly than Locke on the advantages of keeping the legislative and executive powers in different hands; but the separation he thought essential to the rule of law was not so much between the executive and legislative as between them and the judicial power. This doctrine is clearly not the same as Locke's, nor even a development from it. It was suggested to Montesquieu partly by his experience as a French lawyer and judge, and partly by what he saw and heard during his visit to England. In an article published in *French Studies* a few years ago, Mr Shackleton has shown that Montesquieu's doctrine of the separation of powers is much more like what was being advocated in this country by Bolingbroke and his circle than like anything to be found in the writings of Locke. And we know that Montesquieu, while he was in England, saw a good deal of Bolingbroke[1]

'There is', says Montesquieu in the short chapter serving as an introduction to the long chapter on England, 'a nation in this world the object of whose constitution is political liberty. We shall examine

[1] R. Shackleton, *Montesquieu, Bolingbroke and the Separation of Powers. French Studies,* 1949.

the principles on which it established that liberty. If they are good, liberty will appear there as in a mirror.'[1] And then, in the next chapter, he goes on to show that in England the legislative, executive, and judicial powers are separate; that the legislature is divided into two chambers, of which one contains the hereditary nobles (who might otherwise suffer from the envy of their inferiors), and the other is elected by the people generally, except for those whose condition is so low that they are reputed to have no will of their own; that the supreme executive power is vested in a monarch who has the right to veto bills submitted to him; that the legislature has, however, no right to veto executive decisions, but only to call the executive to account for acts done contrary to law; that the popular chamber alone has the initiative in fiscal matters; that it is periodically re-elected; that certain taxes and also the law allowing the monarch to levy and maintain troops are voted for only one year at a time. These provisions of the constitution are not merely described; they are justified as so many means to liberty. In the English constitution, as Montesquieu described it, there is a separation of powers; but there is also a system of checks and balances, and the separation is not complete. The executive is independent of the legislature, but the legislature has the power in certain cases to call it to account; and the executive in its turn has the power to veto legislation. The three branches are separate, but there are devices enabling two of them to impede one another, even in their own spheres.

Montesquieu wrote the chapter describing the English system of government after he had spent two years in England. He was not an obscure foreigner who saw nothing of men in the highest political circles. On the contrary, he was well received in those circles; and he was also an eager and intelligent observer. We must assume that he knew that nearly all the king's ministers were drawn from one or other of the two Houses of Parliament; it is inconceivable that a man moving for two years in the circles in which he moved, and with his interest in government, should not have known it. And yet he does not mention this fact. 'The executive power must', he says, 'be in the hands of a monarch, because this part of government, which nearly always needs to be expeditious [*qui a presque toujours besoin d'une action momentanée*], is better administered by one person than by several. . . .' And he goes on to say, two or three lines further on, that 'if there were no monarch, and the executive power were entrusted to a certain number of persons taken from the legislative body, there would be no more liberty, because the two powers would be united. . . .'[2]

---

[1] Ibid., Bk. XI, Ch. 5.
[2] Ibid., Bk. XI, Ch. 6.

Presumably Montesquieu, like his English hosts, believed that the king's ministers, even though most of them were members of one or other of the two houses, were responsible primarily to the king. They were the king's ministers and not the agents of the legislature. The king exercised the executive power through them, and they were not the less his ministers because it was in practice advisable for the king to govern through men enjoying the confidence of Parliament. As a matter of fact, through the exercise of Crown patronage, it was possible for the king (or whoever exercised that patronage in his name) to provide the government with a substantial following in the House of Commons. It was also generally admitted that the Houses of Parliament ought to co-operate with the king and his ministers, with the executive power. The presence of ministers in the two Houses of Parliament served to make this co-operation easier. But nobody then imagined that, because most ministers belonged to one or other of the Houses, the executive and legislative powers were not in separate hands. It seemed obvious that they were, and Montesquieu probably took for granted what nobody was concerned to deny.

If this is what he did, surely he was right. The king's ministers owed their power to his having chosen them; they were his nominees in fact as well as in name. There was as yet no convention that he had to call upon the leader of the majority party in the House of Commons to exercise this prerogative in his name. It was still truer to say that the king's ministers could get the support of the House of Commons because they were his ministers than that they became ministers because they enjoyed that support. When Montesquieu wrote *De l'Esprit des Lois*, relations between executive and legislature in England were still such that it seemed natural to speak of these two powers as being in separate hands. If it was admitted that the king could not in fact choose his ministers where he pleased, this was seen not as a constitutional so much as a practical limitation on his power. Even the King of France could not choose his ministers where he pleased; even an 'absolute' monarch, if he was to govern effectively, had to look for co-operation and confidence, and the extent to which he got them was apt to depend on his choice of ministers. That a king who was not an absolute monarch should have, in this respect, less freedom than the King of France was only to be expected; but his lesser freedom was not thought to be (and indeed was not in fact) a subordination of the executive to the legislature or a union of the two powers.

Today, when we speak of a separation of powers, we think immediately of the American system of government. There, if anywhere, is a separation of the three powers; there, if anywhere, the doctrine of Montesquieu has been put into practice. And so it comes naturally to us to think of that separation in terms of the most famous system which embodies it. But Montesquieu knew nothing of that system.

When he spoke of the separation of the executive and legislative powers, in the sixth chapter of Book Eleven, he had in mind the English system. He was, no doubt, contrasting it with the French system. In England the executive and legislative powers were separate, and in France they were not. Therefore, if we are to discover what he understood by the separation of powers, we must look, not at a system established after his death (even though its founders were to some extent influenced by him), but at the system which he took to be an example of what he had in mind. His description of this system satisfied not only himself; it also satisfied his English contemporaries. It never occurred to them that a distinguished foreigner had misdescribed their form of government; that he had made a great mistake about it. It was not in his own day but many years later that Montesquieu was accused by Englishmen of having seriously misunderstood their political system. By that time two things had happened: the system had changed, and the United States had come into being.[1]

Where the executive and legislative powers are separate, says Montesquieu, the legislature, though it cannot stop executive action, has the right to satisfy itself that the laws have been duly executed. It has both a legislative and a supervisory power. Montesquieu does not explain either how the supervisory power was in fact exercised in England or how in principle it ought to be exercised; though to assert such a power is clearly to imply that the executive is or ought to be in some way responsible to the legislature. For the legislature cannot exercise its supervisory power effectively unless it can require information about the execution of the laws and can apply some kind of sanction to ensure that its resolutions are not dead letters. Montesquieu says that the legislative body must not have the power to bring to judgement the person 'who executes'. He means, presumably, the chief executive, the monarch, who ought to be, in the old mediaeval sense, above the law, *legibus solutus*. How, then, is the executive to be made accountable to the legislature for how the laws are executed? As to how the legislature is to get the information it needs Montesquieu says absolutely nothing, but he does allude to a right of impeachment, a right of the lower house to bring to judgement before the upper house any citizen who has violated what he calls 'the rights of the people'; who has committed crimes which the ordinary courts cannot, or are unwilling to, punish. Thus we may say of Montesquieu that,

[1] As early as 1776, thirteen years before the United States acquired its constitution, Bentham had argued, in the *Fragment on Government*, that the executive and legislative powers were not separate in England. By their separation he already understood what the American Fathers were to understand: yet his understanding of it was not common in England until the next century; and even as late as 1867, Bagehot, in his *English Constitution*, thought it necessary to insist that the executive and legislative powers were not separate in England.

while he clearly implies that the executive power ought to be responsible to the legislative for how it administers the law, he fails to make clear how it is to be made so.

Montesquieu's conception of the separation of powers is by no means as clear as those critics take it to be who say that, already at the time when *De l'Esprit des Lois* was written, it had ceased (or was ceasing) to apply to the English system. For example, Montesquieu says that the executive power, since it forms part of the legislative only when it exercises the right of veto, must not take part in debates, and then goes on to say, in the very next line, that it is not necessary that the executive should be able to make proposals of law because it can always reject the proposals made by the legislative.[1] He does not say that the executive, where the powers are separate, *must not* make proposals of law but only that it *need not* be able to do this. This implies that, if it were to make them, this would not of itself annul the separation of powers. Montesquieu says nothing about how the executive would make such proposals. It may be that, in this chapter which deals with the constitution of England, he has in mind the king's acting through ministers taken from the legislature. Certainly, his saying that the executive power *does not form part* of the legislative does not exclude this possibility. Montesquieu, whenever in this famous chapter he speaks of the executive, seems to mean the chief executive, the monarch. It is the monarch who is outside the legislature, takes no part in debates and has no share of the legislative power, except when he rejects a proposal of law voted by the two houses. Though he acts through subordinates, his action, no matter who his subordinates may be, originates outside the legislature; it does so even when his subordinates are members of the legislature. This was still the common opinion in the England that Montesquieu knew, and he probably shared it.

I do not wish to suggest that Montesquieu's brief account of the English system of government as it was more than two hundred years ago is altogether correct. He took his opinions about it from the circles in which he moved while he was in England; and no doubt, then as now, there was a wide diversity of opinions. A system of government is always in process of change, and one of the reasons why it changes is that the persons who work it have certain opinions about it, opinions which vary with their prejudices and interests. Even the fullest and most judicious account is only partial and will soon be out of date. Montesquieu's account is one of the most rapid and most summary, and is by no means precise. But it seemed substantially accurate to his contemporaries, English and French; and it probably was what it seemed. Almost certainly, they read into it more than the actual words would convey to someone who knew nothing of the

[1] Ibid., Bk. XI, Ch. 6., p. 405, Pléiade edition.

English system, but that is not to say that they read more into it than Montesquieu intended that they should. A brief account, to those familiar with what it describes, always conveys much more than it literally says; but later, when what it describes has greatly changed, its brevity makes it the more likely to be misunderstood.

But I must not continue on this tack. To the political theorist, it does not greatly matter how far Montesquieu's account of the English political system in early Hanoverian times is correct. The theorist is more concerned with assumptions and arguments than with historical facts. The criticism of Montesquieu interests him less in its details than for the conclusion drawn from it. Montesquieu, say these critics, maintains that the English owe their freedom to the separation of powers, whereas the truth is that the legislative and executive powers are not separate in England. Therefore, unless we choose to argue that the English are not free (and who would choose to be as perverse as all that?), we must conclude that there can be freedom even where these two powers are not separate.

I do not choose to be perverse, and I do not even deny that a people might be free though the executive and legislative powers were not separate. I venture only to suggest that in England they were separate when Montesquieu wrote *De l'Esprit des Lois* and are still separate today. Of course, relations between executive and legislature in England have changed greatly in the last two hundred years, and are much closer than they were. They are also different in England from what they are in the United States; and if we decide that the two powers are not to be called separate unless they are related to one another as they are in the United States, then it is clear that they are not now separate in England. But, then, as we have seen, it is no less clear that they were not separate in England in Montesquieu's day, for the king could and did choose most of his ministers from the legislature, which the American president is forbidden to do. Yet Montesquieu, who must be supposed to have known how they were chosen, said that the two powers in England were separate. I suggest that in England today these two powers, though no longer related as they were in Montesquieu's time, are still so related that they act as checks on one another.

The King's (or Queen's) ministers are so now only in name; the monarch can no longer help to provide them with a majority in the House of Commons. Their relations with the House of Commons are now vastly different from what they were. Yet the ministers, the men who exercise the executive power which once belonged to the monarch, are no more chosen by the House of Commons than they are by the monarch. The Cabinet and the House of Commons (now much the more important of the two Houses) are not the same body, and neither is anywhere near being the mere tool or agent of the other. They are two separate bodies, of which the smaller is emphatically not a committee of the larger, nor the larger an assembly which merely carries out the wishes of the smaller. That the two bodies are related in ways unforeseen by Montesquieu, and much more intimately than ever the monarch was to Parliament in the days when kings governed and did not merely reign, does not make them one; nor does it ensure that the authority of either comes to it from the other. The House of Commons does not decide who shall belong to the Cabinet or what its powers shall be, and has only a limited control over its exercise of those powers; and the Cabinet, though its control over the House is much greater, is far indeed from being able to do what it likes with it. That the same election normally decides both who shall belong to the House of Commons and who shall be invited to form the executive body does not make these two bodies one or make either the subordinate of the other, though it doubtless helps to make relations between the two very different from what they would be if executive and legislature were separately elected as they are in the United States.[1]

When Montesquieu spoke of the executive and legislative powers being united in the same hands, he had in mind the sort of situation which existed in his own country. The King of France was the supreme law-maker and the supreme executive; he, with the help of his advisers, exercised both powers. If, having regard to political realities and not to paper constitutions, we were to look today for a country where the legislative and executive powers are united in the same hands as they were in France in Montesquieu's time, we should find it not in England but in Russia. It is there that the same body exercises in fact (though not in name) both the executive and the legislative powers, the Supreme Soviet having no other function than to applaud the decisions taken by the real rulers of the country. It is in Russia, and not in England, that the making of policy and the making of law are the work of the same body. It is true that in England the more important bills are government bills, but before they become law they must be publicly debated and voted on in an assembly where there is strong opposition to the government. And if the government can put pressure on its supporters in the House of Commons to ensure that they vote for its bills, it must also respond to pressure from them; its relations, even with its own supporters, are very different from what they would be if the House of Commons were the same sort of body as the Supreme Soviet.

In England policy is made by one body in one way, while laws are made by another body in another way. Policy is debated in secret, and the decisions reached are made public only when the body that makes

---

[1] After I had written this chapter I received from Mr L. Branney of the Colonial Office a most interesting paper arguing, though for reasons different from mine, that there is a separation of powers in Britain.

them chooses to publish them or takes action which reveals their nature; whereas proposals of law, no matter where they originate, are publicly debated and publicly opposed, and cannot become law unless they are exposed to discussion and attack. In Russia both policy and law are made, as they were in eighteenth-century France, by the same body, which takes all its decisions in secret. The difference between the English and Russian systems is not merely that in England elections to the supreme legislature are free while in Russia they are not; it is also that in England there is, in reality and not just on paper, a separation of the executive and legislative powers of a kind unknown in Russia. It is, of course, important that power is acquired in different ways in England and Russia, but it is also important that in the two countries it is differently distributed. The ways in which power comes to its possessors are no more alike in Montesquieu's France and Soviet Russia than they are in Soviet Russia and modern England. If we take old France and new Russia together, what distinguishes them from modern England is not the way in which supreme power is acquired but the way it is distributed.

The chapter on the constitution of England is probably, at least in the English-speaking world, the best known in *De l'Esprit des Lois*. More than anything else written by Montesquieu, it influenced writers and jurists in the English colonies and in the mother country. They were so much impressed and flattered by his admiration for English institutions, that they neglected whatever he said about the separation of powers when he was speaking of other institutions. They did not notice that some of his best arguments for an independent judiciary are connected, not with his account of the English constitution, but with the distinction he made beween monarchy and despotism. Even in the eleventh book, which is more concerned than any other with the separation of powers, there are eight chapters devoted to Ancient Rome. There too, according to Montesquieu, there was, during the period when Roman liberty endured, an effective separation of the three powers. His account of it is even more summary (and at times ambiguous) than his account of the English system of government, but he says enough to make it clear that he did not suppose that in Rome under the republic the three powers were so distributed that no person or body having a share of one had a share of the others. For example, he says that while the Roman people, jealous for their liberties, contested the legislative rights of the senate, they did not contest its executive rights.[1] He speaks in a way which suggests that the senate, though it was primarily an executive body, also had some legislative power which the people, for the sake of their liberties, did their best to keep within narrow limits. If, in the eleventh book of

---

[1] Ibid., Bk. XI, Ch. 17.

De l'Esprit des Lois, we compare the one long chapter devoted to England with the several shorter ones which treat of the Roman republic, we may say that, in the two political systems most admired by Montesquieu, there was an effective separation of powers, which was simpler in England than in Rome. And yet in neither system, as Montesquieu describes it, were the three powers so distributed that no body or person had a share of more than one.[1]

We need not agree with Montesquieu's account of English and Roman institutions to see the force of his doctrine about power and liberty. It may well be that to secure liberty there is no need to distribute the three powers as he thought they were distributed in either England or Rome. For though he leaves too much unexplained, it is clear, even from his own account, that there were great differences in this respect between the constitutions of the two peoples whose political genius he praised. If the English system could differ so much from the Roman and yet make liberty secure, why should not some other system differing greatly from both the Roman and the English do so as well? This we may concede, and yet agree with Montesquieu that, to make liberty secure, the political system must be such that power checks power. The rules governing the use of power must be such that, whenever some persons having authority are tempted to abuse it, there are others who can, in a quite regular and legal manner, prevent their doing so. Not only must the courts be independent of the government, but the supreme executive and legislative powers must not be in the same hands, even though they are distributed in such a way that there are several persons and bodies having a share of both.

In every community which is political, which has a regular government carried on by persons recognized as holding public office, all who have authority of any kind exercise it in prescribed ways. So much is implied by the very notion of a form of government or political system. In the widest sense of the word, there is a constitution; there is a body of rules whose general observance by those who govern makes government possible. Therefore, if this body of rules is such that abuses of power can be *legally* prevented, it is likely that they will be so prevented; for the simple reason that all persons and bodies having a share of authority have one interest in common: that the rules in virtue of which they have authority shall be respected. Where others before Montesquieu, for the defence of liberty and against the abuse of power,

---

[1] Notice the last words of the eleventh book: 'But one must not always so exhaust a subject that there is nothing left for the reader to do. It is not a question of making him read but of making him think.' It is astonishing how little it takes to exhaust a subject, in the opinion of Montesquieu! He would have done better to write longer chapters on fewer subjects, taking greater care to make his meaning plain. He asks altogether too much of his readers.

had appealed to natural right and natural law, or to a social contract whose terms oblige both rulers and ruled, or to a right of popular revolt against governments which break their trust, he proclaimed the need for constitutional govermnent: for political power so distributed that anyone having a share of it who is tempted to abuse it finds others having power able and willing to use it to prevent or punish him. Liberty does not flourish because men have natural rights or because they revolt if their rulers press them too far; it flourishes because power is so distributed and organized that whoever is tempted to abuse it finds legal restraints in his way.

These restraints will not be effective unless there is a will to use them – unless the persons who run the system are true to its spirit. But then the system tends to keep them true to it. Montesquieu does not belittle the importance of the political emotions, of loyalty to the constitution and respect for freedom; he merely sees a close connection between these emotions and the institutions they support. As he sees it, men do not first conceive of freedom and then set about looking for the institutions which secure it. Institutions and the sentiments appropriate to them reinforce one another. Those value freedom most who are accustomed to enjoy it, and they cannot enjoy it unless they live in a society whose institutions make it secure. If it is true that freedom will not survive where it is not valued, where men are not ready to defend it, it is equally true that they will not set a high value on it where they have never had, or have long since lost, the means of defending it. And freedom cannot be defended except where there are some at least of the institutions necessary to its defence. There must already be some freedom, and therefore institutions favourable to freedom, before the love of it can grow strong.

From this it follows that freedom is enlarged slowly; it is the fruit of many victories, and the weapons men use, both to preserve the freedom they have and to add to it, are the institutions they already have. Freedom is an effect of many things which are themselves intimately connected: the laws and habits of a people, their temper and prejudices. It cannot survive, in any large and complex community, unless the rules governing the use of power, while serving to make it effective, also prevent the abuse of it. In England, the oldest home of freedom, government is not weaker than elsewhere, not less able to carry out its will; but its functions are so distributed that those who take part in government are both willing and able to prevent the abuses to which all who have power are liable to be tempted.

Montesquieu's doctrine of the separation of powers is not an effect of an unlucky though excusable mistake about the English system of government; it springs from a deeper understanding of what political power is than we can find in all but a few of his predecessors. Power so organized that it checks power without making government ineffective, a system which is self-regulating because it is so organized that no one who takes part in running it can hope to increase his own share of power by breaking the rules of the system: this idea is to be met with before Montesquieu. It was familiar to Harrington, and there are hints of it in earlier writers. But, as Pascal says in *De l'Esprit Géométrique*, 'All those who say the same things do not possess them in the same way. . . . Therefore we must probe to see how this thought is lodged in its author; in what manner, from what angle, and to what extent he possesses it.'[1] This idea was by Montesquieu expounded with greater insight and elaboration than by anyone before him; he possessed it more fully than they did, saw further into its implications and into the conditions, social and psychological, of its being realized. It is his idea by right of conquest.

In this book no social or political theory is studied in all its aspects, but only those parts of it which raise broad issues which cannot be settled without examining fundamental concepts and assumptions. I have discussed Montesquieu's account of the social effects of man's physical environment and what he does to protect himself from it or to adapt himself to it, his views about the interdependence of institutions and modes of thought and feeling, his conception of the supremacy of law, and his ideas about power and how best to organize it to secure freedom. These are the parts of his theory which call for treatment in a book of this kind. Yet his discussion of them occupies only eleven of the thirty-one books of *De l'Esprit des Lois*. There is therefore a great deal left out of account; and when I say this, I have in mind, not Montesquieu's writings which do not treat primarily of social and political theory, but his best-known work which does. Of the twenty books of *De l'Esprit des Lois* which I have not considered only four deal with matters interesting to jurists; the others are all concerned with what is truly social and political theory. Moreover, they deal, not with small matters, but with great ones. They raise important issues, though not of the kind with which this book is primarily concerned, because to consider them it is not necessary to examine critically the basic concepts which we use to explain social and political phenomena or to pass judgements upon them. Of course, in every part of *De l'Esprit des Lois*, in the parts I have neglected as much as in those I have not, Montesquieu uses these concepts, as any one must do who discusses what he chooses to discuss. He uses the concepts, though not in such a way as to move the reader to examine them critically; it is either clear enough how he uses them or his argument

---

[1] *L'Oeuvre de Pascal.* Pléiade edition, p. 383. The French reads: 'Tous ceux qui disent les mêmes choses ne les possèdent pas de la même sorte . . . Il faut donc sonder comme cette pensée est logée en son auteur; comment, par où, jusqu' où il la possède.'

is so meagre or obscure as to make close scrutiny unprofitable. Yet it is to do less than justice to Montesquieu not to draw the reader's attention to how much this particular discussion of his theories leaves out. He devotes two books to considering slavery, its causes and effects in different societies. In the first, Book XV, he considers what is ordinarily understood by slavery, and in the second, Book XVI, what he calls 'domestic slavery' or the extremer forms of the subjection of women. In these two books, and more particularly in the first, the two dominant passions of Montesquieu the social theorist are both very much to the fore: curiosity and the love of freedom. Though his purpose is to explain slavery, he does not trouble to hide his dislike of it. He treats almost with contempt the arguments used to justify it, and is eager to point out its dangers. Everywhere, except in a despotism, it is dangerous to the established order, for where some men have freedom and others are slaves, the qualities on which the survival of freedom depend are undermined; a state which is not despotic but which allows slavery is in danger of becoming despotic. Though Montesquieu sometimes calls all the subjects of a despot 'slaves', he is not, when he does so, using that word in the ordinary sense. In the argument we are now considering, he is not saying that, in a country where there are slaves, in the sense of persons bought and sold on the market, all men are in danger of becoming slaves in the same sense; he is saying rather that, where slavery long endures, even those who do not become slaves in this sense cease to have the rights which distinguish the citizen of a republic or even a monarchy from the subject of a despot.

Montesquieu says that, if he had to defend the right to make slaves of Negroes, this is what he would say:

The peoples of Europe having exterminated those of America have had to reduce the peoples of Africa to slavery in order to use them to clear so much land. Sugar would be too dear if the plant which produces it were not cultivated by slaves. The people concerned are black from foot to head, and they have noses so squashed that it is almost impossible to pity them. It is not to be imagined that God, who is very wise, would put a soul, and above all, a good soul, into a body that was all black. . . . We cannot suppose that such folk are men, because, if we suppose them to be men, people might begin to think that we ourselves are not Christians.[1]

Two books treat of religion, and are written, for the most part, much in the spirit of Machiavelli.[2] The reader is immediately warned that the author will examine the religions of the world only to estimate the

[1] *De l'Esprit des Lois*, Bk. XV, Ch. 5.
[2] They are Bks. XXIV and XV

good that civil society derives from them, and this whether he speaks of the one which has its root in heaven or of those which have theirs in the earth. His tone is cool and ironic; sometimes, no doubt, he is genuinely detached and at other times affects to be so. He even disputes some of the conclusions of Bayle, not to defend the truth of any religion (for that is not his business) but to show that it does not have the effects ascribed to it. He is interested primarily in the utility of various religions, and has little to say about their causes or even their effects other than effects on morals. Islam is, he thinks, better suited to the peoples of Asia, and Christianity to the Europeans, while Protestantism agrees better with the temperament of northern Europeans and Catholicism better with southerners. A new religion accommodates itself to the habits and prejudices of the people among whom it first arises, which makes it unsuited to peoples who differ greatly from them; and this explains why it often begins by making rapid progress over a wide area and then suddenly ceases to spread.

Montesquieu would have governments tolerate religions firmly rooted within their borders but advises them to discourage new religions on the ground that their adherents are usually intolerant. It is a mistake to use penal laws to force men to believe (or to pretend to believe) what their rulers decide they ought to believe, but it may be necessary, in order to preserve peace and good will among men, to discourage the propagation of certain beliefs.[1] Montesquieu does not say what a government should do to discourage such pernicious beliefs. This is one more among many examples of one of the great faults of De l'Esprit des Lois: It touches upon too many topics too lightly and rapidly and prompts too many questions which it never attempts to answer.

Montesquieu was no mean economist. Two books of his greatest work are devoted to commerce, and another to money and exchange. In the seventeenth chapter of Book XXII he explains how money has a price like any other commodity, and how that price is determined by the amount of it in circulation and the total quantity of goods actually in trade. In the tenth chapter of the same book he explains how the rates of exchange between different currencies is determined by the balance of indebtedness between holders of these currencies; and in yet another chapter he condemns the laws against usury as restraints on trade. But he was less interested in the economics of trade than its

---

[1] I must take care to do justice to Montesquieu's dislike of intolerance. One of the most moving and eloquent chapters of De l'Esprit des Lois is the thirteenth of Book XXV. It purports to be a Humble Remonstrance addressed by a Jew to the Inquisitors of Spain and Portugal, inspired by the burning of a Jewish girl at an auto-da-fé. It is beautifully done, and is not the less effective because Montesquieu pretends that he is quoting and even appends a footnote criticizing a sentiment expressed in the remonstrance.

political and other effects. He ascribed the freedom of the English in large part to their being a commercial people.[1]

Montesquieu gave his masterpiece to the world as a finished work, and we know that he spent a long time in the making and perfecting of it. And yet it has less coherence and less unity even than Pascal's *Pensées*. For the *Pensées*, though never made into a book, are nevertheless the makings of a book; they are pieces brought together by a builder of genius who never completed his building, by a vigorous thinker and artist who knew how to put his thoughts together into a coherent, elaborate and elegant whole. But Montesquieu has left us a vast and shapeless building consisting of innumerable small rooms into which he has put furniture assiduously and abundantly collected over many years. He was, like his compatriot Montaigne, both a collector of facts and opinions and more than a mere collector. He had not only an enquiring but a fertile mind. He was an innovator; he had new ideas and attempted new things. He was, in his own very different way, as much an innovator as Hume. But he was not nearly as lucid and acute as Hume; he had nothing like the same ability to say precisely what he meant. If we could ask Hume what he thought he had attempted and achieved as a writer on society and government, he would probably give us a clear and correct answer; if we could put the same question to Montesquieu, we should almost certainly be disappointed with the content of his answer if not with the style.

Montesquieu was the first to attempt a serious study of forms of government in relation to the entire social structures in which they flourish. His information was less reliable and his ignorance vastly greater than he imagined. For so sophisticated a man, he was at times strangely credulous; if he had something of Aristotle in him, he also had something of Herodotus. It took very little to convince him that he had dealt adequately with any subject he discussed. Perhaps he was the dupe of his style, inclining to believe that whatever he had said well he had said truly. Certainly, he spoke without misgivings of

[1] Two of the longest chapters of *De l'Esprit des Lois* treat of the English. The sixth chapter of Book XI I have discussed already. In the twenty-seventh chapter of Book XIX he says (having England in mind) that in a free country there is a natural division between the supporters and opponents of government, their relative strengths varying continually, so that the monarch has to rely first on the one group and then on the other. But, in spite of party conflicts, a free people are not less but more united than others, especially when danger threatens from abroad, and are more willing to make sacrifices and to pay heavy taxes. A free people are tolerant, more given to pride than to vanity, rough in their manners, and in their literature more subtle than delicate. Though in this chapter Montesquieu does not mention the English by name, it is easy to see that he has them in mind. Nor does he merely praise them: like other Frenchmen who have spoken well of the English, he finds them more admirable than attractive. He denies them only one quality which they often boast of possessing, and that is modesty.

matters he knew very little about. Yet he had a considerable knowledge of three very different peoples, the Romans, the English and the French; and, for several of his purposes, they were not a bad sample. His comparative method, applied to them, led to some remarkable results.

Of the great political theorists discussed in this book, only two, Hume and Montesquieu, were much less advocates or critics than observers intent on explaining the facts. They had their preferences, which they did not trouble to hide, but they were quiet preferences. For they lived in quiet times, and had not, like Rousseau, premonitions of unquiet times to come. They were not eager to defend the established order or to change it. They flourished at a time when men were beginning to believe in progress but had not yet become impatient. They did not believe, as Hobbes and Pascal had done, that all that matters is that there should be an order which nobody challenges. The theories which Locke had attacked were discredited, and there was no need for them to assert that legitimate authority derives from the consent of the governed in order to deny that whoever has it is answerable only to God for how he uses it. They knew nothing of radicals and revolutionaries. They were the least dogmatic and the most serene of political thinkers; they wrote in an interval when the sky of politics was unusually clear, with a cloud no bigger than a man's hand in it.

Chapter 8

HUME

LEGEND has it that a Dutch admiral once tied a broom to the mast of his flagship as a boast or as a warning to his enemies. He meant to convey either that he had swept them from the seas or that he intended to do so: I no longer remember which. If philosophers had emblems, Hume's would surely be a broom. Not that he liked to boast or threaten. He was the most polite as well as the most ruthless of critics; he used his broom deftly and quietly, raising little dust, but he used it vigorously.

As a philosopher, an epistemologist, Hume has received his due, and perhaps more than his due, especially at Oxford. As a social and political theorist less than justice has been done to him. It is difficult to explain why this should be so, for he spent as much time and thought on political and closely allied moral problems as on the theory of knowledge. Of all his writings, he was proudest of the *Enquiry Concerning the Principles of Morals*. In that work, as in the third book of his *Treatise of Human Nature*, he tries to explain morality entirely as a social phenomenon. Hume is more important perhaps as an eliminator of the obscure, the inadequate, and the otiose than as a framer of new ideas and hypotheses. He destroyed more than he created. Yet, to the extent that he was creative, he was more so perhaps as a moralist and political theorist than as a general philosopher. In his theory of knowledge he put nothing really satisfactory in the place of what he took away; whereas his account of justice, though it falls short of the truth, is plausible and suggestive; it is also the heart of his social philosophy.

It is true that Hume's account of justice is not entirely original; almost every part of it can be found, somewhere or other, in writings earlier than his own. What is new about it is less the ideas that go to make it up than the clear, systematic, and economical exposition of them. As a moralist, Hume, though not perhaps the equal of an Aristotle or a Kant, is much more than just a discarder of confused or unnecessary ideas.

This is true also of his more narrowly political theory, though to a lesser extent. There is nothing in his strictly political writings to equal the *Enquiry Concerning the Principles of Morals* or the third part of the *Treatise* in the broad sweep of its argument, in the lucid presentation of an elaborate and well-constructed account of a whole area of human experience. Hume wrote treatises about morals and only essays about politics; but his moral theory is at the same time a theory about society. He is interested not only (nor even primarily) in the analysis of moral judgement; he is also, and even more, interested in the social origins and functions of morality. Man is a moral being, a lover of justice, only in society, and needs government to make justice secure.

I. HUME'S REJECTION OF NATURAL LAW AND THE SOCIAL CONTRACT

Hume rejects the traditional account of natural law and substitutes for it the idea of conventions based on the common experience of mankind. He also rejects the notion of a social contract, not merely on historical grounds, but as a tool of explanation. Scarcely any of the contract theorists had been seriously concerned to argue that contracts had actually been made to set up governments; they had mostly used the notion of contract to explain the duty of obedience and how that duty is limited. They had supposed that we can best understand what government is for, why and to what extent it is our duty to obey it, by seeing what kind of agreement men without government would have to make with one another to establish a government capable of giving them security. This was the assumption of the contract theorists which Filmer and other champions of the theory of divine right denied. Some of them found good arguments to support this denial. But their own theories were as little plausible as the theory they attacked; and the conclusions they reached were less popular. Hume's method and purpose are different from theirs. He has no wish to deny the political rights and duties asserted by the contract theorists; he wants only to show that there is no need to postulate a social contract in order to explain them, because there is a better way of accounting for them.

We can get a good idea of Hume's method and purpose by comparing him with Hobbes. In the traditional account of it, natural law sets a limit to all human authority. All government is under that law; so that, where government also makes law, the law it makes is subordinate to a law it does not make. Natural law is the law of God; though not His arbitrary will, because God is entirely reasonable. The law of nature is the law that all men, being God's rational creatures, ought to follow in their dealings with one another. They discover it by reflecting on human nature and on God's purposes for man. It was supposed that, man and God's purposes for man being what they are, men necessarily have certain duties and rights.

Hobbes had taken this notion of natural law and had quite emasculated it; or rather, had taken the phrase and given it a new meaning. His law of nature is not properly a moral law; it consists only of rules which experience teaches men it would be to their advantage to follow if they could be sure that other men would follow them too. The laws of nature, as regards their contents, are only maxims of prudence whose general observance would put an end to the war of all against all. Merely as maxims they are not obligatory, but are so only as divine commands; and they are obligatory in a peculiar sense which does not make them what most people call moral laws. They are the commands of an omnipotent God, whom men, when they see that they are powerless before Him, cannot choose but obey. Hobbes' natural laws do not serve to limit the authority of government. It is usually not safe (and therefore not obligatory) to obey them until there is a sovereign to enforce them; and where there is a sovereign they are contained entire in his actual commands. There is no appeal to them to show that what the sovereign commands is, in some higher sense, illegal. Hobbes' method is to take a time-honoured phrase, put a new meaning into it, and incorporate it in a theory whose purpose is to deny precisely what the traditional doctrine of natural law was meant to assert. Hobbes' method is subversive. It uses the letter of an old doctrine to destroy the spirit. It does not reject but undermines; and to that extent is of necessity ambiguous.

Hume's method is not subversive but openly critical. There are no eternal moral rules, no laws of nature, which man can discover by the mere use of reason when he contemplates his nature as God created it. There are only conventions which men come to adopt because experiences teaches them it is their interest to do so. These conventions are, to begin with, mere maxims of prudence, like Hobbes' laws of nature. Men follow them because it is to their advantage to do so. But they do not remain mere maxims of prudence, for men come to approve the keeping of them and to disapprove the breach of them. It is this approval and disapproval that convert rules of convenience into rules of right. The approval and disapproval are effects of sympathy, of an emotion which is not self-regarding. Though the conventions of morality are rules which it is every man's permanent interest to follow, their moral character does not consist in their utility. It consists in how men feel about them; in feelings men could not have if they were entirely selfish.

The obligation to follow these rules is prior to government. Though Hume rejects the traditional doctrine of natural law, he distinguishes much more clearly than Hobbes does between the moral and the legal. Moral rules are not natural but conventional, and yet man is a moral creature before he is subject to government. What men will put up with from government is limited by the conventions they come to accept as members of society. There are no laws of nature in the sense of universal principles of conduct whose validity is directly apprehended by reason; but there is a law which is not an effect of power and which limits the authority of government; a law which is not command and is prior to the kind of law which is command. Hume, unlike Hobbes, has a good deal of sympathy with the desire to restrain government implicit in the old doctrine of natural law, but discards the doctrine because he thinks he can express whatever is true and valuable in it in another and better way.

We can see similar differences of method and purpose if we compare the attitudes of Hume and Hobbes to the contract theory. Hume rejects it altogether. Hobbes tries to use it to prove the contrary of what the theory was invented to establish. The terms of the contract were supposed to set limits to the authority of the ruler. But Hobbes is bent on showing that it follows from the very nature of a contract capable of ensuring effective government that there can be no such limits. Hume, though he rejects the contract theory, is not concerned to deny that all government rests, in some sense, on the consent of the governed.[1] Power is, he thinks, an effect of obedience. Unless governments were obeyed they would be powerless. The obedience on which power rests must therefore be voluntary.

Yet there is, in spite of these differences, a fundamental similarity between Hobbes and Hume. They agree that no action is right or wrong in itself. It is so only by virtue of some attitude to it. Hobbes has it that an action is wrong if it is forbidden by someone, God or man, strong enough to compel obedience, and right if that someone commands or allows it; while Hume has it that an action if right if generally approved, and wrong if generally disapproved. To explain how it is that there are rules of behaviour among men, both Hobbes and Hume begin by considering what it would be like if there were no such rules. If men were unrestrained in their attempts to satisfy their natural desires, they would repeatedly come into conflict with one another. But conflict is painful and men naturally seek to avoid pain. Reason teaches them, not what is inherently right and inherently wrong, but how they must behave to avoid the pains of conflict. About these rules, as reason discovers them, there is nothing either moral or legal. For reason could as easily discover the means of exacerbating conflict. What gives to the rules which reason discovers the character of law is, Hobbes tells us, that there is someone with the will and the power to compel obedience to them. And Hume tells us that the rules are moral only because men feel as they do about them. In neither case are the rules obligatory because they are rational. The office of reason is not to lay obligations upon us but to discover how we can get what we want. 'Reason is and ought to be the slave of the passions.' The words are Hume's, but the sentiment they express is also the sentiment of Hobbes.

[1] This consent is not agreement or the granting of permission; it is acquiescence grounded in the knowledge that government is in the public interest.

Hume and Hobbes also agree in treating government as a device to ensure that men do not sacrifice their permanent interest to lesser but more immediate advantages. Hobbes is at pains to show that everyone has, on the whole, more to gain than to lose by observing the maxims of prudence, which he calls – rather perversely – laws of nature, provided other people also observe them. He believes that any reasonable man reflecting on his experience will see this. And yet, though everyone can see it, no one can trust anyone else always to act reasonably. If men were so made that they always preferred their own greatest good to every immediate advantage conflicting with that good, there would be no need for government. For then everyone would follow the maxims of prudence and could reasonably trust everyone else to do so. But unfortunately men are not so made. It is not defect of reason in them but the strength of their passions which moves them to prefer a lesser immediate good to their greatest good. Thus, if it is to be worth anyone's while to follow the maxims, everyone must be assured that other people will follow them. And there can be this assurance only where there is a power sufficient to compel obedience to the maxims and a will to use that power. It is always the sovereign's immediate advantage to compel the obedience which is the condition of social peace, because on the preservation of this peace his power depends. The laws of nature, the maxims of prudence, are necessarily contained in the laws of the sovereign; they are the rules which the sovereign must enforce if he is to retain his sovereign power.

Hume uses what is at bottom the same argument when he says that men must palliate their incurable tendency to prefer a lesser immediate good to a greater but more remote one, by setting up over them some persons whose duty and interest it is to compel them, however reluctant they may be, to do what it is in their own long-term interest that they should do. As nearly all men love power, it is easy to find persons willing to undertake the task of government. These persons, whoever they are, will ordinarily be inclined in their own interest to maintain justice, for, unless they do so, their subjects will soon cease to obey them; and justice consists of the rules which it is everyone's permanent interest should be obeyed. Government, as Hume sees it, is not the maintainer of an eternal justice directly apprehended by reason; it is a device which makes it the immediate interest of some persons to promote the permanent interest of everyone.

II. HUME'S ACCOUNT OF JUSTICE AND FIDELITY AS ARTIFICIAL VIRTUES

Justice, or respect for rules of property, and fidelity, or the keeping of promises, Hume calls 'artificial virtues'. Since the 'artificial virtues' are the ones on which the stability of society chiefly depends, it is important to discover just what Hume conceives them to be and how they differ from the 'natural virtues'. The natural virtues are not natural because they are in keeping with any laws of nature in the traditional sense. All virtues, for Hume, are virtues only because they are generally approved of. What, then, makes a natural virtue natural, and an artificial virtue artificial? Hume tells me that 'the only difference betwixt the natural virtues and justice lies in this, that the good which results from the former, arrives from every single act, and is the object of some natural passion; whereas a single act of justice, considered in itself, may often be contrary to the public good.' We have the gist of the difference here; but Hume's statement is too short to be immediately intelligible. It needs to be elaborated.

Let us consider first the natural virtues, and let us take an example. To help the afflicted is a natural virtue. When we see a fellow human being in distress, the sight of this suffering causes us to suffer. We sympathize with him, and this sympathy, says Hume (and here he differs from Hobbes) is not a refined form of egoism. We suffer at the sight of another man's suffering, and not at the thought of ourselves suffering as he does; though it may be because we ourselves have suffered in the past that we understand his predicament and feel sympathy for him. This sympathy is immediately aroused in us by the sight of his suffering; it is a natural passion that moves us to help him. We help him, not from a sense of duty, but because we feel sympathy for him. And when we see anyone else helping a man in distress, we are pleased by the action. This pleasure is also an effect of sympathy. We are pleased, not because we stand to gain anything ourselves by the action, but because we sympathize with the man in distress and with the man who wants to help him. The pleasure we get from seeing one man do good to another, and sometimes even to himself, Hume calls approval. Men are so made that, in the absence of motives causing them to feel otherwise, the mere sight of another's pain gives them pain, and the mere sight of another's pleasure gives them pleasure. Men are by nature given to sympathize with one another; they are therefore also given to feel pleasure at the sight of actions that alleviate pain or cause pleasure, and to feel pain at the sight of actions that do the opposite. They are naturally given to approval and disapproval, and it is these feelings alone which make the actions they are directed to virtuous or vicious.

Approval and disapproval, as Hume explains the matter, are directed not so much at external actions as at the motives which inspire them. When we approve of one man relieving the distress of another, what we approve of is the compassion he feels and his readiness to act. But the motives of other people are not directly known to us, and we can infer their motives only from their actions; and so, in practice, it does not much matter whether we say that approval and disapproval are directed at men's actions or at their motives. Approval and disapproval are essentially unselfish; they are always born of sympathy, which is not a self-regarding feeling. They are not always strong feelings; indeed, though stronger in some people than in others, they are commonly weak if we compare them with such emotions as anger, fear, hatred and love. But they more than make up by their generality for their weakness; they are, as Hume puts it, feelings in which we expect most people to concur with us.

It is easy to see how the natural virtues come to be virtues. The sympathy that moves us to do actions which are naturally virtuous is aroused directly by the thought of other people's suffering or their happiness. To some extent, of course, it depends on experience and reflection; as we cannot know directly how other people feel, we must learn what hurts them and what helps them by reflecting on our own experience. But this we learn quickly, and then sympathy moves us to do what is naturally virtuous and to avoid what is naturally vicious; provided, of course, that there are not contrary passions moving us away from virtue and towards vice. The natural virtues are natural, not because they accord with a law of nature directly apprehended by reason, but because it is easy to see how they arise; how sympathy moves us both to practise them and to approve the practice of them.

In what, then, does the artificiality of the artificial virtues, justice and fidelity, consist? It consists in the different motive that impels us to practise them, and in the character of the experience which causes us to desire that they should be practised. Sympathy alone moves us to do what is naturally virtuous, and the experience needed to enlighten us about the sufferings and pleasures of other people is simple and involves not much reflection. But our motive for being just or for keeping a promise is not sympathy but self-love. It is self-love enlightened by much more than knowledge about how we ourselves feel in this or that situation together with the assumption that other people feel the same in the same situations; it is self-love enlightened by reflection on the remoter consequences of our behaviour to others and their behaviour to us. It is self-love enlightened by reflection on our enduring relations with others; or, in other words, by reflection on our social experience.

Hume's account of the artificial virtues does not require us to assume that man is predominantly selfish; that he nearly always cares more for himself than for other people. It assumes no more than that some of his virtues, justice and fidelity, on which the stability of society chiefly depends, arise *in the first place* from self-love. It does not require us to believe that, once society is well-established and justice is generally recognized as a virtue, men are usually just only from enlightened self-love.

Justice and fidelity are not artificial virtues merely because they arise from self-love, but because their root in self-love is less simple and obvious than the root of the natural virtues in sympathy. They are artificial because, compared with the natural virtues, they rest on more subtle reflection; they are artificial because they are sophisticated and also social. Of course, all the virtues and vices, natural and artificial, are the virtues and vices of rational creatures; they all involve some degree of reflection. The peculiarity of the artificial virtues is that they derive from prolonged reflection on what is involved in men's living together permanently. Not every man need go through this process of reflection; he may be taught the artificial virtues by precept, he may practise them on the mere authority of his parents or teachers. But, then again, not everyone can be taught by precept; some must learn by experience, and in fact most people will do so to some extent.

Let us take concrete examples to illustrate Hume's meaning, for it is best to be clear even at the risk of appearing to labour the obvious. When you see someone in distress, you are quickly moved to sympathy with him, and your first impulse is to help him. But there may be contrary passions at work. If, for example, you are hungry and you see food that someone has set aside for his own use, sympathy will probably not move you to let that food alone. If you take his food, you will cause him pain, and you may sympathize with him on that account; but your sympathy will probably not prevent your taking his food. Hunger will be a more powerful motive with you than sympathy. Not always, of course, but usually. If the food is intended for someone you love, you may prefer to go hungry rather than to cause pain. But love is an emotion you feel for few persons, and will therefore not cause you to respect the property of most people who have what you desire. How, then, does it come about that you do respect their property? You respect it, says Hume, not from sympathy or from fear, but from self-love. For though it is your immediate interest to take from others whatever is useful to yourself, you learn by experience that, in the long run, you have more to gain than to lose by not doing so, provided they in their turn take nothing from you. You learn to do unto others as you would have them do unto you. In other words, you learn to prefer your permanent to your immediate interest; and since other people learn this as well as you, you have good reason to follow the principle you have learned even where there is no government to compel you.

Just as enlightened self-love causes you and other people to abstain from one another's possessions, so it causes you to keep your promises. Experience teaches you how useful it is to be able to rely on other people doing what they said they would do, and also that you cannot expect them to do so unless you do likewise. You learn to value mutual confidence and to play your part in maintaining it. The keeping of promises and respect for property are the most important among artificial virtues; they are artificial because they spring from restraints which the self puts upon itself in its own permanent interest. They arise, not from an uninhibited natural passion, but from spontaneous self-love held in check by enlightened self-love.

But it is not self-love that makes respect for property and the keeping of promises virtues, for whatever is virtuous is so because it is generally approved, and approval always proceeds from sympathy and never from self-love. You desire justice from self-love and you esteem it from sympathy. Justice is not only your interest; it is also the interest of everyone, the general, the public interest. When therefore you see anyone being just, you approve his conduct because you sympathize with the public interest. The moral sentiments are no more self-regarding when they are directed to respect for property and the breach of it, to the keeping and breaking of promises, to the artificial virtues and vices, than when they are directed to the natural virtues and vices.

Since we like being approved of and dislike being disapproved of, we are powerfully and repeatedly influenced by the moral sentiments of other people. These sentiments, though often weak, are also universal. The desire to gain approval and to avoid disapproval is therefore always a strong motive, quite apart from enlightened self-love, to induce people to respect property and to keep their word. That is why justice and fidelity can flourish even in the absence of organized power. Hume has rooted respect for property and the keeping of promises, as Hobbes did before him, in self-love; but he has done so without asserting the universal and invincible selfishness of man, and without concluding that men will not in fact respect property or keep their word unless they are compelled. Though his account of what he calls the artificial virtues still falls short of the truth, it is clearly a great improvement on Hobbes. It does less violence to the facts; it is also more consistent.

So far, I have considered Hume's account of the artificial virtues only in the most general way; I have considered how, in his opinion, men come to conceive of certain rules of behaviour as useful and to desire that people should conform to them, and what it is that makes that behaviour virtuous. I have not yet touched upon Hume's account of the conditions which make the artificial virtues necessary. Would there be such virtues in any conceivable society? Or only in some?

About the conditions of fidelity Hume says almost nothing. Presumably he believes that, whatever the circumstances of men in society, they would always find it useful to make and keep promises and would therefore set a value on the keeping of them. Respect for property is also everywhere in fact a virtue, because the conditions which make

L*

this respect useful in fact hold everywhere. But we can conceive of a society in which these conditions would not hold. We can therefore say that, whereas fidelity is useful in any conceivable society, respect for property is only useful in societies where certain conditions hold. In fact these conditions hold in all societies known to us, and we have no reason to believe that there will ever be a society where they do not hold. But we can imagine such a society.

Rules of property are needed because men's wants are indefinite and the means of relieving them are scarce, and also because human generosity is confined. If whatever we needed to satisfy our wants were to be had for the taking, and always in a form fit for human consumption; if natural resources were boundless and no labour was required to prepare them for use, we could do without property, without rules governing the use of external goods and their transference from person to person. Nature has dealt less kindly with us than with other animals; we need greater protection than they do from the elements and we are physically weaker in proportion to our needs. Fortunately, we are also ingenious animals, and can invent better means than nature provides for satisfying our wants. We can work together intelligently for our mutual advantage; and in society our natural infirmities are much more than compensated for. Though in society our needs multiply quickly upon us, our power to satisfy them grows still more quickly. Society originates in our needs, which we cannot adequately provide for except with one another's help; and we cannot, being the sort of creatures we are and having only limited resources at our disposal, help one another successfully unless we have rules of property.

If men were all so generous as to be always willing to part with anything that another person needed more than they did, they might do without rules of property, even in a world where natural resources were limited. But their generosity is too confined for that; and therefore, since in fact there is not enough of everything to satisfy everybody all the time, men must have rules of property if they are to live at peace with one another.

Scarcity of resources and confined generosity: these are the two conditions which make justice, or respect for rules of property, a necessary virtue. These conditions happen to hold everywhere in our world, and there is no reason why we should suppose that there will ever be a time or place where they will not hold. Only if the conceivable were also in fact possible, only if men were completely generous or if anything a man wanted were to be had for the taking in exactly the form he needed it, could men live happily together without property.

Hume's account of why we need *some* rules of property is certainly plausible. It is when he sets about explaining why we have the particular rules we do have that his explanation suddenly becomes unconvincing. Indeed the passing from sense to fantasy is so sudden as

HUME 309

to be disconcerting. Can the same man who has spoken so much sense still be speaking now?

'That there is a separation or distinction of possessions, and that this separation be steady and constant; this is absolutely required by the interests of society, and hence the origin of justice and property. What possessions are assigned to particular persons; this is, generally speaking, pretty indifferent; and is often determined by very frivolous views and considerations.'[1] We are seriously invited to believe that, though it matters enormously that there should be some rules of property and that they should not change, it does not much matter what they are. Rules of property are like rules of the road; it does not matter whether traffic keeps to the left or to the right, but it does matter that it should keep to the one or the other; it matters that there should be a rule and that everyone should keep to it. True, Hume does not say that it matters not at all what the rules are, provided that there are some and they do not change. 'There are . . .' he admits, 'motives of public interest for most of the rules which determine property; but I still suspect that these rules are principally fixed by the imagination.'[2] He then goes on to mention the principal rules which establish titles to property: present possession, first possession, long possession or prescription, accession or the rule that the fruit or offspring of what you own is also yours, and succession or inheritance. Hume admits that its utility is enough to explain the first rule, present possession; everyone expects to keep what he has, so that the rule that he should keep it is obviously convenient. But first possession, accession, and succession, and perhaps also long possession, arise, he thinks, more from the association of ideas than from convenience. First possession engages the attention most, and we tend to associate things with their first possessors and thus to acquiesce in the rule that who first acquires something should keep it. We also associate things with the persons who have long possessed them, and we therefore acquiesce in prescription for the same reason as we do in first possession. 'We are naturally directed', says Hume, 'to consider the son after the parent's decease, and ascribe to him a title to his father's possessions.'[3] A dead man's property must go to some one. How do we decide who it shall go to? The thought of the father brings the son to our minds, and this association of ideas is the root of inheritance. In the *Enquiry*[4] Hume admits that industry is encouraged by property passing to a man's children or near relations, but this, he thinks, is true only of civilized societies, whereas this rule of inheritance is cherished even among barbarians.

[1] *An Enquiry Concerning the Principles of Morals*, Appendix III, Selby-Bigge, 2nd Edition, p. 301 note.
[2] *Treatise of Human Nature*. Bk. III, Part I, Section III. Selby-Bigge, p. 504.
[3] *Treatise*, Bk. III, Part I, Section III, p. 511.
[4] *Enquiry*, Appendix III, p. 307 note.

When a philosopher gets what he believes is a good idea, he is sometimes tempted to make too much of it. Hume, who had to his own satisfaction used the association of ideas to explain our belief in causality, thought he could also use it to explain how we come by our particular rules of property. His explanation is often pure fantasy. Did it not occur to him that fathers ordinarily want to leave their possessions to their children, and that this is perhaps why it has comes to be thought right that they should do so? Why should the association of ideas have anything to do with the matter? A man who has possessed something for a long time expects to keep it, and this is surely enough to explain the rule of prescription without any reference to the imagination. Though Hume, as I have said, did not deny the utility of his five rules, admitting that there are 'motives of public interest' for most rules of property, he did neglect the obvious for the fantastic. He said that titles to property are often determined by 'very frivolous views and considerations'.[1] There is less frivolity about the rules than about his explanations of them.

It was perhaps because he thought it did not much matter what the rules were, provided there were some, that Hume took it for granted that, whatever they are, they ought never to change. If what really matters is that there should be some rules, and it is more or less indifferent what they are, it is unlikely that there will be good reasons for changing them. At the same time, since men's expectations are formed by whatever rules they have, there is always a good reason for *not* changing the rules. Thus we can actually use the 'frivolity' (as Hume puts it) that attends the choice of the rules as an argument for their being, like the laws of the Medes and Persians, unchangeable. The argument is not illogical, but it is odd and unrealistic. I am less moved to refute it than to wonder how it ever came to be made. I feel about it as I should do if someone were to say: 'I am against divorce, because, while it does not much matter whom we marry, it matters enormously that we should marry and stay married.' There are some good arguments against divorce, but I suspect that this is not one of them.

If Hume had looked more carefully at his five rules of property and had tried to discover just what makes them useful, it might have occurred to him to set limits to their utility. He would then have inquired more closely into the conditions which make precisely these five rules (and not just *some* rules) useful; and might perhaps have concluded that the conditions need not always hold. It might then have occurred to him that, though these five rules are clearly useful in sparsely populated, primitive and agricultural communities, they are not so clearly useful where population is dense or natural resources are scarce or methods of production are elaborate.

[1] *Enquiry*, Appendix III, p. 307 note.

Though Hume's account of property is widely different from Locke's, some of the same objections can be made against it. Admittedly, as a general explanation of how there come to be any rules of property, Hume's account is more convincing than Locke's. It makes property not a natural right but a convention arising out of the social experience of mankind. But Hume's explanation of the five rules of property takes as little account of the economic realities of his own day as does Locke's labour theory of property. He takes it for granted that these rules will be much the same in all societies. No more than Locke, does he consider the possibility that the rules may, in the course of time, have undesirable effects; that they may create such large inequalities as to become intolerable to the unfortunate. He admits, of course, that they do lead to great inequalities, but he quietly takes it for granted that the hardships thus created must always be smaller than the hardships that would follow upon any attempt to change the rules.[1] This assumption is groundless. No doubt, any rules, however well conceived, will cause suffering to some people. Hume admits that it is so and seizes upon it to support his conclusion that the rules must never be changed. But it clearly does not follow that, because any rule involves some hardships, it is always better to keep the rules you have than to change them.

By treating property as a matter of convention rather than of natural right, Hume gains, in theory, a great advantage over Locke. Natural right is immutable, whereas what is conventional can change. This theoretical advantage is, however, thrown away in Hume's treatment of the five rules of property. From eternal right to the association of ideas is a steep descent; the beginnings of the two theories are poles apart, but the conclusion is the same: *Blessed are those that have wealth because everyone is the better off for not disturbing them in the enjoyment of it.*

Both Hume and Locke speak as if every man produced wealth separately, though later he may exchange his product against another man's. Their theories do not assume that there is no division of labour, but they take no account of several men working together to produce something which is the joint product of them all. They speak as if every man produced external goods primarily for his own and his family's use, and secondarily for purposes of barter. To respect property is essentially to abstain from using what other people have set aside for their own use. But, we may ask, how in a society where there is co-operative production are actual titles to property to be justified by Locke's rule that whoever is first to mix his labour with something has the exclusive right to use it, or by Hume's five rules? That there is a

---

[1] Compare this with Hobbes' belief that it is always better to bear with the government that you have than to take the risks involved in putting another in its place.

close connection between methods of production and rules of property never occurred to either of them.[1] The connection may not be what Marx and others have thought it was; but it does exist and is close. Hume believed both in economic progress and in unchanging rules of property. To hold these two beliefs together still seemed reasonable in his time; it was not to seem so much longer.

III. OBEDIENCE TO GOVERNMENT

We saw, when we were comparing Hume with Hobbes, that they both treat government as a device to ensure that men follow their permanent interest even when their passions tempt them to do otherwise.

It is the immediate interest of those who govern that law and order should be maintained, and this is also the permanent interest of their subjects. Hobbes used the notion of the contract to show how it is all men's interest to have an absolute ruler over them; and also used it to try to prove that it is their duty always to obey their rulers. He wanted to establish the legitimacy of government as well as its utility; though on his own initial assumptions he could do only the second and not the first. By his use of the notion of contract, Hobbes confuses questions of interest with questions of right, and also makes an elaborate and difficult case for absolute sovereignty.

Hume avoids both these mistakes. He never confuses interest with right, and is always ready to admit that the power of governments is and ought to be limited. The notion of contract explains nothing that cannot be better explained without it, and Hume quietly rejects it. Subjects obey their governments, not because they or their ancestors have promised to do so, but because it is their interest that there should be government, which there cannot be unless there is obedience. As with justice, so here too, we come to approve of what makes for the common interest and to disapprove of what goes against it; and thus obedience becomes a virtue and disobedience a vice.

To try to ground the duty of obedience in contract, in the making of promises, is to offer an elaborate and less plausible explanation where a simpler and more plausible would do. The duty to keep a promise, Hume tells us, is no more easily explained than the duty to obey governments. Promise-keeping is an artificial virtue like respect for property; it is rooted in self-interest and is made a virtue by being commonly approved. Exactly the same can be said of obedience to government, which is also rooted in self-interest and made a virtue by com-

---

[1] They see, of course, that where there is production and exchange there must be rules of property, but they see no need to alter the rules if methods of production change. Indeed, they take no account of specific methods of production, let alone changes in these methods.

mon approval. As soon as we see that the duties of promise-keeping and obedience to government can both be accounted for in the same way, we are no longer tempted to explain the second by the first. The notion of the social contract, which creates as many problems as it solves, is seen to be superfluous; there is nothing to be gained and much to be lost by holding to it. Justice is prior to government. 'And so far am I from thinking . . . that men are utterly incapable of society without government, that I assert the first rudiments of government to arise from quarrels, not among men of the same society, but among those of different societies.'[1] 'But tho' it be possible for men to maintain a small uncultivated society without government, 'tis impossible they should maintain a society of any kind without justice, and the observation of those three fundamental laws concerning the stability of possession, its translation by consent, and the performance of promises.'[2] Justice is entirely a social virtue, for the very notion of it, the desire for it, and the esteem in which it is held, arise among men in the course of the experience they gain through living together. Though society can exist without government, it cannot do so without a law, though that law is neither 'natural' nor deliberately made but conventional. Society is held together by common interests and conventional notions of justice; and, unless this were so, government could not arise inside it.

Hume thinks it probable that government first arose out of quarrels, not among men in the same society, but among men of different societies, and therefore originated to provide military discipline. The chances are that government began as monarchy, because success in war depends on unity of command. The authority of the military commander was found so generally convenient that it soon outlasted the emergency that created it. The commander became the monarch, and his power grew steadily, partly because it was in the public interest that it should grow and partly because whoever has power tries to increase it. After a time, the defects of monarchy came to be as sharply felt as the advantages, and devices were found to limit the monarch's power, or other forms of government were substituted for monarchy. Hume is as willing as the next man to venture opinions about the probable origins of government; but he does not use these origins to justify authority or to set limits to it. How did government arise? and What makes it legitimate? are, for him, distinct questions.

The power of government is limited by the motives of the obedience which makes government possible. Men obey primarily because it is their interest to do so, and when obedience ceases to be their interest, they soon cease to obey. They disapprove of oppression for the same reason as they approve of government, from regard to the public

[1] *Treatise*, Bk. III, Part II, Section VIII, pp. 539-40.
[2] Ibid., p. 541.

interest. Just as they ordinarily think it their interest and their duty to
obey, so, when government becomes oppressive, they come to think it
their interest and their duty to refuse obedience or actively to resist.
'The common rule', says Hume, 'requires submission; and 'tis only in
cases of grievous tyranny and oppression, that the exception takes
place.'[1]

Hume distinguishes the grounds of the general duty of obedience
from the grounds of the particular duty to obey the persons who
actually rule. Rulers claim the right to govern for all kinds of reasons:
they derive their title from long possession, or statute, or treaty, or
contract, or something else. None of these reasons explains the simple
duty of obedience; they explain only the title to rule of some persons
in preference to others, the title of those who actually do rule or
claim to rule. There may be many people in a country just as capable
of ruling it well as the persons who in fact govern it; and if they did
govern it, their subjects would have exactly the same interest in obeying them. The general utility of government explains how we come
to regard obedience as a virtue; it does not explain why we think some
persons have a better title to govern than others. To explain this title
we always resort to some other principle. But we must not substitute
this other principle for the grounds of the general duty of obedience;
we must not suppose that treaty or contract or election or prescriptive
right can make it our duty to obey when it is not the public interest
that we should obey. A principle of this kind does not determine the
limits of our duty but only the person or persons towards whom we
have the duty. It matters much less what the principle is than that we
should all be of one mind about it; that we should all agree whom we
are to obey. It is usually best to accept whatever principle confirms the
authority of those who actually govern. Government should be stable.
Prudence and justice require us 'to submit quietly to the government,
which we find established in the country where we happen to live, without enquiring curiously into its origin and first establishment.'[2] Hume
thought most disputes about legitimacy absurd and harmful. The wise
man will accept the existing form of government and rule of succession,
and will not contest the authority of rulers who are not oppressive on
the ground that they came by their authority illegally. 'A strict
adherence to any general rules, and the rigid loyalty to particular persons and families, on which some people set so high a value, are virtues
that hold less of reason, than of bigotry and superstition.'[3] Clearly, if
Hume was a Tory, he was a Tory of a peculiar kind.

In the essay on the *First Principles of Government*, Hume distinguishes between what he calls 'opinion of interest' and 'opinion

---

[1] *Treatise*, Bk. III, Part II, Section X, p. 554.
[2] *Treatise*, Bk. III, Part II, Section X, p. 556.
[3] Ibid., p. 562.

of right'. By the first he means the sense men have that government is to their advantage, and by the second their prejudice in favour of any authority or convention that has existed among them for a long time. Opinion of right is not to be confused with the moral sentiments. The moral sentiments arise from sympathy; we approve of obedience to government, as we do of justice, because we sympathize with whatever is in the public interest, and this obedience is clearly in that interest. Opinion of right arises from habit. It is a prejudice in favour of what we have long been accustomed to. The longer a form of government has lasted, the stronger our prejudice in its favour. Opinion of right reinforces opinion of interest and the moral sentiments. We obey our rulers partly because we feel it our interest to do so, partly because we approve of what is in the public interest, and partly because we are prejudiced in favour of whatever kind of government we have.

Fear, affection, and self-interest (in the narrow sense which conflicts with concern for the public interest) are not, thinks Hume, strong motives for obedience. We only obey from fear when we are tempted to disobey and fear of punishment overcomes the temptation, and this is not a frequent condition with most people. We may feel strong affection for our rulers, but ordinarily we do so because they are our rulers or because we think they govern well; so that our affection is more a consequence of the use they make of their power than a motive for the obedience which gives them power. Self-interest in the narrow sense, which is hope of special favours, can inspire obedience in only a few, for most people are in no position to expect such favours. The interest that moves most of us to obedience is therefore not an interest peculiar to ourselves; it is one we share with everyone else. It is the maintenance of law and order, which is the public interest.

Hume is as keen to show that power depends on obedience as Hobbes was to show the opposite. There would be no power worth fearing unless there were motives of obedience other than the fear of power. 'Nothing appears more surprising to those who consider human affairs with a philosophical eye than the easiness with which the many are governed by the few. . . . When we enquire by what means this wonder is effected, we shall find that, as force is always on the side of the governed, the governors have nothing to support them but opinion. It is therefore on opinion only that government is founded; and this maxim extends to the most despotic and most military governments, as well as to the most free and most popular.'[1] The tyrant depends on the opinion of his soldiers; he cannot drive everyone; he must have subordinates who obey him because they wish to do so, because they

[1] Essay on the 'First Principles of Government'. *Hume's Essays, Moral, Political and Literary*. Vol. I, Essay IV, pp. 109-10, 1875 ed.

think it their interest to support him, before he can have power enough to force obedience on the unwilling. This is the sense in which, according to Hume, all government rests on the consent of the governed. This kind of consent involves no contract nor anything that could be called a promise. It is at bottom no more than the willing acceptance of what we see is to our advantage or what we have grown accustomed to. It merely explains what makes government possible; it is not a ground of obligation.

Hume rejects the Tory doctrine of passive obedience just as decidedly as the Whig doctrine that the obligation to obey rests on consent. In the essay on *Passive Obedience*, he argues that, since the duty to respect the law arises from an interest common to all men (i.e., the public interest), law can always be rightly put aside when it endangers that interest. But the danger, he says, must be extraordinary, when public ruin would follow on respect for law or obedience to the established government. Hume is on the side of those who would draw the bonds of allegiance very close; who would justify disobedience only as a last resort in desperate cases. When Hume moves from explanation to advice, he is always strongly conservative; the advice he gives is in substance the same as Burke's. Yet how different the spirit and the style of the giver! Hume is quite without reverence or admiration; he sees nothing divine or majestic about the State; it is merely a contrivance in the public interest. The more we accept it and the less we tamper with it, the more useful it is likely to be. He thinks nothing 'more preposterous than an anxious care and solicitude in starting all the cases in which resistance may be allowed.' Though his tone is sometimes impatient, it is always the tone of the drawing-room or the lecture-room and not of the pulpit or public meeting.

It may be that Hume's conservatism was greatly strengthened by his belief that power rests ultimately on opinion. He seems to have believed that, as knowledge increases and manners grow milder, government, even when it is absolute, must also grow milder since its power rests ultimately on opinion. Time and again, we find Hume repeating that power rests on opinion, and drawing comforting conclusions therefrom and from the growth of knowledge. What he too often forgets is that power does not rest equally or in the same way on the opinion of all the persons subject to it. We cannot assume that, because power rests on opinion, it is scarcely ever used to force unwilling obedience on the majority or to maintain institutions which most people condemn as unjust. Still less can we assume that, as knowledge increases and manners grow milder, power will belong chiefly to the educated and the mild. But Hume made these assumptions because in his day the people most affected by the growth of knowledge and the spread of more humane manners belonged to the privileged classes, who either controlled the government or influenced it. The absolute monarchy of France was, Hume thought, a mild government because of the influence of these classes.

I suspect that Hume plays down the danger of oppression because he makes a false inference from a quite plausible assumption: that social inequalities rest on conventions which must have been accepted to begin with because they were found generally useful. From this premise, in itself not unsound, he draws the doubtful conclusion that the social order resting on inequality is also useful and generally acceptable. But we cannot conclude that the consequences of what was once useful and acceptable are themselves now acceptable and useful. No doubt, society could not subsist without some rules of property, and no doubt too, whatever rules there were, some people would always benefit more from them than others. But to show that the first rules probably arose because they were useful and acceptable to most people is not to show that the inequalities they have led to are so as well. Inequality is, of course, very often accepted by many more people than profit by it; by some from habit and by others from fear. Yet it may be that few except those who profit by inequality actually believe that inequality is useful and just. The others may accept existing laws of property because they can imagine no others, or from mere habit, and yet may deplore the inequalities they lead to; or they may condemn existing laws because they believe that there are others more in the public interest. Government will then rest, not on their opinion, but on the opinion of the rich. As far as they are concerned – and they may be the majority – government rests on force rather than opinion. Now, it may well be that these not very out-of-the-way ideas sometimes occurred to the ingenious Hume. If they did, he was certainly not moved by them to qualify his assertion that government always rests on opinion much more than on force. True, unless it rested on opinion it could not use force; but from this it does not follow that it cannot rest on the opinion of a minority and use force against the majority.

I suspect that Hume, if he had seen the simple argument boldly asserted – that the poor consent to the wealth and power of the rich because the rules which enabled the rich to get power and wealth first arose by being generally accepted – would not have been impressed by the logic of it. But, as he never so put it to himself, he was, I suggest, influenced by it without being aware that he was so. Otherwise, I cannot see what inclined him to make so light of the dangers of oppression. That all power rests on opinion is obvious, but no more so than the fact of oppression. Yet Hume (though without quite saying so) would have us believe that because power always rests on opinion, it must somehow rest with the people generally; as if wealth, knowledge, and influence, however acquired, give their possessors only a small advantage in pursuing their own interest at other people's expense. He speaks almost as if it followed that, because there can be no power where there is no willing obedience, power can be used only to a slight extent to force unwilling obedience.

The matter is not as simple as that. Not only is force not 'always on the side of the governed', for the obvious reason that it can be so organized as to enable a few people to rule great multitudes against their wills; but also habits and conventions can long survive their usefulness. No doubt, while the poor are contented with their lot, we cannot, if we accept Hume's account of justice, say that they are oppressed. For justice, by that account, is respect for conventions whose social function is to prevent people getting in each other's way as they try to satisfy their actual wants. But as soon as the poor cease being contented with their lot, the conventions which protect the privileges of the rich may cease to be generally useful, even though the poor in their ignorance do not question them. These conventions may stand in the way of the poor getting what they want and yet the poor may not know this; they may not understand that, if the rules of property were changed, they might, judging by standards which they themselves now accept, be much better off than they are.

Force does not vary directly with number; and is therefore not always, nor even usually, on the side of the governed. Government is a highly organized form of collaboration, and the persons directly engaged in it are collectively much more powerful than the rest of the community. Even if it were true that government and property first arose from a sense of what was needed in the common interest, it would not follow that they always serve that interest, or that when they change they change to suit it. Yet Hume, without actually saying that it does follow, ordinarily speaks as if it did; he speaks as if what is to the advantage of the rich were also, at bottom, to the advantage of the poor, and even as if the poor really knew this though they might at times behave as if they did not know.

IV. PROPERTY AND PARTY

Hume is less ingenious as a critic of institutions than as a critic of ideas. He helps to teach us how to use the language of politics, and warns us against raising unreal problems. In that capacity, he has seldom been equalled and perhaps never surpassed. But he is by no means as happily inspired when he turns his mind to the realities of politics, to how men actually behave and how social facts are related to one another. This is shown, I think, by what we have already considered; and again by what he says about the connection between property and political power. It is also shown in his account of the dangers of party or faction. This account is worth considering; it strikes some fresh notes in political theory, and raises important issues.

Let us first consider what Hume says about the connection between property and power. He accepts Harrington's axiom that the balance of power in the State tends to vary with the balance of property, and then goes on to add a rider which he thinks of fundamental importance but which spoils the axiom. He says that a large property in the hands of one man will give him as much power as several men get from a larger property shared between them. To put the same point another way, the more widely a given amount of property is dispersed, the smaller the political power attached to it; so that one man with £100,000 a year will have more power than a hundred men with £1,000 a year each. To illustrate his point, Hume takes for examples Crassus in Rome and the Medici in Florence. The fortune of Crassus, immense though it was, was small indeed compared with the collective wealth of Rome, and yet it was enough to make Crassus, for a time, the equal of Pompey and Caesar, much abler men than he was. The Medici successfully used their wealth to make themselves masters of Florence, although their fortune, as a proportion of the total wealth of the republic, was inconsiderable.

Hume's rider, far from improving on Harrington's axiom, detracts from it. It draws attention to single fortunes rather than to broad categories of wealth. There were special reasons which made it easy for Crassus to use his money to buy influence; if he had lived a hundred years earlier or later, he might have been much richer and yet unable to use his wealth to get power. In general, when we are considering the relations of power to property, it is more important to think, as Harrington does, in terms of classes than individuals.

The distribution of power depends directly on the structure of government. This structure, in turn, depends on all kinds of things; among others, on the distribution of property. To the extent that it depends on that distribution, it is affected, not by every difference in wealth, but only by some. Property and income give status, which in turn gives power; but clearly there is not a difference of status for every difference in property and income. Where there is a property qualification for the vote, anyone who has the required amount of property gets only one vote, whether he has exactly the amount required or ten times as much. Again, where a certain kind of expensive education is needed to give a man a chance of getting into Parliament or of holding important office, anyone with parents just rich enough to give him that education has that chance. However aristocratic the society, the more stable its social structure and system of government, the less important the differences of wealth inside it which are not connected with differences of status. In a stable aristocratic society, it may matter a great deal that a man should have £2,000 a year rather than £200, but much less that he should have £20,000 rather than £2,000. Differences of wealth are more important politically

because they lead to differences of status than because the richer a
man is the more he can spend on buying power; and the more stable
a society, the more this is true. Crassus and the Medici could buy
power as they did because they lived in troubled times.

Again, a man's political influence often depends as much (or more)
on the kind of property he has as on the amount. Privileges, social
and political, are usually more attached to some kinds of wealth than
to others; say, more to property in land than to liquid capital, or more
to inherited wealth than to wealth recently acquired. When a new
kind of wealth arises, its possessors may for a long time have little
power. The relations between power and property are clearly much
less simple than Hume imagined.

What Hume has to say about party or faction is not to be compared,
in point of novelty and realism, with the last admirable pages of Burke's
Thoughts on the Cause of Present Discontents. Hume sees parties as
effects of free government which cannot be abolished without abolishing freedom. If you want free government, you must put up with
parties, just as, if you want children, you must put up with noise. Hume
does not see, as Burke was to do, that parties are indispensable to free
government, if it is to survive in large countries; that parties are means
to freedom and not just unpleasant but inevitable consequences of it.
'Factions subvert government, render laws impotent, and beget the
fiercest animosities among men of the same nation, who ought to give
mutual assistance and protection to each other.'[1] This is a more pon-
derous but not less hostile judgement on parties than Trimmer Halifax's verdict on them, that they are 'conspiracies against the nation'.

In spite of this judgement, Hume does not entirely condemn every
kind of party. He tries to classify factions and to show that some kinds
are less dangerous and more useful than others. Some factions, he
says, are held together by loyalty to a person or family, some by
common interest, and some by common principles. The last two kinds
he calls *real* factions to distinguish them from the first kind which he
calls *personal.* A faction can, of course, be both personal and real; it
can be held together by loyalty to a leader or dynasty and also by
common interests or common principles. Personal factions arise most
easily in small states like the Italian republics or the Greek cities; but
real factions often become personal when the interests or principles
that give birth to them are forgotten. This classification is useful and,
as far as I know, new.

I should quarrel with Hume, not about the criteria he uses for
classifying parties, but about his judgements on them. Factions from
interest, he thinks, are the most reasonable and excusable of all; for it
is clearly reasonable that men should combine to promote common

[1] *Essays,* Vol. I, Essay VIII on *Parties in General.* See also Vol. II, Essay XIV:
Of the Coalition of Parties.

interests. Factions from principle, though sometimes reasonable, are more often absurd and dangerous. It does happen, Hume admits, that the principles proclaimed by a party have practical consequences. If they do, then it makes sense to form the party; for it is always reasonable to work with other people to try to get what you otherwise very likely could not get. To combine from principle is then merely to work with people who agree with you in order to achieve common ends. But most of the principles that factions proclaim have, Hume thinks, no practical consequences; they therefore bring people into conflict, not because they want different and incompatible things, but merely because they have different opinions. People then quarrel only because it is intolerable to them that others should think differently from themselves. This kind of quarrel is as dangerous as it is absurd. For how can it be settled in a way acceptable to both parties to it, since each wants to force its own opinions on the other?

Factions from mere principle, which are the most absurd and dangerous of all, are, Hume tells us, peculiar to the modern world. The Greeks and Romans knew nothing of them; all their factions were either personal or based on common interests. Or, if there were differences of principle, those principles had practical consequences. But in the modern world, there are religious factions, which are factions of mere principle, setting people against one another, not because they want different things in this world, but because they want everyone to share certain of their beliefs. Hume admits that religious factions are factions of interest as they concern the clergy, whose power and good living depend on other people believing what they tell them; but as they concern laymen, they are factions of mere principle. There was a time, Hume tells us, when religion was not divisive; when a religion was only a collection of myths and rites peculiar to this or that nation. It was when religion became philosophical that it grew factious. 'Sects of philosophy, in the ancient world, were more zealous than parties of religion; but in modern times, parties of religion are more furious and enraged than the most cruel factions that ever arose from interest and ambition.'[1] Or, as we might put it today, there is nothing more absurd or harmful than an ideological conflict, which is that and nothing more.

We can hardly blame Hume for not seeing what was not properly understood until Burke explained it: that parties are not evils inseparable from free government but are necessary to its survival and efficiency. But he might, I think, have looked rather more closely at his own distinction between principles and interests. Principles and interests are much more intimately connected than he supposed. Indeed, interests common to large numbers of people are nearly always put forward in the shape of principles. No party ever deals only in plain

[1] *Essays*, Vol. I, Essay VIII.

demands; it always says more than just 'we want this'; it also always says, 'this ought to be done in the public interest'. If every party did no more than make bare demands for its supporters' benefit, it would find it inordinately difficult to reach satisfactory compromises with other parties. A party's business is not only to make demands but to find arguments in support of them convincing to as wide a public as possible. It must appeal to principles already accepted, or must propagate principles until they are widely accepted. And these principles lead in turn to the putting forward of new demands. Interests arise from principles just as much as principles from interests. If working men now ask for many things they never dreamt of asking for in Hume's time, it is largely because their conceptions of justice, their principles, have changed. The range of permissible demands is not determined only by conventional morality but also by principles evolved by groups actively engaged in the struggle for power. Men acquire new interests largely because they acquire new principles; and their demands are met without bloodshed largely because groups and classes they do not belong to have come to share some of these principles even when it is not their interest to do so. True, Hume admits that principles sometimes have practical consequences. But he does not see that common interests alone are not enough to hold a group of men together over a considerable period of time, enabling them to deal effectively and peacefully with other groups.

Nor does he see that it is just as true that men acquire common interests and common principles by belonging to organized groups as that they form such groups because they have common interests or principles. In this respect he is less a realist than either Burke or Rousseau. The function of a party, as Burke sees it, is not only to bring together men who share the same principles; it is also to maintain a community of interest and principle among them. Every organized group, Rousseau tells us, acquires a general will, it acquires sentiments and interests common to its members. No doubt, unless they had some notion of an interest or principle common to them, men would not come together voluntarily to form a group, but once they have formed it, they influence one another and acquire more precise and elaborate beliefs which distinguish them from others. It is not merely that they reach a compromise in order to be able to work together effectively; they mostly do not (except the unusually thoughtful among them) have clear ideas of what they want before they come together, and then reach agreement by making concessions to one another. They get clearer ideas (if they do get them) largely in the process of working together as a group. They also acquire a loyalty to the group, which keeps them tied to it even though, as circumstances change, it modifies its principles and alters its conception of its own and of the public interest. Organized groups often outlive the interests and principles which first united them, and it is useful to the community that they should do so. But they do not, when they outlive these interests and principles, become what Hume calls personal factions; they merely acquire other interests and other principles. And yet there is continuity, for the new interests and principles are not acquired at random but arise out of the old ones and the changing circumstances. There are attitudes of mind which persist despite the change, attitudes not the less precious to those who share them because they ordinarily cannot define them.

Where there are such organized groups, they learn in time to do business with one another; they evolve rules which enable them to reach compromises, and they come to set as much store by the rules as by the interests and principles which divide them. That is why in some societies differences of interest and principle are much less dangerous to domestic peace than in others; they are not less dangerous because they are smaller but because the groups that differ have learned how to preserve the peace without giving up the principles or interests which divide them. Burke came close to seeing this, whereas Hume did not, largely because he failed to notice that factions, whether it is interest or principle which divides them, learn from experience that they have some interests in common just as much as individuals do.

Hume was wrong in believing that factions whose disputes are inspired by religious differences do not quarrel about practical matters but are concerned only to impose their beliefs upon one another. True, they are concerned that others should share their beliefs. There is an important difference to which Hume rightly directs our attention between beliefs and interests; we want other people to share our beliefs as we do not want them to share our interests. We accept differences of interest more easily than we do differences of belief. Not all beliefs different from ours are difficult to tolerate, but there are often some beliefs necessary to our peace of mind, and it hurts us to hear them openly challenged. We have to learn to be tolerant, and the learning is unusually difficult. In Hume's time these beliefs were mostly religious, whereas in our time they are mostly political. They are apt to cause the most dangerous and the most unprofitable disputes.

To that extent Hume is right. But he is wrong when he suggests that diversity of religious belief does not create differences of interest giving rise to important disputes about practical matters. If his religion means anything to a man, it deeply affects his conception of how he should live;[1] it deeply affects his worldly interests, the claims he makes on

[1] The man without religion is apt to regard the influence of religion as somehow illegitimate or artificial. If the religious man abandoned his beliefs, his wants would be different from what they are now; and the man without religion is inclined to look upon these wants, if they conflict with his own, as arising not from 'genuine' but from fictitious needs. He tends to discount these needs or to dismiss the endeavour to satisfy them as irrational.

his neighbours and on society in general. These claims are no more spurious or absurd for being rooted in religion than if they had some other source. If I want some things rather than others because I am a Catholic or a Protestant or a Jew, my wants may bring me into conflict with other people wanting different things, even though I am not in the least concerned that they should share my religious beliefs. Nor are men necessarily more intolerant about religious than about other beliefs. No doubt, there are principles from which men draw no practical consequences and about which they quarrel furiously only because they cannot bear it that other people should disagree with them. But I see no reason for believing that religious principles are more liable than others to be thus barren and dangerous.

V. HUME'S CONCEPTION OF A BALANCED CONSTITUTION

Hume's political scepticism was distasteful to many people less because he came to conclusions unwelcome to solid and respectable citizens than because the arguments he used to support those conclusions were untraditional and unattractive. His real bias was towards the Whig rather than the Tory position. If he has been called a Tory, it is largely because, as a sceptic and a Scotsman, he did not accept the official Whig version of the revolution of 1688 which drove a Scottish dynasty from the British throne. He also pulled to pieces the political philosophy used to justify that revolution, the philosophy of Locke, which dealt in ideas that he rejected; ideas like the social contract and natural law. But he accepted the consequences of the revolution from conviction, and not, as many a Tory did, because time and habit had reconciled him to them. He approved of them, and found arguments to support them. It was not his conclusions but his political philosophy, the assumptions and arguments he used to establish his entirely respectable conclusions, which were not to the taste of either Whigs or Tories. He lacked reverence and was slow to admire; he liked to show how people did from interest or prejudice or habit what the good Whig or Tory believed ought to be done from better motives. Human nature, seen through his eyes, is somehow diminished, robbed of its dignity, its depth, and its pathos. Hobbes had sunk it deeper in self-centredness but had also made it tougher and more formidable, and had used magnificent language to describe it. But the lucid and subtle Hume was also prosaic; he saw society, not as a refuge from terror, but as a kind of market for the more efficient satisfaction of wants. He did not see men, as Hobbes had done, driven to calamity, to the war of all against all, by urgent and restless appetites. His was already the Godless and sinless and calculating world of the Utilitarians and economists, where the great business of life is to get as much comfort as possible at the cost of the least inconvenience.

Hume had a habit that is not endearing. It was one of his favourite occupations to point out that other people's quarrels were unnecessary. In the essay 'Of the Coalition of Parties',[1] he does his best to play down the differences between Whigs and Tories. They both, he says, had good arguments when the quarrel between them first began; but the Tories ought now to understand that certain claims to liberty, which were dangerous when they first opposed them because they were then connected with religious fanaticism, are no longer so connected and therefore no longer dangerous. Claims, which they once rightly feared might grow indefinitely till they destroyed the established order, have in fact not been pressed immoderately. Hume warns the Tories that their strongest argument – that what use and practice have established is better than what reason can discover – can now be turned against them; for the system created by the Revolution has endured for several generations. To insist, after so long a time, on recalling a past form of government is to incur the reproach of innovation. The Crown has long since lost many of its rights, and the free constitution we now have does preserve us from evils to which those rights used often to give rise. The impression given by Hume's essay is that the Tories were on the whole nearer being right than the Whigs when first they quarrelled, but that the consequences of the Whig revolution have turned out so much better than anyone could have reasonably expected that the Tories would now be wise to accept them. There is nothing left for the two parties to quarrel about; and the more moderately each puts its case, the more it encourages moderation in the other. Hume's essay is a judicious summing-up in favour of the Whigs by a judge who likes them rather less than he likes their opponents, but feels bound to admit that they are nearer being right, though they are so more by luck than by judgement.

Hume condemned both absolute monarchy and what he called a 'complete republic', meaning thereby pretty much what is today understood by democracy. Democracy, in his eyes, is close neighbour to anarchy. If there were a 'complete republic' in Britain, the House of Commons would become the whole legislature. It would either make itself perpetual; or, if it were periodically dissolved, there would be a risk of civil war at every election. Representative democracy is better than the direct kind; but in a country as large as Britain, any kind of democracy is dangerous. Hume thought that the House of Commons was already as powerful as it ought to be. Enjoying popular support and having the power of the purse, it already had the means of making itself virtually omnipotent. If it had not yet done so, it was only because

[1] *Essays*, Vol. I, Essay VIII.

Members of Parliament, as individuals, had so much to gain by placating the Crown, even though collectively they could reduce it to impotence. Crown patronage enabled the king and his ministers to buy the support of individual members of the House of Commons, and this seemed to Hume the only barrier to the otherwise overwhelming power of the lower house. Luckily, human nature being what it is, the barrier was effective. Hume believed that the odds were in favour of the monarchical in the end prevailing over the popular element in the British constitution. Though he wanted neither to get the better of the other, he took comfort in the thought that, if odds there had to be, they should be in favour of monarchy; for democracy was worse than absolute monarchy was ever likely to be in 'civilized' Europe. Hume did not make lucky guesses about the future; he lacked the gift of prophecy.

Perhaps he was also somewhat deficient in imagination. He preferred a representative to a direct democracy and he knew that the lower house of the British Parliament was a representative chamber. If, then, Britain were ever to become a democracy, it would have to be a representative democracy. The electorate would be enlarged and the House of Commons would gain power at the expense of the monarch and of the upper house. Hume knew this, and yet when he imagined the evils of a future British democracy, he thought of them as being much the same as the evils long attributed to the democracies of antiquity and of Athens in particular. For him, as for so many others in his day, fifth-century Athens was the typical democracy; and he saw British democracy, though he knew that it must have a representative assembly if it were to exist at all, as Athenian democracy many times enlarged and many times worse. He saw only the obvious: that Britain, being much larger than Athens, could never be a direct democracy. He never saw how greatly a large and representative democracy must differ from a small and direct one, both in its institutions and its *ethos*. He did not see, as Montesquieu had done, how intimately the structure and the spirit of government are connected. Though he expressed a preference for a representative assembly over a direct assembly of the people, he had less feeling than either Bentham or Rousseau for the difference between them. Bentham had a keener sense than he had of the advantages of an elected assembly, and Rousseau a keener sense of the disadvantages.

Hume spoke with approval of what he called 'free' government; by which he meant government responsible to the well-to-do and the educated, whom he often referred to, as so many did in his day, as simply *the people* because he took it for granted that their interests were in line with the true interests of the entire community. He could still take for granted what had seemed obvious to Locke. But later Burke could not take it for granted; he had to argue against democracy and for aristocracy, as Hume never felt the need to do. It was no longer possible in the last decade of the eighteenth century to assume that the House of Commons was a popular house. The radicals and revolutionaries were as much opposed to aristocracy as to monarchy, and it even occurred to some of them that kings were better disposed to the people than were the nobly-born or the wealthy.

Hume took it for granted that the classes represented in the House of Commons spoke for the whole nation, that their interests coincided with the public interest. He also believed that the educated and the well-to-do are better judges than the ignorant and the poor of their own and the public interest. It therefore seemed obvious to him that it was best for all classes that government should be responsible only to to the educated and the well-to-do. He thought it 'a just political maxim that every man must be supposed a knave',[1] that he must be supposed to be out for himself and ready to sacrifice the good of others to his own good, and yet he feared no 'sinister interests'. It does not matter, where government is 'free', that those who have an influence on it should be, politically, almost entirely selfish; for their interests are in keeping with the public interest. It is not the interest of all that government should be responsible to all; it is rather their interest that it should be responsible to the enlightened.

Where government is 'free', Hume tells us, authority is effectively limited because those who have power have to seek re-election in order to keep it. Their power is therefore always restrained by public opinion, even where there is as yet no written law but only custom. All government, 'free' or 'unfree', is limited by what Hume calls 'opinion of interest', by the sentiment widespread among the people that it is to their general advantage to obey their rulers. If the rulers weaken this sentiment, they undermine their own authority, which is therefore limited by the rulers' need not to use authority in ways that undermine it. But where government is 'free', there is a further limitation on authority; the rulers have a strong motive to avoid using it in ways that reduce the chances that they will be re-elected. Where government is free, public opinion bears on the actual policies of government, and imposes narrower limits on political power than mere opinion of interest could do.

Hume believed that where government is 'free' (or, as we should say, 'responsible'), written law soon takes the place of custom and of popular loose notions of justice. Experience teaches the people that their security is greater if they require their rulers to apply precisely defined rules. Law therefore, as distinct from custom, arises first under free governments; but its advantages are so obvious that enlightened monarchies soon follow the example of free governments. When Hume opposes government under law to arbitrary government, he is not

[1] Hume's *Essays, Moral and Political*, 1875 edition, Vol. I, p. 118.

thinking of constitutional limits on the legislative power; he is thinking of the obligation, either imposed from without or self-imposed, on
the executive to govern according to precisely defined rules. He is
thinking in terms of the traditional distinction between the 'government of laws' and the 'government of men'.

According to Hume, the arts and sciences first began to flourish
under free governments. Machiavelli had said that they flourish only
(or flourish best) under such governments, but Hume makes a smaller
claim for political freedom. The arts and sciences are not confined to
countries which are politically free, nor are they there necessarily more
vigorous and abundant; though political freedom gives birth to them,
they can thrive apart from it. But they cannot thrive except where
there is personal security, where the individual has well defined rights
which his rulers respect; and personal security is first established
where government is 'free' or responsible. Where the individual has
personal security, where there is the rule of law, industry and trade
flourish. The more secure and prosperous people are, the greater their
leisure. They have time to pursue knowledge and to refine upon their
pleasures. They become curious, discriminating and delicate. They
cultivate the arts and the sciences.

But, though the arts and sciences first grow important under free
governments, the taste for them is later acquired by the subjects of
other governments. Just as the rule of law, though it arises first where
there is political freedom, later spreads elsewhere as its advantages
come to be appreciated by absolute monarchs, so the arts and sciences,
which thrive under that rule, also spread. They thrive under a civilized
monarchy, by which Hume means a monarchy where the king, though
formally absolute, in fact governs according to law. Indeed, the arts
flourish better in civilized monarchies than in countries which are
politically free, for a 'strong genius succeeds best in republics, a refined
taste in monarchies'. This was also the opinion of Montesquieu, who
had said that the English were superior in the sciences and the French
in the arts, and had explained this difference as in part an effect of
different forms of government. Hume agreed with Montesquieu that
the English had greater intellectual vigour and more originality than
the French, and the French more taste and subtlety than the English;
and the first qualities seemed to him, as to Montesquieu, to make for
excellence in the sciences and the second to make for it in the arts.
These ideas about science and art and their political conditions were
never more prominent than in the eighteenth century, which was also
the period when the English and the French, who were then the
richest and the most powerful peoples in the West, were very much
given to bold generalizations often based on nothing better than a
comparison between their two countries.

Belief in progress and in the superiority of western civilization was no doubt less widespread in the eighteenth than in the nineteenth century, but it was perhaps more easy and confident where it was found. Hume shared that belief to the full and with few misgivings. The Benthamites also believed in progress, and so did the early socialists, but they felt that it was strenuous and difficult even though it was certain. They saw misery and stupidity close to them, and felt the need to dissipate them; they saw the light ahead of them breaking in upon the darkness which surrounded them. They were fighters for progress, eager to bring what civilization had to give within the reach of all classes. But Hume merely contemplated progress and took pleasure at the sight of it. He saw himself already among the most fortunate of mankind. He was in the light, and the light was gaining fast upon the darkness, and he was pleased. He was readier to congratulate his fellow men than to exert himself on their behalf. Knowledge and taste were spreading and government was growing milder, absolute rulers saw the advantages of the rule of law, and the influence of public opinion, of the articulate, the educated, and the refined, was greater than ever it had been. In his essay on *Civil Liberty*, Hume says that there were in his time about two hundred absolute princes in Europe, each reigning on an average about twenty years. In the last two centuries, two thousand such princes had reigned, and yet there could not be found among them tyrants as cruel as Tiberius, Caligula, Nero or Domitian, who were four among only the first twelve Roman Emperors. The sun shone high over Europe, and Europe was the centre of the world.

Hume's preferences were much the same as Montesquieu's; he too preferred the English system of government to any other, and thought it the best adapted to preserve freedom in large states. He too saw much to admire in the civilized monarchy of France; he too saw many connections between prosperity, the rule of law, and the flowering of the arts and sciences. He believed in what his century had already learnt to call *civilization*; in the kind of life lived by the more thoughtful and refined among the upper classes in England and France. He believed in the enlightened pursuit of happiness; not of the grosser pleasures, which he thought must quickly disgust the pursuer, but of pleasures that give lasting satisfaction, which he took to be the ones which he and his friends happened to care for most. He wanted the kind of society which enables those who are capable of this happiness to get it; a society where property is secure, where the prosperous and the educated form public opinion, where government respects the law, and where there is freedom of thought for the small part of the nation that can value and use it. He delighted in curiosity, in argument, in new ideas, in good living; he mistrusted zeal and despised obstinacy. He was a friend of the Encyclopaedists of France, more ingenious than they were and less amusing and excitable. He was a very cool customer indeed, except where his vanity was hurt, as it was in his quarrel with Rousseau, when he lost his head a little. Not very much, but just a little; restrained, I suspect, less by a sense of justice than by a desire not to lose face. Though his social philosophy is utilitarian, it is emphatically not the eager and tough radical utilitarianism of Jeremy Bentham. It is cautious, precise, and respectable; unsentimental, unimaginative, sometimes almost unfeeling.

VI. HUME'S IDEAL COMMONWEALTH

Hume was satisfied, on the whole, with English society and English government as he found them. Even if he had not been satisfied, he would probably have been slow to advocate change; for he believed that we cannot reject old forms of government, as we can old engines, in favour of new ones. Men are governed more by authority than by reason, and they attribute authority to what is old and familiar. The wise man will not try experiments upon the credit of mere argument and philosophy; and if he makes improvements will take care to adjust them to what exists.

Yet Hume will not allow that, because innovation is hazardous and ought always to be cautious, there is no use in speculating on what is ideally the best. One of the longest of his essays is deliberately Utopian; it is the *Idea of a Perfect Commonwealth*.[1] Though we must always, when we make changes, take great care how we make them, it can help us to be clearer in our minds what we should do, if we reflect on what would be ideally the best; for we can then strive to bring what exists, gradually and gently, nearer to our ideal, without disturbing society too much.

We have here a conception of reform different from Burke's. Hume does not rule out as harmful and absurd every broad scheme of improvement. Innovation can be large and yet beneficial, provided it is slow and cautious; provided those who undertake it attempt only a little at a time and always take care how what they do affects the people. In Burke's opinion, we understand society so little that to make large schemes for its reformation, however long the time we allow for carrying them out, is patently absurd. Progress is sure because a benevolent God is in control of the universe, but progress, as far as human reason and will are responsible for it, is the cumulative result of many small changes, each made by people who can never see far ahead. I do not want to make too much of this difference between Hume and Burke, for Hume did not in fact want great changes made in England and would probably not have trusted any English govern-

---

[1] *Essays*, Vol. II, Essay XVI.

ment of his day to make them. Nevertheless, the essay on the *Idea of a Perfect Commonwealth* does show that Hume, for all his conservatism, did not think it altogether unreasonable for men to attempt great though gradual changes in their form of government to bring it closer to their ideals.

Of the actual scheme of government imagined by Hume, I need say very little. It owes more to Harrington's *Oceana* than to any earlier model. It is elaborate, ingenious, and moderate. Everyone with a modest property has the vote and there is therefore a large electorate; the voters elect one hundred separate county assemblies which between them have the legislative power; these assemblies elect the county magistrates and also the national Senate, which has the executive power and appoints the Protector, the Secretaries of State, and various councils; all proposals of law are debated in the Senate before they are referred to the county assemblies; the representatives or magistrates of any county may send a law to their senator for proposal to the Senate. Hume thinks that all free government should consist of two councils, a smaller and a larger; because the larger, which represents the people directly, would lack wisdom without the smaller (the Senate), and the smaller would lack honesty without the people. The people, through their representatives, must debate the laws and not merely vote on them. If they were to do this in only one large national assembly, there would be confusion. But divide them into many small assemblies, and they can be trusted, properly enlightened by the Senate, to act in the public interest. Hume's scheme is one of checks and balances meant to give some power to all men of property, but much more to the rich and educated than to the rest. Its purpose, to use Hume's own words, is 'to refine the democracy', from the lower sort of people, who merely elect the county representatives, upwards, through these representatives, to the Senate and the higher magistrates, who between them direct the business of the whole state as distinct from the business of the counties.

Hume was undoubtedly a strong conservative. But he did not stand in awe of what is established; he did not see the mark of God upon it. Nor, on the other hand, did he resign himself to it, as a necessary evil, in despair of better things. He accepted it, partly because he thought it more good than evil, and partly because he had little faith in man's capacity to change his social environment greatly for the better. And yet, when he amused himself by devising an ideal system of government, he took for the model to improve on, not what he found in his own country, but a scheme invented a hundred years earlier by a republican opponent of the Stuart Monarchy.

M

Chapter 9

BURKE

Burke put forward, against the radicals and revolutionaries, conceptions of society and government meant to show how arrogant and stupid their pretentions were. But these conceptions were not original with him. That society is an intricate and delicate structure imperfectly understood by its members; that men can go only a little way towards adapting it to their principles and purposes; that freedom is an empty notion apart from the institutions that give substance to it; that forms of government are slow growths of time intimately connected with the traditions and sentiments of particular peoples: all this was as clearly said by Montesquieu as by Burke. And Hume made a clearer and a logically more rigorous case than ever Burke did against many of the ideas dearest to the radicals: against natural law and natural right and against the social contract. Montesquieu and Hume were both by temper conservative. The difference between Burke and them was that he alone used the positions common to them to launch an attack on others; he alone of the three engaged in controversies as passionate as they were historically important. Montesquieu was primarily a theorist, a student of manners and institutions; he wanted knowledge for its own sake; he was dispassionate though not unprejudiced, for he never troubled to disguise his own strong but calm preferences. Hume was a philosopher, a dissector of ideas, a maker and destroyer of arguments; he was as much a theorist as Montesquieu, though a theorist of rather a different kind.

Burke was an orator who wanted to persuade people to act as he thought best. It takes a good deal of thought, and perhaps even some book-learning, some training in philosophy or in social and political theory, to appreciate the qualities of Hume and Montesquieu. Burke is more familiar and more accessible, and also warmer and more colourful.

Burke's principles need to be considered apart from the practical advice he gives on particular occasions. The task of extracting them out of his voluminous speeches, addresses, and letters is long but not unpleasant; especially if you like his ornate and diffuse style of oratory which is too eager and too passionate to be heavy. I can think of no one who can argue a case at such unnecessary length without wearying the reader. Burke's political philosophy is nowhere systematically expounded; it is revealed, sometimes deliberately and sometimes only by implication, in his writings about particular affairs, English, American and French. To the political theorist the most important of his writings are these: *Thoughts on the Cause of Present Discontents* (1770); the great speeches on America, on *American Taxation* (1774) and on *Conciliation with the Colonies* (1775); the long letter to the Sheriffs of Bristol on the *Affairs of America* (1777); and *Reflections on the Revolution in France* (1790). The last of these, spoilt by excessive passion and also by ignorance of France, makes much the same assumptions about society and government as the others. Burke's temper changed more than his opinions. If he is among the least systematic, he is also among the more consistent of political philosophers.

I. BURKE ON THE USE OF PARTIES IN FREE GOVERNMENTS

In the eighteenth century the House of Commons was not representative of the people, though it was often called the popular house. Only a small minority of the people had votes, which many of them either sold or used as they were told to do by their social superiors. The great landowners had a preponderance of power, which they exercised less through the House of Lords than because they controlled many of the seats in the Commons. Nevertheless, the electorate was varied; for, though only a small part of the people had the vote, there could be found among them all sorts and conditions of men. This system, which to us seems corrupt and unfair, did not seem so then, even to highly respectable and moral persons. It was thought right and expedient both that somewhere or other in the country every kind of person should have a vote, and that the rich and powerful, the educated and articulate, should have a much greater political influence than the poor and ignorant. England was, consciously and proudly, an aristocracy of the well-born, the rich and the successful; an aristocracy limited, on one side and considerably, by monarchy, and on the other side and much less, by the wants and prejudices of the common people. Burke objected neither to this aristocracy nor to the methods it used. The buying and selling of seats and votes was established practice in eighteenth-century Britain; and so, too, was patronage. Without these expedients it would have been impossible to find stable majorities. Even the continental admirers of the English system of government did not prefer it to their own because they thought it cleaner, but because it seemed to provide, on the whole, better security and more freedom. Burke admired it for precisely the same reasons; he always spoke of it with deep respect and spent many years of his life defending it against what he thought were dangers to it. He defended it first against the king, and afterwards against the radicals.

In Burke's opinion, George III, until the loss of the American colonies reduced his prestige, was dangerous to the constitution because he was using Crown patronage to get more power for himself than he had a right to, than kings of England had had since the 'glorious revolution'. Now, patronage is a kind of property; it is a power, however acquired, to bestow office or privilege, either by direct appointment and gift or by influence.[1] Patronage, in this sense, exists under every form of government, and is perhaps as necessary to government as lubricating oil to a machine. How much is needed depends on the nature of the machine. In Burke's time, the need for it was generally admitted, and Burke, a great respecter of property, did not object to it. He objected only to what he thought was George III's misuse of it to upset the balance of power between king and parliament established by the revolution of 1688. Crown patronage had always existed, and had always been much greater than the patronage in the hands of any private person, though less than all private patronage put together.

Under the first two Georges, Crown patronage served to strengthen a succession of Whig governments. These governments were not, of course, party governments in our modern sense; they were aristocratic alliances whose leaders used their own patronage and the Crown's to control a majority of seats in the House of Commons. The alliance in power, as a natural consequence of having power, were opposed by everyone in Parliament who was not with them. Parliament divided into supporters and opponents of the king's ministers, into 'ins' and 'outs'; but there were no organized parties and no settled party principles. If we use the word *party* in the modern sense, it would perhaps be truer to say that, at least until the younger Pitt became Prime Minister, there were no parties in England, or that there were a dozen, than that there were only two. When the Whigs began to suspect George III of trying to make himself independent of them by acquiring supporters of his own in the House of Commons, they called these supporters the King's Friends and accused them of being a *party*.

In those days, to call a group of men a party was to suggest that there was something sinister about them. For party was still denounced, in Halifax's phrase, as a 'conspiracy against the nation'. Kings and politicians affected to be above party; to be patriots and not party-men. The king's ministers could not rule without support in Parliament, which was therefore often divided into parts; but these parts were

---

[1] Patronage is sometimes acquired with office, as it very largely is today in the United States, or else is inherited or bought. Only when the grant of office or privilege is made for the purpose of increasing the power or influence of the giver or of his friends or associates is it properly an exercise of patronage.

not parties. They were loose collections or groups of interests, of which one supported the king's ministers and the other did not. This broad division of Parliament into two parts, unknown before the end of the seventeenth century, was accepted only because it worked. No one had evolved a political theory to explain and justify it.[1] It was understood that the king's ministers were responsible not only to the king but to Parliament as well; it was admitted in practice, if not in theory, that Parliament was more than merely a legislature, for its right to criticize policy was allowed as much as its right to make law. But the responsibility of ministers to Parliament, however broadly understood, was not thought to involve anything that could be called party government. *Party* and *faction* were still more or less equivalent terms; they were still mostly used in a pejorative sense, to suggest something narrow, selfish and unpatriotic.

Burke reacted to the King's Friends much as the other Whigs were doing. He was as convinced as they were that George III, legally and yet surreptitiously and against the spirit of the constitution, was subverting the English system of government as it had evolved since the 'glorious revolution'. The Stuarts had tried to restrain and control Parliament; they had attacked it from without. George III, according to this Whig theory, was undermining its authority from within, without openly challenging the position it had acquired for itself in the seventeenth century. Suspicion of George's motives and resentment at his supposed success caused his political enemies to cry out against party even more loudly than before. What better evidence of the dangers of party than the uses to which George III was putting the King's Friends?

Burke shared the fears of the Whigs, but he was not, as they were, blinded by those fears. Instead of joining in the vulgar outcry against party, he saw in party the only sure defence against royal encroachments. So long as the practice continued of forming governments by striking bargains between aristocratic groups, many of them without settled principles or policies, the king would have an immense advantage over everyone. Disposing of more patronage than anyone else, he could always control the largest single group. The only force strong enough to get the better of him would have to be, not just a temporary coalition of patrons and their political dependents, but a disciplined body held together by common principles and agreed policies. Burke saw no danger at all in the capture of power by a single party, provided that party held power only for a limited period. So long as it could be legally opposed and could be relied upon to give way to a rival when it lost the confidence of Parliament and of the electorate, it

---

[1] Unless we count for a theory a few remarks made by Montesquieu in *De l'Esprit des Lois*, Bk. XI, Chap. 6.

would not be a threat to free government, but would strengthen it by making it effective and responsible.

This is the really important message in Burke's *Thoughts on the Cause of Present Discontents.* Instead of looking upon party as something perhaps impossible to avoid and yet dangerous and potentially evil, or at its best no better than harmless, he welcomed it as a device necessary to responsible government. Instead of treating it, as nearly everyone before him had done, as a 'conspiracy against the nation', he advocated it as something conducive to the public good. To be so conducive, it must be – to use a modern phrase which, though Burke did not use it, does, I think, express his meaning – an *open conspiracy.* Burke was the first to advocate party government as an instrument and preservative of freedom; the first to explain that organizations created for the capture of power are not necessarily obstacles to good and responsible government, but, on the contrary, are means to it, provided they work in the open and respect whatever conventions those who seek or have power are required to respect. Burke did not deplore patronage; he did not suppose that principles and policies alone would hold a party together. He believed in the political ascendancy of the wealthy, well-born, and well-educated, and accepted the methods used to maintain that ascendancy. But he did not want the king to beat the Whigs at their own game, because, if he did beat them, parliamentary government, as the eighteenth century knew it, though preserved in appearance, would be destroyed in fact. Burke wanted government truly responsible to the small part of the nation which he considered politically mature. A government ought to be stable and strong while it enjoys the confidence of the politically mature classes; as soon as it loses that confidence, it ought to abandon power and give place to a successor. This was Burke's ideal, which he thought could best be achieved by means of party.

II. BURKE ON AMERICAN AFFAIRS

Burke was an imperialist. Pride of empire, only a little less than concern for freedom, inspires his writings about America. Pride of empire is merely a form of patriotism, and in itself is entirely respectable, though it may sometimes take dangerous or evil forms. It may lead to oppression or it may be a force making for freedom. It all depends on people's opinions about the best means of holding an empire together. Burke was pro-American largely because he was an imperialist. He wanted to preserve the Empire, though not at any price. He was opposed to George III's American policy for two reasons: because he believed that there were better ways of keeping the Americans loyal to the mother country than the methods the King and his ministers were using; and because he believed that the attempt to coerce the Americans, if it succeeded, would destroy freedom, not only in America, but in England as well.[1]

Though Burke was pro-American, the arguments he used were different from the arguments that excited the colonists. He cared nothing for what he called 'abstract' rights, and could never have composed such a document as the Declaration of Independence. All talk of eternal and inalienable rights was distasteful to him. In his great speech on *American Taxation*, he says:

> I am not here going into the distinction of rights, not attempting to mark their boundaries. I do not enter into these metaphysical distinctions; I hate the very sound of them. Leave the Americans as they anciently stood, and these distinctions, born of our unhappy contest, will die along with it. . . . Be content to bind America by laws of trade, you have always done it. Let this be your reason for binding their trade. Do not burden them by taxes; you were not used to do so from the beginning. Let this be your reason for not taxing. Those are the arguments of states and kingdoms. Leave the rest to the schools, for there only they may be discussed with safety.

Burke did not object, in principle, to Parliament's sovereignty over the colonies, and did not even argue that there were legal limits to that sovereignty. He was willing to vote for the *Declaratory Act* which proclaimed in a general way Parliament's supremacy. He could find no general principle to justify the colonists in their refusal to pay taxes imposed on them by the British Parliament for purposes of revenue, for he admitted that they had for generations allowed Parliament to regulate their trade for the benefit of the mother country; and these regulations were economically more burdensome by far than the new taxes. The colonists were not represented in the Imperial Parliament, and yet they had long accepted Britain's right to make laws that concerned their most vital interests. The colonists were right, not because they were defending general principles valid everywhere, but because they were defending acquired rights. The mother country had for generations regulated their trade but had not imposed taxes on them, either internal or external, for purposes of revenue. The colonists taxed themselves through their own legislatures; they were, in fact, largely self-governing. It was natural and expedient that they should be so; it was natural, because they, as Englishmen, had inevitably carried over with them into America English institutions and political ideas;

---

[1] The war seemed to him a civil war, a war between Englishmen; and also unnecessary and stupid. It was a war that the mother country ought to have been willing to avoid even at great cost, and which she could in fact have avoided at almost no cost.

and it was expedient, because they were separated from England by three thousand miles of ocean. Massachusetts could not be governed from London as if it were an English county. Unlimited though Parliament's sovereignty might be in principle, the English colonies had inevitably acquired a large measure of independence.

How could the British government or the colonists determine the proper measure of that independence? Clearly the government could not do it by insisting on Parliament's sovereignty, nor the colonists by asserting the rights of man. Certain relations had arisen during the last one hundred and fifty years between the mother country and the colonies; relations not easy to define, still less to justify in terms of abstract right. But they had in fact proved acceptable to both parties, and that was their sufficient justification. The ministers and their supporters in Parliament were trying to alter these relations against the wishes of the colonists. The measure of independence the colonists had acquired and learned to value was being threatened. It was absurd, Burke thought, to condemn their resistance on the ground that what was now being asked of them imposed a much smaller sacrifice than, say, the Navigation Acts, whose legitimacy the colonists had never contested. It was no less absurd to try to justify these new taxes on the ground that the money was to be spent for the colonists' benefit. These taxes, light though they might be, seemed to the colonists an innovation, an unprecedented challenge to acquired rights. Just as the English in England valued the rights they had acquired in the course of their history so, too, did the English in America; and the undisputed enjoyment of these rights was what they understood by freedom. Why restrict that freedom? In order to vindicate the sovereignty of Parliament? But the Americans had never contested that sovereignty while it had not seemed to threaten their rights. To attack colonial liberties was to provoke the colonists to deny Parliament's sovereignty. Why put yourself in a position where you have to impose by force a principle which, if only you had stayed your hand, no one would have wanted to question? If your real purpose is to find a revenue, why impose taxes that are bitterly resented? The expense of raising unpopular taxes is out of all proportion to their yield. If American revenues are needed for American purposes, why not begin by asking American legislatures to vote them?

Burke believed that our ability to understand society and to change it to suit our purposes is slight. In the speech on *Conciliation with America*, he says:

> When I contemplate these things, when I know that the colonies in general owe little or nothing to any care of ours, and that they are not squeezed into this happy form by the constraints of a watchful and suspicious government, but that, through a wise and salutary

neglect, a generous nature has been suffered to take her own way to perfection; when I reflect upon these effects, when I see how profitable they have been to us, I feel all the pride of power sink, and all the presumption in the wisdom of human contrivances melt and die away within me.

The colonies were made by the Englishmen who went out to found them and not by English governments at home. Nor were they – to interpret Burke's meaning more exactly – made by the colonists themselves in the sense that they were deliberately contrived. The English colonies in America, like all other human societies, were products of the numberless activities of several generations; of a course of events which, taken as a whole, the human mind could scarcely grasp, let alone control. They were products of a 'generous nature', of the natural wealth the colonists found in their new countries, and also of the qualities of character they brought with them.

The colonists, Burke told the House of Commons, had emigrated when English love of freedom was at its strongest. They were 'not only devoted to liberty, but to liberty according to English ideas and on English principles'. They were undoubtedly very English societies, but they were also different from the mother country. The colonists were mostly not drawn from the classes dominant in the mother country; and they had now long been separated from that country. Burke found the Americans more self-consciously, more aggressively Protestant than the English, with a passion for liberty both narrower and fiercer. He found them more intractable, more legalistic and suspicious; and he attributed these qualities in them largely to the influence of lawyers, who, as he put it, 'augur misgovernment at a distance, and snuff the approach of tyranny in every tainted breeze'. The colonists had their own peculiar temperament, their own spirit, which the mother country must take into account in all her dealings with them. 'The question is, not whether their spirit deserves praise or blame, but what, in the name of God, shall we do with it?' It was not a question of asserting rights of sovereignty against the colonists, or of defending the rights of man against George III, but of restoring peace between two English communities which were like each other and yet also unlike. The prejudices and habits of the Americans made them the sort of people they were. The mother country, even in her own interest, must take her colonies for what they were. If she used force to try to gain her end, she would not gain it; for her end was to have loyal colonies attached to her, and loyalty is not won by force. 'Nothing less will content me than whole America . . . I do not choose wholly to break the American spirit, because it is the spirit that has made the country.'

Burke, the defender of American liberties, was a staunch imperialist.

And yet, much as he cared for the unity of the empire, he cared even more for liberty, English and American. Better, he thought, that the American spirit, which included a passion for liberty, should not be broken than that the empire should be kept together at the cost of breaking it.

III. BURKE ON THE FRENCH REVOLUTION

Burke was in his forties and at the height of his intellectual powers when civil war broke out between the English in America and in the mother country; he was already sixty when the French revolution began. His reaction to that revolution was violent and deep. He hated what the French revolutionaries stood for and attacked them more bitterly and contemptuously than ever he had attacked anyone before. The French Revolution taught him nothing; it only made him cling more fiercely and obstinately to opinions long held.

Nevertheless, *Reflections on the Revolution in France* is a great book. Anyone who reads it for the first time, and who has not read anything else written by Burke, will find in it much that is excellent and well put. But what it contains of social and political theory is for the most part not new; for Burke had already published his most perceptive and luminous ideas about society and government before he wrote the *Reflections*. In his speeches, addresses, and letters on America we can find nearly all the sentiments and ideas most strongly associated with his name: the argument that society is infinitely complex and difficult to understand; the distaste for all talk about universal rights; the respect for what is old and national; the insistence that men cannot greatly alter their institutions except for the worse; the belief that prejudice rather than reason holds society together, so that to destroy prejudice is to undermine society.

Yet Burke's speeches on America do not prepare us for his angry denunciation of the French Revolution. The Americans, no less than the French, had appealed to universal principles and universal rights; and Burke, though he had taken little notice of the appeal, had not been offended by it, but had quickly turned his mind to the grievances that lay behind it. He had not troubled to blame the Americans for the 'metaphysical' nonsense about abstract rights to which, in the course of their dispute with George III, they became every bit as addicted as the French. The doctrine of *the rights of man* is as much American as French. Why, then, did Burke object to it so much in the French and so little in the Americans?

The Americans had enjoyed a considerable independence of the mother country. That independence was embodied in institutions, practices, and habits of thought and feeling that were products of English and American history. The real concern of the Americans, so Burke thought, had been to defend their independence; until independence was threatened, they had not been much interested in the rights of man. Their abstract arguments, little as Burke relished them, were effects of grievances that Burke cared very much about. Provided that particular claims are just, talk about the rights of man, nonsense though it may be, is not dangerous nonsense. Burke believed in the justice of the American cause and therefore quite properly ignored rather than attacked what he called the 'metaphysical' theories produced in defence of that cause. It would have been, from his point of view, a waste of time, and perhaps even bad politics, to attack the American version of the doctrine of the rights of man.

The French revolutionaries seemed to Burke to be using the doctrine of the rights of man for a quite different purpose: not to justify resistance in defence of a traditional freedom, of acquired rights, nor even to support new claims intended to make that freedom more secure, but to subvert society. They were making claims incompatible with the existing social order, the system of existing rights; they were challenging those rights in the name of such principles as equality and liberty, taken in the abstract.

This challenge, in Burke's opinion, was absurd. Equality and liberty, taken in the abstract, are empty notions. If we want to know what people have in mind when they speak of liberty, we must see what specific claims they are making. Freedom is not everywhere understood in the same way; it does not in all societies include the same rights. We cannot, by considering human nature merely as such, outside any particular social order, decide what rights men ought to have. In all societies men have rights and set store by them. Man is by nature a social and a moral creature; and in every society he claims rights for himself and recognizes similar claims made by others. But we cannot discover what claims he makes or ought to make merely by considering his nature, the properties which distinguish him from other creatures. Though it is specifically human to have rights, to make and to recognize claims, there are no *rights of man*; there are only claims which are valid within a particular social order. This, I think, is at least part of what Burke had in mind when he condemned what he called the doctrine of *abstract rights*.

To the doctrine he condemned Burke opposed another. The best of all titles, he thinks, is prescription; if a claim has long been made and long recognized, the presumption is that it serves an enduring need and is therefore valid. Men have not deduced the claims they make and recognize from abstract principles. Their claims arise out of their needs, and their needs out of the situations in which they find themselves. The persistence of claims is therefore strong evidence that they are useful. Burke calls prescription the most *solid* of all titles.

What are we to understand by this? That the most important rights, the ones most cherished, are prescriptive? Is Burke making no more than what he takes to be a statement of fact? Sometimes it may seem so, but at other times it does not. He is not merely telling us how the most cherished claims arise, or what their social function is; he is not merely putting forward an hypothesis. He is also arguing that prescription is the most valid of all titles. He is not merely saying that, as a matter of fact, among the claims that are made, the most cherished, because they serve the most enduring needs, are prescriptive; he is also saying that prescriptive claims take precedence over all others in the sense that they ought to be preferred to them.

This assertion can be interpreted in two ways. It may be held that, since its age is strong evidence that an old established claim serves a useful purpose, the burden of proof rests always on whoever would abolish or curtail it; or it may be held that its age is sufficient evidence that an old established right does serve such a purpose and that therefore it ought not to be abolished or curtailed. We cannot say that Burke took either of these two positions clearly and consistently. Every reader of the *Reflections* will get his own impression. Mine, for what it is worth, is this: that, though Burke sometimes took the one position and sometimes the other, he inclined more to the second than the first.

Burke was moved to wonder, to scorn and to anger by the 'arrogance' of the revolutionaries. They pretended, so he thought, to an impossible knowledge; they pretended to know how a free and equalitarian society could be established, and asserted their right to refashion French society to meet that ideal. The doctrine of the rights of man, as they used it (of the rights of man taken in the abstract outside any particular social order) was not only absurd; it was also pernicious. The French revolutionaries seemed to Burke as pretentious as they were fanatical. They could not, he thought, attain their avowed purposes; they could only ruin France in the attempt to attain them. They were like ignorant surgeons preparing to carry out a major operation on a body whose delicate and nicely adjusted structure they were scarcely aware of; they could use the knife, but only to damage or to kill what they pretended to cure. Burke was not against men's carrying out minor operations on the body politic; he was only certain that they are never competent to do more. The French revolutionaries were, he thought, even more than usually incompetent; their eagerness to make great changes was itself sure evidence of their folly. 'The fresh ruins of France . . . are not the devastation of civil war; they are sad but instructive monument of rash and ignorant counsel in time of profound peace.' He also said: 'When I hear the simplicity of contrivance aimed at and boasted of in any new political constitutions, I am at no loss to decide that the artificers are grossly ignorant of their trade, or totally negligent of their duty.' The wise man knows that society is many-sided and intricate, and that he can do only a little to change it in the way he would have it change. Society is not clay passive to the potter, but a delicate and living whole, more easily damaged than improved.

The French revolutionaries – and the philosophers from whom they took their doctrines – were eager to destroy old prejudices on the ground that they were irrational and were obstacles to progress. Burke thought he knew better. 'We know,' he said (speaking for himself and also, so he believed, for the English generally), 'that we have made no discoveries, and we think that no discoveries are to be made, in morality; nor many in the great principles of government, nor in the ideas of liberty, which were understood long before we were born'. And he went on 'instead of casting away our old prejudices . . . we cherish them because they are prejudices, and the longer they have lasted, and, the more generally they have prevailed, the more we cherish them. We are afraid to put men to live and trade each on his own private stock of reason; because we suspect that this stock in each man is small, and that the individuals would do better to avail themselves of the general bank and capital of nations and of ages. Many of our men of speculation, instead of exploding general prejudices, employ their sagacity to discover the latent wisdom which prevails in them.'

Prejudice is not irrational. It is not belief that cannot be justified; it is only belief that most people never trouble to justify and are perhaps incapable of justifying for not knowing how to set about doing so. They accept their prejudices on trust, and act confidently on them. They acquire them in the process of growing up and getting ready to take their places in society. All people most of the time, and many people nearly all the time, act on prejudice; they act on beliefs they have never troubled to justify. If they waited to justify them, they could not act. To know how to behave successfully, a man need not understand society in the sense of being able to explain it; but he must know what to do in all the usual situations of life. To know this, he must have the sentiments and beliefs appropriate to his condition. If they are appropriate, he will act successfully; he will want what is within his reach, and will be likely to get it. Of course, he will often have to think for himself, and will sometimes come painfully by new opinions; but among the beliefs he acts on, those he takes on trust will be much more numerous than those he acquires by thinking things out for himself. He will avail himself, as Burke puts it, of 'the general bank and capital of nations and ages'.

This 'bank and capital' is not a chance accumulation. It is the fruit of experience and reflection. The beliefs that Burke calls *prejudices* have all, or nearly all, he thinks, been produced by hard thinking; they are beliefs that men have acquired in the past by solving the problems life presented to them. But if every man had to solve all these problems for himself, mankind could never make progress; one of the conditions of progress is that men shall accept ready-made most of the solutions offered to them. They are born into societies whose institutions and beliefs are long established and change slowly. They learn to use the accumulated wisdom of the past much as they learn to put on their clothes; they get the habit of making proper use of what is given to them without troubling their heads about how it came to be what and where it is. Prejudice is not chance or casual opinion; it would never have come into being and been widely accepted if it had not been adapted to men's needs.

Prejudice serves two purposes. It enables the individual to live much better than he could live without it; it enables him to rely on much more than his own wisdom and therefore to satisfy many more wants than he could otherwise do. If the ordinary civilized man lives more commodiously than the savage, it is not so much that his private stock of wisdom is greater as that he has a set of beliefs and habits enabling him to take advantage of the opportunities that civilization offers. Take him out of his environment, and he will be almost as much bewildered, as much lost, as the savage translated from his own society to another quite unlike it. His advantage is that, while he remains in his own civilized community, he can avail himself of an immense stock of wisdom. And he ordinarily does so, not by making it his own in the way that a student does when he understands what he is taught, but merely by acquiring beliefs which he is no more capable of justifying than the savage is capable of justifying his beliefs.

Prejudice also serves to hold society together. Men's prejudices are suited to their institutions. Because of their prejudices men behave as they must if society is to function properly. Every man plays his appropriate part, not because he understands how that part fits into the whole life of his community, but because he has been taught to play it. There are some prejudices common to all the members of society, and others confined to certain classes, groups or professions. The prejudices of a society, together with its laws, customs, rights and obligations, make it the society it is; they help to give it its peculiar character. They form part of a whole system of beliefs and modes of behaviour, and they help to maintain the system. To destroy them is therefore to damage, if not to destroy, society; it is to deprive men of the motives which cause them, though they may not know it, so to behave that the social order, on which their security and happiness depend, does not disintegrate.

Many English philosophers, so Burke tells us, instead of exploding prejudices try to discover the wisdom latent in them. For prejudices, though most people never trouble to justify them, can be justified. They are justified when their social function is explained, when it is shown how they serve to give men security and happiness by preserving the social order. Though Burke praises the 'men of speculation', as he calls them, who make it their business to explain and defend prejudices and not to destroy them, he would much rather have people take them on trust than enquire closely into them. He is not content to say that explanation is a task for which only a few persons have the leisure and the talents, and that most people have no choice but to take society as they find it without hope of ever being able to understand how it functions. He comes at time close to condemning curiosity about it. No doubt, where there are men of speculation bent on exploding salutary prejudices, it is good that there should be other men willing and able to show up their sophistries. The innocent and unreflecting must be protected against those who would argue them out of beliefs necessary to their happiness. But innocence is safer than curiosity, at least for most people. Prejudice is not the enemy of knowledge, but an effect of experience and a substitute for it.

By prejudice Burke does not mean any belief accepted on trust. We normally accept as true an immense variety of statements which we are in no position to verify: ordinary everyday statements made by our friends and neighbours, expert opinions, and scientific hypotheses. Burke, when he speaks of prejudice, has not these things in mind. He has in mind judgements about conduct, beliefs about what is desirable and how men should behave, rather than judgements of fact, though he does not trouble to distinguish between them. When he calls prejudice *latent wisdom*, he does not mean that it is belief capable of verification which most people never verify; he means that it is belief capable of justification which most people never justify. Prejudice is justified when it is shown how it serves to hold society together and to give men security and happiness.

Montesquieu had shown, in *De l'Esprit des Lois*, how men's beliefs and sentiments vary with their institutions. He had argued that every type of government has a *principe* or spring of action appropriate to it; virtue in a republic, honour in a monarchy, fear in a despotism. He had seen that, if a type of government is to survive, it matters less that men should understand how it works than that they should have sentiments which move them to behave in the ways that make it work. What he called the *principe* of a type of government is the psychological or subjective factor whose social counterpart is a whole set of institutions; it stands to those institutions in much the same relation as what Burke called prejudice. Just as for Burke prejudice is more than bare opinion, being opinion backed by emotion, so for Montesquieu virtue and honour are more than bare feelings; they are emotionally charged opinions about how the patriot or the man of honour should behave.

But it is Burke, and not Montesquieu, who gives us much the fuller,

the more eloquent and persuasive, explanation and defence of prejudice and prescription, of traditional beliefs and traditional rights.
Burke did more than reproduce a theme of Montesquieu's; he
breathed upon the bare bones of it and put life into it as Montesquieu
had not done.

IV. REFLECTIONS ON BURKE

1. The Strong Points in Burke's Arguments

There are admirable things in the social philosophy of Burke; things
that are either new or better put by him than by anyone before him.
Radicals at all times too often forget them, and were never more
disposed to do so than in the latter part of the eighteenth century. For
a generation or more before the French revolution, the iconoclasts had
been having it all their own way; they had been writing the books most
read and producing the arguments most widely canvassed. It was they
who were passionate and aggressive, and the conservative writers who
were cool and detached. Burke brought to the defence of the established order passions as strong as any that moved the radicals. He
carried the war into their camp. He made conservatism articulate as
it had never been before; he put into words what many people felt
about the French Revolution but did not know how to say. His was
not the style of the lecture-room or the intellectual salon. If it was not
exactly popular, it was formidable and reassuring. It is doubtful
whether his admirers understood him as easily as people inclined to
radicalism understood Tom Paine. But at least they got comfort from
him; they could feel that here at last was a powerful intellect and an
eloquent voice on their side.

Much that Burke says about the French revolutionaries and revolutionaries in general is well founded. It is true that revolutionaries
nearly always attempt much more than they can achieve, and that
they are bold largely because they are blind. Nowadays we know much
more about revolutions than it was possible to know in Burke's time.
There have been many small and several great revolutions since then,
and they have been carefully studied. Most revolutions lead to results
that the people who start them never wanted. Indeed, it is often
doubtful whether the makers of revolutions know what they want.
They are moved to anger by what they see of the established order,
or they want power and hope to get it by using the anger felt by others,
or they are moved both by anger and ambition. It is the strength of
their feelings, not the depth of their understanding, which moves them
to act. Of course, the successful revolutionary leader needs talents that
are rare; he is not as foolish and improvident as Burke tried to make

him out. In some ways he is less blind than other men; he sees the immediate situation more clearly than they do and is quicker to seize opportunities. Yet the gifts which enable a man to take the lead in troubled times are not the gifts which make the efficient reformer or the deep student of society. It is one thing to know how to get power and quite another to know how to use it to reconstruct society according to plan, and there is no reason to suppose that the two kinds of knowledge often go together. When we say that a revolutionary leader is successful, we ordinarily mean that he succeeds in getting power and keeping it; we seldom mean that he succeeds in changing society to bring it closer to some ideal proclaimed by himself. He may, like Robespierre, have ideas so vague that they cannot be used to estimate how near he comes to getting what he wanted; or he may, like Lenin, have rather more precise ideas, and then it is easier to see how far his achievement falls short of his intention. Indeed, that is putting it too mildly. As Burke saw, it is not that the revolutionary goes only a short way in the direction he wants to go; it is rather that he goes a long way in other directions. He makes great changes but not the changes he wants to make. He is swept along by events into courses undreamt of before he began. He may reconcile himself to the unforeseen effects of his actions, especially if that is a condition of his keeping power. He may even persuade himself that he has wanted all along what in fact he never foresaw. But the belief that he has reconstructed society according to plan is largely an illusion. All this is borne out by history, and Burke saw it when it was less obvious than it is now.

Burke was also right in saying that the social order is maintained, not because people know how it functions, but because they act appropriately; and that they do so largely because they accept traditional beliefs and rights and obligations. Men play their parts in society without understanding how those parts fit together to form a whole system of behaviour. They do so, not by chance or because there is a pre-established harmony, but because they have been *conditioned*. They have been moulded by society and so feel at home in it. If their beliefs and their claims get very much out of line with established institutions, the social order is bound to be disrupted. People then ask much more of society than they have been in the habit of getting, and they complain of oppression; they cease to behave in accustomed ways, thereby upsetting other people and themselves. Conditions are chaotic, or are felt to be so; there is frustration and wasted effort, and men seem to have lost their bearings in the social world. It is not that they have ceased to understand what was once intelligible to them, for they mostly never understood it; it is rather that they no longer accept it because their beliefs and ambitions are not adjusted to it.

Again, as Burke said, liberty and equality are differently understood in different societies. We cannot discover what they are, what rights go to make them up, merely by contemplating the 'essential or universal' nature of man. In no society do all men have the same rights; everywhere there are hierarchy and difference of status. When we claim liberty we are not saying that there ought to be no restrictions, just as when we claim equality we are not saying that nobody must have any right which everyone else does not also have. These two claims, if they were interpreted in this way, would be destructive of society: the first because it would deny the need for social discipline, and the second because it would deny that diversity of function entails diversity of right. When we champion liberty or equality, we are putting some rights forward as more important than the rest; we are saying that everyone ought to have them. What, then, gives these rights their special importance, granted that they are not to be derived logically from man's essential or pre-social nature?[1] Since in no society can man do what he pleases, what decides which forms of discipline are tolerable and which are not? What can it be but current ideas about how men should live, ideas which vary from society to society? Thus it is that restrictions felt to be intolerable in one society can be put forward as conditions of freedom in another.

If by freedom and equality are understood rights long established or cherished, there is no danger in them. But if they are used to press new and large claims, which society cannot in fact meet, they are apt to be dangerous to the very classes for whose supposed benefit they are used, and not only to the privileged. Society is well adapted to meet established claims because these claims are in keeping with what society now is. For that very reason, therefore, it is not well adapted to meeting claims very different from the established ones. By trying to get more out of society than it can give, we risk losing what it has until now given. Or, to use language more like Burke's, by asking for too much freedom we put in jeopardy the freedom that is ours already.

Burke made about as good a case for aristocracy as was made in his time. We may not find it convincing, our assumptions being so different from his, but it is, I think, ingenious. Burke is right in believing that in every society (except perhaps the most primitive and simple) there must be some kind of social hierarchy and not merely a division of labour; there must be differences of power and station which make men socially unequal. Radicals are no longer concerned to deny this. They part company with Burke, not by saying there need be no hierarchy, but by insisting that it can and ought to be made to rest on differences of ability. They attack, not all superiority of power, income and status, but the superiority which is inherited or otherwise unearned. Many of the arguments they use were devised after Burke's

[1] Unless, of course, that nature is so defined as to include these rights; unless, that is, normative statements are 'disguised' by being put in the form of statements of fact.

time, and he never met them. His counter-attack on the champions of equality is therefore rather old-fashioned; it is directed against equality as it was understood before the birth of modern socialism. Burke had never seriously to consider the possibility that society might be so organized, and its economy so controlled, as to ensure that differences of income, power and status, correspond fairly closely to differences of ability measured by standards acceptable to most people. But he did produce arguments for the hereditary principle which are worth considering.

He believed, as Bodin had also done (and the belief is not absurd), that inequalities are often more readily accepted when they rest on birth than on merit. He believed that, in societies where most men expect to die in the class they are born into, they ordinarily do not acquire the ambitions which make them dissatisfied with their lot. Therefore, the less competitive your society, the less envious and the more contented its members are likely to be; from which it follows that to multiply opportunities of rising socially is unlikely to increase happiness. Men feel most secure in stable societies; and the more stable a society, the less movement up and down the social ladder. Burke was not for preventing all movement on it; but he wanted the ascent kept difficult, so as to be beyond the power of all but the most able.[1]

Many people today find this line of argument distasteful and mean; it is against the spirit of our times. But that, though it makes it less persuasive to us, does not weaken it logically. We are not unprejudiced, and for all that we wish it otherwise, it may yet be true that in societies where movement from class to class is difficult, men are less apt to acquire ambitions they cannot satisfy than in societies where such movement is easy. This is an hypothesis not yet tested. Burke may be right.[2]

Burke believed that the upper classes are the chief repositories of the 'collective wisdom' on which the well-being of the community depends. They are the bearers of civilization; they know how to govern; they enforce the rules that hold society together; they set the tone. This does not mean that the lower orders imitate them in all things,

---

[1] Burke took it for granted that men who rise socially are usually able men, and that society is the better for their success. No doubt, they mostly are able, and owe their success to ability as much as to good fortune. But society may not be the better for their success. The qualities that bring success to the few that have it need not be useful, and may even be harmful, to society at large. This is a possibility which seems not to have occurred to Burke.

[2] There is another argument against easy movement from class to class which Burke does not use. The easier this movement the more the successful are estranged from their families, and the more people there are socially ' maladjusted' because they have not acquired in childhood the habits and values needed to put them at their ease in the class into which they have risen.

for they too have their own tastes and customs. If they had not, if they were imitators in all things, they would try to assimilate themselves to the upper classes. The upper classes set the tone when by precept and example they play the largest part in maintaining the standards shared by all classes, the standards needed to preserve the social order. The more they respect the rights of their inferiors, the more secure their own position. Their knowing how to govern, their special skill, is not theoretical knowledge; they need not know how the whole system of government works; they need not be political scientists, any more than the good rider need be learned in the anatomy of the horse. They learn how to govern, partly by actually governing, and partly by acquiring in the process of growing up to be fit members of their class the manner, the tact, and the confidence needed for good government.

The superiority of the upper classes, as Burke conceived of it, is social and not biological. True, he did not believe (as, say, Descartes and Hobbes had believed, or at least had asserted) that men are born with much the same natural abilities, and he did believe that those who rise socially usually owe their success to superior talents. Yet his defence of the privileges of the upper classes does not rest on the assumption that persons born into these classes are better endowed by nature than other people. They owe their superiority less to nature than to social opportunity: by virtue of their position in society, they acquire much the largest share of the wisdom inherited from the past.

It may be objected that Burke's argument is circular. The privileges of the upper classes are justified by a superiority which is itself admitted to be largely, if not entirely, an effect of these privileges. This objection can, I think, be met. First, there is the obvious point that society may not be rich enough to provide these privileges to more than a minority; and yet it may long have ceased to be so simple as not to need the political skills and other qualities which these privileges produce. There is also another argument, subtler and perhaps true, which Burke rather hints at than puts into plain words. He speaks at times as if some of the qualities that make for good government are produced only by a sense of being raised above other people, not by merit, but by birth; as if, even in a society rich enough to educate all its members about as well as the upper classes were educated in his time, these qualities would not exist unless there were an hereditary aristocracy. I may be foisting on Burke an opinion he never held. It is difficult to be quite sure, because he took it for granted that there are in all societies great social inequalities, so that the privileged everywhere owe their privileges more to inheritance than to talent. He never envisaged a society wealthy enough to provide all its members with the amenities and education which the upper classes had in his day, and therefore never really put the question whether even a society of that kind would be the better for having a class with inherited privileges. Nevertheless, my impression is that, if he had put the question, he would have answered it by saying *Yes.* I suspect that he believed that some of the qualities making for good government are hardly ever to be found except among those who from childhood have been used to thinking of themselves as belonging to a superior class. This belief is peculiarly distasteful to radicals. They often willingly admit that inherited privileges may be desirable in a society lacking the means of providing everyone with a good education and a comfortable living; but the idea that they may be valuable in all societies, no matter how great their resources, is repulsive to them.

2. The Weak Points in Burke's Arguments

I have already conceded that Burke was right in saying that revolutionaries are often reckless and blind. But what exactly is the point of this charge against them? Who is the warning addressed to? Is it to the revolutionaries themselves? If it is, they will certainly not listen; for if they did listen they would not be the stuff that revolutionaries are made of. They are out to get power, and will not be stopped in their attempt to get it by doubts about their ability to make good use of it. Is the warning then addressed to the people generally? But revolutions happen at times when the people are in no position to choose their rulers. Only when the structure of authority is breaking down do revolutionaries get their chance. They do not create the situations in which they act; they do not make their chances, they only take them. It is less important to expose the reckless folly of revolutionaries than to discover why the structure of authority is breaking down. Yet this is a question to which Burke scarcely puts his mind.

Again, just what is the point of calling revolutions 'destructive'? All social change involves destruction in one sense; it does more than add to what is already there, it also puts an end to some things to make way for others. If what it makes way for is better than what it puts an end to, it is pointless to call it destructive; and this is as true of violent or illegal (that is, revolutionary) change as of legal reform. No doubt, violence is painful; and peaceful change is nearly always to be preferred to violent change. But what if the change can only be made by violence?

If what comes after a revolution is more acceptable to the people generally than what went before, the revolution is more constructive than destructive. And it may be constructive even though revolutionaries are reckless and blind. It may remedy the grievances that gave birth to it; or else it may, without doing this, so change the aspirations and ideas of the people that they come to like what the revolution has produced, though to begin with they neither desired nor imagined it. Let us give examples.

If we look at the course of events in France from May 1789, when the States-General met for the first time since 1614, until Robespierre's fall in July 1794, we see very little consistency of purpose or foresight among the men who ruled the country; we see one group of in-experienced and excited men giving way to another, with scarcely any of them having time and quiet enough to make up their minds what to do; we see far-reaching decisions taken on the spur of the moment; we see France almost as much a prey to reckless violence and blind hatred as she was during the wars of religion in the sixteenth century. Yet the great revolution did for France what the wars of religion never did; it removed long-standing grievances. True, the revolutionaries did not do what Burke said was impossible; they did not reconstruct France as an architect reconstructs an old house, knowing exactly what he is doing and altering it so as to disturb the people inside it as little as possible. But the fact remains that, as a result of what the arrogant and reckless revolutionaries did, the common people got many things they had wanted before the revolution began and still valued after it was over. The task of reconstruction, if reconstruction there was, was left to Napoleon, who reverted in many ways to the methods of the old monarchy. The people were grateful to him for restoring order, but his actual schemes of government meant little to them. What they cared most about, the destruction of old privileges, was the work of the revolution.

Not all revolutions accomplish even this much. Sometimes popular grievances are used to get power, and nothing is done to remedy them. Sometimes, through the actions of reckless and unscrupulous men who never see more than a move or two ahead, society is changed into something that nobody foresaw and nobody wanted. But this is not, as Burke would have us believe, the *inevitable* character of every revolu-tion merely because revolutionary leaders, hurried along by a course of events beyond their power to control, are mostly blind, except to the immediate chance. The longer views and the tasks of deliberate reconstruction belong, if to anyone, to the leaders of the post-revo-lutionary epoch, when a solid apparatus of power exists once more.

The grievances that bring about a revolution may not be remedied and yet the social order which emerges from it may come to be more generally acceptable than was the social order destroyed by it. A deep and violent revolution, however blind its leaders, in changing society may also change men's ambitions and preferences in such a way that they come to value what the revolution has produced though they never wanted it before it began. If we look at the dissatisfied classes in Russia in 1917, we can hardly say that the Bolshevik revolution has remedied their grievances. The peasants wanted to divide the big estates between them; the middle class mostly wanted constitutional government and civil liberties as understood in the West; and the industrial workers wanted to run the factories and share the profits. These classes, between them the great majority of the Russian people in 1917, never got what they wanted when the revolution was made. Nor did the revolutionaries get what they wanted. True, they got power, but they did not succeed in using it to build the kind of society to which they aspired at the time they took power. Scarcely anyone in 1917 foresaw that Russia would become what she now is; and the few who did foresee it mostly disliked it, condemning the Bolshevik revolution as premature precisely before they foresaw what it would lead to. Yet it may be that the Russian people of today like what they now have better than the Russians of 1917 liked what they then had. I do not say that it is so; I only say that it may be. Certainly, we cannot prove that it is *not* so merely by showing that the grievances of 1917 have not been remedied and that the men who made the October revolution had no intention, when they made it, that Russian society should be what it now is. If the Russians are now satisfied with what they have, we can hardly use the arguments of Burke to condemn the Bolshevik revolution.

Burke attacked the revolutionaries and their friends for being so absurd as to put forward the doctrine of the rights of man. Equality and liberty, taken in the abstract, are empty. In all societies there are some rights which all men have, some respects in which they are equal; and there are rights to which they are strongly attached, and whose loss they would bewail as a loss of freedom.

All this is true, but also, perhaps, beside the point. The revolutionaries were not really concerned to deny it, for it did not affect the claims they were making. They did not demand that everyone, irrespective of age, sex or occupation, should have exactly the same rights; they claimed only that there were some rights which society had not yet granted to all and which all should have. They did not in practice demand unlimited freedom; they understood by freedom some rights which most Frenchmen already enjoyed and some which they did not. As a matter of fact, though Burke did not see it, they wanted to preserve many more rights than they wanted to destroy or to create. Not only conservatives, but radicals and revolutionaries also, are creatures of their age; the plans they make for society are products of their experience in a particular environment. In ways of which they are themselves unconscious, what they can imagine is limited by what they have known. This is even more true of active revolutionaries who catch the ear of the discontented than of Utopian dreamers. To conservatives, and perhaps also to themselves, they look like men who aim at reconstructing the entire social order; but their aims are usually narrower than they seem either to their critics or to themselves. Certainly, the aims of the French revolutionaries, especially while Burke was writing the *Reflections* and before the Jacobins came to power, were not nearly as subversive as Burke made them out to be. The revolutionaries asserted that there were some rights which all men ought to have and which most Frenchmen did not have.

No doubt, they claimed to derive these rights logically from man's nature, his essentially human qualities, his capacity to reason and to make deliberate choices, and therefore called them *the rights of man*. No doubt, too, the securing of these rights entailed larger changes in France than the rebellious Americans had aimed at when they first set up the banner of revolt. But, even if it is true that there are no rights that can be derived logically from man's essentially human qualities, it does not follow that the claims made by the French revolutionaries were invalid. We may reject the arguments used to justify them and still find others to take their place. If there are other arguments in their favour, there is nothing much gained by attacking the particular arguments used by the French to justify them on the ground that they are 'metaphysical'. Burke's purpose, after all, was to deny that the claims made by the revolutionaries were just; he wanted to do more than merely deny that the arguments used to support those claims by the French revolutionaries were valid. He had himself supported the claims of the American revolutionaries without accepting their arguments.

And what is the point of Burke's objection to *abstract* rights? In what does their *abstractness* consist? In the claim made that they derive logically from man's essential nature or his destiny? But that claim, mistaken though it may be, can be made as easily in favour of established rights as of rights not yet legally recognized; it is not in itself a dangerous claim. Or are rights abstract because they are loosely defined, because it is not made clear precisely what people would get or be allowed to do if they were made legal? If that is a disadvantage, it is easily remedied. New claims are often vague when they are first put forward and acquire precision as people set about trying to secure them. Moreover, it is not their vagueness which makes them dangerous. If you confine yourself to saying that everyone should have a living wage you make a vague and harmless statement. You will probably find rich men agreeing with you as readily as poor men; it is only when you go on to define a living wage as something appreciably more than people are actually getting that your claim begins to frighten the rich and to excite the poor. For centuries before the French Revolution philosophers had been saying that all men are by nature equal and free. The French revolutionaries were dangerous – or, if you prefer it, formidable – precisely because they were not content to repeat these abstract claims, but defined them with at least enough precision to make it clear that, if the claims were to be made good, there would have to be great changes in France. Are we then to call claims *abstract*, however definite they may be, merely because they are claims of a kind not made before? But this would be an abuse of language.

Burke's defence of prescriptive right and prejudice – if we interpret it in the most conservative sense (and this is the sense which his actual words often imply) – forbids, if not all change, then at least most deliberate change. If prescription's being the most solid of titles is taken to mean that old established rights must not be abolished or curtailed, then we may do no more deliberately, by way of legislation, than create new rights which take nothing away from old ones. Old rights may, of course, lapse from disuse, and as new needs arise unprecedented claims may come to be made, and, if they are widely recognized, may harden into rights. There can be considerable change though no prescriptive rights and no prejudices are challenged. But not all social change happens in this way. Much of it (except in the most primitive societies) happens because established rights and revered prejudices are openly and deliberately challenged. Wherever there is a legislative function, wherever it is admitted that law can be deliberately made and is not all customary or sacred, prescriptive rights are sometimes abolished or curtailed and prejudices are challenged.

Burke did not exactly deny this. He admitted that reform may be desirable. Nor did he contest the authority of Parliament as it was generally understood in his day. Parliament, in his day as much as in ours, was held to have a prescriptive right to make law; and nobody argued that it had no right to make a law which abolished or curtailed long-established rights. No doubt, most people held that Parliament ought to be very reluctant to make such laws, that it ought not to interfere with long-established rights except where it could make a very strong case for doing so. But nobody, not even Burke, denied that Parliament had a prescriptive right to challenge and even to destroy prescriptive rights, and also to aim at goals not compatible with widely received prejudices. We may say, therefore, that Burke's defence of prescriptive right and prejudice, taken literally, is not consistent either with his own admission that reform may be desirable or with the sovereignty of Parliament which he did not contest. If prescription's being the most solid of all titles is taken to mean that it must be preferred to any title created deliberately, then it is not only wrong to abolish or abridge old established rights illegally or unconstitutionally; it is also wrong to abolish or abridge them legally or constitutionally. There can then be no prescriptive right to challenge and destroy prescriptive rights, and Parliament, even as Burke knew and cherished it, becomes a body claiming an authority it does not rightfully possess.

According to this strange doctrine, it is always wrong to aim at social change. We must not strive for it, but must only let it happen. It must result, not from legislation, but from what men do when they do not intend to change the social order. As a result of their activities their situation changes. They acquire needs they did not have before, and they cease to have needs they once had. They make new claims and they cease making old ones. New rights come into being and old ones disappear; but in all this there is no challenging or destroying of prescriptive rights, no conscious or deliberate making of law.

Now, it may be objected that this is an absurd doctrine, and one to which Burke never adhered. This is certainly true. But it is a doctrine which follows from some of his arguments in favour of prescription and prejudice; he did sometimes speak as if a right's being long established were sufficient evidence of its being useful, and as if prejudice were always a better guide to conduct than reasoned argument.

Burke set a moral, not a legal, limit to Parliament's authority. He wanted only moderate reform, and was opposed to any attempt to make a large social or political change. But he was apt to forget that even moderate reform often involves destroying some old-established rights which those who have them are deeply attached to and challenging some venerable prejudices still widely cherished. The call for even moderate reform finds a response because new needs have arisen and have moved men to make new claims. Being moderate, the reform can be made without interfering with many established rights or challenging many prejudices.

But those who have the prescriptive right (as the king had in France) to make reforms may refuse or neglect to make them. One demand for reform after another may be ignored or refused until nothing less than a drastic change in the entire social system will satisfy any but the privileged classes. If this happens, there is a revolutionary situation which nothing can alleviate except drastic change; and this change, if it is not made according to law, will be made in defiance of it.

It does not really make sense to allow, as Burke does, deliberate change when it is moderate and to forbid it when it is drastic. It would make sense only in a world where reforms are always made in good time, so that there is never a large volume of pent-up demand to be satisfied. Burke had no good reason to believe that he lived in such a world. It is one thing to say that reform ought to be timely and moderate; it is quite another to forbid drastic reforms in a world where reform is not always, or even usually, timely and moderate. Burke's defence of prescription and prejudice, if we take it literally, forbids all deliberate reform of the social and political system. But this Burke did not know, and he therefore allowed moderate reform. He did not see that, given that conditions change and that reform is necessary, there is no good reason why reform should always be moderate and never drastic, unless it is always timely – which it very obviously is not. What is Burke saying in favour of prescriptive rights when he says that age is a proof of their utility? Just what are they useful for? For maintaining the social order? But they are part of that order. To say that they are useful for that purpose is really only to say that if the whole system of rights is to remain what it is, no part of it must be changed. So much is obvious, and nobody will dispute it. It is also irrelevant when the question at issue is: Shall we or shall we not change the system? Or is the proved utility of long-established rights merely their making for happiness or well-being? No doubt, they have seemed worth having to the persons that had them, or else they would not have survived so long. But their long survival does not prove that they ever were, or now are, useful to the whole community; that even those who do not have them are the better off for their existence. They may easily be the worse off. Of course, it can often be shown that rights which only a few persons enjoy are useful to everyone; but this cannot be done merely by pointing to their age. When privileges come to be challenged by the unprivileged, why is the challenge not as much evidence that they are harmful to the challengers as their long survival is evidence that they are useful to the privileged? It may well be that in neither case is the evidence sufficient. The unprivileged may sometimes fail to see what they have to gain by the existence of rights which they do not share, just as the privileged may cling from sheer habit to rights they would be better without. But why should we assume that the first situation is more likely than the second?

A man is happy, I take it, when he leads the kind of life he wants to lead. If he cannot lead it, he is unhappy and feels he is getting less than his due or less than is worth having. His conception of a life worth living depends on his standards, moral and aesthetic. If society seems to him so organized as to prevent his getting what he wants, he will want to change it. If that is his mood, it is no good telling him that the rights he already has make for his happiness. They would only make for it if his idea of a worth-while life were in keeping with his rights. But it is not; and therefore he lacks some of the rights he needs to give him his chance of happiness. It may also be that other people's privileges stand in his way. Perhaps his ancestors, who thought and felt differently, were satisfied with their established rights and were not resentful of privileges they did not share. But what is that to him, and to others like him? If the usefulness of rights is their making for happiness, and if people's happiness depends largely on their living what seems to them a worth-while life, how can established rights be generally useful if they conflict with many people's conceptions of what is desirable? And does it matter how recently those conceptions have been acquired?

Of course, ideals may be beyond attainment. Society may lack the resources needed to give people what they want. Or people may not know how to set about getting what they want. Insofar as Burke was saying to radicals and revolutionaries: 'Do not ask for more than it is possible to get! Be sure you really know what you want and how to get it! Move carefully, because otherwise you may come to regret the disappearance of many things that now seem worthless or harmful to you, or because you may find that much of what you get is not worth having!', he was giving good advice. But the advice does not stand or fall with the principle that long established rights by their mere survival have proved their utility.

Burke failed to see that ideals and abstract theories have a social function just as much as what he called prejudice. He wanted to discover what makes institutions stable, what moves people to behave in established ways. He found a large part of the answer in prejudice. Though he knew that institutions change, and even believed in progress (and therefore admitted that change can be good), he never tried to explain how change comes about. If he had tried, it might have occurred to him that what he called 'metaphysical' doctrines have an important social function. They can, like prejudice, serve to maintain the existing social order, established institutions and prescriptive rights; they can be conservative. But, unlike prejudice, they can also be used to condemn that order and to justify reform.

It is idle to object to them, as Burke did, on the ground that they are empty or false. These theories are not primarily descriptive but prescriptive; it is less important to discover whether they are true or false than how they arose and what they lead to. No doubt, they ought to be subjected to criticism, and to criticism of two kinds: academic and practical. Since they often claim to be descriptive, it is worth while enquiring how much truth there is in them, especially when they have wide currency; because how people think about society affects the claims they make on it. It is also worth while investigating these theories for another reason. Social and political theorists have not been the least important among the creators of the current language of politics, and by looking carefully and critically at their theories, we get to understand that language better and to see how far it is adequate to describe political and social facts. But the really important criticism of social theories, when they are influential, is practical. We must ask: What do they require us to do? How far are the demands they make upon us compatible with one another? How far are we able or willing to go towards meeting them? If we try to show that the theories misinterpret the facts, it is largely because we know that the demands they make are intimately connected with the accounts they give of society. By showing that these accounts are false, we can often go a long way towards showing that the demands are unreasonable.

Man is a theorizing as well as a prejudiced animal. Social and political theories, conservative and radical, are an important part of history. Though they are systems with often a great deal of fantasy to them, especially when they are radical, they cannot be dismissed as the aberrations of cranks. Especially not, if we admit, as Burke does, not only that there has been change, but that it has, on the whole, under Divine Providence, been for the better. We must ask: How does social change take place? How are established ways altered? No doubt, as wealth and knowledge accumulate, institutions inevitably change, and so, too, do prejudices. But new prejudices do not arise directly out of institutions without any need for deliberate thought. How can old prejudices be discarded and new ones take their place, if men must rely, as Burke would have them do, on what he calls 'the general bank and capital of nations and ages'; if they must rely entirely on established opinions about what is proper behaviour and what claims are allowable?

Burke suggests that progress is made through the remedy of 'proved abuses'. But we cannot get social change merely by the remedy of such abuses. At least not unless a 'proved abuse' is something which does not accord with Burke's account of prejudice and prescription. If a proved abuse does no more than violate established rights or offend against current prejudices, to remedy it is to restore the situation as it was before the abuse emerged. In that case, the more successfully abuses are remedied, the less society changes. It is only if we allow that practices which used not to be considered abuses may come to be so considered because they offend against new standards that we can explain social change as the cumulative effect of putting an end to abuses.

Burke makes a tacit and doubtful assumption which is at the root of many of his attacks on the French Revolution. Without saying so in so many words, he takes it for granted that the institutions of a great country like France are all compatible with one another and are also in harmony with a mutually consistent set of prejudices. There may be lesser maladjustments, but none that go deep. A great society develops, according to this view of it, much as a physical organism does; its parts change continually but always in ways that leave them about as well adjusted to one another as they were before. Since there can be only lesser social maladjustments, there need be only modest reforms. Over a long period of time there may be great changes, but they are only the sum of many small ones.

The small changes are made by men as they deal, one after another, with problems not too large and intricate for them to solve; and the whole course of change is controlled, not by them, but by a God who in His goodness wills the happiness of His creatures.

That the whole course of social change is not controlled by man is, I take it, obvious. No one, I suppose, would want to take issue with Burke here. Whether that course is controlled by God is another matter, which the social theorist is not competent to decide. But Burke's tacit assumption that all things social form an harmonious whole is surely quite gratuitous. Burke seems to have believed that because all aspects of social life affect one another and change continuously they must be well suited to each other, so that no really deep-seated tensions and conflicts can arise in the mere course of social development. Institutions and prejudices grow together and so must be mutually compatible.

But a large society consists of many smaller groups, and each of these, though moved by outside pressures, also changes by reason of what people do inside it. The lesser groups, for all that they continually affect one another, may nevertheless change in ways that bring them into conflict. The mere fact that change is continuous everywhere, and that there is always the pressure of group on group, is not of itself enough to maintain harmony. Yet to Burke it seemed evident that, because the social process is intricate and endless, everything involved in it must be fairly well adjusted to everything else, just as the tides smooth the stones on the beach till they all lie comfortably together. It seemed to him that perpetual interaction between the parts must make the whole harmonious. Yet it clearly need not do so, any more in a large society like France than in a small family. True, all the lesser communities, and all the classes, trades and professions, that make up France would not now be what they are if they had not been connected for centuries in the special ways that make them all parts of a unique community. They are tied to one another by an infinity of bonds, most of them invisible. No country in the world has a stronger individuality than France. Yet France is today, as she was when Burke wrote his *Reflections,* a country divided against herself.

Burke would have us believe that France was divided because of the evil influence on her of the philosophers and revolutionaries, who destroyed venerable prejudices, the cement of French society. But why did anyone listen to them? Why were their theories convincing and their denunciations exciting? What other explanation could there be but that French institutions and prejudices were not all well suited to one another; that there were profound conflicts of interest? When everything works smoothly, most people care little or nothing for what philosophers and theorists have to say; they begin to take notice of them only when things go wrong, and they are looking around for explanations and solutions. It is because there is disharmony, either among institutions or between them and current beliefs about what is desirable, that men are inspired to make social theories and to listen to them. And in their turn, these theories work on their minds, exacerbating the tensions and conflicts that gave birth to them. They undoubtedly cause trouble. Burke was right to that extent. But they are also salutary. Whether or not they go on to condemn the social order, they are attempts to understand it. They do not just make people angry and destructive; they inspire thought and deliberate action. True, more often than not, they are lamentably inadequate. This inadequacy can be dangerous, but need not be so. If the champions of a single theory get a monopoly of power, they can do great damage, not only by causing great suffering but by doing violence to commonly received notions of justice. If, however, the champions of no one theory engross all power; if all theories are continually challenged and criticized, they need not be dangerous and can do much good. In any but a static or very slowly changing society, social and political theories are indispensable. Not because any one of them explains society adequately or can be used exclusively to control its development, but because between them they help us to understand society and also to formulate the ideals which inspire us to reform it.

Burke treats social and political theories as if they were somehow external to the course of social change; as if the course would be slow and smooth, except for the influence upon it of perverse theories. But these theories are as much a part of the course of social change as anything else involved in it.

In Burke's time the world changed more slowly than it does now. Still, if he had cared to look, he could have found examples of rapid change. Invasion and foreign rule, which are always disruptive of established rights and prejudices, were as common then as they are now. Before he attacked the French revolutionaries, Burke had attacked Warren Hastings. Did he never reflect on what was happening in India as a result of the sudden irruption into Indian affairs of Europeans whose prejudices, moral and political, differed so widely from India's? Why was India so easy a prey to the European conqueror? If India had been a well regulated society, if her institutions and prejudices had been nicely adjusted to one another, if she had had an effective system of government, the Europeans might never have got their opportunities. What were the Europeans to do in India? Let her alone? If they had chosen to do that, they would have had to leave. They chose instead to make their power effective, and could do so only by making great and rapid changes in India.

Successful revolutionaries are like an invading army whose easy conquest of a country is due, not to superior numbers or better weapons, but to their victim's being a prey to anarchy. Revolutionaries do not take over a going concern; they cannot use the methods of their predecessors. They are faced with urgent problems that require drastic solutions. If they have not made up their minds beforehand what to do, they must improvise. It is pointless to condemn their lack of deep wisdom and keen foresight; they have grasped power from nerveless hands, and cannot hope to keep it except by making large changes quickly. That is not to say, of course, that they are blameless whatever they do; it is only to say that they cannot be blamed merely for taking large and drastic action.

Even a government which has not seized power by violence may have to take drastic action to prevent revolution; as, for instance, Nehru may have to do in India. Though the English brought Western influences to India, and so created new and tremendous problems for her, there were many great and necessary changes which they probably could not have undertaken (even if they had been willing to do so) merely because they were foreigners. It is now for the Indians themselves to undertake them. If they can take thought beforehand, making the changes rapidly and yet also deliberately and carefully, so much the better for them. But that is an opportunity not given to everyone, and especially not to revolutionaries who get power in a disintegrating society.

Burke's conception of society, as a well-integrated whole with long-established institutions supported by venerable prejudices, made it impossible for him to give a convincing explanation of anarchy and revolution. If his conception is true, it must be wrong for any government, even if it has taken power legally, to attempt rapid and far-reaching change. Burke had no alternative but to set France's troubles down to the influence of false and pretentious theories. France had a history as long as England's; her institutions must therefore have been well suited to her needs, and must have been supported by prejudices worthy of respect. If Burke had allowed that the opposite might be true, that the influence of the philosophers and revolutionaries might be as much an effect as a cause of France's troubles, he would have had to revise his ideas about society and social change. Burke could not understand the French Revolution; his assumptions forbade his doing so. If what has long existed is thereby proved useful, and if things that have long existed together always form a well-adjusted whole, the French revolutionaries trying to refashion French society must have been destroying what was, despite surface appearances, an harmonious social order. On Burke's assumptions only a revolution of the kind made by the Whigs in 1688, a neat and effective but modest tilting of the balance between long established powers, is ever desirable—or, indeed, intelligible. Anything else, anything like a deep and rapid transformation of society, cannot be explained; at least not satisfactorily. Burke's account of the French Revolution is in some ways ludicrously inadequate. It is as if we were to say that a ship at sea were storm-tossed because some mutinous sailors on board were troubling the waters. To attribute so much power to the wicked is to do them too much honour. A well-ordered and peaceful France could not have been disturbed so profoundly by nothing but arrogance and ill-will.

The revolutionaries were life-sized Frenchmen in a deeply-troubled France; they were not Gullivers moving recklessly across Lilliput. Society, according to Burke, is the work of God's hands; and so Burke speaks as if persons who aspire greatly to change society are guilty of impiety. But what is society except the living together of men? If God works on society, He does so, presumably, through men. Revolutionaries and theorists are as much men and members of society as are the conservative and the prejudiced. How could Burke know that they are never instruments of God's will? Or that, if they are, they are so only as scourges?

How different are the theories that different men build on similar foundations! Marx, though an atheist, was as certain as Burke that men do not make society and often scarcely understand it, but are carried along on a course of events beyond their control. He too believed that men acquire their needs, interests, and moral prejudices as they grow up to be adult members of society. He too envisaged society as an organic whole, the product of a long evolution. But he described that evolution as a series of conflicts, and put together a theory of social progress which not only allowed for revolution but required it. Far from denouncing philosophers and revolutionaries as disturbers of the peace, moved by envy, vanity and ambition, he explained their activities as a necessary and important part of the historical process.

Chapter 10

ROUSSEAU

ROUSSEAU was much more than a political theorist; he also wrote about religion and education, and his novel, *La Nouvelle Héloïse*, was received with greater enthusiasm than any other published in the eighteenth century. Yet everything he wrote is, in one way or another, related to his social and political philosophy; he was one of the most self-absorbed and emotional of writers, and his political and social theories are deeply affected by his personal difficulties, by his eccentricities and hatreds. What Rousseau wanted was a world fit for himself to live in, a heaven fit for himself to go to, and a God worthy of his love. Nobody who spoke so often of man in the abstract gives so strong an impression that he is speaking always of himself. Rousseau thought of himself as the most human of human beings, unique and yet typical, containing in himself, more purely and intensely than other men, the essence of man. He said in a letter to his friend Bordes: 'Man is naturally good, as I have the happiness to feel.'

Rousseau was a *philosophe* and an enemy of philosophy, a rationalist and a romantic, a sensualist and a puritan, an apologist for religion who attacked dogma and denied original sin, an admirer of the natural and uninhibited and the author of an absolutist theory of the State. Goethe said that with Voltaire one epoch ends and another begins with Rousseau. Nobody in the eighteenth century started as many ideas and struck as many attitudes that caught on with later generations. His book on education, *Emile*, has been called the best of its kind since Plato's *Republic*. It contains the *Profession of Faith of the Savoyard Vicar*, which, condemned by Catholic bishops and Protestant pastors, converted many people to an exalted, vague, undogmatic, and comfortable religion, much less open than orthodox Christianity to attack from the sceptical philosophers. His *Project of a Constitution for Corsica* and his *Considerations on the Government of Poland* show how moderate, ingenious, and practical he could be; they also reveal to us a Rousseau uttering sentiments that might have come from Burke.

I shall confine myself to Rousseau's political philosophy, and even then shall take notice only of its more important aspects. I shall discuss only his account of the state of nature and of the origin of actual societies and states, his belief in man's natural goodness, his conception

364

of a general will, and what he understood by equality. The first is to be found in the *Discourse on the Origins and Foundations of Inequality Among Men*; the second mostly in *Emile*, though several of his other books and essays throw light upon it; the third in the article on *Political Economy* published in Diderot's *Encyclopaedia* and in the two drafts of the *Social Contract*; and the fourth in his political writings generally.

I. THE STATE OF NATURE AND THE ORIGIN OF ACTUAL STATES

Rousseau knew how difficult it must be for a man like himself, formed by society, to imagine what a man might be like who had never lived in society. If men ever lived outside society (and Rousseau seems to take it for granted that they once did so) society must altogether have changed them. He says, in the preface to the *Discourse on the Origins of Inequality*, that 'like the statue of Glaucus, ravaged by time, the sea and storms, until it looked less like a God than a wild beast, the human soul, altered in the bosom of society by a thousand causes . . . has, so to speak, changed so much that it cannot be known'. What he means, of course, is the human soul in its imagined primitive state before society has formed it; that is what cannot be known.

Rousseau begins by admitting that what he would like to discover is not to be certainly known; but he thinks it worth while, if we are to understand what society does to man, trying to reconstruct (though the attempt can be no more than plausible conjecture) man's pre-social past. Rousseau says it is absurd to talk (as so many philosophers have done) of man's deliberately creating society in the light of what have been called 'laws of nature', principles of conduct supposed to be known to man by the use of his reason even before he enters society. Philosophers have always disagreed about these laws; and their disagreements are evidence that there can be no such laws – laws supposed to be so simple and obvious that any sane man can understand them. What the disputing philosophers have proved is not that there are such laws, but that, if there were any, only the most subtle reasoners could know them. Men could not have set up society the better to enforce principles which only a few of them are capable of understanding even after society has civilized them.

Rousseau's argument is not entirely convincing. There are different levels of understanding. We are sometimes said to understand something when we can define or describe it correctly, but this is clearly not the kind of understanding we usually have in mind when we say that a man understands moral rules. To understand them, he need not know how to define them; he need only know how to behave. You cannot prove that there are no principles which have always been accepted by men, in society and outside it, merely by showing that philosophers have never ceased arguing about how such principles should be defined.

But this objection is not really important. What is important is Rousseau's putting forward an idea commonly ignored by his predecessors: that man becomes a moral being only in the process of adapting himself to life in society. Hobbes had, I think, an inkling of this idea, but not more than that. Hume put it forward as emphatically, and more lucidly, than Rousseau; but he understood it differently.

When we say that there is no morality outside society, we may mean only that men have no rights and duties except against and towards one another, so that completely solitary men would need to follow no rules except maxims of prudence; we may mean that there is no scope for morality, no point to it, except among men who come into contact with one another. In that sense, Robinson Crusoe, alone on his island, had no rights or obligations. Or we may mean that it is only in the process of living together in society that men come to conceive of themselves as having rights and duties, that they develop the capacities which make moral persons of them. Hume and Rousseau meant the second and not merely the first; they believed that it is by living together in society that men learn to make claims upon one another and acquire the sentiments which make them respect these claims. Hume, indeed, kept to this position more consistently than Rousseau did; for Rousseau also sometimes spoke, as Locke had done, as if man unformed by society could be moral. Rousseau, as we shall see, was not quick at seeing the implications of any position he took up. He was attracted by new ideas, and was himself at times an innovator; but he often did not discard old ideas incompatible with the new ones. Since he cared little for logical consistency, he felt no need to do so.

But Rousseau also meant something more than Hume when he said that men become moral in society. Hume meant only that social experience teaches them what kinds of behaviour are beneficial or harmful, and that the habits of approval and disapproval which encourage and discourage this behaviour are acquired in society. He admitted that in society we acquire desires and preferences we would not have outside it; but that is as far as he went. He always spoke of moral rules as if they were rules of efficiency; as if their essential function were to enable us to pursue our ends more successfully than we otherwise could. He did not ask himself to what extent the ends we pursue in society are what they are because they are the ends of moral creatures.

Rousseau spoke of our being 'transformed' by society, of our being so deeply affected by it that it is almost impossible to guess what we should be like outside it. We are altogether different creatures for being social and moral; we pursue ends which it is inconceivable we should pursue unless we were moral. The rules of morality are not mere rules of efficiency; they do not make it easier for us to get what we might want even if they did not exist. As moral beings, as creatures who conceive of rights and duties, who have a sense of values, we are psychologically profoundly different from what we should be without this conception and this sense. Moral rules are not therefore rules which experience teaches us are in the general interest, in the sense that they make it easier for us to get what we want; the ends pursued by a moral being are different in kind from those of that entirely imaginary creature, 'natural' or pre-social man. The happiness of a moral being does not consist in the satisfaction of one appetite or desire after another; it is not what Hobbes understood by felicity. It is living in proper relations with others and with oneself; it is the happiness of a self-conscious creature[1] who does not live from hand to mouth but feels the need to live a worthwhile life. These proper relations are relations only possible between creatures that are self-conscious and moral. I shall say more later about how Rousseau conceived of them, when I discuss his doctrine that man is by nature good.

Man in the state of nature, potentially rational but making small use of reason, is neither good nor evil. 'Hobbes', said Rousseau – (and Hobbes, like Rousseau, supposed that men in the state of nature were solitary and brutish, i.e., like the other animals) – 'Hobbes did not see that the same cause that prevents savages from using their reason . . . prevents them from abusing their faculties. . . . So that we can say that savages are not evil precisely because they do not know what it is to be good; for it is neither the development of knowledge nor the restraint of law but their calm passions and ignorance of vice that prevent them from doing evil.' Men in the state of nature are not quarrelsome and have no desire to dominate one another; they are solitary, unreflecting, and easily satisfied; they have no vanity; they have no self-consciousness and no opinion of themselves, and are therefore not governed in what they do by the desire to be well thought of by others. Jealousy, envy, the desire for vengeance, all the emotions produced by vanity, by the desire to please and be admired, are unknown to the quite primitive and unsocial man. While men are in the state of nature, there is neither education, nor progress, nor speech; the generations succeed one another, and men are no different from their

---

1 Rousseau does not use the words 'self-consciousness' and 'self-conscious' as the German Idealists were to do. He does, however, speak of the feelings that we have for ourselves and for other people as feelings accquired in society. (They are feelings that come of our comparing ourselves with others and of our being helped or frustrated by them) They are passions quite different from the natural appetites. They are feelings for or about persons. They involve self-consciousness, and Rousseau sees that they do, though he does not use the word as freely as it came to be used afterwards.

ancestors. There is no inequality, for whatever differences there are between men are without social significance.

It was, says Rousseau, probably growth in numbers that first brought men together into society. They could no longer live isolated, meeting only by chance or under the urge of their sexual appetites. Some time or other, somewhere or other, for reasons that Rousseau admits he cannot know, there were more men than could easily keep themselves alive in the ways common to all wild animals; but precisely because men are not like the other animals, but are intelligent and resourceful, they could adapt themselves to their altered condition. They could change their manner of life. At first, they needed to unite their efforts only occasionally; but as their power to satisfy their wants increased, so too did those wants. Men began to live in families; and gradually, when several families had congregated together, they formed societies. They acquired speech, and with it the power to accumulate knowledge and pass it on to their children. They grew affectionate, anxious to please, to be admired, to be thought better or more formidable than other people. They acquired customs and common standards of beauty and merit.

At that stage of man's development, the family was still more or less self-subsistent, producing the greater part of what it needed. Of course, all social intercourse creates other than material needs, making men dependent on one another for company, esteem, and affection; but as long as families were largely self-supporting, this kind of dependence did not create social inequalities. What inequalities did exist were not so much between families as inside them, where children depended for survival on the care of their parents. This kind of dependence does not, however, have the harmful social effects of some other kinds, because the members of a family are commonly united, at least while the children are small, by strong affections. This dependence is natural and temporary; natural because children are incapable of fending for themselves, and temporary because it ceases as soon as the incapacity ends.

While the heads of families were hunters and fishermen, they worked together only now and then; most of the time, catching or finding food and other necessaries for themselves, their wives, and their children, they worked separately and fitfully. Even when they had to work together, their collaboration was simple and required little or no subordination among them. They needed few possessions: their huts and their weapons were enough. This, according to Rousseau, was the happiest period of mankind's social development; for men had by that time acquired language, and their frequent association had sharpened their wits and quickened their hearts. They had no fixed laws but were already creatures of custom; they had common notions of merit and beauty; they were capable of vanity and envy, but also of love, loyalty, and the desire to please, feelings unknown to the lonely savage. They had become moral, and their goodness (when they were good) differed in kind from that of natural man. This was the happy age when society already existed but men had not yet become the tools or victims of other men.

It was when they ceased to be hunters and fishermen, when they passed to a predominantly *agricultural economy*, when they learned to extract metals and to use them, that grown men became, not merely occasionally, but permanently, dependent on one another for much more than the pleasures and affections of society. When land came to be cultivated, it had to be divided; and crops, unlike the produce of the chase, were not quickly perishable. With continuity of possession and the accumulation of wealth, natural differences in strength and intelligence enabled some men to prosper more than others and to pass on their wealth to their children. These inequalities in their turn created greater opportunities for the prosperous than the unprosperous; and the greater the inequality between men, the more the rich sought to dominate the poor and the poor were filled with resentment and envy. Many of the poor consented to become the servants or clients of the rich, while others preferred to live by plundering them. There followed insecurity and violence, dangerous to both rich and poor, though more dangerous to the rich. It was then that some rich man bethought himself of a device from which all men would profit, but the rich more than the poor. He suggested that men should set up over themselves some power to govern them by wise laws, to protect them from each other, and to defend them against their common enemies. His suggestion was universally approved, and political society was at last established. Rousseau agrees with Locke that government was instituted to protect property, but takes care to add: and especially to protect the property of the rich! Moreover, there is no property in the state of nature, because it is only creatures formed by society who can conceive of rights and obligations, and therefore of rules of property.

In a fragment on the *State of War*, probably written at about the same time as the second *Discourse*, Rousseau says that man 'is naturally peaceful and timid; and at the least danger his first impulse is to flee; he only becomes warlike by dint of habit and experience.' Honour, interest, prejudice, revenge, all the passions that can make him brave danger and death, are foreign to him in the state of nature. It is only after he has formed a society with some man that he decides to attack another; and he becomes a soldier only after he has been a citizen.' The war of all against all is therefore not, as Hobbes said it was, the condition of man in the state of nature; it is, like the other vices and horrors that Hobbes attributed to solitary and brutish man, a product of society. It is communities and not isolated men that are prone to aggression. The war of all against all, which caused men, so

Hobbes tells us, to submit to government in order to put an end to it, is not man's condition outside political society; it is much nearer being the condition of sovereign States in their relations to one another.

The *Fragment on War* does not quite square with the *Discourse on Inequality*. In the *Fragment* Rousseau argues that man is a soldier only because he is a citizen; that war is a relation that can subsist only between organized communities or 'public persons', as he calls them. To say that one man is at war with another is, he says, strictly speaking, a misuse of language. He is also trying to show how it is that man as a social creature becomes quarrelsome. Though this second argument is different from the first, Rousseau runs the two together. Man, he says, becomes the rival and enemy of other men in society, because it is there that he acquires the passions which incline him to aggression; and he also says that the war of all against all is the condition of sovereign States. The connection between these two statements is not made clear. Are States inclined to war because society makes men quarrelsome? That, perhaps, was what Rousseau meant in the *Fragment on War*. But in the *Discourse on Inequality* he is not thinking of relations between States. He imagines a state of anarchy almost as dreadful as Hobbes' war of all against all. It is not, however, the state of nature, but man's social condition just before the establishment of government; it is an effect of social inequalities, of anxiety and arrogance in the rich, of envy and covetousness in the poor. It is the social relations in which men stand to one another which make them rich and poor, and which also give birth to aggressive passions in them. They then set up the State to protect themselves from these passions.

I shall not criticize in detail Rousseau's account of the state of nature and of man's slow progress, through different forms of society, from solitude to the State. I think it an ingenious theory, a better effort at the imaginative reconstruction of the past than any other made in the eighteenth century. The weakest part of it seems to me the account of how the State was at last established. If the rich were really in danger from the poor, why did they not band together and establish a joint ascendancy over the poor? Where was the need to set up government by deliberate agreement with the poor? Or must we suppose, as Rousseau does, that the rich were as suspicious and aggressive towards each other as the poor were towards them. How, then, did they continue to be rich? To keep his wealth, to secure his property, where there is no government, the rich man must have retainers dependent on him. He and his retainers must, therefore, form some kind of rudimentary society together, in which he is the master. If he is in danger, it must be either from other rich men, who also have their retainers, or from the unrestrained poor, who can only be formidable when banded together. That is to say, there can be no great inequalities unless there are already organized communities of some kind (for example, large households) to protect the rich; and the poor can never be really formidable to the rich unless they, too, are organized. None of these communities, these large households, is established by contract. Why, then, should not the State grow out of them slowly and imperceptibly? Whence the need of a deliberate agreement to set up the State? To bring the contract in this way into a long account of how man became a social animal, an account which up to that point has described a course of development uncontrolled by deliberate human purposes, is a crude device; and it is also unnecessary, for it explains nothing that could not be better explained without it. The essential purpose of the contract in political theory is to explain political obligation. But the contract of the *Discourse on Inequality* has no such purpose. It is altogether out of place. In this respect it is quite different from the contract of *Du Contrat Social*, which is used to explain the rights and duties of citizens.

What conclusions can we draw from what Rousseau tells us in the second *Discourse* about the state of nature and man's social development? They are, I think, the following: (1) that man, if ever he lived outside society (and Rousseau is inclined to believe that he once probably did), must have been neither morally good nor bad, but without language, and therefore almost as incapable of sustained thought and reasoning as the other animals, improvident, lazy, and unaggressive; (2) that neither his reason (for he had not yet learned to use it) nor his passions and instincts drew man into society, but that, from some cause unknown to us, it being no longer possible for him to get his subsistence alone, he found himself obliged from time to time to work with other men; (3) that, as this collaboration grew closer, he acquired language, and his understanding and emotions developed until he became at last a rational creature capable of morality; (4) that he did not make society or control its development, but passed from stage to stage without understanding the social process he was involved in; (5) that natural law and natural right, in the traditional sense of the jurists and philosophers, were unknown to him in the state of nature; (6) that, although society alone has made man moral (that is, a creature having a sense of values and recognizing rights and duties), it has made him more inclined to vice than to virtue, and has thus corrupted him; and (7) that this corruption is largely an effect of social inequality, and takes the form of vanity and aggressiveness.

We are not to suppose that Rousseau, because he says that men in the state of nature know nothing of the law of nature, rejects the traditional conception of that law as a moral law which reason teaches us is incumbent on all rational creatures; that he agrees either with Hobbes or with Hume. That he does not agree with Hobbes is obvious. Hobbes' account of the laws of nature does not make them truly moral laws, and he clearly asserts what Rousseau denies, that man can know these laws even in the state of nature. True, Hobbes, whether he calls the laws of nature mere maxims of prudence or insists that they are also commanded by God, says that men in the state of nature do not ordinarily have to obey them; but he also says that they can con-ceive of them in that state, and indeed that they must do so if they are ever to get out of it. Natural man, man unformed by society, is already for Hobbes a rational creature capable of discovering that it would be his interest to follow certain rules if he could be sure that other people would do the same; whereas Rousseau tells us that natural man has no inkling of such rules, and is therefore no more prudent than moral. Natural man lives from hand to mouth, from day to day, forgetting the past and not minding the future, following momentary impulses and appetites that never, or scarcely ever, bring him into conflict with other men.

I have already said that Rousseau, though he agrees with Hume that it is in society that man develops his reasoning powers and also comes to think of himself as having rights and duties, does not treat moral rules as rules of utility. He insists, as Hume does not, that man's nature is transformed by his social environment. There is also another great difference between Hume and Rousseau. What gives to moral rules their moral character is, according to Hume, only how men feel about them or react to them; whereas for Rousseau, as for Locke, they are rules which men ought to obey because they are men. For Rousseau it follows that man, because he has certain capacities, also has certain rights and duties. Man could not know this in the state of nature, but he can know it in society. These capacities are not yet developed in the state of nature; they are so only in society. But once they are developed, man has certain rights and duties. Rousseau perhaps never knew of Hume's dictum, that we cannot derive an 'ought' from an 'is'. At least he took no notice of it. Though he was by no means consistent, much more often than not he agreed with the natural law philosophers that the moral law is a law of reason, in the sense that it consists of rules which can be deduced from our being rational creatures.

There is, of course, an obvious connection, which no moralist denies, between man's being rational and his having duties. Man alone among the animals can compare different courses of action and choose one rather than the others; he alone can discriminate between ends and discover the means to them; he alone can apprehend rules and accept or reject them. Even if actions are virtuous and vicious only because of how we feel about them, these feelings, these moral sentiments, are confined to us alone among animals because we alone are capable of abstract thought and deliberate action. It is common ground to believers in natural law and to moralists like Hume, who call morals an 'experimental science', that justice and reason are intimately connected. The experience which Hume says gives birth to justice is essentially the experience of a self-conscious and rational creature. What Hume and believers in natural law differ about is the nature of the connection. For Hume it is causal. The experience of rational creatures living together in a world where the resources required to satisfy their needs are limited is such as to cause them to conceive of rules of conduct which it is in the common interest should be obeyed, and to have feelings of approval or disapproval towards those who keep or break these rules. For believers in natural law the connection is logical; for them, it follows logically that because we are rational we ought to be just. Neither the morality of our actions nor the goodness or evil of the motives that inspire us can be explained in terms of our feelings about them or any other kind of reaction to them.

Rousseau agrees with the believers in natural law and not with Hume. He thinks that, if we consider what is involved in the rationality of man, in his being a self-conscious, deliberate, purposeful creature recognizing the existence of other creatures like himself, we can know how man ought to behave. Man in the state of nature cannot know it for he is not then in full possession of his reason. It is only in society that he develops to the full the capacities which distinguish him from other animals, and can know and practise the moral law – a law which is eternally valid for all creatures like himself.

Though this is Rousseau's usual position, not everything that he says is compatible with it. He does not, as we shall see later, succeed in squaring his idea of conscience with his account of the law of nature as a law of reason. He sometimes makes a contrast between conscience and reason, and treats the first as the surer guide to morality.

II. MAN'S NATURAL GOODNESS

Sometimes by man's natural goodness Rousseau means the mere innocence of the state of nature, the condition of man before society has made a moral being of him, which is like the condition of Adam before he ate fruit from the tree of knowledge. In proclaiming man's natural goodness in this sense Rousseau is denying the doctrine of original sin. That is not the natural goodness I want to discuss.

But there is in Rousseau another, and a much more important and suggestive, sense of natural goodness, which makes it a moral condition of which social man alone is capable. Many thinkers since Rousseau have used the idea of natural goodness, in this sense, or other ideas closely akin to it. They may not have spoken explicitly of natural goodness; they may have preferred to speak of the fully realized self, of the well-balanced mind, of the integrated personality. All these conceptions have their difficulties. Though there are many versions of

374   MAN AND SOCIETY · VOLUME ONE

them, there is a strong family likeness between them, and they all
have a great deal in common with what Rousseau understood by
man's natural goodness. If then we subject his idea to close scrutiny,
we discover some of the difficulties inherent in nearly all versions of
it. There is no doubting that the idea, in spite of its obscurity, has
been enormously attractive. It has had great vitality; it has had as
many heads as the hydra. Moral and political philosophers are more
sceptical about it than they once were, but psychologists and sociologists still feel the need to use it. It is an idea as old as the Greeks; it
is part of the cultural history of Europe. Rousseau brought it to life
again at a time when it had long been moribund; and he also gave it
its modern character, which owes almost as much to Christianity as to
the philosophies of Plato and Aristotle.

Let me begin with a rough definition of Rousseau's version of it.
When Rousseau calls man naturally good in the moral sense he means
that there is a form of development of man's natural capacities and
passions which enhances his vitality and sense of well-being, and at
the same time disposes him to be benevolent and just in all his dealings
with other men. If man develops in this way he not only becomes
rational and moral; he also achieves true peace of mind, and stable
and satisfying relations with other people. Rousseau also believed
that there is in every man an indestructible impulse or feeling urging
him towards this desirable condition of himself and deflecting him
from courses that prevent his attaining it. This feeling or impulse he
called 'conscience'. Though conscience is indestructible, it is by no
means invincible. Indeed, it is ordinarily too weak to prevent our corruption. But it keeps alive in us the sense that we are 'untrue' to
ourselves; it is the 'voice of nature' in us.

Now, if man is thus naturally disposed to some condition of himself
which is morally good, it might seem that, unless there is some
calamity to prevent his doing so, he must become good. It might seem
that men, as soon as they come together in society and their faculties
are quickened, must become what it is desirable that they should be.
For what is society but the living together of men? If men are by
nature disposed to goodnes, how can society corrupt them? Must we
not suppose a calamity or an intervention of the Devil, something to
take the place of the story of the Fall of Adam, to explain how what
should have gone right none the less went wrong? But Rousseau will
have none of it. Man, he says, is *naturally* good and is yet corrupted
by society, though society is no more than the living together of men
and what follows from it. We have seen how, in the *Discourse on the
Origins of Inequality*, Rousseau describes a *natural*, in the sense of
uncontrolled, course of social development which leads to inequalities
that cripple and diminish mankind, morally even more than materially.
Men are first brought together by the need to satisfy their natural

wants, and this coming together starts a train of events which, through no fault of their own and no calamity, both develops and corrupts their faculties. Society, at least, is not naturally good even if man is so; there is clearly no natural tendency for society to become what it ought to be if men are to attain natural goodness. This conclusion may seem odd, but we are driven to it by Rousseau's own account of the matter. It is only one of several paradoxes, not to say contradictions, in his social and political theory.

To elucidate Rousseau's admittedly vague conception of natural goodness, it is perhaps best to try to find answers to these five questions: (1) What are the natural passions and how do the passions acquired in society arise out of them? In other words, what is the genealogy of the passions? (2) What constitutes the goodness of good passions, and the evil of evil ones? (3) What is the impulse which Rousseau calls conscience? (4) What conditions must hold if man is to attain goodness? And lastly, (5) What can be done to create these conditions?

1. The Genealogy of the Passions

Unfortunately, Rousseau does not make it really clear what the natural passions are, nor how the social passions arise from them. He gives several accounts which do not square with one another. To pursue all his inconsistencies would be tedious, and I shall attend only to a few; not so much to show how careless he could be as to illustrate some of the difficulties inherent in the notion of natural goodness.

In the *Discourse on Inequality*, Rousseau says that there are two primitive passions, self-love and pity, from which arise all our civilized virtues and vices. He does not, however, say which of these passions gives birth to the virtues and which to the vices, nor yet how, if both are needed to generate them all, some of their effects come to be good and others evil. In *Emile* he usually treats self-love as if it were the only primitive passion. What does he understand by it? Clearly not an emotion like anger or pity or hatred. He does not suppose that a man who has self-love feels for himself what he would feel for somebody else that he loved. By self-love he very probably means, after the fashion of his day, not a passion of the self directed to the self, but all of a man's desires whose object is to satisfy his own needs and not other people's. Self-love thus consists of desires which even a creature lacking self-consciousness, lacking the idea of itself as the subject of its own desires, could have. In this sense of it, a dog has self-love just as much as a man has it.

How, then, does self-love give birth to other passions? It does so when the desires it consists of are either thwarted or favoured; and they may be thwarted or favoured either by natural events or by what other people do or fail to do. Clearly, it is the second of these influences which is much the more important. The child does not know how to fend for itself; it is looked after by adults; it is provided for and disciplined. It is never more completely dependent on others than during the first months of its life, when it is still as nature made it, unformed by society. As the child begins to take stock of its environment, as it comes to see that its wants are satisfied by those who take care of it, as it comes to feel that it is itself an object of affection, it ceases to be merely a creature of natural appetites. It acquires emotions, directed towards itself and others, which create new needs in it. It comes to feel affection and to need it; it learns to compare itself with others. It becomes important to it how it stands in the eyes of others and in its own eyes. This comparison of self with others, this self-consciousness, together with the desire to be loved and well thought of and the capacity to love and admire, gives birth to needs less simple and less easily satisfied than the natural appetites. If the child could remain a mere creature of appetite, it might become independent when it grew up, as most animals do. If, in the process of being looked after by others as a helpless infant, man never acquired any needs beyond those he was born with or which came to him merely with physical maturity, he would never become a truly social and moral creature. He would remain in the state of nature; and adult man, in that state, like other fully grown animals, would be independent. It is chiefly because, while he is looked after by others when he still needs care, he acquires emotions and wants which are not mere effects of becoming physically mature, that he is still dependent on other men when he becomes an adult.

This is what Rousseau tells us, in the second book of *Emile*, either in so many words or by implication. He tells us that self-love, which prompts us to do what we must do to keep alive and healthy, is natural, and that it is the mother of all the social passions. It is by ministering to our self-love when we are still unable to fend for ourselves that those who look after us awaken in us the capacities and emotions which make social beings of us. In helping us to satisfy the needs we get from Nature, they transform our nature, creating needs in us which can only be satisfied in social life, even when we are adults and no matter how well-endowed by Nature we may be.

Rousseau, though he often calls self-love the mother of *all* the social passions, sometimes also attributes the virtues to self-love and the vices to vanity. But he clearly does not want us to take vanity for a primitive passion, for he says repeatedly that men come to be vain only in society. Since only self-love is primitive, in the sense of being what it would be even if man were not a social creature, vanity must be born of self-love. What, then, is the point of attributing the virtues to self-love and the vices to vanity? Why call the virtues 'natural' because they issue from self-love, and the vices 'unnatural' because they come from vanity, when vanity itself is born of self-love? Is self-love the 'natural' mother of the virtues and the 'unnatural' grandmother of the vices, having somehow brought forth a monstrous daughter who can bear only deformed children? In the social psychology of Rousseau, self-love stands to vanity as God does to the Devil in certain forms of theology; God creates all things, including the Devil, and then leaves all the dirty work to the Devil while His own hands remain clean.

So far I have been discussing only what Rousseau says in *Emile*. But even if we combine the doctrines of *Emile* and of the *Discourse on Inequality*; even if we suppose that there are two primitive passions, self-love and pity, and that the virtues and vices come from them in the manner described in *Emile*, we are no better off than before. We are no nearer explaining how what is born of self-love is 'natural' and what is born of vanity is not. For the primitive passions, whether they are one or two or more than two, are all *ex hypothesi* equally part of man's pre-social nature; and it is not clear why what issues from one of them should be more or less natural than what issues from another. Besides, Rousseau never says, or even hints at, anything so improbable as that vanity is born of pity. It is clear that, of his two primitive passions, self-love alone could plausibly be said to give birth to vanity.[1]

---

[1] Only in the first of the *Dialogues*, written towards the end of his life, does Rousseau come near to explaining how vanity arises out of self-love. It is not, he says, the strength of our passions but their weakness which makes us corruptible. Our primitive passions keep us alive and healthy, and do not move us to harm one another. In the state of nature they are strong enough to maintain life and health. But in society we find more obstacles in our way, and our natural passions, being weak, are diverted from their objects. We are frustrated, and we become more concerned to get rid of the obstacles than to satisfy our natural passions; we become angry, fretful, and malevolent. It is then that self-love gives birth to vanity, to the comparison of self with others, and to the desire to avenge and dominate.

Rousseau's description is by no means clear. He means, I think, that men, as they strive to satisfy their natural desires, get in each other's way. They become in the end so taken up with their fears and enmities that they are more anxious to get the better of other people than to make the best of their own lives. They are absorbed in their mutual relations, not from affection and trust and the desire to help one another, but from envy, hatred and fear. They become enemies because they lack the strength to be themselves, to come to terms with life. If their natural passions had been stronger, men would have surmounted or removed the obstacles in their way, or would have had the courage to resign themselves to the inevitable, and would not have wasted their energies in bitterness, ostentation, or revenge. The natural passions, self-regarding though they are, do not isolate us from one another. When we are brought together, their inherent tendency, unless they are frustrated, is to give rise to the affections and loyalties that enrich our lives and bind us to each other. Everyone, however strong his nature, needs society to quicken his faculties and to attain true happiness. If he were not cor-

Again in *Emile*, Rousseau distinguishes between two influences work-ing on our primitive passions, the one producing our virtues and the other our vices. The influence that produces vice he calls *external*, but he never makes clear the sense in which he uses that word. If external means 'outside the self', then the influence that makes for virtue must also be external; for Rousseau tells us that it is in society that men become moral beings, which is equivalent to saying that it is in society that they acquire their virtues as well as their vices. What are social influences if they are not external to the self? Neither in *Emile* nor elsewhere does Rousseau show our virtues emerging out of self-love independently of the influence of other people upon us.

(Rousseau says that a good education is essentially *negative*; he often speaks as if the task of the educator were to protect the child from influences which might prevent it developing as it should. He speaks at times as if the moral development of the child were a spontaneous process which must be left to itself if it is not to be vitiated. But this is only a manner of speaking; it is only Rousseau's way of saying that the child must not be taught by precept so much as left to think things out for itself. The things it has to think out are largely social problems: how it should treat other people, and what it can reasonably expect of them. Emile's tutor is clearly an influence external to Emile; he edu-cates the boy by putting him into situations where he has to solve prob-lems for himself, and also by seeing to it that he is not faced with problems, intellectual and moral, which he is too young to solve. In short, Emile's tutor educates the boy by creating the right environment, and that environment is, of course, social. Rousseau's saying that the best education is essentially negative therefore detracts nothing from

rupted owing to the weakness of his passions, he would develop social affec-tions to sustain and comfort him. His mind would be enlivened by conversa-tion, and the sweetest part of his life would be lived in society with others; for man is so made that he cannot enjoy life to the full, cannot possess him-self entirely, except in the society of his own kind.

Rousseau neither affirms nor denies that there are natures so strong as to be incorruptible even in a corrupt society. If he believed that there were such choice souls, he must have thought there were very few of them. And we are not to suppose that he would have counted himself among them. For he tells us in the *Dialogues* that, if he is not corrupt, it is only because, feeling his weakness, he has withdrawn from the world. He is, he says, gentle, com-passionate, peaceful, unambitious, neither vain nor modest, easily excited, but lacking in energy, prudence, and presence of mind. Clumsy, childlike, lazy and timid, he is soon put out of countenance by anyone more ready and force-ful than himself. A lover of virtue, he is too weak to be actively virtuous. He shrinks from evil, lacking the strength to be valiant for good. Over-sensitive and given to dreaming, he avoids action and all unpleasantness. His first move-ments are lively and pure, but he does not persevere. If he is incorruptible, it is from sheer delicacy of soul. He is not innocent, for he knows evil and has sometimes done it, almost inadvertently and from bewilderment, when life has taken him by surprise. His intentions have always, *always* been good.

his assertion that it is in society (that is to say, in the process of learning to live with others) that man becomes rational and moral; and by moral he means, in this context, capable of recognizing that there are rules which he ought to obey.

Man becomes moral in society, and it is also society that corrupts him. These two statements, suitably interpreted, do not contradict one another; the first tells us that only social man is capable of virtue and vice, and the second that he inclines more to vice than to virtue. There is no paradox here. But paradox or no paradox, we are still left uncertain why virtue should be more *natural* than vice. There is neither virtue nor vice outside society, and there is no tendency for man to become virtuous rather than vicious in society. Rousseau's account of how the social passions, vicious and virtuous, are produced out of the primitive passions gives us no clue whatever as to why he believed that man is naturally good and is corrupted by society.

It is easy to see what Rousseau means when he says that primitive man, man in the imagined state of nature, is naturally good. He is denying the doctrine of original sin; he is saying that the passions that man is born with or would acquire even outside society, in the mere process of becoming adult, are neither virtuous nor vicious. He is also denying Hobbes' account of the state of nature; for though Hobbes says that man's natural passions are in themselves no sin, he says that they make man aggressive. Besides these denials, Rousseau also wants to assert something: that man's natural passions serve to keep him alive and healthy. Natural man, having no standards, moral or otherwise, does not praise or blame; but civilized man, contemplating the predicament of natural man, can see that his passions are adequate to his needs, and can approve their being so on the ground that they give him the only happiness he is capable of. Civilized man can say of natural man: he is neither vicious nor virtuous, and yet it is good that he has the passions which he does have. This is the sense in which unsocial man is naturally good.

It is easy to see how Rousseau conceived of this kind of natural goodness. The difficulty is to see how he conceived of the natural goodness which is not innocence, which is not absence of vice as well as virtue, which is not harmlessness; the natural goodness which is a moral condition which only civilized man can imagine and aim at and sometimes attain. It is a condition which, more often than not, he does not attain; but the image of it is always vaguely present to him. When he falls short of it, he is dissatisfied with himself; he is other than he would wish to be, and feels himself to be the victim of his own passions and habits. He expresses this feeling when he says that he is *untrue* to himself. In the *Discourse on Inequality* Rousseau speaks of man as being *outside* himself. There is a condition of himself which man, as soon as he is capable of understanding it, considers more desirable than any other. That is why, in spite of his wretchedness in the society which has corrupted him, he would not wish to return to the state of nature, if that return were possible.

We have seen that Rousseau's account of the origins of the social passions does not tell us what this condition is or what makes it more natural to man than the condition which is actually his. We must therefore pass to the next of the five questions we have put in the hope that by trying to answer them we may discover what Rousseau meant by man's natural goodness. We must ask, What constitutes the goodness of good passions and the evil of evil ones?

2. What constitutes the goodness of good passions? and the evil of evil ones?

Rousseau comes nearer to giving an intelligible answer to this question than to the one we have just considered. The good passions are good because they lead to peace of mind and also to social peace; because they enable us to live without frustration and bitterness, and because they make us well-disposed towards our neighbours. The evil passions are evil because they bring us into conflict with ourselves and with others.

To see how they do this, we must look for a moment at Rousseau's distinction between self-love and vanity, *amour de soi* and *amour-propre*, but this time without troubling our heads about how they are connected. We shall suppose that they are independent of one another. Self-love, you will remember, is in itself neither morally good nor morally evil; it consists of the passions and desires that move us to do what is necessary to keep us alive and healthy. Vanity is always, or nearly always, evil; it is the desire that others should admire us, notice us, and take us into account even when justice does not require them to do so. In the fourth book of *Emile*, Rousseau says : 'self-love, which is concerned only with ourselves, is content to satisfy our needs; while vanity, which always compares self with others, is never satisfied and never can be. For this feeling which makes us prefer ourselves to others demands that others should prefer us to themselves, which is impossible. The tender and gentle passions spring from self-love, and the hateful and angry passions from vanity.' This is an argument immensely important to Rousseau, and he often repeats it. Vanity multiplies our needs, making us depend for our self-esteem on how we appear to others, and creating in us ambitions destructive of their happiness and our own. It makes our neighbours our rivals and enemies, yet binds us to them by chains impossible to break. Vanity makes slaves of us.

The relations between us which arise from what we do to help supply one another's natural wants produce in us affections and needs which draw us more closely together. We are told, also in the fourth book of *Emile*, that 'the child's first sentiment is self-love, and his second, which is derived from it, love of those about him; for in his weakness he is aware of people only through the help and attention he gets from them. To begin with, his affection for his nurse and his governess is mere habit. He calls for them because he needs them and is happy in their presence; it is perception rather than kindly feeling. It takes a long time before he discovers that they are not only useful to him but wish to be so, and that is when he begins to love them.'[1] If we are drawn to other people by the help they give us, or that we give them, we are likely to develop feelings for them which make it easy for us to live at peace with them; but if we come to need them to minister to our vanity, we cannot have easy and pleasant relations with them, for we are bound to ask much more of them than they are willing to give. If the services we expect from others are to satisfy wants which are not rooted in vanity, our demands on them will be modest. They will be willing and able to help us, especially while we are children and most in need of help; and the help given to us will create in us sentiments of gratitude and affection which will make us willing in our turn to help others. Though our affection for others is born of our need of them, it is not a form of self-love. The first persons we love are the persons we most depend on, our parents; but we love them for themselves and not for our own sakes. Love of others springs from self-love, and yet is genuinely altruistic. It enriches life; it enhances the sense of well-being of the person who feels it and of the persons for whom he feels it. When two people are bound together by affection, each needs the other and neither is the mere instrument of the other. Need gives birth to love, which in turn gives birth to other needs; and the needs born of love as much as the needs that give birth to it draw men closer together. Self-love is thus doubly 'natural': because the needs it consists of have to be satisfied if man is to keep alive and healthy, and because the passions it gives birth to nourish and strengthen his mind, making him feel that life is worth living.

Vanity is doubly 'unnatural': because the needs it consists of do not have to be satisfied to keep man alive and healthy, and because the passions it gives birth to (jealousy, arrogance, envy, hatred, lust for revenge) are either insatiable or inordinately difficult to satisfy. While these passions are not satisfied they destroy a man's peace of mind; and yet, if they are satisfied, other people must be hurt or humiliated.

A man is 'true to his nature' when his passions are not insatiable, when they can all be satisfied, and when the attempt to satisfy them

---

[1] *Emile*. Garnier edition p. 248 (my translation).

brings him not enemies but friends. He is then at peace with himself and his neighbours; he is vigorous, free and happy. His freedom is not independence, for he needs his neighbours as much as they need him; it is mutual dependence cheerfully accepted. (Nor is his happiness either the successful pursuit of pleasure or passive contentment with his lot; it is a deep sense that life is worth living, making even the sorrows of life acceptable) The truly happy man is a man of deep feelings, and his peace of mind is not apathy. His kind of happiness is not a happines to be had outside society, nor one for which society merely provides the means; it is inconceivable except to a social, rational and moral being, a self-conscious person who does not live from day to day but sees life in the round. The lonely savage, the amoral and unsocial man, is not happy so much as not unhappy. Anyone who has tasted or even imagined the happiness possible to civilized man could not wish to live from hand to mouth like a savage, whose happiness consists only in his being untroubled by desires beyond his power to satisfy.

Rousseau could have described this condition without calling it *natural goodness*. The name he gave it is misleading; and explains perhaps why he has so often been misunderstood. Natural man, as the eighteenth century spoke of him, is man as he would be if he did not live in society; and the condition we have been discussing is clearly not the condition of pre-social man. True, Rousseau also said that man is good in the state of nature, but the goodness he then had in mind was, as we have seen, quite different from this. And there is, he admitted, no inherent tendency for man to reach this condition in society. On the contrary, his chances of reaching it are small. That, indeed, is the point of Rousseau's dictum that society corrupts man. It is not the condition that man would reach if he were left to develop *naturally*, in the sense of uninfluenced by others, for he can reach it only in society, and to be in society is necessarily to be influenced by others. Nor can it be *natural* in the sense that man alone is capable of reaching it; for it is just as true that he alone is capable of being corrupted by society, and Rousseau did not call this corruption *natural*. In what sense, then, is this condition *natural*? In the sense that man, once the capacities to reason and to will are developed in him by society (and they are capacities that belong only to him), finds life truly worth living only when he has reached it or has hopes of doing so.

I do not say that this obviously desirable condition ought *not* to be called *natural goodness*. The word *natural* has been used in many senses, and there is nothing gained by ruling this one out. But this is only one of several senses in which Rousseau uses the word when he speaks of man's *natural goodness*; and he never clearly distinguishes it from the others, either by definition or by the way he uses it. As often as not, when he calls this condition *natural*, he is speaking of its

origins and not of what it is in itself; but what he is then trying to say,
I cannot make out.

3. What does Rousseau understand by Conscience?

Rousseau ordinarily speaks as if goodness and rightness were qualities
in the things called good and the actions called right; he speaks of
them, not as sensible qualities, but as qualities apprehended by reason.
Reason can therefore tell us what natural goodness is, and can enlighten us about our duties. But reason is not desire; to know the good
is not yet to desire it. What makes us desire it, what inclines us to it,
even before reason has made it fully clear to us what it is and how we
may get it, is conscience. Conscience, indestructible in us but easily
defeated, is the feeling that urges us, in spite of contrary passions, towards the two harmonies: the one within our minds and between our
passions, and the other within society and between its members. Because we have conscience we are never altogether adrift in society.
Conscience is not the strongest impulse in us, but it is always present. It
also serves to put us all on a level with one another, because the weakest
can appeal to it in the strongest, and the appeal, though often unsuc-
cessful, is always disturbing. However corrupted by power or wealth we
may be, either as possessors of them or victims, there is something in
us serving to remind us that this corruption is against nature. When
Rousseau speaks of conscience, his tone is more proper to the sermon
than to the philosophical treatise.

Rousseau would not be Rousseau if he left no room for doubt in the
minds of his readers. There are times when he seems to be claiming
more for conscience than I have just said; there are times when he
seems to be claiming so much for it as to set him apart from believers
in natural law. He tells us in *Emile*, by the mouth of the Savoyard
Vicar, that 'conscience is an innate principle of justice and virtue,
whereby we judge our own or other men's actions to be good or evil'.
Principle does not here mean a general rule; for Rousseau repeatedly
says that conscience is not reason, and he also says that its decrees are
not judgements but feelings. All this is obscure enough. Perhaps the
most plausible interpretation of it is that conscience is a feeling
which draws us towards some kinds of behaviour and away from
others. This would make the role of conscience something like the
role of what Hume called the 'moral sentiments'; actions would then
be right or wrong, not in themselves, but because we were drawn
towards or away from them by conscience.

But, though this is the most plausible interpretation of this particular
passage (and perhaps several others) in Rousseau, I do not think it
gives us his usual position. Morality is not for him, as it was for

Hume, ultimately a matter of feeling. It would, of course, be idle to pretend that Rousseau (who seldom dealt with any matter consecutively and at length, but returned to it again and again in different contexts) made clear what he believed to be the relative functions of reason and conscience in the moral life of man. Nevertheless, in spite of ambiguities, it is almost certain that he did not agree with Hume. The moral law, he believed, can be discovered by reason, and its moral character does not consist in how we feel about it. Conscience moves us to right conduct, but the conduct is not right because conscience moves us to it. Rousseau stands here closer to Kant than to Hume.

We have seen that Rousseau calls conscience innate. Yet in the *Discourse on Inequality*, when he describes the imaginary state of nature, he says nothing about conscience. He clearly does not conceive of conscience as an impulse that would move men even outside society; it is not like self-love or pity. Before conscience can move us, we must be self-conscious rational creatures capable of deliberate choice. We must know what it is to be faced by several possible courses of action and to have to choose one in preference to the others. We must also understand what it is to make claims on others and to have them make claims on us. Only in society do we come to have rules of action and standards of excellence. Therefore, only among men who live or have lived in society can conscience have anything to do.

What then is the point of calling conscience innate? If Rousseau had been asked whether we are all born with conscience, he would doubtless have said that we are; but it is not easy to see what he could have meant by saying so. Conscience, he tells us, is an impulse or feeling which is not active in us in the state of nature. If an impulse or feeling is not yet active, it is not there; it does not occur and therefore does not exist. Is it, then, innate because it exists potentially? But that is only to say that, while it does not exist, it may or will do so; that man is the sort of creature who, under certain conditions, will have this impulse or feeling. Exactly as much can be said of vanity, which Rousseau says is not innate.

I do not think that we should take Rousseau literally. Though he would, if challenged, have said that man is born with a conscience, this is probably not what he was most concerned to say when he called conscience 'innate'. What he meant to convey was rather that conscience is the same in all men, whatever the society they belong to; that its office is everywhere to incline them to forms of behaviour which they cannot but recognize to be right, as soon as they see them for what they are. He also, I think, means to deny that conscience arises out of the primitive passions in the way that the social passions do, though he never explains how it does arise. Indeed, he avoids this explanation by saying that conscience is innate, and simply takes it for granted that his meaning is plain.

{Rousseau denies that conscience is prejudice or socially induced habit or feeling} He feels the need to do so, because he will not have it that the promptings of conscience could differ from society to society, or in the same society from age to age. Nothing, he thinks, can be right in one place or at one time and wrong in another. If, of two exactly similar actions, one is called right and the other wrong, this is only because a mistake has been made about one or both of them. Conscience is always consistent in the sense that, no matter how often men have to act in a given situation, conscience will always prompt them to the same action, provided only that they see the situation as it really is. This is what Rousseau means when he says that, though reason is fallible, conscience is incorruptible.

Conscience is a difficult notion, variously understood. However differently we analyse it, we probably all agree that it is closely connected with the feeling we call shame. Was Rousseau, when he said that conscience is incorruptible and is the same in all men, suggesting that everywhere men are ashamed of the same things? Was he denying that men can be made to feel ashamed, within broad limits, of almost anything? Was he denying that there can be misplaced feelings of guilt and false shame, or, as the French put it, *mauvaise honte*? I am not sure how he would have answered these questions. But I cannot help feeling that an account of conscience which does not face them is inadequate.

4. What conditions must hold if man is to attain goodness?

To be able to live the good life, to attain the proper balance of their faculties and passions, men must either live in the right kind of society or else be made by education immune from the corruptions of corrupt society.

The right kind of society is the society of equals, the society so constituted that men are no longer each other's instruments and victims but are required to obey laws which reason teaches them are just and conscience moves them to obey. This society is described in the *Social Contract*. It is the just society, the only legitimate society, because the only one that conforms to the true nature of man. The laws of this society may thwart some of man's passions; but the better men understand the laws, the weaker the thwarted passions will be. In other words, the better the society, the less its members are tempted to do what they ought not to do. This conception of the just society is the idealist, the Platonic, side of Rousseau's philosophy: it is the idea of a society whose discipline perfects its members. We can discover what that society is by reflecting on the nature of man as a rational and moral being. It is the society in which man is at peace with himself and other men; the society in which he finds it easy to be what he wants to be, and is content to be what he is; the society in which he does not acquire needs and ambitions which move him to live a kind of life that cannot satisfy him and must make him the rival and enemy of other men. Since inequality corrupts man, we have only to discover the social conditions of equality to know what kind of society this should be.

I have said that this conception of the just society is Platonic. And so, essentially, it is. Rousseau, like Plato, assumes that man, by taking thought, can discover the kind of society suited to his nature; a just society very different from the society he lives in.[1] But when Rousseau lays it down that it must be a society of equals, he parts company with Plato and puts us in mind of the Utopias of the nineteenth-century socialists.

Men have also another chance of getting virtue and happiness in this world, though only a few can profit by it. A man can be educated to make the best of a bad world; he can be taught to be morally independent of it, not by cutting himself off from it, but by rising superior to its vanities and prejudices. He can be made, by careful education, nearly immune from corruption, and yet truly sociable, just and kindly in all his dealings with other men. They will be the better for his society, and he will be none the worse for theirs. This education is described in *Emile*. It creates a special environment for the child to protect him from the corrupting influences of society until he has grown strong enough, in his reasoning powers and his character, to resist them. What we find in *Emile* may be called the Stoic side of Rousseau's philosophy: it explains how a child, no better endowed by nature than others, can by training acquire so stable and well-balanced a character as to be almost proof against corruption. Not quite incorruptible, but nearly so; and in any case, better able than others to recover himself when he has temporarily lost balance.

5. What can be done to create the conditions favourable to the good life?

This is the easiest to answer of the questions suggested by Rousseau's account of man's natural goodness. For the answer to it is: Not much.

It is obvious that not everyone can get the education given to Emile. Emile has a tutor to himself alone, and Rousseau says that this must be so if he is to be made proof against the corruptions of existing society.

---

[1] Plato and Rousseau agree that the just society, if it is to exist, must be created deliberately. They also agree that, men being what they are, it is unlikely that this society will be created except on the rare occasions when conditions are favourable. Their idealism is tempered by pessimism.

A scheme of education that requires as many tutors as there are pupils to teach is altogether too expensive; it goes beyond anything the world has yet known, even in Oxford. Moreover, not any tutors will do; they must have the wisdom and patience of Emile's tutor, who was none other than Rousseau himself.

If we cannot change society indirectly by the careful education of each separate child, can we change it directly: can we hope to reform it? How are creatures already corrupt to be induced to set about changing their condition? If they adopt the scheme of government described in the *Social Contract*, they may find themselves unfit to work it. And how can they adopt it? For it can hardly function except in a simple society. Men have all kinds of vested interests in any society, no matter how corrupt it is. They are attached, Rousseau tells us, even to their vices. They may be unhappy; they may be moved by reason and by conscience to alter their social condition and their manner of life. But their vicious appetites are still strong in them, and they lack the will to get the better of them. The transformation of society, even when they acknowledge that it is desirable, is beyond their powers.

In the seventh chapter of Book II of the *Social Contract*, Rousseau says that 'in order that a people should be able to appreciate [*goûter*] healthy political maxims . . . it would be necessary that the effect should become the cause . . . that men should be before they have laws what they are to become as a result of having them.' Or, as we might put it, the wisdom needed to set up or to maintain a good political system is itself the product of that system. Even an uncorrupt people who have never constituted a state, who have never been politically organized, will lack this wisdom. Hence their need of a wise man, a Legislator, to prepare a constitution for them, which they can then freely accept; and the Legislator, unable to use force or to appeal to reason, must use another means of persuasion. He must claim to be divinely inspired. In the *Social Contract*, Rousseau mentions only one people still uncorrupt and 'capable of legislation', the Corsicans. In return for this compliment, he was invited by the Corsicans, then struggling for their independence, to prepare a constitution for them; he was invited to be their Legislator. Let it be said in justice to him that he aspired to persuade only by argument and never claimed divine inspiration.

A man who, believing that there is corruption almost everywhere, offers hope only to the Corsicans and to a few other peoples as uncorrupt as they are, offers little hope to mankind. It is not in the *Project of a Constitution for Corsica*, but several years later and towards the end of his life, in the *Considerations on the Government of Poland*, that Rousseau addresses his mind to the question of how a large and corrupt society, divided into unequal classes, can be brought gradually nearer to the ideal polity described in the *Social Contract*. He advocates a system whereby the Diet or national assembly is elected by provincial assemblies, the executive is appointed by the legislature, and the king has great honour and little power. He wants the serfs emancipated only as they prove their fitness for liberty, because men whose condition has made them servile cannot become citizens overnight. He makes it clear that the Diet, if not the provincial assemblies, must be a representative body, and stipulates only that there be frequent elections and that deputies be closely bound by their instructions. He warns the Poles that their institutions, defective though they are, have made them into a nation distinct from others, and therefore they must not hastily get rid of what is old and national but must change it slowly, aiming always at greater equality and freedom.

Rousseau's scheme of reform for Poland, brief and incomplete though it is, is ingenious. It embodies few illusions about human nature or social conditions; it is realistic and proves that its author could adapt his ideas to circumstances. Yet the scheme, as Rousseau himself admits, is difficult to apply, requiring rare firmness of purpose, patience and intelligence. Moreover, it is a scheme meant for the Poles, and it is not clear how far other peoples could make use of it.[1]

But there is one thing at least that Rousseau does make clear. The society of equals, the society adapted to the nature of man, the society in which man is satisfied with life as he finds it, does not come into being of itself. It must be deliberately created and deliberately preserved. It may be difficult (and at most times and places virtually impossible) to create it. Nevertheless, where it exists, it is an artifact. Nature uncontrolled by man does not produce the society in which man is naturally good.

6. *Plato and Rousseau*

I have suggested that Rousseau's idea of the natural goodness which is not brutish innocence has more than a little in common with what Plato understood by justice. The comparison is worth pursuing for the light it throws on Rousseau's meaning.

In the *Republic* Plato uses the word justice to refer to two different

---

[1] Rousseau's compliment to the Corsicans came before they asked him for advice, but he did not praise the Poles until after they had asked for it. He was then moved to admire their courage and vigour, because, in the midst of misfortune and anarchy, they had all the fire of youth and dared to aspire to government and to laws as if they were a nation just born. No doubt it is difficult for the would-be Legislator not to see it as a proof of courage and wisdom in a people that, in adversity, they should turn to him for advice. Vide: Vaughan, *The Political Writings of Rousseau*. Vol. II, p. 426.

but closely related things. There is a justice in men's souls and a justice also in society; there is an order and discipline proper to their minds as well as an external order and discipline which both preserve the community and enable its members to live as they ought inside it. For Rousseau, as for Plato, there are two orders and two harmonies, each closely dependent on the other: the order that reigns in the mind and the order that constitutes society. Plato does not say that society corrupts man, nor yet that man corrupts society. He is not concerned to apportion blame or to avoid it; he is concerned only to cure men's ills. But to cure those ills he looks to the reform of society as well as of men. Man must be educated into becoming a rational and a just creature, and there is a social environment proper to that purpose. Plato's two kinds of justice are inseparable; and both have as much right to be called natural as the goodness of which Rousseau speaks, for it can be said of both of them that they satisfy a creature having the nature of man. This, at least, is the claim that Plato makes for them. Let man but understand his own nature and he will aspire to them. And again, for Plato as for Rousseau (though Rousseau insists upon it more even than Plato), what is best adapted to man's nature does not come into being of itself; it is not what grows inevitably out of his nature but what is needed to perfect it. Man must discover it, and seek to remould society and himself in its image.

There are obvious similarities between the two theories, as indeed we should expect, seeing how ardently Rousseau admired Plato; but there are differences no less important, though they have been less often noticed. Plato believed that the soul is in good order, that there is justice inside it, when reason controls the passions. But Rousseau, though he sometimes used this Platonic formula or others like it, did not really believe it. He was, after all, a philosopher of the eighteenth century, who had learned from Pascal and from Hume's French disciples that reason alone cannot move men to action. It can compare the passions and know them; it can discover which are insatiable or in conflict with the others and which can be satisfied; it can know justice but cannot desire it. The Platonic idea that knowledge is virtue, that reason not only enlightens but controls, was no longer accepted by many philosophers; and Rousseau, unfashionable though he might often wish to be, was no doubt influenced by prevailing opinions.[1]

He had also another and stronger motive for playing down the

---

[1] But never to the extent of forgetting that the passions of a rational creature are different precisely because he is rational. It is because he is rational that man is self-conscious, that he is a moral being whose happiness depends on how he feels about himself and others. Man needs to feel that he is living in a well-ordered world, and needs self-respect. In many ways, Rousseau was closer to Pascal than to the Encyclopaedists and Hume; he understood, as they did not, man's profound need to feel at home in the world.

sovereignty of reason. He could not hope to prove that one man's reason is no better than another's, that all men are equally intelligent. Now, if reason controls the passions, and ought to rule, it would seem to follow that, since some men are more reasonable than others, they ought to rule and the others to obey them. Again, if it requires superior reason, which only some men are by nature qualified to attain, to discover justice, it follows that not all men are in the same measure naturally good.) These might be conclusions welcome to Plato, but Rousseau, who believed in equality as much as in virtue, could not accept them.

Though Rousseau often spoke of the need to control the passions, he was much less than Plato a lover of discipline. Plato believed that the laws and customs that make society possible also make men good, and that every state, however imperfect, must to some extent impose on its citizens the discipline that makes them virtuous. Rousseau, too, no doubt, believed that every society makes men moral, that life inside it awakens their reason and gives scope to their conscience; but he also said that society corrupts. It makes man capable of virtue and vice, but inclines him much more to vice than to virtue. The restraints it imposes are mostly degrading, and the opportunities it creates mostly occasions of evil. Only a few societies, more similar than most to the ideal society described in the *Social Contract*, are exceptions to this rule; and only a few persons, educated like Emile or born with much more than usual strength of mind, can escape the corruptions of ordinary society. Rousseau believed that most social restraints are imposed on the many for the sake of the few; and also that society mostly restrains men's better feelings while it multiplies and elaborates their evil passions. In the ideal society men would be very little restrained by the laws, because they would not have the passions which put them at odds with justice, or would get only a mild dose of them. They would not need to put a strong curb on themselves, to be perpetually at war with their baser feelings. They would not, like the Christian hero, have to keep down the devil in their own souls. Man is by nature good. That means, to Rousseau, that when he is as he ought to be, he is internally at peace; he does not have to win one strenuous victory after another over himself.

Rousseau loved freedom; and not all his veneration for Plato, who cared for it so little, could diminish that love. That makes a great difference between their two theories. They both thought evil a kind of anarchy, but Rousseau was more anxious to prevent than to restrain it. The good man is not, in his eyes, the strong man armed with virtue perpetually on guard over his soul. He did not want a watchful and strict mastery of reason over the passions, any more than the government of the foolish by the wise. He wanted a society where the passions need little or no restraint, where men need few defences against themselves and each other because they live together under such conditions that it comes easily to them to love and help one another; a society where no man is dependent on a superior but only on friends and neighbours, on an entire community, on a society of equals in whose life he takes a full part.

In his book on education, Rousseau makes Emile's tutor his friend and companion, not his master. The tutor does not punish or scold, he does not impose discipline; he merely creates the environment enabling the boy to discipline himself. He teaches the boy to be self-reliant, and cannot succeed unless his lessons are so discreet that the boy scarcely feels them to be lessons. He does for Emile, in a corrupt society, what man's social environment would do for him in a properly constituted State. He makes him a man of good will, who freely accepts the rules which must be accepted for the public good.

Though there is an illiberal side to Rousseau's social philosophy, it is his love of freedom, and of equality conceived as a means to freedom, which is more often to the fore. This love he tried to reconcile with the need for order through his doctrine of the general will; but he also gave simpler and perhaps more attractive expression to it. There are times when Rousseau comes close to Montaigne, who in his *Essays* tells us to let nature take her course, to deal gently with our neighbours and ourselves, not stifling our passions when they hurt us but finding harmless outlets for them. There is a place in nature for everything; let us follow her example and find a place for everything in ourselves. This, too, is a doctrine congenial to Rousseau, and its influence is often apparent in his writings. Rousseau, like Montaigne, when he finds men trying to impose their preferences on their neighbours, is sometimes moved to ask them by what authority they do so.

III. THE GENERAL WILL

It is in the *Social Contract*, in the first and second drafts of it, that Rousseau gives us much the longest account of the general will. The *Social Contract* describes the just State, the only State that enables men to live as they should do, in accordance with their nature. The *Social Contract* does not offer to tell us, as for instance Hobbes' *Leviathan* does, why it is men's interest to obey established governments; nor does it seek to explain, as Locke's *Civil Government* does, what are the limits of political obligation in actual States. Rousseau's *Social Contract*, like Plato's *Republic*, describes an ideal to be aimed at, but does not tell us what we should do, here and now, in the endeavour to attain it. Practical advice we get only in the *Project for Corsica* and the *Considerations on the Government of Poland*; and very cautious and moderate it is.

Rousseau's purpose in the *Social Contract*, as he describes it himself, is to find 'a form of association that will defend with the whole common force the person and the goods of each associate, and in which everyone, while uniting with all, still obeys himself alone and remains as free as before'. As soon as we begin to consider these words more closely, we find them obscure. If force has to be used, how can the persons against whom it is used remain as free as before? How can a man in society obey himself alone? When he unites with others to form a society, he either agrees to, or soon discovers he must, obey many more people than himself. His having agreed to obey does not ensure that, when obedience is required of him, he in fact wants to obey. When a man agrees to obey, he may make it his duty to do what other people demand of him, but he cannot undertake always to want what they require.

Rousseau's solution is as obscure as his problem. The social contract, which ensures that everyone obeys himself alone and remains as free as before, is thus described: 'Each one of us puts his person and all his power in common under the supreme direction of the general will, and we as a body receive each member as an inseparable part of the whole. At that moment, in the place of the particular person of each contracting party, this act of association creates a moral and collective body, made up of as many members as there are voters in the assembly, and receiving from this act its unity, its common self, its life, and its will.'

This solution raises more questions than it answers. What is the general will? How does it make a man an *inseparable* part of the society he belongs to? How does it make a collective body out of the persons making the contract? And how can that body take the place of those persons?

If we try to puzzle out Rousseau's statement of his problem and his solution of it, or other equally obscure and famous pronouncements from the *Social Contract*, we shall not make much progress towards discovering what he meant by the general will. It is better, I think, to begin by considering the simpler parts of his description of the ideal democracy. These parts, once we have grasped their significance, may make it easier for us to understand what is more obscure. Rousseau was not a metaphysician with a peculiar and difficult conception of what reality essentially is, and so did not use a technical language derived from any such conception. He was not, like Hegel, impelled to use a special vocabulary created by himself for the express purpose of saying what he thought could not be said adequately in ordinary words. Rousseau was obscure for a simpler reason: because he failed to make his meaning plain. His obscure utterances are, if I may so put it, on the same level of discourse as his simpler ones: they do not deal with what is deeper, or 'more true', or 'more real', in a special language unsuited to the superficialities of ordinary discourse. There is no peculiar logic or metaphysic behind his political philosophy; and that philosophy must therefore, in fairness to him, be treated at the level of ordinary common sense. Rousseau thought the French language, as educated and intelligent men used it, sufficient for all his purposes; he always wanted (though he sometimes failed) to be intelligible to educated men who understand ordinary words in ordinary ways. We can therefore probably get closer to his meaning by interpreting what is obscure in his theory in the light of what is intelligible than by reading into it ideas suggested to us by what we know of the later philosophies of Kant, Fichte, or Hegel. For, though German philosophers were deeply influenced by Rousseau, they were also more systematic than he was, using concepts and making distinctions which meant nothing to him.

If we take some of Rousseau's more often quoted statements literally, and try to elicit their meanings, we soon find ourselves caught up in a web of absurdity. Let me give one or two examples of the uselessness of this direct method. In the third chapter of Book II of the *Social Contract*, Rousseau distinguishes 'the will of all' from 'the general will', saying that the first is a 'sum of particular wills', and the second the 'sum of differences' remaining when the 'pluses' and 'minuses' of the particular wills cancel each other out. Now, this account of the general will, if we take it literally, is sheer nonsense. What can the 'pluses' and 'minuses' of particular wills be except what is peculiar to each of them. Let John's will be $x+a$, Richard's $x+b$, and Thomas's $x+c$; x being what is common to them all, and a, b, and c, what is peculiar to each. If the general will is what remains after the 'pluses' and 'minuses' have cancelled each other out, it is x; but if it is the sum of the differences it is $a+b+c$. Whichever it is, it cannot be both; and the second alternative is too absurd to be considered. Beware of political philosophers who use mathematics, no matter how simple, to illustrate their meaning! God will forgive them, for they know what they do, but we shall not understand them.

The first alternative, that the general will is whatever is common to all the particular wills, is not absurd. It makes sense, but it is unrealistic and does not square with Rousseau's account of how that will comes into being. For to discover what is common to particular wills, there is in theory no need for assembly and debate. Each citizen could record his opinion separately, and whatever was found to be common to all opinions could be declared to be the general will. But Rousseau holds that the general will, if it emerges at all, does so in an assembly of equals who freely debate what is of common interest. Even if the general will were a compromise decision reached after a free discussion between people whose opinions differ, it still would not be what was common to those opinions. For in the process of discussion, opinions

change in ways impossible to predict, and the eventual compromise is
not something that could have been discovered by a calculation based
on the opinions that people had before the discussion began.

In the fifteenth chapter of Book III of the *Social Contract*, Rousseau
says that sovereignty cannot be represented, because it consists in the
general will, and will cannot be represented. He puts this forward as an
argument for direct as against representative democracy. The citizens
must make their own laws and not choose persons to make them in
their place; but they may, and indeed ought, to entrust the executive
power to delegates, and not try to exercise it themselves. This statement, that the will cannot be represented, has puzzled several of
Rousseau's admirers. They have tried to plumb its depths, taking it
for granted that whatever was concealed there must be of the utmost
importance. For there is nothing that Rousseau insists on so much as
that the people must never surrender the legislative power into other
hands. To explain what he means by the will's not being able to be
represented is surely to elucidate one of the cardinal maxims of his
political philosophy!

It is certainly a good rule to take the theory you are studying
seriously; but that, I hope, need not involve trying to get blood out of
a stone. Rousseau's dictum, that the will cannot be represented, is
either a truism that has nothing to do with the conclusion he derives
from it or else is plainly false. If what it means is that nobody can do
another person's willing for him, it is true but irrelevant; for it does
not follow from it that nobody can authorize anyone else to make
decisions on his behalf. Strictly speaking, it is not wills but persons
that are represented; and one person represents another whenever he
does what the other has indicated that he desires him to do and what
he has the right to do because the other has so indicated his desire.
Again, if Rousseau's dictum means that no one has the right or power
to appoint someone else to make decisions on his behalf, but only to
carry out decisions he has taken for himself, it is plainly false. The
dictum is empty or useless or false. Do what you like with it, you will
get no pearls of political wisdom out of it. Rousseau, as we shall see,
has some strong arguments against representative democracy, but they
have nothing to do with anything about the will which makes it
incapable of being represented.

Let us deal courteously with Rousseau but let us not be fascinated by
what is obscure and oracular about him. Let us begin by considering
what he imagined a free society would be like; let us first take hold of
what is plain if not exactly simple. We are told that man, unless he
gives up the advantages he gets from society, cannot be independent
of all other men; and we know that Rousseau did not wish him to
give them up. He believed that man can become moral and
rational, can develop his faculties harmoniously, only in society.

/Since complete independence is not desirable, let alone possible, there must be equal dependence./ The free society is a society of equals, where no man is the inferior of another, depending on him in ways in which the other does not depend on him; it is the society where all men depend equally on the community of which they are all active members.

What then, in Rousseau's opinion, is a society of equals? It is a society where, in the first place, every man is entitled to take part in making decisions which all are required to obey; where, secondly, the persons who make these decisions do so as individual citizens and not as members of organized groups smaller than the State; where, thirdly, citizens make the laws themselves and do not elect representatives to do so for them; and where, fourthly and lastly, the body that makes the laws does *not* administer them. If we can discover why Rousseau thought these four conditions indispensable to true equality, we shall be much better able to understand his doctrine of the general will; for it is only in a society of equals that the general will is fully developed.

1. His First Principle

The first condition, *that every man is entitled to take part in making decisions which all are required to obey*, though as important as any, requires the least comment. It is, at bottom, the old doctrine of Locke and the natural law philosophers, that government, to be legitimate, requires the consent of the governed. But Rousseau does not, as Locke and others do, weaken the doctrine by resorting to any such shift as Locke's notion of tacit consent. Sovereign decisions are made by the whole body of citizens.

Notice that the decisions in question are decisions which _all_ are required to obey. It is not said that a man is entitled to take part in making any decision which _he_ is required to obey. For such a decision might be executive or judicial. A man is not entitled to be a judge in his own case when the law is being applied to him either administratively or judicially; he is entitled only to take part in deciding what the law shall be. ⟨He has a right to take part in deciding what shall be required of anyone, including himself, under such and such circumstance⟩ Merely by virtue of being a member of the community, adult, sane, and male, you have a right to take part in the making of law; but the right to take any other part in government you can have only if it has been granted to you according to law. The right to apply or enforce the law is a legal right; the right to take part in making the law is a moral right which can be forfeited only by breaking the law. If you break the law, you may be justly punished, and so deprived for a time or for good of your right to take a part in making the law. But if you have not broken the law, you cannot be justly deprived of your right to take part in making it. A decision of the assembly depriving innocent citizens of their legislative rights would not be law but an attack of one part of the community on another; and victims of aggression have no duty to obey decisions made by aggressors. It may be dangerous for them not to obey; but that is another matter.

2. *His Second Principle*

The second condition, *that the persons making sovereign decisions must do so as citizens and not as members of organized groups smaller than the State, smaller than the entire political community they belong to,* is not so easily explained. It is, of all Rousseau's political principles, perhaps the most completely his own. We are told, in the third chapter of Book II of the *Social Contract*, that ' when factions arise, and partial associations are formed at the expense of the great association, the will of each of them becomes general in relation to its members, and particular in relation to the State: and you can then say that there are no longer as many voters as there are men, but only as many as there are associations . . . there is then no longer a general will, and the opinion that prevails is only particular. It is important, therefore . . . that there should be no partial society in the State, and that every citizen should arrive at his own opinion.'

It was a favourite opinion with Rousseau that men are less divided by private than by organized group interests. The private citizen, who has to rely entirely on himself, on the force of his own arguments, when he tries to get his fellow citizens to adopt some course of action, must speak to them of the common interest. No doubt, he tries to get them to agree to what suits him; he puts forward his own interest as the common interest. But he has no hope of success unless he can persuade them that what he proposes is also in their interest. He has no body of supporters on whom he can rely; he is just one private citizen among others. He neither belongs to an organized group nor is dealing with persons who belong to such groups. He is dealing with a mass of individuals whose private interests are more or less unknown to him; he has a strong motive therefore for appealing to the most general interests. The longer he is so placed, and the more he is in the habit of discussing matters of common concern with others placed as he is, the more he accommodates his private interest to the common interest, and the more attached he becomes to the community. He is persuaded by his own arguments devised to appeal to others, and also by the arguments of his fellow citizens who have the same motives as he has for appealing to general interests.

A private citizen does not ordinarily have his conception of his political interest (of what he wants from the State) ready made in his mind when he comes to discuss matters of common concern with other citizens; what he wants the State to do for him varies with their influence on him. He is usually more persuadable by the others, taken collectively, than they are by him, for he is only one person and they are many. Private citizens who come together to debate public matters and to reach common decisions do not ordinarily have precise and fixed ideas about what should be done; their ideas are mostly fluid and take firmer shape in the course of the debate. It is largely by meeting together to deal with public affairs that they acquire definite political opinions: opinions about what they and others are entitled to ask of the community and what has to be done to meet their claims.

Where a man is in the habit of being concerned with the affairs of his community, he usually has two strong and enduring desires: that the community should flourish, and that he should do well inside it. His idea of what is involved in his doing well will be closely tied up with his idea of what makes the community flourishing. The more he takes part, as one citizen among others, in discussing and deciding matters of common concern, the stronger his attachment to the community, and the more his ambitions are in line with the common interest. He will still prefer his own interest to the interest of most other persons, taken individually; but this does no harm when public affairs are being discussed, for it then pays him to advocate some course which reconciles his private interest with what he can persuade others to believe is the common interest. Others are as good judges as he is of that common interest, and, there being no organized group, he has no pull over any section of them. He is so situated that he is insensibly drawn into accommodating his own to the common interest.

But where there are organized groups in the community the situation is different, because within each group there is at work a process similar to the one which would bind everyone closely to the community if there were no such group inside it. Within each group, citizens acquire loyalties and conscious interests which bind them to the group rather than to the whole community. These loyalties and interests are the stronger for being shared, and for being known to the shared; for it is interests known to be shared which are the most obstinately held to. Men strengthen one another in their common aspirations and resolutions; it is as members of groups, rather than as private citizens, that they make precise and rigid claims on the community. Organized groups are harder, more cynical, more intractable than are private citizens. The process whereby discussion creates a harmony between particular and common interests works much less smoothly where the particular interests are those of organized groups.

Men are most persuadable when they are least committed, when they are not so placed as to be liable to be accused of inconsistency or disloyalty if they change their minds, and when they cannot count in advance on the support of others. If, then, every citizen comes to the assembly uncommitted, his private interests are less likely to stand in the way of a reasonable and just decision than would a policy, or even mere loyalties and prejudices, shared by people who form an organized group. Rousseau knew, of course, that there are in every community interests which are shared by only some of its members. He was not so absurd as to deny that there are sectional interests, and that they are important. He merely said that the people who have them should not form organized groups to push them. Or rather, he said that the ideal, which can be realized only in a small State, is that there should be no such organized groups. But where this ideal cannot be realized, it is better that there should be many such groups rather than only a few.[1]

Though it is in *The Social Contract* that Rousseau tells us that the pursuit of merely private interests is not dangerous to the State, and that he condemns the formation of organized groups in an ideal democracy, some of the points I have been making are better put elsewhere. In some comments written in 1756 on the Abbé de Saint-Pierre's *Polysynodie*, he says, speaking of a private citizen trying to persuade his fellow citizens: 'In an assembly all of whose members are clear-sighted and have not the same interests, each person would seek in vain to bring others over to what suited himself alone: without persuading anyone, he will succeed only in laying himself open to suspicions of corruption and unfaithfulness. No matter how much he may wish to avoid doing his duty, he will not attempt it, or will attempt it in vain, where there are so many to watch him. He will therefore make a virtue of necessity, in openly sacrificing his personal interest to his country's good. . . . For there is then a very strong personal interest, which is concern for his reputation, marching with the public interest.'[2] A few pages further on, speaking of the interests of groups within the State as compared with personal interests, he says that 'they have this added inconvenience, that [a man] takes pride in maintaining, at any cost, the rights and claims of the body he is a member of; and that the dishonesty of preferring himself to others vanishes in favour of a numerous society he belongs to.'[3]

---

[1] Nothing that Rousseau says in *The Social Contract* or elsewhere implies that there should be no parties or pressure groups in the vast democracies known to us. On the contrary, he knew that in large States there must be what he called factions (a term which covers both parties and pressure groups, for he did not distinguish between them); and where there must be factions, he would have people free to form as many as they feel inclined to.

[2] Vaughan, Vol. I, p. 408.

[3] Ibid., Vol. I, p. 422.

Apart from these bad effects of group prejudices and policy, there is another danger. Where there are groups active in politics, it is always possible for several of them to make a compromise at the expense of the others. This is what Rousseau has in mind when he speaks of the evils of intrigue. He has a horror of agreements reached behind the scenes by organized groups who then face the assembly with decisions taken outside it and imposed upon it.

We have seen that, where there must be organized groups, Rousseau prefers many small ones to a few large ones. This is presumably because he believes that a coalition of many small groups will be weaker and more unstable than one made up of a few large ones. What he wants to avoid, above all, is the setting up of a permanent majority, whether it consists of one body only or of several firmly allied with one another. For then everyone outside the majority takes no real part in making the decisions of the assembly. He may cast a vote or even speak, but what he does cannot affect the decision. People who feel that they can affect a decision are disposed to accept it as a common decision, a decision of the entire body they belong to, even when they vote against it; but people who do not feel this are not so disposed.

If no citizen belongs to an organized group, every majority is, so to speak, a chance majority. Nobody knows beforehand who will belong to it. The citizens who make up the majority have no more in common than that they happen, on that occasion, to have voted one way; and next time there is a vote, the chances are that the majority will not consist of the same persons. There is no enduring majority to impose its will on the entire community; there are no enduring minorities to combine against one another. No one need feel that he plays an empty part in the affairs of his community. There are no lesser communities inside the great community controlling it for the benefit of some and to the detriment of others.

This is an ideal model, and we cannot be sure how far Rousseau thought it could be realized in practice. Even a small city state or Swiss canton includes many hundreds, not to say thousands, of citizens. Did Rousseau really believe that an assembly of all the citizens of a state large enough to be self-supporting could function with no organized groups inside it? I do not know. I suspect that he never gave the matter much thought. But, thoughtless though he was in one direction, he was thoughtful, and even original, in another. What he says about organized groups, their interests and their loyalties, though only a part of the truth, is yet an important part.

3. His Third Principle

Rousseau's third principle, *that citizens must make their own laws and must not choose deputies to do so for them,* has been condemned as among the more absurd and unrealistic that he put forward; though he was, as a matter of fact, as well aware as any of his critics that in large states the people cannot make the laws themselves. He was against large states, though he knew that the tendency was for states to grow larger. He merely denied that the tendency was good, and the denial is not obviously absurd. Rousseau believed that in large states inequality is inevitable, and truly popular government therefore impossible. It is perhaps more important to see the force of his argument than to condemn him for lack of realism.

It has often been said that the essence of democracy is the making of sovereign decisions by a process of free discussion between the people affected by those decisions. If people do not take part in reaching a decision that affects them, and also in the discussion leading up to that decision, they may not understand the need for the decision nor the interests and points of view reconciled by it. The decision is therefore likely to appear to them external and arbitrary. They may get used to acquiescing in such decisions; they may even learn to think of themselves as unfit to take part in making them. But it is when they have themselves had a hand in making a decision that they are most likely to recognize it as just or expedient or, if they find it unjust and inexpedient, that they are best able to consider what should be done to get it reversed.

Where sovereign decisions are taken by an elected body, where the most important business of government, the making of the laws, is done by only a small part of the people, the others (so Rousseau would have us believe) never acquire what deserves to be called a political will. The really important decisions are then taken, not by the people, who may not even understand what is done in their name, but by their deputies, whose responsibility to their electors is, at the best, occasional and vague. The English people, Rousseau tells us, imagine that they are free, but they are so only at long intervals, when they take the trouble to elect representatives. There was no point in his passing this judgement on the English people unless he believed that the responsibility of representatives to electors is more apparent than real. The electorate are politically inarticulate; they are mere listeners and voters while the elections last, and afterwards take no part at all in government. They scarcely know what their representatives are doing. Representative democracy is an illusion; it requires the impossible, that the few who make government the business of their lives should be genuinely responsible to a mass of indifferent, if not ignorant, voters. Whenever Rousseau speaks of the people electing deputies to make laws for them, he always speaks as if they were abdicating the most essential of their political rights and duties. When they elect deputies they are not, as he sees it, taking a real part in the government of their country; they are refusing to take it. They are divesting themselves of a power which they alone can exercise properly. To choose someone to make your laws for you is not to assert your legislative right but to renounce it. It is to refuse the greatest service you owe to your country: the duty to think for it. Rousseau speaks of a people that deliberately gives up the burden of legislation and puts it on other shoulders much as the patriot speaks of the man who refuses to bear arms in his country's defence.

Freedom, says Rousseau, is obedience to a law we prescribe to ourselves. But society cannot subsist if every man makes his own law separately. Therefore all must make the law for all. It is impossible that each of us should say, 'I alone have made the law that I obey.' The most we can hope for is that each should say, 'I obey the law that *we* have made' rather than 'I obey the law that *they* have made'. The ideal is that every citizen should identify himself with the community that makes the law, which, Rousseau thinks, he cannot do unless he is a member, on the same terms as all other citizens, of the sovereign legislature. Rousseau knew that this requires that the sovereign community, the State, should be small. He knew also that it was almost impossible to reduce the size of existing States. They had grown bigger in the past and were likely to continue doing so. He knew that the odds were almost everywhere against the people's sovereignty, against equality, against the institutions which he thought make for freedom and social harmony.

Rousseau was as sharply aware as the socialists after him of a process of social change making every man dependent on an always larger number of other men. Society, he knew, was growing vaster and more elaborate; the old small, almost self-sufficing community was fast disappearing. He believed that this increase in the circle of each man's social dependence made inevitably for greater inequality. He therefore condemned the material progress which he thought was the cause of this dependence. It is here that he differs from most, though not all, of the socialists. They disliked inequality as much as he did, but many of them did not see inequality as the inevitable companion of material progress. Conditions, they admitted, might now be growing worse for the poor, but only to grow better afterwards. Rousseau did not share their optimism; he was never tempted to believe that what was wrong with modern society could be put right by workers' co-operatives or the abolition of certain forms of private property or the disappearance of the State. He wanted a property-owning democracy. But real democracy, he said, is impossible in vast and intricate societies. Material progress, by enormously complicating the life of society, leads inevitably to great inequalities of wealth and power. Only where society is simple and small can all its members take an active part in managing its affairs; and unless they can do that, they are neither free nor equal.

It would, I think, be wrong to call Rousseau a reactionary; he did not want society to revert to what it had been in the past. His ideal society is quite unlike what European society had ever been, except perhaps for short periods of time in a few places. But he was passionately against what the modern world calls *progress*.

Rousseau liked to say that the laws must rule and not men, and he also liked to distinguish between independence and freedom. For example, in the eighth of his *Letters from the Mountain*, he says: 'When everyone does what he pleases, he often does what displeases others; and that is not called a condition of freedom. Liberty consists less in doing what we want than in not being subject to another's will; it also consists in not subjecting another's will to our own.'[1]

Now, it smacks of paradox to say that 'the laws must rule and not men'. Laws are customary or are deliberately made, and in either case are enforced or applied by men. As Hobbes might put it, it is always men that rule, whether they make the law or merely apply it. Rousseau uses this paradox, as it often has been used, as a way of saying that governments must not act arbitrarily but must apply the same rules to all their subjects; but he also uses it to give point to the distinction he makes between independence and freedom. Independence, the power to do as you please, is impossible in society. The most you can hope for is that the laws should not seem to you to be imposed on you by others. But they must seem to be so, Rousseau thinks, unless you take an equal part with others in making them. There is a difference between being made to do what other people have decided you shall do and being obliged to do what you have committed yourself to doing. By taking part, on equal terms with other people, in making a decision, you oblige yourself to accept it, even when you actually vote against it. They do not impose their will on you without taking account of your wishes; nor, conversely, when the vote goes your way, do you impose your will on the minority. The situation, where all take part as equals in making common decisions, is not only morally, but also psychologically, different from some people's imposing their will on others. Not only does it create obligations stronger than would otherwise exist, but people feel differently about the decisions. When they are required to conform to these decisions, they do not feel that they are being subjected to the will of others. Other people are as much bound as they are. To express this need that all should feel an equal dependence on the whole community, Rousseau uses the not altogether happy formula that the 'laws must rule and not men'. The rule of law, in this sense, is realized only in the society of equals, which is necessarily small and simple.

It is, I suggest, beside the point to accuse Rousseau of lacking realism. In the *Social Contract* his avowed purpose is to describe an ideal com-

[1] Vaughan, op. cit., Vol. II, p. 234.

munity. Far from pretending that it can be easily established, he goes out of his way to assure his readers of the opposite. In the eighth chapter of Book II, he says that many nations are incapable of good laws, and that even those that have them do so only for a time. Nations, like men, become incorrigible as they grow old. If they do not acquire a good constitution at the only time of their lives when they can adapt themselves to it, when they are neither too barbarous nor too fixed in evil ways, they have no hope of freedom. The Russians are lost to freedom for ever, because Peter the Great tried to ram civilization down their throats before they were ready for it, and they will never be civilized. In the next chapter Rousseau says that the Corsicans are the only people in Europe 'capable of legislation', meaning that they alone can become a properly constituted State. In return for this compliment, they asked him to prepare a constitution for them. In yet another chapter, the eighth of Book III, he goes still further: he implies that there are peoples without even a chance of freedom to miss, if they live in hot countries suited only to despotism or cold ones suited only to barbarism.

Man is born free and is by nature good. If you happen to be a man, do not rejoice too quickly! You can be free and good only if you live in a society of equals, and there is not much chance of your doing that. There is no question here of religious or racial prejudice. Rousseau does not suggest that there is original sin in you or that you are born in any way defective, whatever nation or race you belong to. Merely in virtue of your humanity you are born to freedom. But, unfortunately, you cannot get freedom except in the right social environment, which is not to be had for the asking, but is extraordinarily difficult to create. Those who have it have it more by luck than judgement. I suggest that this is not so much lack of realism as profound pessimism. Rousseau may be wrong about the conditions of freedom; but if he is, we do not prove him so by showing that these conditions can hardly be realized in the modern world. We can refute him only by showing that he mistook the conditions of freedom. This, I think, can be done, though I shall not attempt it here. For the moment, my purpose is only to put the gist of Rousseau's argument as simply, clearly, and forcefully as I can. This is worth doing, because Rousseau was the first to give expression to a feeling that many now share: the feeling that man is lost in a social environment too vast and elaborate for him to control.

4. His Fourth Principle

Rousseau's fourth principle, *that the sovereign assembly must not administer the laws it makes*, looks at first sight like a version of the doctrine of the separation of powers. But the point of it is really quite

o*

different. Rousseau is not concerned that the executive and the legislative should act as checks on one another; he is concerned rather that the legislative should undertake only what it is fit to do.

Rousseau believed that we are ordinarily much more anxious that justice should be done generally than that it should be done on this or that particular occasion. It matters more to us that the laws should be just than that they should be justly applied to a particular person. When we are considering law in the abstract, as a rule that might apply to anyone, we are not moved by the likes and dislikes which nearly always move us when we are dealing with actual persons. Even in a society of equals, the doing of justice to particular persons must be an activity separate from the making of law. Those who do this kind of justice have always a limited authority; the procedures they use are laid down by custom and law; they are trained to impartiality by the very nature of their profession, and there is usually a right of appeal from their decisions. Precautions of many kinds are taken to protect citizens against the errors and prejudices of magistrates and officials; but no such precautions can be taken against a sovereign assembly. The proper task of such an assembly is therefore to do what, in a society of equals, it will have no motive for doing badly; and that is to make laws applying to all citizens equally. Provided the assembly consists of all the citizens, that none are excluded, and that the society is simple and homogeneous enough for no section of it to be felt by the others to be alien, inferior, or dangerous, then the assembly will have no motive for making unjust laws. It will make mistakes, but it will always desire the good of the entire community.

'Every act of sovereignty', says Rousseau in the fourth chapter of Book II of the *Social Contract*, 'that is to say, every authentic act of the general will, obliges or favours all citizens equally; so that the sovereign takes account only of the body of the nation, and does not distinguish any of the persons that make it up'. In the sixth chapter of the same book he says: 'When I say that the object of the laws is always general, I mean that the Law considers subjects in a body and actions in the abstract, never a man individually nor a particular action. Thus the Law may lay it down that there shall be privileges but can give none to anybody by name.' This is what law must be as an expression of the general will; this is why it assimilates the good of each with the good of all. 'Why is the general will always upright, and why do all continually desire the happiness of each, if it is not that there is no one who does not apply the word "each" to himself, and does not think of himself when voting for (what concerns) all?'[1]

If a law, to be properly so called, to be an expression of the general will, must affect all citizens equally, it seems to follow that there can be very few laws. For the vast majority of what are ordinarily called

---

[1] *Social Contract*, Bk. II, Ch. IV.

laws affect some people more than others. Even if we suppose Rousseau to have meant that the makers of law, if what they make is to be genuine law, must not intend to affect some citizens more than others, we are still in difficulties. If the law grants privileges, as Rousseau says it may, to citizens who have deserved well of their country, its purpose is to discriminate. A law that grants benefits to nursing mothers or to widows or to veteran soldiers is not intended to affect all citizens equally. Nor can I, with the best will in the world, when I vote for a law giving benefits to nursing mothers, apply the word 'each' to myself.

If we take Rousseau quite literally, we make nonsense of his arguments, and we also do him less than justice. He was not happily inspired when he said that the law must affect all citizens equally. If, however, we leave out that form of words, we are not left with nothing. For Rousseau also tells us that the law considers subjects in a body and actions in the abstract. In other words, a law is always a general rule of the form: *anyone so and so situated or who has behaved thus and thus shall do this, or not do that, or shall be treated in this way.* When I, as a member of the sovereign assembly, take part in making such a rule, I may know that it can never apply to myself. Yet I know that other rules do apply to me; and I can help make this rule in the same spirit as I would another that did affect me. In an assembly of equals, where all citizens take part in making the rules which apply to whole categories of citizens, each man has an interest in considering every rule as if it applied to himself. The more closely knit and simple the community, and the less inequality inside it, the easier for everyone to act in this spirit.

If I am old, I can never be young again; if I am a man, I can never be in a condition possible only to women, and yet I may take part in making laws that affect only young people or women. If I am poor, I may become rich; if I am rich, I may lose my wealth. There are differences that can never be got over, and others that can. The first are natural, and the second are social. But the natural differences divide men less than the social. It is easier for me, being old, to do justice to the young, or being a man, to do justice to women, than it is for me, being poor, to do justice to the rich, or being rich to do it to the poor. Family ties are the closest of all, and they bind together persons who differ in sex, in age, in health, and in natural ability. These differences, though sometimes divisive, more often serve to bring people closer together. It is much less natural than social differences which make it difficult for people to deal justly with one another. It is inequalities of power and wealth and education that weaken the sympathies of human beings for one another, making it more difficult for them to put themselves in each other's shoes. That, at least, is what Rousseau believed.

*   *   *

Bearing these four principles in mind, together with the arguments that Rousseau used in support of them, we may find it easier to discover what is valuable in his doctrine of the general will, and how he came to distinguish between the citizen's 'general' and his 'particular' will. Let us remember the obvious: that long before Rousseau's time, it had been common practice to speak of groups and communities as if they were individuals; to speak of them as if they had minds and wills of their own. It had also been common practice to speak as if a man could have more than one will. It is often convenient, avoiding clumsy circumlocution, to speak of a class of desires as if they were a will, of a number of people who want the same or similar things as if they shared a single will. The use of metaphors is not confined to the poet or artist; the scientist or philosopher also needs to use them, though for a different purpose. We need not assume that Rousseau, in speaking of the will as he did, was doing anything more than had often been done before him. We need not assume that he was being literal where others had been metaphorical; that he really wanted us to believe that communities have wills in the way that men do, and that every citizen has two separate wills, a higher and a lower, sharing the first with the other citizens and keeping the second all to himself. The trouble with Rousseau is not that he used metaphors so much as that he sometimes used them inappropriately, to give vent to his feelings rather than to help make his meaning plain.

I would not have political theorists keep their feelings out of their books. That would be asking too much of them. But they can, if they take more trouble than Rousseau took, contrive to be clear and yet also warm and colourful. Certainly, we do not help to make sense of Rousseau by taking literally what had always, before his time, been taken metaphorically. His using these metaphors more often and with greater feeling than they were used before him does not prove that he took them literally; it indicates no more than that he used them to say something he had very much at heart. He was not a logician, or a metaphysician, or a psychologist; he was a political theorist using the ordinary language of the educated man, but using it more passionately and less precisely than many earlier political theorists had done.

It is in the first draft of the *Social Contract*, in the second chapter of Book I, in a passage[1] which is not repeated in the second and final draft, that we find the clearest explanation of one, at least, of the senses in which Rousseau used the expression *the general will*. That will is there said to be a set of opinions that a man arrives at when, without being swayed by passion, he reflects on what his neighbours have the right to expect from him, and he from them. The general will is therefore a set of opinions about right conduct. Now, though opinions are not acts

[1] Vaughan, op. cit., Vol. I, p. 452.

of will, Rousseau was not merely careless when he called these particular opinions the general will. He called them *general* because he believed that life in society gives them to nearly all men; and he called them a will because he believed that men feel so strongly about them that their behaviour is powerfully affected by them. Whenever men live together in a society or work together in a group, then, so long as most of them are not mere instruments of the others, so long as they all have a sense of belonging to the society or group, they have these opinions and this feeling. Rousseau believed that a general will, in this sense, exists in every community or association.

No doubt, men can live and work together and yet no general will common to them all arise among them. In the Nazi extermination camps, the killers and the killed lived and worked together; the victims were not passive in the hands of their tormentors, they received orders and obeyed them; there were forms of intercourse between tormentors and victims possible only among rational beings. But they did not therefore form a community together, and there was no general will common to them. There can be no general will common to a group where some remain with the others only because escape is impossible, and do their bidding only because to obey brings lesser horrors than to disobey. If, however, it is not only force that keeps men together, if they are willing associates, if they all feel they *belong* to one community or group, then, however great the inequalities among them, there does exist a general will common to them. In other words, in every society or group, no part of whose members are the mere victims of another part, there are some common notions of justice and there is a sense of community.

But that is only one meaning of 'general will'. In that sense, there is a general will in almost every human society; whereas Rousseau also meant by the general will something much more rare than the common loyalties and ideas of justice which help to hold together nearly every group of men living and working with one another. He also meant by it the decisions taken in an assembly of equals from whose deliberations none are excluded, an assembly where every man casts his vote, uncommitted by decisions taken by some smaller group, where the citizen cannot persuade his compatriots to do what suits himself unless he can show how it also benefits them, where the very conditions of debate incline him to be public spirited and to acquire private interests which accord with the common interest. A man's conception of his own interest is always deeply affected by the values and opinions of the social groups he belongs to. Rousseau was concerned that the group having the greatest influence should be the entire political community and not any class or professional or partial association.

When Rousseau speaks of freedom as the creation of the general will, he means that men, when they take an equal, active, and thoughtful part in making the laws, come to desire justice (i.e. that every man should get his due) as much as their own good; to regard it as so constantly the means to their own good that they learn at last to want it for its own sake, and sometimes even to prefer it to their private ends. Equal and active participation in public business makes for virtue, which is the love of justice, and justice is the common good; so that the virtuous man, even though he sometimes has desires incompatible with justice, wants justice to prevail over all such desires. Justice is a supreme value to him, though not all his desires are compatible with it. Where men feel like this, they also feel that the laws which compel them to be just (should they be otherwise inclined), though they force them to do what they may not, at the moment, want to do, also prevent them from becoming what they would rather not be. These laws, being just because they are made by an assembly of equals, keep men – and I use this phrase to express a feeling and not to state a fact – 'true to themselves'.

If society, instead of depraving man, had developed as it should and had made man what he ought to be, the process of development might be described in these words: Men came together in the first place because it was for some reason necessary for them to help one another to satisfy needs which each man could no longer satisfy for himself; they then found that they could not work together unless each of them acted on the assumption that the needs of others were as important to them as his to himself; this co-operation became in time a habit and men learnt to consider the conditions of it (that is, the behaviour that made it possible) as enjoined upon them, not by maxims of prudence, but by rules of right; and at last, since no great inequalities emerged among them (and we are supposing that they did not), they learnt to prefer justice to the private ends it originally served. They became lovers of virtue, making a difference between the desires and emotions that helped them to live as they wanted to live (that is, as good citizens and virtuous men) and all their other passions. Their general preference for some over others among their passions caused them in time to feel thwarted by the passions which prevented their living as seemed good to them or becoming what they wanted to be; and so it became natural to them to consider the laws that maintained justice, because they satisfied those of their aspirations they valued most, as somehow more truly in accordance with their wills than the temptations to injustice they were sometimes liable to.

Rousseau never described this process as a whole, but he did, at one time or another, describe and approve all the stages that go to make it up.

I have pieced the process together because, in my opinion, it helps us to understand what Rousseau very probably meant by the general will; what he meant by the two (or, if you like, three, though the third derives from the second) most important doctrines he variously asserted when he spoke of it: that in every society men have a sense of justice; that they are nevertheless *habitually* just only when they take part as equals in the making of the laws, uninfluenced except by their own principles and by honest and free debate between them; and that, when they are habitually just, they look upon the laws freely made by an assembly of equals as better guides to conduct and more likely to satisfy them than their personal preferences.

Whether or not these doctrines are true, is open to dispute, but they are, I think, intelligible; and, though they are not simple, they are free from every taint of mysticism. They are what Rousseau meant, or at least the important part of what he can plausibly be supposed to have meant, by his doctrine of the general will. Together with the four principles discussed earlier (with which they partly overlap), they are the heart of his political philosophy. It would be impertinent to suggest that these doctrines are all that Rousseau intended to mean by the many words he used to describe the general will; I will say no more than that they seem to me to represent nearly all that is important and intelligible which can be fairly extracted from what he actually said.

They help to make clearer his conception of freedom, which appealed so strongly to Kant and the German Idealists. 'Whoever refuses to obey the general will will be constrained to do so by the whole body: which means nothing but that he will be forced to be free.' How are we to interpret this paradox? How can a man be forced to be free? As Rousseau himself admits, the 'will cannot bind itself'; or, in other words, our wanting something at one time is no warrant that we still want it at another. If we have agreed to something in the past, it does not follow that we now want to abide by the agreement. How, then, when we are forced to abide by it, can it be said that we are 'forced to be free'?

If we take the words literally, they make nonsense. To get sense out of them, we have to interpret them in a larger context, in the light of the whole doctrine of the general will. The general will is the will to justice, the will to treat the good of others as equally important with our own good. We can distinguish between two kinds of desires in ourselves: those in terms of which we create an idea of what is desirable in ourselves and others or of a life worth living or of a society worth having, and all our other desires. For example, I covet my neighbour's goods, but I also desire to deal justly by him. There is an important difference between these two desires, for I repudiate one of them and hold fast to the other. I desire to be just, but I do not desire to be covetous, though covetous I am. As a moral person I am my own judge. The law, if it helps me to behave as I should like to behave, helps me to be the sort of person I want to be; and at the same time it helps to maintain the kind of society I want to live in. This conception of law as a means to moral freedom is not the conception of Hobbes and the Utilitarians, or of Locke and the school of Natural Law; for it does not say that law preserves freedom merely by preventing people getting in each other's way or by protecting their rights.

Freedom, Rousseau tells us, is obedience to a law we prescribe to ourselves. How then does the general will give expression to a law I prescribe to myself? When I vote against a law, I do not literally choose it as a rule to guide my conduct. If, however, I freely take part in the deliberation and the voting, if no combination is formed to impose its will on me, if I have the right to re-open the question provided I do so in the proper way, then I shall probably want the law to be enforced, even though I voted against it. I shall want this, not merely because the enforcement of law makes for my security, but because I want justice done. I shall acquire greater confidence in the wisdom and justice of the community than in my own, and when I find myself differing from the community, I shall think it probable that I am wrong. I shall not think this because the community is more powerful than I am, but because it allows me and everyone else a free and equal part in the making of the laws, taking full account of me and of everyone. It is likely that the laws as a whole – and I will have voted for many of them – will accord with my deepest convictions about how I and other people ought to behave. Though I shall still sometimes be tempted to break a particular law, I shall look upon the laws in general as rules of right. They will accord with the rules I think I ought to obey, with the rules I make my own. They are my own, not because I invented them, or because I deliberately chose each of them in preference to others, but because I now believe that I ought to obey them. Under the spur of passion I may deliberately break a rule which I believe to be a rule of right; but I cannot believe that it is a rule of right without wanting to be the sort of person who obeys the rule. Even when I am deliberately dishonest, I would rather be an honest person than a dishonest one.

But if I take no part in making the laws, if I am merely obliged to obey laws made by others, or to conform to customs I am powerless to change, the less likely it is that the rules I am required to obey will be rules I accept in conscience because they appear to me to be rules of right. When, therefore, I am constrained to obey them, or am punished for disobeying them, I shall be much more inclined to look upon myself as the victim of others.

This is, I think, too simple an account of the matter. Rousseau greatly exaggerates our aversion to laws imposed on us from without, and perhaps also exaggerates our aptness to consider them just when we have taken part in making them. To a much greater extent than he was inclined to admit, a man's sense of justice is determined by the

because of my son. of how the community decides: never clsd, against anyone.

In my deeper interest to accept the present compromise of my interest, because it is open, even here, to consider interest. I'm enclosed in the dec. even though it doesn't go my way laws and customs of his community, even when he takes no part in making them and cannot change them. We acquire our notions of right and wrong much more because we grow used to a discipline which makes us fit for society than because we take a hand in deciding what kind of discipline we shall have.

Yet there is this to be said in Rousseau's favour: as men's attitude to law changes, as they cease to regard it as eternal and as coming to them from a higher than human source, as statute law supersedes custom, they grow less inclined to accept as just rules which they have had no hand in making and have no power to alter. The more they come to distinguish law from justice, the more concerned they are that law should be just; and the greater this concern, the more it matters to them that they should be consulted about the law. The man who has learnt to make a difference between positive law and justice is disposed to put a high value on moral freedom, on not being obliged to do what he thinks is wrong. For to make this difference is to imply that there are, or may be, better rules than the ones actually enforced; and the man who thinks this is already well on the way to demanding that what he is required to do shall accord with his sense of what is right.

When men come to look upon law as man-made, then, those among them who have had nothing to do with the making of it are apt to see in it the will of others imposed on themselves. While law still seems to them the will of God, to which their rulers are also subject, though they see themselves as bound by a will external to their own, it is the will of an omnipotent Being to whom they owe everything. Clearly, they are then not free, in Rousseau's sense of freedom, for they are bound by a law *not* prescribed by themselves; and yet they are not aware that they lack this freedom, for the idea that they could be makers of law has not occurred to them. But when they begin to look upon law as made by man, they are tempted to ask, Why should we be bound by the will of other men?

This is the question which all the contract theorists tried to answer; but Rousseau stands out among them as the man who took that question most to heart and made the most uncompromising answer. We must have law, we must be bound, but we must be bound willingly, we must bind ourselves, which we can only do if we actually take part in making the law. 'The law is the will of the community, it is the public will touching on matters of common interest.' This was the formula offered in answer to the question, and it was not invented by Rousseau. He is memorable, not as the inventor of the formula, but as the man who tried valiantly to take it literally. All the contract theorists before him, in one way or another, evaded the issue they claimed to settle; he refused to evade it, and in the uncompromising attempt to settle it put forward, if not a viable scheme of government, at least a new conception of freedom.

For reasons we have already discussed, Rousseau believed that free-dom is not to be attained except in small, simple and self-sufficing com-munities. But history teaches us that the demand for freedom, as Rousseau defines it, has not arisen in such communities but in others which are much larger and more intricate. The small and simple community changes slowly and almost imperceptibly; it is the com-munity where custom reigns and the legislator is looked upon more as an interpreter than a maker of law. Rousseau admired both Athens and Sparta (and Sparta more even than Athens); he admired two com-munities which never aspired to democracy as he understood it, and never conceived of his kind of freedom. Neither Plato nor Aristotle, the two great apologists of the small and compact community which Rousseau loved, shared his idea of freedom. In the ancient world, it was the Stoics and the Christians who came closest to sharing it, and they flourished in a cosmopolitan and autocratic empire. And in the modern world, where the demand that men should live under laws prescribed by themselves is widely popular, the type of community in which alone, according to Rousseau, this demand can be met, is clearly impossible. What, then, must we conclude: that the demand for freedom arises only where social conditions forbid its achievement, or that Rousseau was mistaken about the conditions?

If Rousseau had contemplated these two conclusions, he might have preferred the first to the second. For all that he proclaimed the natural goodness of man, he was also much given to pessimism. And certainly, it would be unreasonable to reject the first conclusion on no better ground than its being depressing. Nevertheless, there are good grounds for preferring the second. Let us not forget that Rousseau is not only concerned that men should take part in making the law, he is con-cerned also that they should be able to live according to principles which they can critically and willingly accept. He is concerned that they should be (to use an expression which is true to his meaning though he does not himself use it) morally autonomous. He dis-tinguishes, in the second chapter of Book IV of the *Social Contract*, the *constant will* of the members of the community, their will as citizens, from their particular wishes, and he calls this *constant will* the general will in them. This constant will is the desire for the common good, for justice. It is here spoken of as the desire of every citizen. So the general will, as Rousseau sees it, does not consist merely of those decisions of the assembly which happen to be just; for, if it consisted of them alone, there could conceivably be justice in the State though no one cared for justice for its own sake. Every man might vote from a selfish motive and yet the decision might be just. But Rousseau's doctrine is that, if men are to be free, the general will must be present *in* them; or, in other words, they must have what he calls a constant will. In order to be free, it is not enough that they should take part in making the law; it is also necessary that they should have a constant will in keeping with the law.

⟨Rousseau believes that, unless men take part in making the law, they will not acquire a constant will, and so cannot have freedom⟩ If he is right, then it follows that to take a direct part in the making of law is a necessary, if not a sufficient, condition of freedom. But he is probably mistaken. What matters, if a man is to be free, in Rousseau's sense of freedom, is that he should have a constant will and be able to live in accordance with it, that he should know justice and cherish it, and be able to do what seems just to him and not be forced to do what seems unjust. If the law is contrary to his constant will (or, as we might put it, following Kant, his moral will), he cannot be free; but it is not obvious that he must take part in making the law to ensure that it is in keeping with his moral will, nor yet that, if he does take part, it will be in keeping.

Rousseau is no doubt right in thinking that the constant or moral will is a product of social intercourse, but his belief that that intercourse must be largely political, and political in the way he describes, is mistaken. The man who has a moral will, who is concerned for justice, will want the law to be just, and his ideas of justice will be, at least in part, the fruit of his reflections on established law and custom. Being moral in the sense understood by Rousseau (that is to say, being a man who does not do what is required of him merely from fear or inertia or desire for the good opinion of others), he will necessarily also be critical of himself and of the law. He will want to have his say, he will want to count for something, he will want to be consulted; he will want this, moreover, not for himself alone, but for others also. He will want to live in a community where the makers of law are responsible to those required to obey it. But he will not want only this, he will also want other things not to be had in the small, simple, self-sufficient community in which alone people can make their own laws. Provided the system is one which allows him and others to have their say, either individually or through groups created for the purpose, and provided those who make the laws (and administer them) have a strong motive for taking notice of demands and opinions freely expressed, he may be satisfied. True, he will not believe that all the laws are just, but he may come to believe that the way in which they are made is substantially just; that is to say, about as just as it can be considering how many and how various are the interests that have to be taken into account. Sometimes he will obey the law under protest, he will obey it wishing it were different, and yet he may still obey it because he thinks it right he should do so. He may become, on rational grounds, strongly attached to the political system and think it wrong to weaken it by disobedience even to a law which seems to him unjust, except in extreme cases.

He will not be perfectly free. Indeed, far from it. He would be free only if the laws accorded entirely with his beliefs about justice, which they are never likely to do. Men who think for themselves (and this is what Rousseau wants them to do) are most unlikely to hold exactly the same opinions about what is just. Whoever has a moral will is almost certain to find obstacles to it, not only in himself, but also in established law and convention. But this is as true when he takes a direct part in making the law as when he does not. At least Rousseau provides us with no sufficient reason for thinking otherwise. Even in the small compact community imagined by Rousseau, citizens who vote against a decision accept it willingly, much less because they are convinced that, being in the minority, they are probably wrong, than because they believe it is right that decisions should be reached in that way. The virtue of the system is that it inclines men to accommodate their wishes to other people's because they think they ought to do so and not merely because they find they must do so. It may also be true that, because they are inclined this way, they are the more likely to conclude that when they are in the minority they are wrong; but this (so it seems to me) is more doubtful. They willingly obey because they have been consulted, because their voice has been heard, because the system is such that their wishes and interests count in general for as much as other people's, even though, on this occasion, the decision has gone against them. They willingly obey less because they believe that the law is just than because they believe that it has been justly made.

No doubt, persons accustomed to democracy and who have reflected upon it may come in time to have strong doubts about their own wisdom as well as other people's. As they look back on their past opinions, they may conclude that they were as much or more mistaken than the persons they disagreed with; they may grow attached to the system because experience has convinced them that the decisions taken under it are, on the whole, wiser and more just for being taken in the way they are. But this reappraisal of past decisions goes on as much among those who voted with the majority as among those who voted the other way. It may well be true that when equals take decisions in common their confidence in their collective wisdom increases with time; the more experience has taught all of them that they have been unwise and unjust in the past and may be so again in the future, the more considerately they are apt to deal with one another. Free discussion between equals probably does have some, if not all, of the effects imagined by Rousseau; and this, if it is true, is strong evidence in favour of democracy.

But it is not stronger evidence in favour of the direct democracy described in the *Social Contract* than of other kinds. Democracy does not require that everyone should take a direct part in legislation; it requires only that the discussions and negotiations which lead up to the making of law should be spread wide enough to ensure that all important interests and points of view find free expression and are taken into account, and that there should be general confidence that this is so. It requires, not that everyone should take a part in forming the ' political will' of the community, but that those who do take part should speak for all the sorts and conditions of men in the community, and should have the confidence of those they speak for. Provided these conditions hold, it is just as likely as in a direct democracy that the laws will accord with the *constant* or *moral* wills of the citizens. Admittedly, it is not nearly as likely in a representative democracy as Rousseau says it is in the kind of democracy he favours, but then he greatly exaggerates the merits of that kind.

There is another freedom important to sophisticated man besides moral freedom, and Rousseau, where he does not neglect it, disparages it. Man in society acquires, as Rousseau says, a constant will; he acquires moral principles and, to the extent that he takes them seriously, wishes to live up to them. He finds that his passions, natural and acquired, move him to act against his principles, and he therefore aspires to self-discipline. When he curbs his passions so as not to act unjustly, he feels that he is free, not because his passions are in general weaker than his desire to be just, but because he would rather be a just man than a man whose passions make him unjust; he identifies himself with a part of himself against another part. But love of justice is not all that man acquires in society. He also acquires aspirations which are not moral, and are therefore not what Rousseau understands by a constant will, though they are in some ways similar to it. Man desires achievement; he sets up ideals and strives to realize them. These ideals need not be moral, and yet, if a man is to realize them, he will need as much self-discipline as when he aspires to be just or a good citizen. No matter what a man sets his heart upon, he must make sacrifices to obtain it, and his passions will sometimes stand in his way. Even if he is self-centred and ambitious, as many artists and men of letters are, reason in him may ' rule' the passions; that is to say, he may succeed in imposing upon himself, deliberately, systematically, and over long periods of time, restrictions which serve his ambition. He will be no more a slave to his passions than the just man; for ambition, as much as justice, is possible only in a rational creature who consciously prefers some things to others.

In every society men aspire to other things besides justice or the common good; they have, to use the idiom of Rousseau and Kant, a rational will which is not merely a constant will or a moral will. They admire other than morally good behaviour, they have standards of excellence which are not moral standards. Though it may be true, as Rousseau tells us, that it is not as a mere creature of appetite, but as a creature capable of rational behaviour and having notions of excellence,

that man comes to conceive of freedom and to cherish it, it is not true
that he is free only to the extent that he can live in conformity with
his constant or moral will. He is free to the extent that he can live
as seems *good* to him, and what he thinks good depends on much
more than his moral principles. It depends, as the sociologists say,
on the *values* he accepts, which are only in part moral; it depends,
not only on his ideas about how men ought to behave, but also on his
ideas about (what is worth doing or having.) Man is an artist, an
enquirer, and a lover of power and distinction as well as a moralist;
and his concern for freedom springs also, and largely, from aspirations
which are more properly called aesthetic, intellectual or political than
moral. That man has such aspirations, Rousseau does not deny, but he
has little sympathy for them and takes almost no account of them in
his doctrine of freedom.

Since man aspires to much more than justice and virtue, it may be
that he cannot be satisfied in the small and compact republic described
by Rousseau; it may be that he puts a high value on the much greater
opportunities which are to be had only in larger, looser and more
varied communities. His attachment to such communities may, of
course, be partly due to the causes suggested by Rousseau, to his clinging to vices born of vanity which flourish in such communities, to
insatiable desires acquired in a corrupt environment; but it also has
other causes not less important. He may have a larger conception of
freedom than Rousseau's; he may want what is not to be had in a self-
sufficing and simple community small enough to allow all its members
to take a direct part in making the laws. If he understands what are
the conditions of having what he wants, he comes to accept them; he
comes to accept, and even to value, the legal and political system most
likely to ensure that the rulers of a large community take into account
the needs, the moral sentiments, the aspirations and ambitions of their
subjects. In that case, modest though his own part in that system may
be, he takes it seriously and is a responsible citizen. He is as close to
having a rational political will as the citizen of Rousseau's ideal State.
He does not obey the law from fear only or inertia or self-interest; he
obeys willingly knowing that by so doing he strengthens a political
order which is a condition of the freedom precious to him. Contemplating the State imagined in the *Social Contract*, he might express his
feelings about it in these words: 'I can see that men having only such
aspirations as meet with Rousseau's approval might be happy in such
a community. But I aspire to other things, which are not rooted in
vanity, and Rousseau has said nothing to show that my aspirations are
irrational in the sense that they cannot be reconciled one with another
or must bring me into conflict with other people. I could not be happy
after the fashion of his citizens unless I ceased to be what I now am
and became what I do not wish to be.' He might look upon man's

condition in Rousseau's imagined community much as Rousseau says that the citizen of that community looks upon the condition of man in the state of nature. Man, in that state, had only independence and not freedom, and he had the only kind of happiness of which he was capable. Rousseau tells us that, though there was nothing wrong with him, there were things possible to him, which he could not then know, but which, when he came to know them, would make him think the state of nature well lost.

It is a neat but misleading phrase that freedom is obedience to a law we prescribe to ourselves. If the law we have in mind is the moral law, it is not literally true that we prescribe it to ourselves. We do not decide that there shall be such a law. It arises out of social intercourse between men, it is an effect of their behaviour towards one another, but they do not decide what it shall be. Even when a man, as the saying is, 'accepts it inwardly' or 'makes it his own', he does not prescribe it to himself. He is at first compelled to obey, and then acquiescent, and eventually willing. The process whereby men acquire moral principles has very little indeed in common with legislation. If the moral law is a law we prescribe to ourselves, then it is so only in a metaphorical sense.

And if the law we have in mind is a law deliberately made by men, we cannot define freedom as obedience to it. Though we have ourselves taken part in making it, it does not follow that we willingly obey it whenever we are required to do so. Even though we grant that it is involved in man's being a moral creature that he wants to be the sort of person who chooses to act rightly (though in fact he often chooses to act wrongly), and that the law, where it accords with his moral principles, helps him to be that sort of person, we cannot say that his freedom consists in obeying the law. We cannot say it even though he himself took part in making the law. For, at the time that he is required to obey the law, he may not want to obey it. Moreover, even if he wants to obey it, his freedom does not consist in his obedience; it consists in his being able to do what he wants. We must not say that obedience to law is freedom but rather that law promotes freedom to the extent that it makes it easier for men who have aspirations requiring self-discipline (among which the desire to be moral is only one) to achieve what they aspire to. We can say also that law is the more likely to promote freedom in this way for being made by the persons required to obey it or (and here we part company with Rousseau) by persons responsible to them. And, finally, we can agree with Rousseau that it is only as a rational creature capable of self-discipline that man comes to conceive of freedom and to put a high value on it, though we insist against him that man does not discipline himself only, nor even always primarily, in the name of morality.

Yet Rousseau's account of freedom, though it cannot be accepted in the form he gives it, is still the most valuable part of his moral and social theory. In the *Discourse on Inequality*, and in other places, he explains how man, not yet formed by society, man in the state of nature, a mere creature of appetite, easily puts up with the restrictions that nature places on him. If he cannot get what he wants, he soon ceases to want it, unless he needs it to keep him alive. His desires are free of vanity and are unconnected with rational purposes. He is independent, but he is not free. When he is thwarted, he has no sense of being deprived of what is owing to him, of lacking freedom. He has as yet no idea of freedom; he wants, not freedom, but food, drink and shelter. Only as a rational creature, self-conscious and conscious of his relations with others, does man acquire the idea of freedom. But by then he has ceased to be a mere creature of appetite, who seeks to satisfy each of his desires while it is upon him, giving no thought to the future; he is a creature aware of his own preferences and with a more or less stable way of life. He is housed, both his body and his mind; he has seen himself reflected in many mirrors, he has had judgements passed upon him by others and by himself. He is less concerned that he should be able to do whatever is prompted by his appetites than that he should achieve his enduring purposes; and it is then that he claims freedom. But he must live in a community with others, which he cannot do unless he abides by rules which serve their purposes as well as his. Therefore he cannot be free unless his purposes are in keeping with the rules; and this they are the more likely to be, the stronger his respect for the rules, his desire that they should be obeyed by everyone, including himself. For the rules will then inform his purposes. In the social philosophy of Rousseau justice and freedom are not externally related, as they are for Hobbes or the Utilitarians. Justice is more than a means to freedom, more than a set of rules to prevent our getting too much in each other's way. The law we critically and willingly accept, the law 'we prescribe to ourselves', profoundly affects our conception of a life worth living; and the rights we put a special value on and call freedom are largely determined by that conception.

IV. HOW ROUSSEAU CONCEIVED OF EQUALITY AND WHY HE THOUGHT IT IMPORTANT

In the Middle Ages it had been the fashion to explain both the institution of property and inequality of wealth as effects of corruption. If men were innocent, they would no more need property than government; there would be neither rich nor poor, neither ruler nor ruled. But for several generations before Rousseau, political thought had been loosening its ties with theology. The idea that property and government are effects of sin and remedies for it had steadily been losing ground. The contract theorists had taught that men first set up government for their own convenience; Locke had treated property as a natural right prior to government, and Hume had explained it as an institution which arose among men because they had found it their interest to have stable rules governing the use and transference of external objects. In the eyes of Locke and Hume property and inequality were neither effects nor causes of corruption.

In the eighteenth century, as never before, men had come to believe in progress. They were exhilarated by the quick growth of their knowledge, their power over nature, and their wealth. Mandeville, Hume and the Utilitarians in Britain, and the Encyclopaedists in France, welcomed this great accumulation of knowledge and wealth. They did not deny that knowledge and wealth, for all that they increased so rapidly, were still confined mostly to the minds and pockets of only a small part of the community; they even admitted sometimes that men were more unequal in their day than they had been in the past. But this inequality did not disturb them, for they believed that all classes were gainers from the increase in knowledge, wealth and power, though some gained more than others.

Rousseau reversed the mediaeval argument: instead of saying that inequality is an effect of man's corrupted nature, he said that corruption is an effect of inequality. He agreed with Hume that property is a social institution, and with both Hume and Locke, that it is a means to freedom. There was to be private property even in the ideal society described in the *Social Contract*. He agreed also with Locke and Hume that government serves above all to protect property. But he believed, as they did not, that most governments were in fact much more useful to the rich than to the poor. We have seen how, in the *Discourse on Inequality*, he attributed the first establishment of government to a specious argument of the rich, whereby they induced the poor to adopt an expedient from which they stood to gain much more than the poor. That part of the *Discourse* might almost be called an early version of the Marxian doctrine that the prime function of government is to protect the propertied classes against the classes having little or no property. Only in the ideal society, the society of equals, is the defence of property equally the interest of all.

How, according to Rousseau, does inequality corrupt? It magnifies vanity and its evil effects, and it also makes the poor subservient to the rich. It creates such differences between men, exalting some and debasing others, that they are driven to care more for how they stand in relation to one another than for getting what will satisfy them. At the end of the *Discourse on Inequality*, he says that it is ' to the burning desire to have others speak of us, to the passion to distinguish ourselves . . . that we owe what is best and what is worst among men:

. . . that is to say, a multitude of evil things and a small number of good ones'. Sometimes Rousseau gives us to understand that inequality intensifies vanity, and sometimes that it makes vanity more dangerous. Since these assertions do not exclude one another and might both be true, we can assume, there being no evidence to the contrary, that he accepts them both. Inequality adds to our vanity, but, even if it did not, even if we were no vainer as unequals than we would be as equals, inequality would still make our vanity more harmful to others and to ourselves. Therefore, as inequality grows, the evil effects of vanity grow faster even than vanity itself.

Where men are unequal, every man strives to be superior to others and resents being inferior to them. But, since everyone cannot be superior to everyone else, this striving for superiority is mostly unavailing; men do not achieve what they aim at. They are not satisfied, and yet are moved to behave in ways which are hurtful and humiliating. If they were nearer equality, they would be less concerned to establish superiority and to avoid inferiority; they would be less competitive and less envious, and instead of striving for status would strive for what was more likely to satisfy them.

We have seen that Rousseau attributes to vanity some good effects as well as many bad ones. This explains, no doubt, why he devotes so many pages and so much eloquence to the bad effects and so few to the others. But, despite so many and such harsh pronouncements against vanity, Rousseau admits that it is inevitable. Men are without vanity only in the state of nature, where they lack self-consciousness and have no standards of excellence. In society their happiness always depends greatly on how others think of them, and Rousseau speaks of this concern for reputation as if it were either the same thing as vanity or closely related to it. For example, in his *Project of a Constitution for Corsica*, he says: 'The prime motives which move men to action, if we consider the matter carefully, come down to two, concupiscence [*volupté*] and vanity; moreover, if you take from the first all that belongs to the second, you will find that, in the last analysis, almost everything is reduced to vanity alone. . . . But vanity is the fruit of opinion, is born of it and feeds upon it. Whence it follows that who controls the opinions of a people controls their actions. The people strive for things in proportion to the value they place upon them; to show them what they ought to value is to tell them what they ought to do.'[1] He then continues, only a few lines further on: 'Opinion, when it puts a high value on the frivolous, produces vanity, but, when it turns upon what is in itself great and noble, it produces pride.'[2]

Here, as in so many other places, Rousseau fails to make his meaning clear. Are vanity and pride in themselves the same emotion, differing

[1] Vaughan, op. cit., Vol. II, p. 344, my translation.
[2] Ibid., Vol. II, p. 344.

only in their causes?⟩Are they both equally self-esteem, though the
first arises from a mistaken judgement while the second does not? Does
the vain man take pride in qualities or accomplishments which are
worthless? And is the proud man vain of that about himself which
really has value? Sometimes, as in the last sentence quoted, Rousseau
speaks as if this were what he believed. Yet it goes against the spirit
of most of his teaching, for he says in many places that vanity is the
root of unhappiness and consists in the desire to be admired by others
and to impress them.

We ordinarily speak of pride, when we distinguish it from and
prefer it to vanity, in ways which suggest that the proud man has
stable principles while the vain man has not. The proud man is above
all his own judge; if he falls below his own standards he is ashamed,
even though others do not condemn him. Of course, he is not unaffected by their judgements, especially if they share his principles and
know the facts. The proud man shrinks from the adverse judgement of
his moral peers, of those whose standards are his own, and sometimes
his pride will make a coward or a hypocrite of him. But the need to
meet his own standards, to avoid the shame of being condemned in
his own eyes, may give him courage and sincerity. And he will be little
affected by the blame or praise of persons whose judgement he does not
respect; he will be independent of them.⟩But the vain man does not
have stable principles, or has them so weakly that he fears to abide by
them when doing so would make his neighbours blame or despise him.
He is, as the proud man is not, the slave of opinion; he is driven to
seek admiration by conforming to whatever tastes happen to be
fashionable in the circles in which he moves. He is indifferent to
other men's judgement only if those men are out of fashion. Both the
proud man and the vain man are creatures formed by society; the
proud man does not, any more than the vain one, acquire his principles
and tastes in solitude. But the proud man is independent in a way in
which the vain man is not: he has strength of character and is ready
to ignore or to flout opinion which does not conform with his principles.
This, I think, is the distinction between pride[1] and vanity suggested by
a common use of those words, and it is also in keeping with Rousseau's
account of how society, by exalting men's vanity, corrupts them, producing in them ambitions difficult or impossible to satisfy and making
them rivals for admiration.

No doubt, pride (even when it is not arrogance) can be dangerous
and vanity harmless. Indeed, the proud man, when he is dangerous, is

[1] Of course, pride is often condemned, especially by theologians, but I am here
considering the sort of pride held to be superior to vanity, and am saying no
more about it than seems necessary to explain Rousseau's meaning. It can be
(and indeed has been) argued that pride is worse than vanity: the man who
defies God or the Church is held to be *proud* rather than *vain*.

apt to be more so than the vain one. Pride can be as improper, as misplaced, as any other passion; a man's self-respect may depend on his living up to principles harmful to himself and to others. He may be deeply ashamed of what it would be better that he were not ashamed of. Nevertheless, it may be that pride is necessary to the happiness of a moral being as vanity is not; it may be that society cannot do without it if its members are to find satisfaction in it and to be well disposed to one another. Certainly, Rousseau believed that men, in order to be happy, must have stable principles and tastes and be able to lead a life in keeping with them. He believed that the stronger such principles and tastes in them, the less they are inclined to strive for superiority over others; what is then closest to their hearts is that they should have what they think desirable and be what they think is worth being, and not that they should be preferred to others.

It must be admitted that Rousseau never succeeds in making it clear just what he means by vanity and just why he condemns it. Sometimes he speaks with disfavour of all self-esteem resting on the good opinion of others, while at other times he recognizes that, unless men were moved by the desire to be well thought of, they would not be educable. Man, he tells us, becomes self-conscious in society, acquiring standards of excellence and the desire to excel. If it were not so, he would not be sociable, moral, and rational. Though, as we have seen, Rousseau sometimes speaks of Emile's education as if it consisted in his tutor's protecting him from all social influences, so that he should reach physical, intellectual and moral maturity in a completely natural way, it really consists in his tutor's protecting him from harmful social influences. Emile does not acquire intellectual and moral independence by being taught to think for himself regardless of the good opinion of others; he desires his tutor's good opinion, he desires to excel by standards which he takes from another knowing that they come from another. He is concerned for his reputation, and could not become morally and intellectually independent unless he were so. Rousseau both recognizes this, when he describes Emile's education, and denies it when he condemns all vanity, all self-esteem resting on the good opinion of others, without qualification. It was seldom his way to weaken the effect of his condemnations by qualifying them at the time he made them. He preferred another method; he preferred to unsay in one place what he had said in another. He sacrificed, at least temporarily, the truth as he saw it to rhetoric. I do not say that he did this deliberately; but he did it often, to the great confusion of his readers. Thus we find him at one time condemning self-esteem as vanity, and at another speaking well of it as pride. Thus too we sometimes find him saying that men must be governed through the control of opinion, and at other times setting great store by independence of mind. And though these beliefs can perhaps be reconciled with one another, Rousseau does not see the need to reconcile them. He either contradicts himself or appears to do so, and seems not to notice the contradictions. Nevertheless, he does sometimes provide us in his own writings with arguments to resolve his paradoxes.[1] What he tells us about the education of Emile does enable us to see how he might have distinguished vanity from pride, if he had ever troubled to do so. For Emile, though without false pride, is certainly not without pride. He is not without self-esteem; he has a proper and firm sense of values, and his self-respect depends upon his living up to standards which he has made his own but which are also products of education.

To ensure that men do have strong and stable principles and tastes, Rousseau does not look to education alone; he looks to education and to equality. A proper education teaches men to value what ought to be valued. Children seek to please, to gain approval; they are in their immaturity emulous, having as yet no principles or tastes of their own. We cannot expect them to have independence of judgement until they grow up, and so, since they cannot help but seek to imitate what they see admired around them, since their self-esteem depends entirely on the approval of others, since they are incapable of being their own judges or of questioning the judgements passed upon them, they have to be moulded by others. To put Rousseau's meaning in other words than his own, we have to use the vanity inevitable in children, and which is harmless if not allowed to get out of control, to create a proper pride in them, a pride which does not make them indifferent to reputation but only to the opinions of those who do not share their principles. Pride, though born of vanity, can serve to reduce vanity and to hold it in check.

But the social order must not be allowed to weaken the effects of a good education. It would be absurd to bring up children to respect principles which they cannot practise except at great cost to themselves.

[1] But I must not create the impression that Rousseau's paradoxes are usually resolved or that his contradictions are all more apparent than real. For example, in his doctrine of the general will, he insists that every citizen must think for himself and also says that, where there is such a will, it is likely that all will think alike. He wants both independence and uniformity of judgement, and yet does not really explain how the two are to be had together. Again, what he says of public education suggests that he thinks it more important that citizens should think alike than that they should think for themselves, whereas what he says of private education in *Emile* suggests that he cares above all for independence of judgement. True, he describes public education as it ought to be in a properly constituted State, while Emile is to be made incorruptible in a corrupt society. Does he then set store by independence of judgement only in a corrupt society? I do not think so. I suspect that he takes it for granted that, in a just society, citizens will be found to agree about most matters of importance even though they think for themselves. In his rich, but rather loose and shapeless, social philosophy, there are many things not properly thought out.

Extremes of poverty and wealth, distinctions of rank unrelated to ability and to services done to the community, magnify vanity and its evil effects. They create temptations difficult for even the properly educated man to resist. Inequality undoes much of the good done by a good education. It does even more; it lowers the quality of education. Children are taught to pay lip service to principles which their elders do not expect them to follow in their conduct; they are taught to be hypocrites. Therefore equality, though not a sufficient, is a necessary condition of happiness; it is not enough to abolish inequality, for there must also be a good system of education. But these two things go together: where inequality is great, education is unlikely to be good; and where education is not good men soon acquire passions and tastes which lead to inequality. The well-educated man cares little for wealth; it would seem absurd to him to seek to prove himself superior to others by acquiring greater riches than they have. He is not luxurious and does not advertise himself by a display of his wealth. As Rousseau puts it in the *Considerations on the Government of Poland*: 'So long as the great are luxurious, cupidity will hold sway in all hearts. What the public admires will always be an object of desire to private persons; and if it is necessary to be rich in order to be outstanding, the dominant passion will always be to get rich.' And on the next page we are told ' that simplicity of manners and of the trappings of life is less the fruit of law than of education '.[1]

Equality, in Rousseau's opinion, does not exclude hierarchy or require that no man shall be richer or poorer than another. There must be ranks in society; but men should move from the lower into the higher ranks only as they grow older and more is expected of them, or as their services to the community increase, or when they are elected to a public office. Every citizen should have property of his own and should be, economically, his own master. If men are to be their own masters economically, then some must be richer than others, for some will be abler or more fortunate. Where every farmer owns his own land and lives off it, some farmers will prosper more than others; but this does not matter so long as the rich farmers are not held to be socially superior to the poor ones. So long as distinctions of rank do not spring

---

[1] Vaughan. op. cit., Vol. II, p. 436 and p. 437. As the first passage quoted serves to show, Rousseau, though he puts so high a value on independence of judgement, on not being a slave to opinion, sometimes takes it for granted that most men always will be slaves to it. When he says that what the public admires will always be an object of desire to private persons, the private persons he has in mind are adults. He is not speaking here of the education of children. Clearly, he thinks that men can be influenced for their good through their vanity, for he recommends that they be so influenced. He advocates two courses without being aware how different they are: the reduction of vanity and the substitution for it of a proper pride, and the diversion of vanity from the pernicious to the beneficial.

from differences in wealth but rest on seniority or on services rendered
to the community, so long as mere wealth is not held in honour, Rousseau does not object to some men being richer than others. But where
wealth is held in honour, men are bound to put a value on what is
worthless, on what cannot satisfy; they strive to be as rich or richer
than their neighbours, and they live luxuriously to prove their wealth.
Vanity flourishes and with it all its worst effects.

Apart from magnifying vanity, inequality diminishes independence.
In the *Social Contract*, Rousseau says only that no man should be so
rich as to be able to buy another, nor any so poor as to be constrained
to sell himself; and he has in mind, not the danger of slavery, but of
political subservience. Every citizen must be an independent voter in
the popular assembly, he must not sell his own vote nor buy another
man's. But elsewhere Rousseau launches a more sustained and general
attack on inequality as the destroyer of independence. ' Whoever,' he
tells us in the *Project for Corsica*, ' depends on another and lacks
resources of his own cannot be free. Alliances, treaties, faith between
men, these can all bind the weak to the strong but never bind the
strong to the weak.'[1] He says also that ' everywhere where wealth is
dominant, power and authority are ordinarily separate, because the
means of acquiring wealth and the means of coming by authority, not
being the same, are rarely used by the same persons. It then appears
that power is in the hands of the magistrates, while in reality it is in
the hands of the rich. . . . Thus . . . some aspire to authority, to sell
the use of it to the rich and so get riches for themselves; while the
others, and the greater number, seek wealth directly, knowing that, if
they have it, they are sure to have power some day by buying either
authority or those in whom it is vested.'[2] In the article on *Political
Economy*, Rousseau sets forth in these words what he calls the social
compact between the rich and the poor: ' You need me, for I am rich
and you are poor; let us then make an agreement between us: I will
allow you the honour of serving me on condition that you give me what
little remains to you for the trouble I shall take in commanding you.'[3]
It proves the perversity of established society that the greater a man's
needs, the more difficult for him the process of acquisition, and that it
is precisely ' the superfluities of the rich which enable them to despoil
the poor of their necessaries '.[4] No socialist or communist of the next
century outdoes Rousseau in denouncing inequality of wealth.

Yet Rousseau was neither a socialist nor a communist. He wanted
every citizen to be a man of modest property, a man of independent

[1] Vaughan, op. cit., Vol. II, p. 308.
[2] Ibid., Vol. II, p. 346.
[3] Ibid., Vol. I, p. 268.
[4] From a fragment on *Luxury, Commerce and the Arts*. See Vaughan, op. cit.,
   Vol. I, p. 347.

means; he wanted him to be 'self-employed'. But equality does not maintain itself; and so we are told, in the eleventh chapter of Book II of the *Social Contract*, that 'it is precisely because the force of circumstance tends always to destroy equality that the force of the laws should tend always to maintain it'. How then should it be maintained? Rousseau suggests various devices, not always compatible with one another. In the *Political Economy*, having said that property is the most sacred of all rights, and in a way more important even than liberty because more necessary for the conservation of life, he goes on to say that a man's owning something while he is alive does not give him the right to decide who shall own it after he is dead. Yet he is reluctant to see property pass out of the family, and therefore, instead of drastically limiting the right of bequest, suggests heavy taxes on luxury goods.[1] In the *Project for Corsica*, written some ten years after the *Political Economy*, there is no trace of this earlier reluctance, and we are told that 'the laws concerning inheritance must always tend to restore equality, so that everyone has something and nobody has too much'.[2] All trade, but especially foreign trade, should be kept within narrow limits to ensure that not only Corsica as a whole remains virtually self-sufficing, but that each district in the island relies as much as possible on its own resources. The Corsicans will be the poorer for it; there will be no rich merchants and bankers among them and they will have no large towns. Instead, they will have independence, both national and personal. For the man who is his own master, be he farmer or craftsman, though he has needs which cannot be met by the products of his own and his family's labour, can procure the means to satisfy them at the local market, where he is as well placed as his neighbour when it comes to striking a bargain or fixing a price. Where buyers and sellers are for the most part either independent producers or local merchants well known to them, the terms of trade between all buyers and sellers are more or less equal. There are then no middlemen to control the market and to put producers in a position where they must sell their products on unfavourable terms.[3]

Not only is Rousseau's dislike of inequality as passionate as that of any socialist, it is also justified in much the same way. He agrees with the socialists about the evils which afflict society and about their principal cause, but disagrees with them about the remedy. He does not suggest the abolition of private property in the means of production, distribution and exchange, nor a planned economy, nor co-operative production; he says only that law and government must ensure that all citizens have enough property so that even the poorest

[1] Ibid., Vol. I, p. 259
[2] Ibid., Vol. II, p. 351.
[3] Though I have used here expressions not used by Rousseau, I have endeavoured to be true to his meaning.

of them are independent of the rich. ⟨He is not much of an economist, and many of the expeditions he suggests to achieve his purpose are open to serious criticism, even when his purpose is not questioned. Yet he does hold fast to one belief which he expresses time and again : / the mass of citizens can be economically independent only in a simple and predominantly agricultural society⟩ Freedom is not secure except among equals, and men are equals, not when they have the same incomes, but when each is economically his own master and no man is more dependent for his livelihood on another than that other on him.

The right to property is as sacred in the eyes of Rousseau as in Locke's eyes. Indeed, it is not Locke but Rousseau who applies this word *sacred* to this right.[1] Yet the right of property is differently conceived by Rousseau. What every man has a right to is not the product of his labour but as much property as will secure his independence. The sovereign community, whose legislative authority is unlimited, is made up of citizens who are men of independent property. So jealous is Rousseau of the right of property that he favours, both in the *Political Economy* and the *Project for Corsica* (where he treats of fiscal matters at greater length than in his other writings), the establishment of a public domain whose revenues are to defray the costs of government. This public domain would be worthless unless labour were applied to it, and so he proposes that citizens should be required from time to time to work on it. They should work for the State rather than pay taxes to it. This, he admits, would be an intolerable burden in large states, but in small self-governing communities it has good effects. It leaves the citizen complete master of his estate and yet brings it home to him that he owes service to the community. It preserves independence and enhances patriotism. This is what Rouseau says; though few, perhaps, will accept his reasons for preferring taxes in labour to taxes in money.

We have seen that inequality, in Rousseau's opinion, is an obstacle to political freedom because the citizen who depends on another for his livelihood will not follow his own judgement politically; he will speak and vote in the assembly to please whoever he depends on. But there is another reason why inequality stands in the way of freedom; it weakens men's devotion to the community and so makes it less likely that they will want what accords with the general will. Patriotism, we are told in the *Political Economy*, encourages virtue and 'every man is virtuous when his particular will conforms in all things with the general

[1] In only one place does Rousseau verge on communism, where he says in the *Project for Corsica* (Vaughan, op. cit., Vol. I, p. 337): 'Far from wishing the State to be poor, I would, on the contrary, have it own everything, and that each person should partake of what belongs to the community in proportion to his services.' There are also other ideas which Rousseau takes up in this way to drop them immediately: they do not affect his general philosophy.

will, [for] we want what those whom we love want'.[1] In the eyes of
Rousseau, the most admirable of all peoples were the Spartans and the
Romans, and nothing about them was more to be admired than their
patriotism, their devotion to the community. But devotion to the com
munity is devotion to its laws, its institutions, its traditions, to whatever makes it what it is; it differs both from love of our neighbours and
from love of justice. A man who is indifferent to most of his country-
men, taken individually, may yet be deeply attached to his country; a
man who is shocked by an injustice done to another man may at that
moment be unaffected by patriotism, for the victim of injustice may
not be a compatriot. The Englishman shocked by an injustice done to
a Jew in Germany may dislike both Jews and Germans. And yet – so
Rousseau would have us believe – patriotism deepens our sympathy
for our neighbours and our love of justice.

It is as members of a community to which we are devoted that we
learn to think of other men as neighbours and that we come to know
justice and to put a high value on it. The more equal the members of
a community, the deeper their sense of belonging to it; and the deeper
that sense, the stronger their love of justice and the quicker their sympathies for their neighbours. But where inequality is great, the rich
and the socially exalted look upon the community as their own; they
demand justice for themselves and for others placed as they are but
are not much put out by injustice done to inferiors, while the poor feel
themselves the victims of the community and their devotion to it is
weakened. In a footnote towards the end of the fourth book of *Emile*,
Rousseau tells of a splendidly attired stranger in Athens who, when
asked what was his country, answered 'I am one of the rich'.[2] This, in
Rousseau's opinion, is a very good answer, presumably because it implies that the rich have more in common with one another than with
their poor compatriots. In the *Considerations on the Government of
Poland*, he compares the vigour and generous instincts of the old
Greeks and Romans with what he is pleased to call the feebleness of
the French, the Russians, the English and other 'modern' nations.
Why, he asks, are we not men like the ancients? He gives several
answers, and among them this one, that we lack strong loyalties. The
legislators of antiquity, he says, 'looked for the ties which bind citizens
to their country and to one another', whereas we are divided from
one another by 'our prejudices, our base philosophy, and our passionate concern with little things', and we seek, not happiness, but
'the pleasures that separate and isolate men, making them weak.'[3]

The differences between what Rousseau advocated and what the
French revolutionaries practised are legion. Yet their motto, 'Liberty,

[1] Vaughan, op. cit., Vol. I, p. 250.
[2] *Emile*, Everyman edition, p. 313.
[3] Vaughan, op. cit., Vol. II, pp. 429-430.

Equality and Fraternity', expresses admirably the spirit of his philosophy, and he might even have been tempted to add (for he liked
echoes of sacred texts), 'and the greatest of these is Fraternity'. Patriotism, as he conceives of it, is very closely connected with fraternity;
for fraternity is the feeling that men have for one another, not because
they are drawn to one another as individuals, but because they are
attached to the group to which they all belong, be it a family or a
community or even mankind. Fraternity binds us to one another by
ties which are not oppressive, because the community in which we are
brothers does not so much lay duties upon us as have needs which we
are eager to provide for. Every enduring community must make large
demands on its members; but devotion to the community, far from
making the demands more burdensome, makes some welcome and
others easier to bear.

Rousseau, here as elsewhere, is too extreme. Patriotism can be strong
in communities where there are great inequalities. It was so in Rome
in republican times and in England in the eighteenth century. It is
not true that the more equalitarian a community, the more devoted
its members are to it. In a society where class barriers are breaking
down, men may become more ambitious, more competitive, more
ruthless, more restless and more envious than they were before. An
historian could collect, no doubt, much evidence to put against Rousseau's too simple thesis. And the political theorist, without troubling
to collect evidence, might put a more general objection; he might say
that some inequality is inevitable in any society, even the small agricultural community favoured by Rousseau, and that the degree of
inequality which men will tolerate must depend largely on their
habits and values. If they are brought up to accept their 'station in
society', they may, though that station is inferior, aspire to nothing
different and be devoted to the community they belong to. Or if they
live in times where ambition is thought good and opportunities are
varied, if (for example) they have the tastes and values which most
men have today, they cannot get what they aspire to except in large
and intricate societies where equality as conceived by Rousseau is
impossible, where there must be enormous inequalities of power, if not
of income. If they come to understand this, they may come to accept
with a good will inequalities condemned by Rousseau and yet be ardent
patriots. The idea of equality, of the rights and opportunities which all
men should have, varies from society to society. Except when equality
is taken to mean a complete identity of rights (and it is hardly ever so
taken), it is a concept logically posterior to others, and especially to the
idea of justice. If we want to know what at any time is understood by
equality, we have to ask what the rights and opportunities are of
which it is being said (or denied) that everyone should have them.

Yet there is much to be said in Rousseau's favour. Where men look upon the social order as unchanging and the work of Providence, they put up with inequality readily enough; they are reconciled to their position in society, they accept what God or fate has allotted to them. They are, no doubt, attached to their traditions and they recognize their obligations to their superiors and may feel loyalty to them. Yet they are usually not patriots; their deepest loyalties are to their families or to their neighbourhood and not to a political community which includes both them and their social superiors. They are not patriots in Rousseau's sense of the word, no matter how attached they may be to the corner of the world where they and their ancestors were born. A sixteenth-century peasant far from his native Anjou might have longed for it as poignantly as du Bellay exiled in Rome, but the *patrie angevine* of the poet, which was the *patrie* also of the peasant, was no political community. Devotion to a political community, patriotism as Rousseau speaks of it, is different from acceptance of a social order regarded as the work of Providence and different also from attachment to the ancestral home and region. It may be that devotion to a political community, a State, depends much more than other loyalties on men's feeling that they are, in some important sense, equals. For men are not likely to be devoted to the State they belong to unless they look upon it as a maintainer of justice, and if their idea of equality derives from their idea of justice, then the greater the inequality, the weaker their devotion to the State is apt to be. But this does not mean that devotion to the political community will not be general and strong unless men are equal in Rousseau's sense of equality; it means only that it is likely to be weak unless they are equal in the sense of equality which is in keeping with their notion of justice.

Moreover, men become 'political'; they come to make new claims on their rulers, claims which lead eventually to the emergence of a State, of a solid, intricate, well-defined structure of authority, out of a tribal or a feudal society, as their interests and their notions of justice change. There is no State unless there are citizens, unless there are men who take a different, and a much more hopeful and demanding, attitude to those in authority over them than is taken in a tribal or feudal society. Where society, in this sense, is *political*, and not tribal or feudal, where there is a State, men do not look upon the social order and the laws as the mere work or will of God; they look upon them as something which it is their right to alter the better to achieve their own just purposes. While the social order, which puts some men high above the others, is held to be the work of Providence, then even the most lowly placed in that order may find it easy to resign themselves to it and may acquire deep loyalties inside it, if not exactly to it. But where it is held to be something which men may alter for their own and other men's benefit, then the lowly placed inside it come to question it.

Why should it give so much more to some than to others? The
demand arises that inequality be justified by being shown to consist of
differences in rank or income which are necessary if the community
is to do for its members what they require of it, or to be inseparable
from freedom or from something else generally valued. It comes to be
widely held that, if it cannot be justified, it ought to be abolished. And
if it is not abolished, those who look upon themselves as sufferers from
it feel that justice has been denied to them. They are, in their own eyes,
members of a community which has refused to give them what it owes
to them, and their devotion to it is weakened.

All over the world men are becoming, as they never used to be,
citizens; they are acquiring hopes, fears and loyalties unknown, or little
known, to their ancestors. The demand for equality grows ever wider
and more insistent, and, though the equality demanded is not precisely
what Rousseau understood by the term, it has much in common with
it. It is everywhere agreed that men do not get the equality which is a
condition of freedom merely by being given the vote; they must also
have the security which enables them to use that vote independently
and responsibly. If they are to count politically, if they are to have a
mind of their own which makers of policy cannot afford to neglect,
they must be so placed economically that they are not much more
dependent on others than others are on them. They cannot be expected to be devoted to the community if the community takes little
account of them. These are principles which liberals and democrats in
the West, whose thinking, whatever their party allegiance, has been
deeply affected by socialist doctrines, share with Rousseau, who was not
a socialist, whose conception of democracy differs greatly from theirs,
and who cared nothing for the progress which most of them still believe
in. And these principles, despite their generality, are important.

Yet patriotism, as Rousseau often speaks of it, is not attractive to
western eyes, especially the eyes of a democrat who is also a liberal.
Not that liberals and democrats lack patriotism; devotion to the political community, to the constitution, and to the laws, is probably as
widespread and as deep in the liberal democracies as it is anywhere else.
Democrats who care for freedom are probably as willing as other men
to make great sacrifices in a common cause. But patriotism, as they see
it, is something better taken for granted than made much of. Rousseau
advocates a cult of the fatherland which to many liberals will seem
dangerous to liberty. He praises his heroes, the legislators and other
great men of antiquity, because they established national and exclusive
forms of worship, encouraged games and exercises to increase men's
vigour and self-esteem and to bring them closer together, and provided
spectacles to remind them of their country's past. 'A child', he says,
'in opening its eyes, must see the fatherland and must see it alone to
the day of its death. Every true republican sucks in love of the father-

land with its mother's milk: that is to say, love of the laws and of liberty.'[1] And he advises the Poles not to leave education to foreigners and to priests but to lay down the matter, the order, and the form of it by law. The Poles should establish scholarships for the sons of poor men, gymnasia for physical exercises and games played in common. Public education is better than private, and children are to be accustomed ' to order, equality and fraternity, to compete with one another, to live under the eyes of their compatriots and to desire public approval '.[2] There should be a college of magistrates to control the entire system of education.

Rousseau makes almost a mania of patriotism. It is surely enough that we should love our country, and altogether too much that we should be in love with it and conscious of it every day of our lives. This kind of obsessive patriotism undermines freedom, and so too does a form of education which teaches children what they owe to the community and what it expects of them but does not encourage them to follow their own tastes. This type of education differs from the education given to Emile in much more than merely being public while Emile's education was private; it does not seek to do for many children what Emile's tutor sought to do for only one child. Emile was brought up to be a man of independent judgement and a self-disciplined man; he was brought up to be active and free and therefore eventually became a good citizen, since the free man respects in others what he claims for himself. But these Polish children are to be brought up for the State; the direct aim of their education is to make good citizens of them. No doubt, Rousseau, who takes it for granted that who loves his fatherland and its laws is also a lover of freedom, believes that man cannot be a good citizen without also being a free man. Indeed, this is one of the central tenets of his creed. I have argued that there is a sense in which it is true, and that Rousseau, if he does not make this sense altogether clear, comes at times very close to doing so. The good citizen is also, doubtless, a patriot. We need not deny this. But we must insist, against Rousseau, that the type of public education described in the *Considerations on the Government of Poland* is unlikely to create patriots who are also free men. Admittedly, Rousseau's description is brief and equivocal, and an ingenious advocate might contend that it could be so interpreted as to avoid this conclusion; but this, surely, would be special pleading and not the most natural interpretation of Rousseau's actual words.

Though for patriotism Rousseau has the deepest admiration, he has nothing but contempt for the desire for national glory and aggrandisement. The too-great size of States is the first and principal cause of the unhappiness of mankind, and he advises the Poles to reduce their

---

[1] Vaughan, op. cit., Vol. II, p. 437.
[2] Vaughan, op. cit., Vol. II, p. 438.

frontiers. He is not, in the nineteenth-century sense, a nationalist; he does not put it forward as a principle that all Poles or all Corsicans should be members of the same State. He merely tells the Poles that they ought not to insist on retaining frontiers which bring many foreigners into the same State with them. He takes it for granted that the Corsicans do not want their island divided into several completely independent States, and is therefore content to advise its division into autonomous districts, each with its own popular assembly. Laws affecting only one district should be voted by its assembly, and laws affecting the whole island by all the district assemblies meeting separately. He also supposes that, since all Poles already belong to the same State, they will decide against having a State or States so small that this ceases to be true, and he therefore advises a federal Poland containing only Poles. But he says nothing to suggest that the Poles, if they were minded to it, would be wrong to form a number of independent Polish States.

On the contrary, he tells the Poles that they have two choices. They can choose to be a great European nation, like several others, or they can make a better choice. If they choose greatness, let them cultivate the sciences, the arts, commerce and industry, let them have regular armies, fortresses and learned academies, let them multiply the use of money and promote luxury. They will then become an avid, ambitious, servile and knavish people, and will be counted among the great Powers; they may even reconquer their lost provinces and perhaps also acquire new ones. They will then be able to say 'like Pyrrhus or like the Russians, that is to say, like children, when all the world belongs to me, I shall eat sugar.'[1] But if they make the better choice, they will lead simple lives within even narrower frontiers than they now have; they will not be admired nor reckoned among the great Powers. But they will have what the wise know is worth having, and the foolish do not envy them for having: they will have justice and liberty. They will even have security, being formidable without being dangerous; for who will be tempted to attack a country offering few spoils and defended to the death by resolute patriots?

V. THE ILLIBERAL LOVE OF FREEDOM

The rhetorical dealer in paradoxes is often the victim of his own eloquence. Rousseau who proclaimed his love of freedom so loudly has been accused – and nowhere more than in France – of being an insidious enemy of it. Did he not give to the popular assembly all the powers that Hobbes gave to the sovereign? Did he not leave the citizen helpless against the organized community? Was not what he advocated

[1] Vaughan, op. cit., Vol. II, p. 475.

even worse than the absolute government of Hobbes? For Hobbes
admitted that the subject always retains the right to resist the sovereign
who threatens his life. Besides, the monarch or the aristocratic senate,
however absolute their formal authority, must in practice take account
of the people's moods; their power is always smaller than it seems. But
Demos is apt to be the worst of tyrants, because there is nothing outside him to restrain him. Rousseau speaks of the 'total surrender of
each associate with all his rights to the whole community',[1] and says
that 'the sovereign power has no need to give pledges to the subjects,
because it is impossible that the body should wish to harm all its members, and we shall see later that it cannot harm any of them. The
Sovereign, by virtue of being what it is, is always what it should be.'[2]

It is on the strength of such texts as these that Rousseau is accused of
being an enemy of freedom. The accusation rests on a misunderstanding. Rousseau never speaks of the people as Hobbes does of the
sovereign; he never says that they have the right to command anything they please. He says only that provided certain conditions hold
in a popular assembly, any law made by the assembly is binding on
the entire community for which the assembly legislates.

The people are not sovereign merely by virtue of acting as one body;
they are sovereign only while they act as the body created by the
social contract is required to act, only while they act as an assembly of
equals with no parties or cliques to prevent free debate and voting.
Their sovereignty consists, not in the right to issue any rule, but
in the right to make any law; and a law, in Rousseau's sense of the
word, is a rule of a special kind. To say that the citizen has no
right against the sovereign is therefore not to say that he has no right
against the whole body of citizens, when they do not act in the way
which makes their acts sovereign acts.

If that body were to prevent the citizen taking part, on equal terms
with everyone else, in its deliberations, its act would be a breach of
contract, and therefore by definition not a sovereign act. The body that
is sovereign is so *only while it acts like a sovereign*. Rousseau so defines
sovereignty that the rights of the individual are included in the definition. The citizen does have inalienable rights: the right to take a full
and free part in the making of the laws; the right not to be faced in
the assembly by combinations intent on getting their own way; and
the right that the law shall not discriminate against him. If we bear all
this in mind, the ominous sentence, that 'the sovereign, by virtue of
being what it is, is always what it should be', begins to look harmless.
Rousseau is not to be classed either with Hobbes or Hegel; he has not
in mind actual States. Nor does he say that there could be, anywhere
in the world, a community such that it would be the duty of its mem-

[1] *Social Contract*, Bk. I, Ch. VI.
[2] *Social Contract*, Bk. I, Ch. VII.

bers to do whatever it chose to command; he says only that the decisions of the general will must be obeyed, which is by no means the same thing.

It is largely Rousseau's own fault that his doctrine of obedience has been so often misinterpreted. When he speaks of the sovereign, he uses some of the words and phrases used before him by Hobbes, whose purpose was quite different. Rousseau speaks as if the social contract brought into existence a corporate body against whom the individual has no rights, whatever it may do, whereas what he really means is that the individual has an absolute duty of obedience to that body provided it acts as it should do. The citizen has a right against that body that, when it claims sovereign authority over him, it shall indeed act as a sovereign. It is therefore wide of the mark to say, as some of Rousseau's critics have done, that the ideal State imagined by him is *totalitarian*. Rousseau so defines sovereignty that nobody in his ideal State, not even the popular assembly, can stand to the citizen as the government of, say, Fascist Italy or Nazi Germany (to speak only of totalitarian States which exist no longer) stood to its subjects. The popular assembly cannot silence the citizen; he is free to criticize any proposal brought before it, and, if the proposal is made law, is free to propose its repeal. The popular assembly is an organ of discussion and decision, not of propaganda; it does not seek to mould the minds of its members. Their minds are affected by what they hear and say inside it, but its decisions are never beyond question; for, if they were, it would not be sovereign. According to Rousseau, it is the present will of the people which is sovereign; but their present will cannot be known unless they are free to call in question their own past decisions. The sovereign might, perhaps, without ceasing to be sovereign, forbid criticism of its decisions outside the assembly, but it could not do so inside it and still remain sovereign. This is not merely a conclusion which the reader of the *Social Contract* can properly derive from Rousseau's definition of sovereignty; it is a conclusion reached by Rousseau himself, as is shown by his concern that the citizen should be a man of independent judgement. If the general will is to find proper expression, it is important ' that each citizen should come to his own opinion [*n'opine que d'après lui*] '.[1]

In Rousseau's State nobody can ever speak for the people except the people, and even they are sovereign only as an assembly of equals whose every member has the right against all the others that they shall not so act as to make his opinion count for nothing. This ideal may be unattainable but it is not totalitarian.

In several places Rousseau expresses his abhorrence of the doctrine that justice may rightly be denied to the individual to save the community. 'The pretext of the public good is always the most dangerous

[1] *Social Contract*, Bk. II, Ch. 3.

P*

scourge of the people. What is most necessary in a government, and perhaps most difficult for it, is a strict integrity in rendering justice to all.'[1] He says also that 'the security of the individual is so bound up with the public confederacy that, if it were not that allowance must be made for human weakness, this convention would by right be dissolved if there perished in the State only one citizen who might have been saved, or if only one were kept wrongfully in prison, or if only one lawsuit were lost with obvious injustice'.[2] The law, which is the will of all, may determine what service or sacrifice may be required of a citizen in an emergency, but every citizen at all times has the right against his compatriots that they shall not sacrifice him in disregard of the law, on the pretext that they do so for the public good.

But we must not go from one extreme to another; we must not call Rousseau a liberal because others have called him a totalitarian. There are both liberal and illiberal sides to his philosophy. In the chapter on *Civil Religion*, in the fourth book of the *Social Contract*, he argues that there are certain beliefs which men must have if they are to be reliable citizens: they must believe in a God who is powerful, intelligent, beneficent, and provident, in a life to come in which the just will be happy and the wicked punished, and in the sanctity of the social contract and of the laws. Locke, in his *Letter Concerning Toleration*, argues that atheists are not to be trusted and therefore not to be tolerated. For though nobody should be molested merely because he does not share other people's beliefs, no matter how dear those beliefs may be to those that hold them, the community may rightly refuse to tolerate persons whom it is not reasonable to trust; and atheists are not to be trusted because, not believing in God, they lack one of the strongest motives which make men trustworthy. Rousseau is hardly more illiberal in the chapter on *Civil Religion* than Locke in the *Letter Concerning Toleration*. For though he praises Hobbes for having wanted to unite Church and State, the 'two heads of the eagle', he stipulates that subjects are answerable to the sovereign only for those of their opinions which are important to the community, and then goes on to explain what those opinions are. They consist only of the beliefs contained in what he calls 'a purely civil profession of faith', and amount in practice to little more than the beliefs which a man would need to hold in order not to be an atheist in the eyes of Locke.[3]

---

[1] *Political Economy*, Vaughan, Vol. I, p. 254.

[2] Ibid., p. 252.

[3] Belief in a God indifferent to men, a God who neither rewarded the just nor punished the wicked, would do nothing to strengthen men's motives for acting in ways which make them trustworthy. Locke said nothing about belief in the sanctity of the social contract and the laws, but, given his reasons for not tolerating atheists, we can reasonably conclude what his attitude would have been to persons denying the obligation to keep the contract or to obey the laws.

Both Locke and Rousseau refuse toleration to atheists, and Rousseau differs from Locke merely in proposing that citizens who declare that they hold these minimal beliefs when in fact they do not should be put to death if their lie is discovered.

Yet Rousseau's position, though here scarcely less liberal than Locke's, is certainly less reasonable. Locke does not require subjects to declare publicly their adherence to the beliefs which he thinks necessary to security, he merely says that, if they openly reject them, they ought not to be tolerated. If there are beliefs necessary to security, it is important that people should hold them but not important they should profess them. For if they are to be excluded for not professing them, they are the more likely to profess them when they do not hold them. Rousseau's requirements encourage hypocrisy much more than Locke's do, and not the less so for the terrible punishment he proposes for the hypocrite in the unlikely event of his being found out.

If the just community is as precious to its members as Rousseau says it is, how is it that patriotism and public spirit are not enough to keep citizens faithful to the laws and to justice? It is understandable how someone holding, as Locke does, that governments are set up by men for their mutual convenience should want to reinforce men's motives for keeping faith with one another by having them believe in God. Prudence, taken merely as man's sense of what is to his own enduring advantage in this world, may not be enough to afford security: something more may be needed, and it is not surprising that Locke should seek it in the fear of God. But why would Rousseau seek it there, having quite other and deeper views about the social nature of man? That he should himself incline to religion is not surprising, but his belief that it is unlikely that men will be good citizens unless they have faith in God is not in keeping with what he says elsewhere about the bonds which hold men together in a just society. He would have been more consistent had he held that the more unequal and corrupt a community, the greater the need for religion to maintain security.

In the seventh chapter of Book IV of the *Social Contract*, Rousseau discusses censorship without condemning it; he has in mind, not censorship of the Press, but the supervision of morals. The censors give, as it were, official utterance to public opinion about private conduct; their purpose is to preserve or to purify morals by passing judgements on conduct for which citizens are not answerable to the courts. Rousseau has in mind the censorship in ancient Rome and perhaps also the practice of the Genevan Consistory. He admits that this kind of public supervision of private morals will be effective only when certain conditions hold, but he implies that it is desirable when they do hold. In his other writings he often speaks with approval of the strong pressure of public opinion on the citizen, and he wants Polish children 'to live under the eyes of their fellow-citizens and to desire public approval'.[1] In the *Letter to d'Alembert*[2] he argues that the opening of a theatre would help to corrupt the morals of the Genevese, and he repeatedly gives utterance to his mistrust of intellect and talent.

Rousseau was something of an obscurantist, and every obscurantist is illiberal. He had almost as strong a preference for flatness and the commonplace as John Stuart Mill had for variety and excellence. He praised virtue often and intelligence seldom, and even said that where there is virtue there is no need of talent. Men of talent are, he thought, apt to be heartless, self-centred and vain; and though the world may be the brighter for their presence in it, it is not the happier. For the talented not only often lack virtue, they also undermine it. They hold it in contempt and wither it at the root; they even make men ashamed of it. For the most part, when they moralize, they are sophists who seduce the simple and the sincere, diverting their minds from the truth. They are more than corrupt, they are also corrupters; for society, in its corruption, gives a scope to their talents, and they are eager to preserve the conditions which raise them above their fellows. In the greatest of French comedies, the genius of Molière serves only to make virtue, in the person of Alceste, ridiculous.

Rousseau respected passion but was easily put out by gaiety, unless it was simple; he was afraid of the quick-witted, the sophisticated and the elegant. He had sometimes suffered at their hands, and in the labyrinth of his mind their slights echoed again and again. He was deeply moved by his own ideas, and also mortified by his incapacity to put them easily into words. Other men's talents were oppressive to him, and he was silenced by them. He was most articulate when he was alone, in the privacy of his own mind, and yet he needed an audience. Men of talent, it seemed, were not only the natural enemies of virtue, but of Rousseau, the lover of virtue.

Rousseau spoke slightingly of the arts and sciences. Though he must himself, being one of the great writers of his age, have known the excitement of the artist (an excitement which is in itself quite free of vanity, however vain artists may be), he set no value upon it; he did not see in it, any more than in the excitement of the scientist or discoverer, a moment of excellence in humanity. The dignity of man, seen through his eyes, is entirely moral and not also intellectual and aesthetic. Though he condemned oppression and the manipulation of opinion for private and sectional advantage, he did not condemn it for fear that it should thwart the intellect and the imagination; and it

---

[1] Vaughan, op. cit., Vol. II, p. 440.

[2] In this *Letter* he fastens on *Le Misanthrope* to show how even the best comedy is corrupting. What he says about it proves his ability to appreciate the merits as a work of art of what he attacks as a bad influence on morals; Rousseau as the critic of Molière is altogether more perceptive than, say, Tolstoy as the critic of Shakespeare.

never occurred to him that, even in a society of equals without wealth
or ambition or intrigue to corrupt it, public opinion might be oppressive. He took it for granted that superiority is more pernicious than
mediocrity; he cared little for idiosyncrasy, for experiment, for adven-
ture. Spiritually, he was parochial; he wanted a tight and cosy world
with no room in it for talents great enough to make ordinary men feel
small. He wanted a tranquil and unchanging world, a world without
mysteries or anxiety because its inhabitants lack curiosity, a world
protected by an all-knowing and all-powerful God whose creatures are
comfortable in their ignorance and their mutual trust.

Rousseau has been called a vain, resentful and small-minded man.
No doubt, he was so to some extent, for he sometimes pretended to
despise what he secretly envied. Certainly, Voltaire and the Encyclopaedists thought him small-minded; they were offended as much by his
being the sort of man he was as by his actions, and they spoke of him
contemptuously. They brought out the worst in him, and their ability
to do this was as much his fault as theirs. He was vain and resentful,
but he was also – and this they did not see – a man who aspired to goodness and who was as profoundly dissatisfied with himself as with the
world, even though he blamed the world more than himself. He was
deeply unhappy, not because he was small-minded, resentful and
vain, but because he was not what he wanted to be and could not, for
all his protestations, persuade himself that he was. He was the man who
felt that society had made an outcast of him, and who complained
bitterly of his lot; he was the 'alienated' man become articulate.

If others brought out the worst in him, he too brought out the worst
in them. There is nothing more spiteful and petty in the lives of
Diderot and Voltaire than their treatment of Rousseau. They were
men of the world, as he was not; they were clever, brilliant and self-
confident, as he was not; they were better able to make him look
foolish than he them. He was something of a boor, as they were not;
and the faults of the boorish, though no worse in themselves, are more
painful to contemplate than the faults of the quick and the polished.
Envious though Rousseau was, the fact remains that he had talents
as great as any that he envied. If he was a moralist, so too, in their different ways, were Voltaire and the Encyclopaedists; and of all the
moralists of his age, he was the most eloquent and the most profound.
He was accused of plagiarism, rhetoric, and sophistry by writers who
had less to say that was new and exciting than he had. He suffered
from insane suspicions and made false accusations. There was no plot
against him of the kind that he imagined. But he had enemies. They
were a côterie and he was alone; they supported one another in their
dislike and contempt for him. I would not speak as highly of his
character as Mrs Macdonald does in a book about him written to
defend him against Diderot and his other detractors, but I agree with

her that posterity has seen him largely through their eyes, while most of his contemporaries thought better of him. It is a pity this should be so because, with so personal and passionate a writer, it is difficult to prevent your impression of the man from colouring your estimate of his doctrine.

*   *   *

Rousseau's influence on social and political thought has been immense. We invoke his name less often than Marx's because the revolution which he helped to inspire happened so much longer ago and because there are no powerful bodies who profess adherence to his doctrines, but we use his ideas just as much.

We owe to him a deeper sense of what is involved in man's being a social creature. In the *Discourse on the Origins of Inequality* he describes an imaginary course of social evolution, neither controlled nor understood by man, which makes him a rational and moral being. Man transforms his nature through the activities whose effects are his social environment. In *Emile* Rousseau shows how the child, while its bodily needs are satisfied by those who look after it, acquires feelings towards itself and others which create needs in it different from those it is born with or which arise in the course of mere physical maturation: the emotions and needs of a social, purposeful and moral being. In several of his writings he seeks to show how man can acquire in society passions and needs which society is unable to satisfy; how he can acquire aspirations and needs incompatible with one another and with the social order in which they arise. He turns our minds, as none of the great political and social theorists before him since Aristotle does, to considering how the social order affects the structure of human personality.

We owe him a conception of freedom not to be found in the writings of Hobbes or Locke or Montesquieu. Man, as a rational and moral being, aspires not to being able to satisfy as many as possible of his desires but to being able to live well by his own standards. Man cares deeply for freedom, not because he is a creature of appetites, but because he is a moral person having notions of excellence; because he has an idea (albeit vague) of the sort of person he wants to be and a sort of life which is worth living. He is not the more free the fewer the obstacles to his satisfying his desires; he is the more free the greater his opportunity to be what he wants to be and to live what seems to him a worth-while life.

We owe to him a conception of happiness which is intimately connected with this conception of freedom. To be happy is to be on good terms with yourself and with others, and the terms on which you are with yourself depend largely on the quality of your relations with others, which in turn depend on the social situation. (Happiness, as distinct from pleasure, is possible only to a self-conscious and moral being, having aspirations and able to realize them. Man alone can be 'outside himself', *hors de lui-même* (to use Rousseau's own expression), and man alone can find happiness by 'finding himself': or, to speak less metaphorically, man alone can be made wretched by seeing himself impelled by circumstances to be what he would rather not be, and man alone can attain happiness in being what it satisfies him to be.)

It was the common opinion of moralists that unhappiness is a consequence of vice. Rousseau was eager to show that vice is an effect of unhappiness, and that men are unhappy because they live in the kind of society which makes them so. He ascribed their ills entirely to their environment and not at all to heredity; (he assumed that all men are born with the qualities which would make them capable of happiness in the right kind of society.) Mistaken though this assumption may be, it directs the mind towards discovering cures rather than towards the infliction of punishments.

Rousseau was often given to pessimism. Yet his doctrine is not in itself pessimistic. It does not in the least follow that men, because society has 'corrupted' them, cannot find a remedy for their condition; they can, by taking thought, improve society. They can, despite their vices, set about creating the environment suitable to their nature. For, though Rousseau thought it unlikely that they would do so, he merely gave vent to his pessimism without producing evidence to support it. No matter what society has done to them, men can come to know their condition and to imagine a way out of it; they can discover what suits their nature and are by nature inclined to it. This is Rousseau's doctrine. Why, then, should they not strive to attain it? Why should they not make progress towards it? Because, says Rousseau, their vices weaken their will. But, then, reflection on their condition may strengthen their will. Why should it be supposed that what weakens the will must always prevail over what strengthens it? Rousseau provides no reasons; his pessimism is no better grounded in reason than the optimism of Hegel or Marx.

Rousseau was the first to give passionate expression to man's sense that society has grown too large and too complicated for his own good. Better that the community should be small and stable, with its every member neighbour to all the others, than that it should be vast, restless and quickly changing, with everyone inside it a stranger to all but a few. Man's sense of his own insignificance and his fear of the great society which his own activities have produced, his feeling that he is alone and yet not his own master, his apathy and anxiety is an environment beyond his understanding and control, his feeling that he is lost in an artificial wilderness, man-made but not made for man : these are sentiments which many have uttered since Rousseau but none as eloquently as he did.

Man, to save himself from society, must remake society to his own measure. He must eliminate the inequalities which inevitably make some men the instruments of others. He must create societies of equals, which must be small, because there can be equality only in communities all of whose members can take an active part in the main business of government, which is the making of law. Equality, democracy, and freedom: to these three words Rousseau gave new meanings, and meanings which are important because they express aspirations more and more widely shared since his time. He used old words to say new things and was more original than he knew.

INDEX

INDEX